D1457618

With the
LONC

Tr
AS A

EUROPE
1815–1945

EUROPE
1815–1945

Anthony Wood
HEAD OF THE HISTORY DEPARTMENT
AT WINCHESTER COLLEGE

LONGMANS

LONGMANS, GREEN AND CO LTD

48 Grosvenor Street, London W.1
*Associated companies, branches and representatives
throughout the world*

73400 - 24

*Printed in Great Britain by Richard Clay and Company, Ltd.,
Bungay, Suffolk*

PREFACE

THE purpose of this book is to trace the general course of European history from Napoleon to the end of the second World War. It may be objected that to go as far as 1945 is to deal with events that are still too recent for satisfactory historical study. Not all the sources are yet available and the problem of national bias is considerable. 'Le bon historien,' wrote Fénelon, 'n'est d'aucun pays ni d'aucun temps,' and if the Victorian, who was not inclined to see any great distinction between foreigners, could view the international scene with a certain air of detachment, the British historian of today, looking back on recent decades, finds himself as emotionally involved as any Continental.

These disadvantages seem to me to be outweighed by the great need of the student to understand something of the background of the times in which he lives; in any case, it would be a pity to end the story at 1918, when the problems of the inter-war years can be seen to emerge so directly from the break-down of the nineteenth-century system. Furthermore, although much information is still undisclosed, the major difficulty for the historian of the twentieth century is the quantity rather than the dearth of material. He has more than enough on which to base a tentative assessment. The problem of bias remains, but Professor Renouvin's four volumes in the *Histoire des Relations Internationales* series, the publications of the Institut für Zeitgeschichte at Munich and the agreement reached, in 1951, between French and German historians on the origins of the first World War would all suggest that a dispassionate analysis of the present century is not impossible at a high academic level; at the same time the work of UNESCO, the Historical Association in this country and the Internationales Schulbuchinstitut at Brunswick has made some progress in eliminating the more blatant forms of national prejudice in school textbooks.

To cover a period of such intense development as that between 1815 and 1945 at once poses the problem of method. The aims and difficulties of individual countries are a vital element in the story of these years; and yet it is also a fact that the forces of nationalism, industrialization and social change, and the complexity of languages, peoples, and classes in central and eastern Europe raise questions that cut clean across all political frontiers. Indeed, I believe that these general factors are so essential to the understanding of the period that I have purposely treated the history of the Continent as a whole; I have, however, tried to strike a balance by elaborating the detail of national development within the wider framework, although I have not included the purely domestic history of Great Britain, except where this directly impinges on events abroad.

Over Christian names I have aimed chiefly at the convenience of the reader rather than at any consistent principle, and I have anglicized most titles, although it is not always possible to observe precise distinctions— as, for example, between the German *Fürst* and *Prinz*. Place-names are more controversial, since their different German and Slavonic forms reflect in themselves the rivalries of central and eastern Europe. I have added a glossary of these at the back of the book, and in the text, when no neutral anglicized form existed, I have simply used the one most commonly adopted in this country.

There are many acknowledgements to be made—to my teachers at Oxford, to the London Library and the Deutsches Kulturinstitut who supplied me with many of the necessary books, and to my colleague Count Sollohub who allowed me to make use of his thesis on German nationalism. In compiling the statistics at the end of the book, the publishers have kindly given me permission to quote from the following: *Eastern Europe between the Wars 1918–41* by H. Seton-Watson, published by the Cambridge University Press; *The Struggle for Mastery in Europe 1848–1918*, by A. J. P. Taylor, published by the Clarendon Press, Oxford; *The Growth of the American Republic*, by S. E. Morison and H. S. Commager, published by the Oxford University Press Inc.; *Modern Germany: Its History and Civilization*, by K. S. Pinson, published by the Macmillan Company, New York, C. 1954, by the Macmillan Company; and the 1959 edition of the *Encyclopaedia Britannica*.

In addition to this practical assistance I must also mention debts of a more intangible kind. There is an atmosphere, a background of assumptions, which it is not easy for an English person to grasp in attempting to explain Continental history, and a number of circumstances have helped me to realize, if not to resolve this difficulty. The experience of the second World War seemed at the time to be of little academic value; yet the sight of the shattered orchards of Normandy and the ruin of the German cities did at least give a glimpse of

the stakes for which twentieth-century politics are played. It was as a
student at the University of Basle that I first became aware of the
social and linguistic complexity of central Europe and I take this
opportunity of expressing my thanks to Professor H. Lüdecke for all
his kindness to me while I was there; also to the authorities of Winchester College for later allowing me leave of absence for an invaluable
year as Lecteur at the Sorbonne. Lastly, my greatest debt is to my wife
not only for enduring another bout of authorship, but also for adding a
Scandinavian flavour to my appreciation of European history.

A. C. W.

Winchester 1963

CONTENTS

Part III

THE FAILURE OF LIBERAL REVOLUTION
1848–51

Part IV

THE DESTRUCTION OF THE
VIENNA SETTLEMENT 1851–71

Part V

THE ARMED PEACE 1871–1914

Part VI

THE ECLIPSE OF
NINETEENTH-CENTURY EUROPE 1914–21

Part VII

THE CRISIS OF LIBERAL DEMOCRACY
1921–45

MAPS

THE LEGACY OF THE FRENCH REVOLUTION

'THE truth', said Oscar Wilde, 'is never pure and rarely simple,' a remark which might well be applied to the history of the French Revolution. The most striking feature of the *ancien régime* in Europe in the eighteenth century had been the existence of a highly privileged class of nobility, upper clergy, and *bourgeois vivant noblement*. To belong to this exclusive caste had meant to escape the main burden of taxation and to enjoy the right of entry to the highest posts in the country. This was a system of society so interwoven with the legal and administrative complexities of the *ancien régime* that it is tempting to regard the French Revolution as a concerted effort on the part of the unprivileged to wipe the slate clean and to draw the whole of government and society afresh. Yet throughout the revolutionary turmoil in France there was little unity among the unprivileged. Each small section of society was thinking in terms of a readjustment that would simply enable it to enjoy more fully the benefits of the existing system. The significance of the year 1789 is that each group imagined that its hour had come, and the consequence was a struggle between conflicting ambitions in which the *ancien régime* was torn asunder.

At Versailles, where the Estates General assembled in May 1789, it was the Third Estate, aided by the King's fears of an outbreak from Paris, who threw off the control of the nobility and upper clergy and established the three Estates as an indivisible National Assembly pledged to redefine the governmental structure of France. Yet the Third Estate themselves, representing the ambitions of a mainly professional class, were barely in control of other discordant forces—artisans and unemployed in the towns, who, in Paris, were instrumental in the taking of the Bastille on 14 July, and peasantry in the countryside, who forced the deputies in August to decree the ultimate abolition of all forms of feudal privilege.

Had the King been able to give a firm lead, it is possible that the course of later events might have been entirely different. But the tragedy for Louis XVI was that although, like Charles I of England, he had many commendable personal qualities—deeply religious, a devoted father, a Bourbon without a mistress—none of them were relevant to a monarchy approaching the crisis of its existence. The National Assembly had, by September 1791, devised a constitutional monarchy for France with a representative Chamber elected on an extremely limited franchise, but it was soon clear that they had failed to create a lasting settlement. The reorganization of the Church caused a great rent that cut through every class division in France, creating new support for the *émigrés* who were forming their army at Coblenz. *Assignats*, bills of credit issued against the confiscated lands of the Church, began to circulate as paper currency, and in the consequent inflation the urban poor faced not merely political disillusionment, but also the much sharper prick of hunger, of which the radical politicians were quick to take advantage.

It was the outbreak of hostilities with Austria and Prussia in April 1792 that brought these problems to a head. For the Powers of Europe war meant nothing less than a crusade in defence of the existing order of society. For France it was to mean a struggle for survival which eventually opened the way to democratic republicanism. There were to be three periods when national disaster seemed imminent and each was to have striking consequences on the French domestic scene. In the summer of 1792 the news of military retreats and surrenders led to a *coup d'état* in Paris that ended the monarchy, established a National Convention elected by universal suffrage, and, in January 1793, sent Louis XVI to the guillotine. In the spring and summer of 1793 fresh disasters and the fear of counter-revolution at home brought the two principal political groups into direct conflict. The Girondins had strongly supported the revolutionary war, but wished to preserve a system of political federalism and economic *laissez-faire*, and it was the Jacobins who won the support of the masses in Paris with an emergency wartime policy of centralization, economic controls, and Terror exercised through the Committee of Public Safety and the Revolutionary Tribunal.

By the summer of 1794 the situation at the front had vastly improved. Robespierre and his supporters, who had destroyed two rival factions under Danton and Hébert, were themselves dispatched to the guillotine, and, in the right-wing reaction that followed, the controls were relaxed and the Jacobins became the victims of a new White Terror. For four years a Directory of five attempted to ward off the political extremes of right and left in a series of *coups*, through which they became increasingly dependent upon the army, but when in the summer of 1799 France suffered a number of defeats at the hands of the Second

Coalition of Great Britain, Russia, and Austria, a new Jacobin revival appeared imminent. In fact, the advance of France's enemies was checked and the hopes of the Jacobins with it, but there was little confidence in the power of the Directory to continue to survive such shocks. For the bourgeois the memories of economic controls, reinforced by a policy of Terror, were still too recent, and a small group of conspirators led by Sieyès and Talleyrand looked hastily for a military figure who might stand nominally at the head of a revised constitution which would offer the newly established classes greater security. In the event they underestimated the man whom they chose, for the *coup d'état* of Brumaire[1] brought Napoleon Bonaparte to a position of supreme power which he was to hold for the next fourteen years.

The significance of Napoleon's work within France was not that he created a totally new system of government; rather that he consolidated certain aspects of the Revolution at the expense of others. Constitutional rule based on a separation of powers, decentralization of local government and the great tangle of electoral processes were all swept aside in the creation of a simplified autocracy in which the executive power in the person of Napoleon dominated the so-called legislature and the courts of law, and through the appointment of Prefects in the provinces brought the government of the entire country directly under the central authority. On the other hand, strong rule was able to solve the two great problems which the revolutionaries had created for themselves—the currency and the Church. The *assignats* were abolished, the national finances were re-established through a newly organized Bank of France, and a Concordat with the Pope restored relations between France and Rome. One thing, however, Napoleon knew he could not touch. The Church lands, in which the peasantry and middle classes had been investing during the past ten years, were not given back. Similarly, any reappearance of the old social privileges was out of the question. Equality before the law, a reasonably equitable system of taxation, *la carrière ouverte aux talents* in the army, government service and the professions, all these aims of the early years of the Revolution were now guaranteed by the emergence of what appeared at last to be a stable government. By and large, it was a bargain that suited the French, since it seemed to secure peasantry and middle classes both from a restoration of the *ancien régime* and from the alarming tendencies of revolutionary Jacobinism.

[1] The name of a month in the calendar introduced by the revolutionaries in 1792. The date was actually 9–10 November.

But for Europe there was another aspect of Napoleon's rule that was to be of startling significance. By 1808 the wars in which he had defeated the Continental Powers had placed his country in an absolutely unprecedented position of authority. His relations and marshals occupied the thrones of kingdoms in the Netherlands, Germany, Italy, and Spain; the government of the Swiss cantons had been remodelled and a Grand Duchy of Warsaw created on the borders of Russia. Almost everywhere throughout these territories ran the writ of the Civil Code, embodying the Napoleonic version of the social and political message of the French Revolution.

Napoleon himself was not to last. The fatal attack on Russia in 1812, the retreat from Moscow, and the campaigns against the Powers of the Fourth Coalition in Germany in 1813 led on to the surrender of Paris and the proclamation of the deposition of Napoleon by the French Senate in April 1814. Yet the defeat of France was not to mean the end of the Revolution. It was only twenty-five years since the meeting of the Estates General at Versailles, but in that short time the classes and peoples of Europe had caught a glimpse of a different order of society and government that they could never forget. They had, too, begun to grow aware of a sense of national individuality, partly because of the way in which the Napoleonic conquests had been followed by an immense simplification of the political frontiers of the eighteenth century, but principally because of the antagonism which the imposition of French authority had aroused. Thus Napoleon had bequeathed to Europe more than he could ever have imagined; the history of the nineteenth century is the story of that inheritance and of all the contradictory ambitions to which it gave rise, as a growing economic revolution added strength to the attack on the assumptions on which the old order had been based.

I

EUROPE IN 1815

I

THE CONGRESS OF VIENNA 1814-15

THREE times since 1814 a new map of Europe has emerged from the ruin of the old. Earlier conflicts had often been widespread —in the eighteenth century reaching as far as America and India— but the objectives of the combatants had remained limited and the terms of the subsequent treaties restricted to local territorial readjustments. It was the threat of political and social revolution implicit in the Napoleonic war that gave a different character to the terms of the peace that followed, and in this sense it is easy to imagine a link between the Congress of Vienna and the peace-making of 1919 and 1945 in a new era of European settlements.

Two major features, however, distinguish the treaties of Vienna from those of Versailles and Potsdam. The first point of difference lies in the general aim of the diplomats. After the two World Wars of the twentieth century there was no question of recreating the situation that had existed before the outbreak of hostilities; the statesmen of 1814, on the other hand, were definitely seeking some sort of return to the eighteenth-century system. It was not merely that their pride had been bruised by the impact of Napoleon's armies; the whole basis of the *ancien régime* had been challenged by the extension of revolutionary principles in the lands adjoining France, and for the Allies the purpose of victory was to restore the political and social framework that had been so roughly shaken since 1789.

This determination to re-establish the old legitimate governments helps to explain the second point of difference. All three settlements were primarily the work of the great Powers, but in one respect Vienna was a more genuine congress than the others, since it had been preceded by a logical sequence of agreements with France, restoring the Bourbon monarchy and ending the state of war, so that, when the Congress met, France could take her place alongside the victorious Powers. In contrast to this, at Versailles in 1919, the problems of the peace terms and the redrawing of the frontiers were dealt with in a combined process in which Germany was treated purely as a defeated country. After the second World War, there was no congress at all; the leaders of Germany were all dead, missing, or captive, and the victors already at loggerheads had to content themselves with organizing their areas of occupation in their own ways.

On 6 April 1814 at Fontainebleau, Napoleon, having failed to establish a Regency for his son, the King of Rome, had agreed to unconditional abdication. The terms which the allied Powers imposed on the former ruler of France were by no means severe; he was granted the island of Elba in full sovereignty, as well as an annual revenue of two million francs from France, while the Empress Marie Louise was to hold the Duchies of Parma, Piacenza, and Guastalla in perpetuity, and the numerous members of his family were to retain their titles and to receive annuities, including a pension of a million francs a year for Josephine.

Once Napoleon had been removed, the second problem was to persuade the French that they really wanted a restored monarchy after all. Here they were fortunate in that Talleyrand, the ex-bishop of the *ancien régime*, who had played a leading part in almost every French government since 1789, was able to talk the French Senate into proclaiming the return of the Bourbons and was thus able to contrive the fiction that Louis Stanislav Xavier, Count of Provence, brother of the guillotined Louis XVI, had been recalled by his own country to the throne of France to rule as Louis XVIII. On 23 April an armistice was signed between France and the Allies, and on 3 May Louis made his official entry into Paris. Restored sovereigns should not appear to depend upon foreign bayonets, and this was not an easy moment for Louis with the city full of troops of the Allies. From the Pont Neuf to Notre Dame the route was lined with Napoleon's Old Guard. 'Ces mêmes hommes,' wrote Chateaubriand in his *Mémoires d'outre-tombe*, 'privés de leur capitaine, étaient forcés de saluer un vieux roi, invalide du temps, non de la guerre, surveillés qu'ils étaient par une armée de Russes, d'Autrichiens et de Prussiens dans la capitale envahie de Napoléon.'

The moment passed. Provided that the general principles of 1789 were guaranteed, restoration was acceptable to most of the French, weary of war and of the economic consequences of Napoleon's Continental schemes, and the Allies could move quickly on to the next step —the signing of the Treaty of Paris with France on 30 May. The terms reduced her eastern frontier to what it had been in 1792, with the addition of a part of Savoy, including Chambéry and Annecy, but overseas she had to surrender Tobago, St Lucia and Mauritius to Great Britain and the Spanish half of San Domingo to Spain. In the main, however, this first Treaty of Paris was remarkable for its moderation. Under Napoleon France had imposed her will upon almost every country in Europe, achieving a dominion beyond the wildest dreams of the monarchy of the *ancien régime*, and now at the end, when her power was broken, her original frontiers were respected, no indemnity or reparations were demanded at all, and even the art treasures looted from all over Europe were left in her possession. There was wisdom in such forbearance, for by this means it was hoped that Louis XVIII might be eased on to his throne and Bonapartism die a natural death.

These were the diplomatic preliminaries that preceded the meeting of the Congress of Vienna which in accordance with the Treaty of Paris was attended in the autumn of 1814 by the sovereigns and plenipotentiaries from 'all the Powers engaged on either side in the present war'. Certain questions such as the independence of Switzerland, the creation of a large Kingdom of the Netherlands and the realigning of local frontiers in Germany and Italy had already been discussed among the great Powers, and it was never intended that the Congress should do much more than ratify the final decisions. Vienna, during these months, became a dazzling scene of royalty *en fête*. At a cost of some thirty million florins the Emperor Francis offered a lavish hospitality to most of the reigning sovereigns of Europe, as well as more than two hundred princely families; public balls, banquets, amateur theatricals, sleighing trips through the Wienerwald, all formed a glittering background to the intrigues of the ladies and to Sir Sidney Smith's interminable narration of the siege of Acre, while the great Powers deliberated and the Austrian secret police rummaged through the wastepaper baskets of the diplomats.

To one side of the Hofburg stood Metternich's house on the Ballhausplatz and it was here that the real work of the Congress was carried on. The British delegation consisted of four plenipotentiaries headed by the Foreign Secretary, Lord Castlereagh, an aloof, cold, handsome figure, whose principal aim at the Congress was to bring about a balance of forces in Europe that would remove any danger of expansion by France or Russia. Apprehensiveness over a possible revival of French power was natural, and his wariness of Russia's possible designs westward was a direct legacy from William Pitt's policy during the Otchakov crisis of 1791. Thus for Castlereagh it was essential, first, to guard the eastern frontier of France with a strong Netherlands, Piedmont and an independent Switzerland, and second, to create a central European *bloc* out of Prussia and Austria who might stand firm against France or Russia.

The Russian delegation was large and highly international. The Foreign Minister, Count Nesselrode, and two other plenipotentiaries, Count Razumovski and Count Stackelberg, were accompanied by the German Freiherr vom und zum Stein, the Polish Prince Adam Czartoryski, and the Swiss Laharpe, each to give advice on his own region, while Count Capo d'Istria of Corfu and the Corsican Pozzo di Borgo, Russian ambassador at Paris, exercised a rather more general influence. In fact, Tsar Alexander never relied entirely on any single one of his advisers and the other Powers could never be sure that he would not revoke what his subordinates had just negotiated. Alexander, his round cherubic face shining with benevolence, his tight-fitting uniform almost bursting at every seam, was a strange unpredictable character, oscillating wildly between authoritarianism and liberal gestures, a complicated psychology in which pious aspiration often blended with deep cunning. This duality of outlook was reflected in his schemes for Poland, where he wished to recreate the old Kingdom, granting it a liberal constitution, but at the same time making it part of his own dominions. This would have deprived Prussia and Austria of some of the Polish provinces that they had gained in the partitions of the eighteenth century, and the re-emergence of an undivided Poland completely in the pocket of Russia would have seen the fulfilment of Catherine the Great's original plans before she had had to abandon them in favour of sharing the spoil with Prussia and Austria.

Frederick William III of Prussia, much enamoured of the Russian Tsar, was prepared to accept the idea, tempted by Alexander's suggestion that he should take the Kingdom of Saxony by way of compensation; his delegation, headed by Prince Hardenberg, and mainly bound by the considerations of the Prussian General Staff, was content so long as Prussia's position in Germany was assured. Much stronger objection came from Austria, since Metternich was determined that Russia should not gain Poland, while Count Stadion and Prince Schwarzenberg, although they cared little about Poland, had no liking for the suggested Prussian acquisition of Saxony.

For Talleyrand, now Foreign Minister to Louis XVIII, this quarrel among the Allies offered an ideal opportunity. There was no question of territorial acquisition for France; his sole aim was to restore her prestige and to end her isolation. Before his arrival at Vienna the

Powers had drawn up a *protocole séparé* prescribing a procedure which would have left all major decisions in the hands of the four Powers of the Quadruple Alliance, but it did not take long for Talleyrand to use the Allies' own principle of legitimacy to demolish this scheme. 'The intervention of Talleyrand', wrote Gentz, Metternich's secretary, 'hopelessly upset our plans. It was a scene I shall never forget.' By November Talleyrand had secured the inclusion of France, Spain, Portugal, and Sweden, thus creating a directing committee of the eight signatories of the Treaty of Paris who had convened the Congress.

It was the Polish-Saxon question that enabled him to take the next step. In December he openly supported the Austrians in their resistance to Prussian acquisition of Saxony, and when Hardenberg announced in anger that any further interference with the Prussian claims would be tantamount to a declaration of war, Talleyrand seized his chance during the momentary panic to propose to Castlereagh and Metternich a secret treaty of alliance against Prussia and Russia. The treaty was signed on 3 January 1815. 'The Coalition is dissolved,' wrote Talleyrand in triumph to Louis XVIII; 'France is no longer isolated in Europe.' In fact, neither side would have been prepared to go to war at this moment and the mere shock of such a division among the Allies was sufficient to produce a compromise solution to their difficulties. For Talleyrand, however, it remained a considerable diplomatic victory, since the price of his support had been that France should join the major Powers in the detailed negotiation, and thus during the rest of the Congress the significant decisions were taken by a Committee of Five in which France sat with Great Britain, Austria, Prussia, and Russia.

The treaty was eventually signed in June 1815 by the five great Powers as well as by Sweden and Portugal. Of the Polish territories Prussia was to regain the province of Posen, Austria retained Galicia, while Cracow was to become a Free City. The rest of the Napoleonic Grand Duchy of Warsaw was to become the Kingdom of Poland under the Tsar. Prussia's compensation for this Russian gain was only two-fifths of Saxony, including about 850,000 inhabitants, but she received in addition a large area of the Rhineland, Westphalia, and Swedish Pomerania. Sweden had lost Finland and the Aland Isles after the Russian invasion of 1808, but, in accordance with an agreement of 1812, now received Norway from Denmark, who in return gained only the small duchy of Lauenburg.

No attempt was made to recreate the old Holy Roman Empire, and the thirty-eight sovereign states including the Free Cities of Lübeck, Bremen, Frankfurt, and Hamburg, were loosely linked together in a German Confederation with a Diet at Frankfurt under the presidency of Austria. Within this confederation Hanover was made a kingdom and received small additions of territory, while Bavaria gained Bayreuth and Anspach in return for the territory she restored to Austria. British interests were served by the incorporating of the United Provinces of the Dutch and the Austrian Netherlands into a Kingdom of the Netherlands under the House of Orange, King William I holding the title also of Grand Duke of Luxemburg, although the city itself was to be a Federal fortress with a Prussian garrison.

In Italy no appearance of unity was created at all. The Kingdom of Sardinia rounded off its mainland possessions of Piedmont, Savoy, and Nice with the former territories of the republic of Genoa as a bulwark against French expansion; Austria regained Lombardy and retained Venetia which, until Napoleon's invasion in 1796, had been an independent republic. In central Italy the Papal States including the legations of Ferrara, Bologna, Ravenna, and Forli straddled the peninsula, while to the north of them the duchies of Parma, Modena, and Tuscany were given back to members of the Habsburg family. To the south it was the ruler, rather than the frontiers, of the kingdom of Naples that presented the problem. Murat had fought alongside Napoleon at Leipzig in 1813, but this had not inhibited him from opening negotiations with the Allies, and in January 1814 he had signed a treaty with them, offering his army of 30,000 in return for a guarantee of his throne. By 1815, however, the need that Castlereagh and Metternich felt to conciliate Louis XVIII, who naturally hated any survivor of Napoleon's Europe, had caused them to agree secretly that Murat should be expelled to allow the restoration of the Spanish Bourbon, King Ferdinand, and, in the event, Murat's support of Napoleon on his return from Elba was to give them all the justification that they needed.

In addition to this redrawing of the map of Europe the Powers also reached a number of other more general agreements. In the same year they were to sign a guarantee of perpetual neutrality for the Swiss Confederation, whose cantons the Congress had made up to twenty-two in number with the addition of Geneva, Valais, and Neuchâtel, the last of these being a Prussian enclave. The question of the navigation of rivers which ran through several countries was dealt with by a

EUROPE IN 1810

Territory directly under Napoleon's rule

Dependent States

Scale 0   100   200 Miles

EUROPE AFTER THE CONGRESS OF VIENNA 1815

special committee, and it was established that such rivers should be open to all commerce with no further increase of duties then in force. Another matter that particularly exercised Castlereagh was the abolition of the slave trade. Great Britain, the United States, and Denmark had already abolished it; Sweden and the Netherlands were prepared to do so and Louis XVIII had promised Castlereagh that France would also suppress it within five years. Negotiation with Spain and Portugal took rather longer, but eventually each responded to the offer of a cash payment from the British government by way of compensation.

Castlereagh had been anxious to keep the question of overseas possessions outside the scope of the Congress, mainly because British naval power during the war had enabled her to make great gains at the expense of France and the Napoleonic kingdom of Holland. Here agreement was reached simply through a series of private treaties. Great Britain gave back the East Indies to the Dutch, but retained Ceylon, as well as Cape Colony in South Africa and a part of Dutch Guiana. France had lost Tobago, St Lucia and Mauritius to Great Britain by the Treaty of Paris, but received back French Guiana from Portugal and also Guadaloupe, after Sweden had been persuaded to give up her claim in return for an indemnity of one million pounds from the British.

The diplomatic shifts and quarrels which had inevitably attended this vast readjustment of territories inside and outside Europe were overshadowed towards the end of the Congress by a new and unexpected development. On 1 March 1815, after slipping out of Elba, Napoleon landed in the south of France near Antibes. At Vienna the great pageant of entertainment came suddenly to a halt. 'It seemed', wrote an eye-witness, 'as if a thousand candles immediately went out.' In France the Bourbon restoration, so carefully stage-managed by Talleyrand, fell in ruins, as Napoleon, on his progress northwards, was welcomed by the troops sent to resist his advance. 'I will receive you,' he wrote to Marshal Ney, who had promised Louis that he would bring Napoleon back in an iron cage, 'as I did on the morrow of the battle of the Moskowa,' and Ney found it impossible to resist the old magic. Louis fled hastily to Lille and on 20 March the Emperor once more entered his capital in triumph, while in Naples Murat, hearing the news, declared war on Austria and advanced north towards Milan.

On both sides frantic preparation followed. In France, in order to compete with the Charter[1] already granted by Louis XVIII, Napoleon gave a promise of constitutional government, later embodied in the *Acte additionnel*, and tried to play on the divisions among the Allies by a peace offer to Great Britain and Austria. When this failed, he set off on 12 June with 120,000 troops, intending to strike at Brussels. At Vienna the Allies immediately renewed the Treaty of Chaumont, determined on the expulsion of Napoleon, although doubtful whether they could impose the Bourbons a second time on France; only the British and Prussian forces were immediately available in the Low Countries, since the Russians had withdrawn to Poland and the Austrians were engaged with Murat in Italy, and it was consequently Wellington and Blücher who fought the series of fluid defensive actions that culminated in the battle of Waterloo on 18 June, when the Prussians, whom Napoleon believed he had driven from the field two days before at Ligny, were able to join with Wellington's squares who had beaten back the French attack throughout the whole day, and in the evening the Allied cavalry swept in to victory.

'I hasten to congratulate you', wrote Metternich to Wellington, 'on the brilliant opening of the campaign.' But, as it turned out, Napoleon's fate had depended not on a campaign, but on a single battle. This time it was Fouché, Napoleon's Minister of Police, who played Talleyrand's role in organizing the capitulation of France; the Chamber set up a provisional government and Napoleon fled westwards to Rochefort to avoid being shot by Blücher who was advancing on Paris with his Prussian army. It was four months before any agreement could be reached among the Allies over the terms of the second Treaty of Paris. Prussia, the Netherlands, and many of the smaller German states were in full cry, demanding heavy indemnities as well as the loss of Alsace, Lorraine, French Flanders, and Savoy, but eventually Castlereagh, angered by the brutalities of the Prussian army in France and anxious not to create a lasting sense of grievance among the French, was able, with the support of the Tsar, to bring Austria round, after which the Prussians had to give way. The second Treaty of Paris was finally signed on 20 November; in the north-east, thin strips of territory were surrendered to the Netherlands and the Prussian Rhineland, including the frontier fortresses of Philippeville, Marienbourg, Saarlouis, and Landau; in Savoy, the *département* of Mont Blanc was given to the Kingdom of Sardinia. An army of occupation numbering 150,000 was established in the northern *départements*, the fortress of

[1] See p. 37.

Hüningen near the Swiss border dismantled, and an indemnity of 700 million francs imposed, as well as liability for claims for losses suffered by private individuals.

Thus the Hundred Days cost France dear—and not only France. After his surrender to the captain of *HMS Bellerophon* outside Roche-fort, Napoleon was to spend the remainder of his life, closely watched, on the island of St Helena in the south Atlantic—a poor exchange for Elba. In Italy, a month before Waterloo, Murat had been defeated at Tolentino by the Austrians and had fled to the south of France; in September he returned by sea, landed in Calabria, and attempted to gain support, as Napoleon had done on his return from Elba, but the *coup* failed utterly. He was arrested and later executed by a firing squad on the beach at Pizzo. And even for Louis XVIII, as he wearily retraced his steps back into France, there was the bitter knowledge that the King of France was returning, in Chateaubriand's words, 'derrière ces uni-formes rouges qui venaient de reteindre leur pourpre au sang des Français'.

2

CLASSES AND PEOPLES

A VIOLENT oscillation of frontiers amid more than twenty years of revolutionary war had wrought little fundamental change in the European way of life. All but a small fraction of the 200 million inhabitants were peasantry, and across the great northern plains that stretched from the north-east of France to the steppes of Russia, tiny villages still practised a communal system of farming on the surrounding open fields, where the peasant held his scattered strips. Naturally, there were many local exceptions to this pattern in regions where geography demanded a more individual type of agriculture—among the vineyards of the south of France, in the Alpine districts and the Balkans, and along the shores of the Norwegian fiords. In Finland and the north of Sweden there could be no open fields where the peasant had to struggle against the encroaching forest and the long seasons of heavy snow, while on the polders of the North Sea coast and among the Masurian marshes of East Prussia the farmhouses stood perched along the dykes, each at the head of its own holding.

By any twentieth century standard the cities throughout the entire Continent would seem minute. The population of Paris, the largest of them by far, was 600,000; few others numbered more than 200,000— St Petersburg and Vienna—while the rapid growth of Berlin in the eighteenth century had only brought her to 180,000 by 1815. Commercial towns such as Lyons, Marseilles, and Hamburg could boast 100,000 inhabitants, Genoa rather less, while the Baltic ports were even smaller.

The general aspect of most towns was still of an earlier epoch; houses of timber and plaster formed an untidy pattern of rambling streets around the church and market place; sanitation was primitive and the plash of fountains indicated the main source of water supply. In the larger cities, however, the eighteenth century had brought many changes. The old surrounding walls were coming down and in their place planned vistas of gardens and public walks lent a new air of spacious dignity—in Paris the Champs-Élysées, in Frankfurt the

Palmengarten, in Berlin Unter den Linden. In an age of absolutism the palace had become a symbol of vital importance in the effort to keep up with the Bourbons. Every German prince had toiled at his miniature Versailles. The rococo charm of Frederick the Great's Sans Souci, the simple French style of Drottningholm to the west of Stockholm, the richly embroidered classicism of the Spanish Bourbon Charles III's palace at Caserta, and the still more elaborate splendour of the Winter Palace at St Petersburg were all evidence of this same determination; indeed, the original plans submitted to the Habsburg Emperor Joseph I for the Schönbrunn would have outshone Louis XIV's Versailles, had the finances been equal to it, and even the more modest palace completed in the reign of Maria Theresa was a fair rival.

No single style of building was dominant throughout the eighteenth century. Italian baroque had a marked influence in Austria, Bohemia and the south of Germany, and Vienna itself had been transformed into a city of elaborate façades, in which classical form was almost submerged amid a wealth of fantastic embellishment. The gardens, which were part of the architectural plan of the palaces, tended to imitate the careful geometrical patterns of Versailles, although by the second half of the eighteenth century the artless naturalism of the English park was becoming popular. In the north, on the other hand, baroque never really took root, and the neo-classical style predominated in the Christiansborg at Copenhagen, rebuilt after the fire of 1794, in the rectangular simplicity of the King's palace on the central island of Stockholm, and in the Great Square at Helsinki, which became the administrative capital of Finland under Russian rule.

The system of roads linking the towns varied enormously in quality. The French had long been known to have the best in Europe, and it had been part of Napoleon's Imperial design to extend these beyond the borders of France, so that Paris had become the centre of a great network of paved highways reaching out to Hamburg, Madrid and Amsterdam and over the Mont Cenis and Simplon passes. There was, too, quite a good system of metalled roads linking Vienna with Prague and most of the large towns of south Germany, but to the north and throughout eastern Europe they were little more than stony tracks and a journey by coach was a hazardous and expensive undertaking.

Two particular features emerge from this general picture of the Continent in 1815. The first was a strongly established sense of local feeling, due principally in eastern Europe to the poor communications, and reinforced in Germany, Italy, and Switzerland by the historic rivalries among the old duchies and cantons; throughout most parts of Europe, each large town with its cathedral, university, or trading connections formed an entity in itself with its own leading families and traditions, providing amid the general vagueness of national sentiment a focal point for regional loyalties, strongly emphasized by marked differences in dialect.

This parochialism was to some extent counter-balanced by the second feature, a landed aristocracy for whom the distinction of class cut horizontally across the local and national divisions of Europe; the great mansions on the country estates, the town houses, the lavish entertainments, all pointed to a common way of life based on the assumption of a social pre-eminence, and greatly strengthened, in central and eastern Europe and Scandinavia, by a long process of intermarriage. From Paris to St Petersburg French had become the language of diplomacy and of high society. Count Cavour was happier speaking French than the language of the country that he was later to help create, and it was in French that Metternich, a Rhinelander, exchanged his letters with Madame de Lieven, the daughter of a Prussian family living in Estonia. Allegiance to their class was the dominant loyalty and a foreign origin was of little account; the Duke de Richelieu as Governor of Odessa, Stein in the service of the Russian Tsar and Sir John Acton as Prime Minister to the King of the Two Sicilies were only more recent instances of a social system that had earlier accepted Bouquoys and MacNevens in Bohemia, Hamiltons in Sweden, and Greigs and Barclays in Russia.

Thus far, the natural diversity of regional peculiarities would seem a small detail in comparison with the general factors common to most parts of Europe in 1815. There were, however, within this scene certain profound differences between eastern and western Europe that would suggest a line of demarcation running very roughly down through the centre of Germany.

The first of these differences lay in the general form of society. To the west of the Elbe and in Denmark there had developed between aristocracy and peasantry a complexity of professional, commercial, and industrialist classes, while the middle class to the east of the Elbe was so slight as to be politically and socially insignificant. There was a corresponding difference in the peasantry. To the west the bulk of the land was farmed by a variety of tenants and small owners, whereas the pattern of landholding in the east consisted mostly of vast estates which the landlords farmed with serf labour.

In France royalty and aristocracy had been restored, but without the trimmings of the *ancien régime*. *Émigré* land that had been confiscated by the government since 1789 could be given back only if it had not been sold or granted away, but it has been reckoned that, by 1820, the old nobility had regained about half of what they had lost. Their ancient privileges, however, were gone for ever; they paid taxes, their relationship with their tenants was on a purely business footing, and their estates lay side by side with those of a new aristocracy—merchants, lawyers, and government officials who had seized the chance offered by *la carrière ouverte aux talents*. Restoration France presented a scene of a vigorous *arriviste* society imbued with a belief in 'room at the top'—the France of Balzac's novels. Three-quarters of a population of 29 million were still peasantry, but many now owned their plots of land and consequently had no further interest in revolution, although there was a high proportion of landless wage-labourers and a considerable class of tenant farmers; *métayage*, the system whereby owner and farmer shared the profits, still continued, mainly because it had been practised by the gentry who, on the whole, had tended to survive the Revolution.

In Spain and Italy restoration was distinctly less of a compromise. In both countries the clergy and nobility regained their privileged positions. The Spanish peasantry in the Peninsular War had fought, not for freedom, but in order to expel the foreign invader; in Italy the peasant, sometimes owning a little land, more often a tenant or farming under the *mezzadria* (*métayage*) system, lived in a state of poverty which reached the lowest form of life in the south, and in neither country was the middle class numerous enough to make any effective claim to the fruits of the Revolution.

The Swiss and Dutch peasantry had long enjoyed personal freedom, but their upper classes were of a kind slightly different to the general European pattern. In the large merchant houses along the canals of Amsterdam and in the splendid eighteenth-century baroque mansions of Basle and Berne there dwelt the patrician families whose power lay not primarily in land, but in capital accumulated during a long trading past and in the prestige of their name within the confines of their city. A similar hierarchy of old families was also to be found in the German Free Cities of Bremen, Lübeck, Hamburg, and Frankfurt, still holding fast to the greatness that the days of the Hanse had once given them, although by now conscious of the challenge from a new middle class growing slowly in their midst.

Immediately to the east of the Rhine the relationship of the peasant to his lord varied considerably from serfdom to the payment of a nominal quit-rent. This process of change had already begun in the eighteenth century and the most striking form of emancipation was to be seen in Denmark in the 1780s, where enlightened despotism had abolished personal service and various forms of feudal obligation and had carried through a process of enclosure in the interests of the small farmer rather than of the great landlord. Elsewhere among the states of western Germany the changes had been stimulated by the Napoleonic reforms and were hardly checked by the restoration. But although, throughout the first forty years of the nineteenth century, legal ties continued to be removed or curtailed and feudal payments commuted into rents, the development of an independent landholding peasantry remained very slow, owing partly to the cost of commutation, partly to a land hunger among a growing population.

These social developments among bourgeois and peasantry west of the Elbe contrasted sharply with the scene in eastern Europe. It is true that, since 1807, a series of edicts in Prussia had broken down something of the barrier of caste, enabling nobility to enter commerce and the professions, the middle class to buy manorial estates, and the higher grade of peasant to become the owner of two-thirds of his original holding. But the main effect of this was to provide an economic outlet for the younger sons of impoverished nobility, for whom there had been insufficient opportunities in state service. It did not transform the situation, and although the numbers of bourgeois families increased among the holders of estates, the nobility continued to enjoy pride of place. In the countryside as a whole, the scene was dominated by the Prussian Junkers, a hard-working intensely conservative class of gentry, who farmed their entire estates themselves with serf labour, and, far from breaking up, the tendency was for these great latifundia to increase, as they constantly absorbed new land that had originally been held by the peasantry.

In the Habsburg dominions and Russia the middle class did not amount to more than a tiny section of the population—merchants and civil servants scattered among the towns. Under Habsburg rule ownership of land, which was almost entirely a monopoly of the Crown and the nobility, carried with it considerable control over the resident peasantry, serfs who farmed smallholdings in return for a variety of dues, goods and days of labour-service—the *Robot*. In the German-Slav provinces the peasant did enjoy a certain freedom of movement and some could even dispose of their holding as they wished, but this did not apply in Hungary, where the power of the Crown was more limited and the peasant was almost entirely at the mercy of the magnate.

In Russia the chief positions of state were the preserve of the nobility and although service in the army, navy, or bureaucracy, which Peter the Great had imposed upon them, was no longer obligatory, there were many families for whom such service had become a traditional function. The centre of peasant life was the village commune, the *mir*. 'Crown peasants', who belonged to the State, paid an *obruk* in kind or in cash for the right to cultivate the land; a few of the privately-owned serfs also paid an *obruk*, but the majority had to render *barshchina*, compulsory labour of about three days a week on their lord's land, for which they had to provide the implements. These *barshchina* serfs depended completely upon their masters, who could flog them, send them into the army or to Siberia with hard labour, use them as gambling stakes or sell them outright. 'Landowners do whatever seems good to them on their estates, except inflict capital punishment; that is forbidden,' wrote Catherine the Great to Diderot. The consequence of such a system was that masters sometimes went in fear of their lives; Dostoevsky's father was killed by one of his own peasants, and later, if ever a landowner—as Tolstoy described in his novel *Resurrection*—attempted to introduce reforms, he was often frustrated by the mistrust of the very people that he was trying to help. 'God, how sad our Russia is,' sighed Pushkin, as Gogol read to him the manuscript of his novel *Dead Souls*. One has only to consider the penal code in Great Britain at this time to realize that harshness was a general feature of European life, yet the social inequalities, which in the west might move reformers to anger, were so enormous in Russia that they could inspire nothing but a sense of despair.

Only on the periphery of the Russian dominions were there any regions free from serfdom. Throughout the period of Swedish colonization the Finnish peasant had farmed his land as a free man and now continued to do so. In the Baltic provinces Tsar Alexander I, shortly after his accession, had proposed the emancipation of the serfs, but the scheme had been acceptable to the landlords mainly because serfdom had been found to be a hindrance to effective capitalist farming, and freedom without land was simply to turn the majority of the peasantry into an agricultural proletariat as dependent as before on their masters.

In the Kingdom of Poland serfdom, which had been abolished in Napoleon's Grand Duchy of Warsaw, was not restored, while on the Caucasian frontier the various Cossack communities, whom Tolstoy depicted in an early novel, were also free and in their capacity as military outposts even enjoyed immunity from taxation.

A second point of difference between east and west is to be seen in the varying levels of economic development, for although the great plain-lands gave eastern Europe a surplus of agricultural produce for external trade, the main commercial advantage lay with the west. In the eighteenth century the British, French, and Dutch with their sea power and overseas possessions had developed a considerable world trade, although their relative positions had changed somewhat during the recent war. By 1815 Great Britain's command of the sea routes was unchallenged and her early industrial revolution had enabled her to treble her exports since 1789; French trade now concentrated more on Europe and the Near East, while in the Netherlands it was the Belgians rather than the Dutch who first seized on the opportunities offered by industrialization.[1]

In Germany the desire for greater economic freedom, which had been one of the motive forces of the French Revolution, had led to a considerable weakening of the guilds within which the labour of the handcraftsman had been organized and protected. In the years immediately following 1815, however, industry in Germany was still too undeveloped to keep up the attack on the regulation of labour, and although guilds were abolished in Nassau in 1819, they had by 1830 been re-established in Hesse-Cassel, Hanover, and Oldenburg and retained some power in Bavaria.

National unity, which still eluded central Europe, greatly aided the commercial development of the states of the west in two other ways. The British and French merchant was free from the hindrance of internal customs boundaries. He had, too, a reasonably uniform monetary system. In 1815 the Bank of France, founded by Napoleon, had at first retained an exclusive right of note issue, although a little later under the restored monarchy this was extended to provincial banks; in 1814 the Netherlands Bank was given a similar monopoly; in Scandinavia inconvertible government notes circulated, while in Great Britain the single gold standard had been established in 1816.

In contrast to this the customs barriers between the thirty-eight

[1] See p. 97.

states of the German Confederation, the twenty-two Swiss cantons and the various kingdoms and duchies in Italy seriously hampered the activity of the merchant in his own country, while making a concerted policy of protection against foreign competition highly problematical. This particularism in central Europe was also reflected in a diversity of monetary systems. Twelve different currencies were in circulation in Switzerland, some restricted to their own canton. Among the states and Free Cities of Germany the silver thaler varied greatly in worth and there were differing relations between gold and silver. In Italy every state had its own currency. Such a confusion provided a roaring trade for the money-changers, but in almost every other respect was disastrous for any profound economic development. Thus the idea of unification that came increasingly to occupy men's thoughts in this part of Europe was to be prompted not simply by nationalist aspiration, but by a growing desire to overcome these economic consequences of particularism.

Finally, the third major difference lay in the confusion of peoples and classes that was to be found in eastern Europe. This is not to suggest that the west had yet attained a homogeneity of nation and state. Regional differences in sentiment and dialect have already been noted in Germany and Italy. Three main languages were in use in Switzerland, while German dialect was common in Alsace, and French in parts of Savoy. Yet, with the exception of the Belgians, whose upper and middle classes spoke French rather than the Flemish and Walloon of the peasantry, class divisions in the lands west of the Elbe and in Denmark did not rest primarily on differences of race or language.[1]

The reason for the contrast east of the Elbe lay in the constant shifting of peoples across the great plain-lands of Europe ever since the decline of the Roman Empire. The movement of the German and Slav tribes westwards, the violent incursions of the Huns in the fifth century, the Magyars in the ninth and the Tartars in the thirteenth, and the great surge of the Ottoman Turks through the Balkans, which by the sixteenth century had brought the frontier of Islam to within seventy miles of Vienna, had all to some extent been balanced by a series of movements eastwards—the Swedish colonization of the south coast of Finland, the conquest of the Baltic provinces by the Teutonic Knights, and the peaceful settlement of German farmers and traders

---

[1] This refers simply to the Continent. The social divisions in Ireland with an upper class of Protestant Anglo-Irish stock were not unlike those to be found in eastern Europe.

across the mountains of Bohemia and over the plains of Poland. Except in the lands immediately to the east of the Elbe this interweaving did not result in any general assimilation, and the consequent stratification of conquerors, immigrant settlers and subject peoples, divided by race and language, created social divisions of a type totally different from those found in western Europe.

The situation within the Habsburg dominions provides the most striking instance of this strange medley. The three dominant classes were of totally different origin—German, Magyar, and Polish. The German element were well established in the Alpine regions, the Tyrol, Austria, and the Sudetenland, where the old Bohemian nobility had become germanized since the battle of White Mountain in 1620. From this German group most of the government bureaucracy were recruited and their hold on the towns was everywhere considerable— even in Budapest the local council carried on its business in German until the 1880s. In Hungary, the great nobility were essentially Magyar, but, speaking French, German, or Italian, remained a caste apart, entrenched in their enormous estates with their town and country palaces, and it was only the gentry who maintained a real contact with the peasants, many of whom were by now magyarized, although less than half the total population of Hungary were actually Magyar-speaking. On the other hand, if one excludes the Slovak, Croat, and Rouman peasantry, the thought of a historic past did give Hungary a greater sense of national unity than existed elsewhere in the Habsburg lands. In Galicia, the Polish ruling class had been left unaffected by their transference to the Habsburgs, their peasantry consisting of Poles, Little Russians, and Roumans.

Below these three dominant groups of German, Magyar, and Pole there remained a mass of subject peasant peoples—Bohemians and Slovaks to the north, Slovenes in Carniola, Croats to the south, and Roumans to the east in Transylvania—and among all these the only hope of personal advancement lay in settling in a nearby town and in acquiring a knowledge of the German language.

Along the south coast of the Baltic the same dovetailing of peoples by classes was equally common. In East Prussia and the Polish provinces of West Prussia the German Junker was overlord of a German and Slavonic peasantry. In the adjoining borderland of the Russian dominions this German upper class did not extend into Lithuania, where in the great days of its independence as a Principality there had been a local aristocracy. Their descendants, however, were by now

Polish-speaking and lived in a style very similar to the Polish nobility, working their estates with Lithuanian, Polish, and White Russian peasantry. Farther up the coast still, the upper class became German again, the Baltic barons, descendants of the Teutonic Knights, using the labour of Estonian and Lettish serfs, while to the north of the Gulf, in Finland, centuries of Swedish rule had established a Swedish-speaking nobility divided by language and origin from the peasantry who were almost entirely Finnish.

East of this borderland social differences were equally marked in the major areas of European Russia. The Russian nobility and many of the gentry had become westernized, spoke French, and divided their time between their town houses in Moscow or St Petersburg and their country residences. Yet although they led a life remote from the serfs on their estates, the differences of language and westernization were in a sense more artificial than in the Russian borderlands and the Habsburg territories, and despite the enormous gap between upper and lower classes, a patriotic fervour could still unite them, as Napoleon had learnt to his cost in 1812.

To the south of Croatia, Hungary, and Russia lay all that part of Europe still under the rule of the Turkish sultan. The Balkans were a maze of different peoples, Macedonians, Bulgars, Greeks, Serbs, Vlachs, and Albanians intensely jealous of each other, and speaking a variety of dialects. There had been no great colonization by the conquerors, although about 150,000 Turks had settled in Greece. Religion was the fundamental point of distinction; the mosques of Islam were to be found in most of the towns of the Balkans, particularly among the Albanians who were very largely Moslem, but the Turkish pashas made no attempt to convert the Christian Slavs and Greeks, mostly of the eastern Orthodox Church, whose religion simply marked them as a subject class, liable to heavy taxation. The main feature of Balkan society was the family or small village headed by its local patriarch, and the only people who had been able to establish a general influence outside their own region were the Greeks; they enjoyed a commercial superiority over all the races of the Ottoman empire and their skill in finance and their knowledge of languages, which was forbidden to Moslems, made them invaluable as tax collectors and local officials in the day-to-day government of Turkish territories in Europe. In Greece itself Greek and Moslem poor alike were harried by a Turco-Greek officialdom; since the beginning of the eighteenth century Greeks had been nominated by the authorities in Constantinople as rulers of the Danubian provinces of Moldavia and Wallachia; the Bulgarian Church was by now under their control, and the Bulgars, who were entirely peasant, had almost as great a hatred for the Greek as they had for the Turk.

Thus, in conclusion, while it is undeniable that the statesmen who devised the new frontiers at the Congress of Vienna paid little attention to national sentiment, it is also clear that any political organization of central and eastern Europe could only be on a non-national basis. The problem for the governments was how long such an assumption would remain valid after the excitement of the Napoleonic interlude.

3

GOVERNMENTS AND CHURCHES

1. The governments of Europe

IT is perfectly understandable that the very thought of the Revolution as it developed after 1789 should be anathema to the sovereigns of Europe; yet some of its ideas, at least, had already found expression in their notions of government long before the National Assembly in France had begun its work. The last half of the eighteenth century had been a period of enlightened despotism in which the monarchs had seriously attempted to introduce striking changes aimed at a greater economic and administrative efficiency and at an improvement in the position of the peasantry. These reforms, imposed from the throne, had come up against a dogged resistance from the upper class, and the strength of this opposition revealed the fundamental paradox of the *ancien régime* that there were considerable limits to the power of the sovereigns. Frederick the Great of Prussia and Catherine II of Russia avoided disaster only because they did not try their nobility too far; in the Empire the more radical policy of Joseph II led to open revolt in Hungary and the Austrian Netherlands, while in France it was the attempt of Louis XVI's government to lay a general land tax on the nobility that ultimately brought about the *révolte nobiliaire* in 1788 and the demand for a summoning of an Estates General, which the privileged Orders believed they could control. By 1815 the sovereigns knew well that they had more to fear than a turbulent aristocracy, who by now clung to them for support, and the effect of the Revolution was naturally to make them far more conservative in their outlook. Yet, at the same time, the practical achievement of the French had confirmed the need for a greater efficiency in mobilizing the general potentiality of their states, and the more intelligent of the rulers had realized the importance of anticipating any outbreak by introducing reform themselves, before it was forced upon them through pressure from below.

This need for change was reflected particularly in all those countries whose governments Napoleon himself had not personally altered. It was in Prussia, after the shock of her military defeats in 1806, that the most radical reforms had taken place. Stein and Hardenberg had carried through a partial emancipation of the peasantry from personal servitude to their landlords;[1] the system of education was remodelled, so that the pupil passed through the primary school and the Gymnasium on to the newly founded University of Berlin, and governmental administration was reorganized with a council of state which included the heads of departments under the presidency of the King. At the same time, Scharnhorst and Gneisenau endeavoured to make the best of Napoleon's decree of 1808 that the Prussian army should be no stronger than 42,000 by introducing a short-service system of conscription, from which the citizen passed into the reserve. In the regular army promotion was to be based rather more on merit, although, within itself, the Officer Corps was to retain that character peculiar to Prussian history, whereby it stood apart from the ordinary institutions of government, and thus enjoyed its own personal relationship to the sovereign. The only concessions to liberal hopes consisted of Stein's municipal law of 1808, which allowed the towns their own elected councils, and, in 1823, the recognition of the provincial assemblies, the *Landtage*, based usually on the old division of Estates. Important though these two types of institution were to be later, however, they still did not constitute an effective check, in 1815, on the central executive of King and bureaucracy.

In Russia, government remained entirely in the hands of the Tsar, and although Alexander, who prided himself on his liberal outlook, had carried through various reforms, they were less sweeping than in Prussia. The administrative colleges established by Peter the Great were turned into eight ministries, each with its departmental head. Torture was abolished, as well as serfdom in the Baltic provinces, and there was an extensive promotion of schools and universities. The principal field for Alexander's liberalism, however, was not in Russia itself, but in the newly acquired territories of Finland and Poland.

In 1809, before the four Estates of the Finnish Diet at Porvoo, Alexander promised to maintain 'the religion and fundamental laws of the land as well as the privileges and rights which each class in the said Grand Duchy in particular and all the inhabitants in general, be their position high or low, have hitherto enjoyed according to the Constitution'. This confirmation of the position that Finland had enjoyed under Swedish rule granted rather less than might be imagined, since, although

[1] See p. 21.

Sweden had been a constitutional monarchy throughout the major part of the eighteenth century, the two *coups d'état* of Gustavus III in 1772 and 1789 had considerably strengthened the powers of the sovereign, and Alexander never actually summoned another Finnish Diet, although he constantly talked about it. Nevertheless, Alexander was determined to reconcile the Finns to his rule. He styled himself Grand Duke of Finland, gave back for inclusion within the Duchy the Karelian districts taken by Peter the Great in 1721, appointed a Swedo-Finn Baron Sprengtporten as his first governor, and established a Finnish Committee at St Petersburg to advise him on questions of administration.

In Poland his liberalism went still further. 'Gentlemen,' he said to the Poles at Vilna on his way back from Paris in 1814, 'yet a little patience, and you will be more than satisfied with me.' The constitution, which Alexander granted as King of Poland in 1816, owed much to the Napoleonic system in the Grand Duchy of Warsaw. Poland was to have complete autonomy with her own budget and an army of 40,000, while Polish was recognized as the sole official language, and the Napoleonic Code, freedom of the press and religious toleration were all guaranteed. The Diet was to consist of an upper House, whose members were chosen for life by the King, and an elective Chamber of Deputies with seventy-seven seats for the lesser nobility and fifty-one for the Third Estate. An electorate of 100,000 out of a population of slightly more than three million was a considerably higher proportion than that which existed in Restoration France and was roughly on a par with the British. In fact, the power of the Diet meant little more than the right of petition, and the government of the country was mainly vested in an executive council under the direction of a viceroy appointed by the King. Nevertheless, the Polish constitution was in many ways a remarkable concession, and although Alexander later fell out with the Diet, the only major grievance still outstanding among the Poles in 1815 was Russia's retention of the lands that she had taken in the partition of 1772.

In Denmark the King's power had been absolute ever since 1661, and in 1815 Frederick VI could still rule without the hindrance of any parliamentary institution. In contrast to this, the deposition of Gustavus IV of Sweden in 1809 had been followed by the summoning of the Estates of the *Riksdag*, who offered the crown to Gustavus's uncle as Charles XIII, on condition that they should be able to exercise the constitutional check on the King's actions, of which they had been deprived by Gustavus III's Act of Union and Security in 1789. The Estates retained their influence on the succession, for, on the death of Charles XIII's heir in 1810, they eventually elected as Crown Prince Marshal Bernadotte, who had impressed Swedish envoys favourably while he had been acting on Napoleon's behalf in Denmark. Bernadotte soon adopted the interests of his new country, joined with the Russians in 1812 against his former master, and was chiefly responsible for the taking of Norway in 1814. This was not merely a blow for Denmark; the Norwegians themselves, who had just established their own Parliament, the *Storting*, and elected a Danish prince as their king, had no wish to be absorbed by Sweden and insisted that their constitution should be safeguarded before they would accept a personal union under the Swedish crown.

Of all the governments of Europe there was one essential characteristic that marked the Austrian empire off from the others. Prussia and Russia both included alien peoples within their frontiers, but these were mostly on the periphery of their domains, whose core remained essentially Prussian or Russian. The remarkable feature of the Austrian empire was that it lacked a basic national characteristic. The origin of the Habsburg fortunes had lain in the Alpine lands, but the acquisition of the crowns of Bohemia and Hungary, Galicia, and the Italian provinces of Lombardy and Venetia had given their possessions the character of a vast family estate, in which the separate regions simply owed a personal allegiance to the Emperor. The principal problem in the management of so unwieldy an estate was the precise sharing of government between Vienna and the provinces. Decentralization, which such a diversity of territories seemed to demand, might mean weakness in the face of powerful neighbours, and, in an age of rising nationalism, even disintegration. Instead, centralization, which Maria Theresa and her son Joseph II had attempted to impose in the last half of the eighteenth century, had resulted in overburdening the bureaucracy at Vienna to such an extent that administration moved at a snail's pace. Beneath the Council of State, the *Staatsrat*, there existed a confusion of departments and committees whose responsibilities constantly overlapped and whose work was seldom governed by a clear line of policy. The ministers were the personal servants of the Emperor, appointed and dismissed as he wished. 'He overwhelms me with kindness,' said Metternich of his master in 1829, 'and gives me his confidence, but he does this because I follow the direction which he lays down for me. If I had the misfortune to leave this prescribed path, Prince Metternich would not be Minister of Foreign Affairs for twenty-four hours longer.' At least Metternich, who gained the official title of Chancellor in 1821, knew that he was responsible for foreign policy; the duties of the other ministers varied from month to month and they could never know that the Emperor had not gone behind their backs to deal directly with a civil servant. 'Administration', commented Metternich's colleague Hartig, 'has taken the place of government.' Thus the cumbersome system of centralization not merely had the effect of reducing provincial assemblies to a state of powerless make-belief; it was utterly frustrating for the local officials. 'The want of some all-controlling hand', wrote the British Consul-General in Lombardy in a dispatch to Palmerston in January 1848, 'is most severely felt and is admitted by the local authorities who bitterly complain of the delays of the Government at Vienna from whence they can get no answer to their repeated Representations.'

Only in Hungary was there some check to centralization. The Magyars had always insisted that they recognized the Habsburg as their King, never as the Emperor. This was not a nationalist movement in the nineteenth-century sense. The Hungarian Diet, at which Latin was used as the only acceptable *lingua franca* among so many different languages, was dominated by the nobility and used as a bulwark against Habsburg interference which threatened to undermine their privileges, and even when Francis refused to summon a Diet between 1811 and 1825, provincial government remained in the hands of *comitats* of local nobility which controlled the raising of taxes and recruits for the army.

Other countries could later come to terms with nationalism or liberalism; for Austria no such compromise was possible without jeopardizing her very existence. 'My realm resembles a worm-eaten house,' said the Emperor Francis I to a Russian diplomat. 'If one part is removed, one can never tell how much will fall.' Yet, although the coincidence of differences of class with those of language and origin was to lend impetus to nationalist aspirations, it did also supply the key to Habsburg survival. If any of the dominant groups—Germans, Magyars or Poles—were to present the government with a demand for political autonomy or independence, they seldom had the support of the peasantry, who felt that Habsburg rule, however remote, might to some extent hold their masters in check. On the other hand, any national movement among the subject peoples naturally implied a challenge to the order of society as unpalatable to the German,

Magyar, and Polish landowners as it was to the Habsburgs themselves. 'My peoples are strangers,' commented Francis I. 'Out of their dislike order is born, and of their hatred universal peace.' This realization did at least give the monarchy a policy for self-defence; a final solution to the problem of its inheritance it was never to find. The struggle to do so lies behind much of its history in the later years of the nineteenth century, and its ultimate failure was to bring down a whole European society in the collapse of the Central Powers at the end of the first World War in 1918.

In the lands surrounding France, which had come more directly under Napoleonic forms of rule, the forces of restoration were determined to root out the revolutionary principle. It is true that, in 1815, the Fundamental Law of the Kingdom of the United Netherlands included a States General of two Chambers, one of which was a representative assembly, but this was actually little more than a façade of constitutional government. The Belgians had never accepted it when it had been presented to them for ratification, and despite the fact that the seat of government alternated every year between Brussels and The Hague, they never forgot their resentment at being incorporated with the Dutch[1]. In any case, the new system did not include ministerial responsibility, and the deputies had only a limited control over finance. 'I can reign without ministers,' stated King William I; 'it is I alone who govern and I alone am responsible.'

In Germany, although the general effect of Napoleon's simplification of the map was preserved, the ghost of the Holy Roman Empire still seemed to haunt Europe in the form of the German Confederation devised at the Congress of Vienna. The frontiers of the Confederation, with its thirty-eight states, excluded a part of the Habsburg and Prussian territories and included a non-German element among rulers and populations; Bohemia and Moravia lay within its borders; the King of the Netherlands was Grand Duke of Luxemburg; the personal union of the British and Hanoverian crowns was to last until 1837; and Holstein was governed by the King of Denmark in his capacity as Duke of Slesvig-Holstein.

The most that could be said for the German Confederation was that it had defined a frontier within which the individual states, in time of war, would be unable to sign separate treaties of peace. Beyond this, as with most confederations, the *Bundestag*, the Federal Diet sitting at Frankfurt under an Austrian president, was no more than a collection

[1] See p. 80.

of ambassadors, each concerned to safeguard the sovereignty of his own state. The system of voting in a plenary session was such that a combination of Prussia, Austria and the four major kingdoms of Bavaria, Württemberg, Saxony, and Hanover could destroy any chance of the two-thirds majority needed to carry a measure, while for a change in the constitution itself a unanimous vote was required. The Federal Act, drawn up at the Congress, had authorized the *Bundestag* to organize a military force, as well as some common economic system, but the local jealousies to which the whole system gave full play made it impossible for any executive machinery to emerge at all. The German Confederation represented no more than an arrangement whereby those areas of Germany which lay beyond the frontiers of Prussia and Austria might be sufficiently organized to be drawn within Austria's sphere of influence without becoming a positive political force of their own. Two possible dangers threatened to undermine this scheme—discord between Austria and Prussia over supremacy in Germany, and German nationalism demanding the creation of a stronger central government, which might curtail the sovereignty of the individual states. In fact, particularism in 1815 was strong enough to check either of these dangers. The conservative element in the Prussian government had no wish to become further involved in Germany, for fear of Prussia losing her identity, and consequently had no objection to Austria holding the presidency of the *Bundestag*, while against German nationalism Metternich could rely on the princes, who were determined to preserve their own sovereign power.

Within each of the German states themselves the Federal Act had declared that *eine landständische Verfassung* should be set up. The problem here was that *Verfassung* had a wider connotation than the word 'constitution' in English; it could simply mean a series of governmental edicts of purely executive significance, while *landständische* referred to a gathering of various Estates drawn from different strata of society and often antagonistic to each other—the same difficulties as hampered the full development of the Swedish *Riksdag* and the Hungarian Diet. Thus, many of the thirty-eight governments were virtually absolutist. It would, however, be wrong to apply this judgement to the whole of Germany. A parliamentary tradition of a sort had survived in Württemberg, Saxony, and the Rhine Duchies where the Estates had continued to exercise some control over taxation and the local military establishment; and it was partly owing to this tradition that, in the years following 1815, the princes of the larger states in the south-west, Bavaria, Baden, and Württemberg, governed within the framework of two-chamber assemblies. Yet, while it would be wrong to picture a scene of absolute authoritarianism in every state in Germany, there could be no denying the general weakness of parliamentary life, even where it existed. An upper House of local aristocracy had little contact with a lower House, from whom they regarded themselves as socially apart, while the lower House, elected through an extremely narrow franchise, often consisted of many of the same individuals who composed the local bureaucracy. The existence of such bodies might help to keep alive the idea of constitutional government; they were hardly likely in themselves to constitute a real bulwark of resistance to the prince.

In Switzerland a similar settlement was to emerge. For centuries the Swiss cantons had each pursued their independent policies, only loosely bound by a variety of local agreements, the French-speaking area round the Lake of Geneva and the Italian-speaking communities of the Ticino Valley being generally in a state of subjection to the German-speaking cantons to the north. In 1798 French intervention had cut through all forms of cantonal autonomy and imposed a centralized system which, although it made all individuals equal before the law and was nominally based on an elective principle, really placed all power in the hands of an executive directory. Napoleon's Act of Mediation in 1803 abolished this rigid centralization, which was historically alien to the spirit of Swiss institutions, and established in its place a federal system which restored many of the old sovereign rights of the cantons, while preserving a general Swiss citizenship with freedom of settlement and equality among the cantons.

The fall of Napoleon brought two different groups to the fore. The conservatives wished for a complete restoration of the situation before 1798. Berne was particularly anxious to re-establish her rule over Vaud and Argau, the Alpine cantons wished to return to their old democratic autonomy, and the patrician families of the large towns wanted to regain their privileged position of local authority. The second group, liberals who had enjoyed social freedom under the Napoleonic system and feared the loss of the cantons' new equality of status, pinned their hopes to the maintenance of a strong federal authority, and the conflict between the two became so fierce that it was only the threat of Allied intervention, together with a good deal of negotiation in the Swiss committee at Vienna, that prevented the outbreak of civil war.

The Federal Pact was eventually drawn up in September 1815. The most that the liberals were able to achieve was the preservation of the existing cantons on a basis of equality, including the three additions of Geneva, Valais, and Neuchâtel. Thus, since the French- and Italian-speaking regions were not to be reduced once more to the level of subject cantons, French and Italian remained on a par with German as official languages. Apart from this, the conservatives gained all that they had wanted. In matters of coinage, posts, local customs duties, and education the cantons were to enjoy complete autonomy. They could pursue their own political arrangements, including private military and economic agreements with other countries, provided that these did not affect the Confederation. The recognition of a general Swiss citizenship and of freedom of worship was withdrawn, although Roman Catholic religious houses were to be guaranteed. The central government, the Diet, was correspondingly weak, merely a collection of representatives, each voting on instructions from his canton. There was not even a federal capital, Zürich, Berne, and Lucerne acting in turn as the *Vorort*, the canton representing the Confederation. Unlike the German Confederation, however, the Swiss did have a Federal army, over 32,000 strong, in order to be able to defend their neutrality. In this way, virtually free from any over-riding authority, the patrician families of Berne, Basle, Lucerne, Solothurn, and Fribourg regained their old authority, while even in the cantons which drew up new constitutions the franchise was so restricted by qualifications of property and education that government was mostly in the hands of a local oligarchy. The liberal elements, although defeated, kept up the struggle in the towns, but, as in Germany, they knew that the crux of the problem lay in the creation of a stronger central government which would be in a position to impose their solution on the whole of Switzerland.

Thus, in Germany and Switzerland, only a battered fragment of the Napoleonic régime survived the general restoration. Still less remained in Italy and Spain. Nowhere in Italy was there even the pretence of a constitutional government under the restored sovereigns, who, ironically, had been welcomed back by their subjects. Victor Emmanuel, ruling his enlarged dominions from Turin, the Habsburg princes in the central duchies, Pius VII, the gentle Pope whom Napoleon had carried off into captivity, Ferdinand of Naples who promised a constitution in order to outdo Murat and then suppressed it, all ruled through a handful of ministers who were responsible only to them, while in the north Lombardy and Venetia lay under the control of Austrian governors. In fact, with the exception of Naples, this despotism was reasonably mild, particularly in Tuscany, where the Grand Duke restored the code of his Habsburg predecessor, Leopold, but in the last analysis the strength of most of these governments rested not on the support of their subjects, but on the Austrian emperor, firmly established in Lombardy and Venetia, and with a private agreement whereby he could call for troops from Naples and Tuscany.

In Spain the transformation was as complete. Joseph Bonaparte had at least approved a draft constitution, although it was never put into effect, and the Spanish *Cortes*, summoned by the leaders of the resistance to Napoleon's armies, had produced a constitution in 1812 at Cadiz, which would have established a parliamentary monarchy. Yet, when Wellington's forces had reached the Pyrenees and King Ferdinand VII had returned from a fairly comfortable retirement in France, his first action was to annul the entire constitution by royal decree, after which he proceeded to rule as he wished with all the apparatus of censorship and secret police.

In contrast to this whole-hearted restoration of an earlier system in the territories whose governments Napoleon had completely remodelled, Louis XVIII issued to his people, on 4 June 1814, a Charter whose purpose was to convince all classes that the work of the Revolution would not be undone. The inviolability of property reassured those who had bought their lands since the Revolution, and the guaranteeing of the public debt naturally suited the investing class; there was to be liberty of the press, provided that there was no infringement of the 'lois qui doivent réprimer les abus de cette liberté', and all Frenchmen were to enjoy equality before the law and freedom from arbitrary arrest. The pattern of government came closer to the English system than any of the French constitutions drawn up since 1789. Although the King alone had the right to propose new laws, they had to be passed by a Chamber of hereditary peers and a Chamber of Deputies, one-fifth of whose seats were to come up for election every year. The strength of this lower House, whose size was first put at 258 seats and, after Waterloo, increased to 402, lay in its right to sanction all taxation for one year at a time. The deputies, one-half of whom had to be resident in the *département* that they represented, were drawn from a relatively small class who paid 1,000 francs in direct annual taxation, and the franchise itself was restricted to men of not less than thirty years of age who paid 300 francs a year—an electorate of approximately 100,000 out of a total population of about 29 million.

Within this framework the King had reasonable freedom to govern. As supreme head of the executive he had the right to choose his ministers from within or outside the Chambers and they remained individually his personal servants without any form of Cabinet solidarity. The centralized Napoleonic system of Prefects in the provinces survived the Restoration, and here the King's right to appoint all public officials gave him considerable control over local administration. Certain clauses, too, in the Charter were open to wide interpretation, as, for example, over the Press laws or over the King's power to issue ordinances 'nécessaires pour l'exécution des lois et la sûreté de l'État'. Naturally home or foreign policy might always be criticized in the Chambers, but the royal government had a little room in which to manoeuvre, since there was no limit to the number of peers that the King could create, and his right to dissolve the Chamber of Deputies (provided that a new one was elected within three months) did give him a chance to appeal to the electorate.

On the whole, the Charter represented a serious attempt to heal the wounds of France and to establish a reasonable balance of government, but inevitably it left much to the good sense of the reigning sovereign and to the temper of the upper classes. It was always open to amendment by constitutional means; thus conscription, which it declared abolished, was restored in 1818, and the continual alterations in electoral procedure reflected the various changes in the political outlook of the Chamber of Deputies during the next ten years.[1] The French by now had had ample experience that a written constitution could never be foolproof, but the Charter was at least the best compromise that could satisfy the conditions of 1814, and the average Frenchman could feel that, in France at least, the turmoil of the preceding twenty-five years had not been entirely in vain.

2. Religion

For the Papacy the fall of Napoleon restored rather less than it did for the secular governments. In Spain, Italy, and Bavaria its powers were almost entirely re-established, but the old prince bishoprics in Germany were not recreated, and in Austria Francis I retained a good many of the restrictions imposed on the Church by Joseph II in the 1780s. Louis XVIII's Charter of 1814, had declared that 'la religion

[1] See pp. 58, 63.

catholique, apostolique et romaine, est la religion d'État', but the French clergy were far from regaining the position of a privileged Estate. They continued to be largely dependent upon a salary from the State, and although they were allowed to develop institutions of secondary education parallel to the state system, education still remained technically the monopoly of Napoleon's University of France.

The question of the precise relation of a Catholic sovereign to his own clergy was of long standing in Europe, and the recent trials of the Church at the hands of secular power in France, Italy, and Germany were to give renewed force to the Ultramontane movement, causing the clergy and laity to turn to Rome for practical as well as spiritual leadership. 'Point de christianisme sans le catholicisme,' wrote Joseph de Maistre, 'point de catholicisme sans le pape, point de pape sans la suprématie qui lui appartient.' In France Ultramontanism appealed mostly to the lower clergy as a means of escape from the authority of the bishops; in Germany the movement spread rapidly, particularly in Bavaria where King Ludwig I[1] was determined that Munich should become the cultural and political centre of German Catholicism. But, however much they might differ over the precise relation of the secular and spiritual power, most Catholics believed profoundly that they should work together in a closely knit harmony; the notion of Throne and Altar in some form governed their political thinking. In regions where Catholics were under Protestant rule, no such ideal was immediately within reach, and it was in Belgium and Ireland that the struggle for Catholic independence was later to encourage the rise of a movement of Liberal Catholicism aiming at a divorce between the secular and the spiritual authority.

In Protestant countries the counterpart to Throne and Altar was the doctrine of Church and State. In Great Britain, where there were large numbers of Nonconformists, Anglicans technically held a monopoly of all national and local positions of authority. 'Westminster Abbey', as a contemporary wrote, 'is part of the constitution.' In the State Churches of Scandinavia the monopoly was less irksome, since all but a tiny fraction of the population of Denmark, Sweden, and Norway were Lutheran. In Prussia many of the more conservative saw the union of Church and State as a bulwark against unbelief and supported Frederick William III's advocacy of a common liturgy among all Protestant Churches under the aegis of the State, although one group

[1] See Genealogical table p. 480.

under Schleiermacher strongly resisted the tendency of the Prussian bureaucracy to control the bishops and pastors.

In Russia there was no debate at all over the problem, since the Orthodox Church had long existed within the framework of the State, although there were by now, as a result of recent acquisitions, a variety of religious minorities on the fringe of her territories—Lutheran Finns and Balts, Catholic Poles, Uniate Ruthenians, who observed Orthodox rites, but were obedient to the Pope, and, in the regions of the Black Sea and the Caspian, pockets of Moslem and Buddhist Tartars. It was outside the frontiers of Russia that the political significance of the Eastern Church was most marked. The Orthodox Christian Slavs under the rule of the Turk in the Balkans naturally looked towards the Tsar as their protector, and throughout the nineteenth century Russia was able to use this situation as a means of weakening the Turkish hold. Among the Balkan Slavs as a whole, however, the religious background created considerable division, since the Albanians had largely accepted Islam, the Bulgars resented the hold of the Greeks over their Church, and the gulf between Catholic Croats under Habsburg rule and the Orthodox Serbs was later to make the creation of any large South Slav state extremely difficult.

In contrast to the laxity and secularism of the eighteenth century the early half of the nineteenth does mark an important period of religious revival. This naturally reawakened the old mistrust between the Christian sects, which was to become bitter over the question of national systems of education, and the re-establishing of the Jesuit Order by Pope Pius VII in 1814, followed by their rapid infiltration into most Catholic areas, tended to exacerbate the latent antagonism. In the main, however, this revival did not upset the general tendency towards a toleration of dissenting minorities. The 680,000 Huguenots in France had full rights of citizenship and their clergy even received a salary from the State. Prussia treated her newly acquired Roman Catholic subjects in the Rhineland with reasonable tact, as did Bavaria her Protestant subjects in Franconia. In the southern Netherlands, now under a predominantly Dutch government, the Roman Catholic clergy had complete religious freedom, and in Russia Alexander I went so far as to include a Roman Catholic archbishop and a leader of the Lutheran congregations in the Holy Synod of the Orthodox Church, and even toyed with the idea of a union of the Eastern and Roman Churches.

This ideal of mutual toleration did not extend, however, to the

Jews, who at this time numbered about 10 million in Europe. The reasons for the antagonism from which they had always suffered were partly economic, partly racial—economic, because the laws which forbade them to hold land had caused them to concentrate on commercial enterprise in the towns, at which they were remarkably skilful—racial, because their own religious exclusiveness had prevented their assimilation in the countries where they settled. In the west their numbers were small, and after 1815 they were allowed, in France and the Netherlands, to retain the full rights of citizenship that Napoleon had granted them. In central Europe anti-Semitism was much fiercer. The Catholic states, and particularly the Free Cities of the German Confederation, had strongly opposed the plea which Metternich and Hardenberg had made at the Congress of Vienna for a continuation of the toleration which they had enjoyed under Napoleon. In the end, the matter had had to be left to the Diet at Frankfurt, where no ruling was ever given, and thus, in many towns in Germany, the Jews were once more banished to the ghetto. In the Swiss cantons and the Italian states they lost their civic rights, and although they gained a few concessions in Hungary, none were made in Bohemia and Galicia, while Vienna remained a closed city to them, except for two hundred 'tolerated' families. The Jews were most numerous in Poland; here the hatred was particularly strong, and indeed, throughout the whole of central and eastern Europe, the temporary disorders during successive periods of revolutionary upheaval usually provided an opportunity for a *pogrom* of the local Jewish population.

For the Jews themselves the question of assimilation was as difficult as it was for the Christians who resented their presence. Lacking a country of their own, harried by constant antagonism and frequent persecution, they clung to their religion, their customs, and their use of Yiddish in everyday life as the only means of maintaining their identity. At the end of the eighteenth century the massacres in the Ukraine had given rise to a new conservative sect, the Hassidim, demanding complete isolation from the Christians around them, and the majority of Jews at this time shared this outlook. There were, however, some signs of a desire for assimilation. In Germany Mendelssohn, the friend of Lessing, and, in Russia, Levinsohn each worked towards this end; in Alsace the Jewish population became mainly French-speaking. Some of the more ambitious, such as the poet Heine or the Socialist Lassalle, renounced their Jewish faith—Disraeli and Karl Marx were both the sons of converts—but, on the whole, conversions to Christianity among the Jews were rare—less than 200,000 in the whole of the century. In any case, conversion was a factor of minor importance. The roots of European anti-Semitism lay far deeper than any mere religious antagonism, and the restrictions imposed on Jews were not simply the result of a governmental tyranny; they reflected the general sense of aversion among the non-Jewish peoples themselves and in a century which was to bring greater power to the masses, anti-Semitism was to become a factor of increasing importance throughout the Continent.

4

THE OUTLOOK FOR THE FUTURE

1. Diplomatic considerations

IT was not unnatural that for many decades after the Napoleonic war France should be regarded as the greatest potential threat to the peace of Europe. Her military prowess was obvious, and, with the exception of Russia, her population[1] was still the largest of any state on the Continent. These fears over a possible revival of French acquisitiveness were to have a marked effect on the course of later events. They played their part in the emergence of Belgium as an independent state; they were an essential feature in the story of Italian unification; Bismarck was to make skilful use of them in the three wars with which he created the German Empire, and even after 1870, Great Britain, whose naval bases were planned mainly on the assumption of French hostility, continued to regard France as her major opponent in the colonial field until the end of the century.

The other source of tension lay in Russia. The great circumference of her land frontier through central Asia naturally created a sense of uneasiness among the British with their vast interests in India, and after the building of the Trans-Siberian railway in the 1890s the Far East was to become a new area of rivalry among the great Powers. In 1815, however, it was Russia's expansion westwards that awoke the gravest concern. In Scandinavia her long duel with Sweden throughout the eighteenth century had culminated in her annexation of Finland in 1808. As it transpired, this was to be the end of the struggle, for although the Swedes had accepted Bernadotte as their Crown Prince in the hope that the presence of a Napoleonic marshal might enable them to recover their former position, Bernadotte himself, seeing the futility of any further attempt, had persuaded them to accept Norway as adequate compensation for the loss of Finland; from this time on, so long as some form of balance existed among the Continental Powers, Sweden could reckon to avoid being dragged into the major crises of the nineteenth and twentieth centuries.

[1] See Appendix 7, p. 488.

But if the dispute in the extreme north appeared now to be closed, a new issue had already arisen in the south-east of Europe, where the gradual decline of Turkish rule in the Balkans was to offer a vast field for Russian expansion. The ultimate fate of these Turkish territories in Europe constituted the Eastern Question and particularly concerned two of the Powers—Great Britain and Austria.

For the British the principal aim was to ensure that the Russian Black Sea fleet might not enter the eastern Mediterranean. It had been established by the Anglo-Turkish agreement of 1809 that the Dardanelles should be open to merchant vessels and closed to warships in time of peace, and open to Turkey's friends and closed to her enemies in time of war, and since the absorption of Balkan territories by Russia might eventually rob Turkey of her freedom of action in maintaining this agreement, the policy most likely to be followed by the British government was one of supporting Turkey against Russian encroachment. In this, however, the British were hampered by two other factors —first, the weakness of Turkish domestic government which British ambassadors at Constantinople in the early nineteenth century were constantly endeavouring to reform, and, second, the growing nationalism among the Balkan peoples who, as Slavs and Orthodox Christians, naturally looked to Russia for assistance in throwing off the Turkish yoke. Whenever these factors combined to make the loss of some part of the Turkish dominions inevitable, the only alternative for the British, in order to avoid Russian gains, was the recognition of independent national states in the Balkans under a European guarantee. Over the creation of the kingdom of Greece in 1830, this second course was adopted in agreement with Russia; over the creation of Rumania out of the Danubian provinces of Moldavia and Wallachia it followed her defeat in the Crimean War. Thus Great Britain's support of Turkey was only incidental to her suspicion of Russia; she would not necessarily preserve Turkey's possessions in the Balkans, and when the emergence of the German Empire in 1871 was followed by the gradual succumbing of Constantinople to German and Austrian influence, Great Britain was to swing round to friendship and eventually wartime alliance with Russia, to whom, by 1915, she was even prepared to offer the control of the Straits.

For the Habsburgs any kind of change in the Balkans was bound to be for the worse. They naturally objected to further Russian expansion in their direction; a partition of the Balkans with Russia had little appeal, since it would only add to the complications of Habsburg domestic government which were already considerable; nor did the carving of independent states out of Turkey-in-Europe offer any solution to the problem, since these would become a focal point for the Slav nationalist groups within the Habsburg dominions. The only hope for Austria was the maintenance of the *status quo*, as Metternich's secretary Gentz realized, when he wrote in 1815: 'the end of the Turkish monarchy could be survived by the Austrian for but a short time.'

In fact, Russian policy did not aim at immediate acquisition. The sensitiveness of Great Britain and Austria would make any absorption of Turkish territory an international question which might result in the establishment of greater western interests in the Balkans; there was also the possibility that a smaller Turkey, once shorn of her unwieldy European possessions, might be capable of internal reform and hence become a stronger state on Russia's borders. Thus, although the eventual partition of Turkey-in-Europe remained a talking point in diplomatic circles throughout the nineteenth century, none of the Powers seriously desired it and Russian plans were based rather on a gradual extension of influence throughout the whole of the existing territories of Turkey under the guise of a protectorate over all Orthodox Christians in the Balkans. Besides, other interests which they had in common tied Austria, Prussia, and Russia to a policy of preserving the *status quo*; they were all three autocratic monarchies, mistrustful of western liberalism, and the territories of Poland, which they had earlier shared out among themselves, gave them a considerable stake in the maintenance of existing frontiers.

These various hopes and fears were reflected in two agreements signed in the autumn of 1815. The Holy Alliance drawn up by Tsar Alexander was a personal document to be signed by the sovereigns of Russia, Prussia, and Austria, promising mutual support in the spirit of Christian brotherhood. Despite the scornful amusement with which Metternich and Gentz treated the whole idea, Frederick William and Francis saw no objection to signing an agreement which was too general and high-minded to involve them in any precise commitment. Alexander may simply have seen the scheme as a further guarantee of the existing order, although it is possible that when he suggested that it should be offered to all the other Christian sovereigns in Europe, he may have had some plan at the back of his mind for isolating Turkey, with whom Russia had been at war at the time of Napoleon's invasion in 1812. Whatever Alexander's motives, Castlereagh fought shy of it

and was able to plead the madness of George III as an excuse for standing aside. Nothing very much ever came of the Holy Alliance, but its
name was to stand as a general term for the autocratic governments of
Prussia, Russia, and Austria until the middle of the century.

The second agreement was a more orthodox diplomatic document.
By the Treaty of 20 November 1815 Great Britain, Austria, Prussia,
and Russia renewed the Quadruple Alliance of 1814 for twenty years
as a means of safeguarding themselves against any revival of French
aggression. Castlereagh was careful to insist that the terms should be
limited to an agreement on collective action against any Bonapartist
restoration or any attempted revision of the frontiers of France as
established by the second Treaty of Paris. Once again, Alexander would
have liked to include a general guarantee of all frontiers and governmental regimes throughout Europe, but Castlereagh had no intention
of binding British foreign policy to the requirements of the autocratic
Powers. Article VI of the treaty did contain the famous proposal for
periodic congresses of the signatory Powers 'for the purposes of con-
sulting upon their common interests', but although this was an interesting innovation, the system of congresses, in Castlereagh's view,
was really no more than a convenient method whereby the great
Powers might carry on the normal processes of diplomacy. The autocratic Powers, however, certainly saw them as a possible way of
exercising a *general* supervision and of co-ordinating the suppression of
revolutionary activity anywhere on the Continent, and this divergence
of aim was soon to weaken the united front that the Powers had hoped
to preserve, and, by 1822, had led to Great Britain's withdrawal.

2. *Liberal and authoritarian notions of government*

Political theories are as diverse as the personalities of the men who
produce them and it would be rash to trace the steady development of
a line of doctrine through a whole series of thinkers. It is, however,
possible to outline very generally two attitudes towards the reform of
government which derive from writers before the French Revolution
and whose effects have continued until the present day. Both were
strongly influenced by the new empirical methods of the eighteenth-
century scientists, yet the lines of thought that they suggest were to
run in two entirely different directions.

The first lies at the root of the movements that were to adopt the
course of constitutional government, liberalism, and humanitarian

legislation. The emergence of a limited monarchy in England helped to inspire the theories of John Locke, in which government existed for the sake of a society of property-owning individuals, who were therefore entitled to resist any infringement of their natural rights. The interest that the English pattern of life had held for Voltaire and Montesquieu had been translated in eighteenth-century France into terms of growing criticism of governmental despotism, economic monopolies, and social privilege. Montesquieu's *L'Esprit des Lois*, for example, was strongly influenced by English ideas and his notion whereby despotism might be avoided by a balance of powers between legislature, executive, and judiciary may be clearly recognized in the American and the French Revolutionary constitutions. Naturally, after they had crossed the Channel, these ideas underwent a certain transformation. The rights of the English, rooted in Common Law, were based on a long historical tradition and the events of 1688 never implied any great social revolution. On the Continent, these traditional links had mostly perished and French political thought before the Revolution was a highly literary philosophy, devised by an intelligentsia who lacked all experience in government, and, since it concentrated on the definition of abstract principles, tended to be far more dogmatic, challenging the social as well as the political order.

This first theme is particularly noticeable in the revolutionary mutterings of the early half of the nineteenth century. Within the wide bracket of that general term 'the middle classes', industrialists, merchants, and professional men represented the most active form of discontent, desirous of political power and economic advantage. The degree of subjection against which they protested, the width of the gap between upper and lower bourgeois and the extent to which they concerned themselves with nationalism, all varied from one region of Europe to another; yet, in the outbreaks of 1830 and 1848 there is a striking similarity of demand among these groups—the preservation of monarchy within a constitutional framework, a legislative Assembly elected on a franchise based on a property qualification, freedom of the press, the abolition of social privilege by birth and the removal of internal restrictions on trade and industry—in short, the replacement of absolutism and a privileged aristocracy by a constitutional monarchy ruling in the interests of a business and professional class—the situation established momentarily in France in 1791, and, to some extent, restored in 1814.

The aspirations of this middle-class liberalism naturally represented a growing threat to the established government and society of Europe and in their initial attacks on the old order in the first half of the century liberal and democrat shared a common objective. Like their sovereigns, however, the business and professional classes looked with loathing on the prospect of revolutionary Jacobinism, a republicanism of the masses in which political democracy implied a social equality with all its economic consequences. 'Sir, your levellers wish to level down as far as themselves,' Dr Johnson once remarked, 'but they cannot bear levelling up to themselves.' The same thought is implicit in a statement made by a German liberal, David Hansemann, in 1830. 'By majority . . . we are never to understand one determined by counting heads, but rather the true strength of the nation, which, while it is also to have no interest other than that of the numerical majority, yet differs essentially from it, since by its better education, greater insight and its property, it has a larger stake in the maintenance of a stable, vigorous and good government.' Thus, whenever revolutionary action seemed to be on the point of success, the latent antagonism between the two groups flared up, causing the liberals to retreat towards the old order as a bulwark against extreme social revolution.

The second theme that may be discerned in the eighteenth-century theorists points to a new form of authoritarianism, although the character of the arguments that led up to it varied enormously. For Helvetius the evidence of the senses suggested that pleasure was good and pain was bad, but since men were not sufficiently wise to see how to attain the one and to avoid the other, the aim of government must be to establish through the work of a few enlightened legislators a series of incentives and deterrents by which men would be guided towards the happiest possible life. In contrast to this, Rousseau's ideas were based on a mystical conception of the community. For him the fundamental dilemma lay in the fact that although a man ideally should be completely free, he had to live in a society, which must automatically mean the curtailing of that complete freedom. The solution that Rousseau conceived was a society of naturally good men for whom the expression of their own personal liberty lay in spontaneous surrender to the whole community. Only through this fusing of individual wills in a general will could a society of genuinely free men be established; yet although men should want to attain this state, only a handful actually realized that they did want it. This was the link with Helvetius, for in Rousseau's view it was the duty of those few to lead the rest. Thus Helvetius believed that men must be forced to be happy, Rousseau that they must be forced to be free. Both postulated rule by a small group who knew what was best for all.

Jacobinism and the rule of Napoleon were both instances of this second theme of authoritarianism in the general interest, but it was not really until the second half of the nineteenth century, when the struggle between the classes had become intensified, that it took on a practical form. Nationalists struggling to achieve unification or independence, bourgeois fearful of Socialism, Socialists seeking to transform the whole economic basis of society, all tended to move towards the surrender of freedom to a small group who claimed the right to impose their own solutions on the whole community. This process was to be aided by two further developments of the nineteenth century. First, the startling increase in technical means opened up possibilities of control by the State which was to give the dictatorships of the twentieth century a unique character in the history of the world, and which in all forms of government hastened the general assumptions of collectivism. Second, the need to capture the support of the masses in a new industrial age caused both left and right wings to make increasing use of the doctrine of popular sovereignty. Yet the paradox of this creed was that it accelerated the growth of a simplified form of government under one man, the cult of personality. Mistrust of social extremists caused liberals to fall back on the Second Empire of Napoleon III and the German Reich of Bismarck's creation, just as the fear of Communism in the twentieth century opened the door to the Nazi and Fascist dictatorships; among the Socialists themselves a new highly disciplined organization was to take the place of romantic aspiration, and the Russian revolution of November 1917, which established the dictatorship of the Bolshevik party, was simply another facet of that same argument propounded by Helvetius and Rousseau a hundred and fifty years before.

3. The Romantic movement and its influence on nationalism

Although the calculations of diplomacy and the ambitions of social groups naturally vary according to the circumstances of each epoch, they remain common as general factors to most periods of history. Their distinguishing feature in the early nineteenth century, however, lies in the fact that they became charged with a new intensity through the great emotional storm of the Romantic movement whose repercussions were felt in every side of life and in every region of Europe.

c

It is in the arts that the significance of this extraordinary transformation may be most simply illustrated. The classicism of the seventeenth and eighteenth centuries had established an absolute ideal of beauty only to be realized through obedience to certain rules of balance and harmony, by which the individual promptings of the artist were to be restrained and disciplined. The central theme of the Romantic movement was that it broke violently with these rules and in their place concentrated purely on imaginative insight and emotional impact; thus, in his Preface to the *Lyrical Ballads*, Wordsworth claimed that the purpose of the poems was 'to illustrate the manner in which our feelings and ideas are associated in a state of excitement'. The movement was already clearly established before the end of the eighteenth century—particularly in Germany during the 1770s and 1780s, the period known later as *Sturm und Drang*—and was to gather overwhelming force throughout the first half of the nineteenth. The delight in nature, so marked in the poems of Wordsworth and Goethe, was to be the inspiration of Lamartine, Mörike, Lenau, and Eichendorff; the great outpouring of love poetry of Keats, Shelley, Byron, and Heine; the flamboyance of gesture in the paintings of Géricault and Delacroix; the vast orchestration of Beethoven and Schubert; and the lyrical compositions of Schumann, Liszt, and Chopin, were all later manifestations of this new mood of emotionalism that took possession of every art.

Romanticism, however, went far deeper than any experimenting with new technical forms. The concentration on personal feelings led to a yearning for the unattainable that caused men to look not only within themselves, but also backward in time. Goethe's *Götz von Berlichingen* and Schiller's *Wallenstein* and *Wilhelm Tell* were not simply new types of play, free from the classical rules of the three unities; they heralded that nostalgia for Europe's past from which the historical novels of Walter Scott and Alexandre Dumas were soon to find such a response. In the academic world there awoke an interest in the study of local *patois*—old Provençal and Breton—and Herder's *Volkslieder*, the poems of Robert Burns, the Grimm Brothers' fairy tales, and the great Nordic sagas of the immemorial past appeared as glimpses of some great treasury of regional cultures and folklore. For centuries the deserted monuments of earlier ages had been left untended and often, like the Colosseum at Rome, the shattered Parthenon at Athens or the dissolved monasteries in England, had been plundered by local inhabitants who saw them merely as a quarry of easily available building material. To the tourist of the twentieth century their preservation may seem natural enough; yet it was the Romantic movement, with its passion for ruin, that first caused men to see them with new eyes, stimulating the beginning of serious archaeological exploration in Italy and Greece and turning the English to express a growing love of the medieval in the architecture of the Gothic revival.

In the wider sphere of everyday life whole generations of young people became imbued with the romantic despair of Goethe's *Werther*, a Byronic melancholy in revolt against the orderly assumptions of the eighteenth century. Naturally, in so personal a movement this revolt took a variety of forms. The Romantic might praise Rousseau's 'noble savage', the primitive man uncorrupted by the artificiality of civilization; he might applaud the advent of the French Revolution—'Bliss was it in that dawn to be alive'—or the rise of Napoleon as one of history's great men; or he might succumb to the mystique of royalty, anointed with holy oil and tracing its lineage back through the dim ages. He might proclaim a fierce atheism, or he might retreat from the rationalism of the eighteenth century to a deep reverence for the ritual splendour and historic power of Rome. But whatever the attitude, its expression had always a rich exaggeration, at its best creating a new cultural epoch in Europe, at its worst, morbid, introspective, dallying with drugs and thoughts of suicide.

The most notable consequence of Romanticism was the great stimulus that it gave to the new emotions of nationalism. In France this meant simply an ardent patriotism inspired by the revolutionary ideal and the extraordinary achievement of Napoleon's armies. Although by 1814 the French were glad of peace, the sense of anti-climax among the younger generation in the years that followed is a constant theme in de Vigny's *Servitude et grandeur militaires*, de Musset's *Confession d'un enfant du siècle*, and the early poems of Victor Hugo, and the strength of latent Bonapartism rested not so much on the desire for a new political programme, as on the vague mystical attraction of the Napoleonic legend, a hunger for *la gloire*.

But it was in the regions where national unification had not yet been attained that Romanticism, with its interest in folklore and its sense of a historic past, suggested a new basis for establishing the collective identity of peoples. 'Der natürlichste Staat ist also *ein* Volk mit *einem* Nationalcharakter,'[1] wrote Herder in his *Ideen zur Philosophie*

---

[1] 'The most natural kind of State is therefore a single people with a single national character.'

der Geschichte. The true nation, in fact, was derived from the tribal group knit together by a blood relationship, and this tie, in the opinion of Schlegel and Fichte, was to be recognized in the possession of a common language. 'Whenever a separate language is found,' declared Fichte in his *Reden an die deutsche Nation,* 'there is also a separate nation which has the right to manage its affairs independently and to rule itself.' The doctrine of German cultural and historical unity preached by Schelling at Munich, Dahlmann at Göttingen, Strauss at Tübingen, and Ranke, Fichte, and Savigny at Berlin gave the Universities the leadership of the movement, but the enthusiasm ran far beyond the bounds of the lecture room. In Germany it found practical expression in the war of liberation of 1813; in Italy the new academic interest in the classical past was to blend with the aspirations of extreme Italian nationalists who were later to see Rome as the only possible capital for a united Italy; farther east, although Slovenes, Ruthenians, Letts, and Estonians had been subject too long for the movement to make any immediate appeal, it was soon to have its effect on Bohemians, Poles, Magyars, and Greeks, for whom an awareness of their past was bound to excite thoughts of independence.

The full implications of this nationalist emotion were not to be apparent until the 1840s. Most of the early academic enthusiasts genuinely believed that only good could come of the emergence of a collective identity of national groups. *Frisch, fromm, fröhlich und frei*[1] ran the watchword of the *Burschenschaften,* the student groups organized by Jahn—quasi-religious rather than militant—and it was ironical that much of the revival of the old Slavonic languages was the work of German scholars. Similarly, in Italy the *Carbonari,* a network of secret societies motivated by a hatred of Bonapartist rule, stood for the highest moral ideals, and the complicated ritual of their Lodges, reminiscent of the Free Masonry from which they had sprung, was bound up with the expression of vaguely Christian and democratic hopes for the complete purification of society. Yet it is possible to see in these origins the contradictions that were later to play so great a part in the history of nineteenth- and twentieth-century Europe. The idealists overlooked the competing claims that would be made, when the mystique of *das Volk* came to be translated into terms of nation states with clearly defined frontiers, and when existing differences of language were found no longer to coincide with old historic boun-

[1] 'Brisk, pious, joyous, free.'

daries; more particularly, the overlapping of peoples divided by class and language was to add a sterner note of social revolution to the rhapsody of national self-determination. But, whatever its dangers, the spirit of nationalism, once it was awakened, was too strong ever to be finally denied. 'Art and science are universal,' said Goethe after the battle of Leipzig, 'and in view of these the bonds of nationality disappear. But the consolation they afford is but hollow comfort and cannot replace the proud consciousness of belonging to a great, strong, feared and respected nation.'

II

THE DEFENCE OF THE VIENNA SETTLEMENT
1815–48

5

THE CONSERVATIVE ERA 1815-30

1. The consolidation of the settlement 1815-20

'DEPUIS longtemps l'Europe a pris pour moi la valeur d'une patrie.' This remark of Metternich's to the Duke of Wellington in 1815 throws a profound light on the character of the man who was to attempt to order the destiny of Europe for the next thirty-three years. By upbringing Metternich was a Rhinelander, educated at the Universities of Strasbourg and Mainz; by profession a diplomat, serving the Emperor at Dresden, Berlin, and Paris before becoming Minister of Foreign Affairs in 1809; by birth an aristocrat for whom the *ancien régime* of the eighteenth century meant the very essence of civilization. In many ways there could have been no more suitable representative of the Habsburg empire, resting, as it did, on an utterly non-national structure of classes and peoples. It is understandable that the picture which has been preserved of him is of a great despot; a conservative in a time of irresistible change is hardly likely to be popular. Yet the picture is untrue, for Metternich was neither great, nor a despot. He was a charming cultivated *seigneur*, fond of the lighter side of society, confessing to Madame de Lieven, with whom he carried on a correspondence over the years, that 'la vie d'un ministre est une vie affreuse'. He was conceited, but seldom malevolent. Although suspicious of change, he was fully aware of the need for reform within the system of Habsburg government at Vienna. 'Je passe ma vie à étayer un édifice vermoulu,' he said, but, lacking the brilliance of a Talleyrand, he had to rely on hard work and a constant attention to detail. 'Il prend l'intrigue pour la politique,' Napoleon had scoffed at him; yet the charge was a little unfair, since Vienna imposed not only the objects, but also the methods of government.

In his Political Testament of 1820 the positive aims which he defined suggest an essentially eighteenth-century ideal of balance and harmony. He believed that the only consequence of liberalism would be to shatter an ordered society, after which liberalism itself would

56

succumb to the forces of demagogy—an odd source for an anticipation of Marxist doctrine! He hated, above all, 'the presumptuous man', the term with which he summed up the ambitious bourgeois and the discontented nationalist, and since these two forces directly challenged the old European pattern of society and government, the defence that he planned had also to be on a European scale; 'union between monarchs is the basis of the policy which must be followed to save society from total ruin'. Hence his determination that Austria stand guard over the Vienna settlement in Germany at Frankfurt, and in Italy at Milan; hence his suspicion of the vague liberal whims of Alexander I and Frederick William III.

Certainly, by the end of 1815, Metternich might rest content with the situation in Europe. Napoleon was far away in St Helena; it was already clear that the Diet of the German Confederation at Frankfurt was sufficiently weak to be a mockery of any scheme for more positive unification, and military alliances with Tuscany and Naples had consolidated the control of Vienna over Italy.

France naturally remained suspect, particularly when Louis XVIII, on his second restoration, placed Talleyrand at the head of a government which included Fouché as Minister of Police. 'Le vice appuyé sur le bras du crime' ran Chateaubriand's biting comment in his *Mémoires*, and although Louis may have owed much to Talleyrand's efforts at Vienna and to Fouché's at Paris after Waterloo, royalist opinion was utterly shocked and the appointments did not last long. The narrowness of the franchise and the fury of the royalists after the perils of the Hundred Days resulted in an electoral victory for the Ultras, the extreme conservatives, so overwhelming that it took even Louis XVIII by surprise. *La Chambre introuvable*—out of this world— he called it, and the banishment of Fouché and the retirement of Talleyrand followed almost at once.

The irony of the situation was that Louis was far more shrewd than many of his supporters and during the next year was greatly embarrassed by their ardour, which might well have provoked a Bonapartist or Jacobin reaction. Accordingly, he selected his new ministers from more moderate elements who, together with the Chamber of Peers, which still included many officials of the Empire, might be able to tone down the zeal of the Ultras in the Chamber of Deputies. His principal minister was the Duke de Richelieu, an *émigré* who had already proved his ability in the service of the Tsar as governor of Odessa. 'He is certainly the Frenchman who is best acquainted with

C 2

the Crimea,' sneered Talleyrand at his successor, but, with the inevitably sterner second Treaty of Paris still to be ratified, Talleyrand may not have been entirely sorry to go. In any case, Richelieu proved to be a most happy choice; a bizarre figure with his untidy dress and Russian boots, he was the very man that Louis needed at this time—an aristocrat of whom it could not be said that, unlike many of his contemporaries, he had forgotten nothing and learnt nothing.

For the following twelve months the King and his ministers tried to ride out the storm of the Ultra reaction. Eighteen Bonapartist generals were court-martialled and shot—including Marshal Ney, who was tried before the Chamber of Peers—and if La Bourdonnaye, an Ultra in the Chamber of Deputies, had had his way, there would have been many more. In the provinces an unofficial White Terror claiming some 250 victims raged unchecked; new press laws, passed in November 1815, made liberal newspapers increasingly liable to prosecution, and in December *cours prévôtales* were re-established in the *départements*, summary courts whose death sentences were to be carried out within twenty-four hours. The government did what it could to restrain this Ultra fury, but in May 1816 an unsuccessful Bonapartist outbreak at Grenoble was sufficient warning that the passion for revenge was endangering the whole of the Restoration settlement, and when the British and Russian governments had expressed their concern at the Allied conference of ambassadors, Louis decided, in September 1816, to exercise his right to dissolve the Chamber and to hold a general election.

Apart from the Ultras, there were two principal groups from whom Richelieu might hope for a more moderate Chamber—the Independents, liberal bourgeois suspicious of the old nobility and hankering after the tricolour and the glory of the Empire; and a centre party, the Constitutionalists under Royer Collard and Guizot, Louis' main hope for a balance between extremes. The general election of the autumn of 1816 gave the King and his ministers precisely the moderately royalist assembly that they wanted; the pendulum, however, continued to swing and with each subsequent annual election of one-fifth of the seats the liberal element grew larger, until by 1819 they held 90 out of the 258 seats to which Louis had reduced the Chamber in 1816.

This increase, reflecting to some extent the reaction against the Ultras, was also partly explained by changes brought about with the electoral laws of 1817 and 1818. At first, after 1815, elections had been in two stages, whereby the electors had only exercised an indirect vote at the level of the *arrondissement*, a method which was naturally popular with the wealthier landowning class, since it allowed them to exercise considerable influence. The new procedure, in 1817, reduced the age level of electors from thirty to twenty-five and enabled them to meet in the chief town of the *département*, where they voted directly for all the deputies of that *département*. Thus the working of the electoral system was itself a weapon in the struggle between the political groups, perhaps the greatest weakness of constitutional government under the Charter.

At the time, however, the fortunes of the restored French monarchy were aided by a remarkable national recovery after the collapse of 1814. The finances were placed on a more stable footing than ever before, enabling France to pay off the indemnity imposed by the second Treaty of Paris and thus to rid herself of the army of occupation. Gouvion-Saint-Cyr's conscription law of 1818 added greatly to the forces at the King's disposal to resist any threat of a Bonapartist *coup*, and the Allies, anxious to strengthen the position of the restored monarchy, were well aware that it would gain greatly in prestige from the withdrawal of the Allied army. The final agreement over financial settlement and military evacuation was reached at the Congress of Aix-la-Chapelle in 1818, the first of those meetings envisaged in the Treaty of November 1815. Richelieu was hoping for something more—the inclusion of France in the counsels of the great Powers—and through his Russian connections looked for support from Tsar Alexander who still dreamed of some general political guarantee of all existing régimes throughout Europe. This possibility of Franco-Russian collaboration either within or outside a European concert confronted Great Britain and Austria with a dilemma which resulted in a compromise—the inclusion of France in all future Congresses, balanced by a renewal of the Quadruple Alliance as a safeguard against a re-awakening of French ambitions. 'It is owing to the Emperor of Russia,' wrote Richelieu to Louis XVIII, 'and to his all-powerful intervention that we have attained the end which for the last four weeks seemed always to elude us,' and, on the whole, he could return to Paris well pleased.

Ironically, however, his own position at home had by now deteriorated. He feared that the balance in the Chamber of Deputies was swinging too far in the direction of the liberals. 'Let us think no more of liberal concessions,' he said to Decazes, the Minister of Police. 'We have made enough, and much good they have done us.' But Decazes, together with several others of the ministers, did not agree, and since he was a firm favourite of Louis XVIII, Richelieu, tiring of the situation, decided at the end of 1818 to resign.

The greater liberalism of Decazes, who took his place as Minister of the Interior, was marked principally by the introduction of a new press law. Under Richelieu control of the press had continued to be exercised by the government, even after the dissolution of *la Chambre introuvable*—an untidy system whereby editors had to satisfy both the police and the censorship committee—mainly because Richelieu had feared that an unbridled press might suggest to the Allies that France was not yet to be trusted. The new law of 1819 abolished the police control so that, in future, editors could only be charged with a breach of the penal code, in which case they were assured of a trial by jury. This new freedom of the press, however, remained a matter of interest principally for the middle classes, since a stamp tax, combined with a system of annual subscription, made newspapers too expensive a luxury for the masses.

In Germany Metternich could exercise greater authority, and the maintenance of the restored German princes was less dependent on reconciling the left-wing groups. Yet even here there were tendencies that made him uneasy. Limited constitutions were granted by the rulers in Bavaria and Baden in 1818, and in Württemberg in 1819. In Prussia, although the hopes for a constitutional assembly were dashed, the reform of the educational system, including the creation of a new University at Bonn in the recently acquired Rhineland, seemed unwise to Metternich, since German University professors and students were the driving force behind the criticism of the Vienna settlement. The student societies, the *Burschenschaften*, had spread rapidly from Jena to most of the other Universities, and the violence of their nationalist enthusiasm was most marked at a great festival at Eisenach in 1817, technically in celebration of the tercentenary of Luther's ninety-five theses against Papal Indulgences, but significantly held on the fourth anniversary of the battle of Leipzig.

In fact, few of the German liberals trusted Prussia at this time, regarding her as the home of reaction. Prussia, however, was now to lead the way in a totally different type of movement which challenged the decentralization and consequent weakness of Germany. It has been seen that one of the principal difficulties of the German business man was the continued existence of internal customs barriers between the states,[1] a situation which the Diet at Frankfurt had done nothing to change. Within the Prussian territories themselves, straggling across the north of central Europe, sixty-seven different tariffs hampered the operations of internal trade and made any concerted policy of protection against British manufacturers virtually impossible. 'All states favour home industries by tariffs,' complained a petition of seventy Rhineland manufacturers to Frederick William III in 1818; 'Germany alone fails to protect her children.' A positive answer to their plea was promulgated by the King that same year. Maassen's Prussian Tariff Reform Law, much influenced by the writings of Adam Smith, swept away the variety of internal customs duties within Prussia and established a single unified tariff to be charged at the frontiers. Prussia was not yet sufficiently strong economically to be able to engage in a tariff war, and in any case high tariffs would only have meant a continuation of the smuggling which the law was partly designed to prevent. Import duties were consequently kept low—raw materials to enter free, an average of 10% on manufactured goods, and of 20% on 'colonial' goods such as sugar and tea. Naturally hardships were suffered by small interests when deprived of the protection afforded by local customs, and the industrialists benefited less than the farmers, since the lowness of the tariff on manufactured goods still left them exposed to British competition, but the general advantage derived from the *Zollverein* (Customs Union) was ultimately to be enormous. It was the essential preliminary to economic advance and the process once begun was to affect the whole of Germany. Between 1819 and 1826 the tiny non-Prussian enclaves within Prussian territory, burdened with the expenses of customs collection, found it more attractive to enter the scheme. Then, Prussia's geographical position commanding most of the north–south trade routes enabled her to place heavy taxes on all goods in transit, and through this pressure Hesse-Darmstadt agreed, in 1828, to join the Prussian Union, while in the south and the centre two other Customs Unions were formed in retaliation.

In Italy, at least, Metternich might feel that he could rely on the intentions of the rulers. He was less sure of eastern Europe. In Russia Alexander was in touch with a group of liberal officers who had formed a 'Society of Salvation' in 1817 to debate the possibility of constitutional government and vast land reforms including the emancipation of the serfs. At Aix-la-Chapelle, in 1818, he had shown a keen desire to include France within the Concert of Europe, and in the same year,

[1] See p. 23.

at Warsaw, he had repeated his promises of liberal rule before the Polish Diet. This was naturally very worrying. Metternich constantly lectured princes and ministers on the dangers of unchecked liberalism, and it was poor consolation when, within a couple of years, his worst fears appeared to be confirmed by the first of a series of outbreaks of violence throughout Europe.

2. The first resistance to the settlement

In 1819 a German writer in the service of the Tsar, Kotzebue, was murdered by a theological student at Mannheim. In January 1820 Spanish liberals and army officers combined, under Rafael Riego, to raise revolt in Cadiz and forced King Ferdinand VII to re-establish the constitution of 1812. In February Louis XVIII's nephew, the Duke de Berri, the main hope for the Bourbon succession,[1] was stabbed to death by a lunatic outside the Opera in Paris. In July, in the kingdom of Naples, General Pepe, placing himself at the head of forces raised originally to deal with the local brigands and including a great number of the *Carbonari*,[2] marched on the capital and extracted from King Ferdinand a constitution on the lines of the Spanish one of 1812. Within a month revolt had spread to Sicily, where Pepe was able to retain control only with difficulty. In August an army rising at Lisbon and Oporto against the despotism of the regency council brought a demand for a constitution and for the return of King John VI of Portugal from Brazil. In March 1821 a mutiny of the army in Piedmont was followed by the abdication of Victor Emmanuel in favour of his brother Charles Felix and the appointment as Regent of the young Charles Albert,[3] who had been second in the line of succession and was known to have liberal sympathies. In the same month revolt broke out in the Balkan dominions of the Turks. The Greeks constantly looked to Russia for support and when, in March, the Turks were engaged in putting down a local vassal, Ali, pasha of Janina, a Greek aide-de-camp of the Tsar, Alexander Ypsilanti, took the opportunity to cross the Pruth into Moldavia, occupied Jassy, and called on the inhabitants to rise against their Turkish overlords.

Except in Greece, none of these movements achieved anything lasting and the general outcome was to be a new swing towards

[1] See Genealogical table, p. 478.
[2] See p. 52.
[3] See Genealogical table, p. 483.

conservatism. After the murder of Kotzebue, Metternich summoned a meeting of ministers of the main German principalities at Karlsbad, where he drew up a series of decrees to be imposed throughout the whole of Germany; the press was to be strictly censored, the *Burschenschaften*, as well as all other forms of political gathering, were prohibited, and police officials were appointed to watch over activities at the Universities.

In France the immediate alarm subsided a little when it appeared that the murder of the Duke de Berri was not part of any larger conspiracy, and since the Duchess was now known to be expecting a child, *l'enfant du miracle*, the Bourbon succession might still be secure. The Ultras, however, did not intend to lose such a golden opportunity to castigate the recent liberalism of the moderates, and public opinion forced Louis to dismiss the Decazes ministry. He was able to recall Richelieu, but the new government was inevitably strongly Ultra in character. In the spring of 1820 censorship of the press was restored, and a new electoral law was passed in favour of the upper class. Groups of *arrondissements* were turned into single-member constituencies, where local landed interests might once again make themselves felt more effectively, and, in addition, that quarter of the electorate which paid the highest taxes in each *département* was to enjoy a second vote for the purpose of returning a further 172 deputies to the Chamber. The growing bitterness of feeling between Ultras and liberals soon made it impossible for Richelieu to pursue a central course of action, and on his resignation at the end of 1821 the appointment of the Duke de Villèle increased the strength of the Ultras still more. A few outbreaks in 1822 were easily put down and at the beginning of 1824 the government decided to reinforce its position by holding a general election. The outcome of this appeared decisive. The new electoral procedure, combined with every form of pressure exercised by the Prefects on electors in the provinces, resulted in the return of a Chamber in which the liberals were reduced to fifteen seats—*la Chambre retrouvée*, as the Ultras called it in delight—and Villèle had no difficulty in consolidating this success with a further amendment to the Charter, abolishing the annual elections of one-fifth and prolonging the life of the existing Chamber for seven years.

Meanwhile, the risings in Italy and Spain had presented a more difficult problem, since they were the work of military groups who had momentarily forced the sovereigns to yield to their demands. It was Alexander who suggested a new Congress, which met at Troppau in

October 1820, in order to discuss the means of intervention. Austria and Prussia were only too willing to attend, but, in France, Richelieu, wishing to restrain the ardour of the Ultras, would only agree to send two representatives to act as observers. In Great Britain Castlereagh, who was as suspicious as ever of the intentions that might lie behind general schemes of intervention, had already in May circulated a State paper declaring that his government could never be party to a guarantee of existing régimes in every state in Europe, and emphasizing that the Treaty of November 1815 was concerned only to prevent a Bonapartist restoration in France. Thus the British, too, only sent an observer, and when the three Powers of the Holy Alliance at Troppau published a manifesto claiming the right to intervene when revolutions outside their frontiers appeared to threaten their own internal order, the breach between British policy and the Continent was finally apparent.

In fact, the Powers at Troppau had not been immediately in agreement. Alexander had confirmed Metternich's mistrust of him by first suggesting a liberal constitution for the kingdom of Naples. This may simply have been a scheme for hindering Austria's freedom of action in Italy, but soon the mutiny of Alexander's own old regiment, the Semenovski, and the resistance that he had just encountered from the Polish Diet enabled Metternich's reproachful persuasion to win the Tsar round. The Congress adjourned to Laibach in Carniola, at the beginning of 1821, where Ferdinand of Naples had been invited to meet them. The recently elected Neapolitan chamber had foolishly agreed to his going on the understanding that he would speak on behalf of the maintenance of constitutional government in Naples, but Ferdinand naturally had other plans. Metternich now knew that he could intervene without fear of Russian objections, and in February an army of Croats and Hungarians marched south through Italy, dispersed Pepe's forces in a few hours of fighting and restored Ferdinand as an absolute monarch.

The army mutiny in Piedmont and the abdication of Victor Emmanuel in March 1821 was followed by almost exactly the same pattern of events. The new king, Charles Felix, who was in Modena at the time, had no intention of submitting to the demands for a constitution and appealed to Austria for help. In Turin Charles Albert, who may have been involved in the initial stages of the outbreak, did eventually agree to the granting of a constitution, but he was not prepared to come out openly in revolt, and when Austrian troops entered Piedmont, the rising was rapidly put down, and in September Charles Felix entered Turin to take possession of his kingdom.

The ease with which these two risings in Italy had been crushed is explained principally by the weakness of the rebels. Within each state they had suffered from divided leadership, and, contrary to Metternich's fears of a general conspiracy, there had been no co-ordination of activity between Naples and Piedmont; neither had been thinking in terms of an Italian movement of liberation. The Neapolitan rising had certainly been a popular one; there had been no time lost in the summoning of a constitutional Chamber and if the Neapolitans had not panicked, the resistance to the Austrian forces, which were not large, might have been far more effective. The rising in Piedmont had made little appeal to the masses; no arrangements for a constitutional Chamber ever materialized and the refusal of Charles Felix to compromise doomed the movement from the start. The fundamental reason for the failures, however, lay not in Italy, but in the attitude of the great Powers to Austrian intervention. Alexander had acquiesced in this, and the natural conservatism of the Bourbon government in France, anxious to prove its freedom from any taint of revolution, had ruled out any possibility of French resistance to Austria.

The attitude of France was to be of particular significance in the suppression of the Spanish rising. During the two years following the surrender of Ferdinand VII to the demand for a constitution the liberals had theoretically made considerable headway. Spain had been divided into fifty-two provinces to facilitate the centralizing of administration and the Inquisition had been suppressed. Their lack of unity, however, was clearly demonstrated by the fierce argument in the *Cortes* between moderates and extremists, and the highly conservative attitude of the peasantry, mistrustful of the anti-clericalism of the liberals, gave Ferdinand the hope of popular support in any attempt to restore absolutism. Accordingly, in 1822, Ferdinand made his appeal for assistance to the Powers.

The question of intervention in Spain was the principal subject for discussion at the Congress which met at Verona in October 1822. Who was to intervene? What would be the international repercussions? Metternich was already fully occupied with Germany and Italy and had little liking for Alexander's scheme to send an army across Europe for the purpose. France seemed the obvious choice. Ultra feeling strongly supported such a project and although Villèle, who had by now replaced Richelieu, was doubtful about the financial and military difficulties involved, the French delegates, Chateaubriand and Mathieu de Montmorency, fell in with the general opinion at the Congress that the French army should cross the Pyrenees in support of Ferdinand. The Duke of Wellington, attending the congress in the role of an observer, protested strongly. The State paper of 1820 had already enunciated the British dislike of the Powers' claim to the right to guarantee the governments of 1815 and Castlereagh had accepted the intervention in Italy only as an individual action on Austria's part within her own sphere of influence. The thought of a French army once more invading Spain was a very different proposition; ever since the war of the Spanish succession at the beginning of the eighteenth century the fear that a weakened Spain might fall completely under the influence of France had constantly recurred, and Canning, who became British Foreign Secretary on Castlereagh's suicide in 1822, was even more outspoken in his objections.

Villèle decided to act. Chateaubriand was appointed Foreign Minister and in 1823 a French army, under the command of the Duke d'Angoulême, crossed the Pyrenees. In Great Britain Canning obtained an increase in the personnel of the navy, insisted that there should be no permanent occupation of Spain, no advance into Portugal, nor any interference with the Spanish American colonies now in a state of revolt, and expressed his hope in the Commons that the new régime in Spain would survive the struggle. He was speedily disappointed. This time, in contrast to Napoleon's attempt to establish his brother Joseph on the Spanish throne, the French army acting on behalf of the legitimate sovereign had the support of the local population. The Spanish liberal forces were swept aside. With the capture of the Trocadero fortress at Cadiz absolute rule under Ferdinand was entirely re-established in Spain, and the only consolation for Canning was an agreement with Polignac, the French ambassador at London, whereby France renounced any intention of restoring to Spain her South American colonies.[1]

The victories of the Holy Alliance over all these liberal outbursts were followed by a period of stern repression. In Spain, Ferdinand's revenge was so ferocious that Louis XVIII and Alexander I had to persuade him to desist. In Germany the Karlsbad decrees imposed a close surveillance by the police on all student activity and the powers of the constitutional Chambers in the southern states were seriously curtailed. In Prussia, the long-promised constitution was finally shelved,

[1] See p. 68.

except for the establishment of eight provincial Estates (*Landtage*) in 1823. Pressure was brought to bear on the Swiss cantons, and liberals who had taken refuge there were hounded out. In Italy Metternich went still further, establishing large garrisons at Naples, Alessandria, Ancona, and Florence and covering the whole country with a network of police spies. In Piedmont, the only hope for the liberals lay in the fact that Charles Albert was the heir to the childless Charles Felix. For this reason Charles Felix had demanded at the Congress of Verona that Charles Albert should be excluded from the succession. Metternich, however, had merely suggested that he should make an official denial of any further interest in liberalism, to which Charles Felix added the stipulation that he should serve with the French forces in Spain, reckoning that even if he was not killed in action, he would at least be discredited in the eyes of the liberals.

In Russia, too, Alexander in his last years was moving towards a greater mistrust of liberal experiments and after 1820 adopted a far more conservative attitude towards the press and the Universities. In 1822 he forbade the existence of all secret societies, although this did not prevent a revival, a little later, in the form of a Northern and a Southern Society. Alexander died in December 1825 to be succeeded by his younger brother Nicholas I; the new Tsar, in contrast to his predecessor, was a straightforward soldierly character, quite out of sympathy with liberal movements, and, owing to a peculiar episode at the beginning of his reign, was able to carry out a complete suppression of such activities.

The rising of the Decembrists was due to a momentary confusion over the succession. In 1822 Alexander's brother Constantine, Viceroy of Poland, had renounced his right to the throne. Nicholas, the third brother, much younger than the other two, had, however, been left unaware of the official details of the change and on learning of Alexander's death he proclaimed Constantine emperor at St Petersburg, at the same time as Constantine in Warsaw was proclaiming Nicholas— a show of deference highly unusual in the history of the Tsars. The members of the Northern and Southern Societies at once decided to bring forward the date of their intended uprising in order to seize the opportunity offered by a succession apparently in doubt, and when the troops were eventually summoned to St Petersburg to take the oath of allegiance to Nicholas, who by now knew that he was the rightful heir, the conspirators raised the cry for Constantine and a constitution. They had, however, had too little time to prepare the ground;

many of the soldiers imagined that Constitution must be the wife of Constantine and within a few hours Nicholas had gained control of the situation. Five of the leaders were hanged, many others were sentenced to forced labour or to exile in Siberia, and although the Decembrist movement created the martyrs whose memory was to inspire many later movements in Russia, this liberal failure at the beginning of Nicholas's long reign was a powerful reinforcement for the principles of the Holy Alliance.

Not all the revolts, however, ended in disaster for the liberals. The tie between Spain and Portugal and their colonies in America had been seriously weakened ever since the Napoleonic era, and in 1819 Spain had already cut her losses to the extent of selling to the United States all her territories along the North American coast east of the Mississippi. But in 1821 revolt flared up in her remaining colonies in Central and South America, and in the following year Monroe, the President of the United States, gave official recognition to the new governments of La Plata, Chile, Peru, Columbia, and Mexico. The agreement between Polignac and Canning in October 1823 made it clear that, despite the restoration of absolutism in Spain, Europe would do nothing to help her in the New World. In December, in his annual message to Congress, President Monroe stated the famous doctrine that, while there would be no American interference in European politics nor with any existing colonies, the United States would not tolerate any future colonization or interference by European Powers in the American continents. Monroe's statement aroused little public excitement at the time; yet it did have an immediate effect on British policy. Canning had been holding back from recognizing the new South American republics, but the protective interest shown in them by the United States now forced his hand and at the end of 1824, to avoid their succumbing completely to North American influence, he consented to their recognition.

In Portugal the story was long and confused. In 1821 King John VI, in response to the army rising, agreed to return from Brazil, but it was his two sons who thereafter dictated the course of events. In 1822, the elder son, Dom Pedro, who had been left behind as Regent in Rio de Janeiro, announced the independence of Brazil under his rule, while in Portugal the victory of the French in Spain encouraged the younger son, Dom Miguel, to enter Lisbon in force in June 1823 and to suppress the constitution. On the death of King John in 1826, Dom Pedro, in

Brazil, renounced his own claim in favour of his daughter Donna Maria, who was eight years of age, suggesting a Papal dispensation that would allow her to marry her uncle Dom Miguel. He also promised a restoration of the constitution under his daughter, and when civil war seemed about to break out with Dom Miguel, whose absolutist inclinations were strongly supported by Ferdinand of Spain, the constitutionalist party appealed to Canning. The British Foreign Secretary enjoyed posing as the champion of liberalism, and invoking the traditional British interest in Portugal, he dispatched 4,000 troops with a fleet to Lisbon to ensure that there should be no Spanish intervention on behalf of Dom Miguel.[1]

The turn of events in Portugal and the New World had largely depended on geography and the support of Great Britain and the United States. The Greek question was to be a matter of rather greater delicacy. The original insurrection of Ypsilanti came to nothing; the Moldavians showed little enthusiasm to join him and after the failure of his appeal to the Tsar at Laibach Ypsilanti was forced to flee to Austria in June 1821. His attempt was none the less significant, since it had encouraged the Greeks to the south to rise in a great national movement against the Turks and a savage war broke out in the Morea and soon spread to the Aegean islands. In 1822 a declaration of independence was published by an assembly of Greeks, and a constitution adopted. Moslems and Christians slaughtered each other in great numbers, but it was the sufferings of the Greeks that were seized on by the romantics of western Europe, who, filled with hazy ideas of classical Greece, saw Byron's death at Missolonghi as a martyrdom in a great cause.

The governments were less emotional. For them the major consideration was whether Russia would take advantage of the situation to march in to the aid of the Greeks. Metternich worked hard to persuade Alexander that the principles of the Holy Alliance demanded that the Turks should be allowed to put down the rebels. 'Nothing appeared more in my interests, in those of my peoples, in accordance with the opinion of my country than a religious war against Turkey,' said Alexander afterwards, 'but I thought I observed the revolutionary mark in the troubles of the Peloponnesus', and Metternich could congratulate himself for the moment on having averted Russian intervention on the side of the rebels.

Before long, however, further developments had made some form of intervention inescapable. In 1824, when the Greeks appeared to have

[1] For later events in Portugal see p. 89.

gained the upper hand, the Sultan appealed to his powerful vassal, Mehemet Ali, pasha of Egypt, who sent his son Ibrahim to subdue Crete. Early in the next year Egyptian forces established themselves at Navarino on the mainland of Greece prior to a reduction of the whole of the Morea, where the Greeks were now beginning to fall out among themselves. These events were followed by the death of Tsar Alexander in December 1825. His successor Nicholas might lack the liberal instincts that had made Alexander's policies so hard to gauge, but he had every intention of making full use of the Greek revolt to embarrass the Sultan, as was at once made clear by a Russian ultimatum to Turkey in March 1826.

This intervention by the Egyptians and the Russians convinced the Powers that they could no longer hold back in the hope of a return to the *status quo* before 1821. Mehemet Ali's rule had already set Egypt on the road to becoming a well-organized state, and his plan to follow up his son Ibrahim's victories with an Egyptian colonization of the Morea would create a new Power in the eastern Mediterranean of far greater consequence than Turkey. Alternatively, Russian intervention on the side of the Greeks against the Egyptians could only result in the creation of a Greek state virtually under the suzerainty of the Tsar.

For the other Powers there were two possible courses of action—either to ally with Turkey and Mehemet Ali against Russia, or to act alongside Russia and to impose a compromise settlement over Greek independence through concerted pressure. In London Canning chose the second of these. This was certainly in accord with his own liberal instincts and with public opinion, but the risks involved were considerable, since the expulsion of the Egyptians from the Morea might well open the way to Russian penetration. The Duke of Wellington went at once to St Petersburg and in April 1826 Tsar Nicholas, to avoid the possibility of a European league forming against Russia, signed an agreement providing for joint mediation in establishing Greece as a tributary dependency of Turkey with a reasonable degree of autonomy and freedom of conscience. The Sultan, alarmed at this development, hastily signed the Convention of Akerman with Russia, settling a recent dispute over the government of the Turkish provinces of Moldavia and Wallachia, but still failed to shift the Tsar from his determination to intervene in Greece. In Paris certain groups favoured the idea of an Egyptian colonization of the Morea as a more reliable bulwark against Russia than a semi-independent Greek state, but the French government, suspicious of any Anglo-Russian agreement, signed the Treaty of London in July 1827, associating itself fully with the new scheme for forceful mediation on behalf of the Greeks.

Canning never lived to see the dramatic consequences of his policy. His death in August 1827 was an immense relief to Metternich, and the Sultan felt sufficiently encouraged to reject the demand for an armistice in Greece, presented by the three Powers. British and French squadrons were already in the eastern Mediterranean and in September they ordered the Turkish and Egyptian fleet at Navarino Bay to return under escort to Egypt. Ibrahim refused and in October, after being joined by a Russian squadron from the Baltic, Vice-Admiral Codrington, who was strongly philhellene and whose instructions were sufficiently vague to leave a good deal to his own discretion, decided to use force. The allies entered the bay and in the battle that followed the Turkish and Egyptian fleet was utterly destroyed.

This unexpected development, involving the crippling of Turkish sea power, seemed to play into Russia's hands, and when, in April 1828, the Tsar, claiming a breach of the Convention of Akerman, declared war on Turkey, it was natural that the Duke of Wellington's government in Great Britain should look aghast at this outcome of Canning's policy. The French, acting in accordance with the Treaty of London, dispatched 14,000 troops to the Morea, where Ibrahim was ousted without difficulty, but the eyes of Europe were on the Russian forces as they moved south through the Danubian Principalities, and when they occupied Adrianople, it seemed that the last hour of the Ottoman empire in Europe had come.

The momentary panic proved, in fact, to be needless. Russia had no wish for the dissolution of the Turkish empire, since she knew that partition, which would be the only possible basis for agreement among the Powers, would have far-reaching consequences.[1] The French, for instance, earlier in the year, had suggested an extensive re-arrangement of the Balkans, including, significantly, the creation of a large kingdom of Greece to be given to the King of the Netherlands, after which the Netherlands themselves would be shared between France and Prussia. As a Russian, Nicholas preferred to have a large but weak Turkey as his neighbour, and as a conservative despot he had no wish to bring about a radical revision of the treaties of 1815. He was therefore happy to make peace with Turkey at Adrianople in September 1829 in return for only modest gains that would have no international repercussions—the port of Poti on the east coast of the Black Sea, certain

[1] See p. 45.

islands at the mouth of the Danube, a protectorate over the local government of Moldavia and Wallachia, where a Russian garrison was to be maintained for five years, the demilitarization of the right bank of the Danube and commercial concessions in Turkey.

At the same time the Sultan granted Greek autonomy as laid down in Canning's original agreement with Russia. The Greeks, however, did not gain all that they had wished. By the settlement that was finally reached in 1830 they were not to have Crete and Samos and the frontier was placed fairly far south between the gulfs of Volo and Arta, since none of the Powers wanted to see the emergence of a large state. The only compensation for the Greeks was that they now received their independence outright from Turkey, and the crown of the new kingdom was eventually accepted by Prince Otto of Bavaria, who thus became the first King of Greece.[1]

It was natural that Metternich should regard the whole of the Greek episode as a disaster for the Holy Alliance and already, before it had come to an end, a new threat to his system had appeared from a totally different quarter. In September 1824 Louis XVIII of France had died and the right-wing reaction which had characterized the last years of his reign was to be epitomized by his brother the Count d'Artois, who succeeded him as Charles X. The new king was fortunate in his inheritance—a prosperous country and a stable political situation in which the immediate difficulties of the Bourbon restoration had been successfully weathered by the good sense of Louis and his ministers. But Charles, typical of the Ultras whose views he embodied, was one who had learnt nothing from the Revolution. Divine Right, a great landowning aristocracy, a clergy once more controlling education—this programme to which he was obstinately to adhere was bound to arouse the anger of even the mildest liberals and within six years was to lose him his throne.

A magnificent coronation at Reims with all the ceremonial of the *ancien régime* set the tone to the whole reign. Then, with Villèle as his chief minister and an overwhelmingly right-wing Chamber, Charles embarked on his campaign. Fifty-six lieutenant-generals of the old Imperial army were placed on the retired list. *Émigré* landowners who, on their return in 1814, had failed to regain their estates were to receive financial compensation. In fact, this was not an unreasonable measure,

[1] He was deposed by the Greeks in 1862 and his successor William, the younger son of Christian IX of Denmark, ruled as George I, King of the Hellenes. See Genealogical tables, pp. 480, 482.

but since it was financed by reducing the interest on government annuities from 5% to 3%, it infuriated the bourgeois, who denounced it as the *milliard des émigrés*, although the sum involved only amounted to 650,000,000 francs. Another measure attempted to go some way towards re-establishing the system of primogeniture, thereby finally abolishing the Revolutionary law of inheritance—already modified by Napoleon—which had aimed at breaking up the large estates by stipulating that on the death of the father they should be shared equally among all the sons of the family. Here too, there was something to be said for calling a halt to a process of dismemberment of estates which had considerable economic disadvantages, but such a revision at once conjured up visions of the old privileged landed aristocracy and although the measure was passed in the Chamber, it was thrown out by the Peers.

The religious policy of the government was still more reminiscent of the *ancien régime*. The clergy had been active in attempting to suppress the paganism that had spread during recent years, and Villèle was unable to prevent the passing of a law which made sacrilege committed in any place of worship punishable by death. A more insidious change was taking place in the field of education. Under the Empire this had been a secular monopoly of the University of France. At the Restoration modifications had allowed the establishment of Catholic seminaries, often attended by pupils who, without any intention of becoming priests, simply preferred this form of education, and in 1821 Catholic schools, whose headmasters and teachers were chosen by the bishops, were even granted a status equivalent to the secular colleges. The most significant development, however, was the infiltration of the Church into the centralized system of the State. In 1822 a bishop, Frayssinous, became Grand Master of the University and, two years later, Minister of Education and Ecclesiastical Affairs, and the recapture of education by the clergy went on at such a pace that in 1827 sixty-six out of eighty philosophy teachers in the colleges were priests and, by 1830, about one-third of all the teachers.

It was not long before the intensity of this Ultra programme had awoken a growing hum of criticism in the cafés and *salons* of Paris, which was to find ardent expression in an opposition press, *Le Constitutionnel* and *Le Journal des Débats*, now free from censorship as a result of Charles's one liberal gesture at the beginning of his reign. Moderate and extreme liberals, Bonapartists and even discontented Ultras, such as Chateaubriand, smarting from his dismissal from office in 1824, were moving closer together, partly in a new fervour of anti-clericalism, partly in anger at the lukewarm support that the government appeared to be giving to the Greek cause. Villèle now set about trying to stamp out this opposition, and in December 1826 a new press law, unhappily labelled by its sponsor, Peyronnet, '*une loi de justice et d'amour*,' was introduced in the Chamber. Censorship was reimposed, penalties greatly increased and prosecutions were in future to be levelled against the proprietors of newspapers rather than against the editors; once again, as over the law of inheritance, it was the Chamber of Peers that prevented the passing of the bill by voting so many modifications that Charles eventually withdrew it.

By the spring of 1827 feelings had become so enflamed that cries of '*à bas les ministres*' were raised at a royal review of the National Guard, that symbol of the liberties enshrined in the Charter, and Villèle unwisely advised their disbanding. By November it seemed to Villèle that even the Chamber was no longer reliable and Charles accordingly dissolved it. Seventy-six new peers were created in order to swing the balance in the Upper House, but this time the forces of opposition meant to strike back at the influence exercised by the Prefects in the provinces. Their efforts, through the organization of a society, *Aide-toi, le ciel t'aidera*, raised the numbers of those who came to the polls from 67,000 to 80,000 and when the new Chamber was returned in December 1827, the government found itself faced with a liberal majority of sixty. Villèle's resignation followed in January 1828.

For the next eighteen months Charles attempted unwillingly to work through a government of moderate conservatives under the Viscount de Martignac. 'Je le trouve un peu faible', wrote the King to Villèle, and the tragedy for Martignac was that in his attempts to form a majority out of a centre group he only succeeded in creating the same impression among the opposition. In the spring of 1829 he tried to introduce government reforms which would have placed the appointment of local councillors in the provinces on an elective basis. When this failed to satisfy the Chamber, Charles decided that he would make no further compromise; in August 1829 he formed a new government under his friend Prince Jules de Polignac, the most ardent of the Ultras, and in so doing took a step that was to have a more shattering effect on Metternich's Europe than the affairs of Portugal or the New World or even the creation of the kingdom of Greece.

6

THE REVOLUTIONS OF 1830

THE outbreaks in the streets of Paris, which at the end of July 1830 forced Charles X to give up his throne, set off a series of risings throughout Europe in a chain reaction similar in many ways to the events of 1820–1. This time, however, although the revolts failed in Poland and the German and Italian states, they were successful in France, Belgium, and Switzerland. These liberal victories in the west meant an important modification of the Vienna settlement, but although the republican democrats supplied much of the initial impetus, it was the richer bourgeois groups who made the principal gains.

The key to the liberal victories was the swift outcome of the revolution in France. The risings in the small states on her borders would have had little prospect of success if the monarchy of Charles X had not collapsed, and their ultimate survival was due to the fact that geographically they lay in areas where Great Britain and France could allow no interference by the central European Powers. On the other hand, the British and French governments had less immediate concern with revolution in Poland and the German and Italian states. Here the revolutionaries had to act on their own, and since neither Prussia in Germany nor Piedmont in Italy was prepared to perform the same protective function as Great Britain or France in the west, the revolts came to nothing. The Poles were unique in having a sizeable army with which to operate, but although this enabled them to put up a heroic struggle for nine months, they were bound ultimately to succumb to the greater strength of the Russian forces.

On the whole, except in Poland and Belgium, nationalism played only a small part in the revolutions of 1830. Even in Germany and Italy the principal feature was a violent protest by liberal groups against authoritarian rule. In the risings east of the Rhine, however, the very lack of any national unity meant that the forces of revolution were too scattered and too parochial in outlook to offer any serious threat to Metternich's system. Even the Swiss movements, which were

75

restricted to agitation *within* the cantons, were only saved from external interference by the international guarantee of Swiss neutrality.

For the successful and the unsuccessful alike there were lessons to be learnt from the events of 1830. The successful had shown that a violent change of government could be achieved without either a major war or a prolonged period of internal upheaval culminating in a Terror; while to the unsuccessful, in Germany and Italy, it was becoming increasingly apparent that a liberal movement could not be realistic until it had come to terms with the problem of national unification.

1. The liberal victories: France, Belgium, and Switzerland

The story of the French Revolution of 1830 really begins in the previous year when Charles X dismissed Martignac's government and appointed in its place a group of ministers whose names epitomized the most uncompromising features of the Ultra party. La Bourdonnaye had been responsible for the White Terror of 1815; de Bourmont had deserted Napoleon on the eve of Waterloo; Prince de Polignac, like his king, was an unrepentant *émigré*, whose tendency to allow his policy to be guided by heavenly visions naturally inclined him more to the notion of Throne and Altar rather than to that of constitutional monarchy.

The members of this new government did have sufficient political sense to realize their own unpopularity, and accordingly, during the seven months before the Chamber would have to be recalled to pass the Budget, Polignac made great efforts to achieve a spectacular success in foreign policy. Secret conversations with the Russian Tsar for the regaining of the left bank of the Rhine came to nothing, owing to Prussian objections. Instead, a punitive expedition against the Bey of Algiers was fitted out. The liberals remained unimpressed; *Le Journal des Débats* and *Le Constitutionnel* had been joined in January 1830 by a new opposition publication, *Le National*, edited by Adolphe Thiers, Mignet, and Armand Carrel, and financed by the banker Jacques Laffitte, and when, in March 1830, the Chamber at last assembled, a vote of no confidence was carried by 221 votes to 158. Charles dissolved the Chamber, but in the subsequent election in July, despite governmental pressure on the electors, the opposition was increased from 221 to 274.

So far there was no question of any threat to Charles's throne. The forms of constitutional monarchy would sooner or later demand the dismissal of his ministers, but even if he insisted on retaining them, the deputies had nothing more revolutionary in mind than a refusal to pay taxes. Unfortunately for the future of the Bourbons news of the capture of Algiers had reached Paris on 9 July and Charles fell a dupe to the device with which Polignac had hoped to win general favour. The public remained coolly unmoved; the King, however, imagined that his position was now unassailable and without any attempt to win over the newly elected Chamber resolved upon a royal *coup d'état*.

On 26 July four ordinances were printed in *Le Moniteur*. No newspaper or periodical under twenty pages was to be published without royal permission. The Chamber was dissolved and arrangements for a new election were announced. The most significant change of all was a modification of the franchise which reduced the effective electorate to about 25,000, excluding most of the industrialist and commercial class. It seemed clear that these measures could be nothing less than a preliminary to annulling the Charter, yet at this crucial moment in his reign Charles demonstrated the full extent of his political incompetence. He had chosen to act when the Paris garrison numbered rather less than 11,000, owing to the military operations in Algeria; the Minister of War, de Bourmont, was absent; his deputy minister, Champagny, had received no warning and Marmont, who had been given command of the troops in Paris, knew nothing of the ordinances until he read them in *Le Moniteur*. Charles himself had gone off hunting at Rambouillet.

In fact, not even the publication of the ordinances caused the deputies to turn immediately to violence. It was the republicans—Godefroy Cavaignac, Trélat, and Raspail—who, seeing their chance to end the monarchy and to bring in universal suffrage, were determined to fight, and they were joined almost at once by Lafayette, who was in his own person a somewhat elderly symbol of the early years of the French Revolution. By 27 July they were mobilizing the discontented elements, such as the printers for whom the suspension of the freedom of the press would mean unemployment, and students in the Latin Quarter who were always ready for a revolution, and soon the barricades began to go up in the narrow streets. The gun shops were raided, and on 28 July it became clear that the revolution was in earnest when the Hôtel de Ville was taken by the rebels, recaptured by Marmont's troops and then taken once again on his withdrawal. On 29 July the Louvre and the Tuileries were attacked and occupied, the palace of the

Archbishop of Paris was sacked and two regiments of royal troops deserted to the rebels.

In three days of fighting the republicans in Paris had revealed the flimsiness of the King's rule, but in doing so they also forced the hand of the liberal deputies. These, much as they disliked Charles X, had wished to avoid violent revolution, since this might open the door to republicanism, but by 30 July it was clear that they would have to throw in their lot with the insurgents. Early that morning a group of liberals including Mignet and Adolphe Thiers, whose tiny bird-like figure was to be a gift for nineteenth-century cartoonists, met at the house of the banker Laffitte. Certainly Charles would have to go. What alternative, then, could they find to a republic? Quickly the plot was hatched, and while the men at the Hôtel de Ville looked to Lafayette and dreamed of a republic, anonymous posters appeared in Paris declaring that Louis Philippe, Duke of Orleans, would be the most appropriate successor to the Bourbon Charles X.

The hopes of the liberal monarchists now rested on two men. Could Louis Philippe, who had not yet been consulted, be persuaded to pick up the crown? Would Lafayette allow him to do so? It was Thiers who found a way through the difficulties. Riding out to Neuilly he assured Louis Philippe that his moment had come and that he alone could prevent the creation of a republic which, among other things, might well mean the exile of the Duke himself. At the same time Laffitte had organized a meeting of some sixty of the Chamber of Deputies who, together with a few peers, agreed that Louis Philippe should be invited to Paris and appointed Lieutenant General of the Kingdom. That evening, while Lafayette hesitated over accepting the responsibility of becoming President of a new republic, the Duke entered the city, making his way unobtrusively through the barricades to the Palais Royal; on the next morning, after the deputies had duly appointed him Lieutenant General, he proceeded to the Hôtel de Ville for the fateful interview with the republicans. Here the crowd saw him accept the tricolour and publicly embrace Lafayette, and with that 'republican kiss' the Orleanists knew that they had won the day.

After this there were few complications. By now Charles knew that he had lost his crown and was mainly concerned with aiding his ministers' flight. In an effort to keep the succession in his family he nominated Louis Philippe Lieutenant General, instructing him to proclaim the Duke de Bordeaux, the son of the Duchess de Berri, as King

Henry V of France. Louis Philippe chose to ignore this and on 3 August the news that a mob was on the march to Rambouillet convinced Charles that it was time to quit his kingdom. The royal party, including the young Duke de Bordeaux, made a stately progress to Cherbourg, from where Charles sailed to his final exile, and on 7 August the Chamber announced that the throne was vacant and offered the crown with the title of King of the French to Louis Philippe.

The amendments to the Charter which the deputies drew up at the same time certainly established the fact that the new king had been granted his throne on terms, but in themselves they were remarkably mild. Extraordinary courts of law and censorship of the press were prohibited. The tricolour was proclaimed once more the national flag of France. The Chambers were to share with the King the right of initiating legislation and the King was deprived of the power to suspend or to dispense with existing laws. The essential question, however, lay in the composition of the Chamber and here the new Charter said extremely little, simply reducing the minimum age of deputies to thirty and their length of tenure to five years. It was not until a year later, in July 1831, that a new electoral law revealed the extent to which the richer bourgeois had triumphed. The tax qualification for deputies was lowered from one thousand to five hundred francs, and for voting from three hundred to two hundred francs; thus the previous electorate of 100,000 only rose to rather less than 170,000 out of a population of 32 million.[1]

A republican viewing the final outcome of the hectic days of July might reasonably speak of a great betrayal. The bourgeois, represented by the liberal deputies, had feared in Charles a return to some form of *ancien régime* in France, but it had been the people, as depicted in Delacroix's famous picture of Liberty on the barricades, who had fought the royal troops in the streets at the cost of some five hundred dead; yet at the end they had gained virtually nothing from the revolution of 1830. The fruits of victory had been adroitly seized by the commercial and industrialist classes. This realization was to lead to a growing antagonism between middle and lower classes throughout the reign of Louis Philippe, and when the monarchy succumbed once more in the revolution of 1848, it was to take more than a republican kiss to settle the issue between them.

For the absolutist Powers, the revolution of 1830 in France was not merely an affront, but a threat to the whole system which they had

[1] See Appendix 4, p. 486.

been at such pains to restore in 1815. To the rulers east of the Rhine a rising *bourgeoisie* was as detestable as a lower class movement, and the angry mistrust which the July monarchy inspired appeared almost at once justified by the spate of revolution that followed the events in Paris.

At the end of August the Belgians rose in revolt against the government of the Kingdom of the Netherlands in which they had been incorporated by the diplomats at the Congress of Vienna. Dutch sentiment in the past had sometimes regretted the division of the Netherlands which had been the price of their freedom from Spain in the seventeenth century; but the main purpose of the reunification of the Netherlands in 1815 had been to shut off France from making any encroachment in the north-east. Indeed, by the nineteenth century, their only unity was geographical. They did not share the same mother tongue, while in religion the Dutch were predominantly Calvinist, the south Roman Catholic. This sense of difference was aggravated by the fact that the government of the kingdom was carried on largely in the interest of the Dutch.[1] The Belgian numerical preponderance was not reflected in the States General; Dutch was the official language, and Dutch officials held about four-fifths of the executive posts. Belgians complained bitterly that they had been saddled with too great a share of the Dutch national debt; economic policy, tending towards low tariffs, favoured the commercial classes, and although the Belgian merchants had no wish to lose the market that existed in the Dutch colonial empire, the rapidly growing industry of Belgium[2] needed protection against British competition.

The chief difficulty that had stood in the way of any Belgian national movement had been the antagonism that existed between the Catholic party, strong in the rural areas, and the liberal bourgeois group, open to French influence and highly anti-clerical. The essential preliminary to any Belgian rising was agreement between these two, and it was only after 1828 that the influence of Lamennais' ideas of Liberal Catholicism[3] began to make a compromise possible, whereby the liberals would allow the Catholics their schools and the Catholics allow the liberals freedom of the press.

On 25 August, while the Paris rising was still of recent memory, rioting in the Brussels Opera House gave the local bourgeois their opportunity. Their aims did not run as far as national independence; like their counterparts in Paris, they were uneasy over latent republican-

---

[1] See p. 33.   [2] See pp. 97, 98.   [3] See pp. 105–6.

ism and would have been well content with an administrative separation, while retaining a personal union of the two countries under
William I. Unlike the revolution in France, however, resistance spread
rapidly through the provinces and William resolved upon taking
Brussels by force. Four days of fighting left the Belgians still in possession of their capital, but after such bloodshed there could be no
further question of treating with William, and the liberals found themselves committed to the side of the extremists. The recent alliance of
Catholics and liberals made it possible to form a provisional government and on 5 October this government proclaimed Belgium independent of the Kingdom of the Netherlands.

By the end of October an armistice had been signed with the Dutch
and early in November a National Assembly, chosen by some 30,000
electors, met to draw up a constitution. Monarchy was to be retained,
but the House of Orange was excluded for ever. The executive was
placed under the control of a bi-cameral legislature; all forms of
political and social liberty were guaranteed and considerable rights of
local government were left to the provinces. The franchise was
extended to all who paid a tax of 20 florins—some 46,000 out of a
population of four million.

Thus, in a few weeks the Belgians had shaken off Dutch control
and devised a form of government that was to be the envy of liberals
throughout Europe. The question of their ultimate survival, however,
lay not in their own hands, but in the attitude of the great Powers confronted by this violation of the 1815 settlement. At the end of September 1830 William I had appealed to the other governments to assist
him in putting down his rebellious subjects. Metternich was too concerned about possible dangers in Italy to act; Tsar Nicholas I and
Frederick William III would have been glad to intervene, yet dared
not, since they knew that if they sent an army into the Low Countries,
Louis Philippe, who was under great pressure from powerful groups in
Paris to annex Belgium, would have no option but to bring assistance
to the Belgian liberals. In fact, neither Louis Philippe nor his government had any wish to embark upon a new adventure in Europe, and in
September Talleyrand, now making his final return to public life,
hastened to England to convince the British government of the need
for a general agreement on non-intervention. As a result the Duke of
Wellington proposed an immediate conference of the five Powers at
London.

It was soon clear that the Dutch could not bring their Belgian

D

subjects to heel on their own, and on 29 November the likelihood of intervention by the autocratic Powers on behalf of the Dutch king was still further diminished when the outbreak of revolt in Warsaw turned their attention eastwards. In Great Britain the Duke of Wellington's government had fallen while the conference was still in session and the principal concern of Lord Palmerston, Foreign Secretary in the new Whig administration of Lord Grey, was to forestall any attempt by the French to annex Belgium. Thus, on 20 December a Protocol was issued by the Powers in conference announcing the plan to create an independent Belgian state, and this was followed in January 1831 by two further Protocols sharing the national debt of the United Netherlands between the two countries and defining a frontier which excluded Maestricht, Dutch Limburg, and any part of Luxemburg from the new Kingdom of Belgium.

At this point British fears over French intentions appeared to be suddenly confirmed. William I was prepared to accept the January Protocols, but the Belgians were furious at the decision over the frontier and in retaliation precipitated a new crisis by electing, on 3 February, a younger son of Louis Philippe, the Duke de Nemours, as their King. Fortunately Louis Philippe, feeling that his newly established régime was hardly ripe for war, wisely took note of Palmerston's anger, rejected the candidature of his son and replaced Laffitte with the more cautious government of Casimir Périer.

By June the Belgians had been mollified by the promise of further negotiation over Luxemburg and had agreed to offer the crown to Leopold of Saxe-Coburg. This choice, however, caused some resentment among the French, since Leopold had a personal link with Great Britain as the widower of George IV's daughter, Charlotte, and in August Anglo-French hostility flared up once more, when William I invaded Belgium again and Louis Philippe, in response to Leopold's appeal, marched in to repel the Dutch attack. Palmerston at once suspected the worst, particularly when Talleyrand spoke of the possibility of partitioning Belgium, and Prussia too began actively to prepare to come to the assistance of William, now that the French had intervened. The French accordingly withdrew their troops, and after this Anglo-French relations improved, although there was to be one further round with William, when a combined British and French force captured Antwerp from him in December 1832.

Haggling over the precise details of the frontier continued until the final agreement was signed in 1839. The province of Limburg was shared between the two countries; the Belgians were allowed the freedom of the navigation of the Scheldt, while the Netherlands retained control over the mouth of the river. Luxemburg presented an intricate problem, since as a separate duchy in the hereditary possession of the House of Orange it was a member of the German Confederation and the capital was a Federal fortress occupied by a Prussian garrison. The local inhabitants had, however, joined with the Belgians in the rising of 1830 and now a part of the duchy was given to Belgium, while the rest, including the city, remained under its Grand Duke William. Lastly, by the treaty of 1839, the neutrality of the new Belgian state was recognized by the five great Powers of Europe.

Meanwhile, the events in France had also stimulated a movement among the Swiss cantons. The growth of Swiss industry had already strengthened the opposition to the cliques of conservatives and in 1819 a student society, *Zofingia*, had been formed after the pattern of the German *Burschenschaften*, aiming at breaking down the particularism of the cantons on which the power of the patrician families depended. In the summer of 1830 the example of France, the return of six Swiss regiments from the French army, and the initiative of local leaders, lawyers, schoolmasters, and business men, resulted in a series of demonstrations which ultimately caused the ruling cliques to make great constitutional concessions.

As elsewhere, the changes were liberal rather than democratic. Equality before the law and the liberty of the press were guaranteed, but the local franchise, although considerably extended, was still left dependent upon a property qualification. The course of the revolutions varied from canton to canton. In Zürich and Geneva the change came peacefully; in Schwyz there was violence and in Basle the clash between the two parties could only be resolved by a division of the canton into two—a rural area, Basselland, dominated by the liberals, and the city of Basle, where the patrician families retained their power. In Neuchâtel[1] there were to be further complications, since the canton was still a hereditary possession of the King of Prussia. All this activity, however, was confined to the individual cantons and the form of the central federal government remained as yet unaffected.

[1] See p. 11.

2. The liberal defeats: Poland and the Italian and German states

Throughout the summer and autumn of 1830 the rulers of the three autocratic Powers had watched the course of events in France and Belgium in an agony of frustration. Metternich and Nesselrode, the Russian Foreign Minister, had both been on holiday in Bohemia when the news from Paris first arrived; they conferred at once and agreed that they should not interfere, provided that no other country was affected. Yet when the Belgians rose, the subsequent diplomatic imbroglio still held them powerless to intervene and in September Metternich was sufficiently depressed to confide to Nesselrode his belief that it meant the beginning of the end for the old order in Europe.

Tsar Nicholas, however, was still determined on action and was pushing ahead with his military preparations, when he was suddenly confronted by a revolt within his own dominions. The major theme of the Polish insurrection, which began in Warsaw on 29 November, was a romantic nationalism coloured by a dislike of being under the rule of a Russian viceroy and by recent disputes between the Tsar and the Diet. The outbreak was principally the work of a handful of junior Army officers who gained control of the garrison of 10,000 in Warsaw. Superficially this was a more promising start than any of the revolts in the west, but it pointed also to the real weakness of the Polish rising, which never succeeded in turning a military *coup* into a social movement. Russian rule during the previous fifteen years had been sufficiently mild to deprive Polish nationalism of any widespread grievances that might have momentarily united the Polish peasantry and their own landed aristocracy. As it was, the peasantry did not join the rising and the middle class was still too small to constitute a significant factor. The rebels suffered also from a fatal cleavage within their own ranks; the moderates under Prince Czartoryski thought mainly of reclaiming the eastern provinces that Russia had taken in 1772 and had little love for any form of social change, while the radicals talked in terms of agrarian reforms and national independence.

At the outset, at least, the rebel army, far stronger than the available Russian troops, was able to drive out the Grand Duke Constantine, and when the Russians counter-attacked early in 1831 under Field Marshal Dybicz, the Polish forces, now 70,000, were able to hold them off in the lands east of Warsaw, until they suffered a defeat at Ostroleka[1]

[1] See map, p. 158.

on 26 May. This military disaster brought about the collapse of the moderate government under Czartoryski in Warsaw, but although a new general Krukowiecki was able to restore order in the capital, the days of the Polish revolt were numbered. Cholera, making its first appearance in Europe from the east, played havoc with both armies—particularly disastrous for the Poles who had few reinforcements—and on 8 September the Russians entered Warsaw. The radicals were prepared to fight on, but separate units of the army were beginning to desert and on 5 October the remnant of 20,000 marched over the frontier and surrendered to the Prussians.[1]

The possession of an army had enabled the Poles to make a spectacular resistance, but without assistance from the west their cause had been hopeless from the start. They had certainly believed that such assistance would come, although they had little reason for thinking this. In a general appeal issued in April 1831 the Polish government had pointed out that Poland had far more historic right to national independence than Belgium or Greece. What they ignored was that Belgium and Greece lay geographically in areas where Great Britain and France could not allow permanent occupation by the great Powers and where the creation of independent states was the only possible compromise that would avoid political gain by either side. The tragedy for the Poles was that they lay outside the British and French spheres of action.

In Italy the chances of successful revolution had also hinged on the question of intervention. A young lawyer of Modena, Enrico Misley, had devised a scheme for the creation of a constitutional Kingdom of Central Italy under the rule of Duke Francis of Modena whom he had won over to his ideas. The original plan for the rising, whereby tension between Austria and Russia over Greece was to have prevented Metternich from interfering, had been shattered by the Russo-Turkish treaty of 1829,[2] but the events in France in 1830 helped to revive Misley's hopes, and when Sebastiani, the new French Foreign Minister, announced in September that France would oppose any intervention by Austria outside her frontiers in Italy, the leaders decided to take the risk and, in February 1831, revolt broke out in Bologna. This realization that Italian hopes depended upon the attitude of the French was perfectly sound and pointed to the means whereby success was ultimately to be achieved in 1860. On this occasion, however, the conspirators were to be betrayed by the French King and the Duke of

[1] For the consequences of the revolt in Poland see p. 123.   [2] See p. 71.

Modena. Louis Philippe had informed Metternich privately that the French proclamation had only served to satisfy public opinion and that he would not oppose Austrian action in Italy. In the same month Laffitte's belligerent government was dismissed and the cautious administration of Casimir Périer which replaced it had no more intention of intervening on the side of the rebels in Italy than it had in Poland. Francis of Modena had by now turned his face against any further plans of revolt, and although he and Marie Louise of Parma had to escape from their duchies, he arrested the local leaders before he left and took them with him to Mantua.

Thus, Metternich had no hesitation in sending his troops south where the revolts were swiftly crushed. It was, nevertheless, a delicate situation and they were withdrawn as soon as their work was done. When a second rising in Bologna brought them back again, Louis Philippe felt that his government was now sufficiently well established to justify a gesture and, in February 1832, French troops proceeded by sea to occupy Ancona. There they remained for six years—as long as the Austrians stayed in Bologna—but this move was merely due to the need to preserve French prestige and it meant little for those who wished to bring revolution to Italy.

In Germany revolt was inspired as much by the Polish example as by the French, but its extent was limited in the main to the confines of particular states, although a meeting of intellectuals at Hambach in the Bavarian Palatinate did go so far as to discuss the question of German unification. Local risings imposed liberal constitutions on the rulers of Brunswick, Hanover, Saxony, and Hesse-Cassel; in others, where elective Chambers already existed, liberal opposition grew more outspoken. All this, however, was short-lived. Prussia and Austria, acting through the Diet of the German Confederation, were able to re-establish the situation in most states, and when, in April 1833, German students, encouraged by Polish *émigrés*, tried to carry out a *coup* at Frankfurt in order to bring pressure to bear on the Diet, they were easily defeated. In June 1834 Metternich was able to put fresh heart into the princes assembled at Vienna with added restrictions on liberal activity, and for the moment he could feel that the threat of further revolution was no longer immediate.

7

THE DIPLOMATIC SCENE 1830-48

THE pattern of liberal successes and failures in the revolutions of 1830 might at first suggest the division of Europe into two camps —the constitutional governments of the west and the autocratic Powers of the Holy Alliance—each with their own accepted spheres of influence. From the point of view of economic development and the general tone of domestic affairs this might be a valid distinction; it is seldom, however, that diplomacy can run in accordance with common political ideologies. Indeed, the most striking feature of these years was a growing discord between Great Britain and France, due partly to commercial competition, but mainly to British uneasiness over the increasing independence of French policy in the Mediterranean.

Another factor at this time was a change in Russian policy towards Turkey. The crisis of 1827-9 had shown Tsar Nicholas that there was no slackening in the nervousness of the great Powers over the possibility of Russian expansion at Turkey's expense. Accordingly he began now to wonder whether friendship rather than enmity with Turkey might not offer greater rewards. Metternich and Frederick William III would probably favour this as part of the maintenance of the Vienna settlement, but Nicholas naturally realized that the consequent growth of Russian influence at Constantinople would be bound to create distrust in Great Britain; thus, since British disapproval could really only be effective with French military support, the Tsar was particularly pleased at the poor state of Anglo-French relations. These aims, however, were purely Russian. Nicholas was perfectly ready to move outside the circle of the Holy Alliance to gain the friendship of Great Britain in order to keep her separated from France; equally, when Anglo-French relations had finally collapsed in 1846, Metternich was prepared to open negotiations with France.

The debate over the Belgian frontier was still continuing when a new crisis in the Near East arose out of the settlement of the Greek question. In 1831 Mehemet Ali, angered by the Sultan's decision to give him Crete instead of Syria, as originally promised, in return for his services in Greece, invaded Syria with 30,000 men and after taking the fortress of Acre swiftly overran the whole country. In 1832 he advanced into Asia Minor and when the Turkish army was defeated at Konieh, it seemed once again that nothing could prevent the collapse of the Ottoman empire.

The reaction of the Powers to this new situation varied. France was not unfavourably disposed towards Egypt, but the monarchy of Louis Philippe was too recently established to face with equanimity the complications that the dissolution of Turkey would involve. Great Britain, on the other hand, was definitely opposed to Mehemet Ali, since her lines of communication with India made her anxious, like Russia, to prevent the emergence of any strong Power in the Near East. Neither Great Britain nor France, however, immediately warmed to Metternich's proposal of forceful mediation, until the Sultan in despair appealed to Russia, and Tsar Nicholas, seeing a chance to develop his new policy of friendship towards Turkey, agreed to come to her aid. The arrival of a Russian fleet in the Bosphorus and the occupation of both sides of the Straits by Russian troops in February 1833 naturally made diplomatic intervention by the other Powers of Europe inevitable, and they hastily imposed a settlement whereby Turkey granted Mehemet Ali the pashaliks of Egypt, Crete, Syria, Damascus, and Tripoli for his lifetime.

The withdrawal of Russian forces was at once followed in July by the Treaty of Unkiar Skelessi between the Tsar and the Sultan. The terms of this defensive alliance, which was to last eight years, promised Turkey Russian aid if she were attacked; on the other hand, the only assistance that Russia would demand in the event of war would be the closing of the Straits to her enemies' warships. This was a significant revision of the Anglo-Turkish agreement of 1809, for although it did not allow Russia to enter the Mediterranean, it did enable her to shut off the Black Sea to her enemies in wartime. These clauses, although secret, were soon known everywhere in Europe and caused considerable indignation in London and Paris. Any collective protest, however, seemed to be ruled out after September 1833, when a meeting took place between Tsar Nicholas and the Emperor Francis at Münchengrätz and a convention was signed between Austria and Russia agreeing on collaboration in central Europe and guaranteeing the maintenance of Turkey.

One consequence of this reaffirming of the principles of the Holy

Alliance at Münchengrätz was a slacking of tension over the Eastern Question, much assisted in January 1834 by the withdrawal of Russian forces from the Danubian principalities.[1] A second more positive effect was a short-lived *rapprochement* between Great Britain and France. Since 1831 both countries had been sending unofficial aid to the constitutional party of the Portuguese Queen Maria whose throne had been usurped by her uncle Dom Miguel. In Spain another young Queen, Isabella, succeeded her father, Ferdinand VII, on his death in 1833, but the government under the regency of her mother had been challenged by her uncle, Don Carlos. Thus civil war was now raging in Spain and Portugal between the forces of the rightful Queens who were supported by liberal opinion, and the two wicked uncles whose views were purely autocratic. Palmerston had for long been suspicious of French intrigues in Spain, and when Talleyrand proposed an Anglo-French military alliance for joint action on behalf of the Queens, he converted it in April 1834 into a Quadruple Alliance with Spain and Portugal. This he hoped might restrain the French from acting on their own initiative and 'would serve as a powerful counterpoise to the Holy Alliance of the East'.

Naturally, Palmerston was exaggerating. The Quadruple Alliance did succeed in defeating the uncles and in establishing the Queens on their thrones. On the other hand, the subsequent worsening of Anglo-French relations precluded any chance of an effective league against the autocratic Powers.

The reasons for this latest hostility lay in the strategic and economic implications of an active French policy in the Mediterranean. Palmerston certainly hoped for a lasting friendship and was careful not to make an issue of the establishment of French power in Algeria, where by 1836 they had begun to occupy the interior.[2] This strengthening of France's position in the western Mediterranean did, however, cause a greater sensitiveness over Spain, and the Quadruple Alliance was virtually disrupted by British endeavours to achieve commercial connections there, which might compensate for any political influence that the French hoped to gain south of the Pyrenees.

France's interest in North Africa also brought about a clash over policy in the Near East. The British reaction to the Treaty of Unkiar Skelessi was to offer the Sultan assistance in reforming his navy, but without any positive alliance, since that might have encouraged him to renew the war with Egypt. In return, the British received commercial

[1] See p. 72.   [2] See p. 117.

concessions in 1838, whereby their merchants might trade freely throughout the Turkish dominions—a blow for Mehemet Ali who was attempting to develop Egyptian exports through state monopolies of cotton, tobacco, and indigo. In contrast to this British friendship with Turkey, France had greater sympathy with Egypt who was thus able to make considerable use of French technicians in the modernizing of the Egyptian army and the beginnings of industrialization. This raised something more than questions of commercial rivalry. The Red Sea route to India was of permanent importance to Great Britain, and the growth of French influence in Egypt, coupled with the efforts of the French consul at Basra to interfere with the use of the overland route through Mesopotamia, naturally seemed to the British like a revival of the plans that Napoleon had once entertained for cutting their direct line of communication with the east.

In the circumstances it was not surprising that the next crisis in the Near East should reveal the full extent of British and French antagonism over Egypt. In 1838 Mehemet Ali, encouraged by the French, refused to pay his annual tribute to the Sultan Mahmud, who promptly sent an army against him into Syria. The outcome was disastrous for Turkey. The Egyptians under Ibrahim won a decisive victory at Nezib[1] in June 1839; the Turkish fleet changed sides and sailed for Alexandria, and it seemed that Turkey lay once again open to conquest by Mehemet Ali.

Metternich's hope was to bring about a form of collective mediation by the five Powers—much to the relief of Constantinople, where the sudden death of Mahmud shortly after the battle of Nezib had put the government somewhat at a loss. In August, however, Tsar Nicholas announced that he would have nothing whatever to do with the scheme, and it looked as if Russia was about to make use of the Treaty of Unkiar Skelessi to embark upon an independent course of intervention in aid of the Turks. But this was not Nicholas's intention. He was by now disillusioned over the value of an alliance with Turkey and in the recent events he had seen an opportunity to aggravate the ill feeling that already existed between Great Britain and France. Accordingly, in the autumn of 1839, knowing full well that the French would prefer to give their support to Egypt, he opened negotiations with Palmerston for imposing a settlement in the Near East which would check Mehemet Ali's ambitions.

His policy was highly successful. Whereas the Austrian and Prussian

[1] See map p. 13.

ambassadors in London joined in the new scheme, the French hung back and in March 1840 a new government under Thiers attempted to bring about a direct settlement between Turkey and Egypt on its own. This convinced Palmerston that the Powers must go ahead without France and in July the four of them signed a treaty at London imposing their own settlement in the Near East. Mehemet Ali was presented with an ultimatum promising him the hereditary possession of Egypt and the pashalik of Acre for his lifetime, in return for the restoration of the Turkish fleet and the evacuation of northern Syria. Mehemet Ali, still putting his faith in French support, made no reply and in the autumn of 1840 a combined naval and military force of the Allies landed near Beirut. Mehemet Ali was already faced with a revolt of the Christians in the Lebanon; Ibrahim was defeated in the mountains above Junieh, Beirut surrendered to the Allies and, farther south, Acre was bombarded and taken. Despairing of any assistance from France, Mehemet Ali now agreed to terms, restored Syria, Crete, and Arabia, as well as the Turkish fleet, and agreed to pay annual tribute to the Sultan in return for his recognition as hereditary Pasha of Egypt.

In France the treaty of the four Powers in July 1840, from which she had been excluded, awoke a tremendous patriotic fury in the boulevards and Thiers' government was at one with public opinion in denouncing a pact so reminiscent of the Quadruple Alliance of 1814. 'Si l'Europe veut avoir affaire à nous, elle n'a qu'à essayer,' Thiers had said in April, and when it was apparent that the Powers intended to act against Egypt, hotheads spoke of challenging Europe with a revision of the treaties of 1815. 'La France doit se souvenir que, même étant seule, elle a tenu tête à l'Europe,' declared the *Revue des Deux Mondes*, and the government now embarked on military preparations, including the fortification of Paris.

In fact, neither Louis Philippe nor Thiers was keen to thrust France into a general European war. A corresponding surge of German nationalism throughout the states of the Confederation seized on the memories of the war of liberation against France in 1813; the songs *Die Wacht am Rhein* and *Deutschland über alles* and the hope which King Ludwig of Bavaria expressed that Strasbourg might again be a German city, all suggested that another form of revision of the treaties of 1815 might involve the loss of Alsace, and clearly pointed to the need for caution. Palmerston was convinced that France was bluffing, and in October 1840 Louis Philippe decided to hold out no longer and secured the resignation of Thiers. With this France rejoined the Concert of Powers, and took her part in the final agreements with Mehemet Ali. In July 1841 the settlement of the Near East was rounded off with the signing of the Straits Convention whereby Russia gave up the special terms that she had gained from the Treaty of Unkiar Skelessi, and the situation reverted to the ruling laid down in the Anglo-Turkish arrangement of 1809.

Nicholas had certainly been successful in his attempt to use the Egyptian crisis as a means of finally breaking up the alliance of 1834 between Great Britain and France, but it was Palmerston who could claim to have scored the greatest success in this episode. Realizing that Russia was bound to oppose the capture of the Ottoman empire by such a powerful ruler as Mehemet Ali, he had been able to rely on her support for his policy, and sensing the anxiety of the French over the resurgence of German nationalism, he had known that he could call their bluff. Thus he had cut short Egyptian expansion, undermined the extension of French influence in the eastern Mediterranean, and with the Straits Convention of 1841 had seen Russia abandon the policy of Unkiar Skelessi in favour of continuing friendly relations with Great Britain.

Many of these features of the international scene were to hold good until the revolutions of 1848. Nicholas continued to nurse his new friendship with Great Britain, and in 1844, when he feared that Anglo-French relations were on the mend, he came to England to warn Lord Aberdeen, Foreign Secretary in Sir Robert Peel's administration, that the collapse of Turkey would offer France the chance of gains which only close Anglo-Russian collaboration could prevent. No positive alliance resulted from these conversations, but relations between Russia and Great Britain remained favourable and there was little indication that within ten years the two countries would be at war.

Nicholas, however, had been right to suspect the renewal of some sort of *entente* between Great Britain and France. New personalities, Guizot in Paris and Aberdeen in London, were convinced of its importance and worked hard to heal the rift between the two countries—a policy in which Queen Victoria played her part with two visits to France in 1843 and 1845.

There were, however, still too many bones of contention for their efforts to achieve much more than an uneasy truce. In the policing of the Atlantic against the slave trade, the French suspected the British of attempting to increase their control of the sea. There was, too, considerable tension over the opening up of the Pacific at this time, and it had been mainly due to fears of the possibility of annexation by France that the British government had placed New Zealand under British sovereignty in 1840. This decided the French, in 1844, to take possession of the island of Tahiti, where an English missionary, Mr Pritchard, had been carrying on a lonely struggle to persuade Queen Pomare to put herself under the protection of the British Crown, and although Aberdeen was determined to leave well alone, the arrest of Pritchard by Admiral Dupetit-Thouars caused a minor sensation, which Louis Philippe finally settled by a personal payment of £1,000 to the missionary.

As before, however, the key to continued Anglo-French discord lay in the Mediterranean. In Athens the ambassadors of the two countries intrigued against each other. In Tunis the British hoped to see Turkey re-establish firm rule as a bulwark against French expansion from Algeria, and when the French intended, in 1844, to march on Fez in Morocco, where the local potentate had been assisting the Algerians against them, it was only strong British objections that held Louis Philippe back. The final breakdown in their relations occurred over Spain. By 1840 Queen Isabella was ten years of age and a long wrangle ensued when Louis Philippe put forward a scheme for her marriage to one of his sons. The British government, reacting strongly against this, suggested a Coburg husband for the Queen, but Guizot regarded this with equal suspicion owing to Coburg connections with Great Britain and Belgium. The two governments, anxious to preserve the somewhat battered *entente*, handled the problem as tactfully as possible and were moving towards a compromise involving a double marriage—the Queen to a Spanish cousin and her sister to one of Louis Philippe's sons—when Peel's government fell and Palmerston replaced Aberdeen as Foreign Secretary. Palmerston at once took up the Coburg candidature again in no uncertain terms, whereupon Louis Philippe refused to negotiate any longer. In September 1846 he declared the Queen of Spain betrothed to her cousin and her sister to his son, the Duke de Montpensier, and the fury of indignation to which this announcement gave rise in Great Britain marked the end of any further attempt to keep up even the pretence of an Anglo-French *entente*.

It may seem odd that a simple dynastic issue should bulk so large in nineteenth-century diplomacy. Yet when the dispute is placed in the wider context of rivalry in the Mediterranean, the question of French or British influence at the Court of Madrid naturally assumes a greater significance. It is possible that France was moving towards a new and enterprising foreign policy linking her with the two Bourbon kingdoms of Spain and Naples in a league that could have freed her from any dependence on Great Britain and might even eventually have enabled her to challenge Austrian power in Italy—as the earlier expedition to Ancona in 1832 had suggested.[1] The full extent of Guizot's possible aims must remain a matter for speculation. The immediate outcome of the breakdown of the *entente* was the beginning of a friendship between France and Austria—France, because she feared isolation, Austria, because Metternich wished to present a united front to Palmerston whom he suspected of favouring the gathering forces of liberalism and nationalism. Contacts between the two remained purely tentative; Louis Philippe, mindful of the left wing in the Chamber, hesitated to announce a definite *entente* with a country that stood for the maintenance of the settlement of 1815, and Metternich had little confidence in the stability of any parliamentary government. As it turned out, their doubts were not unfounded; within a year the revolutions of 1848 had driven them both from power and the scheme for a Franco-Austrian alignment had ceased to have any practical relevance.

[1] See p. 86.

8

THE ECONOMIC TRANSFORMATION
OF EUROPE

IN their outcome the revolutions of 1830 had shown that, although its original aim had been European-wide, the system of Metternich was really only effective in central and eastern Europe. Great Britain had always fought shy of it; France had been suspect as the home of revolution. But the west in these years was to offer something more than an example of political nonconformity; it was the point of origin of an economic revolution which was to be fundamentally more destructive of the old order than any local insurrection and which in its later developments has continued to transform the European scene to this day.

The first factor in this period of change was a remarkable growth in population,[1] due mainly to a great reduction in the death rate of new-born children through advances in medical science. In 1800 the population of Europe as a whole stood approximately at 188 million; by 1850 it had reached 267 million. This sharp increase was reflected variously in different countries, most marked in the British Isles and in Germany, more gradual in France, who by 1850 had already been surpassed by Germany. The immediate significance lay, however, in distribution rather than in total size. In Great Britain and France industrialism caused towns to grow out of all proportion to the general increase in population; in the first half of the century Paris and Lyons were doubled, Toulouse and Marseilles rose by 75%, and in the industrial regions of the north-east a small town such as St Étienne expanded from 16,000 to 56,000. East of France this urban development was much less striking. Thus, in Germany, the 73·5% of the population classed as rural in 1816 had only dropped to 72% by 1846; in Prussia, as late as 1850, the factory workers amounted to no more than 4% of the total population, and in Hungary, out of 11 million people, there were by 1839 only 117,000 engaged in any form of industry. Nevertheless, the pressure of a growing population in the countryside

[1] See Appendix 7, p. 488.

95

was causing the peasantry to move into the towns. Berlin and Vienna each doubled their size between 1815 and 1848, and in central and eastern Europe, although the numbers of middle class and proletariat were still small, the advent, in many of the towns, of peasants speaking their own dialects was to be an important factor in the awakening consciousness of national loyalties.

The far greater urban development in the west is largely explained by the second characteristic of economic change at this time. By 1815 the new industrial processes affecting the production of iron and textiles, the manufacture of machinery and the application of steam power had given Great Britain an enormous lead over all other European countries. With the return of peace it was unlikely that her principal economic competitors would allow one country to remain the workshop of the world; an effective response to the British challenge, however, could only be made in the west, where capital was available and small forms of industry were already in existence. Even here the type of industrialism which developed in the years following the war and which began to accelerate after 1830 was distinctly dependent upon the technical experience of British engineers and workers who played a considerable part in this first phase of the Industrial Revolution on the Continent.

The major economic difficulty for France in 1815 was the loss of the Belgian coalfields which, until the tapping of the fields of northern France after 1850, left her with only those of the Upper Loire and the edge of the Belgian fields around Valenciennes. This meant that in 1815 her coal output was little more than that of 1789, although by 1847 it had been raised from 900,000 to 5,153,000 tons. The use of coke in the smelting of pig-iron was only seriously developed after 1815 through the aid of English experts and capital, and although output rose from 221,000 tons in 1821 to 591,000 in 1847, the enormous demands made by the building of railways in the 1840s could only be met by considerable imports of coal and iron from Great Britain. Cotton-spinning mills, which had begun to appear during the Napoleonic period, grew throughout the first part of the century until by 1847 there were in Mulhouse in Alsace 1,150,000 spindles and another 550,000 in the cotton area of Lille, Roubaix, Tourcoing, and Armentières. The power-loom developed much more quickly and by 1846 there were 10,000 in operation in France. Other textile industries made less use of steam power, but machinery was gradually affecting many trades such as riveting, leather-cutting, and nail-making, and since chemical science was advanced in France, Paris could boast its gas burners for street illumination by 1844.

Compared with the fairly slow pace in France the industrialization of Belgium advanced with astonishing speed, both under Napoleon and during the period of Dutch rule. Rich in coalfields, the Belgians were working some 300 collieries and raising more than 6 million tons of coal a year by the time they struck out for independence in 1830. They had long been skilled in metal work—Liège had been one of Napoleon's great munitions centres—and a considerable immigration of British engineers and workmen after the war helped them to build up a great industry of machine-making with a market in Holland, Russia, and Germany. In 1817, for example, John Cockerill founded the famous iron and machine works at Seraing which within twenty years was employing 2,000 workers—a very large labour force for those times. In these years Belgium was second only to Great Britain, and in the words of the report of an English commission: 'Belgium surpasses in proportion to her size and population every nation in the world.'

The only other part of Europe seriously affected by industrial development was Germany. Like Belgium, she was rich in coal resources and the existence of thousands of tiny establishments gave her a long tradition and experience in the working of metals from the Harz mountains. There was, however, not much attempt made to exploit the coalfields in the Ruhr and the Saar until after 1815, nor in Silesia until about 1840, and by 1846 the total output of coal in Prussia was barely more than 3,200,000 tons, a figure which compares unfavourably with Belgium. The Prussian government was certainly alive to the need to industrialize and in 1821 the *Gewerbe Institut*—an institute of trades—was set up to encourage industrial enterprise. This, together with the services of British technicians, helped to foster the development of machines in factories, but in Berlin itself the lack of any coal nearby made progress slow, and in the rest of the Confederation insufficiency of capital and the confusion of frontiers and local laws hampered any speedy development. In the Rhine provinces the firms of Krupp at Essen and Haniel, Huyssen and Jacobi at Ruhrort and Oberhausen were indications of a greater power to come, but these were very early days for German industry and in the 1840s Belgium was still producing more iron than the whole of the *Zollverein*.

The greatly increased volume of goods circulating within Europe

naturally demanded sound communications and the third characteristic of this period of economic transformation was a revolution in
transport. Even before the railway age striking improvements had
been made in the use of roads, canals, and rivers. In France the restored
Bourbons and Louis Philippe continued to develop an invaluable
heritage of good highways, as well as undertaking a great programme
of canal building. Similarly, the Prussian government benefited greatly
from its acquisition of the Rhineland roads, although communications
in the eastern provinces of Prussia remained poor. River transport in
Europe had always been problematical, since waters were often shallow
or rocky or dangerously swift, and in Germany the local river tolls
continued to be a hindrance to trade until 1834. The invention of the
steam-boat, however, overcame some of the physical difficulties,
making it possible as early as the 1820s to run services on the Rhine, the
Weser and the Elbe, as well as across the Danish Belt and the Sound to
Sweden, and farther north from Stockholm to St Petersburg. In
1830 the Austrian Danube Steam Navigation Company was formed
with the intention of opening up a great waterway which until then
had been little used, but the reefs and rapids of the Danube and the
sand-bars at the delta were always to prevent it from becoming a great
economic artery.

It was, of course, the railways that were to bring about the real
revolution in European communications. Much of the initial impetus
and knowledge came from Great Britain, where independent companies had been experimenting with various forms of steam locomotion
in the 1820s, and among Continental countries it was once again Belgium that jumped into the lead. With their thriving industry and geographical situation, the Belgian Parliament quickly recognized the
potential value of a well-planned railway system and in 1834 voted in
favour of entrusting the whole project to the State—in contrast to the
British pattern of authorizing individual companies by Act of Parliament. In the next thirteen years, as a result of the work of Lebeau
and Rogier, a network of railways connected Belgium with Holland,
Germany, and France; they proved expensive—an average of £16,500
a mile—but the indirect gain in terms of increased export of coal and
pig-iron made it an investment of incalculable national profit.

In France the approach to the whole question was far more cautious.
Torn between systems of State control and private enterprise, the
French Chamber spent most of the 1830s in discussion over funda-
mental principles. In fact, a few concessions to private companies did

result in the laying of 350 miles of track in this decade, but it was not until 1842 that a compromise solution was reached whereby private companies could build the railways according to a national pattern, on the understanding that they would eventually become State property and that in the meantime the State would supervise rates and safety precautions. After this there followed a great boom in railway building, attracting British capital through the banker Edward Blount and bringing to France a whole army of British engineers and railway workers, and by 1848 over 1,200 miles of track had been laid in France.

The enthusiasm for railway building was spreading fast in the 1840s. In Germany the southern and western states tended to rely upon governmental direction, while Prussia, after at first hanging back, began to work in cooperation with private companies, and by 1848 the completion of 3,000 miles of track had brought Germany within reach of a national network. By the same date Vienna was linked with Prague and Warsaw, and Amsterdam with The Hague and Rotterdam. The Swiss made little progress with railways at this time; a mountainous countryside created great engineering difficulties, the conservative element foresaw a dangerous threat to the independence of the cantons, and farmers anticipated a fall in local prices with the increase of foreign competition. In the industrial north their development was seen in a more favourable light, but was hampered by the rival railway schemes of Zürich and Basle, and it was not until 1847 that the first Swiss line was opened between Zürich and Baden.

In north Italy small local lines were completed between Venice and Milan, Turin and Genoa, and Pisa and Leghorn, but it was the Kingdom of Naples, always decried as the most backward state in the peninsula, that actually produced the first railway in Italy. In 1839 a line between Naples and Portici was officially opened by King Ferdinand, who had stipulated that there should be a chapel at every station and no tunnels, which he regarded as conducive to immorality.

The enormous demands made on capital to finance these developments helped to create a fourth characteristic of the economic revolution—the enhanced position of banking on an international scale. The tendency in each country was for the government to rely upon one bank as an agent for its own financial transactions and as a means of controlling the fiscal economy of the country. The difficulty of performing the second function was greatly increased by the existence of many private note-issuing banks, and it was the struggle to restrict the right of issue that marked banking history in England, France, and Prussia during these years. In Holland the Netherlands Bank had enjoyed a monopoly of note issue from the time of its establishment in 1814, while in Belgium the rivalry between two houses—the Société Générale and the Banque de Belgique—ended in the government granting each the right to issue notes. Another problem was the standardization of currency. The uniform French franc system was introduced in Belgium in 1832 and, later, in Switzerland, but in Germany a variety of local currencies was still in circulation at the end of the 1830s.

The most striking feature of all was the growth of international financial operations. The notes of the Bank of England enjoyed an unrivalled position in Europe after the Napoleonic war and the immense amount of capital available in England, due to her earlier industrialization, combined with a long experience in the handling of credit, the development of cheques, and the clearing-house system, made London the financial centre of the world. Merchant bankers in the City, the great houses of Rothschild and Baring Brothers, were the sources to which governments and business men all over the Continent and in North and South America increasingly turned for the floating of loans to finance new industrial developments and the building of railways. The activities of these London bankers, together with others such as the Hopes of Amsterdam and the Parishes of Hamburg, spun across the political frontiers a delicate web of international credit so sensitive to the rise and fall of public confidence that the economy of one country became inextricably involved in the economy of the others.

Two periods of distress were to illustrate this new interdependence. In 1833 President Jackson deprived the Bank of the United States of its function as a central financial agency for the government, and the investment of Federal funds in a number of state-chartered banks led to a period of speculation, followed by a panic in 1837 in which the failure of many banks involved a loss of European capital in America. The consequent shock to credit in Europe meant bankruptcy for many firms, unemployment for the workers, and a frantic search for capital as Belgian financiers fell back on the Bank of England, which in its turn had to rely on the Bank of France. Prosperity returned in the 1840s with the era of railway building, but the potato blight and bad harvests of 1845–7 caused a draining away of capital on imported foodstuffs from South Russia and America and the sudden drop in available money brought a fresh collapse of confidence with its usual accompaniment of bankruptcies and unemployment.[1] Great Britain, as the most highly industrialized country in Europe at this time, suffered the greatest dislocation in these two slumps, but as industrialism grew, so subsequent crises in the century were to reveal the new closeness of economic relationship throughout the entire Continent.

These four principal characteristics of the economic transformation of Europe suggest a great variety of consequences of growing significance during the rest of the century. National commercial policies were directly influenced by the strengthened position of the commercial and industrial classes after the revolutions of 1830 in France and Belgium and the Reform Act of 1832 in Great Britain and were all based on the assumption that in open competition the British industrialist had an enormous advantage over his counterpart on the Continent. Free Trade, as Bismarck once said, was the weapon of the strongest nation. Thus, whereas in Great Britain the tendency was to continue to lower or to remove import duties, a policy of protection for the new industries prevailed on the Continent.

In this respect there was little difference in France between the policy of the Bourbons and that of Louis Philippe's government. In the years following the Restoration duties on imported cotton and iron as well as on corn had constantly mounted. Louis Philippe, who would have liked to lower them, did succeed to some extent at the beginning of his reign, but in 1841 he had to pander to the interests in the bourgeois Chamber with an increased tariff and it was the resistance of French manufacturers, coupled with strong British objections, that forced him to abandon the scheme for a Customs Union with Belgium.

In Germany the most significant change was the merging of the Prussian *Zollverein* with the Unions of the centre and the south, which took effect on 1 January 1834.[2] The establishment of a general protective tariff for German industry, the abolition of internal customs enormously facilitating local trade, the beginnings of a uniform currency, and the rapid growth of a network of railways, all formed part of the theme constantly reiterated by the economist Frederick List, that Germany might one day accomplish the economic conquest of the world; and although List committed suicide in 1846, the foundations

[1] See pp. 133–4.
[2] Oldenburg, Brunswick, Hanover, and the Hanse cities still remained outside the scheme, but most of them had joined the *Zollverein* within the next twenty years.

of a great German national economy had in fact been laid before his death. In Switzerland Berne strongly supported the demand of the liberals to follow the example of Germany and, in 1835, cantonal customs were abolished, although a complete economic union did not come until the victory of the federalists in 1848.[1]

Unlike the bourgeois liberals of western Europe who gained state legislation in their own interest, the new working class was left unprotected by any governmental action. In the industrial towns France was beset with the same ills as in England—child labour, long hours, starvation wages and appalling living conditions in slums lacking all means of sanitation, where the great cholera epidemics of 1832 and 1848 spread like wildfire. In England the efforts of Lord Ashley and other humanitarians had succeeded in restricting child labour in the mines and factories and in establishing a ten-and-a-half-hour day in certain forms of industry by 1850. In France a Factory Act of 1841 also restricted the use of child labour in concerns employing more than twenty persons, and in Prussia, after complaints from the army that physical defects were having a serious effect on the intake of recruits, Frederick William III, in 1839, forbade the employment of children under nine years of age and decreed a ten-hour day for those under sixteen. These French and Prussian measures, however, were largely vitiated by the absence of an adequate system of inspection.

Among the workers themselves there was little success in organization. In France the penal code forbade any association larger than twenty, striking and picketing were criminal offences, and the workman's *livret*, instituted by Napoleon, gave the employer a considerable hold over his labour force. The harshness with which this control was exercised varied, but an average of two hundred workmen a year were sentenced to imprisonment between 1825 and 1847, and two attempts to establish the right of association—in 1831 and 1834 among the silk workers at Lyons[2]—frightened the government of Louis Philippe into treating them as armed rebellion which was put down by military force after bitter fighting. Two fundamental weaknesses hampered the French proletariat in these years. First, there were still too few of them—only a million by 1846 throughout France; second, large forms of industrial enterprise had not yet developed on the Continent even in the west. The scene was one of thousands of tiny workshops. In 1848, for example, there were 64,000 private concerns in Paris—50% of them consisting of no more than the proprietor either on his

[1] See p. 148.   [2] See p. 118.

own or aided by one workman—and in these circumstances the organization of workers was difficult to achieve.

Thus, by 1848, the full implications of the economic revolution were far from being completely worked out; yet they were ultimately to create a situation that would utterly shatter the assumptions of the *ancien régime* so carefully pieced together again at the Congress of Vienna. Industrialism, finance, the growth of railways, the improvement of postal services and the development of the electric telegraph were all to bring various regions into far greater closeness of contact and within the countries themselves to exert a strong centralizing influence. The size and armament of military forces and their systems of mobilization were to be transformed, and areas of Europe, rich in minerals, were to acquire a new strategic significance. In the east, a growing urban population in greater touch with the provinces was to hasten the awakening of nationalism; in the west, a proletariat was eventually to become capable of organization, and throughout the whole Continent, even as early as the 1840s, there was evidence of a new pressure of social and political aspiration bearing inexorably against the foundations of the Holy Alliance.

9

REVOLUTIONARY TENDENCIES 1830–48

'EUROPE is racing towards democracy,' wrote Chateaubriand in 1834, '. . . the most audacious doctrines concerning property, equality and liberty are proclaimed night and morning in the face of monarchs trembling behind a triple guard of unreliable soldiers.' If the language was exaggerated and the monarchs trembled slightly less than Chateaubriand imagined, the 1830s and 1840s were none the less a time of audacious doctrines. In the west, the issues were primarily social and political; in Germany and Italy, the hopes of the new middle class for constitutional government and economic liberty fused with the longing for national unification; in the east, among the peoples of the Austrian and Turkish empires, the aims were almost entirely national. The very diversity of these ideas almost precludes any coherent systemization, yet one feature they shared in common; an intoxicating air of romanticism blows through these Utopian schemes, the delight of poets, philosophical visionaries and University students, impatient of piecemeal legislation and compromise, envisaging not simply reform, but a total regeneration of society.

'The name of Paris', wrote Alexander Herzen on his arrival from Russia in 1847, 'was closely bound up with all the noblest enthusiasms of contemporary humanity. I entered it with reverence, as men used to enter Jerusalem and Rome.' It was not long before he was recording his disillusionment—'death in literature, death in the theatre, death in politics, death in the Chamber'—yet despite the heavily bourgeois instincts that sheltered beneath the umbrella of Louis Philippe, his original comment was not inappropriate. Paris at this time was the centre of a literary scene as brilliant, perhaps, as France has ever known, one in which romantic novelists and poets made a colourful, if somewhat uncoordinated contribution to political and social ideas through their warm sympathy with the working class. 'The proletarian question,' said Lamartine, who became a member of the Chamber in 1833, 'is one that will cause the most terrible explosion in present day society, if society and government decline to fathom and resolve it.' In Great

Britain poets were more wary of becoming directly involved in political life than they were in France, yet an interesting parallel exists between the writers of the two countries in these years of social adjustment. In *La Comédie humaine*, that great cycle of novels in which Balzac set out to portray every aspect of Restoration France, there is the same awareness of the vast gulf between the rich and the poor as one finds in Charles Dickens, and Hugo's poem *Melancholia*, written in 1846, is completely in harmony with Elizabeth Barrett Browning's *Cry of the Children:*

> *Où vont tous ces enfants dont pas un seul ne rit?*
> *Ces doux êtres pensifs que la fièvre maigrit?*

The conventional picture of George Sand as a pipe-smoking Bohemian, the maternal guardian of Chopin on Majorca, might not immediately suggest a parallel with a West Country vicar like Charles Kingsley; yet, just as Kingsley expressed the indignation of the Christian Socialists in *The Water Babies* and *Yeast,* so the ideas of Pierre Leroux were proclaimed in the Socialist novels of George Sand, who was a close friend of Michel de Bourges, the lawyer who had defended the leaders of the Lyons riots of 1834.[1]

There was thus no lack of revolutionary sentiment in the periodicals and literary circles of Paris; they provided an atmosphere of romantic enthusiasm and they were passionately sincere. 'Le poète aujourd'hui,' wrote Victor Hugo in 1824, 'doit marcher devant les peuples comme une lumière et leur montrer le chemin.' Yet it is important not to rate them too highly, for even in France they were to some extent a class apart. A more significant movement is to be found in Liberal Catholicism, since it affected an infinitely wider range of the French public. Amid the tumult of the nineteenth century the Church of Rome stood as a guarantor of the established order of society. Throne and Altar remained its ideal and as a consequence the sense of a great cleavage between the Catholic right and the republican left, which had torn France asunder in the French Revolution, persisted. This was a simplification, however, that not all Catholics could accept. In Ireland Daniel O'Connell had worked furiously against Protestant rule from Westminster; in Belgium Catholics and liberals had combined to expel the Dutch,[2] and these efforts were now to inspire a Breton priest, the Abbé de Lamennais, to lead a movement that combined Catholicism with

---

[1] See p. 118.   [2] See p. 80.

liberal reform. In a series of writings culminating in his *Paroles d'un croyant* in 1834, he demanded that the Church should separate itself from the State, that the press and education should be free from secular control and that elections should be more frequent and the franchise extended. Gradually Lamennais fell away from the Church, partly because it condemned his ideas, partly because it would give no support to Polish nationalism, one of the great emotional cries of the French romantics. Liberal Catholicism, however, was to have important consequences not only in France, but also in Germany and Italy. Firstly, it opened up an alternative road for those who, while remaining devout Catholics, believed in the need for change; secondly, those who supported it fell back on the direct authority of the Pope and thus greatly strengthened the cause of Ultramontanism.

This was not all. As well as the writers, poets, and religious controversialists there was, mainly in Paris, a hard core of dedicated professional revolutionaries. Of these it is indeed strange that the man whose ideas were in the end to come closest to the European scene of the mid-twentieth century was born almost three decades before the outbreak of the French Revolution and died in 1825, when Continental industialism was still in its infancy; stranger still that he should have been a direct descendant of the memorialist of Louis XIV's Versailles. The central problem that puzzled the Count de Saint-Simon was how to find a new spiritual unity in an industrial age which he sensed was to transform the world. In his view these changed circumstances must mean a society organized 'in the manner most advantageous to the largest number'. This, however, did not imply egalitarianism; Saint-Simon, as an aristocrat, naturally thought in terms of a graded society, but for him the aristocracy of the future, based not on privilege but on ability, would consist of scientists, technicians, and bureaucrats, a class dedicated to improving the lot of the poor. It is this understanding of the extraordinary increase in *technical* means at the disposal of the State that gives Saint-Simon his astonishingly modern note. Others certainly reflected upon the possible consequences of the new power in the hands of a government; Herzen wrote gloomily of 'Genghiz Khan equipped with telegraphs, steamships and railways'; de Vigny in his *Servitude et grandeur militaires*, published in 1835, speculated on the dangers of 'quelques aventuriers parvenus à la Dictature' taking over the machinery of State at a stroke—a method later adopted by Louis Napoleon and Adolf Hitler. Yet it was the remarkable quality of Saint-Simon's thought that in acknowledging the fact he went on to conceive the totally different pattern of a technological society that must result.

Saint-Simonianism spread rapidly through France, Belgium, and Germany, but the movement was not greatly helped by the antics of his disciples after his death. Perhaps this was partly his own fault. His last advice to them on his death-bed was: 'il faut être passionné', and they certainly took it to heart. There had been a strong religious element in Saint-Simon's writing which the new leaders Bazard and Prosper Enfantin now stressed. Before long, however, the leaders had fallen out, since Enfantin, seizing on Saint-Simon's belief in the equality of the sexes, decided that the movement could not be complete without a Woman Messiah, an idea which Bazard, a married man, found unacceptable. Styling himself as 'le Père', Enfantin established a community of about forty of the disciples, where amid hymn-singing and the tilling of the soil they were to await the arrival of 'la Mère'. 'La Mère' did not arrive and after a year's imprisonment for organizing an illegal society, the Saint-Simonians set out east to look for her, but the nearest that they ever came to their goal was a meeting with Lady Hester Stanhope at Beirut. Fortunately this phase of silliness did not last, for in Egypt their natural technical interests caused them to divert their energies to the possible construction of a Suez canal and of a Nile dam. Neither scheme came to anything for the moment, but on their return to France the Saint-Simonians reverted to a more normal social life and many of them were later to play a leading part in the development of French railways and banking.

Thus the Saint-Simonians, standing for a creed which was to prove a most acute prognostication of mid-twentieth century society, ended by coming to terms with the nineteenth. There remained, however, a strange variety of professional revolutionaries whose whole lives were dedicated to an attack on the existing system. Of these the most colourful was the Russian Michael Bakunin, a colossus of mob oratory, who castigated every form of injustice and indeed every form of restraint or government. 'This Columbus without America and without a ship' Herzen called him, an appropriate epithet, since Bakunin in his passion for destruction was less interested in any constructive alternative; for him all systems were equally oppressive.[1] Something rather more positive lay behind the aims of Auguste Blanqui who demanded the abolition of private property, but he, too, was essentially a man of the barricades. A *Carbonaro* in his youth, he gained a medal from the

[1] For the later development of Anarchism see pp. 254-6.

government of Louis Philippe for his part in the revolution of 1830, but from then on Blanqui was always on the losing side. With Barbès he organized the *Société des Saisons* in Paris which, in 1839, attempted an armed rising that was put down by the National Guard, and after this he was to spend a large part of his life in prison, only to emerge as the unrepentant apostle of revolution in 1848 and in the Paris Commune of 1871.

Others were more constructive in their views. The ideas of Charles Fourier were motivated by a revulsion against the competitiveness of unrestricted capitalism, a state of economic war in which the casualties were always suffered by the working class. Cooperation was the doctrine that he preached, but because he was deeply suspicious of all central authority, he conceived a whole series of small communities whose members would share the produce of their work. Like Saint-Simon, he was obsessed with the possibilities of the technological application of scientific knowledge, envisaging a society that would offer both congenial work and a great deal of leisure. Much of this thought was wrapped up in fantasy, and to the world Fourier appeared as a queer old man wending his way each morning to feed his cats in the garden of the Palais Royal, before returning to his room at midday to await the arrival of the imaginary millionaire who was to finance his schemes. Yet something of his ideas found expression in the English Cooperative movement that began with the small store opened at Rochdale in 1844; his writings spread as far afield as Russia, and in America several experimental Fourierist communities were established, just as Robert Owen had attempted to create his own model society at New Harmony in Indiana.

This need to strike out on virgin soil and to create a totally new form of ideal community was a natural consequence of the more far-fetched schemes of Utopian Socialism. Yet even those that were rooted in the immediate surroundings of industrial Europe sometimes ended on a note of vague hopefulness. In 1839 Louis Blanc published his *Organisation du travail*, a short book which grew steadily longer as successive editions included the comments of his critics and his answers to them. Blanc regarded the State as the 'supreme regulator of production', responsible for organizing all branches of industry in *ateliers sociaux*, in which workers, grouped by trades, would govern themselves democratically and share their wages according to an agreed proportion. There is, however, a touch of Utopianism even in Blanc, for he believed that capitalists too would be prepared to join the *ateliers sociaux*, although he denied that he was envisaging the State as the owner of all property and the controller of all enterprise. In fact, Blanc never really thought out the later stages of his scheme: 'la machine une fois montée, elle marcherait d'elle-même.'

In contrast to all these, the revolutionary theory of Karl Marx was striking in its completeness, springing from an analytical appreciation of the contemporary scene and based not on a new religion of humanity, but on a philosophy of history in which romantic aspiration was replaced by a cold sense of logical inevitability. Marx, a German Jew, the son of a lawyer in Trier, had studied at the Universities of Bonn and Berlin, where he had been profoundly influenced by the teaching of Hegel. For a short while he was editor of the *Rheinische Zeitung* in Cologne, in which he criticized the Prussian government and the German landowning class to such effect that the paper was suppressed in 1843, and after this he moved to Paris. Here he met and quarrelled with most of the leading Socialists. 'His voice was disagreeably harsh,' wrote an acquaintance at this time, 'and he spoke of men and things in the tone of one who would tolerate no contradiction and which seemed to express his own firm conviction in his mission to sway men's minds and dictate the laws of their being.'

There are innumerable echoes of his predecessors and contemporaries in Marx's writing. Trier had been a centre of Saint-Simonianism; his own father as well as his professors at Berlin had been influenced by it, and ideas of social regeneration, of association replacing antagonism, had all been common parlance long before Marx. Yet for Marx these similarities were superficial and irrelevant, since the whole basis of his thought was utterly different. To him it was a waste of time to draw up a blue-print for a perfect society or to argue that the present society was unjust or unpleasant. All that mattered was to discover the laws of historical change and then to direct a revolutionary movement so that it ran in accordance with those laws. Throughout the past the principal feature of society, as Marx saw it, had been the domination of one class over the rest through its control of the means of production, until the circumstances of that domination eventually produced an economic situation out of which a new class rose to replace the old. Thus the medieval aristocracy based on a system of feudal land tenure had been ousted by a commercial *bourgeoisie*. But the process did not end there, for the competition to produce had led to an industrial revolution bringing in its wake the growth of a vast factory-worker population. The continued competition of capitalism would cause the

economy to oscillate between boom and slump, would bring war between nations in the search for markets and raw materials, and eventually create the circumstances in which the working class would rise
against their masters and establish a new ruling class of the proletariat.
Thus for Marx a capitalist society was not merely unpleasant. It was
doomed. To compromise, to bring in humanitarian reforms, to incorporate the capitalist in a moderately Socialist state, all this was simply
to attempt to prolong a moment in history that was already passing
and for this reason he had nothing but furious contempt for most of
his fellow revolutionaries.

In Germany, where a working-class movement was only just beginning to develop, the atmosphere of growing discontent and agitation was centred mainly on questions of liberalism and nationalism. A
numerous middle class, impatient of a system in which the landed class
was still socially and politically predominant, continued to demand
constitutional forms of government, but the regional and historical
differences between the German states, made any united effort almost
impossible. In 1837, for example, it was simple for the new King of
Hanover, Ernest Augustus, Duke of Cumberland and uncle of Queen
Victoria, to suppress the Hanoverian constitution, and when seven professors of the University of Göttingen, including the Grimm brothers
and Dahlmann, published their protest and were dismissed, there was
nothing that the liberals could do; the Federal Diet refused to intervene and the only consolation for the professors was the offer of chairs
at other German Universities.

This powerlessness against a system which rested on Austrian control
led to an overlapping of thought between German liberals and nationalists, since the successful experiment of the *Zollverein* naturally seemed
to lend the force of practical argument to the emotions of nationalism;
'. . . . we have instead of one Germany thirty-eight German states,'
wrote the *Düsseldorfer Zeitung*, 'an equal number of governments,
almost the same number of courts, as many representative bodies,
thirty-eight distinct legal codes and administrations, embassies and
consulates. What an enormous saving it would be, if all of that were
taken care of by one central government.'

Yet within the span of these aspirations there remained many difficulties. The general mistrust of Prussia, and the sense of rivalry between
the Lutheran states and the Catholic south and Rhineland were still
strong. The precise definition of a unified Germany's frontiers was

highly debatable.[1] Many of the liberals, suspicious of the social implications of democratic republicanism, thought in terms simply of a
stronger federal state (a *Bundesstaat*[2] rather than the *Staatenbund* of 1815),
or if a unitary state were to be created, hoped for the retention of
monarchy and looked with some misgiving at the more radical sentiments suggested in a verse of Ferdinand Freiligrath:

> *Dass Deutschland frei und einig sei,*
> *Das ist auch unser Dürsten,*
> *Doch einig wird es, nur wenn frei,*
> *Und frei nur ohne Fürsten!*[3]

These complications, however, did little to check the ardour of
German nationalism which derived much of its emotional force from
the manifold aspects of the Romantic movement,[4] considerably aided
by the intellectual leadership of the Universities. A great flowering of
poetry, philosophy, history, and philology combined to demonstrate
the unique character of the German people and to create in the imagination a sense of spiritual unity, *der Volksgeist*. 'Venerable Barbarossa,'
wrote Geibel in 1835, referring to the legend of the medieval Emperor
Frederick I, 'when will the eagle disperse the ravens that hover round
the summit of the Kyffhäuser and thus herald your return to earth?'
The publications and lectures of the historians in particular helped to
build up a highly coloured version of Germany's role in Europe. Her
historic mission was to check the Slav onrush from the east and, by
conquest, to civilize them; her undoing had been due to the machina-
tions of the French who had undermined her unity in the Thirty Years'
War, robbed her of Alsace under Louis XIV, and of still more under
Napoleon. Thus, while Metternich's system was the immediate obstacle to unification, extreme German nationalism looked far beyond
Austria for its ultimate fulfilment. Its greatest hatred was for France,
'the hereditary foe, the eternal, tireless, destructive enemy', as Stein
wrote in 1815, and the flaming of German patriotism in the war of
liberation in 1813 was to find continued expression in Fallersleben's
Deutschland über alles, Becker's *Sie sollen ihn nicht haben, den freien
deutschen Rhein*, and Schneckenburger's *Die Wacht am Rhein*. In the east
it was a question not of frontiers, but of peoples, and here no river

---

[1] See pp. 52, 144.   [2] See Glossary of technical terms, p. 493.
[3] 'It is also our desire that Germany should be free and united; she can be united only
when she is free, and only free when she is without princes.'
[4] See p. 49.

marked the goal of German nationalism—only a mystic sense of destiny, whereby the racial purity of the *Volk* might be preserved.

There are several striking parallels between German and Italian nationalism at this time. In Italy Napoleonic rule had carried through a highly beneficial rationalizing of the old system, at the same time awakening a strong sense of Italian national feeling in opposition to foreign interference; and resentment at the reimposition of Austrian influence throughout the peninsula after 1815 had found thinly veiled expression in the historical novels of Manzoni and the early operas of Verdi. As in Germany, resistance to the Vienna settlement had been hamstrung by the particularism of the Italian states, jealous of each other and especially nervous of the ambitions of Piedmont. There was one further problem that was peculiar to Italy in that the existence of the Papal States remained the supreme obstacle to unification that Machiavelli had deplored centuries before. For the Italian nationalist Rome was the only possible capital of Italy; for the Popes the Temporal Power was inviolable and any interference with it was certain to incur the wrath of Catholic opinion throughout Europe. On the other hand, geography which provided the nationalists with one of their principal arguments left little doubt where the general line of an Italian frontier would lie, and in the Italian *risorgimento* there was much less of the mystique of the *Volk* with which the Germans challenged the various forms of Slav nationalism.

Amid the constant discussion and literary activity in Italy during these years three main streams of thought may be discerned, two of them moderate and liberal in their social programme, the third radical and democratic. The first was embodied in *Il Primato*, the work of the Abbé Gioberti, a Piedmontese priest, who had been banished in 1833 and who published his great scheme ten years later from Brussels. The essence of Gioberti's plan was that the predominance of Piedmont and the antagonizing of Catholic opinion might both be avoided by the creation of an Italian federation out of the existing states under the presidency of the Pope. The second group, in which Massimo D'Azeglio and Cesare Balbo were significant personalities, turned instead to the leadership of Piedmont, reckoning to establish a North Italian Kingdom as a beginning. Both movements hoped for the usual liberal reforms of constitutional government and freedom of the press; neither of them had very much idea of how the blow was to be struck.

In contrast to these sane, cautious schemes, 'Young Italy', the movement of Giuseppe Mazzini, the son of a University professor at Genoa, had all the fire of a crusade. For Mazzini there could be no compromise with Rome or Piedmont; the only solution for Italy lay in a unitary republic. An early flirtation with the *Carbonari* had led to his exile from Piedmont in 1831, and after two unsuccessful attempts to stir up revolt in Piedmont from France and Switzerland he eventually came to England in 1837 to work ceaselessly for the great day. 'Religion and politics are inseparable,' he wrote, and Mazzini, solemn-eyed, clothed always in black and consumed with a sense of personal dedication, was indeed like some high priest of a new religion of humanity in which all national sentiment must find expression and in which all social ills would be solved by the brotherhood of man.

In eastern Europe the principal motive force was literary. The Romantic enthusiasm for salvaging local *patois* and bringing to light remote heroic epochs gave rise to the publication of a host of grammars, dictionaries, and histories of literature, striving to create formed languages out of what for centuries had been no more than peasant dialects. In this medley of submerged peoples language was the only means of individual identification and swiftly became a political symbol, since the conscious cultivation of a national tongue was an essential step in establishing the unity of a national group. The effect of this linguistic movement was mostly confined to the towns, where it was to prove a powerful instrument of national pride, raising questions of the language to be used in the law courts and taught in the schools, and exacerbating local antagonisms where difference of class coincided with difference of racial origin.[1]

In Hungary two movements were at work. One group under Count Széchényi, an extremely wealthy member of the Magyar aristocracy, recommended the end of immunity from taxation which the nobility enjoyed, together with an improvement in the position of the peasantry and agricultural reforms which might increase the economic output of the country. The second group, led by Louis Kossuth, one of the lesser nobility, embraced most of these suggestions, but went further in demanding a greater economic independence for Hungary. Before long, social jealousies had created a considerable cleavage between the two, and at the same time both were regarded with profound mistrust by the non-Magyar people within Hungary, as, for example, when the Croat deputies refused to accept the innovation of Magyar as the official language of the Hungarian Diet of 1844. It was a situation symbolic of the incompatibility of all the great aims quickening into life in

[1] See pp. 25, 52.

E

central and eastern Europe, a mutual intolerance that was to be the ruin of the risings of 1848.

In Norway and Finland the hope of greater independence was in-evitably bound up with the question of language; in the early 1840s Jörgen Moe and Peter Asbjörnsen worked together to edit a series of Norwegian fairy tales and poems, while Ivar Aasen began collating and combining the local Norwegian dialects to produce a national language which might oust the predominantly Danish tongue spoken by the urban and bureaucratic classes. Meanwhile, in Finland Elias Lönnrot, a Karelian doctor, had compiled a written version of the Finnish saga *Kalevala*, and Johan Snellman was voicing the demand for the use of Finnish in educational institutions. 'The bulk of the nation,' he said in 1840, 'can never be raised so long as Swedish remains the language of administration.' The situation in Finland was thus more complex than in Norway, for whereas the growth of Norwegian national conscious-ness simply created a greater impatience at Swedish control, the resent-ment of the Finns towards the local Swedish-speaking upper class only confused the issue of independence from Russia, and Tsar Alexander II was later able to make use of this in attempting to reconcile the Finns to Russian rule.[1]

In Russia herself the atmosphere of political repression tended to make movements of reform a matter of purely intellectual discussion. Very broadly two groups of thinkers and writers began to emerge in the 1830s, each drawing a different conclusion from their common realization of the peculiar nature of Russian history. To the western-izers it seemed that Russia had been too long cut off from the rest of Europe. 'Isolated from the European family, we sought our moral code in miserable Byzantium,' wrote Peter Chaadayev in a letter first published in 1836, 'and while the world was being built anew, we re-mained as before cowering in our hovels of mud and straw, cut off from that universal movement in which the social idea of Christianity was formed and developed.' Thus the westernizers drew their inspira-tion from European sources, particularly from German philosophy, and it was not surprising that several of their leaders such as V. S. Pecherin, Nicholas Ogarëv, and Alexander Herzen should eventually leave Russia to spend their lives in the west.

In contrast to them the Slavophils saw the future in terms of the individual character of Russian society. They did not hate the west; they were conscious that much was wrong in Russia, but they believed

[1] See p. 230.

that the solution must be worked out in accordance with her own particular destiny. 'These native foundations which we previously ignored on account of our blind partiality for western civilization, our reckless neglect of our own past history (regarding it as barbarous),' wrote Kireyevsky, 'are quite distinct from those elements which compose the civilization of western European peoples.' The Slavophils based their faith on the Orthodox Church and the small decentralized social unit of the *mir*, the village commune; it was out of these, they argued, that a new Russian society must be shaped. This sense of isolation from the rest of Europe did not in itself create an organized movement, but as a general attitude it was to lend added impetus to the ideas of the Populists[1] in the 1870s, and in the twentieth century a strong Slavophil thread was to run through the development of Russian Communism.

[1] See p. 255.

10

THE ATTITUDE OF THE GOVERNMENTS
1830–48

THE growing sense of dissatisfaction through Europe, aggravated by the inevitable tensions of a period of economic transition, was naturally reflected in the problems that confronted all governments in the years following the revolutions of 1830. In France it might well have seemed that no royal prince could have been more suitable for the role of constitutional sovereign than Louis Philippe at this particular moment in French history. The testimonial which Thiers and his companions had produced for their candidate in July 1830, and which was at least partly true, had already indicated this. A son of Philippe Égalité, he had fought for the Revolution at Jemappes in November 1792 and had only gone into exile in 1793, when the Revolution was fast ceasing to be respectable. After the Revolution he had shown little interest in the extravagance of the Ultras, preferring to devote his energy to regaining the Orleans estates until, by 1830, through tireless litigation and highly skilful investment, he had become one of the richest men in France. His orderly domestic life, his large family to which he was devoted, the umbrella which he carried under his arm, were all symbols of bourgeois virtue. Daumier in his cartoons might mock the fleshy pear-shaped face, but there was no escaping the fact that in many ways Louis Philippe was a monarch ideally of his time.

The leading political figures of his reign—bankers, journalists, and University teachers—were also symbolic of the victory of 1830. There were in the main two groups—a party of resistance which regarded the revolution as no more than a change of king and, beyond that, wished for law and order within France and peace with the rest of Europe; and a party of movement which contemplated further social reforms and wished to give active assistance to the revolutionaries outside France's boundaries. Throughout most of his reign Louis Philippe was to rely on governments drawn from the party of resistance, few of which lasted long until his appointment of Guizot, a University professor, who after 1840 remained his principal counsellor. Only on three occasions did he entrust himself to more venturesome spirits and each time he secured their resignation within a few months, when a serious international crisis seemed to be developing—Laffitte in 1831 over the Belgian question,[1] Thiers in 1836 when he wished to intervene more forcefully in Spain, and again in 1840, when war over the Near East appeared imminent.[2]

Caution and common sense were thus the hallmark of the reign of Louis Philippe, its principal monument in the Place de la Concorde an Egyptian obelisk of an epoch sufficiently remote to avoid controversy.[3] '*Enrichissez-vous*', an unfortunate phrase wrenched from its context in a speech made by Guizot, was a satisfactory formula for many of the electorate of less than 200,000. The membership of the National Guard was restricted to the middle class, and the Chamber was one in which the business man could successfully resist Louis Philippe's schemes for the lowering of tariffs, or a Customs Union with Belgium. In education, at least, the government did make some headway, with Guizot's law of 1833 setting up primary schools in every commune of more than 6,000 inhabitants, as well as *écoles normales* for the training of teachers. Schooling was to be free, but not compulsory, and by 1847 the number of primary schools had increased from 33,000 to 43,000. Clergy were not prohibited from teaching in these schools and since no State monopoly was imposed, the Church enjoyed reasonable freedom of education at the primary level. The King was, however, disappointed in his hopes of being able to extend this freedom to secondary levels, which for the moment remained purely secular and strongly anti-clerical in outlook.

Only in one field did Louis Philippe make a bid for *la gloire*—the colonization of Algeria; thus Charles X's expedition against the Bey of Algiers was prolonged throughout the entire reign in a bitter campaign of conquest which constantly demanded more and more troops— 64,000 by 1840, 101,000 by 1847. In 1841 27,000 French immigrants were settled there as a conscious means of consolidating France's hold and by 1845 their numbers had grown to 75,000. Yet the acquisition of Algeria failed to awaken any patriotic pride. Rather, the expense of the war, the viciousness of the fighting, and the appalling ravages of disease became objects of criticism, and the part played by five of Louis

[1] See p. 82.   [2] See p. 91.
[3] From a diplomatic point of view, however, it was significant that it should have been a gift from Mehemet Ali.

Philippe's sons in Algeria, instead of adding honour to the royal family, only associated them personally with an unpopular military adventure.

It was, however, within France that the principal discontents were to grow. At a parliamentary level an obvious grievance was the smallness of the electorate, for the paradox of the bourgeois monarchy of Louis Philippe was that its electoral regulations left so many of the bourgeois unrepresented. The pressure increased, but the government would not budge. 'I cannot find among us today,' said Guizot in 1842, 'in the actual state of society, any real and serious motive, any motive worthy of a free and sensible country, to justify the proposed electoral reform.' There was, too, among the deputies themselves, a dissatisfaction at the degree of control which Louis Philippe attempted to exercise over the Chamber; between 1830 and 1847 the number of officials who sat as deputies rose from 142 to 193 out of a total of 459 seats, and although this cultivation of a Court party had been a time-honoured practice during the development of constitutional monarchy in Great Britain, it hardly accorded with the axiom that Thiers had stated in 1830: 'le roi règne et ne gouverne pas.'

The King and his bourgeois allies might quarrel over powers of government; they remained united in the face of a restless working class. As Chateaubriand pointed out, 'l'opposition devenue industrielle . . . ne veut pas renverser ce qu'elle a créé et ce par quoi elle vit: deux frayeurs l'arrêtent, la frayeur du retour à la Légitimité, la frayeur plus grande du règne populaire.' Two outbreaks in Lyons towards the beginning of the reign appeared to underline this second danger. In 1831 a period of unrest during the summer, due to a slump in the silk trade, led to a series of strikes and lock-outs in November, after the workers had attempted to establish a minimum wage scale, and in the subsequent fighting, during which some six hundred casualties were suffered, the city was for a short time in the hands of the workers. When order was eventually restored, the government was sufficiently restrained to impose only slight sentences of imprisonment on the leaders, but in April 1834 another slump, together with disputes over a new law restricting the right of association, caused a further outbreak of fighting in Lyons, and at the same time the *Société des Droits de l'Homme* attempted to stimulate a sympathetic rising in the east of Paris. This time the repression was sterner. At Lyons the rioting was crushed after three days of battle, and eighteen of the leaders were sentenced to transportation; in Paris the troops played havoc in the working-class districts with a ferocity which Daumier recorded in his gruesome lithograph of the massacre of the rue Transnonain.

In fact, despite all the moderation to which Louis Philippe aspired, there was an undercurrent of violence throughout his reign. No less than six attempts were made on his life—the most spectacular being in 1835, when an infernal machine killed forty-one people but only slightly wounded the King. The police had to watch constantly for conspiracy by republicans or by Bourbon legitimists, and in addition to all other revolutionary activity there always remained the shadow of Bonapartism.

It could be argued that Napoleon Bonaparte's most effective work was accomplished after his exile at St Helena. The Napoleonic legend, inspired by his memoirs and the record of his conversations on the island, wafted through the Continent during the following decades, creating an entirely imaginary picture of what might have been—a constitutional government for France, which would have given full rein to national aspirations in other parts of Europe. Napoleon himself died in 1821; there remained his son, the Duke de Reichstadt, a frail figure hemmed in by the aura of his father and the fearful suspicion of his father's enemies, who kept him in a form of decorous imprisonment in Vienna until his death in 1832. The Emperor's family, however, had been Italianate in its proportions and there was always to be a Bonaparte Pretender. Napoleon's brother, Louis, had married Hortense, Josephine's daughter by her first marriage, and of their two sons the elder had died during a *Carbonaro* escapade in the Italian revolt of 1831, leaving to his younger brother the somewhat insubstantial inheritance of the Bonaparte clan. An upbringing in exile, tinged with the excitement of romantic conspiracy, set its mark on the early activities of young Louis Napoleon. From Switzerland, where he served for a time as an artillery officer in Canton Berne, he embarked in 1836 on a forlorn attempt to rally revolutionary sympathies in Strasbourg. The *coup* failed, but the government of Louis Philippe thought it wiser not to give him the publicity of a public trial and dispatched him instead to the United States. In 1838 he settled in England and in the following year gave practical form to the legend in a little book, *Des idées napoléoniennes*, at the same time as Disraeli found him a useful model for one of the characters in his novel *Endymion*. In 1840 his next attempt at greatness, however, far outran the imagination of the novelist—a Channel crossing by paddle-boat with a few companions and an eagle in a cage, an unsuccessful effort to inflame the Boulogne garrison with the memory of his uncle's name, ending in a desperate swim from the shore and an ignominious arrest. This time the French government did risk putting him on trial and he was sentenced to perpetual imprisonment in the fortress of Ham in the north-east of France, where he busied himself with another book, *L'extinction du paupérisme*, before he finally made his escape to England in 1846.

On the whole, Louis Philippe had dealt lightly with Bonapartism; indeed, in terms of symbols he had been positively favourable. In 1833 Napoleon's statue had been placed once more at the top of its column in the Place Vendôme; in 1840 the French king had secured agreement with the British government whereby Napoleon's body might be brought back from St Helena to lie eventually in the church of the Invalides. Yet symbols were not enough. 'If you reject peaceful reform, then you will have reform by violence,' Victor Hugo warned the King. A welter of newspapers preached the same message, appealing to different sections of the population; *Le National* had by now grown more moderate, advocating only a gradual extension of the franchise, but a more radical group under Ledru-Rollin founded *La Réforme* in 1843, while Louis Blanc's short-lived *Revue de progrès* and its successor the *Revue indépendante* under George Sand and Pierre Leroux helped to spread ideas of Socialism. The publication of Michelet's *Histoire de la Révolution* in 1846 and of Lamartine's *Histoire des Girondins* in 1847 awoke thoughts of their revolutionary tradition among the discontented bourgeois at a time when an economic slump[1] and a new unpopular foreign policy[2] of friendship with Austria were playing havoc with the fortunes of the monarchy. But the conservatism of old age left Louis Philippe impervious to the growing barrage of criticism. 'In God's name,' cried de Tocqueville in a debate on electoral reform in January 1848, 'change the spirit of the government; for, I repeat, that spirit will lead you to the abyss.' But the Chamber, as blind as its king, rejected the proposals for an extension of the franchise by 228 votes to 189, and disaster now lay only a few weeks away.

Outside France the frustration of the bourgeois in countries where constitutional government had been established was rather less marked. In Great Britain the Parliamentary Reform Act of 1832 settled the grievances of the new wealthy middle class. The movement towards Free Trade, strongly supported by the industrialists, was to become intensified throughout the next forty years, and the repeal of the Corn

[1] See p. 133. [2] See p. 94.

Laws by a Conservative Prime Minister in 1846 was a symbol of the decline of the agricultural interest in an industrial age.

On the Continent Belgium remained the model liberal constitutional state. King Leopold retained a personal control over foreign policy, carrying on a considerable correspondence with his niece Queen Victoria as well as with Metternich and the King of Prussia, and fostering the dynastic interests of the Saxe-Coburg family through the arrangement of marriages with the ruling houses of Great Britain, France, and Portugal. In home affairs, however, he kept meticulously to the ideal of constitutional monarchy. Unlike Louis Philippe, he made no attempt to engineer a submissive majority in the Chamber, worked mainly through coalition ministries and on one occasion horrified the autocratic Powers by accepting in the Belgian army a Polish general who had taken part in the Warsaw rising of 1830. His happy relations with his subjects were assisted by a thriving economy[1] and by the continuation of that compromise between the liberal and Catholic parties which had facilitated the movement for independence in the 1830 rising—a harmony that survived even the establishment of State schools and did not begin to break up until 1847.

In the Netherlands the constitution of 1814[2] gave the Dutch considerably less share in the government of their country and King William showed little inclination for any change. The example of the Belgians, however, after gaining their independence, brought increasing pressure on the King and in 1840 he was forced to give way. In response to the demands of the second Chamber a limited form of ministerial responsibility was granted; in future each department was to submit its own financial requirements every two years and the legislature was to have the right to alter the franchise, although, in fact, no alteration was made. These changes were hardly revolutionary, but King William was too much of an autocrat to relish this new situation and since he had already shocked his subjects by his proposal to marry a Belgian Catholic, he decided to abdicate in favour of his son in 1841. William II was perfectly prepared to work with the revised constitution and a cautious liberalism began now to weaken the hold both of a rigid Calvinist orthodoxy and of the old conservative classes.

The same tendencies were to be found in Scandinavia. In Sweden the representative assembly still met in the old form of the four Estates, but although the middle class pressed for the establishment of a unified Parliament, constitutional revision was successfully resisted by the

<hr>

[1] See pp. 97, 98.   [2] See p. 33.

clergy and the nobility. By 1840 Bernadotte, reigning as Charles XIV, had been forced to pay some attention to the wishes of the *Riksdag* in selecting his ministers, and the general economic improvement of the country did much to mollify liberal ambitions. In 1834 the Göta Canal created a shorter link by water from the North Sea to the Baltic; centres of technical education were established, mining and forestry developed, and the agricultural yield of Sweden was so increased that despite a rising population no further importation of grain was necessary after 1850. In 1842 primary schools were established in every parish. On Bernadotte's death, in 1844, his son succeeded as Oscar I and the new king, Swedish-speaking unlike his Gascon father, was more popular with the Swedes and had stronger liberal instincts. In 1846 the trade guilds which had hampered the new business classes were abolished and in the following year the first Poor Law was established. Meanwhile, in Norway, the constitutional assembly, the *Storting*, had fought stubbornly to resist Bernadotte's proposals that the royal veto on its proceedings should be absolute, and after a serious crisis in the relations between the two peoples in 1836 Bernadotte came to terms with the Norwegian demands for a greater independence in their own affairs.

In the countries where no constitutional rule had yet been established the struggle was to take a different form, partly because there were few accepted organs through which the liberals could work, partly because in central Europe the issues were complicated by questions of nationalism.

In Russia, under the rule of Nicholas I, there could be no question of constitutional development. The new Tsar, who liked to refer to his empire as his 'command', had soon subordinated the existing central organs of government to a system of secret committees and police agents, but despite his militarist approach, Nicholas was not averse to reform, provided that it was imposed from above. Speransky carried out a great codification of existing laws and a new department was established under Kisilev through whom the position of the Crown peasants was considerably improved. Nicholas himself was particularly concerned with exerting a greater control over the nobility and gentry and did make some progress in regulating their relations with their serfs. He restricted the punishments that they could inflict, introduced measures whereby it would be possible for serfs to acquire property, and, in 1845, prohibited night work for children under twelve years of age in the factories which some landowners had set up on their estates;

but the full effects of all these decrees were largely nullified by the passive resistance of the proprietors.

For Nicholas, however, a benevolent interest in the serfs was not to be confused with any sympathy with the wider movements in favour of pan-Slavism or constitutional reform, and the Tsar who could not even accept the idea of Louis Philippe as King of the French, naturally imposed the sternest censorship on all forms of liberal writing. Gogol did manage to gain permission to perform his play *The Inspector General*, which mocked Russian officialdom, but a little later he felt so stifled by the atmosphere of repression that he emigrated to Rome, and in 1852 Turgenev was arrested and confined to his country residence simply for calling Gogol 'great' in an article on his death. In Poland the rising of 1830 had confirmed all Nicholas's worst suspicions of Alexander's experiment in liberalism and in 1832 an Organic Statute abolished the Diet and the constitutional liberties that had been granted to the kingdom. Technically Poland retained governmental autonomy, but the period of repression that followed involved an intensive process of russification. Tribunals confiscated about one-tenth of Polish property and distributed it to Russians. The sons of the rebels were sent to Russian military schools; the Russian language was established in all institutions of primary and secondary education, the Universities of Warsaw and Vilna were closed, and in the Russo-Polish border districts the new policy included the transportation of thousands of suspects to the east and a fierce persecution of Jews and Uniates.[1]

At Vienna the succession of the Emperor Ferdinand on his father's death in 1835 brought no change in the stagnant atmosphere of repression. The new Emperor was so utterly incapable of rising to his responsibilities that the work of government was managed by a State council over which Ferdinand's uncle Archduke Ludwig presided; here Metternich had to contend with his rival Kollowrat, a Bohemian nobleman whose skill in financial matters had added enormously to his influence since his entry into the administration in 1826. Such a group was hardly likely to hammer out a positive solution to the problems of serfdom and tariff reform which were becoming insistent, and proposals for reform from any other source were made unlikely by a vigilant police supervision. In the 1840s, however, the provincial Diets did begin to give some expression to discontent. The Bohemian Diet raised a demand for the right to vote taxes; the Estates of Lower Austria agitated for agrarian reform, and since they met in Vienna, began to

[1] See p. 40.

find support in the *salons* of the capital. The most vigorous criticism came from the Hungarian Diet in their demands for equality for Protestants and for the use of Hungarian at their meetings, but their efforts were weakened by the antagonism between the magnates' party under Széchényi and the gentry under Kossuth.[1]

Prussia presented a very different scene. Until 1840 there had been little trouble, mainly because the government could rely on an efficient bureaucracy and a good army, and Frederick William III had, on the whole, been prepared to follow Metternich's advice. In 1840, however, a new king ascended the throne. Like Tsar Alexander I and Charles Albert in Piedmont, Frederick William IV was one of those sovereigns of the first half of the nineteenth century who were torn between conservatism and a romantic desire to be accepted as a liberal monarch. On his accession he released many of the political prisoners of the previous reign, abolished the censorship and appointed to the Council of State Boyen, who was one of the leaders of the party for reform. Disliking the more modern type of constitutional Parliament, he granted greater power to the provincial Diets which met on the basis of Estates, allowing them the right to publish their debates. These concessions at once ended the period of relative quiet that Prussia had known since 1815. Middle-class liberals in the Rhineland, the most industrialized region of the Prussian dominions, began to agitate for a constitution of the Belgian type; in 1841, at Cologne, Karl Marx opened his attack on the existing governmental and social system in the *Rheinische Zeitung*; handcraftsmen seriously affected by the new industrialism, and peasantry often unable to keep up the payments on their commutation of feudal dues, became more openly restive. The conservative Junker class watched the activities of the King with growing doubt and at Berlin found spokesmen in a pietistic Court circle led by Leopold and Ludwig von Gerlach, who turned to the heir to the throne, the King's brother William. Frederick William IV wavered, and then swung towards the conservatives. The *Rheinische Zeitung* was suppressed in 1843. Freiligrath, to whom he had given a pension, was banished, and by 1845 he was requesting the French government to expel German writers from France. His vacillation was finally exemplified by the summoning of the United Diet at Berlin in 1847. Liberal hopes were raised since the declared purpose of the Diet was to vote a loan for the building of a railway to link East Prussia with Berlin. Yet they were simultaneously dashed by the realization

[1] See p. 113.

that the United Diet was to be no more than a combination of all the provincial Diets of Prussia, based on the division into social Orders, and in his opening speech Frederick William made it clear that he would go no further in the direction of constitutional government. 'Never will I permit a written sheet of paper to come between our God in Heaven and this land, as if it were a second Providence, to rule us with its paragraphs and supplant the old sacred loyalty.' As a result the United Diet came to nothing. The liberals demanded a national legislative assembly, as had been promised after the Napoleonic war, and when this was refused, rejected the loan. The Diet dispersed in June 1847 and within a few months Frederick William was to find himself confronted with a far more dangerous situation.

In Denmark the liberal movement had gained no more than the establishment of consultative provincial Estates in 1831—on the Prussian model of 1823[1]—but social and political antagonism here was less bitter owing to the enlightened despotism of the Danish kings. Liberal feelings was concentrated far more on the question of Slesvig. Since the Middle Ages the King of Denmark had ruled over the duchies of Slesvig and Holstein as their Duke. The Union was a purely personal one and its significance in the nineteenth century rested on the fact that while the population of Slesvig was partly Danish- and partly German-speaking, the Holsteiners were almost entirely German. By now German nationalism in Holstein was becoming outspoken, supported by the local nobility who resented the absolutism of the Danish kings, and by the students of the University of Kiel where Dahlmann was teaching after his expulsion from Göttingen in Hanover. The immediate complication was that the Salic law, excluding succession through a female line, applied in the duchies, but not in Denmark; thus if a Danish king was actually to succeed through a female line, the way would be open for German interests to establish a duke of their own in the duchies. Such a possibility was now not far distant, since Christian VIII, who ascended the Danish throne in 1839, had only one son Frederick, who was childless, and beyond him the Danish succession would have to pass through a female line.[2] Foreseeing this eventuality, German nationalists insisted on the indivisibility of the two duchies and began to look to the Duke of Augustenburg as their future candidate. The Danes, determined that they should at least not lose both duchies, began to emphasize the distinctness of Slesvig from Holstein. This policy was finally stated in 1846, when Christian VIII published

[1] See p. 29.   [2] See Genealogical table, p. 482.

an open letter in which he declared that Slesvig was governed by the same laws of succession as in Denmark. This clearly suggested an intention ultimately to absorb Slesvig within the kingdom and awoke a storm of indignation among the Germans in the duchies and throughout most of Germany. The full significance of the dispute is that it illustrates the fatal confusion of liberal and nationalist ideals that was to bedevil the revolutionary movements of central Europe. For it was the German liberals who maintained most fervently the indivisibility of the duchies which might one day be under a German prince, while the liberals at Copenhagen, who hoped to extract a constitution from their king, fell in whole-heartedly behind Christian VIII with their demand for Denmark up to the Eider, the southern boundary of Slesvig.

This excitement over the future of the duchies was indicative of the heightened emotions everywhere in Germany. Working-class unrest in the new industries of Saxony, a mounting antagonism between Protestant and Catholic in the Rhineland, a new wave of anti-Semitism among the radicals of the southern states, all formed a background of latent violence to such political developments as the forcing of a liberal ministry on Grand Duke Leopold of Baden at the end of 1846 or the unsuccessful attempt on the part of the Elector of Hesse-Cassel to restrict the local constitution in 1847. At the same time, in Bavaria, old King Ludwig had become completely captivated by the charms of a dancer of partly British extraction, who, after assuming the name of Lola Montez, had already enjoyed an exotic career throughout most of the Continent, and her interference in the work of government led to an outcry that was later to lose Ludwig his throne.

In Italy the old order appeared reasonably entrenched in most of the states, but the advent of two rulers was to undermine the control that Metternich hoped to maintain here. In 1831 Charles Albert had ascended the throne in Piedmont. After his experiences in 1821[1] he knew that he must disarm the suspicions of Metternich and this he attempted, first by a military alliance with Austria, and then by the ostentatious severity with which he crushed Mazzini's conspiracies to raise a mutiny in the Piedmontese army in 1833 and to invade Savoy in 1834. In the second part of his reign, however, Charles Albert began to win back a little of the sympathy of the liberals, who by now had come to regard him as a creature of Metternich's. A noble of liberal tendencies, Count Pes di Villamarina, was appointed Minister of War

[1] See pp. 64, 67.

in 1835 and in the ten years following 1837 a series of codes of a
Napoleonic type, abolishing feudal practices in Sardinia and encouraging commerce, were introduced. Tariffs were considerably reduced,
guilds abolished, and the University of Turin expanded. A new short-
service system for the army enabled Piedmont to put 70,000 troops in
the field in 1848 and plans went ahead for the development of railways.
This modernizing of the kingdom was naturally in tune with liberal
aspirations, and at the same time it was noticeable that good relations
with Austria were deteriorating in the 1840s through a number of disputes over the sale of salt to Canton Ticino and the plan for a railway
line which would link Genoa with Lake Maggiore—in conflict with
the Austrian scheme for a line by-passing Piedmont from Leghorn
to the Brenner pass via Florence and Trieste. To the end Charles Albert
remained an enigmatic figure—the Hamlet of Savoy, as Mazzini called
him; the weakness of Piedmont against Austria forced him to dis-
semble and, in any case, he never entirely knew his own mind. Yet, by
1845, the moderate Italian liberals were looking to him with new hope.
'Tell these gentlemen to remain peaceful, not to move,' he said to
D'Azeglio, who visited the King to sound him on his intentions,
'because at present there is nothing to be done; but let them rest assured
that when the opportunity comes, my life, the life of my sons, my
treasure and my army will all be spent in the cause of Italy.'

Ominous though this might sound for the settlement of 1815, it was
nothing compared with the shock that Metternich was to suffer within
the next few months. In June 1846 Pope Gregory XVI died and a wave
of excitement swept through the liberals at the election of Cardinal
Giovanni Mastai-Ferretti, who assumed the title of Pius IX. For it was
known that the new Pope, a man of great personal charm, was favourably disposed towards liberal ideas and was familiar with the writings
of Count Balbo and particularly Gioberti's *Primato*. They were not disappointed. Pius at once embarked on a much needed plan of reform in
the Papal States; an amnesty for political prisoners was declared, the
press was to enjoy a greater freedom, and a Civic Guard and an advisory body, the *Consulta*, each consisting of laymen, were established.
A liberal Pope was the one thing that Metternich had never anticipated, and his fears of the possible consequences soon appeared to be
not entirely unfounded. Pius IX's liberalism was essentially cautious,
but in the secret societies the republicans saw their chance to foment
public excitement and the agitation for reform began to spread. In
1847, in Tuscany, Grand Duke Leopold II was impelled to abolish the

secret police, and in Lucca a Civic Guard was formed. Hastily Metternich ordered the reinforcing of the garrison at Ferrara. On this Pius
appealed to the Powers of Europe, and when Charles Albert placed the
Piedmontese army at the Pope's disposal and began to speak in terms of
a war for the independence of Italy, this dangerous situation, coupled
with the persuasion of Lord Palmerston, the British Foreign Secretary,
caused Metternich to withdraw his troops from Ferrara.

Meanwhile, in 1846, there had been a further outbreak of Polish
nationalism in eastern Europe. The milder rule of Frederick William
IV at the beginning of his reign had encouraged Polish patriots in the
province of Posen, to the south of West Prussia, to prepare an insurrection under the leadership of Mieroslavski, but in February 1846 the
Prussian police got wind of the scheme and imprisoned the leaders, so
that the insurrection never came to anything more than an unsuccessful attack within the city of Posen itself. The movement, however, did
spark off a republican rising in the Free City of Cracow, and it appeared
to the Habsburg government that the unrest was about to spread to
their own Polish province of Galicia. Polish nationalism in these regions, however, was a sentiment largely confined to the landowning
class. To deal with this threat, therefore, the Habsburg authorities decided to exploit the hatred that the local Ruthenian peasantry felt for
their Polish landlords and actually urged them on to a great mass rising
in which the gentry were massacred and their mansions destroyed. In
Western Galicia alone it was reckoned that about two thousand were
killed. At the same time the rising in Cracow had been suppressed
within ten days by Russian and Austrian troops, and in the following
year the city was annexed by Austria. The entire episode had been
hopeless for the Poles from the start, but these events do have a bearing
on the revolutions that followed in 1848. The Polish nationalists were
to enjoy a short-lived alliance with the Prussian liberals, who saw them
as a possible ally against the conservatism of Russia, and when revolution finally broke out in Berlin in March 1848,[1] one of the first acts of
the crowd was to release Mieroslavski and the other Polish leaders from
the Moabit prison. Another aspect, more sinister for the liberals, was
the skill with which the Habsburgs had been able to make use of the
antagonism which existed between the subject peoples and their immediate overlords.

There was to be further disorder within Metternich's sphere of interest before the end of 1847—the outbreak of civil war in Switzer-

[1] See p. 142.

land. Political dispute here had recently centred itself not merely on the cleavage between liberals desirous of a stronger federal authority and conservatives who took their stand by the independence of the cantons, but also on a more bitter struggle between a Catholic Ultramontane party and a group of free-thinking radicals. The decision in Argau to dissolve the monasteries, two unsuccessful attempts by radical forces in 1844 and 1845 to march on Catholic Lucerne, and the installation of the Jesuits at Lucerne in November 1845, were all stages in a civic strife that culminated in the formation of the *Sonderbund*, a league of seven Catholic cantons—Lucerne, Schwyz, Uri, Unterwalden, Zug, Fribourg, and Valais. The Protestant liberals held ten cantons, and the gaining of Geneva and St Gallen by May 1847 gave them the majority that they needed in the Diet. Berne had already appointed as President of the Confederation Ulrich Ochsenbein, who had led the 1845 expedition against Lucerne, and in July the radicals used their majority in the Diet to set up a committee for a revision of the federal pact and to demand the expulsion of the Jesuits from all cantons as well as the dissolution of the *Sonderbund*. On the refusal of the Catholic cantons the Diet declared war on them in the name of the Confederation. The war lasted twenty-five days, at the end of which the *Sonderbund* forces surrendered, completely out-manoevured by General Dufour who commanded the troops of the Diet.

Metternich had fully understood that defeat for the *Sonderbund* would mean an open challenge to the conservative principle in Europe, but the swiftness of the liberal victory, together with Palmerston's refusal to countenance intervention, stopped him from taking effective action. 'Today,' said Metternich in December, 'the Powers are faced with radicalism in control.' He was not alone in realizing the significance of the Swiss Diet's victory. The news was greeted with wild enthusiasm in Rome, Florence, and Prague. 'May Europe be inspired by your great example', wrote Michelet and Quinet from France to the Swiss Diet, and they had not long to wait. Within a couple of months Switzerland was to be saved from any further threat of foreign intervention by a series of revolutions throughout the whole of Europe, in which the Swiss have always considered that they led the way.

III

THE FAILURE OF LIBERAL REVOLUTION
1848–51

II

THE OUTBREAK OF REVOLUTION
IN 1848

1. The immediate causes

IN 1848 all the smouldering grievances of the Continent suddenly flamed up in the greatest conflagration of revolt that Europe has ever known. The 'year of revolutions', more violent and widespread in its effect than those earlier outbreaks of 1820–1 and 1830, marks the climax of that period of constant unrest which characterized Metternich's Europe. Nearly all the risings failed. The governmental pattern of Europe, which in the spring of 1848 seemed everywhere in dissolution, had within eighteen months been almost completely restored. Yet all was not entirely fruitless. The movements of 1848, unsuccessful as they were, provided lessons both for the governments and for their opponents, and through that new experience a period of change was to ensue in the middle decades of the nineteenth century as revolutionary as the events of 1848, although utterly different to what the revolutionaries themselves had anticipated.

The complicated history of the years since 1815 might well suggest the possibility of a revolutionary outbreak almost anywhere in Europe, but the mere existence of general unrest does not explain why the 'year of revolutions' should happen as and when it did. The ruling classes were convinced at first that they were faced with a European-wide conspiracy and this fear lies behind much of the initial success of the risings. 'Je ne puis pas monter à cheval contre les idées', said William of Württemberg to Prince Gortchakov, the Russian minister at Stuttgart. In fact, there was no general conspiracy at all. 'Le 24 février', said Proudhon speaking of the revolution in Paris, 'a été fait sans idée', and his remark could be applied to the whole of the European scene, for the revolutions of 1848 were utterly confused and lacking in any preconceived plan, a series of spontaneous explosions which often took the leaders of revolutionary thought completely by surprise. Karl Marx and Bakunin were both in Brussels when the Paris revolution broke out; Mazzini was in London; and even after they had hurried to the centres of action, they had little success in gaining control. In June Bakunin in Prague only heard by chance that a new insurrection was just about to break out in the city, and in May 1849 he was on the point of leaving Dresden when he found the barricades up in the streets. This helplessness of the so-called leaders was best summed up by Ledru-Rollin during a fruitless rising in Paris in May 1849: 'Je suis leur chef, il faut que je les suive.'

Most striking of all is the lack of any organized Socialist movement at this time. The masses in the towns manned the barricades, but most of their leaders are unknown and in some cases were non-existent. By chance the *Manifesto of the Communist Party*, drawn up at the request of the London centre of the Communist League, had been published in January 1848. This remarkable document, based on Marx's theory of history and couched in language that makes it one of the world's greatest masterpieces of propaganda, closed with its ringing challenge: 'The workers have nothing to lose but their chains. They have a world to win. Workers of all lands, unite!' Yet the only tangible consequence of its publication was the expulsion of Marx from Belgium. It is true that in Paris and, later, in Frankfurt he hoped that a momentary alliance between bourgeois and workers would enable the workers ultimately to gain the upper hand, but everywhere in Europe the fear of Socialism was to drive the bourgeois back into the arms of their rulers. Marx denounced them furiously in his newspaper, the *Neue Rheinische Zeitung*; this led to his being charged with incitement to treason, and although his impassioned speech before a Cologne jury secured his acquittal, he found, by August 1849, that England was one of the very few countries that was still open to him.

Thus, personal leadership does little to explain the revolutions of 1848. The most important cause lies in an agricultural and economic crisis that affected every region of Europe. Poor corn harvests in the years 1845 and 1846 coinciding with a blight that ruined the potato crop from Silesia to Ireland sent the price of food soaring, and soon hunger had led to violence in France, Belgium, the Rhineland, Württemberg, and northern Italy. Then typhus broke out—to be followed, in 1848, by the second terrible visitation of cholera. All this misery was soon to be increased by mass unemployment, when shortage of capital brought a sharp curtailing of credit that turned the boom of the mid-1840s into a slump.[1] In France and Belgium, on the railways alone,

[1] See p. 100.

750,000 men found themselves without work; in many of the larger towns of southern Germany almost one-third of the inhabitants became dependent upon charity, and the general despair in central Europe was reflected in the figures for emigration which leaped up from 34,000 in 1840 to 93,000 in 1846 and 100,000 in 1847.[1] This dislocation of every-day life was felt most keenly in the cities—a significant factor, since the revolutions of 1848 were essentially urban movements—and although the worst aspects of the crisis were passing by 1848, the hunger, the hopelessness of the unemployed who turned to machine-breaking, and the innumerable bankruptcies of the smaller business concerns, all formed a more compelling motive for rebellion than the watchword of any revolutionary theorist.

2. The succession of outbreaks

The basis of any study of the year 1848 must be the chronological sequence of events. In many ways it might seem simpler to consider each country or region in turn. This method, however, would obscure the most significant element in the whole imbroglio. The revolutions did not happen in the neat isolation of local history. They happened within days of each other and the news of revolt in one city after another was the greatest general motive force in the story of this tumultuous year. Another important factor is the order in which the risings occurred. The chances of successful revolution in small states depended ultimately upon the attitude of the governments of France and Austria; thus, the abdication of Louis Philippe on 24 February and the dismissal of Metternich on 13 March are crucial dates in the early months, since they were at once followed by fresh outbreaks, or by more drastic action in states where revolt had already taken place.

The sequence begins in the first days of January 1848, when the citizens of Milan suddenly gave up smoking. This was not simply a New Year's resolution. It was a concerted attempt to be a nuisance to the Austrian authorities in Lombardy who enjoyed a monopoly of tobacco, and the situation quickly became explosive. On the one side were Radetzky's troops, who had been taunted mercilessly since clashes in the previous autumn, on the other the Milanese pining for a smoke, and a series of incidents in the city, the 'tobacco riots', culminated in a cavalry charge in which several people lost their lives.

Then, on 12 January, in Sicily, an attack by the crowd on the garrison of Palermo ultimately forced King Ferdinand II to offer the islanders

[1] See Appendix 9, p. 490.

an independent administration, but when the Sicilians would only accept a fully constitutional government the fighting continued until, by the end of January, the Neapolitan army had been driven out of most of the island and the rebels had re-established the constitution of 1812, declaring Sicily's independence. Within a few days Ferdinand, unsure of his position on the mainland, hastily proclaimed a constitution for the whole of his kingdom, including an Assembly with two Chambers, one of which was to be elective. These events in Naples naturally gave rise to fresh demands on the rulers farther north. On 8 February Charles Albert appointed a commission to draw up a constitution, while three days later the Grand Duke of Tuscany yielded to revolutionary pressure centred on Leghorn and agreed to allow representative government.

Few of these changes in Italy could have survived long if the major capitals of Europe had remained untouched by the movement towards revolution. Within a couple of weeks, however, the whole outlook was changed by a sudden rising in Paris. The fall of the July monarchy in February 1848 was as much a surprise to the opponents of the King as it was to Louis Philippe himself. A growing opposition in the Chamber, reinforced by attacks in the press, had been demanding a slight extension of the franchise, but the middle-class liberals were not seriously thinking of ending the monarchy. Left-wing propagandists had been active in advocating social changes in the interest of the working class, and the mass unemployment had lent strength to the cry 'le droit au travail'; yet even here there is little evidence of any concerted plan of attack at this moment. 'On ne renversait pas le gouvernement,' wrote Alexis de Tocqueville two years later, 'on le laissait tomber.'

A reform banquet had been prohibited by the government; a protest march through Paris on 22 February and the appearance of a few barricades on the next morning persuaded Louis Philippe that the time had come to dismiss Guizot. Count Molé took his place, but that evening another procession had an encounter with royal troops cordoning off the Foreign Office, which resulted in the death of sixteen of the crowd, and by the morning of 24 February Paris was once again in the throes of revolution. Molé, unable to form a ministry, resigned. Louis Philippe turned to Thiers and at the same time gave Marshal Bugeaud the task of subduing the city by military force. The troops might have succeeded, but Thiers, not wishing to involve his new administration in further bloodshed, ordered a cease-fire; the barricades remained untaken and many of the soldiers, sensing the weakness of higher authority, began to go over to the rebels. Thiers' own scheme was for the King to leave Paris without further resistance and to wait at St Cloud until the middle-class opposition fell out with the working-class element. His instinct was sound, but Louis Philippe rejected the advice. He preferred to rely upon the National Guard, but when later it seemed that the Tuileries were about to be attacked, their cries of '*à bas le systèmé*' revealed a wavering loyalty that robbed him of any further intention to resist. He seemed unmindful of the army of 80,000 regular troops at his disposal. For Louis Philippe the National Guard was a symbol of the bourgeois on whose support his monarchy had rested; with that support apparently lost, he yielded to the persuasion of the Duke de Montpensier to abdicate in favour of his grandson, and a little later the monarch who had entered his capital on foot on a July night in 1830 took his leave of it in a brougham—ahead of him the road to exile in England, behind him the Tuileries abandoned to a fury of looting and destruction by the mob, which Flaubert was to describe in his *l'Éducation sentimentale*.

The fall of Louis Philippe was in many ways similar to that of Charles X. 'Comme un autre en trois jours,' wrote de Vigny, 'il tombait en trois heures.' Both had lost the support of a significant element of the middle class. Both had been caught off guard by the strength of the outburst of opposition, although Charles X had less excuse since he, at least, had attempted a *coup d'état*, whereas Guizot had only forbidden a banquet. Both had sought escape in abdication in favour of a grandchild, neither of whom was destined to rule. Two points of difference, however, were to give the events of 1848 a more radical twist. First, the working class of Paris were more powerful and articulate than they had been in 1830; second, there were no further branches of the royal family to whom the bourgeois could turn in order to avoid the extremes of republicanism. These two factors explain the far greater caution exercised by the bourgeois in the weeks immediately following Louis Philippe's abdication and their apparent readiness to work in some sort of accord with the extreme left-wing leaders.

The Chamber would probably have been prepared to accept the accession of the Count de Paris with his mother as Regent, but a mob broke in on them and insisted on the proclamation of a republic, thus extinguishing the last flicker of hope for the survival of kingship in France. Armand Marrast, the editor of *Le National*, who had hurried to the Chamber as soon as he had heard the news of the abdication, persuaded Lamartine to announce the establishment of a republic. There and then, before the mob had dispersed, seven republican deputies were nominated to form a provisional government—Lamartine, Marrast, Ledru-Rollin, Arago, Crémieux, Marie, and Garnier-Pagès. These seven were at once swept off to the Hôtel de Ville in accordance with revolutionary tradition, but here they were met by a crowd from *La Réforme* who were only prepared to accept them if three others were added—Louis Blanc, Flocon, the editor of *La Réforme*, and Martin, a mechanic, better known as Albert, all of them spokesmen of the left-wing movement.

Thus from the beginning the provisional government consisted of an indigestible amalgam of two utterly different political groups. For a short time this ill-assorted team jogged along together, each group too unsure of the strength of its own position in the turbulent capital to risk attempting to dispense with the other. It was part of the irony of the situation that Bakunin, who had rushed to Paris on hearing the news, soon appeared almost embarrassingly revolutionary even for the extremist section. 'On the first day of a revolution,' remarked Caussidière, the new left-wing Prefect of Police, 'he is a perfect treasure; on the second he ought to be shot.' Before long, however, Bakunin had scented greater excitement farther east and Flocon was only too happy to grant him a loan for a journey to Posen. Meanwhile, on 26 February, Lamartine, in an impassioned speech in favour of the tricolour had managed to avoid the adoption of the red flag—to Blanqui's disgust. At the beginning of March, the various political and financial restrictions on the press were removed, and between March and June well over two hundred journals entered upon a brief and uncertain life; on 5 March the government announced that elections to a Constituent Assembly would take place on 9 April, in which every adult Frenchman should have the right to vote—a gigantic leap in the size of the electorate from 241,000 to about 8,000,000.[1]

The left-wing members of the government were naturally not slow in pressing on with their own programme of social reform, and as early as 28 February the government almost fell apart over the question of reducing the length of the working day. A compromise was eventually arranged whereby a *Commission du gouvernement pour les travailleurs* consisting of 242 workers and 231 employers under the presidency of Louis Blanc was to meet in the Luxembourg Palace. Through the efforts of the *Commission* hours of work were reduced to ten hours in Paris and eleven in the provinces. A more significant achievement was

[1] See Appendix 4, p. 486.

the establishment of the *ateliers nationaux* whereby the unemployed were organized in a whole hierarchy of military-sounding formations under Émile Thomas, a young engineer, to be given work at 2 francs a day or to be paid a dole of 1½ francs. The general dislocation of economic life consequent on the recent revolution had added enormously to the number of unemployed in Paris, and by April 70,000 had enrolled in the *ateliers nationaux*. They were not entirely ineffectual; they did produce some constructive work—including the preparation of the hall in which the Constituent Assembly was to sit—but the main object of Marie, the right-wing Minister of Public Works, was simply to keep this large body of men away from political activity, and the final form that was given to the scheme was a far cry from Louis Blanc's original plan of workers organized in a vast federation of trades.

For the moment both sides, liberal parliamentarians and republicans, were simply manoeuvring so as not to lose the unexpected opportunity that the fall of the monarchy had given them. The crucial issue remained the elections to the Constituent Assembly. How would the provinces of France view the recent events in Paris? It was the left wing who were most worried about this, for, as Blanqui realized, they needed time in which to spread their propaganda among the peasantry. Accordingly, the Minister of the Interior, Ledru-Rollin, who stood closer to the left than many of his colleagues in the provisional government, dispatched carefully chosen *commissaires* to the provinces to give impetus to the left-wing movement, while two demonstrations in Paris on 17 March and 16 April attempted to force the government to postpone the elections. The first of these did succeed in getting the date of the elections shifted to the end of April; the second failed, mainly because Ledru-Rollin chose to support the bourgeois and called out the National Guard against the imminent insurrection.

If anything, these efforts on the part of the left wing proved harmful to their cause. In 1830 it had been a small group of bourgeois in Paris who had defeated the extreme republicans. In 1848 it was almost the whole of France that spoke against them. The French peasant, mistrusting any Socialist schemes that might rob him of his land, showed himself once again to be the most conservative element in nineteenth-century French politics, and the news of mob violence in Paris only confirmed him in his fears. When the elections did finally take place in April, 84% of the vast new electorate went to the polls to return an Assembly of 900 deputies, overwhelmingly right wing in outlook—lawyers, teachers, landowners, and army officers, middle-class men of

established position, four-fifths of them over forty years of age—and
with the emergence of this new factor in the French revolution of
1848 a fresh stage in the struggle between right and left was about to
open.

Meanwhile, as in 1830, the news from Paris had sent a wave of revolutionary fervour throughout Europe. In Belgium the economic
crisis during the two preceding years had resulted in the formation of
a liberal ministry under Charles Rogier in June 1847. On 28 February,
four days after Louis Philippe's abdication, Rogier proposed a lowering
of the property qualification for voters, thereby increasing the parliamentary electorate from 46,000 to 79,000, and this measure, coupled
with the suppression of the stamp tax on newspapers, the exclusion of
government officials from the Chambers, and the regulating of the
King's power to nominate burgomasters, ended the likelihood of any
continued discontent among the middle classes. A Belgian Legion,
formed in Paris, on which the extremists relied, was easily defeated
in March by government troops, and by June the country was sufficiently quiet for the government to hold an election in which the
moderate liberals were completely successful. Three factors help to
explain this controlled liberal victory in Belgium at a time of rampant
revolution. First, the Catholics and liberals, in the face of radical
republicanism, had recreated the union which had been the essential preliminary to national independence in 1830. Second, many of the working classes in Belgium still lived in rural districts where the Roman
Church was powerful and Socialist ideas had not spread at all. Third,
the wisdom of Charles Rogier in granting a wider suffrage—in contrast
to Guizot's obstinacy in France—had robbed the extremists of any
chance of an alliance with the middle class.

A similar policy of concession was to enable the Dutch to make an
appreciable step in the direction of constitutional monarchy. Warned
by the news of Louis Philippe's fall, William II attempted, first of all,
to impose reform from above by a series of suggested revisions of the
Fundamental Law, but when these had met with little response, William
set up a Royal Commission which included several of the liberal
leaders, and in the course of the year a new scheme of government involving many radical alterations was worked out and eventually put
into operation. The Second Chamber was no longer to be elected by
the provincial States, but by direct suffrage, the right to vote being
dependent upon a certain level of taxation—a franchise that was also

to apply in the elections to provincial States. Ministerial responsibility was acknowledged and annual budgets were to be presented to the States General, whose powers were also to include some control over colonial affairs, education, and provincial administration. These measures opened the way to later constitutional development, such as the growth of political parties and further extensions of the franchise, but for the moment they still left considerable power with the sovereign and, in any case, the modifications were mainly in the interest of the richer middle class.

The same unrest now threatened the position of the princes in the German Confederation. As in the Netherlands, the demands were mostly middle class in character and except in the Rhineland, where industrialism had already gone some way, any Socialist tendencies were weak. Nevertheless, the pressure was such that the rulers of Baden, Württemberg, and Brunswick, and the patrician families of Lübeck, Bremen, Hamburg, and Frankfurt all found themselves assailed and were forced to give ground.

These movements in the German states, however, were as local as they had been in earlier decades. The hope for the creation of German national unity which might overcome this particularism found expression in a scheme put forward by Heinrich von Gagern, the minister of Hesse-Darmstadt. He was responsible for a meeting of fifty liberals, mostly from the south-west, on 5 March at Heidelberg, where it was decided that invitations should be sent to all past and present members of state legislatures in Germany to confer at Frankfurt at the end of March. When it met, this preliminary gathering, the *Vorparlament*, 600 in number, worked in conjunction with the Federal Diet and set about organizing elections throughout Germany for a National Constituent Assembly in which representation was to be on the basis of one deputy per 50,000 inhabitants, although the extent of the franchise varied from state to state.

Thus, by the middle of March, the fall of the monarchy in France had had repercussions far outside her frontiers, and it was natural that an enthusiast like Bakunin should imagine that a new world was dawning throughout Europe. Already, before leaving France in March, he had written in *La Réforme*: 'Soon, perhaps in less than a year, the monstrous Austrian empire will be destroyed. The liberated Italians will proclaim an Italian republic. The Germans, united into a single great nation, will proclaim a German republic. The Polish democrats after seventy years of exile will return to their homes. The revolutionary movement will stop only when Europe, the whole of Europe, not excluding Russia, is turned into a federal democratic republic.' In fact, the pattern so far seemed little different from that of 1830, and it is difficult to assess what might have been the course of events, if Metternich had been free to act. But this time Metternich himself was to succumb, for on the very day that Bakunin threw out his great prophecy, revolution burst in the heart of the Habsburg dominions themselves.

On 3 March, in the Hungarian Diet at Pressburg, Louis Kossuth had demanded the abolition of serfdom, the end of absolute rule from Vienna and the establishment of virtual independence for Hungary, a speech so violent that it had seriously alarmed the party of the nobility led by Széchényi. Within a week it had been echoed in similar demands by the Lower Austrian Estates and, a little later, by the Bohemians in Prague. Vienna itself was in an uproar of excitement and, on 12 March, after two professors had presented a petition from the University, the State council agreed to summon a meeting of delegates from the provincial Estates.

The storm broke on 13 March. Students and workers swarmed into the Ballhausplatz to hurl abuse at Metternich standing with his family at the windows of the Chancellery. They swept on to the Hofburg and when, amid the usual confusion, the troops opened fire, a new fury led to further outbreaks of fighting and destruction throughout the city. Now at last, at the very centre of his government, Metternich was face to face with those forces of popular violence which he had hated and dreaded ever since he had watched the pillage of the Hôtel de Ville at Strasbourg in 1789. To the end he refused to make terms. Immaculate in his green top coat and light grey trousers, contemptuous of the mob and indifferent to his colleagues, the Chancellor came to give his last advice at a Council of State. The troops must disperse the crowd; to avoid the fate of Louis Philippe, the Emperor had only to stand firm. But Metternich had his enemies inside as well as outside the Hofburg. Amid the whispering of archdukes and ministers throughout the rest of that day the notion predominated that the monarchy might be saved by the sacrifice of the Chancellor himself, and in the evening, when Metternich returned, he was informed that the answer to the crowd was to be his own resignation. 'Tell the people that I agree to everything', said the Emperor Ferdinand. With those words the career dedicated to the service of the Habsburg monarchy came to a close, and under cover of darkness the Chancellor of Europe made his escape as best he could from the city that had rejected him.

The fall of Metternich was to bring the revolutions in Europe to their climax. A manifestation at Budapest encouraged the Diet of Pressburg in March to pass measures, ending serfdom and establishing parliamentary rule with an electoral property qualification, and henceforth the only link with the Habsburg empire was to be a purely personal one in the King-Emperor himself. Louis Batthyány became the head of the government in Hungary, Deák Minister of Justice and Kossuth Minister of Finance, and in the following month Ferdinand gave the royal assent to all these changes, accordingly known as the April Laws.

In Vienna, on 15 March, he had already promised to grant a constitution, but the lack of leadership among the Viennese rebels made it possible for the initiative to remain in the hands of a succession of elderly Court officials, first Kollowrat, Metternich's great rival, then Ficquelmont, and after him Pillersdorf. The Imperial ministers delayed taking action and eventually drew up a constitution on their own, in which there were to be two Chambers, one of which would be elective, the vote being severely restricted by a high property qualification. Then further revolt in May forced them to agree to the summoning of a single-chamber Constituent Assembly, elected by universal suffrage, and a little later this body, predominantly middle class, met in Vienna. Long before this, however, on 20 May, the Court had fled to Innsbruck, from where it might be free to stem the tide of revolution.

As in Hungary, so in Germany and Italy Metternich's fall was to bring the national question out into the open. In Prussia Frederick William IV, who in a confused way had always regarded himself as a liberal monarch, was confronted with a rising in Berlin on 18 March and within twenty-four hours, after one engagement in which 230 of the crowd were shot down by his troops, he ordered a cease-fire and promised the summoning of a Constituent Assembly, thus attempting to place himself at the head of the revolutionary movement in Prussia. But by now revolution in Germany was turning towards something more than local revolt; German deputies were already being elected to the *Vorparlament* that was to meet at Frankfurt, and Frederick William impulsively coming to terms with the situation rode through the streets of Berlin beneath the new German flag of black, red, and gold. 'Henceforth,' he announced in a proclamation, 'Prussia will be merged in Germany.' With Metternich gone, even the monarchs of Europe could speak differently.

The same acceleration of events was to be seen in Italy. In Rome, on 15 March, Pius IX granted a constitution for the Papal States—the accepted pattern of two Chambers, one of which would be elective, the vote dependent upon a property qualification. In Venice a Civic Guard was formed which at once gained control of the arsenal, and on the withdrawal of the Austrian troops the Republic of Venice was proclaimed under the presidency of Daniele Manin. In Milan street fighting broke out, and after five days Radetzky, the commander of the Austrian garrison, withdrew his troops to Verona. The climax came on 24 March, when Charles Albert took his great decision at last and declared war on Austria. Four days later the Piedmontese army crossed the frontier to join forces with the Milanese rebels and made a swift advance over the Lombard plain towards the Austrian army, which had fallen back east of Lake Garda.

12

THE CLASH OF AIMS

METTERNICH dismissed; Prussia to be merged in a new Germany; Piedmont at open war with Austria in the struggle for Italian independence. It looked indeed as if the early months of 1848 were to be 'the springtime of nations'. Yet the upsurge of revolution had been so spectacular that it was easy to over-estimate its significance. 'Oui, ma chère,' said Metternich to his wife on the night of his dismissal, 'nous sommes morts.' In fact, very few of the rulers in Europe had lost their thrones. Louis Philippe and Ludwig I of Bavaria had been compelled to abdicate; the Dukes of Modena and Parma had fled. Otherwise, the rulers had wisely given way to the demands that had been presented with such sudden violence; they still retained command of their military forces and they had only to wait to see whether the revolutionaries could maintain the united front with which they had won the first concessions.

It was precisely here that the weakness of the revolutions of 1848 lay, for the clash of aims made any constructive achievement virtually impossible. Middle-class liberals desiring constitutional monarchy and a restricted parliamentary franchise came into conflict at once with the egalitarianism of the radical republicans. In France, where there could be no turning back to monarchy for the moment, this was to mean a pitched battle between the two. In Italy and Germany, the same question, complicated still further by regional jealousies, bedevilled all efforts to achieve national unification. Was there to be a unitary republic, or a compromise with the existing duchies and kingdoms within a federal government? In central Europe there was the additional problem of the geographical definition of national frontiers. The claims of language and history were so confused that it was self-evidently impossible for any frontier to be drawn on which all would agree, and the larger national groups—Germans and Magyars—energetically pressing their claims, had no patience with the aspirations of smaller groups such as Bohemians, Slovaks, Croats, Serbs, and Roumans, whom they firmly intended to include within their new frontiers. It is consequently not surprising that these smaller groups should soon deplore the apparent break-up of the Habsburg dominions, preferring to remain within the old non-national structure of central Europe rather than to become subject peoples of new nation states.

In France it was with considerable relief that the moderate element in the provisional government found that the Constituent Assembly, which first met on 4 May, represented such a triumph for the right wing. Their nervousness until this moment was highly understandable. Since the fall of the monarchy almost 450 clubs had been formed in Paris, and a flood of newspapers had spread ideas of Socialism; the National Guard had been thrown open to those who could not afford to buy their own arms and equipment, and although the *ateliers nationaux*, which by now had absorbed well over 100,000 unemployed, had mostly remained uncommitted during the demonstrations of March and April, their very existence represented a potential weapon of mass power of which the extremists might yet gain control.

Both sides knew at once that the election of such an Assembly meant an end to the uneasy truce between the bourgeois and the left wing. The first action of the Assembly was to replace the provisional government by an executive commission of five—Arago, Garnier-Pagès, Marie, Lamartine, and Ledru-Rollin—all of them moderates except Ledru-Rollin, whose action against the demonstrators on 16 April[1] had nevertheless won him the trust of the bourgeois. On 12 May it prohibited the direct presentation of petitions, thereby depriving a crowd of its main excuse to invade the hall of the Assembly, and this stimulated the left wing to make one further desperate move. On 15 May the crowd burst in on the Assembly, declared it dissolved, and then marched off to the Hôtel de Ville to proclaim a new government. But it was too late for a Paris mob to influence the course of the 1848 revolution. The existing government stood firm and the National Guard dispersed the crowd. The leaders, Blanqui and Barbès, were placed under arrest, and the executive commission took the opportunity to close the revolutionary clubs, purge the National Guard, and remove Caussidière, the radical Prefect of Police.

The next step in the right-wing reaction concerned the *ateliers nationaux*. They were expensive and it had been noticed that the workers enrolled in them had taken some part in the activities of 15 May. The main problem was that their abolition would almost

[1] See p. 138.

F

certainly have violent consequences. On 26 May, however, the government took the risk of dispatching Émile Thomas to Bordeaux and on 21 June a decree was issued giving all enrolled workers who were unmarried and under twenty-five years of age the option of joining the army, and warning the rest that they were to be sent out into the provinces—where, of course, they could easily be dispersed.

The outcome was as Émile Thomas had predicted. Once again, on 22 June, barricades began to go up in the narrow streets of Paris—mainly in the eastern districts between the Place de la Concorde and the Hôtel de Ville. Lamartine, who had opposed the abolition of the *ateliers*, hastened round the city appealing to the rebels in a vain attempt to avoid bloodshed, but only succeeded in earning the mistrust of both sides; poetic romanticism had no further part to play in the French revolution of 1848. Fighting had already begun on 23 June and the Assembly, by now frightened that it was about to suffer the same fate as Charles X and Louis Philippe, hastily vested supreme power in General Eugène Cavaignac, a veteran of North Africa. Troops were rushed in by train—a new factor in governmental action—and for three days a savage war raged in Paris. The workers fought virtually without leaders, since Blanqui and Barbès were already under arrest and Louis Blanc and Ledru-Rollin refused to become involved; and the pathetic hopelessness of the whole insurrection is perfectly captured in some of the short stories of Turgenev, who was living in Paris at the time. At the end, when the rising had been utterly crushed and Cavaignac had received the thanks of the Assembly, it was reckoned that 1,460 of the insurgents had been killed, but this figure ignores the numbers of those who were shot in summary executions.

The June days finally enabled the right wing to consolidate their position; 15,000 suspects were arrested, 4,000 deported, and Louis Blanc fled to England. Many of the clubs were closed and the press laws reimposed. *Le droit au travail* as a fundamental principle of society came increasingly under attack until it had been whittled away almost to nothing, and in September the length of the working day was increased to twelve hours in Paris.

By November the Assembly had completed the constitution of the Second Republic. The legislature, a single Chamber of 750 deputies, elected by universal male suffrage, was to sit for three years, but was not to include any minister or public officials. Executive power was to be vested in a President, also elected by universal suffrage to hold office for four years, but not eligible for re-election. The whole scheme was based on a separation of powers, which in the minds of the theorists was still the accepted formula for the avoidance of despotism. In fact, they should have known by this time that such a separation made it impossible to overcome a deadlock between the legislature and the executive. The President was forbidden to dissolve the Assembly before the three years had expired; nor could the Chamber dissolve itself. If a deadlock did arise, neither side would be able to refer to the electorate. On the other hand, while both could claim to have been elected by the country, it would obviously be easier for a President to mobilize public opinion and to act decisively than for an Assembly of 750 consisting of many shades of opinion; thus, a skilful politician, once installed as President, might be able to use his executive power to overthrow the legislature with all the justification of public support.

Clearly a great deal would depend upon the personality of the first President, and it was here that the memory of the June days proved highly significant. The working-class movement had been defeated, but there were many among the bourgeois and peasantry who wondered whether any parliamentary republic could effectively resist another left-wing rising. By now all faith had been lost in the men of the centre such as Lamartine, and no leader had yet emerged on the right to capture the popular imagination. It was at this moment that there appeared on the scene a new figure, quite unassociated with the preceding events of the year. Prince Louis Napoleon[1] had been allowed to return to France in the summer. At first sight he would not have seemed the man who was eventually to rise to supreme power in France. The heavy moustache, the dull expressionless eyes, the shy clumsiness on public occasions, the French spoken with a German accent, all convinced the deputies of the Constituent Assembly at least that there was no danger in allowing this head of the house of Bonaparte to stand as a candidate in the approaching presidential election. And yet, as a number of by-elections to the Constituent Assembly had already shown, at this precise moment in the revolution of 1848 Louis Napoleon was in the remarkable position of appealing to almost every class. His uncle's name suggested *la gloire;* for the peasantry he seemed to stand for strong orderly government; to the workers, deprived of any other leadership, his essay on *L'extinction du paupérisme*, written in 1844, offered a hope that seemed to exist nowhere else; to the bourgeois of the extreme right he seemed a useful stopgap to enable them to prepare the ground for a restoration of

[1] See p. 119.

monarchy. On 10 December the presidential election took place and 'Poléon' was swept to victory with 5½ million votes, a majority that utterly overwhelmed the other four republican candidates. The elections to the Chamber of the new constitution had yet to be held, but the French had already chosen the man who was to destroy the republic in which most of them had already lost faith.

The basis of the struggle in France had remained purely social. In Switzerland the fundamental problem was the establishment of a stronger central government, although this too implied a social read-justment, since it meant a surrender of power by the local patrician families. The success of the Swiss in reaching a solution was due partly to the speed with which the liberals had overcome their opponents in the *Sonderbund* war of 1847, partly to the common sense, willingness to compromise and experience in local government of the victorious group.

At first, the commission set up by the Diet in August 1847 to revise the federal constitution was bound to proceed cautiously owing to the possibility of foreign intervention. The revolutions in Paris and Vienna released them from this fear; a successful rising in Neuchâtel ended the existence of a Prussian enclave within Swiss territory,[1] and the way was now open for the reconstruction of a unified Federal State. The new scheme was drafted in the early months of 1848, and debated in the Diet in May and June. It was accepted by a considerable majority of the cantons and by the autumn the new constitution was already in opera-tion.

Under the new system a Federal legislature was to consist of two Chambers, a Council of States, with one deputy from each canton, and a National Council, elected by universal manhood suffrage, with seats allotted in proportion to the population of the cantons. The arrange-ment naturally satisfied the larger cantons, which had previously never had a representation relative to their size. The two Councils were together to elect the seven members of a permanent Federal executive. The Federal government, now with a revenue of its own, became responsible for diplomacy and national defence, public works and the maintenance of a postal service. It had the right to approve cantonal constitutions, prohibited political treaties between cantons, and estab-lished a Customs Union, together with a uniform currency, through-out the country. On the other hand, local forms of government,

[1] See p. 83.

provided that they respected civil rights, were left entirely in the hands of the cantons. Thus the Swiss, despite the existence of three different languages within their frontiers and a deeply rooted local patriotism among the cantons, succeeded in finding a permanent solution to their difficulties out of the turmoil of 1848.

In comparison with the Swiss the problems that faced Charles Albert were infinitely more complex. The Habsburg dominions were in uproar and Radetzky had fallen back east of the Mincio. The Austrian forces, however, now firmly based on the four fortresses of the Quadrilateral—Peschiera, Mantua, Verona, and Legnago—the key to the valley of the Po, had still to be defeated in the field, while the precise relationship of Piedmont, Lombardy, and Venetia in any new system was a problem fraught with local jealousies and conflicting aspirations and greatly complicated by the attitude of Great Britain and France.

At first the general weakness of the Habsburgs forced Radetzky to remain on the defensive and by the end of April Charles Albert, reinforced by Piedmontese reservists and about 5,000 Tuscans and Modenese, had laid siege to Peschiera and actually defeated an Austrian army under General D'Aspre at Pastrengo ten miles farther east. This promising beginning, however, was deceptive and was immediately followed by three major setbacks. First, on 29 April, Pius IX issued a Papal Allocution in which he stated that it was impossible for the Papacy to lend itself to a military operation, thus robbing Charles Albert of vital moral support and of the Papal forces that had been on their way northwards. Next, on 1 May, urged on by his ministers at Turin, who stressed the political necessity for a rapid victory, Charles Albert made a hasty attack at Santa Lucia, but was repulsed—only a slight defeat, but one which caused a storm of criticism at the military leadership among the radical elements in Turin. Third, in the middle of May, King Ferdinand of Naples felt sufficiently sure of his army's loyalty to revoke the promises that had been extracted from him in February; the constitution was quietly ignored and the Neapolitan troops—of whom 40,000 had originally been promised—were recalled southwards.

These ominous signs did little to check the activity of the politicians. In Turin Count Cesare Balbo, the Premier, was presiding over a fury of constitution-making which depended both on the defeat of Austria and the suppression of any Mazzinian democratic movement. The future state of North Italy still remained a political unknown, since Lombardy and Venetia, having each declared their independence, were doubtful about surrendering it at once to a new kingdom of North Italy centred on Turin, but by the beginning of July something tangible had emerged, when all the duchies, including Lombardy and Venetia, did agree to union with Piedmont.

This agreement had a considerable bearing on the attitude of the western Powers, since, although Great Britain and France would have been glad to see the Habsburgs removed from Italy, any mediation on their part was governed by the distrust that each had for the other over the gain that might be made out of the changed situation. Palmerston's aim was to negotiate a settlement with Austria before the French could march to the assistance of Charles Albert as a means of revising the frontiers of 1815, and since a North Italian kingdom would act as a bulwark against France, proposed the union of Lombardy and Venetia with Piedmont. Pillersdorf in Vienna was also fearful of possible French intervention, and in May an Austrian under-secretary, Hummelauer, was sent to London to discuss the terms of a pacification. Hummelauer, however, would not go beyond an offer of independence for Lombardy and autonomous rule for Venetia under an Austrian archduke. 'The Emperor cannot surrender Venetia without virtually giving up the Italian Tyrol,' he pointed out to Palmerston, and there for the moment the matter rested. In Paris, however, the notion of intervention was really only supported by the left-wing element; Lamartine had no wish to start a general revolutionary war, still less to launch the French army against the Austrians. 'La France,' he said, 'interviendra seulement si l'Italie l'appelle,' a safe promise, since he knew that Piedmont had no wish for French intrusion. 'Italia farà da sé,'[1] Charles Albert had said. The principal aim of the French government was to avoid the aggrandisement of Piedmont and this could only mean the creation of Lombardy and Venetia as independent republics—which, by July, seemed to be ruled out by the decision of the two provinces to fuse with Piedmont.

The common assumption behind all these negotiations was military victory for Charles Albert. In July, however, this assumption was abruptly shattered. The loss of Papal and Neapolitan reinforcements, coupled with the notable absence of Lombard troops, had seriously affected Charles Albert's prospects. At the same time the hard-pressed Austrian government was able to dispatch 20,000 men under Count

[1] 'Italy will do it on her own.'

Thurn and another 15,000 under General Welden, and on 22 July Radetzky launched a great attack on Charles Albert's forces, 30,000 of whom had been engaged in besieging Mantua. For the next five days there raged the highly fluid battle which takes its name from the nearby village of Custoza, ending with the retreat of the Piedmontese army. Charles Albert hoped at least to make a stand before Milan, but when this project appeared hopeless, he agreed to an armistice which would allow him twenty-four hours to withdraw his troops into Piedmont, and by the end of the first week of August Lombardy was once more under Austrian rule.

In central Europe the social struggle between liberal bourgeois and radical republicans was complicated by the further question of defining national frontiers. The German National Constituent Assembly, elected through the efforts of the *Vorparlament*, had met in the Paulus-kirche, the church of St Paul, at Frankfurt on 18 May, but the weakness of this body soon became apparent. Its members were drawn almost entirely from the upper ranks of the professional middle classes —University professors, school teachers, lawyers, and civil servants— and they spent most of this exciting year under the presidency of von Gagern debating the general principles, the *Grundrechte*, on which a constitution for a united Germany should be based. The main division of opinion was between moderates who wished for some sort of compromise with the existing states of Germany, and extremists who demanded a centralized republic. The practical problem which they could hardly hope to solve was the immediate creation of an armed force with which to defend their newly-found freedom, and in due course, when confronted with the outbreaks of left-wing extremists and with the requirements of their own nationalist policy, they were to become dependent upon the armies of Austria and Prussia.

Actually, left-wing activities in Germany were more noisy than dangerous. A German Legion formed in Paris by the poet Georg Herwegh, envious of Lamartine's prominence in the revolutionary scene, set out to march on Baden in April, in order to establish a republic, but on encountering the forces of the princes, scampered to safety over the Swiss border. Karl Marx had moved to Cologne early in the year, but he took no active part in any of the risings, since he believed that from a working-class point of view they were premature. Nevertheless, in the larger cities of Germany workers' movements were sufficiently in evidence to cause alarm to the bourgeois, particularly in Frankfurt itself.

It was the national question that really occupied the deputies sitting in their pews in the Pauluskirche. The definition of the frontiers of the new Germany gave rise to a controversy that was to recur throughout all subsequent German history. One group favoured the conception of *Grossdeutschland* (Great Germany), maintaining that wherever German was spoken was German territory and thus demanding that a large part of the Habsburg dominions, excluding Hungary, should come within the frontiers of the new state. This would mean the inclusion of a number of Slav minorities under German rule, and the resistance of the Bohemians to such an idea was made clear at the very beginning when Palacky, a professor at the University of Prague, refused the invitation of the Germans to attend the *Vorparlament* at Frankfurt. It would also mean the partition of Habsburg territories, which was hardly likely to be acceptable to Vienna, once order had been restored. The other group, headed by Professor Dahlmann, advocated a *Kleindeutschland* (Little Germany), which would exclude the whole of the Habsburg lands. The weakness here was that it would leave Prussia by far the strongest element within Germany and few of the liberals from the south had much confidence in Frederick William's assertion that Prussia would be merged in Germany. The idea was equally unacceptable to Austria who could not allow her own permanent exclusion from German affairs.

This concern with frontiers was to give the German liberal movement an intensely nationalist flavour lacking in English and French liberalism, and two issues, the Polish provinces and Slesvig-Holstein, came increasingly to occupy the time of the Frankfurt Parliament. After the demonstrations in Berlin Frederick William had agreed to Polish autonomy in Prussian Poland, but the resident German population had objected so violently that by April local German domination had been re-established. In Denmark the new king Frederick VII had lent full support to the nationalist claim to Slesvig and the Germans in the duchies had declared their independence and appealed to the Frankfurt Parliament. In both these issues an ambitious nationalism among the Frankfurt liberals triumphed over counsels of moderation. In Slesvig-Holstein the claims of the German language were said to override the historic rights of the Danish king; in Posen precisely the reverse argument was used to reject the appeal of the Poles.

The Danish question revealed the fundamental weakness of the

Frankfurt Parliament, which, lacking any military power, could only rely on the armies of others. It was the Prussians who, on behalf of the Frankfurt deputies, marched into the duchies to the assistance of the Germans there against the Danish forces, and the full ineffectualness of the Frankfurt liberals was revealed when Prussia, alarmed at the possible international consequences of this invasion, signed a truce with Denmark at Malmö on 26 August without any reference to them. Worse was to follow. The recently established ministry at Frankfurt fell during the subsequent debate in the Parliament, but when the truce of Malmö was finally accepted by a narrow majority, a left-wing revolt broke out, on 16 September, in the city itself and the Parliament was only saved by the intervention of Prussian and Austrian troops from the federal fortress of Mainz.

Thus, by the end of the summer of 1848, the hopes of the German liberals had been shown to depend not upon any great movement of the people throughout Germany but upon the governments of Berlin and Vienna. Yet by this time the revolutionary force that had momentarily threatened these centres was already waning, and although Frederick William had not yet finally made up his mind to break with the movement, the position of the Habsburgs had changed noticeably for the better. In Prague any alliance between Germans and Bohemians had been short-lived. On 2 June the Bohemian leaders had opened a Slav Congress—in retaliation to the German Parliament at Frankfurt—at which their allegiance to the Habsburg dynasty was reaffirmed. *Grossdeutschland* seemed a greater menace than Vienna, and the smaller Slav groups had realized that complete national independence for them would be meaningless, since they would never be strong enough to defend themselves against an independent Germany or Hungary. 'If the Austrian Empire did not exist,' Palacky had said, 'it would be necessary to create it,' and the aim of the leading Bohemian politicians was no more than a greater independence within the framework of Habsburg rule. Farther east, other minorities were also growing aware of the need for Habsburg support. Magyar nationalism under the influence of Kossuth had led to the attempted absorption of Croats and Serbs to the south, and of Roumans in Transylvania. The Croat Diet at Zagreb consequently looked to the governor of Croatia, Jellačić, appointed by the Emperor and extremely pro-Austrian, while the Roumans declared at a meeting in Blaj Cathedral that the Rumanian nation would always remain faithful to the Emperor of Austria.

F 2

All these divisions naturally pointed the way to Habsburg recovery—
Bohemians to be played off against Germans; Croats and Roumans
against Magyars; liberals against social extremists. In June, a nationalist
revolt broke out in Prague, strongly disliked by the moderate Bohemians, and this gave Windischgrätz, the Imperial general who had
withdrawn there from Vienna, the opportunity to subdue the Bohemian movement with military force—a suppression which was actually
viewed with approval by the Frankfurt deputies. In July, the news of
Radetzky's victory at Custoza gave the Court sufficient confidence to
return to Vienna. Here the Pillersdorf administration had been replaced
by Wessenburg, and Schwarzer, the Minister for Public Works,
decided that the moment had come for the reduction of the industrial
wages of women and children. This was at once followed by the Viennese equivalent of the June days in Paris, and on 23 August, after a
pitched battle with the police and the National Guard, the working-
class movement in Vienna was crushed. The only other major force
that the extremists might have used was the peasantry, but when, on
7 September, the Austrian Constituent Assembly granted them their
one serious demand—the abolition of feudal tenure—they lost all
further interest in revolutionary action.

Meanwhile, the situation had been deteriorating for the Hungarians.
Elections in June had produced a National Assembly consisting mainly
of nobility, interspersed with a certain number of professional men,
but by this time relations with the Serbs and Croats had become so bad
that within eight hours of its first meeting on 4 July Kossuth had to
proclaim 'the country in danger'. In Croatia Jellačić, first dismissed
at the request of Hungary, was reinstated in September by the Imperial
government. He immediately declared war on Hungary, and on
11 September his troops crossed the Drave river in an advance on
Budapest.

Hungary at once appealed to Vienna and a momentous debate took
place in the Austrian Constituent Assembly. The extremists and the
Germans supported Hungarian independence, since this was the surest
way of undermining the Habsburg power; the conservatives and
Bohemian deputies, each conscious of their need to maintain the Habs-
burg dynasty, formed a majority and the appeal of Hungary against the
Croat invasion was thus rejected. The government consequently felt that
it was unlikely to be hampered by any pro-Hungarian movement in
Vienna and, on the assassination of Count Lamberg who had gone to
Budapest as an Imperial intermediary, Latour, the Minister of War,

actually sent reinforcements to Jellačić's Croats. In Hungary Batthyány, who had genuinely tried to reconcile the Croats, had already tendered his resignation as head of the government and on 3 October Ferdinand appointed Jellačić—of all men—in his place and dissolved the Hungarian Parliament. This was an ultimatum. The Hungarians, in reply, rejected the royal decree and set up a National Defence Committee under the chairmanship of Kossuth, who thus became virtual ruler of Hungary.

The troubles in Vienna, however, were not yet over. On 6 October the extremists who considered rightly that Hungary's fate was bound up with their own, fomented a great revolt in the city, determined to prevent the dispatch of any more troops to the Croats. Latour was hanged from a lamp-post, and when, on the next day, it seemed that the city was completely out of hand, the Court fled once again, this time to Olmütz. With them went many of the conservatives and Bohemians of the Austrian Constituent Assembly, and this second rising in Vienna was supported mainly by workers and University students. They were able to muster a force of about 40,000, but after the Hungarian army had made a half-hearted attempt to come to their assistance, the Viennese rebels were left to their fate. Jellačić, repulsed in Hungary, marched westwards against them, but the main counter-attack was carried out by Windischgrätz, and by 31 October, after a series of violent encounters, his army had broken the resistance and the city was given over to an orgy of looting and slaughter.

In November a new government under Prince Schwarzenberg, Windischgrätz's brother-in-law, was set up in Vienna. An abdication was arranged in order to get rid of Ferdinand, whose personal acceptance of the April Laws would be an embarrassment in any further action against Hungary, and on 2 December his nephew, the young Francis Joseph,[1] was proclaimed Emperor in his place. Thus, by the end of the year, although there was still to be trouble in Hungary and Italy, the ruling classes of Habsburg Europe surveying their battered dominions might reckon that they had weathered the worst part of the storm that had burst upon them only ten months before.

[1] See Genealogical table, p. 480.

13

VARIETIES OF LIBERAL DEFEAT 1849-51

1. The struggle in central Europe

WITH these recent changes in the situation in central Europe the rulers of Prussia and Austria now felt sufficiently encouraged to impose their own solution within their dominions. In Berlin the conservative Junker party finally gained the ear of Frederick William and after the city had been occupied by General von Wrangel and a new Prime Minister, Count Brandenburg, had dissolved the Prussian National Assembly, the King simply proclaimed a new constitution, the *octroyierte Verfassung*, on 5 December. There was a shadow of consolation for the liberals, since the most startling aspect of this constitution was the manner of its birth; in content it came close to the aims of the Prussian National Assembly and even included the election of a lower Chamber by universal suffrage.

In Austria the government of Schwarzenberg under the new Emperor Francis Joseph had, in November, already drawn up a new programme for establishing strong centralized rule from Vienna, and on 19 December an army under Jellačić entered Hungary, where the abdication of Ferdinand had naturally not been accepted. Budapest fell on 4 January 1849 and after an Imperial victory at Kápolna on 27 February, Schwarzenberg decided that it was time to follow the example of Prussia. The Constituent Assembly, which had been dispatched to Kremsier to complete its labours, was dissolved and on 4 March a new constitution, drawn up principally by Count Stadion, the Minister of the Interior, was proclaimed. As in Prussia, some account was taken of the aspirations of the constitutionalists; a Parliament of two houses as well as elective local councils had the correct revolutionary ring, but their rights were carefully circumscribed and the essence of this dictated constitution was the establishment of a unitary state cutting across the historic divisions of the provinces and thus ending the hopes for the federal solution which the deputies at Kremsier had devised at the beginning of the year.

For the Austrians, however, the struggle was not yet at an end. In

North Italy Charles Albert re-opened hostilities with Radetzky in March, but was crushed almost at once in the disastrous Novara campaign.[1] The Hungarians, who knew that all was lost if the Stadion constitution should triumph, fought back with greater success. An army equipped under a Polish general, Bem, in Transylvania repulsed the Austrian troops at every point and regained Budapest, while, on 14 April at Debrecen, the Hungarian Parliament, shaking off its earlier restraint, declared the complete independence of Hungary from Habsburg rule, and elected Kossuth as governor of the new state.

It was this turn of events in Hungary that decided the Austrian government to look for assistance outside their dominions, and on 21 April 1849 Francis Joseph made his personal appeal to Nicholas I of Russia. Ever since the beginning of 1848 the Tsar had been an agonized spectator of events throughout Europe, fearful lest the excitement of revolution would spread to Russian Poland, and now the Austrian Emperor's invitation to him to intervene released him from his frustration. Louis Napoleon's expedition to Rome[2] removed any remaining need for caution, and on 1 May Nicholas announced his intention of coming to the aid of his fellow sovereign. From this moment the fate of the Hungarians was sealed. Like the Poles in 1830, they could only hope for assistance from the west, but once again geography and the dictates of diplomacy ruled out this possibility. In vain Kossuth offered Palmerston markets for British goods in an independent Hungary, including even free ports on the Adriatic and the Danube. For Palmerston, much as he might admire the Hungarian efforts and abhor the Russian intervention, the maintenance of the Habsburg empire seemed of greater importance to British interests, and his views were echoed by Louis Napoleon whose Foreign Minister, de Tocqueville, made it clear to the French ambassador at St Petersburg that France was not to be drawn into a contest alongside Hungary. As a consequence the new state of Hungary did not survive the summer. Eighty thousand Russians under Paskevich crossed the Carpathians at the same time as General Haynau penetrated along the Danube and Jellačić drove through in the south. The Hungarians were surrounded, out-numbered and torn by internal rivalries, despite Kossuth's desperate sacrifice in surrendering political as well as military power to the Hungarian commander-in-chief, Görgey, and three days after a defeat at Temesvar on 10 August, Görgey surrendered his army of 30,000 to the Russians at Világos.

[1] See p. 164.   [2] See p. 165.

The Tsar, desirous only of the restoration of the *status quo* in central Europe, had no interest in any territorial acquisition as a reward for his intervention. The concentration of the Austrians on Italy and Hungary

CENTRAL EUROPE AND ITALY 1848-71

in 1848 had, however, left them open to a new threat to their position in Germany. The Frankfurt Assembly under von Gagern had, by the end of 1848, drawn up a list of fundamental rights on which the new German constitution would be based, and which the parliaments of the various states seemed prepared to accept. The constitution itself, which was completed by 27 March 1849, established a central Federal government with a Parliament of two Chambers, one representing the states, the other a House of Representatives elected by universal suffrage on a secret ballot. Executive power was to be vested in a hereditary German emperor with command of the military forces, a suspensive veto and the right to dissolve the lower House for new elections.

It is easy to mock the lack of realism of the deputies at Frankfurt; they had, in fact, seized their opportunity when it came, and although they were to be robbed almost immediately of their constitution, to whose general principles they had devoted so much thought, they had, nevertheless, laid a foundation of ideas on which later generations in the twentieth century might hope to build. In fact, a federal scheme was not unrealistic—the solution which Bismarck was later to adopt under a different guise. This represented a victory for the more cautious right-wing groups. They had, too, faced up to the problem of whether to include Austria—*Grossdeutschland*—or to exclude her—*Kleindeutschland*—and here the temporary setbacks suffered by Austria at this time in Italy and Hungary played their part in events. The Frankfurt deputies settled for the exclusion of Austria, and it was Frederick William IV of Prussia whom they elected as emperor on 28 March. Twenty-eight of the German states accepted these proposals and for the moment it seemed as if Austria, despite her denunciation of this new step and the withdrawal of her delegates from the Frankfurt Assembly, was to have no part in the new government of Germany.

Salvation, however, came from an unexpected quarter. At Berlin Frederick William, mistrustful of the democratic nature of the new Federal constitution and now strongly in sympathy with the conservative elements, looked askance at a crown granted to him by the people. On 27 April he refused the Assembly's offer. At the same time he dissolved his own Parliament who had appealed to him to accept, and by a decree divided the electors into three classes, based on a tax qualification that would ensure the predominance of the richest section of society in any future Prussian Parliament.

Shortly after this the Frankfurt Assembly, powerless as ever, disintegrated, as the delegates were summoned home by their various governments. The struggle between Austria and Prussia, however, continued. Frederick William might have rejected a crown offered by the people, but he was not averse to a new federal arrangement in Germany which might allow Prussia to enjoy what had previously been Austria's position of influence. On 26 May 1849 in a 'Union of the

Three Kings'—Prussia, Saxony, and Hanover—he accepted a new proposal put forward by a Prussian Catholic conservative, General von Radowitz. This was similar in many respects to the Frankfurt scheme, but with one highly significant difference. Prussia, instead of being merged in Germany, was to establish her own leadership over all the states of *Kleindeutschland*. The moment was certainly propitious; Austria was still tied down in Hungary, and a series of radical republican outbreaks in Saxony, the Palatinate and Baden forced the German princes to turn to the protection of the Prussian army, which by the end of July had restored order in their territories. By the beginning of September, although mistrust of Prussia caused Bavaria and Württemberg to hold themselves aloof, twenty-eight states had agreed to accept the new Union and in March 1850 a German Parliament assembled at Erfurt to discuss the final details of the Prussian scheme.

By now, however, Schwarzenberg had his hands free from trouble in Italy and Hungary and was determined to wreck this Prussian bid to usurp Austria's position in Germany. Accordingly he put forward a scheme of his own—a *Grossdeutschland* including the *whole* of the Habsburg dominions, in which the government of Germany would be entrusted to a Directory consisting of delegates from Austria, Prussia, and the larger states. Before long the tide was running fast against Prussian ambitions. In May 1850, at a meeting with Frederick William and Schwarzenberg at Warsaw, Tsar Nicholas insisted on friendly relations between Prussia and Austria, and when he remarked that 'the aggressor is not always the one who attacks, but the one who causes the quarrel', Frederick William realized that in any continuation of the dispute Russian sympathies would be with Austria. In July this desire for a restoration of the *status quo* was underlined by an agreement between Great Britain, France, and Russia confirming the position of the Danish king for the future as Duke of Slesvig-Holstein:[1] Hanover and Saxony had by now begun to move away from dependence on Prussia, and in October Schwarzenberg formed a military alliance with Bavaria and Württemberg.

The immediate crisis which was to test the strength of the two groups occurred in Hesse-Cassel, where the Elector was threatened with internal disorder. The Prussian army prepared to intervene; Schwarzenberg replied with an ultimatum, insisting that intervention should only come from the forces of the old German Federal Diet. In the first week of November there was a little skirmishing between Austrian and

[1] See p. 213.

Prussian troops in Hesse, but the new Prussian Prime Minister, Otto von Manteuffel, was anxious to avoid the development of hostilities, and von Radowitz who had become Foreign Minister in September had already resigned. The Minister of War, General Stockhausen, had no faith in Prussia's chances in a war with Austria, and in the diplomatic field Great Britain and France had both made it clear that they would remain neutral. As a consequence, Manteuffel agreed to a personal meeting with Schwarzenberg at Olmütz and here, on 29 November, Prussia agreed to abandon the Erfurt scheme. This victory for Austria, however, did not mean that the way was open for Schwarzenberg's own proposals. The smaller German princes were aware that their survival must depend upon the maintenance of a balance between Prussia and Austria in central Europe and at a conference held at Dresden in 1851 Prussia was now able to put herself on the side of those who wanted a return to the *status quo*. Schwarzenberg, somewhat disgruntled, had to accept a revival of the German Confederation of 1815, and on 16 May an alliance between Austria and Prussia rounded off a settlement which appeared to nullify the efforts made on all sides in Germany during the past three years.

2. *The collapse of Italian hopes*

The defeat of Charles Albert at Custoza, followed by the armistice of Salasco in August 1848, had not meant the immediate end of the movements in Italy. It did, however, bring them to a new period of crisis in which the spirit of optimism and of common purpose faded before the old local jealousies and divergence of aim among the revolutionaries. To the radicals it seemed that the Piedmontese armistice simply marked the defection of Charles Albert from the revolutionary cause, in line with Ferdinand of Naples' recall of his troops and Pius IX's Allocution. In Naples, Ferdinand, sure of his army, was able to crush a Sicilian rising, during which his bombardment of Messina in September earned him the nickname of King Bomba, and by 1849 there was little left of the Neapolitan constitutional experiment. In Piedmont, Tuscany, and the Papal States, however, the rulers still remained uneasily at the head of liberal governments which had increasingly to come to terms with the angry vehemence of the radical element. Venice under Manin was unsubdued; the Piedmontese army remained fully mobilized, and while the Habsburgs still had to give much of their attention to central Europe, it was not impossible to hope that some reshaping of Italy might yet emerge from the confusion.

In Turin the news of the retreat through Lombardy had brought down the government of Count Casati, and between August and December the new cabinet in which Count Revel and Dionigi Pinelli were the dominant personalities was assailed by a growing demand from the left for a renewal of war, which the government knew to be impossible owing to the condition of the Piedmontese army. Struggling to find a way out of the dilemma in which a negotiated peace could only bring about their own downfall, while a continuation of the war must mean military disaster, the cabinet was assisted at first by the new difficulties that confronted the Habsburgs in Vienna. At no time, however, would the Austrian government offer anything more than Home Rule for Lombardy and Venetia—unacceptable to the Piedmontese radicals —and after Windischgrätz had crushed the October rising in Vienna[1] and Prince Schwarzenberg had assumed control, determined on the full restoration of Habsburg power, there was little chance of any further delaying tactics. In December the government, in a last effort to restrain the war party, revealed the true state of the army at a secret session of the Chamber, but the only consequence of this was to bring about their fall. Gioberti now accepted office as premier.

Meanwhile, to the south of Piedmont, extremist pressure had also become more marked. In Tuscany the Ridolfi government fell after the news of Custoza, and its successor collapsed in October when Montanelli and Guerrazzi took over as the only leaders acceptable to Leghorn, where radical sentiment was so strong that the city appeared to be on the verge of seceding from Tuscany. In Rome Pius was faced with a similar scene of mounting violence. His Allocution of 29 April had already robbed him of much of his popularity with the masses, and he had by now lost confidence in his own liberal Premier who seemed to wish to deprive him of temporal power in the Papal States. In September he appointed Count Rossi, a liberal who, but for his sudden death, might have played a great part in this phase of Italian history. Rossi not only reckoned to stabilize the situation in Rome; he had a plan for Italy, the Gioberti scheme of federation under the presidency of the Pope. Negotiations were opened up with Turin, but the delicate position of the Pinelli–Revel government made it impossible for them to abandon the idea of a North Italian Kingdom. It will never be known what Rossi might still have achieved. The radicals in Rome had

[1] See p. 155.

already seen that here was a man who might be strong enough to capture the revolution for the moderates and on 15 November, on his way to attend the opening of the Chamber, he was stabbed to death by the guard of honour that lined the steps to the entrance.

For Pius this murder of his premier meant the end. He stayed long enough to accept a new cabinet including Dr Sterbini, who was afterwards suspected of having had a hand in Rossi's assassination, but he had by now made up his mind to flee from Rome and on 24 November he slipped out of the Quirinal and was driven by coach to Gaeta in Neapolitan territory. This flight of the Pope was the final blow for any moderate movement south of Piedmont. In itself it was an appeal to all Catholic opinion in Europe and it shattered the hopes of the liberals as effectively as his election in 1846 had awoken them.

In Rome the road was now open to the Mazzinian republicans, and after elections in January 1849 the Chamber proclaimed a Roman Republic, declaring the abolition of the Temporal Power, but guaranteeing the Pope his spiritual prerogatives. There had already been a hope at this time that Tuscany and Piedmont would send deputies to Rome so that a Constituent Assembly might be created for a new united Italy. In Tuscany Guerrazzi yielded to the pressure of public opinion and for a short time even managed to persuade Grand Duke Leopold to agree. Leopold, however, could not side against the Pope, who had already denounced these latest developments, and in the first week of February he fled to Siena and thence to Gaeta. This was naturally followed by further excitement, but strong action by Guerrazzi, supported by the moderate deputies in the Assembly at Florence, prevented the extremists in Tuscany from gaining power, and for the moment the duchy remained only half committed to the republican movement in Rome. In Turin, Gioberti, who might have been prepared to collaborate with the scheme of Rossi, turned his face against the Mazzinian republicanism of Rome, and believing that Piedmont must keep Tuscany by her side before the war with Austria was renewed, he actually prepared an expedition to restore Grand Duke Leopold to power. Neither Charles Albert nor the cabinet would support him in this and since his refusal to recognize the Constituent Assembly in Rome had already lost him the left-wing deputies in the Chamber, he was forced to resign on 21 February.

After Gioberti, Charles Albert could hold off the extreme nationalists no longer; a new cabinet was formed, dominated by Urbano Rattazzi, and on 12 March the truce with Austria was denounced. It is easy to understand the determination of the war party; the repression of the Lombards by Radetzky's troops after the Piedmontese withdrawal the previous summer had caused considerable emotion: Schwarzenberg seemed unlikely to accept any compromise, and the overwhelming cost of keeping an army inactive in the field meant that Piedmont must either demobilize or seek a final decision in war. Yet the renewal of hostilities was a hopeless project from the start. The failure of the Italian states to come to any agreement among themselves condemned Piedmont to fight entirely alone, and there was little likelihood of any assistance from Great Britain or France, both of whom wanted only a peaceful settlement in Italy. Nothing daunted, however, the Piedmontese government placed the army under the command of a Polish general, Chrzanowski, and staked everything on a last throw.

The war lasted less than a week. On 20 March Radetzky crossed the Ticino and advanced on Mortara. Chrzanowski seemed at first to attempt a direct advance on Milan, but then had to pull back to meet Radetzky's thrust. On 21 March Mortara was taken by the Austrians and by 23 March Chrzanowski had fallen back to a position in front of Novara. Here Radetzky attacked and after a day of fierce fighting Charles Albert's generals confessed that they could not continue the action and that a surrender must be negotiated. Radetzky's terms, however, were so heavy that Charles Albert preferred to abdicate rather than to accept them. 'Since today I have failed to find death on the battlefield, I make my last sacrifice for my country: I lay down my crown and abdicate in favour of my son, the Duke of Savoy.' He set off at once, escaped undetected through the Austrian lines, and travelled through France and Spain to Oporto, where he died the following July—a Hamlet who, having cast aside his doubts, had still failed to find a solution to his problems in resolute action.

The revolutionary movement in Italy did not long survive Novara. Piedmont suffered no territorial loss in the final peace treaty, since Schwarzenberg was anxious not to antagonize Great Britain and France, and the principal demand was an indemnity of 75 million lire to Austria. Within Piedmont, Victor Emmanuel duly succeeded to the throne and agreed to retain the constitution which his father had granted. In April the moderates in Florence managed to overthrow Guerrazzi's government and declared for the return of the Grand Duke. Leopold had, meanwhile, appealed to the Emperor Francis Joseph, and in May the Austrian army, advancing south to occupy Modena, Parma, and Lucca, moved on into Tuscany, forced its way into Leghorn against the resistance of the populace, and on 25 May occupied Florence. Venice continued to hold out, but the withdrawal of the Piedmontese fleet made the end inevitable and in August the city surrendered, although Manin and Pepe were able to make good their escape.

In Rome, too, the revolution went down fighting. In March, Mazzini, shortly after his arrival, had been elected by the Assembly as one of the Triumvirs with full power to defend the Republic. During his short period of rule he did his best to preserve law and order, only confiscated some of the land of the religious houses, which was shared out among farmers at nominal rents, and in his treatment of the clergy tried to give substance to the claim that the new republic would not interfere with the Pope's spiritual authority. There was a wilder note in the presence of the Italian patriot, Guiseppe Garibaldi, whom the news of the events in Europe had brought back from an adventurous career in South America, and Mazzini was careful to keep his red-shirted Legion away from the city of Rome. But the Roman Republic had not long in which to demonstrate to the world that its republicanism was an orderly form of government that respected private property. On 25 April a French expeditionary force under Oudinot landed at Civita Vecchia and within a few days began its march on Rome.

Louis Napoleon's decision to intervene in Italy—apparently so contrary to the ideals of the new French Republic—was dictated by domestic and diplomatic considerations.[1] At home he had become increasingly aware of the general sympathy with the Pope, a feeling by no means restricted to the right-wing deputies of the French Assembly; and in Italy itself he dared not allow the Habsburgs to use the flight of Pius as an excuse for an advance as far south as Rome. Similarly, Mazzini's decision to fight to the last was purely political. There could be no hope of a successful resistance for long, but he believed that the mere fact that their enemies would have to crush them by force would be a proclamation to the world that the Republic of Rome, the only possible capital for a united Italy, had lived and suffered and one day would rise again.

In fact, the French were hoping not to fight at all, but when on 30 April they were bloodily repulsed at the western gates of the city, military self-esteem made it essential that Rome should be taken. If Mazzini wanted glory for his doomed Republic, surely he had it now. The Austrians were approaching from the north, the Neapolitans from

[1] See p. 167.

the south, and there was a Spanish army at Gaeta. Garibaldi, who had brought his Legion back into Rome in time to drive off the French on 30 April, dominated the military scene. In May, while a French envoy, de Lesseps, negotiated with Mazzini—a lull during which Oudinot was able to build up his reinforcements at Civita Vecchia—Garibaldi turned south to check the Neapolitan advance. Then, on 3 June, the French, now 20,000 strong, began their assault and for the rest of that month the fighting raged as Garibaldi's troops were gradually driven back from the Villa Corsini, then to the western gate, then to the Aurelian wall; they were amateurs, hopelessly outnumbered, fighting without any chance of success, and on the last day of the month Garibaldi, battle-stained but still defiant, had to report to the Triumvirs that no further defence was possible.

With the surrender the French occupied Rome. The Assembly was dissolved and the keys of the city were sent to Pius, who appointed three cardinals to rule until his return in April 1850. Mazzini escaped and made his way to London. Garibaldi in an epic journey northwards, during which his wife Anita died, eventually reached the coast of Tuscany, from where he sailed to Tangier and later to the United States.

Thus, by the summer of 1849, the great hope of Italian unification seemed utterly crushed. It could be argued that the Italians had never deserved to succeed, for they had remained a prey to local jealousies which even their hatred for the Austrians could not overcome. Yet two other factors lie at the root of their failure. First, the military effort of Piedmont had shown that Charles Albert had been wrong to believe that *Italia farà da sé*; the Quadrilateral was too strong a bastion for the Italians to act without a powerful military ally. Second, the Pope's refusal to give his support had ruled out any possibility of a compromise solution that might have had the blessing of Catholic Europe. Yet with that refusal a further emotional factor had emerged, which until this time the extremists had lacked. The Mazzinian republicans had lost their city of Rome, but they had created a legend and in history legends often count for more than hard realistic facts.

3. The life and death of the Second Republic in France

In attempting to assess the French revolution of 1848 it is easy to assume that a republic which lasted for less than four years was doomed from the beginning. Certainly among the right wing and even the moderates there was little belief in a form of government which only the unexpected fall of Louis Philippe had forced upon them. The Spanish ambassador described France at this time as a country 'filled with monarchists who cannot establish a monarchy and who groan under the weight of a republic which has no republicans to defend it'. In the circumstances it might seem simple, indeed inevitable, that the newly elected President should soon establish himself in a more permanent and resplendent position, and the enigmatic melancholy of Louis Napoleon lends strength to the notion of the conspirator about to take his final step to absolute power. He was inscrutable. 'Les paroles qu'on lui adressait étaient comme les pierres qu'on jette dans un puits,' wrote de Tocqueville in his *Souvenirs*; 'on en entendait le bruit, mais on ne savait jamais ce qu'elles devenaient.'

Yet a republic, which, in Thiers' famous phrase *nous divise le moins*, was not an inappropriate *modus vivendi* for nineteenth-century France. Even during its short lifetime there was very little likelihood of the monarchists or the Socialists gaining their ends, and although there is not much doubt over Napoleon's intentions, it would be wrong to under-estimate the difficulties that confronted him at this decisive stage in his career. He had constantly to walk a tight-rope. His greatest strength lay in the fact that he could claim to represent the choice of the French people. He dared not alienate that support, yet at the same time he needed the goodwill of an influential section of the upper and middle classes who had only accepted him as a temporary expedient against some left-wing form of government.

This state of dilemma was well illustrated by his action over the Roman Republic in 1849. After Charles Albert's defeat outside Novara in March 1849, the prospect of Austrian influence becoming established in Piedmont was naturally abhorrent to France, and it was out of consideration for this that the Austrians imposed only the mildest terms. Within a month, however, the restoration of Habsburg rule in Tuscany pointed clearly to an impending attack by the Austrian forces on the Roman Republic. Traditional French interests in Italy and Louis Napoleon's own instincts as a former *Carbanaro* were in accord at this point in the orders to Oudinot to sail for Civita Vecchia on 21 April with 7,000 men. The Austrians were to be forestalled, but the problem of the expedition's ultimate role remained unresolved. Was it to be a reinforcement for Mazzini's Republic? Or was the Republic to be crushed and Pope Pius IX restored? The answer was provided by the energetic repulse of Oudinot's troops by Garibaldi when they attempted to enter the city, and by the election in France, on 13 May, of a new Assembly in which Bonapartists collaborating with monarchists created a right-wing majority of 500 out of 750 seats. The clericals were to have their Pope restored, and the hopeless failure of Ledru-Rollin's rising in Paris on 13 June meant the end of Mazzini's last hope.

During the following twelve months the conservatives in the Chamber continued to make good their position. In March 1850 *la loi Falloux*, named after the minister who introduced it, established liberty of teaching for any person or institution, thereby allowing complete freedom for the religious orders to establish their own secondary schools and institutions of advanced education.[1] In the same month some thirty by-elections to fill the place of those deputies who had been arrested for their part in the rising of the previous June resulted in the return of twenty candidates of Socialist or extreme republican views. To the bourgeois this awoke all the fears of a new left-wing insurrection, and in May they made use of a loophole in the constitution to decree a three-years residential qualification for all voters—a refinement which had the effect of disfranchising about three million of the poorer classes.

In the summer of 1850 all sides were thinking in terms of a régime which would supersede the Second Republic. The extreme left, contrary to expectation, disregarded any possibility of insurrection and centred their energies on preparations for the election of a new President and Assembly, due in 1852; monarchists paid visits to their respective sovereigns, Orleanists to Louis Philippe at Claremont in Surrey, Legitimists to the Bourbon Count de Chambord, 'Henry V', at Wiesbaden. It was, however, the President who embarked upon the most significant campaign. The developments of the last eighteen months had been something of an embarrassment to Louis Napoleon, who could never be sure that public opinion would not associate him exclusively with a right-wing movement, and in August and September he made two journeys throughout France stopping at many of the larger cities to preach the Bonapartist gospel.

On his return he felt sufficiently sure of his position to challenge the Assembly; yet he did attempt at first to gain his ends in cooperation with the deputies. Between May and July 1851 he struggled to pass an amendment to the constitution which would have prolonged his tenure of office, but failed to win the necessary majority of three-quarters. By the autumn of 1851, however, when the expiry of his term of

[1] These schools were, nevertheless, to be under the supervision of the University of France—a fact which angered the extreme Ultramontanes.

office was not far distant, he was already thinking in terms of a *coup d'état*. In November his attempt to gain the repeal of the electoral law of May 1850 was defeated by the Assembly—possibly a cunning means of enhancing his own popularity at the expense of the Assembly, although there are indications that he genuinely wished the measure to be passed. In the same month an attempt by the right wing, by now highly mistrustful of their President, to secure control over the military forces of the country, was defeated by the republicans in the Assembly, who saw the measure simply as a monarchist manoeuvre. And then in the early hours of 2 December—the anniversary of his uncle's proclamation of the first Empire and of the victory at Austerlitz—Louis Napoleon struck. The announcement of a conspiracy against the State, his opponents divided and surprised, the control of the necessary military forces at the disposal of the President, all made the outcome a foregone conclusion; and within forty-eight hours Louis Napoleon had no need to trouble himself any further with the restrictions imposed by the constitution of the Second Republic.

IV

THE DESTRUCTION OF THE VIENNA
SETTLEMENT 1851–70

14

THE CHANGING BACKGROUND

THE practical outcome of the revolutions of 1848 might well seem depressing to liberals throughout most of the Continent. The national movements had failed utterly; after the collapse of the Second Republic the character of Louis Napoleon's government remained as yet an unknown quantity, and outside France the advance of constitutional rule was restricted to only a few small regions of Europe. In Belgium and the Netherlands the powers of the existing legislatures and the size of the electorates had been increased. The Danish king had bowed to the demands of a popular Convention which tempered the royal despotism with a two-chamber Assembly elected on a limited franchise. In Prussia and Piedmont, although the forms of parliamentary government recently granted by Frederick William IV and Charles Albert had survived, the Prussian system, after the modifications of April 1849[1], weighted representation heavily in the interest of the richest class, while the Piedmontese rested on an extremely narrow franchise. Beyond this, only the Swiss could claim a fundamental revision of their whole constitutional pattern—the establishment of a strong federal authority based on universal manhood suffrage.

To the north and the east nothing had been challenged. Sweden had been relatively untouched by the revolutions and despite a gradual trend towards a greater liberalism it was not until 1866 that the four Estates of the *Riksdag* were transformed into an elective bi-cameral Parliament. In Russia there had been no chance of any outbreak. Tsar Nicholas's police had even pounced upon what was little more than a politically-minded literary society and twenty-two of the suspected rebels—Dostoevsky among them—had reached the scaffold on a winter's morning in 1849 before the news of their reprieve was announced and they were dispatched instead to Siberia.

In Italy and central Europe much indeed had been challenged, but to little avail. 'From Rome, which fell before a people which betrayed humanity, to Hungary sold to the enemy by a general who betrayed his fatherland, everything in 1849 has been sinful, gruesome

[1]See p. 159.

and vile,' wrote Alexander Herzen. In Italy, Lombardy and Venetia remained under military rule until 1857 and the lands of *émigrés* were confiscated. Austrian garrisons in the northern duchies and legations ensured the suppression of all forms of constitution, while in the Kingdom of Naples absolutism had already been restored. French troops continued to occupy Rome until 1870,[1] and although Pius IX did retain the *Consulta*, he had no wish to attempt any further experiments in constitutional government.

In Germany all traces of the Frankfurt Parliament were quickly swept away; the German flag of black, red, and gold was removed from the hall of the Federal Diet, and the ships of the national fleet which the liberals had begun to create were sold by public auction. Among the states themselves recent constitutional changes were virtually wiped out in Mecklemburg, Saxony, Hanover, and Hesse-Cassel, and throughout Germany leading liberals were executed, imprisoned or forced to escape abroad. Even in Prussia, where the constitution survived, local self-government was strictly curtailed, the power of police surveillance greatly increased, and in 1854 the upper Chamber was transformed into a House of Peers.

In Hungary there were over a hundred executions including thirteen generals and Count Batthyány; the separate identity of the Kingdom was smothered in a new policy of centralized absolutism, whereby Schwarzenberg and Alexander Bach gave full expression to the tendencies already suggested in the constitution of 1849,[2] which was itself revoked in December 1851. Everywhere throughout the Habsburg dominions German was to be the official language, and in 1855 a Concordat restored to the Roman Catholic Church its old power of supervision over education, a privilege of which it had been deprived by Joseph II in the 1780s and which had not even been revived in the settlement of 1815.

It has been seen how the liberals had only known success in the 1848 revolutions where they had been able to gain their ends without becoming dependent upon the forces of the urban masses, and how failure had inevitably followed when their fears that the working class might gain too great a control over the revolutionary movement had quelled the liberal attack on the old order. To the governments it seemed that there was a further lesson to be learnt; they were confirmed in their determination to make use of the natural conservatism of the peasantry. In France it had been the small farmer on whom Louis Napoleon had

[1] Except for a short interval in 1867, see p. 234.   [2] See p. 156.

been able to rely for his strongest support; in Austria, the peasant, once he had gained the abolition of feudal tenure in September 1848, had lost all interest in the later efforts of the revolutionaries, and in the Hungarian revolt the mobilizing of the Croat peasantry against their Magyar overlords had merely been a repetition of the Habsburg stratagem of 1846 in Galicia.[1]

The idea had already been formulated before the revolutions. 'Our princes have not yet exhausted the resources with which they may survive the struggle against triumphant mediocrity,' commented Radowitz in 1846. 'Let them but have the courage to turn to the masses.' Thus, throughout central Europe in the 1850s the governments did not rest content with the suppression of liberal activity; they embarked upon a deliberate policy of encouraging the peasantry and the handcraftsmen in the face of a growing industrialism. In those parts of Germany where the process of rural emancipation from feudal obligations had not yet been completed, it was greatly accelerated. In Prussia government measures passed in 1850 entitled *all* peasants to commute their manorial dues and established special banks offering credit facilities to farmers. Thus, whereas by 1848 only 70,000 Prussian peasants in the regions east of the Elbe had obtained their freedom, a further 640,000 were to do so between 1850 and 1865.

Similarly the governments attempted to bolster up the craftsmen's guilds whose intricate regulation of labour might act as a brake on *laissez-faire* capitalism. 'Handcraftsmen,' wrote Bismarck in October 1849 at the beginning of his political career, '. . . constitute the backbone of the burgher class, of an element whose survival is essential to a healthy national life and whose maintenance seems to me to be fully as important as was the creation of a free peasantry at the beginning of this century, for the sake of which the authorities did not boggle at serious infringements of law and property.' Nassau and Saxe-Gotha in 1849, Frankfurt in 1850, and Bavaria in 1853 all decreed greater control over the practice of crafts. In Prussia guilds were restored as early as February 1849; in the following years some 4,600 craft corporations were re-established and after 1854 they came more directly under State supervision. In Prussia another stroke in the governmental campaign against the new capitalist class was to benefit the industrial worker. In 1853 a Factory Act prohibited the employment of children under the age of twelve in factories and mines; those between twelve and fourteen were not to work more than seven hours a day, were to be

[1] See p. 128.

free from night work and were to continue their education in factory schools. Such a measure, reinforced by a system of inspection, gave far greater protection than had yet been extended to the young in Great Britain, France, or in most other parts of Germany.

Benefit there might be for many, yet the assumptions behind these measures remained utterly impracticable. This conservative trend throughout central Europe in the 1850s was the last stand of a social order which, although it had survived the assaults of 1848, could not hope to resist the cumulative forces of economic change with which it was sooner or later bound to come to terms.

The statistics of the production of coal and iron[1] show clearly how the tide of industrialism was moving progressively eastwards across the Continent in the years between 1850 and 1870. In Great Britain the increase in the annual output of coal from 57 to 112 million tons still kept her economy comfortably in a class of its own; the most significant change on the Continent was to be seen in Germany, where the annual output rose from 6 to 34 million tons, whereas in France, although trebled, it stood only at 13 million tons in 1870. Similarly, in the manufacture of pig-iron Great Britain still remained well ahead with an output of slightly less than 6 million tons in 1870, while Germany in these two decades raised hers by 1,185,000 to 1,300,000 tons as against France's increase of 78,000 to 1,180,000. In 1856 Great Britain was to be the home of another fundamental discovery, the Bessemer process for the manufacture of modern steel, and by 1870 she was turning out 700,000 tons—more than double the production of either France or Germany.

Equally striking was the continuing revolution in communications. The 14,000 miles of railway track that had been laid in Europe by 1850 had grown by 1870 to 65,000 miles, and the international network across the whole Continent encouraged the development of a cheap postal service. At sea the development of the steamship had halved the time for the crossing of the Atlantic as early as 1838, and the general bulk of world freight had risen from 10 million nautical tons in 1840 to 25 million in 1870. The most startling conquest of the ocean, however, was represented by the electric telegraph; a cable from Dover to Calais was laid in 1851, and Europe had been linked with the United States by 1866 and with India and Australia by 1871.

All this astonishing increase in the tempo of economic life naturally

[1] See Appendix 10, p. 491.

stimulated a greater borrowing of capital. Banks for the promoting of companies sprang up in profusion—*Crédit Lyonnais, Crédit Industriel,* and the *Société Générale* in France, *Kreditanstalt* in Austria, and many others in the German states; the international ramifications of banking were well illustrated by the French *Crédit Mobilier* under the Péreire brothers, one-third of whose shares in the 1850s were held by British investors and whose promotion of industrial joint-stock enterprises eventually led to the acquisition of considerable interests in Austrian and Russian railways. Governments, too, availed themselves of the new facilities and between 1848 and 1872 the total public debt of European states rose from £1,730 million to £4,605 million—much of it raised from outside the frontiers of each state.

Another aspect of the economic scene was the general growth of the population of Europe[1] which rose steadily in the 1850s and 1860s from 266 to 296 million. This increase is all the more remarkable in that some five million emigrants left the Continent during these years— predominantly central European and Irish peasantry moving to the United States[2]—the annual average reaching 350,000 in the early 1850s, dropping to 200,000 and then rising to 400,000 a year by 1870.

The rate of increase within the various regions of Europe differed enormously. In 1850 France and Germany had each numbered slightly less than 36 million, yet the French, even after the acquisition of Savoy and Nice in 1860,[3] were only 37 million by 1870, in contrast to 41 million Germans; thus in population, as well as in industrial output, these were the years when Germany clearly began to outstrip her rival across the Rhine. The most startling change, however, was to be seen in Russia where an additional 20 million had brought her to a total of 77 million in 1870. Another feature, common to most regions of Europe was the growth in the size of the urban population. The eighteenth-century streets and squares were becoming a historic core about which new residential areas sprawled out over the surrounding countryside, and as the old walls and fortifications were swallowed up by the towns that they had once defended, they were gradually demolished to make way for broad encircling boulevards—such as the Ringstrasse in Vienna, the great thoroughfares of Napoleon III's Paris, and similar roadways in Florence and Turin.

The general economic pattern of the period was one of rising prices, due to the greater volume of trade, and particularly to the enormous increase in the world's output of gold after the discoveries in California

---

[1] See Appendix 7, p. 488.   [2] See Appendix 9, p. 490.   [3] See p. 203.

and Australia. This tendency was interrupted by two great slumps in 1857 and 1866 which illustrated the growing closeness of economic relationship throughout the whole world, already suggested by the earlier crashes of 1837 and 1846.[1] Prosperity seeped down only very slowly to improve the condition of the poor, and the fine new façades of the towns often served to mask the appalling slums that lay behind. Still, the position of the working class *was* changing slightly for the better in these years, since wages did rather more than keep pace with prices and continued to rise until 1873.

Another aspect of the economic pattern was a movement towards free trade. Great Britain had long espoused this policy; the Netherlands and the *Zollverein* slowly lowered their tariffs; in 1850 Belgium repealed her Corn Laws, and in 1857 Denmark's agreement to abolish her Sound dues was another step in the same direction. Unlike their counterpart in Great Britain, however, continental industrialists were seriously divided over the question of protection, and the governments accordingly approached Free Trade with considerable caution, preferring to make private trade agreements with individual countries, rather than to adopt a general principle. Thus, as early as 1851, Cavour[2] as Piedmontese Minister of Agriculture, Commerce, and Marine had completed Free Trade treaties with Great Britain, France, and Belgium, while France's famous treaty with Great Britain, as a result of Richard Cobden's visit to Paris in 1860, was paralleled by others with Belgium, Turkey, the *Zollverein*, Italy, the Netherlands, and Austria.

The full consequences of industrialism were far more than purely economic. The growing concentration of the working classes in the factories was soon to facilitate their political organization, while in central and eastern Europe the drift of the peasantry into the towns lent strength to the development of nationalism. For the governments, new techniques were to bring greater powers and wider problems. French engineering skill, for example, which had accomplished the cutting of the Suez canal by 1869, not merely shortened the commercial route to the east; it opened up political issues over the future control of the canal, which had originally caused the British to oppose its construction. Military and naval forces, too, were to be revolutionized as muskets were gradually replaced by rifles, muzzle-loading cannon by breech-loaders, and wooden sailing ships of the line by screw-driven ironclads. 'To move an army now is to move a great city', commented *The Times*

[1] See p. 100.   [2] See p. 195.

in 1861, and on the Continent General Staffs were growing increasingly aware of the strategic significance of railways. Troop movements by rail had played some part in the suppression of the revolt in Cracow in 1846 and in Hungary in 1849, and in the 1860s the varying speeds with which countries could mobilize their armies were not merely to alter decisively the balance of military power, but were also to become a factor in diplomacy of which Bismarck was to make devastating use.

All these changes pointed to an eventual alliance between the rulers and the new forces of industry and commerce. In the west and in Scandinavia this alliance had been slowly forcing itself on the governments since 1815, gradually weakening the chances of survival for Metternich's Europe. In Piedmont Cavour was to seize on it from the beginning of his political career. In central Europe the change came late and then with a dramatic suddenness, as the realization dawned on the governments that an obstinate determination to resist the advance of the new capitalist classes by encouraging the peasantry and the handcraft guilds was not only useless but positively harmful.

In Prussia the anti-liberal reaction lasted until 1858, when the insanity of Frederick William IV could no longer be disguised and his brother William took over as Prince Regent. The conservative government of Manteuffel and the Gerlachs, already discredited by the failure of an attempt in 1857 to regain control of the Swiss canton of Neuchâtel,[1] had been weakened still further by the economic slump of the same year and was now replaced by a more liberal ministry under Prince Karl Anton von Hohenzollern-Sigmaringen. In the following years Prussian parliamentary elections lent impetus to this swing away from the right, and the subsequent tendency to ease restrictions on industry in Prussia was reflected almost immediately afterwards in the legislation of more than a third of the other German states—as well as in Austria after the shock of the Italian war of 1859.[2]

Nor was this change limited to the attitude of the governments. The awareness of their economic strength had enabled the Italian and German middle class to recover from their recent disillusionment and to dream once again of the commercial advantages that they would derive from national unification. Yet they, too, had learnt their lesson from 1848. This time they did not intend to succumb to the romance of political idealism divorced from the hard facts of power; with a new realism they began to look to Piedmont and Prussia as the only possible leaders who might accomplish their aim through a process of diplomacy

[1] See p. 148.   [2] See p. 199.

and war, without at the same time letting loose the radicalism of the masses. The year 1859 marked not only the beginning of Cavour's great venture to form with French help a North Italian Kingdom, but also the organization of the *Deutscher Nationalverein* (German National Association) which aimed at the creation of a united Germany under Prussian leadership. A new social alliance was in the making, and events to which it soon gave rise in Italy and Germany were finally to destroy the pattern of central Europe devised at the Congress of Vienna.

15

THE FRENCH SECOND EMPIRE 1852-70

1. *The domestic scene in France*

IN France the Second Republic had succumbed almost without a blow to Napoleon's *coup d'état* of 2 December 1851. In Paris the only serious street fighting two days later had been crushed in an afternoon; in the provinces left-wing republicans had held out for a while in the south-east, but the major cities remained firmly under control. Thus, within three weeks Louis Napoleon could gamble on a plebiscite, and although some of the 7,481,000 votes approving his action and accepting the need to redraw the constitution may have been due to official pressure, the bulk of them were no more than a confirmation of the election that had carried him to the presidency three years before.

The new constitution was completed in January 1852. It opened with a resounding guarantee of the principles of 1789 and then proceeded to name Louis Napoleon as President for ten years. This office was entrusted with the fullest executive powers, including command of the armed forces, the initiation of all legislation and the appointment of ministers and officials. There were to be two Chambers—a Senate of a hundred and fifty selected by the President and with its functions limited to a right of veto on all laws that might violate the constitution; and a *Corps Législatif*, elected by universal suffrage every six years and only able to vote on new laws without discussion. This representative Chamber was not to contain any ministers and the chairmen of both were to be appointed by the President.

It might well seem that Louis Napoleon had provided himself with an instrument admirably suited to the establishment of autocracy. Certainly he envisaged a form of strong personal rule; the deliberations of the Senate were not to be public, while those of the *Corps Législatif* were only to be published in an official summary. For the elections the constituencies were carefully arranged in the conservative interest, and the Prefects and mayors received instructions for the promotion of official candidates. On the other hand, Louis Napoleon's system clearly depended upon much more than a mere power of repression. The members of the Senate were irremovable and after the initial creation there would be no further possibility of his packing the House. The *Corps Législatif* might not be able to discuss the laws and the budget, but they did at least have the right of voting on them. Furthermore, they were elected by universal manhood suffrage on a secret ballot, and later political developments were to prove this to be much more than an empty form. Had Louis Napoleon stood at the head of a highly organized Bonapartist party, this would not have been so. In fact Bonapartism was more of a mood than a party and he had instead to rely upon that general appeal which had already taken him so far. 'When one bears our name and when one is at the head of the government', he wrote, 'there are two things one must do: satisfy the interests of the most numerous classes and attach to oneself the upper classes.' Thus, in the first elections the official candidates were not selected by those Bonapartist committees that did exist, but by the Prefects, and were drawn from a wide range of political views including a number of Legitimists, Orleanists, and men of recent wealth. In the outcome, over six million voters went to the polls, five-sixths of the official candidates were returned and only six opposition candidates were successful, four of whom were republican. For the moment, at least, Louis Napoleon had the situation that he needed, but the broad base for which he hoped could never be entirely stable, and the authoritarian nature of his government remained very much at the mercy of public opinion in an age when the technical means of controlling it were still comparatively weak.

It was typical of Louis Napoleon's whole conception of his rule that he should revert once again to a plebiscite before taking the final step in his venture. In November 1852 seven million voters agreed to the restoration of hereditary rule, and on 2 December the Prince President became the Emperor Napoleon III—a style that took a leaf out of the royalist book in emphasising the myth that Napoleon I's son, the Duke de Reichstadt, had reigned after his father's abdication. The Emperor now had only to find an Empress, and there followed in January 1853 Napoleon's marriage to Eugénie de Montijo, a Spanish noblewoman, who in 1856 gave birth to a son and thus provided an heir to the Imperial throne. Yet for all his efforts to acquire respectability Napoleon never quite succeeded in living down the origins of the Second Empire. As a monarch he remained to the end a *parvenu*, a conspirator who had made good; always there was a touch of theatre about this re-appearance of a Napoleonic court at the Tuileries and in the popular imagination the memory of the Second Empire is essentially a romantic one, a world of petticoat influence and elegant licence amid the flickering gas-lamps of Paris.

None of this, however, should obscure the fact that Napoleon's reign marks a time of immense energy and activity for the domestic economy,[1] a time when Saint-Simonian influences found their most powerful practical expression. A new institution, *Crédit Mobilier*, under the Péreire brothers undertook the financing of a variety of industrial concerns, while *Crédit Foncier* provided much of the capital needed for urban development. The government was particularly concerned to extend the railway system, and by 1870 the length of track in service had grown to 11,000 miles. The value of French imports and exports rose from 2,615 million francs in 1851 to 8,008 million in 1869, and the Paris Exhibition of 1867 proclaimed French industrial advance to the world. Paris itself was the greatest advertisement of Napoleon III's rule. Under the masterful direction of Baron Haussmann, the Prefect of the Seine, great broad boulevards cut through the tangle of narrow streets which had earlier resounded with the excitements of the Revolutionary years, and across which the barricades had been thrown up in 1830 and 1848. Twenty thousand houses were demolished; more than double that number were erected, and the great shopping centres, the new Opera, the market of *Les Halles* and the development of the Parc Monceau, the Buttes de Chaumont, and the Bois de Boulogne, all date from this period. The city which the twentieth-century tourist sees today is largely the Paris of Napoleon III.

Authoritarian rule proved not only efficient; it was also mild. The laws controlling the press had in principle been inherited from the Second Republic, but did at least allow an editor two indiscretions, and although tribunals had had to deal with 26,000 persons arrested after the *coup d'état*, 10,000 of these were acquitted or simply placed under police surveillance. Of the rest who were imprisoned or transported to Algeria, only 6,153 were still unpardoned by 1853, while in 1856 all who were prepared to accept the existing government were allowed to return.

Nevertheless, by 1860 there were signs that the general popularity on which Napoleon based his government was beginning to be seriously weakened. He had always hoped to retain the support of the clericals, but the Ultramontane group was becoming increasingly

---

[1] For comparative figures see pp. 175–6 and Appendix 10, p. 491.

impatient of the Concordat, and the growth of Church schools, consequent on *la loi Falloux* of 1850,[1] added fuel to the conflict with the secular state system of education. It was, however, over Napoleon's foreign policy that the issue really came to a head. In the Crimean War clerical interests and national aims went hand in hand, but in 1859 Napoleon embarked upon an Italian adventure in which his support of Cavour seemed to threaten the whole basis of the Temporal Power of the Papacy; the liberal sentiments of the Emperor and the conservatism of the clericals had clearly become irreconcilable. Then again, Napoleon's desire for greater freedom of trade had aroused the hostility of many business interests, particularly the smaller ones who still depended upon a system of protection, and the Anglo-French commercial treaty of 1860, which reduced import duties on British coal and manufactured goods and on French wines and brandy, proved to be the forerunner of similar treaties involving reciprocal reductions with Belgium in 1861, the *Zollverein* in 1862, Italy in 1863, Switzerland in 1864, Spain and the Netherlands in 1865, and Austria and Portugal in 1866. Lastly, the expansion of industry had naturally led to the considerable growth of a proletariat concentrated in large towns where republicanism began actively to revive.

Napoleon's response to these dangers was to veer towards the left. In 1859 the remaining exiles were allowed to return without the imposition of any condition, although a few, such as Victor Hugo in the Channel Islands, still refused to live under Bonapartist rule. By a decree of 24 November 1860 liberal changes were introduced into the constitution, permitting the Senate and the *Corps Législatif* to vote a reply to the Emperor's address at the beginning of each session and to publish the record of their debates. In 1864 the working class were granted the right to strike. In 1867 both Houses were allowed to interrogate ministers, and the Senate acquired a more parliamentary role when it was given a suspensive veto over legislation passed by the *Corps Législatif*. In 1868 a relaxation of the press laws resulted in the appearance of an additional 150 newspapers, the vast majority of which were hostile to the government.

This tendency towards a greater liberalism was a calculated risk which, although it inevitably offered greater scope for the forces of opposition, might have gone far to preserve the Second Empire. Unfortunately it was accompanied by other factors. Napoleon's health was failing fast in the 1860s and his own personal control over events

[1] See p. 168.

at home and abroad during these years was gravely weakened. The system of official candidates was no longer so effective; the mayors were becoming more independent and a pamphlet published in 1868 commented: 'the Prefect is no longer the dazzling star who alone spreads his light on the *département*.' More disastrous still, the Emperor's foreign policy encountered one check after another and for a Napoleonic régime this meant a serious loss of prestige.

The consequence of this decline was to be seen in the elections of 1863 and 1869. The republicans who had only gained five seats in 1857 were able to add to their numbers, capturing many of the larger cities, and were strengthened by the appearance of such personalities as Léon Gambetta, Jules Ferry, and Henri de Rochefort. To the right of the republicans a new Third Party under Thiers demanded greater concessions in the direction of parliamentary government—winning 35 seats in 1863 and 116 in 1869. At no time did the government positively lose an election, but the voting in 1869 convinced Napoleon that the moment had come to take a further step towards constitutional rule.

The outcome was that short-lived period known as the 'Liberal Empire'. The changes decreed in the autumn of 1869 granted the *Corps Législatif* the right to initiate legislation, completed the transformation of the Senate into an upper House and allowed ministers to be drawn from the members of either Chamber. As his Prime Minister, Napoleon selected Émile Ollivier, one of the five republican deputies of 1857, a superb orator, who had by now become less extreme in his political outlook. In January 1870 Ollivier formed a ministry from official candidates and moderates, and after the right of confirming any constitutional revision had been transferred from the Senate to the people, a plebiscite was held in May in which the electorate were asked to accept all the changes that had been introduced since 1860. Once again the government gained the approval that it sought with an overwhelming vote of seven million, although the two million abstentions suggested some doubts and the one and a half million who opposed reflected the republican hold on the cities.

It can never be known whether these concessions would have given a new lease of life to the Empire. Certainly they had not yet satisfied all political aspirations, for the ministers remained responsible primarily to the Emperor—a situation more reminiscent of eighteenth-century England than of a modern parliamentary democracy—yet the responsiveness of the Empire to political forces does suggest an elasticity that might have been equal to further domestic tensions. As it turned out, Napoleon's fate was sealed ultimately by defeat in war. 'More than ever before,' he said in May, 'can we look forward to the future without fear', but before the summer was out, his country had been overrun by the Prussian army and in September the abdication of the Emperor brought this colourful epoch of French history to a close.

2. The Crimean war 1854–6

Little more than a year after the establishment of the Second Empire France found herself once again at war with Russia, this time with Great Britain as her ally. The siege and capture of Sebastopol, the great Russian naval base in the Crimea, did not perhaps wipe out the memory of the retreat from Moscow; yet the eventual surrender of Russia followed by the imposition of terms at the Congress of Paris in 1856 marked a restoration of political prestige for France that she had not known since the days of the first Napoleon.

The initial circumstances of the quarrel had already been developing in the last years of Louis Philippe. The French supported the claims of the Latin Catholics, and the Russians those of the Greek Orthodox over the Holy Places in Jerusalem and Bethlehem, and after the accession of Napoleon III the Turkish government was subjected to mounting pressure from both sides. Concessions were made to the Latins and then revoked in a secret agreement with the Greeks, whereupon the French ambassador, La Valette, coming back to Constantinople in April 1852, insisted on his ninety-gun screw-driven battleship, the *Charlemagne*, sailing through the Dardanelles, and in July a threatened bombardment of Tripoli by a French naval squadron forced the Turks to give way.

As usual, however, these details had little to do with the fundamental issues at stake. Religious disputes in the nineteenth century did not in themselves lead to international hostilities. Nor, for that matter, was the Crimean war simply the continuation of a vendetta between a Bonaparte and the Russian Tsar; it arose out of a question of far wider import—the extent to which the Powers should allow the extension of Russian influence in the Balkans. In January 1853 Tsar Nicholas began to sound British reactions to proposals for a partition of Turkey, but these came to very little and in any case he did not push them too hard. His real interest was in the special mission of Prince Menshikov to Constantinople, who after some preliminary negotiation virtually

G 2

presented the Turks with an ultimatum in May. Control of the Holy Places was to be granted to the Greeks and a Russian protectorate was to be recognized over all Greek Christians under Turkish rule. It was this second demand that revealed the full extent of the Tsar's ambitions, since this would enormously increase Russia's influence over the whole of Turkey without the embarrassment of a partition among the Powers. In Great Britain Palmerston had been dismissed from the Foreign Office in December 1851 after his over-hasty acceptance of Louis Napoleon's *coup d'état* and the coalition government formed under Aberdeen in December 1852 seemed unlikely to intervene. From Austria Nicholas expected positive support; the Habsburgs were already indebted for Russian assistance in Hungary in 1849, and as recently as February 1853 they had had a dispute of their own with Turkey whom they had forced to abandon a projected invasion of Montenegro. Thus, Nicholas was convinced that he was now well placed to impose his demand for a protectorate with the threat of an occupation of the Danubian Principalities.

It was a serious miscalculation. In March 1853 Napoleon had already dispatched the French fleet from Toulon to Salamis, and Stratford Canning, the British ambassador at Constantinople, encouraged the Turks to reject the proposal for a protectorate, although he still hoped for negotiations to continue. The British government was certainly more cautious than the French, but when on the departure of Menshikov Nicholas repeated his threat, the Malta fleet was ordered on 2 June to Besika Bay outside the Dardanelles. Nicholas, however, still felt sufficiently confident to send Russian forces across the Pruth on 2 July, and the occupation of Jassy and Bucharest, the capitals of Moldavia and Wallachia, followed at once.

Now, at last, the Tsar learnt that he had really overplayed his hand. Both Vienna and Berlin reacted strongly against this invasion. In Austria Count Buol, who had become Foreign Minister on Schwarzenberg's death in 1852, made it clear that no moral obligation to Russia would allow his government to countenance such an alarming outcome of the Menshikov mission, and turned at once to Great Britain and France. Nicholas, faced with this disappointment, began a diplomatic retreat in accepting the Note which the other four Powers drew up at Vienna in July, whereby Turkey was simply to be asked to guarantee no change in her rule over her Christian subjects 'without previous understanding with the Governments of France and Russia'. This agreement was partly the work of Napoleon and it naturally enhanced his own position both in Europe and among the clericals in France. It was, however, doomed to failure; the Turks refused to accept it and in September a 'violent interpretation' of the Vienna Note by Nesselrode, the Russian Foreign Minister, still maintaining the original aims of the Tsar, suggested that they had been wise to do so.

Throughout the autumn the crisis slowly mounted. On 22 September the French proposed to the British cabinet that their combined fleets should sail through the Dardanelles, and although Stratford Canning resisted this for as long as he could, he had eventually to summon the British fleet to Constantinople in October. Meanwhile, Nicholas was painfully conferring with Francis Joseph and Frederick William IV, but could draw neither of them from a policy of neutrality. In Constantinople the belligerence of Mehemet Ali,[1] the Turkish Minister of War, was strongly supported by the anti-Russian feeling that had been growing steadily and on 4 October the Sultan declared that there would be war unless the Principalities were evacuated within two weeks. The Russians did not move and by the last week of October Russo-Turkish hostilities had opened north of the Danube. Stratford Canning was still able to hold the Turks back from sending their fleet into the Black Sea, but on 30 November a light flotilla was destroyed by the Russians at Sinope. Although this was a perfectly legitimate operation of war, it had a startling effect upon public opinion in the west—particularly in Great Britain—and in France a £2 million loan was immediately raised for Turkey, while Napoleon declared that if the British fleet would not enter the Black Sea with the French, he would act alone. In January 1854 the British gave way to this pressure, the two fleets passed through the Bosphorus and after Nicholas had been presented with a demand that his fleet should take no further action against the Turks, the Russian ambassadors were withdrawn from London and Paris. War was officially declared on 31 March, but although Great Britain and France had already signed a treaty with Turkey a fortnight before, they did not actually become allies themselves until 10 April.

None of the participants had seriously expected the outbreak of a major war. Diplomatic miscalculation and the pressure of public opinion had combined to create a situation in which neither side had been able to pull back. Yet behind all the concern for prestige there had been a very real issue in the proposed Russian protectorate over the Balkan Christians, and the occupation of the Principalities,

[1] He is not to be confused with Mehemet Ali of Egypt who had died in 1849.

followed by the outbreak of a Russo-Turkish war, had confronted the western Powers with the old threat of a Russian advance on to Constantinople.

It was in order to meet this threat that by the beginning of June 1854 the first British and French contingents were being landed at Varna, a Bulgarian town on the coast of the Black Sea. The key to the situation, however, lay not in the military action of Great Britain and France, but in the attitude of the Central Powers. 'If Prussia and Austria go with us,' commented Prince Albert, 'matters are different and the war becomes impossible for Russia.' By now Nicholas was only too aware of such a danger. On 20 April Austria had formed an alliance with Prussia, in May her army on the Turco-Hungarian frontier was mobilized, and in June the two Powers demanded that Russia should evacuate the Principalities. More ominous still, by July the Austrians were in consultation with the French in drawing up the Four Points on which peace might be negotiated. These were finally established early in August, stipulating a European guarantee of the Principalities, the freedom of the navigation of the Danube, the revision of the Straits Convention of 1841 'in the interests of the Balance of Power in Europe', and the abandonment of the Russian claim to a protectorate over the Christian subjects of Turkey.

Russian policy was inevitably governed by this fickleness on the part of the Austrians. Nicholas dared not allow them to move any closer to the west and accordingly by August his troops were already evacuating the Principalities, which were occupied by Austria during the remainder of the war. The danger, however, was not yet past. In November the Austrians seemed about to join with the Allies in insisting on the Four Points and Nicholas had once again to give way, instructing Gortchakov, the Russian ambassador at Vienna, to open negotiations on them while the war continued. Fortunately for Nicholas, Buol, the Austrian Foreign Minister, intended to do no more than to fish in troubled waters. It was only after the Russians had made it known that they were prepared to negotiate that he made Austrian military intervention dependent upon their refusal to do so, and then duly collected his reward from Napoleon III in the form of a convention signed on 22 December guaranteeing the territorial *status quo* in Italy. This convention, however, did not prevent the Allies from turning to Piedmont where King Victor Emmanuel, aided by the French ambassador, compelled his Prime Minister Cavour against his own judgement to join the western allies in January 1855, and a small

Piedmontese army of 15,000 was dispatched to the Crimea in return for which Cavour was only able to gain a promise of a place at the subsequent congress. In fact, this Piedmontese alliance represented the principal achievement of the diplomats, since Austria would not be drawn any further, and despite two Allied naval expeditions to the Baltic when the fortifications of the Åland Isles were destroyed and Sveaborg, the island fortress outside Helsinki, bombarded, Sweden refused to be enticed out of a cautious neutrality.

Meanwhile, by the autumn of 1854 the revision of the Straits Convention of 1841, the third of the Four Points, implying an Allied aim to neutralize the Black Sea, had become the main issue of the war. This had not played any part in the circumstances of the outbreak, but it was indirectly relevant, since the removal of a Russian fleet from the Black Sea would obviously greatly strengthen Turkey's security. Thus, when the Russian evacuation of the Principalities deprived the Allied forces at Varna of any immediate objective, they were dispatched in September to the Crimea across the Black Sea, preparatory to an assault on Sebastopol. The British and French armies, commanded respectively by Lord Raglan and St Arnaud, numbered together over 50,000. Marching south they imposed a retreat on the Russians at the battle of the Alma, but then instead of making at once for Sebastopol moved inland round the port and eventually took up siege positions on the south side. There followed the appalling winter of the Crimean war; the British drove off the Russian attacks at Balaclava on 25 October and at Inkerman on 5 November, but the troops suffered frightfully on the exposed plateau. Military leadership was hopelessly incompetent on both sides, but it was clear that of the Allies the French army was better supplied and administered than the British. In May 1855 the Kerch peninsula was captured, but it was not until 9 September that the final assault on Sebastopol was successful.

Tsar Nicholas had died earlier that year and his son, who succeeded as Alexander II, was determined to bring the war to an end. An armistice was signed in February 1856 and in the same month a peace congress assembled in Paris. By the terms of the treaty signed in March Russia lost southern Bessarabia, and Kars, which she had taken from Turkey in the Caucasus, was restored to the Sultan. The Black Sea was to be neutralized and the Straits were to remain closed to warships while Turkey was at peace. The Danube was placed under international control, and Europe, instead of Russia alone, assumed a protectorate over the Principalities and the Christian subjects of the

Turks. Finally, by a separate treaty with Great Britain, the Åland Isles in the Baltic were to remain unfortified. Only Piedmont failed to gain any positive advantage, and although it was doubtless pleasant to hear the British Foreign Secretary attack Austria's rule over her subject peoples at the peace congress, Cavour was unable to acquire the duchies of Modena and Parma whose rulers he had suggested might be compensated with Moldavia and Wallachia.

The war had cost the combatants dear. The British lost nearly 33,000 men, and the French 32,000, the vast majority of these through sickness. The Russian losses were heavier, although the figure of 500,000 given by their medical department seems excessive. Both Great Britain and Russia attempted to remedy some of the deficiencies that the war had revealed; the medical and administrative services of the British army were overhauled, and in Russia Tsar Alexander II embarked upon a great programme of general reform.[1] These were perhaps the most lasting results of the war, since the neutralization of the Black Sea which was the most significant change engineered by the victors was only to hold good until 1871.[2]

Nevertheless, it was precisely in these next fifteen years that the Vienna settlement was finally to be destroyed and the circumstances that made this possible sprang directly from the diplomatic conse-quences of the Crimean war. First, the Holy Alliance which, if it had any meaning at all, must rest on friendship between Austria and Russia, was utterly shattered, and as a result of Buol's policy of playing off one side against the other Austria was condemned to a fateful isolation. Second, Russia, exhausted by the war, temporarily abandoned any forceful intervention on the European scene and began to look for an ally in France and then later in Prussia. Third, the Congress of Paris marks the opening of a period of French predominance which until 1863 appeared to make Napoleon III the diplomatic arbiter of Europe.

3. The foreign policy of Napoleon III

In the period between the two empires French foreign policy had been fundamentally conservative. The expeditions to Spain in 1823, to Ancona in 1832 and to Rome in 1849 had all been in defence of the established order; caution had prevailed in the crises over Belgium in 1831 and Egypt in 1840, and although there had been an extension of French influence in the Mediterranean during the reign of Louis

[1] See p. 226.   [2] See p. 244.

Philippe, this policy had been developed largely within the limits of the Restoration settlement. The essential factor in the momentous changes of the mid-century decades was Napoleon III's desire to make use of the short-lived pre-eminence of France after 1856 to attempt a radical revision of that settlement. The irony of the story is that he was not equal to such a task and it was Cavour and Bismarck who seized the opportunities with which the Emperor's revolutionary foreign policy provided them.

The habits of the conspirator died hard and historians share the same uncertainty as his contemporaries over the precise aims of Napoleon's diplomacy, which was always a highly personal matter, *un secret de l'empereur*. Indeed, it has been suggested that he was none too sure of them himself—a sphinx without a riddle, as Bismarck called him. There were, in fact, a variety of motives that inspired the cloudy workings of Napoleon's political imagination. Not all of them were entirely compatible and it was never certain which of them would predominate in the Emperor's mind at any one moment. No Bonaparte could be indifferent to *la gloire;* no ruler in France dependent to some extent upon conservative support could ignore the French clerical concern for Rome and the survival of the Temporal Power. His old interest in nationalism was perfectly genuine, yet it did at times blend with a more practical aim to cause embarrassment for other Powers and to create a series of client states. 'On est plus grand par l'influence morale qu'on exerce,' he said in 1859, 'que par des conquêtes stériles.' Most of all, he longed to revise the treaties of 1815—hence his passion for European congresses and his determination to remain on good terms with Great Britain.

It was unfortunate that his greatest successes in the realm of *la gloire* were overseas where they excited little interest in France. By 1860 Algeria, whose conquest was now complete, had a European settler population of 290,000 and the native areas were largely under military rule. To the south the coast of Guinea and Dahomey was occupied and under the governorship of Faidherbe the interior of Senegal was opened up and the port of Dakar founded. The greatest French achievement in Africa was the building of the Suez canal, begun in 1859 and completed ten years later under the direction of Ferdinand de Lesseps, a fitting expression of the Saint-Simonianism which had earlier influenced him. In the Far East Saigon was captured in 1859 and France later assumed sovereign rule over parts of Indo-China and a protectorate over Cambodia, while in 1860 she joined forces with the

British in an expedition to Pekin to gain greater trading privileges in China. In 1861 another French expedition intervened in Syria after a massacre of Christians, but withdrew shortly afterwards to avoid offending British susceptibilities.

Napoleon's most grandiose performance overseas was in Mexico. Here French forces, which had been sent out in 1861 together with British and Spanish on a debt-collecting expedition, remained behind at Vera Cruz in an attempt to oust the anti-clerical reforming Mexican leader Juarez and to establish in his place the Habsburg Archduke Maximilian. This was certainly contrary to any nationalist principle, but naturally it pleased the clericals in France. A puppet French empire in Central America might well act as a bulwark against the growing penetration of the United States and offered a prospect of *la gloire* which did capture the imagination of French public opinion. This was unfortunate, since the Mexican venture turned out to be an appalling fiasco. By 1863 the French commander, Bazaine, who was sufficiently enamoured of the project to acquire a Mexican wife, had established Maximilian on a somewhat unstable throne, but the long resistance put up by Juarez eventually involved over 38,000 French troops, of whom 6,000 died. In 1865, with the end of the American Civil war, the United States government was at last in a position to object strongly to this serious infringement of the Monroe Doctrine, and Napoleon, already worried by the course of events in central Europe, had to cut his losses. In 1867 his troops were withdrawn and Maximilian paid the price of the French emperor's ambition before a Mexican firing squad.

In Europe, however, it was the encouragement of suppressed nationalities that seemed most likely to produce a practical reward in the form of French satellite states and a revision of the treaties of 1815. During the Crimean war Napoleon had toyed with ideas of fostering Finnish independence and at the Congress of Paris had wanted to hasten the emergence of a Rumanian state out of the Danubian Principalities, which were actually placed under a single governor three years later. This duality of purpose was particularly marked in his attitude towards Italy, for although his belief in the need for Italian independence had romantic undertones, his support of Cavour in 1859 was motivated by a desire to create a federation dependent on France.

In fact, Napoleon's determination to alter the *status quo* was ultimately to enable others to bring about changes seriously to the detriment of France. The united kingdom of Italy that had emerged by the end of 1860 was a far cry from what he had originally intended; the predominance that France enjoyed after 1856, followed by her acquisition of Savoy and Nice—the price of her assistance to Cavour—only aroused suspicions which thrust her into isolation. And in the 1860s Napoleon's dream of gaining Belgium as a puppet state in the Rhineland led him constantly to play into the hands of Bismarck who was thus aided in his own work of national unification and the eventual defeat of France.

16

THE UNIFICATION OF ITALY UNDER
CAVOUR 1859–60

PERSONALITIES are easier to visualize than social tendencies, and when in the middle decades of the nineteenth century political developments are seen to centre round three such fascinating individuals as Napoleon III, Cavour, and Bismarck, it is tempting to oversimplify the course of European history at this time. The historian often finds the attraction of success irresistible; thus, while the ultimate failure of Napoleon merely reinforces his charm as the romantic conspirator, the remarkable achievements of Cavour and Bismarck have too easily encouraged the cult of the master-mind shaping the destiny of modern Europe. In recent years, however, this conception has been attacked from two points of view. First, their personal success has been set in the context of a growing economy and technical development; second, the interpretation of their efforts has been brought down to a more human level at which it is possible to see that they sometimes made miscalculations and, unlike the historians, were quite unable to anticipate what was going to happen next. Despite this, the fact remains that the map of central Europe was utterly changed in less than a dozen years; economic and technical developments alone do not create a nation state in the face of opposition, and the triumphs of Cavour and Bismarck may appear the greater when viewed, not as the inevitable workings of a master plan, but as the outcome of the day-to-day perplexities that govern political action.

Count Camillo Benso di Cavour was born in 1810 of an old and distinguished Piedmontese family. The full rounded line of the face encircled by the short fringe of beard, revealed in the photographs taken in later life, appears at first sight benign and paternal; it is the features, the strong set of the mouth, the eyes shrewd and narrowed behind the spectacles that suggest the sharp mind of the *Realpolitiker*. As a younger son he was educated at the Military Academy of Turin and later served for a few years as an officer in the engineers. He did not remain in the army long, but his interests remained technical and scientific in the development of his estates and soon brought him into contact with the business world. He became a director of the railway laid between Turin and Genoa, and of the Bank of Turin, and was an active member of the National Agricultural Society founded in 1842. One of the great formative influences on his outlook was a visit to England in 1835; the growth of the first railways, the sense of commercial and industrial expansion encouraged by the emergence of Free Trade, the atmosphere of the debates in the House of Commons which he attended, the common assumption of political liberty under a constitutional monarchy, all helped to shape the policies that he was later to advocate in his own newspaper *Il Risorgimento*, which he started in 1847.

In the summer of 1848 he was elected to the Chamber of Deputies. His opposition to a renewal of the war with Austria led to his failure to be returned in January 1849, but in the elections of the following July, after the final defeat, he won a seat for Turin which he was to hold for the rest of his life. Under the premiership of D'Azeglio he rapidly made his mark as a shrewd debater and an excellent administrator, and in October 1850 he entered the cabinet as Minister of Agriculture, Commerce and Marine, to which he added the post of Minister of Finance in April 1851. Early in the next year, however, a protest from Louis Napoleon at Piedmontese press comments on the *coup d'état* of December 1851 led the government to bring in the Deforesta Press Law making the press liable to trial without jury in actions involving foreign Powers. Cavour supported the government on this measure, but realizing the need to retain the sympathy of the liberals, came to a working agreement on his own initiative with the centre left group under Rattazzi, an agreement that became known as the *connubio* (marriage). Shortly after this, D'Azeglio and Cavour fell out; Cavour, lacking the King's support, had to resign in April 1852, but by October D'Azeglio, confronted by the forces of the *connubio*, could carry on no longer and at the beginning of November Victor Emmanuel found that he had no option but to nominate Cavour as premier at the head of a coalition of centre parties, a post that he was to hold until his death in June 1861, except for one short break in 1859.

Much of the later Cavour can be seen in his behaviour during this astonishingly rapid rise to power—his refusal to support the renewal of war by Piedmont alone against Austria in 1849, his series of Free Trade treaties with Great Britain, France, Belgium, the *Zollverein* and Holland, and his determination to build a strong centre liberal group, even to the point of undermining the Prime Minister in whose cabinet he was serving. His fundamental ambition was the creation of an Italian Kingdom through the extension of Piedmont's frontiers, although it is open to doubt whether he believed that he might succeed in gaining the Kingdom of Naples or the Papal States. The first essential was the transformation of Piedmont into a modern state, and here he owed a great deal to his business experience and his knowledge of western Europe. He seized upon the importance of railways, hoping to make Piedmont part of an international network, initiating a scheme for the piercing of Mont Cenis by a railway tunnel, and turning Genoa into a great commercial port. This, of course, necessitated heavier taxes, but although much of this revenue was being used on capital expenditure, prosperity was such that the national deficit had been reduced to 25 million by 1854. At the same time a considerable reform of the army and of the state administration was carried out, and the Civil Code reorganized. The boldest stroke of all was the considerable reduction of the Church's secular power. The Siccardi laws of 1850 had already openly defied the authority of Rome by ending the existence of ecclesiastical courts, and in 1855 all religious orders were declared abolished except those concerned with teaching, preaching, or helping the sick. It was natural that such a policy should earn for Cavour the lasting mistrust of Pius IX, who watched events in Piedmont with increasing wariness, but Cavour was far from being an enemy of the Church; his attitude was merely that of Liberal Catholicism maintaining that the Church's role should be confined to the purely spiritual side of life.

This policy of modernizing Piedmont while avoiding any suggestion of revolution or republicanism was simply a preliminary to the greater aim of some form of Italian independence. Yet Cavour never fell into the error that Italy could achieve this on her own. War with Austria would be inevitable. For this he must have the active assistance of a great military Power, and from the beginning he knew that such assistance could only come from France.

The hope was not vain, since Napoleon's need for glory and his inclinations as an old *Carbonaro* would both be satisfied by assisting in the realization of Italian liberty; at the same time the expulsion of Austria from Italy, together with the French acquisition of Savoy and Nice as a reward, would form an attractive revision of the treaties of 1815. On the other hand, although Napoleon had said in 1852: 'Je suis résolu à faire quelque chose pour l'Italie que j'aime comme une seconde patrie', he was well aware of the dangers that would attend such a policy. Clerical opinion in France demanded that Rome should remain inviolate; a coalition of the central Powers might lead to an attack on France's north-eastern frontier, and even if the issue was brought to a successful conclusion, he had no desire to see a strong united Italy on France's borders. It was these considerations that governed the whole of Napoleon's vacillating policy throughout the Italian adventure.

Piedmont's participation in the Crimean war on the side of the Allies was certainly a step in the right direction, but Cavour was unable to obtain any territorial concession in return for her services[1] and the really decisive change came about in a totally unexpected manner. In January 1858 an Italian revolutionary, Felice Orsini, made an attempt on the life of Napoleon as he was about to enter the Opera in Paris. The bomb killed many of the bystanders, but left untouched the man whom Orsini blamed for the Oudinot expedition against the Roman Republic in 1849. There was understandably a strong French diplomatic reaction against Great Britain, where Orsini had prepared his plot, and against Piedmont, his country of origin. In Great Britain Palmerston cooperated to the extent of introducing a new Conspiracy Bill; in Piedmont Cavour, although resisting the immediate French demands, passed a measure for the prosecution of journals that attacked foreign states, and ostentatiously threw the blame on the Mazzinians. Surrender to pressure from a foreign state at a time of heightened national feeling could be a hazardous matter for a constitutional government. Palmerston actually fell from power over his Conspiracy Bill owing to the fervent public sympathy for the Italians; Cavour dared not risk losing the support of Piedmontese liberals, as D'Azeglio had done over the Deforesta Press Law in 1852, although at the same time he knew that he had to retain the friendship of France. The final outcome was a complete surprise. Napoleon was deeply impressed by Victor Emmanuel's letter to him rejecting any French dictation to Piedmont, and his entourage began to reflect that there might be further attempts on the Emperor's life unless he took a more positive lead in Italian affairs. Whatever the reason—and there is a point beyond which Napoleon's thoughts defy analysis—the scales now tipped definitely in favour of supporting the Italians. Orsini's appeal to the Emperor to assist Italy in gaining her liberty was read out at his trial and later published, and when Victor Emmanuel's

[1] See p. 190.

emissary was leaving Paris for Turin, Napoleon assured him that in case of war with Austria France would stand beside Piedmont.

There followed a meeting between Napoleon and Cavour at Plombières in the Vosges on 20 July 1858. As one might expect from these two conspirators, nothing was signed, but a great deal was agreed. France was to supply 200,000 men and Italy 100,000 to fight in a combined effort against Austria, who was to be driven out of Italy. Cavour was to engineer the outbreak of hostilities in such a way that Austria would appear to be the aggressor, and after the victory Italy was to become a federation of four states under the presidency of the Pope—a kingdom of Upper Italy under Victor Emmanuel including Piedmont, Lombardy, Venetia, Modena, Parma, and the Romagna; a kingdom of Central Italy including Tuscany and a large part of the Papal States, all under the Duchess of Parma; Rome and the Patrimony of St Peter; and the Kingdom of Naples. In return, Napoleon was promised Savoy and, rather more vaguely, the hand of Victor Emmanuel's daughter Clothilde for his cousin Jerome.

Cavour naturally left Plombières highly delighted. Napoleon, too, returned to Paris satisfied with the terms of the bargain. A marriage alliance with one of the oldest reigning houses in Europe was in accord with the *arriviste* tendencies of a Bonaparte; the gaining of Savoy would be a moral blow at the Vienna settlement and the re-emergence of the federalist solution to the Italian problem might mollify the French Catholics, at the same time ensuring that a new great Power did not suddenly emerge on the French frontier. In January 1859 an ominous remark by Napoleon to the Austrian ambassador was followed some ten days later by a warlike speech from Victor Emmanuel in the Piedmontese Chamber, in which he announced that 'we cannot remain insensible to the *cris de douleur* that reach us from so many parts of Italy'. In the same month a definite treaty was signed between France and Piedmont, adding Nice to the territory that France was to gain, but making no mention of the proposed Italian federation, after which the projected wedding of Prince Jerome and Princess Clothilde took place in the Chapel Royal in Turin.

Yet there were anxious months ahead for Cavour. Rumours and speculation on this latest intrigue in European diplomacy ran from chancellery to chancellery, and Napoleon began to have serious doubts over the acquiescence of the Powers. Lord Derby's ministry in London was openly pro-Austrian, but public opinion, strongly supporting the Italians, made any effective British intervention unlikely. Napoleon had hoped that Russia might have been prepared at least to threaten the Habsburg eastern frontier, but in a secret treaty of March 1859 Alexander II would promise no more than benevolent neutrality. The attitude of Prussia gave the least satisfaction of all, since the Regent Prince William, suspicious of Napoleon's desire to revise the 1815 treaties, held firmly to friendship with Austria. This inability to gain a promise of support or even of neutrality awoke all Napoleon's fears of a Prussian attack from the Rhineland, and his ministers were by this time strongly encouraging him to drop the whole scheme.

At the same time as the Emperor was reflecting on these diplomatic difficulties, Cavour was struggling to find some means of provoking Austria into an aggressive act. In fact, no independent issue ever existed—merely a growing tension in the north Italian plain, particularly after the publication of Napoleon's article 'Napoléon III et l'Italie'; Piedmont and Austria piled up their military preparations, and it was only through the attempts of the Powers to mediate that Cavour found his excuse. By April the question of a congress had been raised; Cavour, almost at his wit's end, found that his partner was growing increasingly lukewarm and when Napoleon agreed to a proposal made by the British government that both sides should demobilize simultaneously as a preliminary to a congress, Cavour had no option but to accept such a reasonable suggestion. But for Buol it was all too reasonable; needing a diplomatic and if possible a military humiliation of Piedmont before any congress assembled, the Austrian government dispatched an ultimatum to Piedmont on 19 April demanding that Piedmont should demobilize immediately and unconditionally. Thus, at the last moment the Austrians had played into Cavour's hands. He had only to point out the intransigence of Vienna in the Chamber—and hence to the world—reject the ultimatum and await the Austrian attack. On 29 April Austrian forces under Gyulai crossed the Ticino into Piedmont and on 3 May Napoleon, satisfied that Austria could be stigmatized as the aggressor, declared his intention of coming to the defence of his Piedmontese ally.

The war of 1859 lasted little more than two months. The Austrian forces available in Italy numbered only about 90,000, since the government in Vienna fully expected a French attack through south Germany, and Gyulai decided on a speedy advance against the 50,000 Piedmontese before they could be reinforced by the French. Napoleon's troops, however, had been on the move since the last week of April and by the beginning of May almost 10,000 a day were entering Piedmont either across the Mont Cenis pass or by sea to Genoa. The Austrians acted too slowly and by the middle of May the allies were ready to advance on the northern front, thereby turning the Austrian right flank. On 4 June the first major encounter took place outside Magenta to the east of the Ticino and after heavy fighting the Austrians withdrew to the south of Lake Garda. This left most of Lombardy open to the allied advance, and Napoleon III and Victor Emmanuel riding together through the streets of Milan received an ecstatic welcome from the crowds. Sterner fighting, however, lay ahead, and on 24 June a long bloody battle among the hills around the village of Solferino cost the French 17,000 men against Austrian losses of 22,000. At the end Count Schlick, who had replaced Gyulai a few days before, fell back on the Quadrilateral and by 2 July the French had crossed the Mincio.

Then suddenly all Cavour's hopes were dashed. On 5 July, without any previous consultation, Napoleon proposed an armistice, and a week later at Villafranca met Francis Joseph to discuss the terms whereby France would withdraw from the war. Lombardy was given to Piedmont, but Venetia and the fortresses of Mantua and Peschiera were to remain in Austrian possession; the hereditary rulers of Tuscany, Parma, and Modena, all of whom had fled to the Habsburg camp after the news of Magenta, were to be restored to their duchies, and all parts of Italy were to be included in a new Confederation under the presidency of the Pope. Cavour had not been present at Villafranca, and when late at night Victor Emmanuel brought the terms to him, it was hardly surprising that he should give way to a passion of vituperative rage. For him the war had been pointless; Lombardy alone meant nothing, with Austria still in possession of Venetia and the Quadrilateral and Habsburg influence re-established in Tuscany and Modena. He stormed at his king, offered his resignation, which was accepted on the spot, and returned in despair to Turin. A few days later Napoleon set off for France, agreeing to let the question of Savoy and Nice drop in return for Piedmont paying the expenses of the war.

Francis Joseph, whose dislike of the war had been reflected in the appointment of Rechberg in place of Buol as Foreign Minister in May, had been only too glad to accept the terms of Villafranca. Magenta and Solferino had revealed the weak state of his army and the significance of this affected more than Italy. The draining of any further reinforcements into the Lombard plain would have made Austria utterly dependent on the Prussian army in Germany, and the arrival of

Kossuth at Napoleon's headquarters suggested a recurrence of trouble in Hungary. As Cavour had seen, the loss of Lombardy was a relatively small price for Francis Joseph to pay for retaining Habsburg power in Italy—a better bargain, probably, than any congress would have given him.

Why had Napoleon deserted Cavour at this moment? One reason was that swift military victory was an essential requirement of mid-nineteenth century *Realpolitik*; Europe had to be presented with a *fait accompli*. One may see Bismarck urging his generals on to bombard Paris in January 1871 for precisely the same reason. To Napoleon, shocked at the toll which the Austrians had taken of the French army at Solferino and alarmed at the thought of diplomatic reactions to his latest adventure, the prospect of a long siege of the Quadrilateral fortresses was unthinkable. The decisive factor was the reappearance of the original difficulties that he had recognized before entering into the compact with Cavour. The failure to gain a promise of Prussian neutrality meant that the diplomatic preparation had been incomplete. It is true that Bismarck was using all his influence to let 'Austria's war against France eat deeply into her substance' as a means of substituting Prussian for Austrian hegemony in Germany, but Bismarck was only ambassador at St Petersburg and the Prince Regent was determined to support Austria. On 24 June the Prussians mobilized six army corps in the Rhineland and this threat to his north-eastern frontier meant the realization of Napoleon's worst fears.

Then, again, there was the question of the future state of Italy. Did Cavour really mean to rest content with a federation under the Pope? Napoleon had begun to doubt it. After the flight of the hereditary rulers Cavour had been quick to dispatch Count Pallieri to Parma, and Farini to Modena, where they were to act as royal commissioners to organize pro-Piedmontese governments; similarly, the withdrawal of the Austrian garrisons from Bologna and Ancona after Magenta had opened the door to the Romagna. None of this was contrary to the agreement of Plombières, but when the Piedmontese ambassador at Florence engineered Ricasoli into the position of dictator, Napoleon began to see that Cavour had hopes of incorporating Tuscany also into the kingdom of Upper Italy—thus undermining the federal scheme of Plombières, which had earmarked Tuscany for inclusion in a Central Kingdom. 'Je ne veux pas l'unité,' remarked Napoleon after Villafranca, 'mais l'indépendance. L'unité me procurerait des difficultés en France à cause de la question romaine; et la France ne verrait pas avec plaisir surgir à son flanc une grande nation qui pourrait diminuer sa prépondérance.' Napoleon was right in suspecting Cavour's plans which were really as great a breach of Plombières as Villafranca where Napoleon, even if he deprived Piedmont of the hope of Venetia, did at least reaffirm the federal plan to which Cavour had originally agreed.

But Villafranca only affected the major actors in the drama. France had withdrawn, Cavour had resigned, and Piedmont was at peace with Austria. It was the question of the duchies that remained unsettled, and here Ricasoli and Farini were to play a great part in the story of Italian unification. Although it had been agreed at Villafranca by France and Austria that the hereditary rulers should be restored, the royal commissioners there refused to stand down, and since Napoleon had stipulated that there should be no military intervention on Austria's part, they remained in control of the duchies. Farini united Modena, Parma, and the Romagna under the title of Emilia, but was dissuaded from a scheme of union with Tuscany by Ricasoli who pointed out that this would be tantamount to creating a possible kingdom of Central Italy as envisaged in the federal scheme. Instead, each organized their governments to petition for annexation by Piedmont; yet without the consent of the Powers Piedmont could make no move. The result was deadlock.

Two factors enabled Piedmont to gain her end. In Great Britain a general election in 1859 had brought Palmerston back into power with Lord John Russell as Foreign Secretary. These 'two dreadful old men', as Victoria called them, strongly favoured the creation of a unitary state in Italy and in January 1860 Russell put before Napoleon four points which would allow the duchies to vote on annexation through elected assemblies. The second factor was Napoleon's own change of mind. His failure to gain any territorial acquisition appeared to make the war of 1859 a senseless adventure; at home he had lost rather than gained prestige, at the same time infuriating Italian nationalist sentiment. To forestall the British in gaining influence at Turin; to annex Savoy and Nice after all; these now became his new objectives.

Cavour returned to power in January 1860 and it was typical of his skill to use the British offer to tempt Napoleon to a new bargain— Savoy and Nice against Tuscany and Emilia. There were dangers involved for both of them. Austria might be angry at this change of front by Napoleon; the British were particularly anxious to prevent France from gaining Savoy and Nice—hence Russell's four points.

However, a careful sounding of Habsburg opinion showed that Austria would be prepared to acquiesce in such a re-arrangement, provided that Venetia and the Quadrilateral remained untouched, and Cavour was prepared to brave the displeasure of the British government, knowing that in the last resort the support of France was the decisive factor. On 24 March a treaty between France and Piedmont settled the bargain. Plebiscites in all the affected territories followed—not a great obstacle to two such realists as Cavour and Napoleon—and thus only ten months after Villafranca, Victor Emmanuel found himself king of the whole of north Italy, except for Venetia, while the French frontier had moved eastwards into the Alps.

The most colourful episode in the history of the Risorgimento was yet to come. Garibaldi had taken a typically hazardous but successful part in the extreme north in the war of 1859, and had later been responsible for holding the southern frontier of the duchies, causing constant alarm in official circles that he was about to invade the Papal States. To Garibaldi it seemed that the great moment of Italian liberation had arrived; he had little patience with parliamentary practices, mistrusted Cavour's reliance on France, and hated the cession of Savoy and Nice to Napoleon, particularly since Nice was his own birthplace. Then in April the chance of further action came with the news of revolt in Palermo, and Garibaldi at once began to collect arms and volunteers, until in May he had a force of a thousand with which he set off in a couple of paddle-steamers from Genoa. The outcome was beyond the wildest romantic dream. The landing at Marsala was unopposed; Neapolitan troops sent out to meet them were defeated in an untidy soldiers' battle at Calatafimi, and with his forces now raised to three thousand by local recruiting Garibaldi advanced through pouring rain on the army of 20,000 holding Palermo. Through cunning feints and the aid of the local population he fought his way into the centre of the town and by the end of May negotiation with General Lanza had resulted in the withdrawal of the Neapolitan garrison to Naples, thus leaving Garibaldi free to mop up the rest of Sicily.

Cavour, however, was not a romantic. Historians are divided over his precise attitude towards the embarkation of the expedition. One view is that he publicly disowned it, while secretly allowing it to go forward. 'The argument was—', wrote Hudson, the British ambassador at Turin, to Russell in June, 'if he fails, we are rid of a troublesome fellow, and if he succeeds, Italy will derive some profit from his success.' A more recent view is that he genuinely tried to stop the expedition while it was at sea, but could not act openly, since he dared not offend both the King and public opinion in the new North Italian Kingdom. Whatever he thought, there is no doubt that Cavour was seriously worried. There had been no diplomatic preparation for this latest development in the south; he could not be certain yet of the possible political repercussions of the cession of Savoy and Nice to France, and Garibaldi's activities might well convince the Powers that the changes in the Italian peninsula were assuming such proportions that they must intervene. Events in Rome in 1849 had linked Garibaldi's name with that of Mazzini in the public imagination, and whereas the revolutionary movements in the central duchies had been under Cavour's control, those in the south owed their inspiration to Mazzini; Garibaldi's anger over Nice might well incline him towards the establishment of a republic, thus making foreign intervention highly probable, followed by a congress at which Piedmont might lose some of her recent gains.

By the beginning of June Cavour's mind was more at ease. Garibaldi had adopted the cry of 'Italy and Victor Emmanuel' and the capture of Sicily was a hard fact that appealed to realist and romantic alike. The problem now was to hold the ring. For this he had simply to play on the mutual suspicions of the great Powers. Palmerston and Napoleon were each convinced that the other intended to make capital out of events in southern Italy, and when Napoleon proposed in June that a separate independent Kingdom of Sicily should be created, the British government rejected the suggestion, fearing that it might become a satellite of Napoleonic France, endangering British naval bases at Gibraltar, Malta, and Corfu. For the same reason Napoleon's plan for an Anglo-French naval force to prevent Garibaldi reaching the mainland was rejected and on 18 August Garibaldi set off unopposed across the Straits of Messina.

So far, so good; but it was clear now that Garibaldi would stop at nothing, and Cavour knew that no diplomacy could prevent Austrian and French intervention if Garibaldi marched on Rome—as he had every intention of doing. How was that to be avoided? Cavour's first plan was to forestall him by stirring up a revolution of his own in Naples, but the scheme failed, since the Neapolitans were content to await the arrival of Garibaldi. The only other possibility was for the Piedmontese army to march south through the Papal States and to interpose itself between Garibaldi and Rome. This would also enable Cavour to recapture the initiative; but for Napoleon the essential

element in the enterprise was that it would relieve him of the unpleasant necessity of sending more French forces to the rescue of the
Pope in Rome, and he secretly assured Cavour that it would be safe to
proceed. It was not a moment too soon. Garibaldi had swept up through
Calabria before the crumbling resistance of the Neapolitan troops and
by 7 September he was in Naples. Four days later the Piedmontese
army, coming nominally to the assistance of revolts in the Papal
States, crossed the frontier. It defeated the small Papal army at Castel-
fidardo, rapidly occupied Umbria and crossed the Garigiliano into the
Kingdom of Naples just after Garibaldi had fought his first serious
engagement with the Neapolitans on the Volturno on 1 October.
Other fears were soon silenced. Cavour was able to convince the
British that French acquiescence had not been bought with the promise
of the cession of Genoa, while at Warsaw Francis Joseph found it
impossible to reach agreement over concerted action with Prussia and
Russia, without which he was not prepared to act. Plebiscites in
Naples, Sicily, Umbria, and the Papal marches brought an overwhelming vote for union with Piedmont, and the disapproval which
the Powers had been swift to express was soon shown to be without
substance, when Russell took the lead in a famous dispatch at the end
of October in which he spoke of 'the gratifying spectacle of a people
building up the edifice of their liberties and consolidating the work of
their independence'. Early in November Garibaldi officially handed
over his conquests to Victor Emmanuel and on the day after the King
and he had made a state entry into Naples, he set off for his home on
the rocky island of Caprera, after refusing all honours and rewards.
In January 1861 the first national Parliament met at Turin.

Thus only a dozen years after the collapse of Italian hopes in the
risings of 1848-9 a united kingdom of Italy had been created, lacking
only Venetia and the Patrimony of St Peter, the enclave of territory
round Rome. The key to success had been careful diplomatic preparation based on a realization of the need for military assistance from
France, rather than reliance upon a general revolutionary situation.
What revolutionary feeling there had been in the north had been carefully controlled by Cavour and his agents—almost as artificial as the
circumstances of the outbreak of the 1859 war—and he had been
determined to avoid any public association with the Mazzinians,
although he had found them a useful diplomatic threat as the grisly
alternative if he did not get his way. Two other advantages Cavour had
had over the leaders of the 1848-9 movements. There was no question

this time of the leadership of the Pope; the only essential was that Rome should be left unmolested—here lay the difference between *Realpolitik* and romantic nationalism. The second advantage was that a system of parliamentary government had already been firmly established at Turin and there was no need for the furore of constitution-making that had crippled the activities of 1848–9.

Yet however great may have been the part that Cavour played in the unification of Italy, he was undoubtedly aided by extraordinary good luck. 'How many times', he wrote afterwards, 'have I not exclaimed: Blessed be the peace of Villafranca.' Napoleon still lacking Savoy and Nice, Ricasoli's and Farini's efforts in the central duchies—these factors gave him a North Italian kingdom as a continuation of the war might have failed to do. Nor did he ever imagine the possibility of Garibaldi's swift success in the south, for that desperate venture of a thousand men might do well enough in South America where Garibaldi had served his apprenticeship, but could hardly seem a worthwhile gamble under the nose of the chancelleries of Europe. On the other hand, the way in which Cavour seized his opportunity, when it seemed that the impossible had happened, is a supreme testimony to his diplomatic skill, and it is on the whole a just verdict that links the names of these two men in the last act of the Risorgimento.

17

THE DEFEAT OF AUSTRIA 1862–6

1. Bismarck's rise to power

FROM the moment when, in November 1852, Cavour had become premier in Piedmont, it had taken him little more than eight years to accomplish the unification of Italy; almost exactly the same length of time was to elapse between Bismarck's appointment as Minister President of Prussia in September 1862 and the proclamation of the German Empire in the Hall of Mirrors at Versailles in January 1871. Both men made a calculated use of war to attain an end which the liberals of 1848 had hoped to achieve in a different form by different methods; both were enabled by the mistakes of their enemies, in Bismarck's phrase, 'to assume the role of the injured'. One cannot, however, press the parallel too far. Whereas Cavour saw his work completed with a dramatic suddenness and then died within a few months of his success, the road for Bismarck ran through a whole series of short wars—with Denmark in 1864, with Austria in 1866 and with France in 1870. Although more fortunate than Cavour in that the excellence of the Prussian army gave him greater independence of action, he still had to ensure that his enemy of the moment fought alone; the implications of his policy raised infinitely wider diplomatic complications, and the ultimate emergence of the German Empire so transformed the balance of power in Europe that for the subsequent twenty years it needed all his skill to control the situation which he had created.

The personality of Count Otto von Bismarck was far more complex than the popular conception of the 'Iron Chancellor' would allow. Outwardly he might seem a typical son of the old Junker family from which he sprang; as a University student at Göttingen he had duelled, drunk, and run into debt; all his life he loved good food and wine, and his military bearing, thick moustache and stern heavy-lidded eyes might well suggest a Prussian officer whose life was bounded by his regiment and the management of his estates. Yet the appearance and the myth both, to some extent, belie the inner character of the man.

207

He had the temperament of an artist—although without any interest in art—quick-thinking, infinitely flexible, and so highly strung that in moments of tension he could find relief only in tears or the smashing of china. An authoritarian himself, he could not endure to be under the authority of others; thus he hated his year of military service at Potsdam; he resigned from the Prussian civil service, because, as he said, he could not 'put up with superiors', and later as a diplomatic representative his dispatches read like general statements of higher policy. During his early manhood he spent long periods on his family estates, first in Pomerania, later at Schönhausen in Brandenburg, but the peace of the countryside only bored him to distraction, driving him into escapades that earned him the name of 'the wild Bismarck'; and until the age of thirty-two, his tremendous energies still unharnessed, he seemed no more than a neurotic failure. Then, in 1847, two events changed the whole course of his life. His marriage to Johanna von Puttkamer brought him a new background of personal happiness and encouragement; and with his election to the Prussian United Diet[1] a new ever-absorbing interest awoke within him.

Bismarck's politics at this time were those of a staunch Prussian conservative, strongly hostile to any change in the existing situation. In the United Diet he constantly attacked the liberals, and in the spring of 1848 he rushed to Berlin to put heart into the Court to resist the revolutionaries. Naturally he gained no place in the Prussian National Assembly, elected by universal suffrage in that year, but under the terms of the constitution which Frederick William promulgated in December he was able to find a seat in the new Chamber by a narrow majority, and here he poured scorn on the proposed Frankfurt constitution of 1849 and welcomed the defeat of Radowitz's scheme at Olmütz.[2]

It was this apparent belief in the maintenance of the old system of the German Confederation, based on Prussian cooperation with Austria, that led to his being selected as the Prussian representative at the Federal Diet in 1851. The beginning of his diplomatic career, however, was to bring about a fundamental change in his outlook. The Austrian assumption of superiority at the Diet naturally irked his own arrogant individualism, and before long he was moving towards the attitude that had prompted Radowitz's attempt in 1849—the conception of a Prussian-dominated *Kleindeutschland* from which Austria would be excluded. 'Germany is too small for both of us,' he was writing by 1856, 'both plough the same contested field.'

[1] See p. 124.   [2] See p. 161.

This new attitude was reflected in his personal reactions to all the diplomatic moves in the 1850s. During the Crimean war he advocated neutrality, noting how Austria's wavering was antagonizing all her possible friends,[1] and deploring the idea of 'tying our trim and sea-worthy frigate to the worm-eaten and old-fashioned Austrian man-of-war'. In 1859 he was dispatched as ambassador to St Petersburg, and from there he watched impotently as the Prussians mobilized on the Rhineland in support of Francis Joseph against Napoleon III, instead of taking advantage of Austria's embarrassment to end her control over the German Confederation.[2]

In fact, as it turned out, the indirect consequences of this policy were eventually to serve Bismarck well. The mobilization in the Rhineland in 1859 had revealed certain weaknesses in the Prussian military machine. The reforms at the beginning of the century had established a system of compulsory military service including three years with the colours and two in the reserve, after which the citizen passed into the *Landwehr*, a form of militia. The size of each year's intake of recruits had, however, remained fixed, despite Prussia's rising population, and the three years active service was in practice no more than two. The Regent, Prince William, a keen soldier, strongly supported by von Roon, the Minister of War, and von Moltke, the Chief of the General Staff, now proposed that, in order to exploit the full military potential of the country, all young men should serve for the full three years, and that the reserve should be greatly increased at the expense of the *Landwehr*. These changes, raising Prussia's war establishment from 230,000 men to 450,000 and involving the creation of forty-nine new regiments, would have to be financed out of additional taxation, and when the scheme was put before the Prussian Parliament, it encountered considerable opposition from the liberals—not simply because of the cost, but because they mistrusted the whittling away of the *Landwehr* which, as a citizens' army with its own non-aristocratic officers, represented a military force remote from the conservative instincts of the Prussian Officer Corps. The debates in the Chamber soon exposed the deeper social and political implications that lay behind a simple reorganization of the army, and after two years of unsatisfactory bargaining the crisis was reached in 1862 when it became clear that the Chamber was not prepared to accept the budget.

For some time the conservative elements had known that Bismarck

[1] See p. 188.   [2] See p. 201.

H

was the man to handle this situation, but William, who in 1861 had finally succeeded to the throne on the death of his brother,[1] mistrusted Bismarck's outspoken views on Prussia's relations with Austria and held back as long as he could. Recalled from St Petersburg in March 1862, Bismarck was dispatched to the embassy at Paris. Here he awaited the call of destiny and when, in September, he received a telegram from von Roon—'Periculum in mora. Dépêchez-vous'—he knew that the moment had come. He hastened to Berlin and on 22 September he emerged from an interview with the King which gave him at last the power for which his imperious nature longed—a Prime Minister whose appointment depended upon his ability to overrule a constitutional Assembly, a conservative now able to give free rein to a revolutionary foreign policy. It was a situation completely in harmony with the contradictions of his own character.

2. The Slesvig-Holstein question

The crisis was reached almost at once, for on the day after Bismarck's appointment the Prussian lower House finally rejected the budget. As soon as he had formed an extremely conservative Cabinet, he made some attempt at negotiation, insisting, nevertheless, on a reform of the army as a vital necessity for Prussia. 'Nicht durch Reden und Majoritätsbeschlüsse,' he lectured the deputies on 29 September, 'werden die grossen Fragen der Zeit entschieden—das ist der grosse Fehler von 1848 und 1849 gewesen—sondern durch Eisen und Blut.' ('The great questions of the day are not decided by speeches and resolutions of majorities—that was the blunder of 1848 and 1849—but by iron and blood.') The statement has echoed down the years in every assessment of Bismarck's career, and, whatever cynicism it may seem to imply, it was perhaps the most honest thing that he ever said, and despite the shock that it may have caused the deputies in 1862, they were more than willing to accept the fruits of its application in 1866 and 1871. It was indeed a simple statement of fact, as Cavour had already shown.

But for the moment it had no persuasive appeal, and when deadlock had been reached over the budget Bismarck fell back on a demonstration of the flimsiness of parliamentary institutions in Prussia at this time. There was no problem over the actual collection of taxes, since the government's right to this was part of the existing constitution; the budget was only concerned with the control of expenditure.

[1] See p. 178.

Technically this should have been an effective safeguard, but Bismarck argued that a profound disagreement between King and Parliament could not be allowed to prevent the government from continuing to run the country. In other words, he proposed to ignore the opposition of the Chamber, and during the next four years taxes were collected and the army reorganized as if the Prussian Parliament did not exist. William I watched with considerable alarm at first, convinced that he and his minister would meet the same fate as Charles I and the Earl of Strafford. The fact that they did not is one of the many differences between the pattern of English and German history, and with the apparent success of the policy the King found himself increasingly dependent upon his remarkable Minister President.

Even for Bismarck, however, such a course could only be a temporary expedient, but he believed that he would find the justification for it by bringing about a Prussian solution to the German problem at the expense of Austria. It so happened that early in 1863 there occurred three developments in Germany, Poland, and Denmark, each of which threatened to undermine the structure of the 1815 settlement, and although none of them was of Bismarck's making, he was able to turn them all to his own advantage. The first move was initiated by Austria when Anton von Schmerling[1] decided on a remodelling of the German Confederation. Despite the resistance of the Austrian Foreign Minister, Rechberg, whose conservatism favoured the maintenance of the Metternich system, he was able to gain the ear of Francis Joseph, and a meeting of the German princes was summoned at Frankfurt in August 1863. The essence of the new scheme was the creation of a *Grossdeutschland*, reminiscent of Schwarzenberg's abortive proposal at Dresden in 1851.[2] An executive Directory of six states, including Austria, Prussia, Bavaria, and three others chosen in rotation, was to be set up under the presidency of Austria, while a Federal Assembly was to consist of 302 delegates elected indirectly by the representative bodies of the German states.

Such a plan was really no more than a device on Austria's part to win over liberal sentiment, now greatly excited by the recent success of Cavour and Garibaldi in Italy. It is doubtful whether it would ever have amounted to much, and in any case Bismarck was determined that it should not succeed. The key to the whole problem was the attitude of King William. Twice Francis Joseph attempted to persuade William to attend the meeting of the princes at Frankfurt—once in personal

[1] See p. 225.   [2] See pp. 160-1.

conversation with him at Gastein, and again in August, when the King of Saxony approached him at Baden as an emissary from the congress. Each time it was the passionate opposition of Bismarck that held him back, and when the princes realized that Prussia would not enter the proposed scheme, they too refused to go any further, since they feared that the absence of Prussia in the reshaping of central Europe would entail their own submission to Austria. As at the Dresden Conference of 1851,[1] they saw rightly that their survival depended upon a balance between the two great Powers of Germany. This failure of the congress at Frankfurt not only marks the last positive attempt of Austria to gain the initiative in preserving her own position; it gave Bismarck a chance to outbid her in winning liberal support for Prussia, for on 15 September a Prussian envoy to the congress justified the absence of King William by demanding that in any new scheme a Federal Assembly must be based on *direct* elections by the German people.

At the same time as this debate in Germany, the Powers of Europe had been closely concerned with the diplomatic repercussions of a very different issue—the great Polish rising against Russian rule,[2] which broke out in January 1863. Bismarck had long made it clear that he had little sympathy with the Poles; Prussia's own Polish territories gave her a common bond of interest with Russia in this respect and at the beginning of March General von Alvensleben was dispatched to St Petersburg to conclude a convention with the Tsar, whereby it was agreed that the military forces of the two countries would cooperate within their own territories in putting down the Polish rebels.

Until now the Powers had on the whole been prepared to let the Polish question rest; in 1856, for instance, Prince Czartoryski had tried in vain to have the matter discussed at the Congress of Paris. The liberation of Poland, however, had remained a great cry of the liberals throughout Europe, and the deliberate assistance which Bismarck was lending the Russian government fired the western Powers to make a positive attempt at intervention. A joint note from Great Britain, France, and Austria contained proposals which would have given the moderate Polish party much of what they wanted, but when neither the Tsar nor Bismarck showed any inclination to accept this as a basis for negotiation, the mutual suspicions among the mediating Powers prevented them from continuing to insist upon a settlement. Napoleon offered an alliance to Austria, but Rechberg was too mistrustful of his

[1] See p. 161.   [2] See p. 231.

sympathy with the submerged national groups of Europe to allow Austria to be bound to France; similarly, the British, much of their attention taken up with the economic and maritime complications of the American Civil war, regarded Napoleon's acquisition of Savoy and Nice as a warning of further designs that he might have on the Rhineland; and when Napoleon bolstered up his proposal for a European congress in the autumn with a public statement that the treaties of 1815 were no longer in effect, the British government made it clear that this was not their view and the negotiations went no further. Thus, whereas the failure among the great Powers to agree on intervention had been an essential factor in the success of the Italians in 1860, a similar lack of agreement sealed the fate of the Poles, who were now condemned to the isolation that had wrecked their hopes in 1831, and by the beginning of 1864 the Russians had crushed the rising.

Nor was this all. The diplomatic exchanges of these months had revealed the dangerous lack of cohesion among the Powers that was to be an essential element in Bismarck's success. Austria had repeated her blunders of the Crimean War—antagonizing Russia without finding a partner elsewhere. An alliance with France might have saved her from her later defeat by Prussia, but Napoleon's schemes for Venetia and the Balkans put this out of reach. Equally significant, France's attempts to organize intervention in the Polish crisis brought to a close the *entente* with Russia which had made French assistance to Cavour possible in 1859,[1] and it was natural that Russia should now rely increasingly on her friendship with Prussia.

All these circumstances were to play their part in the third issue that arose in this troubled year—the reopening of the Slesvig-Holstein question. The earlier attempt of the Danes in 1848 to incorporate Slesvig within their kingdom[2] had come to nothing in the general restoration of the *status quo* after the year of revolutions. In an act of mediation between Denmark and the German Confederation a settlement of the Danish problem had been signed at London in 1852 by the great Powers, when it had been agreed that Christian of Glücksburg[3] should eventually succeed the childless Frederick VII as king of Denmark and, despite the complications of the Salic Law, should also inherit the duchies to which Christian of Augustenburg would give up his family's claim in return for financial compensation. The Danes, on the other hand, agreed that the duchies should remain

[1] See p. 199.   [2] See pp. 125, 152.   [3] See Genealogical table, p. 482.

indivisible, promising 'not to incorporate Slesvig within the kingdom' and not to take any steps 'tending towards that end'.

There were two weaknesses in the Treaty of London. First, Christian of Augustenburg's renunciation of his claim had not been explicit, since the Danish government had never admitted that he had any rights to renounce; and through a legal quibble his eldest son, Frederick, who had not been of age in 1852, was later able to revive the claim for himself—with the additional justification that the Estates of the duchies had never actually ratified the eventual succession of the Glücksburg Danish king as their Duke. Second, the treaty had disappointed both Danish and German nationalists. The German Confederation had not been a signatory to it, and the Danes soon showed that they had little intention of keeping their part of the bargain.

By a number of governmental measures, including a new constitution in 1855, Frederick VII strove to divide the two duchies, constantly stressing the closeness of Slesvig to the kingdom. The final step came in March 1863 when Frederick decided to take advantage of the general uproar over the Polish rising to propose a further constitutional revision. The March Patent substituted a bi-cameral Parliament for a single representative Chamber, but its principal significance lay in the fact that although the Estates of Holstein would be able to exercise control over legislation within their own duchy, their opposition would have no effect upon measures passed in Denmark and Slesvig. German feeling in the Confederation, still determined on the indivisibility of the duchies, was at once violently outspoken, but the Danish government, encouraged by a treaty of defence with Sweden in August, refused to retract. Then, in November 1863, Frederick died before he had actually signed the new constitution and the final decision was left to his Glücksburg successor. Christian IX knew that the Patent was bound to be considered a breach of the Treaty of London of 1852 to which he owed his title as Duke of Slesvig-Holstein, but the force of Danish public opinion left him little option and he accordingly gave his consent to the new constitution.

No sooner had this been announced than angry voices in the Diet of the German Confederation demanded the immediate occupation of Holstein, and Frederick, the son of the Duke of Augustenburg, took up his claim to the duchies. The events of 1848 were not, however, to be repeated in their entirety, since this time Prussia was not to lend her assistance to the Confederation. Bismarck had to insist upon this decision against the strongest opposition. 'Sind Sie denn nicht auch ein

Deutscher?' cried William in fury, but being still dependent upon his minister, the King had to accept his policy. The Danes had put themselves in the wrong, as the British Foreign Secretary, Lord Russell, pointed out to his ambassador at Copenhagen in December; on the other hand, Frederick of Augustenburg's claim, in contravention of the Treaty of London of 1852, was an equally aggressive step, and Bismarck did not intend throwing away this diplomatic advantage. Certainly he meant to resist the Danes, but not on behalf of Frederick or the German Confederation. Instead, he took his stand on the Treaty of London and turned to Vienna for cooperation. In fact, this was a moment when Austria might very well have strengthened her position by placing herself at the head of German nationalist feeling in support of Augustenburg, but after the failure of the Frankfurt meeting of princes Francis Joseph had lost faith in the ambitious schemes of Schmerling and preferred to listen to his Foreign Minister. Rechberg, as a conservative, was only too anxious to preserve the existing map of Europe and, conscious of Austria's isolation, responded gladly to Bismarck's proposals, which seemed to represent a far more respectable policy than what he had feared from Prussia.

On 16 January 1864 a treaty was signed between Austria and Prussia providing for joint military intervention if Denmark would not retract. Bismarck was careful to exclude from its terms any mention of the Treaty of London, claiming that his King's sympathies with German nationalism would not allow this, and it was simply stated that the future of the duchies would only be settled by mutual agreement between the two countries. This gave Bismarck precisely what he wanted, although the Austrian *Reichsrat*[1] showed itself to be considerably more alert to Prussian ambitions than Rechberg. 'Prussia has scarcely digested Silesia,'[2] argued one of its speakers, 'and now she is getting her claws into the duchies, while we are leading her into them with drum and trumpet. But what music will get her out again?'

Forces of the German Confederation had already moved into Holstein, where the Danes withdrew without resistance. The independent ultimatum presented jointly by Berlin and Vienna was, however, rejected at Copenhagen; on 1 February a combined Prussian and Austrian army entered Slesvig and by the middle of April had driven the Danes back into Jutland. Naturally these events were watched with some alarm by the Powers, but there was little that they were prepared to do by way of concerted action. Russia still felt in need of friendship

---

[1] See p. 225.   [2] Annexed by Frederick the Great.

with Prussia during the last stages of her suppression of the Polish rising. The attention of Great Britain was still partly distracted by the havoc which British suspicions of Napoleon's designs on the Rhineland had wrought on Anglo-French relations during the Polish crisis, and this made any cooperation unlikely. Sweden, too, hung back, since the attack by Austria and Prussia suggested a greater commitment than she had envisaged at the time of her treaty with Denmark in 1863.

The only contribution made by the Powers was the summoning of an international conference at London in April. For Bismarck it was essential that the conference should break down through the apparent intransigence of the Danes. Accordingly he changed his ground, maintaining that since a state of war existed with Denmark, the treaty of 1852, of which she, Prussia, and Austria had all been signatories, was no longer valid, and Prussia and Austria were therefore free to impose new conditions. By these means he was to ensure that Denmark would continue the fight, and he was assisted in this by the hopes that the Danes still entertained of foreign aid. Originally they had had some grounds for imagining this. In the summer of 1863 only a few months after the marriage of Christian IX's daughter Alexandra to Edward, Prince of Wales, Lord Palmerston had uttered a rash threat in the British House of Commons to the effect that Denmark would not fight alone; in Paris there had been rumours that Napoleon intended an attack on Austria over Venetia early in 1864. 'It is quite possible', the Italian minister had told the Danish ambassador, 'that we will be able to make a diversion in your favour next spring.' But no treaties of alliance existed with either Great Britain or France and by April 1864 the Danish government should have been able to read the signs.

They did not read them, and Bismarck was able to attach so many qualifications to a suggested personal union of the duchies with the kingdom of Denmark that the Danes rejected such a compromise. Only now did Bismarck take up the cry of the German nationalists, proposing independence for the duchies under Frederick of Augustenburg. 'We must let the whole pack howl,' he said, and howl they did, as the war continued and the Prusso-Austrian forces thrust on through Jutland. Augustenburg's hopes naturally lifted, but they soon fell again when Bismarck made it plain to him in conversation that he would be little more than a puppet of the Prussian government. In fact, Bismarck had no intention that he should become even that. 'At the London conference,' he said to Beust, the Saxon Prime Minister, a year later, 'I hitched the Prince to the plough as an ox to get it moving. Once the plough was in motion, I unhitched the ox.'

For the moment the renewal of the war was all that he needed. By the end of June the army had completed the overrunning of the mainland and the Prussians had crossed to the island of Alsen off the east coast of Slesvig. Diplomacy could do nothing to save the Danes. A mild Russian attempt at mediation came to nothing. The British toyed with the idea of gaining French support, but still could not quieten their fears of Napoleon: '. . . what will France require as the price of her alliance with England?' wrote Lord Russell to Queen Victoria on 23 June, 'and is it in the interest of England to pay that price?' As a consequence the British cabinet decided two days later not to intervene. With its last hope gone, the Danish government resigned on 8 July, and on 1 August preliminary peace terms were signed whereby the two duchies were surrendered to Prussia and Austria.

3. The war of 1866

Thus far, Bismarck's skill had lain in strengthening his position while acting within the framework of what was superficially a conservative foreign policy. For although his outbidding of Austria at Frankfurt in 1863 with a demand for a German Parliament elected by universal suffrage and his momentary support of Augustenburg after the failure of the London conference were calculated appeals to liberal feeling, his actual diplomatic moves—the defeat of the Austrian attempt to create a *Grossdeutschland*, the Alvensleben convention with Russia, and the treaty of January 1864 with Austria against Denmark's rejection of the existing settlement of the Slesvig-Holstein question—could all claim to represent the attitude of a Metternich rather than a Cavour.

In the following two years, however, this apparent conservatism was sharply modified as he manoeuvred for the position from which he might effect the transference of power in Germany from Vienna to Berlin. In the joint occupation of the duchies he had an excellent situation in which to pick a quarrel with Austria; with the Prussian expulsion of the troops of the German Confederation and the gradual conversion of Kiel into a Prussian naval station, he showed scant regard for his ally, and in May 1865, at a meeting of the Crown Council, he openly stated his intention of annexing both duchies and of reorganizing the German Confederation. By the summer of that year Prussian activity in the duchies had become so overbearing and the dispatches from Berlin to Vienna so violent that the Austrians began to anticipate the severance of relations between the two countries. In an endeavour to avoid this Count Mensdorf, who had replaced Rechberg after the Danish war, arranged a meeting of an Austrian envoy with King William and Bismarck while they were taking the waters at Gastein, and by the convention that was signed in August it was agreed that the condominium in the duchies should end. Instead, Austria would administer Holstein, and Prussia Slesvig. This 'papering over the cracks', as Bismarck called it, was simply one step nearer to annexation, as most foreign governments realized; it did not render Austria any more secure in her relations with Prussia, and by dividing the duchies it confirmed the impression among the states of the German Confederation that Francis Joseph was the accomplice of Bismarck in destroying the cause of Frederick of Augustenburg.

It was not enough, however, simply to prepare the way for a breach with Austria. 'If war in alliance with France against Austria is banned,' Bismarck had declared at the Crown Council in May, 'then a Prussian policy is no longer possible.' In fact, what he wanted from France was not a firm alliance—that might be dangerous and costly—but simply neutrality in the event of an Austro-Prussian war. On the other hand, an alliance with Italy—less dangerous and costly only to Austria— would serve him well. In both these aims he had the extraordinary good fortune to be assisted by the mistakes of the Emperor of the French himself.

As has been seen, Napoleon III had not been content to follow the foreign policy of his predecessors. His encouragement of foreign nationalism and his hopes of revising the French frontier of 1815 had caused him to develop a policy in striking contrast to that which had shaped the French government's attitude towards Germany in the crisis of 1840 and towards Italy in 1848. Amid a confusion of hesitancy and rashness he had at least acquired Savoy and Nice for France in 1860, but only at the price of developments in Italy far beyond what he had originally intended, and in France there were already many voices raised in dissent. Thiers pointed out that by assisting Italian and German unification France was only creating a rod for her own back, and added the prophecy that one day the two of them would combine against France. It was the folly of Napoleon that he did not realize that, for France too, the Vienna settlement represented a guarantee.

In October 1865 Bismarck visited Napoleon at Biarritz. Exactly what they discussed is unknown, but before he left Berlin, Bismarck had hinted to the French *chargé d'affaires* at the possible acquisition of Belgium by France. Nothing positive emerged from their meeting; Napoleon, whose powers of decision were declining as his health deteriorated, remained uncommitted, but Bismarck could feel that he had forestalled the likelihood of any immediate French alliance with Austria.

So far Napoleon had been cautious. Over the negotiation of the Prusso-Italian treaty, however, he revealed both the extent of his hopes and the serious misconceptions on which his policy was based. The Italian government had recently failed in a bid to purchase Venetia from Austria and at the beginning of 1866 began to respond to Prussian suggestions of an alliance. They were at first extremely mistrustful over the use to which Bismarck might put this, but their doubts were eventually overcome by Napoleon's persuasion. 'Italy will get Venice,' he remarked to Nigra, the Italian ambassador in Paris, 'and France will benefit by the conflict of the two Powers whose alliance hems her in. Once the struggle has begun, France can throw her weight into the balance and must obviously become the arbitrator and master of the situation.' Here in a nutshell lay his two fundamental mistakes. He believed that the gaining of Venetia would take Italy's eyes off Rome, to whose defence the Catholic interest in France committed him. More particularly, he believed that in any Austro-Prussian war the two sides would be so evenly matched that there would be time for him to bring off a diplomatic *coup*.

The secret military alliance between Prussia and Italy was finally signed on 8 April 1866. Italy promised to declare war on Austria as soon as hostilities between Prussia and Austria had begun, and as a reward was to receive Venetia without the Trentina district. The agreement was to be valid for only three months and Bismarck lost no time in attempting to goad Austria into violent action by a proposal at Frankfurt on 9 April that a German Parliament should be elected by universal suffrage. He had already played this card before in September 1863, but his own treatment of the Prussian Parliament had by now made German liberals highly suspicious of the honesty of his intentions. 'Universal and equal suffrage, direct election and a German Parliament are fine words,' commented the *Nationalzeitung*, 'but what have they to do with Count Bismarck or the Diet?'

Despite this disappointment, however, two factors gave Bismarck the whip-hand in drawing Austria into what Prussia could claim was a defensive war. First, the speed with which Prussia could mobilize on her southern frontier was so much greater that, as the tension between the two steadily mounted, Austria had to take the apparently aggressive step of mobilizing before Prussia. Second, her diplomatic position was so weak that she dared not rely upon a proposal for international mediation which Prussia, in order to keep herself in the right, would not have been able to reject. Thus it was Austria who refused the suggestion for a congress put forward by Great Britain, France, and Russia—to the wild relief of Bismarck who had unwillingly had to accept it. Similarly, Bismarck did not obstruct the efforts of a Prussian deputy, Anton von Gablenz, whose mission of pacification to Vienna also came to nothing. The only positive diplomatic move that Austria did make at this time was a treaty with France, whereby French neutrality was purchased in return for the surrender of Venetia and a promise of the creation of a new Rhineland state. This was naturally in accordance with Napoleon's schemes at this time, while Austria hoped to gain Silesia from Prussia in compensation for her loss of Venetia.

The Franco-Austrian treaty was signed on 12 June. Relations between Austria and Prussia had already collapsed at the beginning of the month when Austria had referred the question of the duchies to the German Diet—an open break of her treaty of January 1864 with Prussia. Bismarck had replied with the occupation of Holstein. To his disappointment this did not lead to immediate conflict. He followed it up with an amplified version of the Prussian proposal for a new German constitution and then, on 14 June, when the Federal Diet passed a Bavarian amendment of an Austrian proposal for a Federal mobilization, the Prussian representative announced Prussia's withdrawal from the German Confederation. On the following day Prussian troops marched into Hanover, Hesse-Cassel, and Saxony, all of whom had sided with Austria, and without any more formal declaration the war began.

The die was cast, and the whole future of Bismarck now rested in the hands of the Prussian generals. 'If we are beaten', he said to the British ambassador, 'I shall not return. I can die only once and it befits the vanquished to die.' He was not left long in suspense. The defeat of the Italians at Custoza on 24 June made little difference to the course of hostilities in the north. To prevent the Austrians from gaining time to organize their defence, Moltke took the deliberate risk of crossing the

Bohemian frontier on 23 June with three separate armies; on 3 July the centre army under Prince Frederick of Prussia encountered the main forces of the Austrian commander Benedek outside Königgrätz, and with the arrival of the Crown Prince's army on the Prussian left wing the Austrians suffered a staggering defeat with a loss of 44,000 men—almost five times as many as the Prussian casualties.

'Excellency,' said a Prussian general to Bismarck afterwards, 'you are now a great man. But if the Crown Prince had come too late, you would now be a great villain.' This was certainly true. Yet the victory at Königgrätz was not entirely complete, since Benedek had still been able to withdraw a large part of his forces. It was Bismarck's statesmanship that now ensured that Königgrätz alone should be the decisive battle. All that he wanted from Austria was freedom of action for Prussia in north Germany. 'We need Austria's strength in future for ourselves,' he said, and the chances of a revived friendship for which he looked, once Prussia had the upper hand, would only be damaged by territorial annexation. In any case, a quick peace was essential if he was to forestall any attempt on the part of Napoleon to make some profitable form of mediation.

To achieve this he had to fight on a good many fronts. His appeals to Czech and Magyar nationalists, coupled with the prospect of moderate terms, soon had their effect on Vienna. Almost more difficult was the resistance of King William, who had now tasted military triumph and saw himself as 'the conqueror at the gate of Vienna'. Eventually Bismarck had his way and on 26 July a preliminary peace was signed at Nikolsburg, to be followed a month later by a final settlement at Prague. The terms were primarily concerned with the remodelling of Germany along Prussian lines. Prussia herself was to absorb Slesvig and Holstein as well as Hesse-Cassel, Hanover, Nassau, and Frankfurt. All the other states north of the Main—including the kingdom of Saxony whose autonomy Austria did at least manage to preserve—were to become members of a new North German Confederation under Prussian leadership. The states south of the Main were to form a vague union of their own—a political expression of no significance, since Prussia immediately signed secret treaties of military alliance with Bavaria, Württemberg, and Baden. Paradoxically Austria's only territorial loss was in the theatre of operations where she had enjoyed complete success. Her military victory over the Italians was followed in August by the annihilation of the Italian fleet in the Adriatic, but despite these disasters, Bismarck kept his word and

Venetia was surrendered indirectly through France to Italy. It was, however, the territories that she did not lose which pointed to the full significance of the Austrian defeat, for her exclusion from the new North German Confederation meant that the point of control in German affairs had shifted from Vienna to Berlin, and the way was open for the creation of that *Kleindeutschland* which the Habsburgs had previously been able to resist.

18

THE FRUITS OF VICTORY AND DEFEAT

1. The North German Confederation

KÖNIGGRÄTZ was not the only victory that Bismarck could claim on 3 July 1866. On the very same day elections held in Prussia reflected the patriotic excitement of war in a great increase of conservative seats from 38 to 142. The most significant aspect of the Prussian political scene, however, was a change in the attitude of the liberals. A policy of 'blood and iron' seemed about to achieve the unification which they had sought to no avail in 1848 and many now found themselves unable to resist the attraction of Bismarck's success. The issue was put clearly before them when, in September, Bismarck introduced in the new Chamber an Indemnity Bill excusing the government for having ruled without a constitutional budget since 1862. Only seven votes were cast against it and in the subsequent split among the Progressives a new National Liberal party was to emerge, including leading members of the former opposition who were prepared to support the Prussian government over foreign policy.

This abdication by the liberals was to bring about a new harmony between Bismarck and the Prussian Chamber. Gratuities were voted for the victorious generals and Bismarck himself received 400,000 thalers—approximately £60,000—with which he purchased Varzin, a large estate in Pomerania. All parties agreed to the annexation of Hanover, Hesse-Cassel, Nassau, Frankfurt, and Slesvig-Holstein by Prussia. The deposition of King George of Hanover aroused objections among the right wing of the conservatives, but there could be little effective resistance, even when in 1868 the government confiscated the King's personal income, thereby creating a useful private source of financial supply known as the *Welfen-Fonds*.

By the autumn of 1866 Bismarck was completely worn out, but in December he had recovered sufficiently to return to Berlin to begin work on the drafting of the constitution of the North German Confederation (the *Norddeutscher Bund*), which was promulgated in July 1867. The President, who was the King of Prussia, had the right of concluding all treaties and declaring war and was commander-in-chief of the Federal forces. A Federal Council (the *Bundesrat*) consisted of delegates voting on instructions from the governments of the member states who had appointed them. Here Prussia, owing to her now greatly increased size, enjoyed seventeen votes, while twenty-six votes were shared among the other twenty-one states in the Confederation. The lower House (the Reichstag) was a single representative Chamber elected by direct universal manhood suffrage, and with the right to veto the budget and all legislation. The sole Federal minister was the Chancellor, Bismarck, who, since he was only directly responsible to the President, could not be dismissed through a parliamentary vote.

The new constitution thus differed significantly from that of the old German Confederation of 1815 since, within the limits of north Germany, it had created a far stronger federal executive. It was equally remote from the proposals of the liberals at Frankfurt in 1849; the predominance of Prussia was barely disguised at all and, as Napoleon III had already shown, universal suffrage by itself was no serious obstacle to authoritarian rule, so long as the powers of the representative Chamber were carefully restricted. 'Let us put Germany into the saddle', Bismarck had said during the debate on the constitution; 'she will know how to ride.' It was a memorable figure of speech, but hardly exact, for in reality it was German political sentiment that had been placed in harness and Bismarck who sat in the saddle.

2. The Ausgleich: *the creation of Austria-Hungary 1867*

If the Prussian victory had opened the way to the remodelling of Germany, the two Austrian defeats of 1859 and 1866 had had an equally profound effect upon the government of the Habsburg empire. The loss of Lombardy had forced Francis Joseph to realize that it would be dangerous to refuse to come to terms with the political and social forces that had been suppressed since 1849, and the system of centralized autocracy[1] which Bach had continued to administer after Schwarzenberg's death in 1852 had accordingly been modified in a succession of constitutional experiments.

Bach was replaced by Count Goluchowski, a Polish aristocrat, and in 1860 the March Patent increased the membership of the *Reichsrat* with an additional thirty-eight representatives from the *Landtage*. This simply gave rise to demands for greater regional autonomy which were then hurriedly granted in the October Diploma of that year,

[1] See p. 173.

since Francis Joseph wished to strengthen his position at home while he was in consultation with the Russian Tsar and the Prince Regent of Prussia at Warsaw.[1] The Diploma, together with a number of rescripts, re-established the position in Hungary as it was before 1848 and re-instated institutions of local government including the Diets of Transylvania and Croatia. It met, however, with little success, since the Magyar leaders insisted upon the validity of the April Laws of 1848[2] and German and Magyar opinion objected generally to the concessions which had been made at the same time to the other nationalities. Goluchowski was dismissed in December and succeeded by Anton von Schmerling, who had earlier testified to his liberal instincts by resigning from the post of Minister of Justice at Vienna when the Austrian constitution of 1849 had been abolished in 1851. His attempted solution, the February Patent of 1861, simply revised the October Diploma in the direction of slightly greater central control. The *Reichsrat* was to consist of 343 deputies elected by the various Diets, but with the balance heavily weighted in the favour of the Germans. This, too, proved unacceptable and Schmerling eventually dissolved the Hungarian Diet which had refused to send its delegates to the *Reichsrat*. The Croat Diet, which objected to the exclusion of Dalmatia from Croatia, was also recalcitrant and was dissolved in the following November.

Nevertheless, during the next few years Francis Joseph's negotiations with Hungary did make some progress and would have made still more but for his appointment of a Bohemian aristocrat, Count Belcredi, in place of Schmerling. Belcredi still hankered after a federal scheme which would include other national groups as well as the Magyars, but it was at this point that Austria suffered her great defeat by Prussia in 1866 and to the Hungarian extremists it seemed that the moment for independence had come. Francis Joseph was fortunate, however, in that Deák and Count Andrássy both recognized the need to retain a connection with Austria in order to stand firm against the Slav elements within the Empire, and the negotiations between these two on the Hungarian side and the Saxon Count Ferdinand von Beust, who had now entered the Austrian government, eventually led to a settlement in 1867.

The *Ausgleich*, the Austro-Hungarian Compromise, established a dual monarchy in which Hungary was to enjoy constitutional independence within her historic frontiers[3]. The union between Austria and

[1] See p. 205.   [2] See p. 142.   [3] See map, p. 158.

Hungary, however, was to be more than a personal one, since foreign policy, military and naval affairs, and certain financial matters were to be regulated in common by a joint ministry and an assembly of delegates from the two parts of the empire. Similarly, commercial affairs, monetary standards and railways, although not administered in common, were to work upon uniform principles. The Compromise was significant not merely as the surrender of the Habsburg monarchy to the claims of Hungarian nationalism; it marked the abandonment of the old Habsburg principle of playing off the subject peoples against the master races, for although a new Austrian constitution published at the end of 1867 granted equality of rights to the nationalities still under the direct rule of Vienna, the rehabilitation of the Hungarian kingdom now made the Magyars politically dominant throughout the south-eastern half of the Habsburg lands.[1]

3. The reforms of Tsar Alexander II 1855–81

In March 1855 death brought the long reign of Nicholas I of Russia to a close. 'I hand over to you my command', said the dying Tsar to his son Alexander, 'but unfortunately not in such order as I should wish.' There was good reason for his sense of despair. The despotism which for thirty years he had exercised through secret committees and the agents of the Third Section had proved itself unequal to the tasks of government. At home the constant risings of the peasantry pointed to the fact that the great problem of serfdom had still to be solved; in the realm of foreign affairs a dangerous isolation had forced Russia to fight alone in the Crimea and at the moment of Nicholas's death Sebastopol lay invested by British and French troops.

With this uneasy inheritance Tsar Alexander II was to embark on a vast programme of reform that involved the greatest transformation of Russian society and government since the days of Peter the Great. When, in April 1856, Alexander announced to a gathering of the Moscow nobility: 'better to abolish serfdom from above than to wait till it begins to abolish itself from below', he put in a nutshell the two assumptions on which he was to govern. Reforms must come in order to anticipate revolution; yet he knew that they *could* only come if they were imposed by Imperial decree. The backwardness and conservatism of the peasantry, the smallness of the middle class, Tsardom's mistrust of a nobility gaining greater power, and the problems of control over

[1] See pp. 270–1.

such an enormous land mass, are all constant factors which explain the despotic character of the great periods of cataclysmic change that punctuate Russian history. Thus the paradox of Alexander's reforms was that although they moved towards greater social freedom and constitutional development, they could never be allowed to interfere with the authority of the Tsar, and the reign which began on a high note of optimism was to grow increasingly conservative and was to end with an assassin's bomb.

For Alexander the memory of the revolutions of 1848 appeared less ominous than the deficiencies revealed in Russia's system of government by her fortunes in the Crimean War. So pressing did this need for internal reform seem to him that he was prepared to cut his losses and to accept the terms of the Treaty of Paris in March 1856.[1] This left him free to concentrate on the emancipation of the privately owned serfs. He was not entirely without support in this. Some of the larger land-owners in the south were beginning to prefer wage labour, and it was clearly essential in the gradually developing factories; among the liberals and writers emancipation had long been an accepted aim and the Tsar himself may have been influenced by the publication of Turgenev's *Sportsman's Sketches* in 1855. Yet among the bulk of the nobility and gentry and even many of the peasantry the idea awoke a suspicious hostility, and it took all of Alexander's determination to keep the pro-ject alive through four years of discussion in the various committees and provincial commissions. There were in fact many practical difficulties. The experience of emancipation in the Baltic provinces under Alexander I[2] suggested that freedom without land might well reduce the peasantry to an even worse position than before; if, on the other hand, the peasantry were to be given some of the land, the landowners would require compensation which could only come in the first place from the government.

Eventually, however, Alexander achieved his object and in March 1861 the emancipation of the serfs was proclaimed by Imperial decree. The legal position of serfdom was declared abolished without com-pensation to the owners. The peasantry were to receive a portion of the estates of their landlords at an agreed price, four-fifths of which was to be advanced by the government, who would recover this outlay through redemption payments by the peasantry during the next forty-nine years. The peasantry gained about three-fifths of the land in all, but the actual division of the estates and the amounts to be paid in

[1] See p. 189.   [2] See p. 22.

compensation varied greatly from province to province, being settled by Arbitrators of the Peace, drawn mostly from the nobility and gentry. Thus compensation was everywhere fixed at a far higher level than the existing land-prices; this discrepancy was particularly marked in the central and northern regions where the soil was almost exhausted, while in the fertile black-soil regions, where the rate of compensation came closer to the real value, the landowners retained a far larger share of their estates.

The emancipation of the Russian serf was probably as fair a compromise as could be imposed from above, but like most compromises it was highly unsatisfactory to both sides. Many of the 262,000 landlords had been in debt, with a high proportion of their serfs mortgaged to State credit institutions; hence, much of the financial compensation due from the State was retained to pay off these debts, and even the government bonds that they did receive were found to depreciate in value in the course of time.

For the majority of the 20 million privately owned serfs the economic consequences of emancipation came as a considerable shock. Household serfs received no land whatsoever and were forced to look for employment elsewhere. The partitioning of the estates gave the farming serf less land than what he had actually been able to cultivate before 1861; on average, this loss has been calculated as much as one-fifth, and in the more fertile southern districts it was even higher. The redemption payments to the State were another source of resentment among the peasantry, who in a confused way had always regarded the land as theirs and now found themselves compelled to pay for it. In fact, it was the *mir*, the village commune to which the peasant belonged, that became financially responsible to the government and would ultimately possess the land. The *mir* had always played a large part in Russian peasant society in allotting the strips of serf-land. Now this conception of collective ownership gave it a further hold over the peasant, since it decided what each individual's share of the *mir's* redemption payment should be, and through the system of passports it could prevent the peasant from leaving the district or from separating himself economically from the community, unless he was able to guarantee his share of the whole of the outstanding debt. Thus, although the peasant was now legally free from his old master, this dependence had been largely replaced by the *mir*.

The full consequences of emancipation, however, did not end here, since the change in the legal relationship between landlord and peasant was bound to involve modifications in local government and the judiciary. In January 1864 Alexander decreed the establishment of representative assemblies at two levels in local government—district and provincial. By a method not unlike the Prussian electoral system landowners, townsmen, and peasantry chose their deputies for the district *Zemstvo* separately—the peasantry by a system of indirect election—but the distribution of seats was so arranged that no single class had an absolute majority, although in the higher assembly, the provincial *Zemstvo*, whose members were elected by the district *Zemstva* from their own deputies, the landed class did tend to predominate. Within three years this new type of institution had been established in twenty-seven provinces and soon brought about striking local improvements in medical and veterinary services, hospitals, asylums, and various forms of fire insurance. Their most remarkable achievement lay in encouraging the growth of elementary schools which, between 1856 and 1880, increased in number from 8,000 to 23,000. In 1870 a similar system of self-government in the towns established municipal councils whose functions corresponded roughly to those of the *Zemstva*. From the point of view of their immediate practical consequences these governmental reforms were more beneficial than the emancipation of the serfs, yet the restrictions that constantly hampered the activity of the assemblies pointed to the caution with which a Tsarist régime was bound to regard all such experiments.

Meanwhile, another edict in 1864 had proclaimed a totally new system of judicial procedure whereby petty cases were to be heard by the equivalent of Justices of the Peace elected through the *Zemstva*, while criminal cases were to be tried in regional courts by appointed judges before juries chosen from lists prepared by the *Zemstva*. Trials were to be in public and the provision of salaries for the judges made them less liable to bribery. The Third Section still retained its powers of 'administrative arrest', enabling it to exile any suspect to Siberia without trial, but the general improvement in the tone of judicial proceedings after this time was clearly observed by impartial observers. At the same time Golovnin at the ministry of education was working to improve the quality and number of secondary schools, and the relaxing of the censorship created a new sense of freedom in the Universities. At the Ministry of War Miliutin abolished the most brutal forms of punishment in the army, equipment was brought up to date, and the education of army cadets improved. His greatest struggle was to introduce a system of universal conscription, a burden which until then had been borne almost exclusively by the peasantry, and it was not until 1874, after the warning of Prussia's victories over Austria and France, that the measure was actually proclaimed. All men of twenty years of age were to be liable to perform six years with the colours, but the actual selection was to be by ballot—with considerable reductions in length of service according to the level of education which the recruit had attained before joining the army.

It was perhaps in Finland that Alexander was to see the most successful aspect of his rule. At the beginning of his reign his official visit to Helsinki, where he was Chancellor of the University, and the reestablishment of the Finnish committee at St Petersburg through the efforts of the Finnish Secretary of State, Count Armfeldt, indicated the Tsar's interest in the Grand Duchy. In 1863 the first Diet to be summoned in Finland since 1809 was opened by Alexander himself at Helsinki, and by 1867 had drawn up a Fundamental Law which meant nothing less than the restoration of constitutional rule in Finland. There was a highly conservative note in the preservation of the old form of the four Estates, instead of a modern parliamentary assembly, but the franchise was extended, the agreement of three of the Estates was needed for the passing of any new law, and the Diet was to meet at least once every five years. Liberal ambitions were encouraged by currency reform, the weakening of the guilds and the ending, in 1869, of the Church's control over schools; and plans were made for a railway line linking Helsinki with the inland provinces. All these reforms in the economy and administration of the country were naturally facilitated by a long tradition of local self-government and the absence of any serfdom. Alexander's principal aim, however, was to reconcile the Finns to Russian rule, and here the social antagonism between Finns and Swedo-Finns suggested that the fostering of a growing Finnish national spirit might be an effective means of quelling those who still looked to Sweden. In 1863 the Finnish language was granted equality with Swedish in the law courts and government offices, and in 1865 notice was given that by 1872 it would be compulsory for all officials throughout the Grand Duchy. Despite the greater conservatism of the later half of his reign, Alexander never went back on his word to the Finns and it is a remarkable fact that even today, long after the gaining of Finnish independence and two desperate wars with Russia in the twentieth century, the statue of Alexander II still stands in the Great Square in Helsinki.

In Poland the same liberal policy led to disaster, in striking contrast to its success in Finland. This was partly because the more recent memory of Polish independence encouraged the Poles to take advantage of the general relaxation of control to make more violent demands; also partly because the upper classes were the leaders of national feeling. Alexander began in 1857 by authorizing the establishment of an Agricultural Society for the consideration of agrarian reforms, and in 1861 a Polish magnate, Alexander Wielopolski, was given ministerial powers to introduce a number of measures including the recognition of Polish as the official language, the establishment of new schools, and the emancipation of the Jews. A growing national excitement in Warsaw, however, led to violent demonstrations on the anniversary of Kosciuszko's death; Wielopolski resigned and Russian military rule was established until June 1862, when Wielopolski was reinstated. The situation continued to deteriorate, however, when an attempt on the life of the new Governor-General, Alexander's brother Constantine, was followed by public executions, and a new levy of army recruits finally provided the spark for the great Polish rising of 1863.

'This much is certain,' wrote Marx to Engels in February, 'that the era of revolutions is now once more fairly opened.' He was completely wrong. The Polish revolt did not spread and was doomed by almost exactly the same factors as in the rising of 1830.[1] First, the peasantry, hating their masters, refused to take much part in the struggle. Second, the rebels were still divided among themselves. Even in exile there had been two centres of resistance; the moderates under Prince Czartoryski, living in his splendid seventeenth-century mansion on the Ile St Louis in Paris, concentrated on the frontiers of 1772 and the constitution of 1791, while the radicals, who demanded the emancipation of the peasantry and the Jews, were led by Mieroslavski, who in 1861 had established a training school for his movement at Cuneo in Piedmont and was in touch with a Polish society organized by Joseph Conrad's father at Kiev. Each party accordingly established its own military dictator throughout the fighting in Poland and Lithuania. Third, the rebels were not only divided, but also outnumbered—10,000 Poles against 80,000 Russians—and the refusal of the western Powers to do more than protest, coupled with Prussia's active assistance to Russia,[2] sealed the fate of the revolt.

By the spring of 1864 resistance had been crushed and the inevitable executions, deportations, and heavy fines for the rebels followed. From now on Alexander decided that the conciliation of Polish national

---

[1] See pp. 84–5.   [2] See p. 212.

sentiment was an unworkable policy. Instead, he would revert to his father's plan of 'russification', and in the hope of winning over the peasantry, complete emancipation granting them about one-third of the land was proclaimed in March 1864; redemption payments were made considerably lower than in Russia and were to be financed by a general land tax, which meant that the Polish landowner actually had to contribute to his own compensation. Polish institutions soon disappeared. Russian became the official language in all schools, and in 1866 the Kingdom of Poland was renamed the Vistula Region. It was a sad end to the hopes of the Polish patriots; yet it is hard to escape the conclusion that by antagonizing Alexander's initial goodwill they had thrown away a splendid opportunity and brought disaster on themselves.

19

THE DEFEAT OF FRANCE 1870-1

1. The Franco-Prussian war

SIGNIFICANT though the constitutional changes in Germany and Austria-Hungary may have been, the diplomatic consequences of Bismarck's success in 1866 were still greater. Only the southern states remained to be brought within a new Germany from which Austria had been excluded; in Italy only Rome and the patrimony of St Peter still lay outside the frontiers of Victor Emmanuel's kingdom. For Napoleon III it was now vital that he should regain the initiative in the revision of the Vienna settlement; on the other hand, the clerical interest at home forbade him to abandon Rome, and the realization that Königgrätz implied a defeat for France made it essential to resist any further step towards German unification. Thus the years immediately following the Peace of Prague saw a duel between Napoleon III and Bismarck, in which the Emperor of the French, weakened by failing health and still torn between conflicting policies, was simply no match for the Chancellor of the North German Confederation.

For Napoleon the need to regain prestige was an over-riding consideration. He sought first some territorial gain which might make less obvious the contrast between Bismarck's recent success and his own failure in Mexico.[1] A bid to purchase the Grand Duchy of Luxemburg from the King of the Netherlands came to nothing; through Benedetti, the French ambassador at Berlin, he opened fruitless negotiations over the possibility of acquiring a part of the Palatinate, and a proposal whereby France should absorb Belgium achieved no more than to place in Bismarck's hands a highly incriminating document of which he was to make good use in 1870.

A second more sensible aspect of his policy in these years was an attempt in 1868 to create an active alliance with Austria-Hungary and Italy against Prussia. It was not unreasonable to assume that Francis Joseph might have been ready to seize an opportunity to reverse the decision of 1866, but here again Napoleon was to be disappointed. The

---

[1] See p. 192.

233

mildness of the terms which Bismarck had imposed on Austria made her unwilling to embark upon a hostile policy. 'What our monarchy wants,' wrote Beust, 'is the maintenance of peace.' And over Italy the problem of Rome remained insuperable. Napoleon had actually withdrawn the French garrison there in December 1866, but the subsequent raids into Papal territory had forced him to send it back in November 1867 and the principal condition on which Victor Emmanuel insisted—the evacuation of Rome by the French—was a price that Napoleon knew he could not pay.

These hopes that Napoleon entertained of creating an alliance against Prussia naturally have a bearing on the outbreak of the Franco-Prussian war in 1870, since they might suggest some justification for Bismarck getting his blow in first. Indeed, the causes of the war still remain a matter of controversy. The story begins in Spain in 1868 when a military junta headed by General Prim drove Queen Isabella from her throne and the *Cortes* in the following year agreed upon the establishment of a liberal form of government under a constitutional monarchy. This presented an immediate problem. 'Finding a democratic king in Europe,' remarked Prim, 'is like looking for an atheist in Heaven.' In the event it proved to be not only difficult but also highly dangerous, for the choice of a sovereign for the Spanish throne was of particular concern to France, who had been well satisfied with the pro-French policy of Queen Isabella. The danger became still more apparent when the choice of the Spanish government eventually fell on Leopold, a son of Prince Karl Anton of Hohenzollern-Sigmaringen— highly suitable from the Spanish point of view, since his family was Roman Catholic. It was hardly likely, however, that the thought of a Hohenzollern on the throne of Spain would commend itself to the French. For this reason Prim was anxious to keep the negotiations secret, but when by March 1870 Leopold had twice refused the offer, it seemed that Prim and his agent Salazar would have to look elsewhere.

For long after the Franco-Prussian war the Prussians always maintained that the negotiations had only concerned King William in his capacity as head of the Hohenzollern family. Towards the end of the century, however, evidence emerged to show that Bismarck, while remaining quietly in the background, had fostered the Hohenzollern candidature even to the extent of using the *Welfen-Fonds*, the confiscated income of the King of Hanover, to bribe the Spanish *Cortes*, and had worked hard to persuade both Leopold and King William to fall in with the idea. But even if this is established, there remains the question of his motive. Napoleon III had informed him that he would never tolerate a Hohenzollern on the Spanish throne, and in view of later events it would be tempting to assume that Bismarck intended to use the issue to provoke war between the two countries, after which France would be unable to prevent the incorporation of the south German states within Germany. Certainly he must have seen this as one possibility. On the other hand, a Hohenzollern candidature was not a good emotional cause with which to rally the south German states, among whom considerable antagonism existed towards Bismarck, and it may well have been that he would have been satisfied simply to see a peaceful solution with Leopold on the Spanish throne. The presence of an ally on France's southern frontier would be useful for the future and a diplomatic success here might well have the effect of further undermining Napoleon's prestige at home. In any case, at the end of 1869 Napoleon had embarked upon the experiment of parliamentary government and Bismarck could well afford to wait to see whether this would improve his chances of including the south German states within the Confederation.

In May 1870, however, a strongly anti-Prussian Foreign Minister, de Gramont, took office in France and Bismarck at once revived the question of the candidature. Leopold was persuaded to accept and King William agreed 'mit schwerem, sehr schwerem Herz'. The essential for Bismarck now was speed, but when on 19 June Salazar sent the news by telegraph to Madrid, a mistake in the deciphering of the message led Prim to believe that Salazar's return was not imminent and he accordingly prorogued the *Cortes*. This fatal error played havoc with the plans of Bismarck and Prim, since on Salazar's return to Madrid, the *Cortes* had to be summoned again to carry out the election of Leopold to the throne, and in the general delay and excitement the secret leaked out to the French. Thus, before the election could take place, there was time for France to protest and for King William to have second thoughts.

In Paris there was at once a fierce reaction in the press and de Gramont's speech before the *Corps Législatif* made it clear that France could never allow 'a foreign power, by placing one of its princes on the throne of Charles V, to disturb to our detriment the present equilibrium of Europe'. Instead of remonstrating with Prim the French government resolved to cut through any subterfuge by negotiating directly with King William at Ems. William at once responded to this approach by Benedetti, the French ambassador, and it was mainly due to his efforts that on 12 July Prince Karl Anton agreed to withdraw the candidature on his son's behalf. This decision was communicated from Sigmaringen to King William at Ems, Prim at Madrid, and the Spanish ambassador at Paris. Thus by two o'clock in the afternoon the French government could relax, while Bismarck, who arrived at Berlin from Varzin a few hours later that day, found that he was faced with a major diplomatic reverse.

Then, at the very moment when Bismarck claimed afterwards that he was contemplating resignation, the French threw away their moral advantage by over-reaching themselves. Not content with the withdrawal, Napoleon and de Gramont sent instructions to Benedetti that he should demand of King William that the Hohenzollern candidature would never be renewed. Benedetti's fateful interview with William took place on 13 July on the Brunnenpromenade at Ems and resulted simply in an emphatic refusal by the Prussian king to acquiesce in this attempt to bind his actions for the future. A telegram describing this new turn of events was at once dispatched to Bismarck who was authorized to publish it. Bismarck later made much of the historic scene when the telegram reached him that evening as he was dining with Moltke and Roon; a rapid editing of the text made the incident at Ems appear like a heated argument ending with a direct snub to the French ambassador, and its publication in the press and in the foreign courts worked official and public opinion up to a fever pitch in France and Germany, culminating in a French declaration of war on 19 July. Whatever Bismarck's intentions may have been previously, war had certainly been his aim at the end as the only way out of a diplomatic crisis in which the stakes had become too high for either side to surrender, and the sensitiveness of the French to possible Prussian schemes had ultimately played into his hands.

Like Bismarck's earlier opponents, France soon learnt that she must fight this war without allies. In March 1868 Russia had already promised that she would intervene on Prussia's side if Austria-Hungary joined France, and the knowledge of this was sufficient to keep Francis Joseph neutral; in any case, the Germans and Magyars of the Dual Monarchy were strongly opposed to going to the assistance of the French. Danish public opinion favoured war against Prussia in the hope of regaining Slesvig, but the government wisely waited to see how militarily effective France would be as an ally. In Italy Victor Emmanuel put up his price, demanding not merely the evacuation of Rome by the French, but also freedom for Italy to modify the position of the Papal territory, and once again Napoleon dared not accept. 'France', said de Gramont, 'cannot defend her honour on the Rhine and sacrifice it on the Tiber.' British mistrust of France was still considerable and was greatly heightened when, on 25 July, Bismarck published in *The Times* the text of Benedetti's earlier proposal that Belgium should be annexed by France.

Once again Bismarck's diplomacy was aided by the immediate success of the Prussian army. Napoleon himself had had an inkling that the French army was in need of reform and had struggled unsuccessfully to establish universal military service, although he did at least secure the adoption of a new rifle, the *chasse-pot*, by the infantry. Yet not even he could have anticipated the appalling confusion of the French mobilization which produced only 200,000 troops, in contrast to the Prussian staff work which transported 380,000 men to the front in eighteen days. With this numerical superiority Moltke thrust into Lorraine and defeated the French right wing at Wörth on 6 August. The rest of the German forces swept on to the south of Metz and after two indecisive battles at Vionville and Gravelotte in the middle of August, Bazaine withdrew into the fortress of Metz. A fresh army which had been organized under Marshal MacMahon at Châlons had now to advance to the aid of Bazaine, but when it encountered the German Third Army at Sedan near the Belgian border, three-days' fighting ended in the surrender of the French army on 1 September. Among the 82,000 prisoners was Napoleon III himself who had hoped in vain for death on the battlefield. He now had one last conversation with Bismarck at a wayside cottage before his ensuing internment at Wilhelmshöhe. Here he remained for six months, after which he crossed the Channel to exile once again in England where he died in January 1873.

Indeed, Sedan was to mean more than the end of any serious chance of victory for France; the official publication of the news in Paris on 4 September brought about the fall of the Second Empire. Crowds invaded the Chamber, and in response to their demands the opposition deputies under Jules Favre and Gambetta agreed that a Republic should be proclaimed at the Hôtel de Ville; by now revolution had its own well-established traditions. An American dentist engineered the escape of the Empress Eugénie, whom Napoleon had appointed as Regent during his absence, and a provisional government of National Defence was formed by the deputies of Paris under the presidency of General Trochu.

The new government was determined to continue the fight. 'We shall yield neither an inch of our territory, nor a stone of our fortresses,' announced Jules Favre, now Foreign Minister, but by 19 September the German army was besieging Paris and the conduct of the war rested almost entirely with a few of the deputies who had been sent to Tours before the capital was invested. They were greatly strengthened by the arrival of Gambetta, who escaped from Paris by balloon in October, but the hastily organized Army of the Loire attempting to relieve Paris was thrust back by the Germans and in December the delegates had to leave Tours for Bordeaux. A second effort failed to strike effectively at the German communications across northern France and the army had eventually to seek refuge in Switzerland. Meanwhile, at the end of October, Bazaine had surrendered at Metz with 173,000 men and on 28 January 1871 Paris, which had been bombarded and was near to starvation, finally capitulated. The government of National Defence now negotiated a three-weeks' armistice during which national elections were to be held throughout France, and when the new Assembly had met on 12 February at Bordeaux, it became clear that a peace settlement would not be long delayed.

2. The consequences of the war

A. THE CREATION OF THE GERMAN EMPIRE

On 18 January 1871 Bismarck finally brought his work to its triumphant climax, when in the Hall of Mirrors at the palace of Versailles he proclaimed William I German Emperor. The date was in a sense the Hohenzollern counterpart to the Napoleonic 2 December, for it had been on 18 January 1701 that Frederick III, Elector of Brandenburg, had assumed the title of King-in-Prussia; the place, too, was significant, for the proclamation of the German Empire in the palace of the *roi soleil* appeared to mark the final victory of Prussia in her long struggle over the years with France.

There was also much that was symbolic in the actual negotiations which had led up to this moment. At the beginning of the war the fear of invasion by France had caused the south German states to turn to Prussia, and as popular opinion swung round in favour of their inclusion within the victorious German Confederation, it was soon apparent that the only issue was to be their actual method of entry. Bismarck was determined that the offer of the Imperial crown should not, as in 1849, emanate from the people of Germany; it must come from the

German princes, and in October 1870 he opened discussions along these lines with the representatives of the four south German states who had arrived at the army headquarters at Versailles. By playing off one against the other he brought Württemberg, Baden, and Hesse to agreement with his terms and a little later Bavaria was won over with a few meaningless concessions. Then Ludwig II of Bavaria was prevailed upon to invite King William of Prussia to become German Emperor. Ludwig had little respect for the Hohenzollerns, but the orgy of building with which he attempted to enhance the glory of the Wittelsbachs and which later in the twentieth century was to be a godsend for the Bavarian tourist industry, had put him in such debt that he was glad to accept an income of £15,000 a year from the *Welfen-Fonds* and allowed himself to be deluded into imagining that the Imperial throne would be occupied alternately by a Hohenzollern and a Wittelsbach.

It was only after his fellow princes had joined with Ludwig in his proposal, that William consented to receive a deputation from the German Reichstag who made the same request on 19 December. Strangely enough, their President, Eduard Simson, had been the spokesman of the Frankfurt Assembly which had originally offered the Crown to Frederick William IV in 1849, but there the similarity with the epoch of liberal revolution ended. The entry of the south German states had been negotiated by Bismarck alone; the constitution of the new Empire was to be little different from that of the North German Confederation, an autocracy only slightly held in check by democratic forms, and the Imperial crown had been granted, as William II claimed in 1910, 'by God's grace alone and not by Parliaments, popular assemblies and popular decision'.

B. THE PARIS COMMUNE

France's settlement of her affairs was to be rather less tidy. Initially the speed with which the deputies had acted in Paris on 4 September had forestalled any immediate threat of social revolution, and the government of National Defence under Trochu was far more homogeneous than the executive committee that had been set up in February 1848. Within Paris the tension was nevertheless considerable; the working-class clubs and societies were highly suspicious that the middle-class republicans were half hearted in their resistance to the Germans, and on two occasions during the siege the new government almost succumbed to an assault on the Hôtel de Ville—first, at the end of October, when the failure of an attempt to break out from Paris coincided with the news of the surrender of Metz and the arrival of Thiers who, after the failure of his diplomatic mission to London, Vienna, and St Petersburg, wished to arrange an armistice with Bismarck; then again on 22 January after a further *sortie en masse* had come to nothing.

In fact, the extreme left wing were proved correct in their doubts. The propertied classes had by now lost all faith in the continuation of the war, and when elections had been held during the three-weeks' armistice following the surrender of Paris, the attitude of the National Assembly which met at Bordeaux on 12 February 1871 made it clear that the provinces were determined on peace. This time the pattern of 1848 *had* been repeated, since the Assembly was predominantly right wing with some 400 monarchists and conservatives against 200 republicans, many of whom were moderate; Gambetta, who had demanded a continuation of the war, had to admit defeat and Thiers, who at the age of seventy-three had enjoyed an overwhelming electoral triumph, was nominated as 'Chief of the Executive Power of the Republic of France'.

Thiers lost no time in carrying out his policy of making peace with the Germans. The preliminaries which had been completed by the end of February included the surrender of Alsace and Lorraine, an area rich in iron ore and agricultural land, although Bismarck's motives were largely governed by strategic considerations. In addition to this, France was to pay a war indemnity of five milliard francs in the next three years, during which various *départements* were to remain under German occupation. Despite all his arguments Thiers could gain no more in concessions than a slight reduction of the indemnity and the retention of the fortress of Belfort in return for a ceremonial entry of the German Army into Paris. These were hard terms, and the annexation of Alsace and Lorraine was to rankle for many years afterwards, but the National Assembly had no choice; on 1 March the preliminaries were duly accepted and formed the basis of the Treaty of Frankfurt signed later that year.

For France, however, the end of the conflict was to be followed almost at once by the horrors of civil war. The extreme left-wing elements in Paris had never accepted the decision for peace which had been imposed upon them; Thiers himself was regarded as an enemy of the working class and the parade of German troops on 1 March brought emotions in the capital to boiling point. Furthermore, the National Assembly's decision to end the moratorium which had been declared on commercial bills and house rents appeared as a new move on the part of the bourgeois, and at the same time a decree stopping the payment of one-and-a-half francs a day to the National Guardsmen deprived many of the poor of their principal means of support.

On 18 March Thiers, who had established his government at Versailles, gave orders for the guns of the Paris National Guard at Montmartre and Belleville to be seized. It is uncertain whether he intended this as a deliberate provocation, but when the attempt led to violent local resistance, he followed the course which he had originally suggested to Louis Philippe in 1848 and ordered the government authorities to evacuate the city. This abandonment of Paris gave the left-wing elements their chance to organize, on 26 March, a municipal government known as the Commune, and to prepare a desperate resistance to Thiers' forces at Versailles. Although the rebellion has all the characteristics of class conflict, heightened by the bitterness of defeat in war, it would, however, be wrong to consider it a manifestation of organized Socialism. There was a diversity of political groups within the Commune, and the haziness of their attitude towards capitalism is exemplified by the orthodox way in which they financed their activities by raising loans from the Bank of France, which at the same time was making similar advances to the government of Versailles. The Paris Commune represented no more than an explosion of anger, an echo of the June days rather than an anticipation of Marxist conspiracy.

It was, nevertheless, an appalling episode of bloodshed and cruelty. At Versailles Thiers built up his forces, negotiating with Bismarck for the release of prisoners of war, while the German army forming an outer ring looked on at this object lesson in the working of French democracy. Already in April government troops were shooting prisoners captured in the clashes and the Commune seized hostages preparatory to retaliation. On 8 May the main attack on the city was launched under MacMahon and by the middle of the month his forces were fighting within Paris. For a week the battle raged through the streets; prisoners were massacred on both sides, and eventually the Commune ordered the shooting of fifty-six hostages, including the archbishop of Paris. By the last week of May the government forces had conquered—after a final stand by the Communards in the cemetery of Père-Lachaise, where on the following day 147 of them were executed. In the whole course of the struggle some 20,000 had perished, although the precise figure will never be known, and subsequent trials condemned 13,450 to terms of imprisonment and 7,500 to deportation.

I

Only at this fearful cost did the National Assembly once more become master of Paris, a city devastated and shocked by the ferocity of a holocaust in which the Tuileries and the Hôtel de Ville—twin symbols of French political antagonism—had both gone down in flames.

C. THE QUESTION OF THE SPANISH MONARCHY

The continued search for a new monarch was to bring almost as much tribulation to Spain herself as it had already done to France. With the events of July 1870 Prim turned from the Hohenzollerns and the Crown was eventually accepted by Amadeus, the second son of Victor Emmanuel of Italy.[1] The short reign of King Amadeus, however, was hardly a success. Prim, on whom he depended, was assassinated at the end of 1870 and to the majority of Spaniards their new king was simply a foreigner whose father had just shocked Catholic sentiment with his occupation of Rome.[2] Within a year the republicans, excited by the Paris Commune, had greatly strengthened their hold on the municipalities, while at the same time the supporters of Don Carlos, the grandson of the original claimant,[3] seized their opportunity to raise Catalonia and the Basque provinces in rebellion. Amadeus tried for a time to work in conjunction with the liberal and republican elements, but eventually gave up the struggle, abdicated, and returned to Italy in February 1873.

The republic which the *Cortes* now attempted to establish was no more successful. The Carlists were still holding out in the north and the introduction of a federalist system, coupled with a rapid succession of presidents in a single year, so weakened the authority of the Spanish government that in January 1874 General Pavia overthrew the *Cortes*, which was replaced by a group of generals. The new administration did not immediately succeed in crushing the Carlists, but it did at least bring an end to the republican period. The deposed Queen Isabella had eventually abdicated in favour of her son Alfonso, who was now sixteen years of age, a cadet at Sandhurst, and in December 1874 General Martínez Campos proclaimed him king to his troops at Saguntum. This restoration was supported by Primo de Rivera at Madrid and in 1875 the reign of Alfonso XII duly began. By February 1876 the Carlists had been driven back across the Pyrenees and in the same year a constituent Assembly devised the system under which Alfonso was to rule. The legislature was to consist of a bi-cameral Assembly, the upper House being partly elected, partly nominated by the King, the lower

[1] See Genealogical table, p. 483.   [2] See p. 243.   [3] See p. 89.

elected on a franchise based on a property qualification. By this means the Bourbons in alliance with the upper classes continued to govern Spain until 1923, when Primo de Rivera, nephew of the general who had assisted in the restoration in 1874, carried out the *coup* which was to reduce the king of Spain to a mere figurehead.

D. ROME AND THE BLACK SEA

The year 1870 was to be of profound significance also for the Roman Catholic Church. Already in 1864 Pius IX had issued the Syllabus of Errors which had formally defined the Papal attitude towards the growth of modern secular systems of government. It condemned Socialism, Communism, and the subordination of the Church to the State; it denied the validity of public opinion as the fundamental sanction of civil society and insisted upon the exclusive right of the clergy to control the education of the young. Then, in 1867, Pius announced his intention to summon a General Council and in the autumn of 1869 there began to assemble at Rome some 700 bishops from all over the world. One purpose of the Vatican Council was to consider the precise nature of the Pope's authority and on 18 July 1870, as a thunderstorm raged outside, there took place the final vote and promulgation of the constitution *Pastor Aeternus*. The controversial doctrine of Papal Infallibility was now explicitly stated, and the Pope speaking *ex cathedra* on matters of faith and morals was held to be 'possessed of that infallibility bestowed by Christ on his Church and therefore such definitions of the Roman Pontiff are irreformable of themselves and not from the consent of the Church'.

The Franco-Prussian war broke out on the next day and although Napoleon III would enter into no positive political agreement with Victor Emmanuel, military requirements necessitated the withdrawal of the French garrison from Rome at the beginning of August. With the news of Sedan and the capture of Napoleon, Victor Emmanuel had nothing more to fear from France. His troops entered the Papal enclave and on 20 September the bombardment of Rome began. Pius, however, insisted that there should only be a token show of resistance and with the occupation of the city Rome had at last become the capital of the kingdom of Italy. In November the Law of Guarantees accorded the Pope all the attributes of sovereignty, allowed him to retain the Vatican, the Lateran, Castel Gondolfo, and his Swiss Guard, and granted him an annual income of 3,225,000 lire. Catholic opinion throughout Europe did at least secure this much for the Pope; it could not prevent the loss of all his territories together with the final separa-tion of secular and ecclesiastical affairs in Italy, and although Pius refused to accept the Law and placed the King and his government under the ban of the Church, this only served to exacerbate their relations until the signing of the Lateran Treaty with Mussolini in 1929.

One other European Power was able to take advantage of the French disaster. Russia was at once aware of her opportunity to denounce the neutralization of the Black Sea which had been imposed on her by the Treaty of Paris in 1856, and her decision to do so was communicated to the other governments at the beginning of November 1870. France was not in a position to object and Bismarck regarded such a concession as a small price to pay for continued Russian friendship and acquiescence in the intended German annexation of Alsace and Lorraine. Great Britain was more concerned about the possibility of a secret agreement between Russia and Germany, and Gladstone's government merely took a stand against the denunciation of an international treaty by one of the signatories. A compromise was reached at a conference held in London from January to March 1871, when the Russians accepted the general principle that international agreements could not be revised by unilateral action, and were then granted their wish with a formal abrogation of the Black Sea clauses of the Treaty of Paris. For the Russians the victory was largely theoretical, since they could not yet contemplate the creation of a great naval power on the Black Sea, and it was Bismarck who made the greatest capital out of the conference. The British were by now considering a friendly alignment with the new power of Germany on the Continent, and although Bismarck avoided any positive alliance with them, he was able to profit by their attitude when Great Britain and Russia, who was naturally satisfied with the outcome of the London negotiations, agreed that the peace settlement with France should not be a matter for general European negotiation. Thus the French were left in isolation to the end, and the revision of the Treaty of Paris and the Italian occupation of Rome form an appropriate accompaniment to the downfall of the empire of Napoleon III.

V

THE ARMED PEACE 1871–1914

20

THE GROWTH OF COLLECTIVISM

1. Forces of social and economic change

BETWEEN 1815 and 1870 the course of European history might be summed up as the impact of forces of social and economic change upon the settlement of Vienna. The new situation which had been emerging in the 1850s and 1860s implied more than a radical alteration in the balance of power in Europe; it was a consequence of the fact that the governments had been prepared to take into partnership the rising *bourgeoisie* whom Metternich had stigmatized as the 'presumptuous' men. In the outcome it was not unnatural that during the forty-three years which elapsed before the outbreak of the first World War the middle-class liberal whose discontent had lain behind so much of the unrest of the earlier part of the century should imagine that the fruits of the earth were now his to inherit.

Indeed, to some extent they were. The aristocracy of central and eastern Europe might still be socially predominant; yet optimism and materialism were to be the predominating themes of a great period of middle-class affluence—'the world of security' Stefan Zweig called it, when from the middle of the twentieth century he looked back wistfully on the years of his youth in Austria. In Germany the new sense of power and wealth was reflected in the rapid expansion of Berlin, now becoming one of the great cities of Europe. In Paris it consolidated the position of the sophisticated upper stratum of new rich mingling with old aristocracy that Proust depicted in *À la recherche du temps perdu*, and at the same time it helped to create the *petit bourgeois* society of Georges Duhamel's chronicle of the Pasquier family; over them all loomed the Eiffel Tower, constructed in the Champ-de-Mars for the industrial fair of 1889, a symbol of the new engineering skills whose social and economic implications were changing the face of Europe.

Secure and benevolent the world might seem to those who did not live at the lowest economic level; yet the paradox of the liberal victory for greater personal freedom was that the continued development of the very forces that had given rise to it were seriously to curtail the individual's liberty of action. In diplomacy a new balance had to be found against a background of sharpened mistrust and more specialized techniques of warfare. On the domestic scene the requirements of social organization in an age of the masses and the tentacular complexity of growing industry imposed new forms of collectivism with which every government had to come to terms whatever its political complexion.

This collectivism was the cumulative effect of a number of social and economic factors which had already been at work throughout most of the century. First, the population of Europe,[1] aided by improvements in medical science and public sanitation, mounted extraordinarily in the last three decades of the nineteenth century, despite the emigration of 21 million overseas. Although this rate of increase was not maintained, the 293 million inhabitants in 1871 had risen to 490 million by 1914. Between 1870 and 1910 Great Britain rose from 31 million to 45, and Germany from 41 million to 65; France, on the other hand, was not only surpassed, but lagged still further behind with a relatively slight increase to 39 million, a figure which put her only slightly ahead of Italy's 35 million. The most prodigious increase was in Russia who over the same period rose from 77 to 111 million. In an age when men were becoming more and more conscious of statistics, numbers implied strength; thus it was natural that France should appear to be in decline, and that while the west kept a watchful eye on the growing population of Germany, the Germans themselves should look eastwards with still greater apprehension at the rising man-power of their Russian neighbour. In fact, a balanced population in terms of age groups may be more advantageous than a rapidly rising one which is bound to be unbalanced, and in Russia, where the change was most marked, the increase from 50 million peasantry in 1861 to 100 million by 1917 played havoc with the successful working of Tsar Alexander II's division of the estates.

The effects of the general rise in population were accentuated by the drift towards the towns. This tendency, which had already long been a feature of western development, became far more noticeable throughout central Europe after 1871 and was particularly striking in Germany, where the enormous growth of her industry raised her urban population to 60% in 1910. The concentration of so many thousands of people in the cities involved something of a social revolution in itself. When Elizabeth of Bavaria married the Emperor Francis Joseph in 1854, she found not a single bathroom in the Imperial Palace of the Hofburg;

[1] See Appendix 7, p. 488.

yet in the last decades of the century local civic authorities were everywhere interesting themselves in the problems of plumbing and main
drainage and attempting to safeguard the health and welfare of town-
dwellers through a host of local regulations which, twenty years earlier,
would have seemed an intolerable infringement of the rights of
property. Where the architect had previously been employed to build
palaces and churches, he now turned his attention to main thoroughfares, municipal buildings and railway stations, many of them designed
in a heavily ornamented neo-classical style. The effect was not only
local; improvement in communications through the invention of the
telephone and the growth of the railway network throughout Europe
from 140,000 miles in 1890 to 213,000 in 1913 added enormously to the
closeness of control from the capital city and enabled all forms of
association to work with greater discipline and strength.

The general consequence of this collectivism in the organization of
social life was to create far greater uniformity on a national scale. This
was assisted by two additional factors—schools and newspapers. Before
the outbreak of the first World War almost every country in Europe had
established its own system of primary education, compulsory and free,
while the curricula of secondary schools were beginning now to include
the study of modern languages and science. The growth of literacy and
the prospect of a wide circulation in the cities encouraged the development of a national popular press. In 1896 Alfred Harmsworth founded
the *Daily Mail* in Great Britain; in the same year the prices of *Le Petit
Parisien* and *Le Matin* were lowered to appeal to a larger public in
France, and 1898 saw the launching of the Ullstein venture of the
Berlinermorgenpost. Naturally all these influences represented a tremendous challenge to the parochialism which had always been the very
essence of European life, and the local barriers of tradition and dialect
were to be still further weakened in the twentieth century by the
development of radio and the cinema. Yet at the time, startling though
they must have seemed to contemporaries, they only marked the beginning of a process of change which was inevitably slow. In his novel
Buddenbrooks Thomas Mann made much of the gulf that still existed
between a north German and a Bavarian, while Daudet's *Lettres de mon
moulin* and *Tartarin de Tarascon* and Pierre Loti's study of Breton fisher-
men in *Pêcheur d'Islande* suggest that in many parts of the Continent life
was still relatively unchanged.

A fundamental factor in this new pattern of European life was a remarkable acceleration in the industrial revolution. The development of

coal mines, iron foundries, and textile factories which had formed the
basis of the transformation of western Europe in the first half of the
century[1] was now spreading fast eastwards. Germany, which by 1870
had already surpassed France, was by 1914 seriously challenging Great
Britain as the principal industrial Power in Europe. More striking still
was the rapid industrialization of Russia, particularly after 1890. The
1,000 miles of railway track, which was all that she could claim in 1860,
had grown to 44,000 miles by 1914, and it was not inappropriate that
Sergius Witte, who became Russian Minister of Finance in 1892, should
earlier in his career have been a provincial station-master.

Between 1870 and 1914 coal production[2] in France rose from 13·3
million tons to 40 million, in Austria–Hungary from 8·6 million to 47
million and in Russia from three-quarters of a million to 36·2 million.
The French were still hampered by a comparative poverty of coal
deposits and these figures for Austria-Hungary and Russia indicate how
previously non-industrial countries were beginning to catch up with
her. In the whole of Europe Great Britain remained in the lead, rising
from 112 million tons to 292, but German production from 34 million
tons in 1870 came close to equalling Great Britain with 277 million in
1914. In 1913 12 million tons were raised in the Saar alone and 43
million in Silesia, and by 1906 more than half a million men were employed in the mining of German coal and lignite.

The same tendency is to be observed in the manufacture of pig-iron.
France rising from 1·2 million tons to 4·6 million was being challenged
by Russia whose output of half a million in 1870 had increased to 3·6
million in 1914, although Austria-Hungary had attained no more than
2 million by this date. Great Britain had risen from 6 million to 11
million, yet despite this advance she was by 1914 no longer the leading
producer in Europe, owing to a prodigious increase in Germany from
1·3 million to 14·7 million, aided by the geographical proximity of her
coal and iron ore. Similarly, the British went ahead with the production
of steel with the new Bessemer process, which depended upon the use
of non-phosphoric ores not easily available in Germany, but after the
work of Gilchrist and Thomas in 1879 had shown how this limitation
might be overcome, the prosphoric ores of Lorraine enabled Germany
to produce 14 million tons of steel in 1914 as against the British 6·5
million.

In ship-building Great Britain still remained in the lead; in 1910 her
steam tonnage was more than four times as great as Germany's. None

the less, the German advance was significant and opened up many avenues for the future. Naval rivalry between the two countries was to be an important political factor from the beginning of the twentieth century, and by 1913 the Hamburg-Amerika line had 172 steamships operating in competition for the new passenger services. The general increase was staggering, for between 1893 and 1913 the world tonnage of merchant fleets was actually doubled.

All this growing production, together with an enormous expansion of textile factories, was simply due to the development and refinement of the techniques which had first launched the industrial revolution on the world. There were, however, at this time a number of discoveries and inventions which gave a further impetus to the transformation of the economy. The generation of electricity, facilitated by Siemen's invention of the dynamo, provided a new source of power for the factories. In 1882 the first generating station was operating in New York, and in the following year in Germany Emil Rathenau laid the foundations of what was to become the AEG (*Allgemeine Elektrizitäts Gesellschaft*). Electric cable linking the continents multiplied, and before 1900 wireless communication, pioneered by Marconi, was already an established fact. Another sphere in which there was a tremendous advance at this time, particularly in Germany, was the chemical processes which were to have an astonishing effect on commercial life with the production of synthetic dyes, fertilizers, margarine, and soap, and whose new drugs were to be an important ally for medical research, leading to a better understanding of malaria, cholera, and tuberculosis and the development of antiseptic methods in hospitals. Most striking of all was the invention of the internal-combustion engine which was to be followed by the diesel engine in 1895. The motor car had made its appearance before the end of the century and in 1903 the Wright brothers in America made their first successful flight in a propeller-driven aeroplane.

Such a profusion of industrial activity combined with the development of technical means of control and communication was bound to have consequences that were entirely in keeping with the general tendency towards collectivism. The concentration of thousands of workers in the factory and mining towns facilitated the organization of trade union movements on a scale that had been impossible before. In the incessant economic struggle small industrial firms were absorbed into bigger concerns, local shops succumbed to the mammoth store, provincial banks became amalgamated and everywhere larger and larger units appeared to dominate the scene. Soon, both in the United States and Europe, these large units themselves began to merge with others. Sometimes the method was to develop what was known as a vertical combine, where the various stages of production from the ownership of the raw materials to the distribution and retailing of the finished article were all brought under the control of a single authority. Another type was the horizontal combine known as a Cartel, which consisted of a working agreement between large industries dealing with the same commodity. By this means the amount of production might be regulated, the market shared on a rational basis and a common selling price fixed—very often at two levels, one for home consumption, the other much lower for selling abroad. In France a metal industries trust, the *Comité des Forges*, was virtually controlled by six major firms; in Germany the Rhenish-Westphalian Coal Syndicate, created in 1893, controlled half the coal production of the whole country, and the *Stahlwerkverband* almost the entire steel industry in 1904. By 1900 there were 275 German Cartels, and in 1906 the Austrian consul at Berlin commented in a report: 'never before was economic Germany so entirely under the absolute rule of a group of men barely fifty in number.'

These concentrations were largely on a national basis. A further consequence of the industrial and technical advances, however, was to draw the whole world into a single economic unit. Everywhere the demand for capital added to the ramifications of international finance. In this field Great Britain retained a position which sheltered her for the moment from the full consequences of German industrial advance; thus, although in 1895 her imports exceeded her exports by £130 million, this difference was more than compensated by the interest from enormous overseas investments. France and, to a lesser extent, Germany were the other principal creditor nations, and the rapid growth of industrialization outside western Europe meant enormous loans to the Balkan countries, Turkey, Japan, and the South American states. Within Europe the most significant feature was the immense investments in Russia, where by 1897 48% of her national debt and by 1914 one-third of the stock of her joint-stock companies were in the hands of foreigners —predominantly French.

This growing closeness of relationship was bound to exercise a unifying influence upon the economic pattern throughout the world. In the mid-century prices had been rising, but between 1870 and 1893 they tended to fall. There were two main reasons for this. First, the amount of precious metal in the world had not kept pace with the vastly increased quantity of commodities on sale; this shortage was bound to have a deflating effect, and after 1871 Germany, the Scandinavian countries, the Netherlands, Portugal, and the United States all abandoned the gold standard. Second, there was a relative glut on the European market, since the use of farming machinery had enormously increased American production of corn, which could now be distributed by railways and steamships, while refrigerator ships could bring frozen meat from South America. The subsequent drop in the European farmers' selling prices naturally reduced their own purchasing power, which in turn had its repercussions on industry; this helps to explain three particularly bad periods of depression—in 1873, in the early 1880s, and in 1893—when bankruptcies were followed by widespread unemployment, although the actual moment of impact varied slightly from country to country.

In the twenty years before the outbreak of the first World War, prices began to rise again. This was due partly to the discovery of the deposits of gold in South Africa, Western Australia, British Columbia, and Alaska, partly to a return to a policy of Protection in Europe. There was, however, no escape from the cycle of boom and slump and further depressions in the periods 1900-1, 1907-8, and 1912-13, all added to the militancy of the working-class movements which were making an increasingly effective use of the strike weapon. The violence of these economic oscillations pointed to the great paradox of the modern industrial world—that the more the inventiveness of the human mind opened up the resources which might raise the general standard of living, the more the life of the ordinary individual was placed at the mercy of economic forces that he did not understand and could not control. The world might be becoming a single economic unit; yet the principle by which the men of Europe still governed their affairs was increasingly one of national survival in a state of haphazard competition, and within Europe the conflict of national commercial policies led to the growth of tariff walls, thereby creating new obstacles for the interflow of goods, just when railways and steamships had broken down the old.

In fact, the governments did not lightly abandon the old ideal of moving towards Free Trade. In France, after an initial period of wavering at the end of the Franco-Prussian war, there was a short-lived return to the policy of the Second Empire; in Germany von Delbrück, the Minister of Finance, worked for the continued reduction of tariffs, and in 1873 duties on the importation of iron and shipbuilding materials were abolished. Gradually, however, the governments were won over by the appeals of farmers and industrialists, made more insistent by the crash of 1873 and the general fall in prices throughout the 1870s, and as each country retaliated against the others, so the tariffs began to rise.

In Germany duties on corn and manufactures were reimposed in 1880 and in France a tariff law of 1881 established mild Protection for industry, although not for the farmer. Russian tariffs rose sharply in the 1880s, and by 1887 they had become extremely high in Italy. In 1891 a referendum in Switzerland produced a vote of 220,000 against 159,000 in favour of heavier duties, and in 1894 the return of an agriculturalist majority in the Swedish *Riksdag* ensured a return to Protection. The principal method of adjustment was still by treaty with individual countries, but in 1892 the French Chamber placed restrictions on this by establishing a minimum rate for commercial friends and maximum rates for others. In 1902 a new German law decreed a high minimum rate on agricultural goods, and although raw materials were still to enter free, the rate was gradually to increase on manufactured articles according to the degree to which they were finished.

By 1914 only Great Britain and a few of the smaller countries such as Belgium and the Netherlands still clung to Free Trade. It is true that ideas were at work for bringing an end to these tariff walls that threaded their way across the Continent. Bismarck had once discussed with the French ambassador the possibility of a central European Customs Union which might include France, and in 1897 the German Emperor William II suggested to Tsar Nicholas II the formation of a general European union against American competition. But nothing came of these schemes and the continuing economic conflict was often bitter. The trade treaty between Germany and Russia in 1894 was almost like a peace settlement after a period of keen tariff war. The passing of the Italian tariff law in 1887 involved the denunciation of a French commercial treaty, and the sharp drop in trade between the two countries was translated into terms of political animosity. 'France must now forget the history of the supremacy and influence which she once possessed on this side of the Alps,' declared the Italian premier Crispi,[1] and the French *chargé d'affaires* at Rome discovered that Italian children believed firmly that the Italians had defeated the French at the battle of Solferino in 1859! Thus a general tendency towards collectivism did not necessarily unify; if anything, it created a more highly charged atmosphere of rivalry in which the issues became ever more dangerously complex.

[1] Quoted from D. Mack Smith: *Italy 1860–1960.*

2. *The world of Socialism*

'Liberalism is but the accomplice of demagogy and serves, very often unconsciously, to drive a road for it and often to level it most conveniently. Liberalism shares the fate of all forerunners. Once the true lord appears, it is almost impossible to find any traces of the forerunner. Nothing is further from liberalism than demagogy; this latter is categorical, tyrannical in its ends as in its choice of means.' Naturally these remarks made by Metternich earlier in the century were uttered from a very different standpoint from that of Karl Marx; yet in their belief that the victory of liberalism would only mark a temporary stage on the road to the rule of the masses Metternich and Marx were in striking agreement. The decades preceding the outbreak of the first World War confronted the established society with a threat far more serious than anything before, since the multiplication in the numbers of industrial workers greatly increased their power of collective resistance, and there developed a considerable corpus of Socialist philosophy imbued with a keen sense of political realism and intellectual analysis quite remote from the Utopian excitement of the barricades of 1830 and 1848. For the Socialists there was, however, one weakness in this new precision in the definition of revolutionary aims in that it tended to sharpen the points of difference between the various groups.

The two major forces at work at this time were Anarchism and Marxism. The essence of Anarchism was a hatred for the State as a political organization; the Anarchist ideal was a loose federation of small communities in which the natural goodness of man would allow the individual to enjoy a full personal development. 'All exercise of power perverts and all submission to authority humiliates,' wrote Bakunin, who had taken up the leadership of the movement again after his escape from Siberia in 1861. Anarchism, in fact, despite its more modern and extensive organization, still retained a good deal of an outmoded Utopianism, and the terrorist methods of its more extreme supporters were reminiscent of the individual acts of violence of earlier revolutionaries. Indeed, between 1881 and 1901, they singled out the political Heads of State with a remarkable pertinacity; a Russian Tsar, a President of the French Republic, an Empress of Austria, a King of Italy, and a President of the United States, all figured in their record of assassination, a performance at which the crowned heads of Europe could hardly fail to be impressed.

One of the more positive features of Anarchism was that it had its attractions for a rural as well as an industrial society. In Russia the Populist movement appealed strongly to the Slavophil outlook,[1] since it seized on the collective unit of the village community, the *mir*, as an essentially Russian phenomenon on which future society could be based. 'History is fond of her grandchildren,' said Chernyshevsky, one of the great exponents of the movement, 'for it offers them the marrow of the bones which the previous generation had hurt its hand in breaking,' and to the Populists it seemed that the development of the *mir* as a local unit of industry and agriculture might enable Russia to by-pass both the horrible living conditions of mass-industrialism and the dictatorship of a new technical bureaucracy. Their propaganda was successful in recruiting a large number of enthusiasts who set out in 1873–4 on a great mission to the provinces to educate the peasantry for their new role, but these *narodniki*—men of the people—soon encountered the same mistrust and lack of comprehension among the peasants that the earlier reforming landowners had experienced, and this, coupled with the hostility of the government, who regarded the whole thing as highly subversive, led the more extreme members to fall back on a policy of sporadic violence.

In France the memory of the June days in 1848 and the Paris Commune of 1871 lent considerable emotional support to Anarchism and its impatient insistence on direct action, but with the growth of industry the movement was to become affiliated with a new doctrine of Syndicalism. First inspired by Fernand Pelloutier, then developed into a positive philosophy by Georges Sorel in his *Réflexions sur la violence*, published in 1905, Syndicalism desired a pluralist type of industrial organization in which federations of trade unions would replace the bourgeois parliamentary system. The Syndicalists were consistent in refusing to fight for their aim through the existing organs of government, and their principal weapon in the class struggle was to be the general strike through which the whole community could be brought to heel.

In Spain both the peasantry and the industrial workers were strongly influenced by Anarchism. It was particularly active during the unrest of 1873 and although General Pavia temporarily banned all working-class organizations when he seized power in the following year, the movement continued to grow in the rural districts and gained a hold on the trade unions of Catalonia, later to be reinforced by Syndicalist theory. In 1892 peasantry marched into Jerez and had to be dispersed by cavalry, and in 1909 the proclamation of a general strike in the north led to a week of civil war in which there was fierce street-fighting in Barcelona. The working-class movement in Spain remained strongly Anarchist long after the movement had faded away in the rest of Europe; it was dominant in the *Confederacion Nacional del Trabajo,* which by 1919 had 700,000 members, and although it never made its peace with other left-wing movements it was to play a considerable part in the resistance of the Spanish government to the advance of General Franco in the Spanish Civil war of 1936–9.[1]

The gulf between the aims and methods of Anarchism and Marxism was one of the most significant aspects of the Socialist movement in the 1880s and 1890s. Anarchism wished to destroy the State at once; Marxism accepted the State as a necessary evil until the final stage of social development had been reached. Anarchism believed in a policy of terroristic violence; Marxism regarded this as futile, a last sputter of revolutionary romanticism. Anarchism was prepared to accept the peasantry as a fundamental force of revolution; Marxism looked unequivocally to the workers who would take over the development of a bourgeois economy—although Marx himself towards the end of his life was beginning to wonder about the role of the peasantry in a Russian uprising.[2]

The argument between the two sides raged throughout the remainder of the nineteenth century. This was a time when the improved communications and the involuntary closeness of relations throughout the world had encouraged the growth of a whole range of organizations devoted to international cooperation; the Red Cross Convention had been signed in 1864; a Postal Union was formed ten years later, and an Inter-Parliamentary Union in 1889, as well as various pacifist associations, and in 1899 and 1907 the Powers themselves held conferences at The Hague, where it was agreed that a Court of International Arbitration should be established, although efforts to achieve an all-round reduction in armaments were unsuccessful. It was consequently hardly surprising that a Socialist organization should develop along the same lines; in 1864 Marx was largely responsible for the founding of the International Working Men's Association, the First International, whose congresses continued to meet until it was finally dissolved in 1876 at Philadelphia. In 1889 this was succeeded by the Second International which remained a significant Socialist organization until 1914.

[1] See pp. 435–7.   [2] For the general doctrine of Marxism see pp. 109–10.

The seriousness of the split between the Anarchists and the Marxists was naturally emphasized in the congresses of both the First and the Second International. Indeed, the First was virtually destroyed by it, but although the meetings of the Second in the 1890s were often hampered by the virulence of the dispute, the Marxist element predominated largely through the discipline of the German party—the *Sozialdemokratische Partei Deutschlands* (SPD)—under Wilhelm Liebknecht and August Bebel.

There were, however, other issues of disagreement that were eventually to shatter the effective political strength of the Second International. The Marxists rejected the theories and tactics of the Anarchists; on the other hand, although they were for the moment prepared to accept the continued existence of the State, they could not countenance any form of gradualism. This was the hope of moderate Socialists, who believed that their ends could be attained by a policy of cooperation with liberals through Parliaments and negotiation by trade unions, an idea that was naturally anathema to the Marxists who saw that it would win the working class over to the acceptance of a society which would still be fundamentally bourgeois. The hopes of the gradualists were greatly strengthened by the growth of social and industrial legislation improving working and living conditions throughout most of the Continent. In Germany Bismarck's laws for social insurance in the 1880s,[1] in France the limitation of the working day to ten hours in 1900 and the enforcement of a six-day week in 1906, in Austria the establishment of factory inspection in 1883 and the general regulation of industry in 1907, and in Great Britain the extension of earlier Factory Acts followed by the Liberal administration of 1906, all had their counterpart in smaller countries such as Switzerland, Belgium, and the Netherlands. Many of the concessions by the governments were grudgingly made, and the alternation of boom and slump continued to stimulate the class antagonism in the labour disputes of these years and lent strength to the Marxist thesis; yet the Social Democrats remained deeply concerned over the growing attraction of gradualism. 'The idea of a social democrat must not be a trade union secretary, but a tribune of the people,' warned Lenin in his pamphlet *What is to be done?* in 1902. 'A trade union policy of the working class is simply a bourgeois policy for the working class.'

It was in those countries where parliamentary practice was strongly established that gradualism made its greatest appeal. The English trade

[1] See p. 285.

unionists were incorrigibly bourgeois in Marxist eyes, an idea epitomized by an occasion at the London congress of the International in
1896 when the English president threatened to end an Anarchist distur-
bance by summoning the police. In France there were inevitably a whole
variety of political sects, and while the Marxist element stood firm
under Jules Guesde, there were many such as Paul Brousse and later
Jean Jaurès and Viviani, who were prepared to work through the party
machinery in the Chamber, and in 1898 a French Socialist, Alexandre
Millerand, actually became Minister of Commerce under Waldeck-
Rousseau. Similarly, at the beginning of the twentieth century Socialists and liberals were cooperating in the Italian Parliament as well as in
Belgium over the establishment of universal suffrage. In Germany the
tendency was less marked, partly because the deputies in the Reichstag
had little control over the actions of their government, partly because,
in contrast to France, the German Socialist movement was monolithic
in its structure and predominantly Marxist. Nevertheless, it was a
German, Eduard Bernstein, who in 1899 produced a positive doctrine
of gradualism in a formal criticism of Marx's arguments. This attempt
to revise the basic tenets of the faith was strongly resisted by Karl
Kautsky and its rejection by the German Social Democrats was duly
ratified at the Amsterdam congress of the International in 1904.

Another issue which exercised the minds of the International during
these years was the question of their attitude towards a European war.
Fundamentally they were in agreement that the idea of such a conflict
in which the working classes of different nations would be forced to
slaughter each other was utterly abhorrent; yet, when the extremists
urged that the governments of the Powers should all be immobilized
at the moment of outbreak by a general strike and by a unanimous refusal to vote war credits and to serve in the armed forces, various nationalities found that under certain circumstances they would have to align
themselves with their governments. 'If Russia, the champion of cruelty
and barbarity, the enemy of all human culture were to attack Germany,'
said the German Bebel in 1891 '. . . we are as much and more interested
than those who stand at the head of Germany, and we would resist
Russia, for a Russian victory means the defeat of social democracy.'
The conflict with the submerged nationalities was also reflected in his
remark in 1897: 'A good comrade who only knows German is more
use than an incompetent Polish-speaking one.' Similarly, at an Austrian
Social Democrat congress in 1899, a German Austrian remarked:
'German will remain a language of culture and communication whether

we like it or not and regardless of the likes and dislikes of our Czech comrades.' And in the countries where gradualism was an active force, Socialists who were fighting to win the votes of a parliamentary electorate had to be even more outspoken in their patriotism. 'We shall at no moment forget', announced Millerand in France, 'that at the same time as being internationalists we are Frenchmen and patriots.'[1]

National emotions were one serious obstacle in the preparations for averting the outbreak of war, but there was another in the very doctrine of Marxism itself. Marx and Engels had declared categorically that the whole course of historical development made a vast capitalist war inevitable, indeed essential, for it was through this catastrophe that the bourgeois governments would topple and the dictatorship of the proletariat emerge. Yet for the men who would have to endure the horror of general war on the Continent the prospect was so appalling that despite their national differences they continued to think in terms of the impossibility of such a contravention of the brotherhood of the working class, and at the congress of 1913 at Basle, amid a frenzy of wishful thinking, they made a solemn affirmation of faith at a great gathering in the old cathedral of the city.

Many of the divisions within the International had consisted of a struggle between the Marxists and their opponents. There was, however, at the same time a considerable debate within the Marxist party itself over revolutionary methods. This finally came to a head in 1903 at a Russian Social Democrat congress which began in Brussels and then, owing to the attentions of the Belgian police, had to be transferred to the Tottenham Court Road in London. Under the presidency of George Plekhanov, a former Russian Populist who had turned to Marxism, the meeting was to debate the statutes of the party and at once issue was joined between Lenin and Martov.

Lenin whose real name was Vladimir Ilyitch Ulyanov was the son of a school inspector at Simbirsk. His work as a student of law at the University of Kazan had been interrupted owing to the mistrust of the authorities after the execution of his elder brother for participating in a plot to assassinate Tsar Alexander III. He turned, instead, to reading Karl Marx, whose first volume of *Das Kapital* had been translated into Russian as early as 1868—to Marx's surprise—and when he was eventually allowed to qualify in 1891, he devoted the next four years to the dissemination of Socialist propaganda. This led to his arrest and a spell

[1] This selection of quotations is taken from *The Second International 1889–1914*, by James Joll.

of exile in Siberia, where he was able to continue his studies, and shortly after his release in 1900 he left Russia for the greater freedom of the west. By the time of the Brussels congress Lenin, as he now called himself, was thirty-three years of age, a persuasive speaker, a skilful antagonist in argument, and utterly dedicated to the cause of revolutionary Socialism.

The clash over the first clause of the party statutes was due to Lenin's insistence on the restriction of membership to those who accepted the party programme and who supported it 'both materially and by personal participation in one of its organizations'. His conception of the party, in fact, was of a disciplined *élite* whose authority was essential for the accomplishment of the revolution in Russia—an attitude which possibly owed something to his training as a lawyer and to the hereditary influence of his Volga German mother. Martov, on the other hand, wished to frame the clause so as to include the milder liberal elements who merely sympathized, and it was his motion that won the day. Later, however, some of Martov's supporters left the congress, and Lenin's group, who were thus able to secure the election of their candidates to leading positions in the party, became known as the *Bolsheviki* (the men of the majority).

Despite this temporary victory Martov had considerable backing in the Socialist world from Axelrod and Trotsky, as well as Kautsky and Rosa Luxemburg among the Germans, while Plekhanov, although he had supported Lenin at the congress, could not agree with him entirely. Indeed, the *Mensheviki* (the so-called men of the minority) felt themselves sufficiently strong to denounce the Bolshevik Central Committee, and as other issues arose, so the split widened. The Mensheviks were absolutely orthodox Marxists in that Russia's peculiar difficulty in their eyes was that the bourgeois revolution which must, according to their theory of history, precede the proletarian, had not yet taken place. Thus they believed that since the historical process was inexorable, their immediate role must be to facilitate this bourgeois revolution—hence Martov's wider definition of party membership; then a long interval of time must elapse during which the victory of the bourgeois would create the conditions from which their own downfall would automatically follow. The emergence of a large proletariat was the essential factor for the Mensheviks and they did not envisage the peasantry playing an effective part at any stage of the revolutionary process.

To Lenin, however, the very peculiarity of the situation in Russia demanded a different technique which he outlined in *Two Tactics of*

Sound Democracy in the Democratic Revolution in 1905. First, he recognized the existence of a revolutionary element among some, at least, of the peasants. Second, he felt that this possible reinforcement for the proletariat might be lost if the bourgeois revolution were allowed to consolidate itself, and although he clearly emphasized the distinction between the two revolutions, he declared that the second must follow upon the first almost at once. As soon as the Russian *bourgeoisie* had embarked upon their revolution against Tsarist absolutism, the proletariat, aided by some of the peasantry, must capture it for themselves. 'We stand for uninterrupted revolution,' he wrote in an article in 1905. 'We shall not stop half-way.'

Thus, in a sense, the doctrine of the Bolsheviks was as much a revision of Marxism in the direction of accelerating the revolutionary process as Eduard Bernstein's proposals had been in the direction of gradualism. Yet, of all the schools of thought that divided the Socialist world, the emergence of Bolshevism was to have the most startling effect—and this mainly because of the original issue that had split the Russian congress of 1903. For, unlike any of the other sects, Lenin's creation of a disciplined *élite* gave them a striking power in 1917 out of all proportion to their numbers, which was to enable them to accomplish the second revolution within eight months of the outbreak of the first.

21

SOURCES OF NATIONAL TENSION

1. The new realism

'FACTS, not emotional pleas,' wrote Émile Zola, when he was making the preliminary notes for his novel *Germinal*, published in 1885. These words sum up a remarkable change of outlook in the last half of the nineteenth century, a change undoubtedly stimulated by the emergence of a modern technical society; in place of the romantic imagination which had inspired both art and revolution, the new trend was set by a clear sense of scientific realism and there were few sides of life that were not to be deeply affected by it.

Germinal itself was one of a series of twenty novels in which Zola traced the influence of heredity and environment on two branches of a family, the Rougons and the Macquarts, observing the effects of corruption, poverty, and disease with a dispassionate ruthlessness. This was something more than a photographic technique; it was an attempt to turn the writer's desk into a sociological laboratory. The same desire for a careful documentation of life is to be found in Flaubert's *Madame Bovary*, published as early as 1857, and was the basis, later, of the novels of the de Goncourt brothers and the short stories of Guy de Maupassant. It was as a consequence of this new mood that the translation of the great Russian novelists made such an impact on France in the 1880s. 'Quel peintre et quel psychologue!' wrote Flaubert to Turgenev in thanking him for a copy of Tolstoy's *War and Peace*, and although the Russian novels were less harsh in tone than the French, the delicacy of human observation in the great works of Tolstoy, Turgenev, and Dostoevsky certainly made them part of this new school.

On the stage the predominating influence came from Scandinavia. *A Doll's House*, *Ghosts*, *The Wild Duck*, and *An Enemy of the People*, written by the Norwegian Henrik Ibsen in the 1870s and 1880s, were set against a modern bourgeois background and eschewed such artificial devices as the soliloquy. Neither he nor the Swede August Strindberg, however, was content to remain a detached spectator, Ibsen constantly attacking the complacency and hypocrisy of middle-class respectability,

Strindberg obsessed with the tensions of family life. In contrast to this, the plays of the Russian Anton Tchekov—*The Seagull, Uncle Vanya,* and *The Cherry Orchard,* all written at about the turn of the century— simply suggest an overwhelming sense of acceptance and resignation, although as drama they too depend on a power of wry observation. All three writers were linked by a common attitude towards their art and it is significant that Tchekov had been trained as a doctor and that Strindberg should devote a good deal of his time to chemical research.

The same swing away from romanticism was to be discerned in other spheres. In France a new school of poets who called themselves the Parnassiens shunned all forms of high-flown phraseology, insisting on simple concrete images. In painting, a new technique known after 1874 as Impressionism attempted a scientific approach to the problem of conveying a sense of light. Like the playwrights, these painters—Manet, Monet, Renoir, Pissarro, Degas, and Sisley—tended to use everyday scenes as their subject matter, and were to create one of the great periods of French art, although their work was recognized abroad, particularly in Germany, long before it was accepted in France.

This attitude, which at a popular level found expression in the vogue for the science fiction of Jules Verne and, later, H. G. Wells, was also reflected in various forms of intellectual activity. The study of history was becoming more and more dependent upon the examination of the archives; the *Cambridge Modern History* edited by Lord Acton, the *Dictionary of National Biography* edited by Leslie Stephen, and the massive works of Ernest Lavisse, Alfred Rambaud, and Gabriel Hano-taux pointed to a growing professionalism, while Jacob Burckhardt's *Civilization of the Renaissance in Italy,* published in 1860, suggested a new comprehensiveness of approach. At the same time there were serious attempts to promote economics and sociology to the level of exact sciences—as, for example, in the work of the Germans Max Weber and Werner Sombart on the development of capitalism, in Fréderic Le Play's analysis of family life in Europe, in Charles Booth's survey of living conditions in London, and in Sidney and Beatrice Webb's research into the history of the working class.

This awareness of the potentiality of scientific method in its application to the arts and society was only one aspect of the change. It was the actual message of the scientists that had the greatest consequences. The new theories of the time seemed to place the whole conception of mankind in an utterly changed perspective. For many years the researches of the geologists had clearly suggested that the earth had been in existence for millions of years, contrary to the literal interpretation of the Old Testament already coming under the critical scrutiny of German Biblical scholarship, and with the publication of Darwin's *Origin of Species* in 1859, followed by his *Descent of Man* in 1871, the biologists finally brought the whole issue out into the open. Darwin in attempting to explain the diversity and development of species propounded a theory in which the emergence of man in the world was not due to a cataclysmic act of divine creation, but simply to a process of selection through a relentless struggle for survival. This sense of the haphazard was strengthened—among the experts, at least—by the revolutionary notions of the mathematicians and the physicists when, early in the twentieth century, Albert Einstein's theory of relativity added a fourth dimension of time to matter and energy, suggesting a continuous process of change.

Of all these intellectual developments it was Darwin's theories with their implication that man was simply the product of the law of the jungle that really fired the public imagination and led to the long dispute between the scientists and the theologians. But this was not all. It so happened that at about the same time the archaeologists were beginning to publish their discoveries of substantial traces of hitherto unknown civilizations. Throughout the nineteenth century work had continued on the Egypt of the Pharaohs, assisted by the deciphering of the hieroglyphics on the Rosetta stone. Then in Mesopotamia in the 1840s Henry Layard uncovered the cities of Nineveh and Nimrud, and the deciphering of cuneiform opened the door to a knowledge of the Assyrians, which in turn established that there had been a still earlier Sumerian civilization at the mouths of the Tigris and the Euphrates. In 1872 a German business man, Heinrich Schliemann, discovered not merely the site of Troy, but a whole series of cities one upon another, and his later excavations at Mycenae were afterwards to lead Sir Arthur Evans on to the discovery of the Minoan civilization with its centre at Knossos in Crete. At the same time there was hazier evidence of others —the Hittites, the Ceylonese, the Incas west of the Andes, the Maya in Yucatan, and the ruins of Angkor lost in the forests of Indo-China.

The glimpse which these discoveries gave of a history of mankind far richer and more complex than had previously been imagined naturally suggested that forms of human society developed, flourished, and decayed in accordance with the Darwinian theories of the struggle for survival. This did not deter several thinkers from continuing to discern a sense of purpose in the history of the world. In Great Britain, now at the height of her prosperity, Herbert Spencer considered that the theory of evolution in its application to society encouraged a belief in progress, while the Russian Kropotkin in a series of articles in the 1890s stressed the essential element of cooperation and mutual aid in humanity's successful survival. Alternatively, it was natural that Darwin's hypothesis should appeal to Karl Marx, who had been living in the direst poverty in London since 1849, working on his interpretation of history as a class struggle,[1] and when the first volume of *Das Kapital* was completed in 1867 he proposed to dedicate it to Darwin who, however, was careful to refuse.

Utterly different though the social aims and assumptions of these three men may have been, they did all nevertheless share a certain optimism in envisaging a positive goal towards which mankind was evolving. For others, however, the conclusions to be drawn were pessimistic. Among the most significant of these was the son of a German pastor, Friedrich Nietzsche, who at an early age became Professor of Classical Philology at the University of Basle. The basis of his philosophy, gradually developed in a series of works published in the 1870s and 1880s, was a feeling of despair at the meaningless process of change in the universe. To Nietzsche it seemed that the only hope for man was to impose his will upon this chaos by violence, and in place of Christianity whose doctrine of humility and love he despised as inculcating a 'slave-morality', he postulated the rule of certain individuals whose ruthless strength qualified them to govern the rest. 'Formerly one spoke of God when contemplating distant seas. But today I enjoin you to say: superman. . . .'

A similar note of despair was to be heard much later in Oswald Spengler's *Der Untergang des Abendlandes* (*The Decline of the West*) which, although completed in 1914, was not published until after the first World War, when its pessimism was entirely in tune with the disillusionment of German intellectuals. 'Man is a beast of prey,' wrote Spengler. 'For me humanity is a zoological quantity. I see no progress, no goal, no way of humanity—except in the heads of western philistines who believe in progress.' The only pattern that he observed was a cycle of world cultures, each passing through a series of phases from spring to winter, and the conclusion which he drew was that the western democracies had reached the final stage of their decline and that the time was ripe for the emergence of a new Caesarism.

This rejection of any idea of rational progress was matched by other

[1] See p. 109.

aspects of scientific advance. The beginnings of the study of psychology, the behaviourist theories of William McDougall, the work on conditioned reflexes by Ivan Pavlov in Russia, the new techniques of psycho-analysis developed by Sigmund Freud, Karl Jung, and Alfred Adler, the experiments in hypnotism carried out by Charcot in Paris, all threw a new light on the extent to which human action was dependent upon the emotional and the irrational.

Thus scientific realism had almost come full circle. Like early nineteenth-century romanticism, this stress on instinct and intuition manifested itself in a variety of forms. It encouraged the concentration on the self, as in the excesses of the Decadents in their exploration of every kind of sensation during the *fin de siècle* period, and it played its part in inspiring the elusive hints and emotive images of the Symbolists, the school of writers who succeeded the Parnassiens. It lent an extraordinary significance to Raskolnikoff, the character whom Dostoevsky created in his novel *Crime and Punishment*—the student who commits a murder to prove to himself that he is great enough to be above the rules of conventional morality. It encouraged the growth of the philosophy of the absurd and the unpredictable within the general systems of thought known as existentialism. The desire to plumb the depths of the subconscious led to the development of Surrealism, a new movement in art and writing, which the originators described as 'the dictation of thought in the absence of all control exercised by the reason and outside all aesthetic and moral preoccupations', and although their pictures sometimes appeared almost light-hearted, they suggested more often a delving into the darker sides of the mind, the stirring of a muddy pool.

2. Nationalism in central and eastern Europe

'The wars of peoples will be more terrible than those of kings', said Winston Churchill in the House of Commons in 1901, and indeed the cult of the irrational was to lend itself to something far more sinister than the encouragement of an erratic individualism. A new ferocity of emotion took possession of extreme racial and national movements, playing some part in the ultimate disaster of 1914 and opening the way for the new Caesarism of the inter-war years with its shrill emphasis on the power of the group and on the weakness of liberalism and intellectualism.

In 1894 a French army officer, Captain Dreyfus, was charged with selling military secrets to Germany and the debate over his guilt, complicated by the fact that he was the only Jew on the General Staff, raged throughout France for more than ten years.[1] In 1912 Leonardo da Vinci's *Mona Lisa* was stolen from the Louvre by an Italian determined that the picture should be returned to its country of origin. These are only two instances that point to the heightened sense of pride and antagonism in the years before the first World War, but it was essentially in central and eastern Europe that the theory of the struggle for survival now gave the most ambitious turn to these emotions. The effect was to be seen on subject and dominant peoples alike. On the one hand, it lent force to the small groups still partly submerged under Habsburg, Hohenzollern, and Romanov rule, and in the Balkan countries whose national evolution was not yet complete; on the other, it led the governments to impose a far greater uniformity within their frontiers, while at the same time the conflicting doctrines of pan-Germanism and pan-Slavism aimed at a radical revision of those frontiers which far outran the more cautious aspirations of the professional diplomats.

Some four years before the publication of Darwin's *Origin of Species*, a Frenchman, Arthur de Gobineau, had published his *Essai sur l'inéga-lité des races humaines*, in which he gave a precise formulation to racialist ideas that had previously been no more than a vague Romantic notion. Gobineau's fundamental assumption was the superiority of the white over the black races and of the Aryan people among the whites. The yellow races Gobineau explained away as an unfortunate attempt on God's part to create the white. 'Évidemment le Créateur n'a voulu faire qu'une ébauche.' This superiority of the Aryan involved among other things a new interpretation of history, for Gobineau saw the decline of the Roman Empire as the collapse of an unworthy Latin world before the revitalizing onrush of the Nordic tribes—a conception which is still implicit in many German history books.

The natural right of a group to express its will to power, a mystical patriotism and a racial pride encouraging a contempt for the Slavs and a hatred for the Jews—these were the principal themes of German nationalist writing in the years before the first World War. In 1874 Heinrich von Treitschke became professor of history at the University of Berlin and, although a Saxon himself, never ceased to proclaim the glory of the Prussian hegemony over the rest of Germany and the right of the State to demand the sacrifice of the individual in war. 'He must renounce his whole ego for the sake of the great patriotic idea.

[1] See p. 283.

Therein lies the moral sublimity of war.' The series of operas that Richard Wagner composed around the *Nibelungenlied* were a musical panegyric to the German race, and when Wagner wished to explain how the descendants of Siegfried had until recently been surpassed by the peoples of the west, he wrote: 'we should seek to take earnest account of this [degeneration] if we wish to explain the decay of the German folk which is now exposed without defence to the penetration of the Jews.' The same anti-Semitism is to be found in the writings of Houston Stewart Chamberlain, an Englishman who adopted Germany as his country and married Wagner's daughter Eva. His *Foundations of the Nineteenth Century* was devoted to inveighing against the mixing of blood and to exalting German greatness. 'And because the German soul is indissolubly bound up with the German tongue,' he wrote in a letter to the Emperor William II in 1901, 'the higher development of mankind is bound up with Germany, a mighty Germany spreading far across the earth the sacred heritage of her language, affirming herself everywhere and imposing herself on others.' With Eugen Dühring the argument is even more strongly anti-Semitic, but concentrating on Germany's need 'to free herself from the curse of English economic theory under the firm of Adam Smith, Ricardo, Malthus, Stuart Mill, Cobden' by the establishment of Protection and State control.

The outcome of this more fanatical form of nationalism was twofold. At a governmental level it encouraged the imposition of a policy of germanization on the non-German people within the Reich. In Slesvig, and in Alsace and Lorraine, known as the Reichsland directly under the authority of the Emperor, this was largely a matter of the acquisition of business interests and the use of the German language in schools and law courts. In the Polish provinces an official commission for colonization—the *Ansiedlungskommission*—first established by Bismarck in 1886 and later assisted by the *Deutscher Ostmarkverein*, stimulated an influx of German settlers. This had the effect of reinforcing the position of the German upper class who held some 59% of the great estates in Posen, West Prussia, and Upper Silesia, although the total Polish population of the provinces remained a growing challenge, rising from 67% in 1867 to 71% in 1910.

Various other patriotic associations operated at an unofficial level, although not without influence on the government. The Colonial League, founded in 1887, the Navy League, the All-German Association, which later became the Pan-German League, the writings of Friedrich Lange and Karl Lamprecht, all preached the same fundamental doctrine of German greatness and of the need for all peoples of Germanic origin to be included within the frontiers of the Reich. Pan-Germanism with its racial assumptions went far beyond the claims of *Grossdeutschland*, and in the years immediately preceding the first World War became far more specific in its demands, as in the work of Otto Tannenberg and Friedrich von Gerhardi. 'Our aim is the creation of a powerful, world-embracing German empire,' wrote Eduard Weber in 1913, '. . . if England stands in the way, then let the cannon speak!'

This intensified sense of nationalism was by no means restricted to Germany. It was becoming increasingly active among the subject peoples on the periphery of the Russian dominions, at first largely cultural, then more political in its expression, as the Tsarist government attempted to counter it with a policy of russification.

In Finland the growing influence from St. Petersburg was already noticeable in the last years of the reign of Alexander III; later, when in 1898 the appointment of General Bobrikov as governor-general was followed by the drafting of Finnish recruits into the Russian army and of Russian officers into the forces of the Grand Duchy, Finnish local authorities refused to comply. By 1903 Bobrikov had taken over most of the administration of the country and the constitution had been suspended. Bobrikov was assassinated in 1904 and the short-lived revolution in Russia in 1905[1] did bring Finland some relief, when in the following year the old Diet of four Estates was replaced by a single-chamber Assembly elected on a wide franchise for both sexes, the first instance of votes for women in any country in Europe. The Tsarist government, however, continued to press on with its policy of russification. This only served to encourage the growth of Finnish nationalism, which had been still further excited by the success of the Norwegians, when in 1905 the Swedish *Riksdag* agreed to the repeal of the union and a separate Kingdom of Norway was created under Haakon VII, a prince of the Danish house.[2]

In the lands on the south coast of the Baltic there had been a considerable revival of local Estonian, Latvian, and Lithuanian cultures. Here, however, the domination of the German upper class over Estonians and Latvians and of the Polish over the Lithuanians inspired as much antagonism as the fact of Russian rule. The implications of these grievances were thus social as well as political, and local Social Democrat parties took the lead in the various separatist movements.

[1] See pp. 289–93.   [2] See Genealogical table, p. 482.

But the German and Polish upper classes too were hit by the policy of russification. Russian became the official language in the schools, which in 1886 were placed under the Russian Ministry of Education; the German university of Dorpat became a Russian university renamed Yuryev, and at the same time the Orthodox Church embarked on a great campaign for expansion in the Baltic lands.

In Poland the Russian government had hoped to blanket national feeling by means of industrial development, but the effect of this was lost through the recurrent slumps and the decline of agricultural prosperity.[1] To the south there were growing demands for autonomy among the Georgians, the Volga Tartars, and the Rumanians of Bessarabia, while in the Caucasus Russia found herself actually working in cooperation with the Turkish Sultan in repressing the Armenians. This was also a period of fierce anti-Semitic legislation by the Russian government. The local *pogroms* which followed the assassination of Alexander II in 1881 were succeeded by a series of enactments against the five million Jews who lived within Russia, excluding them from many professions, restricting their attendance at secondary schools and universities, and often expelling them from their place of residence; and it was hardly surprising, in view of the growing anti-Semitism throughout Europe at this time, that the Jews, under the leadership of an Austrian Jew, Theodor Herzl, whose *Der Judenstaat* was published in 1896, should themselves contrive to form the movement known as Zionism which dreamed of a national home in the region of Palestine.

Nationalism in its most uninhibited form was to be seen in the Balkans, where the newly formed states were free to indulge in all their patriotic rivalry. The creation of Bulgaria after the Congress of Berlin in 1878[2] awoke a fierce animosity among the neighbouring peoples, since both Serbia and Greece feared Bulgarian expansion into regions still Turkish which they hoped eventually to gain for themselves. Among the Serbs there was, too, the desire to acquire Bosnia, and although their dislike of the Catholic Croats made this difficult of realization, a movement of reconciliation aiming at a federal southern Slav state—Yugoslavia—had been initiated as early as 1861 by the Catholic bishop of Zagreb, Strossmayer.

This growth of national aspirations in the Balkans naturally exercised an enormous attraction for the subject peoples under Habsburg rule, and here there was to be a marked difference of governmental attitude between the two sections of the Dual Monarchy. When in 1868 auto-

[1] See p. 251.   [2] See p. 301.

nomy was granted to the Croats, including the use of the Croatian language in the Diet at Zagreb, it seemed as if the Magyars might be prepared to grant their subjects terms as good as they had themselves received from Vienna, but in the following years they began to impose an overwhelming policy of magyarization in political, economic, and cultural spheres on Poles, Slovaks, Transylvanians, and even on Croats, despite the agreement of 1868. In contrast to this enforced uniformity the Austrian government was moving towards greater liberal reforms extending the franchise and offering wider representation to its subject peoples.[1] 'Only by cultivating the Slavs can Russian influence be paralyzed,' wrote the Crown Prince Rudolph a few years before his death at Mayerling in 1889, and Austrian mildness was a conscious attempt to find some answer to the attraction of Russian pan-Slavism.

This movement in Russia was parallel in some ways to pan-Germanism, but whereas the pan-Germans thought in terms of conquest, the Russian pan-Slavs saw themselves as the liberators of subject Slav peoples. Like the pan-Germans in Germany, they did not actually represent official Russian policy, but their view was akin to the claim to a protectorate over Orthodox Christians under Turkish rule which had contributed to the outbreak of the Crimean war, and thus had a bearing on the Tsarist government's rivalry with the Habsburgs in the Balkans. Many of the Slavs themselves, however, had doubts about succumbing to the embrace of Russian protection, and in the years immediately preceding 1914 Russian pan-Slavs had developed a modified scheme known as Neo-Slavism, aiming at no more than close friendship between all Slav countries, including Austria-Hungary.

This certainly appeared less ominous and gave some encouragement to political groups in Austria who hoped for 'trialism', a reorganization of the Empire whereby the south Slavs might be promoted to equal partnership alongside the Germans and Magyars. The idea was supported by Francis Ferdinand,[2] the heir to the throne after Rudolph's death, yet even if he had lived to become Emperor, it is doubtful whether he could have won over the Germans and Magyars within his dominions who would have strongly resisted trialism. To the end, the future of the Habsburg Empire remained at the mercy of its own complexity, and amid the mounting tensions of eastern Europe it seems improbable that any lasting Habsburg solution would have been feasible. Ironically, it was the circumstances of Francis Ferdinand's death that precipitated the final collapse, for his assassination at Sarajevo in June

[1] See p. 287.   [2] See Genealogical table, p. 480.

1914 led indirectly to the outbreak of the first World War, and although the eventual destruction of the Russian, German, and Austrian empires could not automatically solve the problems of eastern Europe, it did mean that a solution to them must be sought along totally different lines.

3. Imperialism

Until the 1870s there were only five countries in Europe which held overseas possessions of any significant size—Great Britain, France, the Netherlands, Spain, and Portugal—and of these only two had made any substantial gains in the nineteenth century. France had fostered a considerable colonization of Algeria as a means of consolidating her hold there; in the 1840s she had laid claim to Tahiti and the Marquesas in the Pacific, and under Napoleon III had established interests in Africa and Indo-China.[1] British acquisitions had been far more extensive; in addition to the empire which had already been hers in 1815, Natal, Singapore, New Zealand, and Hong Kong had all been settled during subsequent decades, while imperial rule had been established over parts of Burma and large regions of the north-west of India. Of the other three, the Dutch, after losing the Cape to the British in the course of the Napoleonic war, now simply retained their possessions in the East Indies. Spain and Portugal had suffered great losses in South America[2] and now held only a fraction of their former empires—Spain in the Philippines, Cuba, San Domingo, and Porto Rico; Portugal in the African colonies of Angola and Mozambique, where her actual settlements did not reach far beyond the coast.

Although, as has been seen, these developments had had some bearing on international relations, their significance for European diplomacy had been largely peripheral. In contrast to this, the last decades of the nineteenth century saw an extraordinary intensification of national concern over the acquisition of colonies, which now came to occupy a central position in political negotiation. The most dramatic feature of this new period of expansion was the opening up of Africa, whose enormous territories were almost entirely shared out among European states in the space of about twenty years. A second feature was that the old colonial Powers were now joined by several new competitors—Germany, Italy, and Belgium in Africa, the United States and Germany in the race for the Pacific Islands, Russia and Japan in the demands for territorial and commercial concessions from the decadent Chinese empire—while the presence of oil in the Turkish dominions of the Middle East created a new source of rivalry among British, American, German, and Russian interests.

Few of these gains would have been possible or even desirable, had it not been for the recent advances in science and industry. Improved medical knowledge now enabled white men to spend prolonged spells in the tropics; with the development of light weapons, such as the machine-gun, comparatively small numbers of Europeans could shatter the resistance of local native peoples, and the new techniques of engineering and railway construction facilitated the exploitation of raw materials which would otherwise have been out of reach. All these factors were essential prerequisites, but they do not in themselves explain this remarkable acceleration in imperial enterprise.

The causes were extremely varied. Much of the exploration of Africa had been inspired by genuine scientific interest, coupled with missionary and humanitarian zeal to spread the Gospel and to stamp out the Arab slave trade. In an age in which colonialism has grown unpopular it is fashionable to treat these disinterested motives with a certain cynicism; yet it is a fact that in Africa, Madagascar, and the Pacific explorers and missionaries were active long before the diplomats had any interest in their whereabouts, and far from being political agents were sometimes a source of embarrassment to their own governments—as in the episode of Mr Pritchard on the island of Tahiti.[1]

A more commonly accepted explanation is that the scramble for territory was stimulated by the mounting economic competition between the countries of Europe, since a growing industrialism had created a demand for the rarer types of raw material that were not available in Europe. It has also been suggested that colonies would supply new markets and greater scope for emigration at a time when populations were rising sharply. None of these arguments, however, are decisive. The gaining of raw materials did not necessitate the acquisition of such vast territories; the tropical climate was unlikely to attract a large number of immigrant settlers; and if there were any hopes of developing new markets they were soon to be disappointed; even by 1913 Germany's trade with all her colonies amounted to no more than 0·5% of her total foreign commerce.

A more persuasive economic thesis was put forward in 1902 by J. A. Hobson in his book *Imperialism*, in which he claimed that the expansion

[1] See p. 93.

K

of empire was due to the need of financiers to find a new outlet for the investment of their surplus capital. British investments overseas, for example, rose from £785 million in 1871 to £3,500 million in 1911, and it was natural that an apparent link between capitalism and imperialism should be seized upon by Lenin whose pamphlet *Imperialism, the Highest Stage of Capitalism*, published in 1916, was largely based upon Hobson's book. Yet this argument, too, is fundamentally unsatisfactory.

A more detailed analysis of the figures for these years shows that the bulk of overseas investment was attracted to regions other than those seized by the Powers after 1870. The enormous increase already cited for Great Britain is largely explained by mounting investments in the United States, Canada, Australasia, India, and the South American countries. Similarly, although South African gold and Rhodesian copper offered good prospects, the total public and private investment in the whole of British, French, German, and Belgian territories between the Sahara and the frontier of northern Rhodesia amounted to no more than £237 million by the end of 1913. Naturally there were considerable economic advantages to be gained from certain imperial developments; yet the facts would not seem to suggest that they operated as a decisive influence in the shaping of this remarkable expansion of Europe throughout the world.

Indeed, the political moves of the governments in negotiating territorial frontiers and spheres of influence appear to have been based on a series of *ad hoc* decisions rather than any general principle. The regions of Africa, Asia, and the Pacific under debate offered a field for diplomatic manoeuvring which was no longer possible on the Continent, entangled as it was towards the end of the century in a network of alliance and counter-alliance. Strategic considerations tended to predominate. The opening of the Suez canal and her concern for the route to India drew Great Britain into Egypt and East Africa despite the greater economic significance of West Africa, while France hoped that the recruiting of native troops might bolster up her failing man-power; eventually, once the race was on, ambitions were often governed simply by the desire to prevent a rival from gaining an advantage. In fact, the most striking motive was irrational—the desire for prestige in which the new mass electorates and the popular press entered with enthusiasm. Sir John Seeley's lectures on *The Expansion of England* and the writings of Rudyard Kipling, the hunger of the French for *la gloire* after the humiliation of 1871, and the aspirations of the German Colonial League were all indications of this new fever; all were in accord with Treit-schke's remark in 1879 that 'every virile people had established colonial power'.

Bismarck himself had little interest in colonies and saw the race for empire purely from the point of view of its impact on continental politics. 'My map of Africa lies in Europe,' he said. 'Here lies Russia and here lies France and we are in the middle. That is my map of Africa.' Nowhere was this attitude more clearly demonstrated than in the African territories north of the Sahara. It was his encouragement that led France to annex Tunis in 1881, for by this means he hoped to lull the French into forgetting their loss of Alsace and Lorraine, and to create a lasting division between them and the Italians, who had hoped to gain Tunis for themselves. The French did not forget Alsace and Lorraine, but at least he was able to profit from the anger of the Italians with the Triple Alliance of Germany, Austria-Hungary, and Italy which was concluded in 1882.

At the same time Bismarck had been urging Great Britain on to the annexation of Egypt, which would certainly create bad feeling between the British and the French. The opening of the Suez canal—a French engineering project—in 1869 had introduced a new factor in the inter-national significance of Egypt. Throughout the century the British had been extremely suspicious of possible French designs on their route to India. This had partly governed their attitude towards Mehemet Ali in the 1830s,[1] and in 1875 it had been in order to forestall French financiers that Disraeli had bought up from the Egyptian Khedive Ismail seven-sixteenths of the shares in the Canal Company. The two countries, however, did cooperate in the following years in setting up a dual con-trol of Egyptian finances. Ismail, who had announced virtual bank-ruptcy, was deposed to be succeeded by his son Tewfik, and in 1882 a rising Egyptian nationalist movement under Arabi Pasha, determined to oust European influence, prompted the dispatch of an Anglo-French naval force to Alexandria. In the event, however, the British acted alone. The French premier, Freycinet, was defeated in the Chamber, fearful lest French forces should become too deeply involved far from home, and while the French fleet steamed away, the British bombarded Alexandria and after landing an army which defeated the Egyptians at Tel el Kebir on 13 September, occupied Cairo. Initially the British had had no intention of staying in Egypt, which never became formally a part of their empire; yet once they were in occupation, concern over the

[1] See p. 90.

control of the canal which had brought them in prevented them from leaving. This new acquisition naturally aroused the animosity of both France and Russia, and thus in the realm of diplomacy it was Bismarck who had made the principal gain.

South of the Sahara the penetration of the vast territories of the interior by British, French, and German explorers in the 1850s and 1860s was followed by the growth of claims to possession. In the 1870s the French were pushing inland through Senegal towards the upper Niger; de Brazza was exploring the regions to the north of the mouth of the Congo, and in 1883 French forces undertook the conquest of Madagascar. At the same time private British interests were developing on the lower Niger and in East Africa. In addition to this, there were three newcomers in the colonial field. In 1876 King Leopold of the Belgians formed an International African Association and employed H. M. Stanley to act for him in exploring the Congo basin, which Leopold hoped to develop as a personal concern, an aim which soon brought him into collision with the French and the Portuguese. In 1883 Italy took possession of Eritrea and in 1884 Germany suddenly embarked upon a bid for German colonies in South-west Africa, Togoland, the Cameroons, and East Africa. This startling change on Bismarck's part was still motivated by European considerations, since his aim was to furnish himself with grounds for a quarrel with Great Britain. He had two reasons for this. The first was based on the hope of forming a friendship with France, who bitterly resented the British occupation of Egypt. The second was due to his fear that on the death of William I, which could not be far distant, his son Frederick who was married to Queen Victoria's daughter would embark on a liberal pro-British policy. 'When we entered upon a colonial policy,' he explained years later, 'we had to reckon with a long reign of the Crown Prince. During this reign English influence would have been dominant. To prevent this we had to embark upon a colonial policy because it was popular and conveniently adapted to bring us into conflict with England at any given moment.'

The outcome of this new period of competing imperial aims was a Congress held at Berlin in December 1884. Here agreement was reached over the general area of expansion, the suppression of the slave trade, and a rather vague formula for free trade in the Congo basin until various regions had been definitely annexed. The Berlin conference, however, only set the stage for the next act in the scramble for empire. By now the central regions were gaining a significance of their own in that their acquisition might enable one country to develop a band of territories right through the continent, either north–south or east–west, at the same time foiling similar designs of others.

Thus, in 1885 Great Britain annexed Southern Bechuanaland in order to prevent a possible link-up between the Boer Transvaal and German South-west Africa which would have blocked the way to her own expansion northwards. The road was thus open for Cecil Rhodes's South Africa Company, formed in 1889, to found two colonies— North and South Rhodesia—beyond the Transvaal. All political aims were now converging on these central regions. In 1888 Sir Donald Mackinnon founded the British East Africa Company in an attempt to counter the growth of German interests there, and the British government, now saddled with the problem of Egypt, was anxious to prevent the headwaters of the Nile falling into foreign hands.[1] At the same time a quarrel had developed between Great Britain and Portugal, who feared that British infiltration into Mashonaland and Nyasaland would prevent any eventual link between Angola and Mozambique.

Most of these disputes were satisfactorily settled in 1890. In Germany the Emperor Frederick III had died a few months after his succession in 1888 and Bismarck had by now swung round to the idea of friendship with Great Britain. Accordingly it was agreed that the British should safeguard the Nile by holding Kenya and Uganda and should assume a protectorate over Zanzibar; in return they ceded the island of Heligoland in the North Sea which they had held since 1815 and recognized Germany's possession of Tanganyika. At the same time the British made two other treaties—with France recognizing her seizure of Madagascar and certain of her West African boundaries, and with Portugal who gave way over the establishment of Nyasaland and Mashonaland.

The race between Great Britain and France, however, was not yet over. In March 1896 the Italians suffered a great defeat at Adowa at the hands of the Abyssinians from whom the French hoped for cooperation, and the British government decided that the moment had come for the conquest of the Sudan. In September 1898 Kitchener occupied Khartoum after having defeated the dervishes under their Khalifa at Omdurman, and a few days later encountered Captain Marchand who had just reached Fashoda with a small French force at the end of an epic

[1] The same anxiety affected the British government's attitude towards Italy's invasion of Abyssinia in 1935—although not sufficiently to bring about any intervention. See p. 428.

journey through the heart of Africa from the west in an effort to cut off the British from further expansion southwards. Marchand, however, was too far from his base to present any effective resistance and in March 1899 the two governments agreed upon a dividing line between the basins of the Nile and the Congo.

Meanwhile, there had been considerable activity in the Pacific, where, apart from Australia and New Zealand, colonial claims had been limited to a few islands held by Great Britain, France, and Spain. In 1884 Germany had annexed the Bismarck archipelago and the north-eastern segment of New Guinea, to which the British responded by taking the south-eastern segment of the island. Then at the end of the century the United States began to move into the Pacific. In 1898 Hawaii was finally annexed, in 1899 the Samoan group was shared with Germany, and on the conclusion of the Spanish American war of 1898 the former Spanish colonies of the Philippines, as well as Cuba and Porto Rico, were established as American dependencies.

In most parts of Africa and the Pacific the absence of any highly developed systems of government had resulted in direct territorial acquisition by the Powers. In Asia the struggle took a different form. Here the goal was to establish terms of preferential treatment from the existing local governments which would protect national, economic, and strategic interests. Along the northern frontier of India the British and the Russians intrigued for influence over Afghanistan and Tibet, while in the Turkish dominions of Mesopotamia and in Persia Great Britain, Germany, Russia, and the United States competed for concessions which would enable them to develop the rich deposits of oil.

In the Far East the weakness of China had already been demonstrated in the wars of 1839-42 and 1857-60, which, although fought primarily by Great Britain, had enabled several other European Powers and the United States to obtain considerable concessions for their own economic interests. Shortly after this the Chinese government attempted to carry out some sort of modernization of its military and naval forces, but was still unable to prevent further encroachments, including the French acquisition of Annam in 1885. The challenge to the position of the western Powers came ultimately not from China, but from the emergence of a new Power. In 1894 Japan gave sudden proof of the efficacy of her own programme of modernization on which she had embarked in the 1860s, when she fought a short successful war with China who by the Treaty of Shimonoseki in 1895 was forced to recognize the independence of Korea and to surrender Formosa, the Pescadores, and the

Liao-tang peninsula, which included the harbour of Port Arthur. This victory for the Japanese was naturally an affront to the other rivals for power in the Far East, and almost at once France, Germany, and Russia imposed their own revision of the treaty insisting that Japan should at least relinquish the Liao-tang peninsula in return for a heavier indemnity.

The emergence of Japan was of particular significance for Russia, since it was an immediate challenge to the political and economic hopes centred on the Trans-Siberian railway which had been under construction since 1891, and the Russian foreign ministry took a sufficiently serious view of it to suggest a policy of cooperation with her over the partition of Manchuria. Nicholas II, who had succeeded as Tsar in 1894, preferred, however, to cultivate friendship with China, and in 1896 his government concluded an agreement with her whereby Russian warships could use the ports of the Liao-tang peninsula, a port in Shantung was leased for fifteen years, and the Trans-Siberian railway was to take a short cut through Manchuria to Vladivostok. These Russian gains at once stimulated further demands from the other Powers for corresponding concessions. In 1897 Germany used the excuse of the murder of two German missionaries to extract a ninety-nine year lease of Kiao-chow, whereupon Russia obtained in 1898 a twenty-five year lease of Port Arthur, which was to be linked by a branch line with the Trans-Siberian railway. In the south France gained Kwang-chow-wan, while the British government yielded to the pressure of public opinion and accordingly secured Wei-hai-wei. 'It will not be useful and it will be expensive,' commented the British Prime Minister, Lord Salisbury, 'but as a matter of pure sentiment we shall have to do it.' It would be an over-simplification to say that his remark sums up the whole of the great Powers' race for empire, but it does certainly stress one very compelling motive.

22

THE DEVELOPMENT OF
PARLIAMENTARY GOVERNMENT

IN the decades before the outbreak of the first World War the new social and economic power of the middle classes was reflected in varying degrees in the growth of parliamentary institutions throughout the Continent. The most striking aspect of this development was the extension of the franchise. Universal suffrage was established in the German Empire and the French Third Republic and was later granted in Bulgaria, Greece, and Norway. In 1874 the Swiss even introduced a system of direct democracy by referendum, which in 1891 came to include proposals for individual legislative changes. Other countries proceeded more cautiously in lowering tax and property qualifications. In Austria there were extensions of the franchise in 1882 and 1896 and it was finally made universal in 1907, although remaining severely restricted in Hungary. In Belgium an electorate of 116,000 out of a population of five and a half million was increased in 1893 to 1,370,000, half of whom were to enjoy two or three votes, while in 1913 the franchise was made universal—each concession being prompted by the threat of a general strike. In Italy the quadrupling of the electorate in 1882 only enfranchised 7% of the population, but in 1912 most adult males were granted the right to vote. In Russia, after the revolution of 1905, a national Parliament, the *Duma*, was to be elected on a system that nominally came close to universal suffrage.

At first sight it might seem that the age of democracy had dawned. For conservatives this only justified the gloomy comment of Jacob Burckhardt in 1842: 'This frightening accentuation of the rights of the individual consists in this: *cogito* (whether correctly or falsely doesn't matter) *ergo regno*.' And for many liberals now safely ensconced among the established classes it revived the old dread of 1848 that their own success would open the way to the working-class masses among whom Socialist ideas were now rife.

In fact, these concessions were not as startling as they might appear.

The franchise in itself was only one element in the full exercise of democratic power; what mattered was the extent to which the distribution of seats represented the balance of political opinion among the electorate, and, more important still, the degree of control which the elected assembly could exert over the government of the country. The practice of democracy rests not simply on the granting of votes, but on the general evolution of a parliamentary tradition at a local as well as a national level. In this respect the study of the franchise alone is misleading. In central and eastern Europe, where executive power had been virtually absolute, the development of parliamentary assemblies made only a minor impact upon the authority of the State. In Germany, Austria-Hungary, Russia and the Balkan countries, government remained largely in the hands of the ruling few, and only in the west and in Scandinavia, where constitutional limitations had already been imposed before the days of universal suffrage, did these considerable extensions of the franchise have any great meaning.

1. The French Third Republic

In France the debate over the future form of government continued for some four years after the Franco-Prussian war. At first all the indications suggested a restoration of the monarchy. The National Assembly elected in 1871 was strongly royalist; in 1873 Thiers was replaced by the devoutly Catholic and conservative Marshal MacMahon as President of the Republic, and when Bismarck embarked upon his campaign against the Catholic party in Germany,[1] the French clericals were able to strengthen their cause with a patriotic antagonism towards the Imperial Chancellor. Monarchy, however, was not to be restored. Paris had been worth a Mass for Henry IV, but for the Bourbon claimant, 'Henry V', Count de Chambord, it was not worth a tricolour. He insisted on the adoption of the white Bourbon flag, and MacMahon himself, conscious of the revival of republican ardour reflected in recent by-elections, knew this to be an impossible condition. Nor would the disappointed Legitimists join forces with the Orleanists, and in 1875 a series of 'Organic Laws' established the Third Republic for lack of any other solution.

There were to be two Houses, a Chamber of Deputies elected by universal suffrage, and a Senate of 300, a quarter of whom were elected for life by the National Assembly, the remainder for nine years by the

[1] See p. 284.

départements and colonies. The most that the conservatives could do was to gain equal legislative powers for the Senate and to hope to strengthen the position of the President, who was to be elected by the two Houses and to hold office for seven years. Over this second point they were to be defeated, for a new Chamber elected in 1877 forced MacMahon to dismiss the government which he had formed under the Duke de Broglie, and the constitutional predominance of the lower House was confirmed two years later when MacMahon resigned and was replaced by Jules Grévy under whom the presidency was reduced to a more nominal position.

This victory for the republicans was followed by a renewed assault upon the position of the Church. Since the middle of the century religious orders had greatly increased in numbers, authorized communities held property worth a total of 421 million francs—nearly £17 million—and as a consequence of the *Loi Falloux* of 1850[1] two-fifths of all French school children now attended Catholic schools. To the anti-clericals the Syllabus of Errors and the doctrine of Papal Infallibility[2] appeared to represent a declaration of war, and although the Senate rejected a law forbidding members of unauthorized congregations to teach anywhere in France, a precise interpretation of the existing Concordat did enable the government to dissolve a certain number of unauthorized communities. In 1882 Jules Ferry made primary education compulsory, free, and secular, thereby prohibiting religious instruction in State schools; *écoles normales* were instituted for girls, and Catholic universities were deprived of the right to confer degrees.

By the end of the 1880s, however, the republicans were once again in danger of falling between two stools. They had based their power on the support of the *petite bourgeoisie*, ending the system of life-membership of the Senate in 1884 and loosening the central government's power to the extent of allowing all mayors except those in Paris to be elected by local councils. By now, however, the radical forces of the industrial proletariat were becoming far more coherent, and the death of Napoleon's son, the Prince Imperial, in Zululand in 1879 and that of the Count de Chambord in 1883 might have made it possible for all monarchists to fall in with the Orleanists. In fact, the right wing—Catholic, anti-parliamentary and strongly represented in the army—were by this time ceasing to be royalist and were developing a more sinister tendency to look simply for a strong man who might

[1] See p. 168.   [2] See p. 243

seize power. In the years 1887–9 it seemed as if they might have found him in General Boulanger, the Minister of War, who won tremendous popularity both with the right and with a section of the radicals in one of those instances, common in French history, when the two extremes join forces against the centre. Boulanger, however, was not the man for a *coup d'état* and his loss of nerve and eventual flight to Belgium in 1889 discredited both sides and enabled the Third Republic to enjoy a new lease of life.

Indeed, despite the rapid changes of government and the general sense of mediocrity in political life the new Republic had shown a remarkable resilience. It demonstrated the total recovery of France from the war with the great Paris Exhibition of 1889; it survived the financial scandal of the Panama scheme in which several members of the government were found to be involved, and remained unshaken by the assassination of one of its Presidents, Sadi Carnot, in 1894. After the Boulanger incident a greater harmony between the moderates of the left and right suggested that the Republic might be moving into calmer waters, but these hopes were to be wrecked by the storm of the Dreyfus *affaire*. In 1894 Alfred Dreyfus, a young Jewish staff officer, was court-martialled for selling military information to Germany and was later sentenced to imprisonment on Devil's Island. Dreyfus's family continued to fight to establish his innocence, and when the authorities refused to accept new evidence that seemed to clear him, political opponents of the government began to take up the case. The controversy reached its height when in 1898 Émile Zola published in Clemenceau's newspaper *L'Aurore* an open letter to the President of the Republic, '*J'accuse*', and eventually after fresh developments Dreyfus was brought back to France, retried by court-martial at Rennes, found guilty again and then granted a pardon from the President.

The *affaire* had torn France apart with all the passions of conservative anti-Semitism and republican hatred of the Catholic military high command, and the possibility of a coalition of moderates faded amid a new governmental onslaught on the Church. In 1903 Pope Leo XIII had been succeeded by Pius X, less prone to compromise with the forces of secularism, and after the new Pope's denunciation of President Loubet's visit to the King of Italy, the French government passed legislation in 1905 that brought the Concordat to an end. The State was now to be entirely separate from all forms of religion, and consequently the Catholic Church was no longer to be subsidized and lost practically all its property by confiscation. Thus although the impact of the Franco-Prussian war had been relatively brief, the wounds which France had inflicted upon herself more than a hundred years before still remained unhealed.

2. *The domestic scene in Imperial Germany*

The constitution of the German Empire made it impossible for the Reichstag to play such an active part in political life as the Chamber of Deputies in France. The Chancellor remained purely dependent upon the Emperor, and Prussia's position in the *Bundesrat* enabled her to block any undesirable legislation. However, the Reichstag did have certain negative powers and although Bismarck usually managed to retain the initiative, he had always to make sure of forming a working majority among the various parties.

It was perfectly natural that after his recent victories he should maintain his alliance with the National Liberals led by Rudolf von Bennigsen who had earlier presided over the *Deutscher Nationalverein*,[1] and this alignment was strengthened by Bismarck's mistrust of the Catholic Centre party under Ludwig Windthorst with about seventy seats in the Reichstag. There were a number of reasons for these doubts over the political reliability of the Catholics. The Syllabus of Errors and the declaration of Papal Infallibility was to create considerable tension between Church and State in Germany, but in addition to this the Catholic party was sympathetic towards the Poles in West Prussia and Posen and towards the French in Lorraine, while the Catholics of south Germany still supported the notion of *Grossdeutschland* on which Bismarck had turned his back.

This period of alliance with the National Liberals, which lasted until 1879, was marked by a great onslaught by the government on the Catholic Church in Germany—the *Kulturkampf*. In 1872 the Jesuits were expelled from the Reich; in 1873 the May laws brought all ecclesiastical education and appointments under State control; in 1875 civil marriage became compulsory and, later, Catholic rights of assembly were restricted and their publications severely censored. Bismarck had been determined to win; 'we shall not go to Canossa', he had boasted, but the passive resistance of the Catholics eventually forced him to submit to his first political defeat; bishops and priests went to prison rather than obey and by 1876 nine Prussian sees were

[1] See pp. 179, 223.

THE DEVELOPMENT OF PARLIAMENTARY GOVERNMENT

unoccupied and 1,400 parishes had no legally appointed priest. What worried Bismarck still more was the possibility of an alliance between the Centre party and the Socialists against the government, and in any case he was coming to dislike the increasing dependence on the National Liberals which the *Kulturkampf* imposed upon him.

Thus, when in 1878 the pacific tendencies of the new Pope Leo XIII seemed to open the way to a settlement with the Catholics, Bismarck began to move round to a new alignment with the Centre party and the conservatives, whose position was now strengthened by a growing alliance through inter-marriage between the Prussian landowning class and the great industrial magnates of the Rhineland. For the Catholics this was eventually to mean a considerable modification of the laws that had weighed so heavily on them; for the conservatives it meant the introduction of a policy of economic protection for agricultural goods and manufactures.[1]

This abandonment of the tendency towards lower tariffs signified the final break with the National Liberals; it also aroused the antagonism of the Social Democrats, whose party had been founded in 1875,[2] since Protection meant dearer food for the worker. In fact, Bismarck had already opened hostilities with an anti-Socialist law in 1878, and although the left wing of the National Liberals were able to reduce its legal life to two-and-a-half years, so that he had constantly to renew it, serious restrictions were now placed on the political activity of the Socialists. His handling of the campaign was more subtle than the *Kulturkampf*; by laws passed in 1883, 1884, and 1889 he even attempted to steal their thunder by the introduction of an extremely modern scheme for social insurance against accident, sickness, and old age. Yet here, as with the Catholics, he was again to encounter defeat. Despite all his efforts the electoral vote of the Social Democrats rose from 500,000 in 1877, to 763,000 in 1887 and to 1,427,000 in 1890, and on his dismissal the anti-Socialist laws gradually lapsed.

The old Emperor William I died at last in 1888 and was succeeded first by his son Frederick III, who only survived him by three months, and then by his grandson William II.[3] Unstable, conceited, and struggling with a deep inferiority complex, the young Emperor was determined to assume a personal control of government which Bismarck had kept so long to himself, and in 1890 the Imperial Chancellor was virtually dismissed. Retiring to Varzin Bismarck continued to nurse his sense of grievance until his death in 1898, while

---

[1] See p. 253.　　　[2] See p. 257.　　　[3] See Genealogical table, p. 481.

William pushed ahead with his self-conscious gestures and ill-judged interventions in foreign policy, which were ultimately to contribute substantially to the disaster of the first World War and the end of the German monarchy.

In home affairs he toyed at first with liberalism. During the chancellorship of General von Caprivi tariffs were lowered, the length of service with the infantry was reduced from three to two years, and the régime was made less oppressive in Alsace and Lorraine and in the Polish provinces. All this, however, was not to last. William's policy failed to prevent the growth of the Social Democrats and only served to antagonize the Prussian landowners. Extensions of the social insurance laws and certain concessions to the trade unions were made under the next two Chancellors—Prince Hohenlohe (1894–1900) and Prince Bülow (1900–9)—but the general tendency was a return to a conservative and nationalist policy. In 1902 the landowners and industrialists gained their demand for an increase in tariffs, and in the following years governmental pressure on the French in Alsace and Lorraine and on the Poles in the eastern provinces was renewed at a time when national feeling was becoming ever more pronounced throughout Europe.

3. Austria-Hungary

At five o'clock in the morning the Emperor Francis Joseph would rise and toil at his desk throughout the day on the minutiae of Habsburg administration. He was a man of simple tastes, totally uninterested in the luxury and comfort that were his to command. In the Schönbrunn palace the Emperor slept on an ordinary iron bedstead and in an age of gas and electricity preferred his oil lamp. He was a devout Catholic and every Maundy Thursday would solemnly wash the feet of a dozen old men brought to the Hofburg from a local almshouse. No ruler could have been more dedicated to the government of his dominions than Francis Joseph; no man more unfortunate in the tragedies of his personal life.

The unflinching sense of duty and decorum that sustained him played havoc with his relationship with his family. His wife, Elizabeth of Bavaria, rebelling against the strictness of court formality, was drawn towards the greater flamboyance of the Hungarians and spent much of her later years in travel around Europe. His son, the Crown Prince Rudolph, was opposed to him on political grounds; his nephew Francis

Ferdinand, had offended him by marrying Countess Sophia Chotek, a Czech lady whom the Emperor did not consider sufficiently high-born for such an honour, and even after Francis Ferdinand had become heir to the throne on Rudolph's death, the couple were constantly on their guard against real or imagined slights.

The end was violent for all of them. There had been signs of mental instability in Rudolph, whose relative on his mother's side, King Ludwig II of Bavaria,[1] had eventually gone mad and drowned himself with his attendant, and although Rudolph's death at the hunting lodge at Mayerling in 1889 remains something of a mystery, it seems probable that he and his mistress died in a suicide pact; the Empress Elizabeth was stabbed to death in 1898 by an Anarchist on the shore of the Lake of Geneva, and in 1914 Francis Ferdinand and his wife were shot down in the fateful assassination at Sarajevo. Thus in the end Francis Joseph outlived them all, a bearded patriarch symbolizing the past, an old man burying himself in the details of a riddle to which neither the nineteenth nor the twentieth century could find a satisfactory answer.

In December 1867 the creation of a constitution for the Austrian half of the Dual Monarchy opened a new liberal era. The press was granted greater freedom, elementary education was made free and compulsory and, with the abolition of the Concordat of 1855[2] in 1871, was removed from the control of the Catholic Church. Concessions for the Czechs were also planned, including equality of status for the German and Czech languages in Bohemia, and Francis Joseph even suggested that he might be crowned at Prague, but the objections of the Germans and the Magyars brought all this to nothing. Gradually, however, non-German nationalities were enabled to play a greater part in parliamentary and governmental life and eventually, in 1907, universal suffrage was established in the Austrian lands, although the parliament thus elected had little control over the administration. None of these measures could overcome the mounting antagonism among the different nationalities, and a fresh attempt by Count Badeni in 1887 to grant equality for the Czech language led to a serious outbreak of rioting and eventually forced him to resign.

In the Hungarian half of the Dual Monarchy a new generation of Magyars, impatient of the moderation of the older leaders, Deák and Andrássy, began to adopt a far more intransigent attitude both towards the suppressed nationalities and the Habsburg monarchy.[3] In 1874 the electoral law concentrated the vote almost entirely in Magyar

---

[1] See Genealogical table, p. 480.　　[2] See p. 173.　　[3] See p. 271.

hands; in 1875 the Slovak cultural organization was dissolved, and by 1905 the number of Slovak schools had been reduced from nearly 2,000 to 241. At the same time strong Magyar demands were being made for economic independence and for a separate Hungarian army, and when István Tisza, leader of the more moderate Liberal party, was defeated in the election of 1905, Francis Joseph had to use the threat of introducing universal suffrage in Hungary to bring the opposition to terms. Tisza regained power in 1913, but even under his premiership the fate of the Dual Monarchy seemed to hang by a thread, and the message of Kossuth was still as active a menace to the Habsburgs as it had been when Francis Joseph had first ascended the throne.

4. Russia and the revolution of 1905

It might well have seemed that the reforms of Tsar Alexander II would at last set Russia on the road to western constitutional development; yet this was not to be. The bomb which was flung at Alexander on 13 March 1881 as he was driving in his carriage through the streets of St Petersburg, not only killed the Tsar; it confirmed all the conservative tendencies of his son who now succeeded as Alexander III.

The old note of unrestricted autocracy sounded unmistakably in the accession manifesto drawn up by Alexander III's tutor, Pobedonostsev, who regarded western liberalism as alien to the spirit of Russia; and the late Tsar's most recent scheme for elective commissions working in consultation with the government was never put into operation. In 1884 the universities were deprived of their autonomy. In 1889 changes in the electoral system gave the landed gentry complete control over the *Zemstva*, and in 1890 the administration of the peasantry was placed under the supervision of Land Captains who were appointed by the Ministry of the Interior from among the poorer gentry and who took over the functions of the local justices previously elected by the district *Zemstva*. In 1892 similar amendments brought the municipal councils under the control of the central executive. Thus, the whole delicate relationship between the bureaucracy and regional interests which Alexander II had hoped to foster was abruptly shattered, at the same time as a policy of russification in the outlying provinces[1] and a harrassing of the Jews emphasized the return to an uncompromising centralized autocracy.

Nevertheless, Alexander III and his son Nicholas II, who ascended

[1] See pp. 269-70.

the throne in 1894, saw their system as one of enlightened paternalism, and certainly this was a remarkable period of economic change for Russia. Railway construction which proceeded at an extraordinary pace under Serge Witte, the Minister of Communications, and the raising of foreign loans were both essential factors in the startling development of textiles, metallurgy, ship-building on the coast of the Black Sea, and oil in Baku. As in the west, the growth of an industrial proletariat raised the problem of working and living conditions, and in the early years of Alexander III's reign Bunge, the Minister of Finance, introduced factory laws protecting women and children, which were to be enforced by inspectors. Bunge's liberal tendencies also led him to abolish the poll tax on the peasantry, and it was perhaps not surprising that the more conservative elements in the government secured his dismissal in 1887. After this the factory laws were simply evaded, until industrial unrest led to a decree in 1897 imposing a working day of no more than eleven-and-a-half hours, or of ten if it included night work.

Indeed, paternalism could never be equal to all the implications of the vast process of change that Russia was undergoing. The new proletariat offered a great opportunity for the Social Democrats, who founded a secret newspaper *Iskra* (the Spark) under an editorial board consisting of Plekhanov, Axelrod, Vera Zasulich, Lenin, and Martov. At the same time bitterness was growing in the countryside, where the rapid increase in population was reducing the average size of holdings for the majority of peasants on whom the bad harvests of the 1880s and the famine conditions of 1891–3 weighed heavily; this was further accentuated by a new division between rich and poor peasantry, since a minority were beginning to prosper, renting the land of the gentry and purchasing more of their own through a peasants' bank founded by Bunge in 1884. Conscious of these pressures Witte, who had become Minister of Finance in 1892, attempted some ten years later to take the *Zemstva* into partnership, but his efforts simply enabled Plehve, Minister of the Interior since 1902, to oust him from office and the policy of reaction continued unchecked.

It was the outbreak of the Russo-Japanese war in February 1904[1] that brought to a head the discontent from land hunger and industrial conditions. The war was unpopular in itself, and when Plehve was assassinated in July, his successor, Prince Svyatopolk-Mirsky, a man of liberal views, consented to the holding of a *Zemstvo* conference in

[1] See p. 316.

November, where a unanimous demand was made for greater personal and political liberty. In January 1905, however, the fall of Port Arthur to the Japanese saddled the government with all the odium of military defeat. A few weeks later Father Gapon, who had been organizing a workers' movement under police supervision in St Petersburg, led a great deputation to the Winter Palace, where the troops opened fire, killing a great number of the crowd. This was followed by a wave of strikes and the murder of police officials throughout Russia, and in February the Grand Duke Serge, the Tsar's uncle, was assassinated. Nicholas II now declared himself ready to consult representatives on the government of the country, although still insisting on the maintenance of autocracy, and a series of conferences were held among the reformers during the summer to discuss the demands which should be put to the Tsar. These hopes were to be quickly disappointed, however, when the constitutional concessions which the government announced in August proved to be purely nominal; a national Parliament, a *Duma*, was to be set up, but its consultative functions were to be so hedged about and the franchise so narrow that it proved quite unacceptable.

By now more extreme elements were beginning to seize their chance. In June the crew of the battleship *Potemkin* mutinied and conducted a short campaign on the Black Sea before seeking refuge in a Rumanian port; at the same time the Social Revolutionaries had stirred up the peasantry with the cry: 'all the land for the peasants', and there had ensued a great rising in the provinces in which landowners were expelled and their estates taken over. In October a general strike virtually paralyzed all civic life in St Petersburg, where a little later in the same month Trotsky, who had hurried back from Switzerland, was elected vice-president of a workers' Soviet (council) whose executive included Mensheviks, Bolsheviks, and Social Revolutionaries.

Witte had just returned from the United States after the conclusion of the peace treaty with Japan, and was convinced by these developments in Russia that the Tsar must offer further concessions which would divide the liberals from the extremists. The outcome was the issue of the October Manifesto. A *Duma* with the right to veto legislation was to be elected on a wide franchise, and the committee of ministers under their president was to acquire something of the character of a cabinet, although remaining independent of the Duma. In November the St Petersburg Soviet called an end to the strike, Finland's old rights were restored to her, and preparations were made for the general election. This, however, was followed by demands in Warsaw for Polish autonomy, and when Witte, who was now head of the government, imposed martial law in Poland, the St Petersburg Soviet ordered a fresh strike in sympathy with the Poles.

This activity on the part of the Soviet might well seem to foreshadow the revolutions of 1917. In fact, the revolution of 1905 has far more in common with those of 1848. In spite of mutinies at Kronstadt and Sebastopol, the monarchy still retained control over the bulk of its armed forces and the clash of aims between the various political and social groups gave Witte his opportunity to restore the situation. He attempted to conciliate the peasantry by promising the reduction and eventual abolition of their redemption dues, and in December he made a gesture towards the liberals by decreeing a further extension of the franchise so that it became virtually universal. Simultaneously martial law was declared in St Petersburg, most of the members of the Soviet were placed under arrest, and a fierce campaign in the countryside put down the peasant rising, culminating in a savage social war in the Baltic provinces. Thus, the extreme elements were crushed and the liberals were fobbed off with a constitution which was not the work of a constituent Assembly, but had simply been decreed from above; this was apparent from the details of the new system, which not only left the Tsar absolute control over the armed forces but even allowed him to raise loans on his own initiative, so that it was perfectly possible for him to escape from the *Duma*'s control of the budget. Even so, the conservatives found it highly alarming; Witte's efforts to win over the liberals had created many enemies for him at court, and as soon as he had raised an enormous loan from France he was dismissed.

Once order had been restored, the original form of the constitution did not survive long. The first *Duma* which met in May 1906 in the Tauris Palace was dominated by the Constitutional Democrats (Cadets) who hoped for further concessions, and was dissolved in July after they had led a great attack on the government Official pressure during the elections to the second *Duma* succeeded in reducing the number of liberal deputies, but the left-wing representation was increased and the session, which only lasted from March until June 1907, was disrupted by an incessant struggle between the conservatives and the Social Democrats. By now the government felt sufficiently strong to introduce a modification of the franchise which greatly favoured the interest of the country gentry and reduced the representation of the non-Russian peoples, so that when the third *Duma* met in November 1907, the Octobrists—so called because they were content with the provisions of the October Manifesto—held a commanding position. This third *Duma* and its successor in 1912, which was almost identical in personnel, were consequently both far more acquiescent; yet they did voice criticism, encouraged a good many minor measures of administrative reform and, within their limitations, did suggest the beginnings of parliamentary life in Russia.

Meanwhile, under Peter Stolypin, who became President of the Council of Ministers in 1906, the process of restoring the Tsar's authority had been completed; revolutionary elements in the cities were rounded up, fifteen members of the St Petersburg Soviet, including Trotsky, were sent to Siberia for life, although Trotsky succeeded in escaping almost immediately afterwards, and in the provinces a series of field court-martials imposed hundreds of death sentences. Stolypin, hated though he was for these measures, was not simply a senseless reactionary. Industry and commerce were encouraged through contact with a federation of leading industrialists and business men, and he had, too, a positive policy for the peasantry. Stolypin's aim was to create greater support for the existing régime through a system of peasant proprietorship. 'The natural counterweight to the communal principle is individual ownership', he said; 'it is also a guarantee of order, since the small-owner is the cell on which rests all stable order in the State.' Thus he set out to break the hold of the *mir* over the individual peasant which Alexander II's reforms had actually strengthened,[1] and before the end of 1906 decrees had been issued allowing the peasant to leave the *mir* when he wished, or, if he remained, to consolidate his strips of land in one place and to hold them permanently. Communal responsibility for taxation was ended and this general weakening of the position of the *mir*, coupled with a more extensive use of the peasants' bank, hastened the development of a richer class of peasant farmers, the *kulaks*, so that by 1917 some 1,300,000 peasant households had been established with their own consolidated farmlands.

Social tensions and political agitation continued to trouble the Russian scene and in 1911 Stolypin himself was assassinated. It is not impossible to imagine that with these governmental and economic changes Russia might have been able to find her way towards the

[1] See p. 228.

modern western type of constitutional state, but the roots of this transformation were still all too shallow; what was needed was time, and when by 1917 military disaster, as in 1856 and 1905, seemed to threaten the whole basis of Russian government, the changes had not gone far enough to create a powerful alternative to the extremes of revolutionary Socialism.

23

BISMARCK'S EUROPE 1871–90

'THE worst of all this is not the present war,' wrote Jacob Burckhardt in 1870, 'but the era of wars upon which we have entered.' From a long-term point of view this was a remarkable prophecy; in fact, the subsequent forty-four years were to be a period not of war, but of armed peace, as each great Power, mindful of the efficiency of the Prussian army on which Bismarck's success had ultimately rested, sought to improve and expand its own military forces. Ironically, Bismarck himself reckoned that the creation of the German empire marked the limit of his ambitions in Europe, and after 1871 his diplomacy was aimed almost entirely at preventing the outbreak of further wars from which Germany could have nothing to gain. 'We have no further demands to make,' he said in 1890. 'Germany does not need the three million Dutchmen who have no desire to be absorbed by us, nor the Baltic countries, nor Poland, nor any other territory. We have enough annexed populations.'

The new policy of defensiveness presented him with two fundamental problems. First, he had to ensure that France should remain without an ally so that she might be discouraged from attempting a war of revenge. The British certainly looked with some anxiety at the change in the balance of power on the Continent; 'Napoleon III', remarked Odo Russell in 1872, 'was not more powerful than Bismarck is in this moment.' Yet their traditional suspicion of France, aggravated by colonial rivalry, made an Anglo-French alliance highly unlikely, particularly at a time when the British government wished to avoid any continental commitments.

Second, it was essential that he should preserve good relations between Austria-Hungary and Russia, because if war broke out between them, Germany would almost certainly find herself drawn into it. This would not only be disastrous in itself, but would also have a direct bearing on the French question, since in the inevitable scramble for alliances France would be able to escape from the isolation that

Bismarck was determined to impose on her. The principal danger here lay in the heightened significance of the Eastern Question. Austria-Hungary, excluded from Italy and Germany, could not remain indifferent to Russian ambitions in the Balkans. The possible creation of Russian satellite states out of the territories of Turkey-in-Europe affected more than Austrian foreign policy; nationalist feelings among the Slavs were becoming a factor in themselves and the emergence of a strong independent Slav state would represent a considerable domestic danger, since it would act as a focal point of resistance for all the subject Slav peoples of the Habsburg empire. Thus, the Austrian government remained ever mindful of Gentz's prediction in 1815,[1] and the growing menace of nationalism in the Balkans gave a new urgency to her fears of Russian pan-Slavism. Until 1879 Bismarck's method of dealing with these problems was based on the avoidance of any system of international alliance. Instead, he attempted to create a league of friendship between Germany, Austria-Hungary and Russia, and several meetings between the sovereigns in 1872 and 1873 helped to consolidate this *Dreikaiserbund*. After the revision of the Black Sea clauses in the Treaty of Paris in 1871 Russia was satisfied for the moment; Francis Joseph had abandoned any thoughts of undoing the results of the war of 1866 by alliance with France, and Count Andrássy, a Magyar aristocrat who had replaced Beust as Foreign Minister, wished to base his policy on friendship with Germany. Naturally the League of the Three Emperors, reminiscent of the earlier Holy Alliance and prompted by the same motive of conservatism, did not attempt to settle any of the deeper issues, since that would only have invited its disruption; it merely fostered a deceptive sense of unity, and its flimsiness was soon made apparent in two successive crises.

The first—the French war scare of 1875—was mainly the consequence of the speed with which France seemed to be recovering from her recent defeat. As early as 1873 the indemnity of five milliards of francs had been paid off and the German occupation force had accordingly been withdrawn. In the same year relations between France and Germany became cool when a right-wing pro-clerical government was formed in Paris at the very time when Bismarck had begun to mount his *Kulturkampf*.[2] The crisis came to a head in January 1875 when the French Chamber began to discuss a bill for the reorganization of the French army, including the addition of a fourth battalion to each regiment, and when the bill was passed in March, the German press—largely through Bismarck's encouragement—embarked upon a great campaign, accusing France of preparing for war. In fact, William I was adamant that all talk of military hostilities was absurd, but the French government, keen to seize the opportunity for a diplomatic success, flung back the charge of chauvinism, declaring that Bismarck was determined on a preventive war against France and giving full publicity to some indiscreet remarks made by one of his political agents to the French ambassador at Berlin. The whole incident was really only a war of nerves, a technique which was to become highly familiar in the twentieth century, but it had the effect of bringing Tsar Alexander and his Foreign Minister, Gortchakov, to Berlin in May to warn the German government to go no further. After this the German press campaign was called off and the excitement very soon died down.

Artificial though it was, the crisis was nevertheless not without its significance. Probably Bismarck had intended no more than to frighten the French into dropping their plans for military reform. It is idle to speculate on how far he would have gone, if he had been able to gain the acquiescence of the great Powers. The fact was that he had failed to do so. Both Great Britain and Russia had made it clear that they objected strongly to any suggestion of the waging of a preventive war by Germany against France; only on Austria, apparently, could Bismarck safely rely. The alignment was momentary, yet it demonstrated how easily Bismarck's hopes for the *Dreikaiserbund* and the isolation of France could be shattered. He was in a sense the victim of his own success; the pattern of events whereby the German empire had been created had awoken a deep mistrust among the governments of Europe, and not even Bismarck's skill could avoid the instinctive workings of the balance of power.

There was nothing artificial about the second crisis, which at its height seemed likely to bring about a major war between Austria and Russia. In 1875 the Christian Slavs of Bosnia and Herzegovina rose in revolt against their Turkish masters, and as unrest continued to spread, all the old problems implicit in the Eastern Question came to the fore once again. Would Russia take advantage of the situation to carve a new Slav state out of the Balkans?

Fortunately for Bismarck Gortchakov, the Russian Foreign Minister, was equally aware of the delicacy of the situation; Alexander II did not allow himself to be impelled by pan-Slav enthusiasm within

Russia, and to Bismarck's relief the Powers of the *Dreikaiserbund* did at first act in some degree of unison.

Mediation was attempted unsuccessfully in the summer of 1875; in December Andrássy's Note put forward a scheme for the reform of Turkish rule in the Balkans, which the Turks accepted, but failed to apply. In May 1876 the three Foreign Ministers agreed on a fresh proposal of reforms, the Berlin Memorandum, and offered to include France, Italy, and Great Britain in their negotiations. France and Italy accepted, but Disraeli, suspicious that some plan for a general partition of Turkish territories in Europe was in the making, refused.

By now Ottoman fortunes had taken a turn for the worse; the Sultan had been deposed, the Bulgarians had joined in the revolt, and at the end of June Serbia and Montenegro declared war on Turkey. Yet even this did not bring about the threatened split between Russia and Austria-Hungary. In July Gortchakov and Andrássy met at Reichstadt and agreed that there should be no intervention, but that if Turkey did fail to re-establish control over her Slav subjects, Austria-Hungary was to take Bosnia, while Russia should regain that southern part of Bessarabia which she had lost in 1856.

By the autumn of 1876, however, Turkey had recovered. The Bulgarian Christians were put down with a murderous brutality that inspired Gladstone to publish his pamphlet, *The Bulgarian Horrors and the Question of the East*, a fierce indictment of Turkish rule in the Balkans. More significant from Russia's point of view was the defeat of the Serbian and Montenegran armies, which seemed to presage a revival of Turkish power throughout the Balkans, and before the end of the year Tsar Alexander had swung round to the pan-Slav view that Russia must take military action against Turkey.

This Russian decision to intervene presented her diplomats with a new set of problems, since it was essential that, once the attack had been launched, Turkey should not find an ally in Great Britain or Austria-Hungary. With the British they felt that they could take a chance; in January 1877 at a conference at Constantinople Lord Salisbury and Ignatiev, the Russian ambassador, had been in accord over further proposals of reforms which the Turks had once again blocked, and the effect of Gladstone's pamphlet on the British public had created a storm of anti-Turkish feeling that Disraeli could not ignore. With Austria-Hungary the difficulty was overcome by secret military and political treaties—the Budapest conventions—signed early in 1877. In return for observing benevolent neutrality in the forthcoming Russo-

Turkish war, she was to receive Bosnia and Herzegovina, the continued existence of Serbia and Montenegro was guaranteed, and, most important of all, no large Slav state was to be set up in the Balkans. Both sides could be satisfied with this. Russia had ensured that an Anglo-Austrian alliance would not be formed against her; Austria-Hungary had been able to exact compensation and a guarantee as the price of her acquiescence in a course of events which Andrássy in any case did not feel he could prevent.

Thus far, Bismarck, who had refused to commit himself, could feel that the worst had been avoided, since Austro-Russian relations had survived even this latest development. In the last weeks of April 1877 Russia declared war on Turkey and with Rumania as an ally advanced into Bulgaria. The Russian diplomats, like Bismarck in his earlier days, now depended upon the generals for a swift victory. In this they were disappointed through the stubborn resistance of the Turkish fortress of Plevna under Osman Pasha, who did not surrender until December. The Russian advance was swift after this; at the end of January 1878 Adrianople fell to their forces and once more—as in 1828—it seemed that nothing could save Constantinople. But the long siege of Plevna had taken its toll; the Russian army was by now not in good shape, and during the nine months that the war had lasted British public opinion, alarmed by the Russian advance, had had time to swing round to the side of the Turks. At this point the Russians wisely decided to call a halt and an armistice was signed.

Continued doubts over Russian intentions led to the dispatch of the British fleet through the Dardanelles into the Sea of Marmora in the middle of February, and the crisis came to a head at the beginning of March with the signing of the Treaty of San Stefano between Russia and Turkey. This was not the work of Gortchakov, who had favoured a moderate peace settlement, but of Ignatiev who was a pan-Slav enthusiast. By its terms the independence of Serbia, Montenegro, and Rumania was recognized by Turkey and all three were allowed to extend their frontiers, although Rumania's acquisition of the Dobruja was a poor compensation for the loss of Southern Bessarabia, which Russia now regained as well as making an extension of her frontier in the Caucasus. There was no mention of Austria-Hungary's right to annex Bosnia and Herzegovina—only the imposition of governmental reforms within Turkey-in-Europe that had been agreed upon at the Constantinople conference; worst of all, Bulgaria was to become a large autonomous principality under a Christian governor, while paying tribute to Turkey, and her frontiers were to run west into the Balkan mountains and as far south as the coast of the Aegean.

Thus the Treaty of San Stefano awoke all the worst fears of Great

THE BALKANS 1878–1913

Britain and Austria-Hungary; it completely ignored the Budapest conventions, and through the creation of a large Bulgarian state almost certainly under Tsarist influence appeared to be the fulfillment of Russia's hopes of gaining substantial control over the Balkans without the embarrassment of a partition among the Powers. This was naturally unacceptable to Austria-Hungary, and for Great Britain the advance of the Russian frontier in the Caucasus represented a threat to British communications with India.

During the next three months anxious negotiations, culminating in the Congress of Berlin, led to a complete revision of the Treaty of San Stefano. This diplomatic retreat by Russia is explained by a number of factors. Gortchakov was furious at Ignatiev's clumsiness in over-reaching himself, and in the last resort Tsar Alexander II was not prepared to go to war for the maintenance of the treaty. There was no hope of military support from Germany. Bismarck's concern through-out the crisis was to maintain a complete neutrality, and in December 1876 he had announced in the Reichstag that the issues contained 'no German interest worth the bones of a Pomeranian musketeer'. There was no immediate cooperation between Great Britain and Austria-Hungary, since Andrássy would have preferred to reach a private agreement with Russia, but his negotiations with Ignatiev at Vienna came to nothing, simply because it was impossible to devise any formula that would be adequate to compensate Austria-Hungary for the creation of a large Bulgaria. It was the British government who forced the pace. Disraeli, now Lord Beaconsfield, summoned 7,000 Indian troops to Malta; Lord Salisbury, who was determined on a firm stand, replaced Lord Derby as Foreign Secretary and on 30 May signed an agreement with the Russians who abandoned the project of a large Bulgaria. This was followed on 4 June by an Anglo-Turkish treaty whereby Great Britain agreed to defend Turkey-in-Asia against Russia in return for the purchase of Cyprus as a military and naval base, and on 6 June by an understanding with Austria-Hungary over her right to annex Bosnia.

The Congress of Berlin in June was thus largely concerned with tidying up the details of these fundamental decisions. It was the first time that Berlin had been the scene of an international settlement and Bismarck, who presided in his capacity as 'the honest broker', plainly delighted in the glamour of a great diplomatic occasion amid a round of receptions and gargantuan meals. Even so, there was a bizarre note in this evocation of the great days of Vienna and Paris. Lord Beacons-field, who headed the British delegation, had to be persuaded to address the Congress in the Radziwill Palace in English, and in a letter he described how 'Prince Bismarck, with one hand full of cherries and the other of shrimps, eaten alternately, complains he cannot sleep and must go to Kissingen.'

The details were eventually settled, although not without considerable negotiation. The autonomous principality of Bulgaria was to consist of no more than the area immediately to the south of the Danube; below this, Eastern Roumelia was to be a Turkish province under a Christian governor, while the southernmost regions were to remain directly under Turkish rule. As Bismarck said, the diplomats were not there 'to consider the happiness of the Bulgarians, but to secure the peace of Europe'. Austria was to be allowed to occupy Bosnia and Herzegovina and to garrison the Sanjak of Novibazar which separated the frontiers of Serbia and Montenegro. Russia was to retain southern Bessarabia and Batum, but agreed to concessions along the Caucasian frontier. In addition to this, in accordance with the terms of the Cyprus Convention, Great Britain supported her guarantee of Turkey's Asiatic frontier with a scheme for posting British military consuls in Armenia, and declared her freedom to send a fleet through the Straits virtually whenever it suited her.

On the face of it the Treaty of Berlin was a resounding diplomatic defeat for Russia. The Treaty of San Stefano had been wiped out and during the Congress the Russians had even been unable to prohibit the Turkish military occupation of Eastern Roumelia owing to Beaconsfield's stubborn insistence. Yet the gains with which they were ultimately left were very similar to the claims which Gortchakov had originally envisaged. Great Britain and Austria-Hungary could feel that they had preserved Turkey-in-Europe, even though she had suffered certain losses, and each had to some extent strengthened their own position for the future—the British by increasing their power in the eastern Mediterranean, the Austrians by opening the road to a far greater influence over the western Balkans.

Bismarck himself was content that a highly explosive situation had not led to an Austro-Russian war, even though the outcome was little more than a process of what Gortchakov called 'replastering'. The Balkan crisis, nevertheless, made a turning point in the shaping of his policy. The significance of the negotiations at Berlin was that although to outward appearances Bismarck had maintained his neutrality, he had by his very refusal to uphold the Russian claim to a large Bulgaria revealed that, if forced to decide, Germany would favour Austria-Hungary. This attitude was finally confirmed in October 1879 by the Dual Alliance, a treaty signed between Germany and Austria-Hungary promising mutual aid if either of them were attacked by Russia and benevolent neutrality in the case of an attack by any other Power.

From Austria-Hungary's point of view the creation of the Dual Alliance is simple to understand; it meant that she had at last escaped from the isolation which had been so disastrous for her since the Crimean war, and for Andrássy, who had always hoped for such an agreement with Germany, it was the culminating triumph of his career. For Germany there is rather more to explain, since the treaty meant the abandonment of her policy of freedom from diplomatic alliance; Bismarck had now openly committed her to the defence of the Habsburg empire—the very system which he had fervently denounced during his years at Frankfurt in the 1850s. It is clear that he feared that the Balkan crisis had seriously prejudiced the continued working of the *Dreikaiserbund*; an anxious Austria-Hungary might turn to France, and he hastened to offer a firm promise of support, in order, as he said, to 'dig a ditch between her and the western Powers'. There was, too, the chance that the Russians, who now blamed Bismarck for the failure of their plans in 1878, might be sufficiently alarmed at this new development to forget their resentment and to bid once again for friendship with Germany. Nevertheless, the Austro-German treaty was something of a gamble for Bismarck. It might equally well wreck the whole of his policy by driving Russia into alliance with France. It could also encourage Austria-Hungary to embark on a much more venturesome course in the Balkans, and indeed after his departure in 1890 the weakness of German foreign policy did later allow Germany to become harnessed to Austrian requirements.

From this first step much was to follow; for the next eleven years Bismarck strove to strengthen Germany's position in Europe through a web of written treaties of which Berlin was the central point, while at the same time doing his best to frustrate the creation of any counter system of alliances. In this last he was assisted greatly by the anti-Austrian attitude of the Gladstone administration formed in Great Britain in 1880, and by British anxiety over Russian expansion southward in Central Asia. He was, too, in a strong position to exploit the colonial rivalries of the other Powers, since he had had no intention of involving Germany in Africa or Asia. The only interest that he ever expressed in colonial acquisitions was due mainly to his domestic policy in 1884–5.[1] Thus, he was delighted when in 1881 the French, to the

[1] See p. 276.

anger of the Italians, occupied Tunis; and he was perfectly prepared to encourage Great Britain to take Egypt in 1882, since this might exacerbate her relations with Russia and France.

This mutual antagonism of others enabled him to develop his own system. In June 1881, despite the objections of Austria-Hungary, he managed to renew the *Dreikaiserbund*, which guaranteed a benevolent neutrality if any of the three should find themselves at war with a fourth great Power, including as well a vague understanding over both the annexation of Bosnia by Austria-Hungary and the union of Bulgaria and Eastern Roumelia under Russian influence, both at an unspecified date in the future. By this means he had undone some of the harm that Russo-German relations had suffered through the Congress of Berlin, and could now rely on Russian neutrality in a Franco-German war in return for German neutrality in an Anglo-Russian war.

In May 1882 a Triple Alliance was formed between Germany, Austria-Hungary, and Italy. The Italian government, conscious of Italy's isolation and piqued by the French annexation of Tunis, was only too keen to make a treaty with Germany and hoped that an alliance with Austria-Hungary might assist them in their domestic difficulties with the Pope. Austria-Hungary wanted to silence Italian propaganda attacking her rule over Italians in the South Tyrol and was glad of the promise of Italian neutrality in the event of a war with Russia. Germany, anxious at the momentary improvement in Franco-Russian relations, reckoned to enlist a possible ally against France. The treaties that were signed were to last for five years and were essentially defensive in character. Italy and Germany were each to help the other in the event of one of them being attacked by France. Austria-Hungary was also to help Italy defend herself against France, but here the agreement was not entirely reciprocal, since Italy's assistance to Austria-Hungary against Russia would depend upon Russia's being joined by France.

Although the implications of the Triple Alliance looked both east and west, it did not seriously involve Germany in new commitments. It was the separate agreement of the Dual Alliance of 1879 that continued to draw her into the Balkans. Already in 1881 Austria-Hungary had signed a secret treaty with Prince Milan of Serbia, whereby Serbia became bound to her economically and politically, and in return the prince was allowed in 1882 to assume the title of King. Then in October 1883 Rumania, soured by the loss of southern Bessarabia after her support of Russia in the Turkish war of 1877, signed a secret treaty of mutual defence with Austria-Hungary and Germany. For Austria-Hungary this was a diplomatic *coup*, for not merely had she weaned Rumania from Russia, but also Germany had by this last agreement guaranteed the defence of Austrian interests in the Balkans.

The development of a new crisis in the Balkans soon put this intricate network of German commitments to the test. The trouble began in September 1885, when a revolt against Turkish rule broke out in Eastern Roumelia and the inhabitants declared their intention to be included within the frontiers of Bulgaria. This might well have seemed to be in accordance with Russian ambitions, but by now the attitude of the Powers had changed. Prince Alexander of Battenberg, who had been established as the ruler of Bulgaria, had resisted Russian attempts to make his country a satellite state, and as a consequence in 1885 it was Russia who objected to the enlarging of Bulgaria, while Austria-Hungary and eventually Great Britain—after some hesitation on Lord Salisbury's part—supported it. The situation grew more tense in the autumn, when King Milan of Serbia, determined on compensation for the increase in the size of his neighbour, invaded Bulgaria and was decisively defeated at Slivnitza. At this point Austrian intervention prevented the overrunning of Serbia and in the spring of 1886 the Powers agreed on a personal union of Bulgaria and Eastern Roumelia.

But the crisis was not yet over. In August 1886 the Russians organized the kidnapping of Prince Alexander, who abdicated a few days after his return. Despite considerable pressure, however, it seemed unlikely that Bulgarian nationalists would submit to a Russian nominee on their throne and the Powers began hastily to prepare for a new contest over the Balkans.

In February 1887 Great Britain and Italy signed a treaty in which they were joined by Austria-Hungary in March. This was a purely defensive agreement, no more than a vague promise to cooperate over the maintenance of the *status quo* in the Mediterranean. On the other hand, the renewal of the Central Powers' Triple Alliance, also in February, included additional treaties which went much further than the original arrangements of 1882. Austria-Hungary had hoped to gain a definite promise of Italian assistance in the event of an Austro-Russian war; Bismarck, anxious lest such an agreement would encourage Austria-Hungary to embark on a warlike course, was able to avoid this, and the Austro-Italian treaty simply provided for Italian compensation in the Balkans in the event of any Austrian gains. The Italian treaty with Germany was more positive, for it was agreed that if Italy went to war with France as a result of any further French expansion along the north coast of Africa east of Tunis, she would receive military support from Germany and would be entitled at the end to annex Corsica and Nice.

Naturally this treaty with Italy suggested a far more dangerous involvement for Germany, but it was Bismarck's hope that the recent Mediterranean agreement between Great Britain and Italy could hold France back from making any move along the north African shore. He had wanted to strengthen the position of the Central Powers, if possible without antagonizing Russia, who might otherwise turn to France. It was consequently with Russia that he now embarked upon the most delicate negotiation of all. The terms of the Reinsurance Treaty signed between Germany and Russia in June 1887 had to be woven carefully around all other existing German obligations. It stated that each would remain neutral if the other went to war with a third Power, but the agreement would not become operative if Germany attacked France or if Russia attacked Austria-Hungary. Bismarck had no intention of attacking France and he hoped that the treaty might discourage aggressive action by Russia against Austria-Hungary. Thus the Reinsurance Treaty was not strictly a contravention of the Dual Alliance, which was purely defensive, but it was nevertheless a slightly dubious transaction in that the distinction rested simply on Germany's power to decide whether Austria-Hungary or Russia was the aggressor, if war did break out between them—and the history of Bismarck's own wars had shown how debatable such a definition of aggression could be.

The crisis in the Balkans finally came to a head in July 1887 when the Bulgarians elected Ferdinand of Saxe-Coburg as their prince. Ferdinand, who was a grandson of Louis Philippe and had served as an officer in the Hungarian army, was naturally acceptable to Vienna and it seemed as if Russian intervention was bound to follow. In December a second Mediterranean agreement between Great Britain, Austria-Hungary, and Italy provided for limited support of Turkey against Russia, but when the Austrians requested the assistance of Germany, Bismarck warned them that he could not agree to an Austrian attack on Russia unless they were 'absolutely certain of English cooperation'. His final step to preserve peace in February 1888 was the publication of the Dual Alliance. This was a warning both to Russia if she should attack Austria-Hungary, and to Austria-Hungary, since it revealed to the world that the Dual Alliance was purely defensive and that Austria-

L

Hungary would fight alone if she took the initiative in attacking Russia herself.

After this the tension relaxed. The Russians contented themselves with asking the Sultan to declare the election of Ferdinand illegal. In this they were supported by France and Germany and opposed by Great Britain, Austria-Hungary, and Italy. The Sultan acquiesced in the Russian demand, the Bulgarians ignored the declaration, and since none of the Powers intended to take the matter any further, the crisis could be considered safely past. 'Bulgaria, that little country between the Danube and the Balkans,' declared Bismarck in the Reichstag, 'is not by any means a matter of sufficient importance to justify an all-European war from Moscow to the Pyrenees and from the North Sea to Palermo; at the end after such a war nobody would know just what he had fought for.' His words have a prophetic note; they are a tribute to his common sense, and at the same time a warning against the dangers that his own efforts had helped to create.

24

THE END OF THE ARMED PEACE 1890–1914

1. The break-down of the Bismarckian system 1890–1907

IN 1890, within a year and a half of the accession of the Emperor William II, the long career of Bismarck came abruptly to an end. The fundamental reason for this was that the young emperor and the elderly statesman who had created his empire were temperamentally incompatible. The practical issue over which they split was Bismarck's desire to attack the growing forces of Syndicalism and Socialism within Germany, but it so happened that their clash coincided with a further development in foreign policy—the expiry of the three-year Reinsurance Treaty signed with Russia in 1887.

The treaty had admittedly been a somewhat desperate attempt on Bismarck's part to preserve friendship with Russia alongside the alliance with Austria-Hungary and among the inner circles of the German government there had developed a considerable opposition to it. Baron Fritz von Holstein, the most significant figure at the German Foreign Office from 1890 until 1906, believed that it actually contradicted the terms of the Dual Alliance of 1879, and that in any case it was unlikely to ensure Russian neutrality in the event of a Franco-German war. The German General Staff merely reckoned that in any future war they would have to contend with both Russia and France and were therefore keen to strike at Russia before she became any stronger. With the resignation of Bismarck in March 1890 the government of his successor, General von Caprivi, came markedly under the influence of Holstein, and when shortly afterwards the Russians proposed a renewal of the Reinsurance Treaty for six years, the offer was rejected.

The new German government was thinking of turning from friendship with Russia to alliance with Great Britain and in July 1890 the Anglo-German agreement over Heligoland and East Africa[1] gave some encouragement to these hopes. Unfortunately for the heirs of Bismarck the Russian government drew the same conclusion; 'the

[1] See p. 277.

entente with Germany has virtually been accomplished', the Russian ambassador in London warned St Petersburg, and it was natural that Russia should begin to look in the very direction which Bismarck had always attempted to block. There was already considerable French investment in Russia;[1] France was only too anxious to escape from her own isolation and in August 1890 General de Boisdeffre was invited to attend Russian army manoeuvres.

The formation of a positive Franco-Russian alliance was not yet, however, the immediate aim of either side. The French, like the Russians, would in many ways have welcomed an agreement with Germany, but the somewhat tactless behaviour of William II's mother on a visit to Paris at this time turned public opinion firmly against such an idea; other French groups would have preferred a British alliance, but rivalry over Africa put this out of reach. The Russians themselves still thought wistfully of the Reinsurance Treaty, but when in June 1891 the Triple Alliance of Germany, Austria-Hungary, and Italy was renewed and the Italian premier, Rudini, went out of his way to stress his country's good relations with Great Britain, the Russians and the French finally became convinced that the British were about to join the Central Powers. This was enough to send a French naval squadron on a courtesy visit to Kronstadt, where it was officially welcomed by Alexander III who actually stood up for the playing of the *Marseillaise*. Tsardom could make no greater gesture, and yet military conversations had advanced so little beyond the expression of good intentions during the next twelve months that by July 1892 *Figaro* was demanding 'alliance ou flirt?'

Eventually, in August 1892, a positive military agreement was signed between the two countries. In future, if France were attacked by Germany or by Italy supported by Germany, Russia would attack Germany; alternatively, if Russia were attacked by Germany or by Austria-Hungary supported by Germany, France would attack Germany. If any member of the Triple Alliance mobilized, then France and Russia would both automatically mobilize without further consultation, the French force to number some 1,300,000, the Russian between 700,000 and 800,000. In October 1893 a Russian naval squadron paid a return visit to Toulon and in January 1894 the French government gave its approval of the alliance which had already been officially accepted by Alexander III the previous month. Since it was technically a military agreement, it did not have to be presented to the

[1] See p. 251.

French Chamber, and thus, although its existence was soon common knowledge, the actual terms of the treaty remained secret.

On the face of it the Franco-Russian alliance was not offensive; it mentioned no positive aims such as the return of Alsace and Lorraine and was really little more than an escape for both countries from isolation. As a military agreement, however, it was particularly concerned with the question of mobilization which both sides recognized as a highly significant step. 'Mobilization is declaration of war', remarked General de Boisdeffre. 'To mobilize is to oblige one's neighbour to do the same,' and although the two systems of alliance balanced fairly well during the next twenty years, the obligations that they involved, coupled with the requirements of a speedy mobilization, were to be an essential link in the chain reaction that led to the outbreak of war in 1914.

The immediate consequence of the Franco-Russian alliance was to confirm the recent calculations of the military in Germany and of the naval experts in Great Britain. The German General Staff had long been resigned to the thought of war on two fronts, but their plans for meeting this threat had recently undergone considerable changes. Moltke had reckoned that the repetition of an invasion of France as in 1870 was out of the question and had accordingly planned to hold a defensive position in the west, while making for limited objectives in the east. In 1891, however, Count Alfred von Schlieffen took over as Chief of the General Staff and the whole plan of battle was reversed. Schlieffen disliked the idea of possibly having to give ground in Lorraine and turned instead to the preparation of an attack on France through the Vosges. Much later, however, he devised a new scheme for a great out-flanking movement through Belgium and northern France eventually wheeling south to the west of Paris and enveloping the French forces. This would entail placing so much strength on the German right wing that the French might be able to make some advance in the south and thus the whole line would pivot. In six weeks, however, Schlieffen believed, all would be over in the west and then the German armies could be rushed across Germany by railway to deal with the Russians whose mobilization would have been considerably slower.

The Schlieffen plan, based on the current theory of the sudden 'knock-out blow', has all the completeness of an essentially academic theory, and provides an interesting insight into the totally unpolitical cast of Schlieffen's mind. As a professional soldier it was unthinkable to him that the resistance of the French could continue after they had suffered defeat in the field, although the experience of the *francs-tireurs* during the Franco-Prussian war ought to have taught him caution here. He was indifferent to the diplomatic consequences of the violation of Belgian neutrality which was certain to involve British intervention. More surprising, he seems to have utterly ignored the possibility that the Russians might be able to launch a diversionary attack in the east—as indeed they did in August 1914. Schlieffen remained at the head of the German General Staff until 1906; under his successor, von Moltke, the nephew of William I's Chief of Staff, his plan continued to dominate all German military thought and preparation until 1914, and this was to affect far more than the opening moves in the first World War, for it created a strange diplomatic complication in that, although the most dangerous crises were likely to arise to the east of Germany, any full-scale mobilization would be bound at once to threaten France.

For Great Britain her lack of a large conscript army and the sense of detachment with which she could view events on the Continent were luxuries dependent upon a naval supremacy that had not been challenged since Trafalgar. The problem for the British admirals was whether that supremacy could be maintained in the face of the growing fleets of France, Italy, and Russia. The French construction of ironclads had been a particular source of alarm in the naval scare of 1888 and in the following year Parliament passed a Naval Defence Act which authorized the expenditure of £21,500,000 for the construction of ten new battleships and many smaller craft. It was the near certainty of a Franco-Russian alliance, advertised by the Russian naval visit to Toulon in 1893 that brought the next scare to a head. France and Russia had been Great Britain's two most likely opponents throughout the nineteenth century. Would her naval forces be able to maintain themselves in the Mediterranean and to hold the Straits against their combined fleets? Joseph Chamberlain, for one, had serious doubts. 'The British navy', he remarked, 'would have to cut and run—if it could run,' and in December 1893 Lord George Hamilton formulated the two-Power principle that 'our fleet should be equal to the combination of the two next strongest navies in Europe'. In fact, this was the minimum requirement of the admirals; what they would have liked was a five to three superiority, but this might be difficult to get even under the Conservative government that was formed in 1895.

It was this same sense of insecurity that now caused the British to concentrate on some means of escape from their diplomatic isolation.

Alliance with France was for the moment ruled out by continued antagonism over Egypt and Central Africa. On the other hand, the British were quite open at this time to the thought of an alliance with Germany. Indeed, so far as diplomatic issues were concerned, nothing stood in the way of the two countries becoming firm friends—just as the Russians themselves had imagined at the time when they had retaliated by turning to France. The German government, however, believed that the British were becoming increasingly dependent upon gaining an alliance with them and accordingly made their terms high, insisting that Great Britain should join the Triple Alliance.

Certainly British isolation was to be greatly emphasized by several diplomatic moves in the next few years. In 1895 the pressure which was brought to bear on Japan to make her surrender her mainland gains from China[1] was due to a Continental group formed by France, Germany, and Russia, from which Great Britain was pointedly excluded. In January 1896 she suffered a far greater affront. In South Africa Dr Jameson, a close associate of Cecil Rhodes, had just failed ignominiously in a raid from Southern Bechuanaland into Transvaal territory and William II now sent a famous telegram to the Boer President Kruger congratulating him on having overcome this danger 'without appealing for the help of friendly Powers'. William's intention with this heavy hint was to convince the British government of their isolation and to force them to accept Germany's terms for an alliance. In fact, like most of William's excursions into *la haute politique*, it was based on a misconception of the situation. All that he achieved was to anger public opinion in Great Britain, where a flying squadron was hastily prepared in case of active German intervention, and when he turned to the other Powers for moral support, he found that none of them had the slightest interest in involving themselves in a quarrel with the British over the Transvaal. On two further occasions William strove to bring home her isolation to Great Britain—in August 1897, when he suggested to Tsar Nicholas II that they should act in unison against her, and in June 1898, when he made a similar unsuccessful proposal to the French.

Meanwhile, other significant events were taking place within the Ottoman empire. Between 1893 and 1898 Sultan Abdul Hamid set about crushing a growing nationalist movement among the Armenians, and when the numbers slaughtered appeared to be approaching 200,000, Great Britain, France, and Russia all sent official protests. The Sultan

[1] See p. 279.

did not have to pay much attention to this, since he knew that there was little likelihood of unity among the Powers; Russia herself had little love for the Armenians and in any case would never have agreed to Lord Salisbury's suggestion that a British naval force should be sent through the Straits to the Armenian shore of the Black Sea. The episode, however, was important in two ways. First, it created considerable anti-Turkish feeling in Great Britain; second, the fact that Germany did not send a protest opened the way to closer diplomatic relations between Berlin and Constantinople.

The next event in this part of Europe was the outbreak of war, in 1897, between Turkey and Greece over a revolt of the Greeks under Turkish rule in Crete. At first the Powers had reckoned simply to hold the ring, but a Turkish advance across the plain of Thessaly in April made intervention inevitable and in June an armistice was imposed. By 1898 it had been agreed that Crete should have autonomy, although still technically under the Turkish flag, but the most important outcome of these negotiations lay elsewhere. It sprang from the fact that Russia was by now wanting to concentrate on her Far Eastern policy without being hampered by any complications in the Balkans. France, however, refusing to go beyond the letter of the treaty of 1894, was not prepared to stand guard for Russia. She 'would not regard herself as at all committed in a conflict which sprang from the question of the Black Sea and the Straits', the Russian ambassador was informed in December 1896, and on this Russia turned instead to her most likely opponent. Negotiations during the Cretan war in 1897 revealed that Austria-Hungary was only too anxious to preserve the *status quo* in the Balkans, and in April Russia reached a firm agreement with her over this, fully accepting the situation created by the Treaty of Berlin in 1878, including the Austrian occupation of Bosnia and Herzegovina. Thus the Russians were free to concentrate entirely on the Far East and from now until 1905 there was to be a diplomatic truce in the Balkans.

This change of direction in Russian interests had a marked effect upon Great Britain. Until now, although no longer so confident over her isolation, she had not tried very hard to escape from it, but the growth of Russian influence in the Far East, coupled with the granting of territorial concessions to France and Germany on the Chinese coast,[1] made it important for her to find an ally who would safeguard her own interests in these regions.

[1] See p. 279.

There followed as a consequence two serious attempts by Great Britain to gain a positive alliance with Germany. The first was mainly the work of Joseph Chamberlain in 1898. It failed because William II believed rightly that Germany had no fundamental interests to defend in Africa or the Far East. 'The Niger and the Gulf of Pechili concern us less than Alsace–Lorraine.' And for this reason, knowing that Russia was Great Britain's principal opponent, he was anxious not to become a cat's-paw for the British. 'Chamberlain must not forget', he remarked, 'that in East Prussia I have one Prussian army corps against three Russian armies and nine cavalry divisions from which no Chinese wall divides me and which no English ironclads hold at arm's length.' And so although they reached a minor agreement over British control of the Portuguese Delagoa Bay railway, the first attempt came to nothing.

Further developments in the intervening years before the second attempt made its success extremely unlikely. It is true that the Fashoda episode[1] had heightened Anglo-French antagonism and had been followed by a re-affirmation of the Franco-Russian alliance which was now slightly extended in its stated aims to include 'the maintenance of the balance of power'. In every other respect, however, the likelihood of an Anglo-German alliance receded. Germany herself was continuing to cultivate her friendship with Turkey. In 1898 William II paid a second visit to Constantinople and plans were discussed for the building of a Berlin–Baghdad railway. Long afterwards this scheme was often quoted as an instance of German economic imperialism stretching out a tentacle into the Middle East. At the time it was only Russia who made serious objections, since such a line seemed likely to cut her off from the Balkans, whereas the British and French governments were, on the whole, not displeased to see German interest diverted from Africa. A further incident was the outbreak of the Boer war which made Great Britain intensely unpopular on the Continent, although the other Powers had to swallow their indignation when they found themselves in need of cooperation with Great Britain over the quelling of the Boxer rising against foreign influence in China.

More decisive than all these events, however, was the German decision to build a navy. The policy of adopting a somewhat distant attitude towards Great Britain, which the politicians had mistakenly imagined would drive her into a German alliance on their terms, had begun to create a sense of rivalry between the two countries and the

[1] See p. 277.

L 2

dispatch of a British naval squadron in 1896 in response to William's telegram to Kruger had naturally lent force to the demands of the German naval enthusiasts. In 1897 Bülow replaced Marschall as German Foreign Minister and Admiral von Tirpitz became Minister of Marine; there followed in 1898 the first German Navy Law which laid the foundations of a large battle fleet, and the excited approval with which this was greeted may be gauged from the creation of the German Navy League financed by the industrialist Krupp and gaining 240,000 members within three years. For the British it was understandable that such a step should seem a considerable challenge. Their army, although reformed, was tiny by Continental standards; the building of a German navy naturally seemed like a direct threat to their own security, and William II's personal attitude certainly gave some justification for alarm in Great Britain. 'I am not in a position to go beyond the strictest neutrality,' he said at the time of the Boer war, 'and I must first get for myself a fleet. In twenty years' time, when the fleet is ready, I can use another language.'

The passing of the second German Navy Law in 1900, making provision for a still larger fleet, did not in itself prevent Lord Lansdowne from attempting a new approach to Germany in 1901. As in 1898, however, this came to nothing. The British government was still primarily concerned with the Far East, and the Germans, convinced that a war between Great Britain and Russia was imminent, had no intention of being drawn into it. They still believed that if they waited long enough the British would be bound to turn to them and they ignored the warnings of the German ambassador in London who suggested that the British might look elsewhere—a threat which Holstein dismissed as 'an absolute swindle'. As it turned out, this second rejection was to prove the crucial miscalculation of German foreign policy. The loss of the chance of an alliance with Great Britain was to deprive Germany of room for diplomatic manoeuvre and to throw her back on to entire dependence upon Austria-Hungary. Thus Great Britain moved into the orbit of her opponents, and the growing excitement of public opinion in both countries over the naval question, coupled with William II's almost pathological mistrust of Edward VII, made any reversal of this situation extremely unlikely.

Eventually, in 1902, Great Britain found in Japan the partner that her particular interests required. Both of them had reason to mistrust the growth of Russian influence in Manchuria, particularly after the suppression of the Boxer rising; both had recently failed to reach agreement with Russia, and a treaty was duly signed between them on 30 January 1902. Each recognized the other's interest in China; if either were involved in war with a third Power, the other would observe strict neutrality; if either were involved in war with *two* Powers, then the other would lend active assistance. For the British this treaty simply forestalled any Russo-Japanese alliance aimed at a partition of economic interests in China, and it fortified the Japanese sufficiently to contemplate an attack on Russia. The terms of the treaty were published at once, thus making French support of Russia in such a war much less likely, since this, according to the Anglo-Japanese treaty, would bring France into direct conflict with Great Britain— over an issue in which no French interests were seriously at stake.

This last factor was to play an important part in the next develop-ment in European diplomacy, since the French, anxious to avoid being dragged into a Russo-Japanese war, began to look for an alignment that would help to keep them out. This clearly pointed to some sort of agreement with Great Britain. There was a further motive for the French in that Delcassé, the Foreign Minister, was aiming to establish direct control over Morocco; he had already gained Italian acceptance of such a move in 1902 by promising French acquiescence over the future annexation of Tripoli by Italy, but Spain was not prepared to agree without the assent of Great Britain, who was bound to be con-cerned about the security of Gibraltar.

British motives were rather less precise. They were still hoping to find a European ally without entangling themselves in excessive commitments, and the growth of German naval rivalry now naturally inclined them a little more towards France. Even so the process was a slow one. Shortly after King Edward VII had paid a famous State visit to Paris in May 1903, private negotiations were opened, but it was not until a year later that agreement was reached on a number of specific points. As well as a settlement over the frontier of Gambia and over spheres of influence in Siam, this included a mutual recognition of British interests in Egypt and French interests in Morocco, although over this last the British were careful to stipulate that they should enjoy commercial equality with the French and that the Mediterranean coast-line opposite Gibraltar should remain unfortified. Thus, the Anglo-French *entente cordiale* of 1904 involved no treaty of alliance between the two countries; yet these highly limited political agree-ments between them were to form the basis of a remarkable psycho-logical reconciliation which subsequent events were to strengthen.

Before the agreements had been signed, it suddenly seemed to the French that the worst had happened. The Japanese, despairing of ever being able to persuade the Russians to evacuate Manchuria, launched a naval attack on Port Arthur on 8 February 1904 without any official declaration of war. The course of the fighting was governed by the fact that the Russians failed to gain control of the sea, and the Japanese were thus able to build up their reinforcements; in January 1905 Port Arthur fell to them and, as they advanced northwards, General Nogi succeeded in out-manoeuvring the Russian forces drawn up in defence of Mukden. There is an element of fantasy in the last act of this drama when the Russian Baltic fleet, having sailed all the way round the Cape of Good Hope to come to grips with the enemy, duly did so on 27 May 1905 and was annihilated in the Straits of Tshushima. American mediation now led to the signing of the Treaty of Portsmouth in September 1905. Inevitably this meant considerable cessions to Japan—Port Arthur, the southern half of the island of Sakhalin, part of the railway in Manchuria and Russian recognition of Japanese supremacy in Korea. On the other hand, hardly any indemnity was charged and no lasting bitterness created, so that in the next few years Russia and Japan were able to draw closer together over the division of Manchuria into spheres of influence.

The most striking aspect of the war had been the effectiveness of the Japanese forces against a major European Power, and at a technical level naval experts had duly noted the psychological effect of the torpedo and the mine, even if the practical efficiency of both still left a good deal to be desired. But although it was fought on the other side of the earth, it also had considerable political repercussions in Europe. Germany regarded the situation with some satisfaction, since she was convinced that the long anticipated war between Great Britain and Russia was now about to break out. Indeed, there had been a moment of great tension in October 1904 when the Russian Baltic fleet at the beginning of its fateful voyage to the east opened fire on British fishing boats off the Dogger Bank in the North Sea under the impression that they were Japanese torpedo boats. However, the Germans' hope that the Russians would now turn hastily to them for an alliance was shattered by the determination of the French to prevent a war in which they would have to choose between their alliance with Russia and their new friendship with Great Britain. The crisis came to nothing. The Russians were too occupied in the Far East, and for the British there was by now not the slightest need for war with Russia; their Japanese alliance gave them the support that they needed in China and the Anglo-French *entente* had helped to quieten their fears of the combined French and Russian navies—particularly after the Japanese had dealt so effectively with the Russian fleet at Tshushima.

Thus, despite the fears of the French, the Russo-Japanese war did not seriously endanger the new alignment. There were, however, other trials ahead. The German government, conscious of having lost their immediate chance of a British alliance, began to take positive steps towards both weakening the Anglo-French *entente* and working towards some sort of agreement with Russia. The obvious trouble spot that might still split Great Britain and France was Morocco, and on 31 March 1905 William II landed at Tangier and made a public statement that Germany would regard Morocco as an independent country. The purpose of this artificially stimulated crisis was to cause an international conference to be convened, where the Germans hoped that the weakness of the Anglo-French *entente* would be revealed to the whole world. A little later, in July, William II sailing in his yacht in the Gulf of Finland had a consultation with Tsar Nicholas II at Björkö, where the two sovereigns agreed on a treaty of defensive alliance against attack by any European Power in Europe.

In the event each of these schemes failed. The Björkö agreement was ratified by neither government, Bülow in Germany fearing that it would be too great a liability, the Russian ministers apprehensive of offending France on whose support they now felt far more dependent after Russia's poor showing in the war with Japan. Over Morocco the Germans did get their conference. It was held at Algeciras in January 1906, but it failed conspicuously to strengthen Germany's hand. The *entente* Powers remained undivided, whereas Germany found herself supported only by Austria-Hungary. Thus, with the defection of Italy the Powers of the Triple Alliance had themselves been revealed as the weaker group; on the other hand, Germany's initiative in provoking this conference now led the British and the French to begin a series of purely informal military conversations which were later to be of considerable significance.

The failure of the German emperor's diplomacy was to be followed by another remarkable development—the formation of the Anglo-Russian *entente* of 1907. Russia's weakness as revealed by her war with Japan made her anxious to find another friend, and her fears of German influence in Persia through the building of the Berlin–Baghdad railway suggested that it would be as well to end her differences with Great

Britain. On the British side there was the desire to prevent Russia from drifting back to her policy of a Reinsurance Treaty with Germany, and when Sir Edward Grey became Foreign Secretary in the 1906 Liberal administration in Great Britain, negotiations began almost at once.

The convention between the two countries was finally signed in August 1907. Like the Anglo-French *entente*, it simply took the form of the settlement of a number of disputes without the creation of a positive alliance. A striking feature of the negotiations was the new freedom with which the British, now firmly based on Egypt, felt they could discuss the opening of the Straits, and although Grey did not intend to throw in such a concession immediately, he did suggest a vague promise for the future. This was sufficient to give the British the best of the deal in Central Asia, where it was agreed that Tibet should be a neutral state, while Russia renounced her interests in Afghanistan. In Persia the spoil was to be shared—a northern zone including the capital, Teheran, to be a Russian sphere of influence, a southern zone on the north side of the Gulf to be a British one, while the area in the middle was to be neutral.

The news of the *entente* was not well received in Great Britain, where public opinion was strongly anti-Russian; liberals and radicals disliked the *pogroms* of the Jews and the crushing of the revolution of 1905,[1] and the cry went up that Russia had gained too much from the bargain. In fact, the agreements represented a reasonably fair settlement of a number of outstanding disputes and in the area in which Russia seemed to have done best—in Persia—it was no more than a recognition of the existing situation. In Germany reactions were still stronger. In 1885 Bismarck, commenting on the possibility of an Anglo-French-Russian alliance, had remarked: 'it would provide the basis for a coalition against us more dangerous for Germany than any other she might have to face'. The terms of the Anglo-Russian *entente* make it clear that there was no conscious attempt at the encirclement of the Central Powers here; yet it was perhaps understandable that many Germans should think so, and there could be no denying that Germany's diplomatic position had deteriorated greatly since the departure of Bismarck in 1890.

[1] See p. 291.

2. The approach of war 1907–14

From now until the outbreak of the first World War European relations were dominated by two general factors—the renewal of rivalry between Russia and Austria-Hungary over the Balkans, and the growing naval competition between Great Britain and Germany.

There were in the main two reasons for the end of the diplomatic truce between Russia and Austria-Hungary. First, Russia's defeat by Japan and the settlement of many of her disputes with Great Britain along her Asian frontiers turned her attention back once again to the Balkans. Second, there had recently been a radical change of policy in Serbia. Until 1903 under the rule of King Alexander Obrenović this had been pro-Austrian, but in that year a group of officers carried out a palace revolution in Belgrade, assassinated the King and his Queen Draga and established a new king, Peter Karageorgović. This meant much more than simply another bloody chapter in the story of a Balkan feud, since King Peter introduced parliamentary government and embarked upon a pro-Russian policy, at the same time drawing money and munitions from France.

At first, Austrian reactions to this change in Serbia were only mild, but in 1906 with the appointment of Aehrenthal as Foreign Minister and Conrad von Hötzendorff as Chief of the General Staff a far stiffer attitude was adopted. For the moment relations with Russia were not upset; in September 1908 Aehrenthal and the Russian Foreign Minister Izvolski met at Buchlau, where they agreed that Austria-Hungary should proclaim the annexation of Bosnia and Herzegovina, which had in fact been under Austrian military occupation since 1878;[1] thus, without moving a single soldier, an effective blow would be dealt to the pride of the Serbs who had long hoped to gain these provinces for themselves. In return, Aehrenthal agreed that Izvolski should canvass the governments of Europe on the opening of the Straits.

Unfortunately for their future relations Austria-Hungary allowed Russia very little time in which to make sure of her side of the bargain. Izvolski had just come up against objections to the Russian proposals at London and Paris, when he heard on 6 October that Aehrenthal had openly proclaimed the annexation of Bosnia and Herzegovina. Taken by surprise, Izvolski swung round and supported the Serbs in their indignation. The crisis lasted several months, but this time— unlike Algeciras—it was the Central Powers who won the day. Great

---

[1] See p. 301.

Britain condemned the annexation, but had no military commitment; France, who had ultimately, was hesitant in her support of Russia, whereas Germany took her stand positively by Austria-Hungary. 'The moment Russia mobilizes,' wrote Moltke to Conrad in January 1909, 'Germany also will mobilize and will unquestionably mobilize her whole army.' Thus, in March 1909 Russia decided to accept the situation and the only remaining formality was for Turkey to receive an indemnity of £2,400,000.

The Bosnian crisis was, on the face of it, a victory for the Central Powers—an outcome that was to have a significant effect on Russia's attitude in 1914. Yet it was a victory that entailed certain disadvantages, since the very realization of the fact soon brought the *entente* Powers closer together. Nor from Germany's point of view was the new turn in diplomacy an entirely happy one, since the Moltke–Conrad correspondence, supported by William II, seemed to bind Germany to underwriting the whole of Austria-Hungary's activities in the Balkans—an interpretation of the Dual Alliance of 1879 of which Bismarck would never have approved. 'There exist specifically Austrian interests which we cannot undertake to defend,' he had said in the Reichstag in 1887, 'and there are specifically German interests which Austria cannot undertake to defend. We cannot each adopt the other's special interests.'

A further outcome of the Bosnian crisis was the stimulation of anti-Austrian feeling in Serbia. A new society for national defence, *Narodna Obrana*, was founded to encourage the training of spies and saboteurs and the dissemination of anti-Habsburg propaganda in Bosnia. In 1909, after Austrian objections to its activities, this had to be turned into a purely cultural organization, which, however, could still act as a screen for a secret society—the Black Hand—continuing to work at the original objectives. One of the leaders of this secret organization, Colonel Dragutin Dimitriević, who acted under the code name of Apis, was chief of the Intelligence Department of the Serbian General Staff and had earlier participated in the assassination of King Alexander in 1903. The Black Hand, which received a good deal of support in high places, while remaining essentially unofficial, was extremely successful in establishing contact with Serb and Croat students from Croatia; in 1910 and 1913 it was responsible for two abortive attempts to assassinate the Austrian Governor of Bosnia, and in 1914 was to accomplish the most resounding political murder of its career.

At the same time as this reawakening of hostility in the Balkans the

British and the Germans were continuing to compete over the size of their respective navies. In Great Britain Sir John Fisher, First Sea Lord from 1904, was realigning the whole disposition of British naval forces, basing them on Malta, Gibraltar, and the home ports, particularly in the north of Scotland, and despite the desire of the Liberal government to limit naval rearmament the development of long-range gunnery and the torpedo necessitated the laying down of a new design of all-big-gun ship—the *Dreadnought*. In Germany, in 1908, an amendment to the Navy Law raised the number of capital ships to be constructed from three to four a year, but it was not until 1909 that the Liberal government in Great Britain was prepared to retaliate, alarmed by the rumours of ship-building in Austria-Hungary and Italy.

The next crisis in Germany's relations with the west came in 1911— once again over Morocco. A local rebellion had driven the Sultan out of his capital at Fez, which French troops proceeded to occupy in order to restore order, and Germany, determined on compensation for any French gains in this area, declared that France's action nullified the Algeciras agreement and on 1 July sent a German gunboat, the *Panther*, to Agadir as a token of her interest in the affair. The German demand for the French Congo was rejected by France, but the Prime Minister Caillaux was known to be friendly towards Germany and the British government was alarmed lest France and Germany might strike a private bargain which might include the cession of Agadir to Germany as a naval base on the Atlantic coast. Thus, when the British Chancellor of the Exchequer, Lloyd George, announced in a speech at the Mansion House on 21 July that Great Britain could not be indifferent to these possible changes, the warning may have been addressed as much to France as to Germany. The war scare mounted throughout August, but in September there was a financial panic in Germany and by the beginning of November a new agreement had been negotiated, whereby Germany recognized France's right to establish a protectorate over Morocco in return for a small part of the French Congo with access to the sea.

War for the moment had been averted, yet the second Morocco crisis was followed by a succession of developments that continued to threaten the peace of Europe. Italy, regarding the establishment of French power in Morocco as imminent, now resolved to seize Tripoli from Turkey. She had already gained the assent of the French[1] and the British over this and at the end of September 1911 embarked upon a

[1] See p. 315.

war with Turkey in which the Italian fleet bombarded Beirut and carried out the occupation of some of the Aegean islands. By the spring of 1912 her activity in these waters had so alarmed the British that they intervened diplomatically, and in October 1912 the Treaty of Lausanne was signed between the belligerents, whereby Italy gained Tripoli and Cyrenaica, but not the Aegean islands, which were to be evacuated—although the Italians never actually complied with this last condition.

A further consequence of the second Morocco crisis was the dissatisfaction of the naval enthusiasts in Germany. Tirpitz considered that they had 'suffered a diplomatic check and we must solve it by a supplementary naval bill'; he was thinking now of attaining naval parity with Great Britain by 1920 and he did succeed in gaining increases in plans for construction. All this, however, was in conflict with the advice of the German ambassador in London, Count Metternich: 'if we now state bluntly to the British government the alternatives: either you remain neutral or we increase our fleet, the result will be an even closer attachment to France—if the relations between England and France could be closer than they are at present.' Indeed, the politicians of Germany and Great Britain were by no means happy about this growing naval competition; Bethmann Hollweg, the Chancellor, did not care greatly for Tirpitz's programme and as a matter of principle Asquith's Liberal government objected to an armaments race. It was this attitude that led to the visit of Lord Haldane to Germany in 1912, but although negotiations continued over colonial questions and a Mesopotamian railway agreement, Germany's price still remained far too high for any definite political alliance to be achieved.

The news of the Haldane visit did, however, have a marked effect upon French diplomatic activity. Military conversations between the British and French General Staffs had concentrated on the dispatch of a British military force to the Continent in the event of war and now a co-ordination of naval strategy led to a revolutionary change in British dispositions in that the French in future were to be responsible for the Mediterranean, thus leaving the British free to concentrate on their home waters and the Channel.

At the same time France was anxious to strengthen her ties with Russia, which had not shown themselves to be particularly effective during the crises of 1908 and 1911. The Russians, too, were conscious of the need to reinforce their position, since they were anticipating further complications in the Balkans. The tension here was due to the formation of a Balkan league. In March 1912 Serbia and Bulgaria had signed a treaty for the partition of Macedonia and in May this had been joined by Greece and Montenegro. Russia herself had become involved in these negotiations, since Turkey's performance in the recent war with Italy suggested that she was now no longer strong enough to guard the Straits, which were a vital trade route for Russia's economy. The Tsar's government did not care greatly for the projected partition; yet they did not wish to offend the Balkan *bloc* on whom the security of the Straits might soon depend.

In August, shortly after these developments in the Balkans, the French Prime Minister, Poincaré, visited Russia, and the subsequent conversations were to be of immense significance in attaching a far wider interpretation to their existing agreements. According to the military treaty of 1892 French aid to Russia would only follow an attack on Russia by Germany or Austria-Hungary supported by Germany. The Bosnian crisis of 1908, however, had made it clear that the problem was hardly likely to be so clear-cut. If Serbia were threatened by Austria-Hungary, Russia might well find herself attacking Austria-Hungary in Serbia's defence, and if a German attack on Russia then followed in accordance with the Dual Alliance of 1879, whose terms had been made public by Bismarck in 1887, it might have been possible for France to argue that Russia had brought this upon herself by her own action and that the Franco-Russian alliance therefore did not become militarily operative. The Poincaré visit now established the fact that if such circumstances should arise, France would regard herself as bound to support Russia. Thus the agreement supplied a fatal link in the chain of diplomatic commitments; for, when it is taken in conjunction with the Moltke–Conrad correspondence of January 1909,[1] it is clear that the situation had been finally created whereby a Balkan crisis could lead automatically to a general war. This was certainly not intentional. It is true that certain historians of the post-war period seized on the agreement as a dastardly plot by French and Russian politicians, but it is by now generally accepted by German as well as French historians that it did not represent a warlike policy. It sprang simply from a desire to bolster up the Franco-Russian alliance which without this further interpretation would have been virtually meaningless in the circumstances of 1912.

Within a couple of months the Russians were proved correct in their

[1] See p. 320.

anticipation of a new Balkan crisis, when in October Montenegro, swiftly followed by Bulgaria, Greece, and Serbia, declared war on Turkey. They were everywhere successful. The Bulgarians attacked through Thrace and were only checked before Constantinople, while the Serbs drove south and the Greeks north into what was left of Turkish territory in Europe. This was a crisis entirely of the Balkan states' own making—a novel situation for the great Powers, who found themselves watching a radical alteration in the *status quo* contrary to their own interests. Russia had no intention of letting Constantinople fall to Bulgaria, while Austria-Hungary was determined to prevent Serbia from gaining a part of the Adriatic coast, and on 3 December 1912 the Powers cooperated to impose an armistice which was followed by a peace conference at London. Here they were able to agree to the creation of a new state, Albania, which effectively prevented Serbia from extending her frontiers to the Adriatic and a peace treaty was finally signed on 30 May 1913.

Once again, however, the Balkan states showed that a mere agreement among the great Powers was now no longer sufficient to decide their fate. Serbia, demanding compensation for the loss of the territories involved in the creation of Albania, insisted on retaining areas of Macedonia that were to have been part of Bulgaria's share of the spoil. Bulgaria, confident of her own military powers, declared war on Greece and Serbia and at once encountered disaster. Rumania joined her two opponents; Turkey was able to recapture Adrianople, and in August 1913 the Treaty of Bucharest robbed Bulgaria of some of her recent gains as well as the region of the Dobruja, which was taken by Rumania.

The Powers accepted the Treaty of Bucharest, but the emergence of a greatly enlarged Serbia suggested to the government at Vienna that the hour might not be far distant when she would attempt to adopt the role of Piedmont in 1859 or of Prussia in 1866. From now on, Conrad, the Chief of Staff, and Count Leopold von Berchtold, who had become Austrian Prime Minister in February 1912, thought to seek a solution in a short war, followed by the partition of Serbia. Italy seemed unreliable, but William II made it clear that Austria-Hungary could count on German support. 'You can be certain I stand behind you and am ready to draw the sword whenever your action makes it necessary,' William told him in October, '. . . whatever comes from Vienna is to me a command.'

This subservience of German policy to Austrian requirements was all the more dangerous because of the mounting armaments race between the Powers. Already in January 1913 a new German Army Law had increased the annual intake of conscripts from 280,000 to 343,000; in March the German government had ignored Winston Churchill's proposal for a short truce in naval construction, and the widening of the Kiel Canal for the larger German battleships was proceeding with all speed. In August 1913 France extended her period of military service to three years—the only way in which she could compete with Germany's greater population. Russia, too, was planning an expansion of her military forces, and in Great Britain measures were taken for the defence of the new naval bases at Cromarty and Scapa Flow.

Even so, it was not impossible for the Powers to reach agreement over some of their difficulties. When Russia protested at the appointment of a German general, Liman von Sanders, as head of a military mission at Constantinople with command of a Turkish army corps, Germany was prepared in January 1914 to make his post purely advisory. And even later in 1914 relations between Great Britain and Germany actually seemed to be improving with conversations about Africa and an agreement over the south of Persia.

Everything rested on the situation in the Balkans and it was here that the Black Hand organization in Serbia brought about the last fatal crisis. For some time Colonel Dimitriević—Apis—had been determined on a fresh assassination attempt; a plan to strike down General Potiorek, the Austrian Governor of Bosnia, came to nothing, but when in the late summer of 1913 Potiorek invited Francis Ferdinand, the heir to the Habsburg throne, to attend army manoeuvres in Bosnia in June 1914, Apis decided that here was a more illustrious victim. In April 1914 he had selected three of the youths who were to take part in the attempt and by the end of May they had already secretly crossed the frontier from Serbia into Bosnia. At this point in the drama Pašić, the Prime Minister of Serbia, seems to have heard something of the plot and was consequently faced with a highly unpleasant dilemma. To denounce it might lead to his own assassination by the Black Hand and would in any case place Serbia in a difficult diplomatic position; on the other hand, to let it go forward might have the most appalling consequences. His reaction to the problem was to send a guarded warning to Vienna—so guarded that it never penetrated to the relevant authorities. As it was, Francis Ferdinand duly attended the manoeuvres in June 1914 and on the last day of his visit proceeded with his wife to pay a formal visit to Sarajevo. On the way to the City Hall the bomb that was thrown at their car did not harm them, but on the return journey, owing to a remarkable series of mischances, their car actually came to a halt within a few yards of the spot where Gavrilo Princip, one of the young conspirators, was standing on the pavement. Princip shot them both with his revolver and at such close range it was inevitable that their wounds should be mortal.

Nearly all those involved in the plot were captured by the police. Their Serbian origin was undeniable and although they declared that they were not acting on orders, Berchtold and Conrad at once believed that fate had presented them with a justification for the war which would enable them to crush Serbia. The German government supported them, simply envisaging a local war between the two countries, and on 23 July Austria-Hungary presented Serbia with an overwhelming ultimatum. A few minutes before its expiry Serbia accepted almost all its conditions, but the Austrians were determined not to hold back. They were still unable to prove conclusively a positive link between the Sarajevo conspirators and the Serbian government, and diplomatic intervention by the other Powers might rob them of what seemed a golden opportunity. On 28 July Austria-Hungary, insisting that she was simply engaging in local hostilities in self-defence, declared war on Serbia.

For Russia this new crisis was too reminiscent of the Bosnian episode of 1908. She had failed Serbia then, and if she failed her again, her influence at Belgrade would finally be lost. On 26 July the Tsar had already reassured the Serbian Crown Prince that 'Russia will in no case be indifferent to the fate of Serbia', and on 28 July Russia began a partial mobilization against Austria-Hungary. On the following day Germany warned Russia that if she did not desist, German mobilization would be bound to follow. But by now technical considerations were beginning to predominate. The Russian General Staff could not carry out their plans properly without a general mobilization, and on 30 July the Tsar, convinced that the only alternative was the abandonment of Serbia, consented to this.

In Berlin Bethmann Hollweg, highly alarmed at the course that events were taking, was beginning to urge caution on Vienna; yet at the same time Moltke was demanding more positive action. On 31 July Germany began general mobilization and when Russia refused a further request to check her own measures, Germany declared war on her on 1 August. The problem here was that German mobilization automatically involved the Schlieffen plan which was based on the assumption of war against France. The French were accordingly asked to promise their neutrality in a Russo-German war; this was known to be extremely unlikely and even if they had agreed, the Germans intended to force the issue by asking for the surrender of Verdun and Toul. In reply, the French Prime Minister, Viviani, stated simply that 'France will act in accordance with her interests'; a German declaration of war followed on 3 August, and when the opening stages of the Schlieffen plan led on naturally to the invasion of Belgium by Germany, Great Britain declared war on 4 August.

Few historical issues have been the subject of such detailed analysis and controversy as the outbreak of the first World War. Colonial and economic rivalries, the chauvinism of public opinion, and the quickening of the armaments race have all been suggested as fundamental causes of which diplomacy was merely the reflection. All these had added greatly to the air of tension, yet none of them can be seen to have been particularly decisive in 1914. Indeed, the settlement of colonial disputes by peaceful means had been one of the most remarkable achievements of the period; nor can economic factors be simplified sufficiently to account for the military conflict. In fact, the immediate political circumstances point to the fundamental cause. Serb nationalism was ultimately incompatible with the continued existence of the multi-national Habsburg state, and the Austrians, believing that they must learn their lesson from the events of 1859 and 1866, resolved to crush Serbia while they had the support of Germany. Certainly there were wild elements at work in Serbia; the assassination of Francis Ferdinand was from a European point of view an act of the utmost folly; yet the virtual acceptance of the Austrian ultimatum by Serbia does place a heavy burden of responsibility for the war on Austria-Hungary.

Beyond this, the fate of Europe had become bound up in the workings of a diplomatic machine of rival alliances. Local war could only be prevented from becoming general if one of the two groups was prepared to give way and this time neither would do so. A consequence of Germany's diplomatic arrogance in the previous years had been to leave her utterly dependent on her alliance with Austria-Hungary, a crucial factor, since the policy of Berchtold and Conrad might well have been different, had they not had the unqualified support of Germany. For Russia the problem was the maintenance of her own influence in Serbia. Without this the changing situation in the Balkans might well mean the eventual control of the Straits by a hostile Power. For France the principal fear remained the armed might of Germany; hence Poincaré, now President of the Third Republic, on a visit to St Petersburg in July reaffirmed the Franco-Russian alliance, although it is true that on 30 July the French government was urging caution on her Russian partner.

Great Britain was not directly involved in this tangle of diplomatic retaliation and it has sometimes been suggested that war might have been averted, if Sir Edward Grey, the British Foreign Secretary, had made it clear to the Central Powers that Great Britain would come to the aid of France. This criticism ignores Grey's difficulty that, whatever his personal views, he could not hope to convince the Liberal cabinet of the need to intervene in a continental war over Serbia; only the invasion of Belgium would stir British public opinion sufficiently to accept this step. In fact, an earlier British intervention would have made no difference at all. The German cry of encirclement presupposed British enmity, and in any case Germany had little interest in the tiny British army; when the British expeditionary force did cross the Channel to France in August, Moltke told the German navy not to stop it, since he wished to destroy it on land. Furthermore, while an announcement of British intervention would have had no effect upon the Central Powers, it might well have encouraged the French and the Russians to take an even firmer line at a time when Grey was hoping that negotiation might still be possible.

It was, however, not diplomacy alone that was responsible for the final stages in the story. The most significant factor in these last fateful days was the surrender of the diplomats to the needs of the General Staffs. The final moves in Austria-Hungary, Germany, and Russia were dictated by the technical requirements of military programmes all constructed round the launching or the parrying of the vital 'knock-out blow'. Long ago Bismarck had foreseen the danger when he had advised the Austrian government: 'we must both take care that the privilege of giving political advice to our monarchs does not in fact slip out of our hands and pass over to the General Staffs'.

Diplomacy had failed and the military staffs had had their way. Yet there was, too, another failure at this time—the collapse of the scheme of the Second International to paralyse all efforts to wage war. It had been their hope that in all countries a general strike and a refusal to join the colours would cause the machinery of war to break in the hands of the belligerent governments.[1] Yet to the chagrin of the leading Socialists they found that the rank and file of the Socialist parties only echoed the cries of their governments. 'We will not have our women and children sacrificed to the brutality of the Cossacks,' remarked the editor of *Vorwärts*, the German Social Democrat newspaper, and when Hermann Müller, a member of the central executive, rushed frantically to Paris on 1 August, he found that the French Socialists were prepared to vote in favour of war credits against German attack. Only in Serbia did two Social Democrat members of parliament have the courage to vote against war credits, while in Russia Mensheviks and Bolsheviks abstained. Otherwise, although the summer of 1914 had been a time of considerable industrial unrest, the governments found that Socialists were prepared to fall in obediently behind them. Of the two great forces that had exercised such power over men's minds during the past century, nationalism had proved stronger than Socialism.

The whole Continent was now to be torn by a long and desperate war; yet even on the brink of the catastrophe the spirit of the nineteenth century preserved its civilized forms. In London the authorities provided meticulously for the safe departure of the German and Austrian ambassadors and their staffs, while in Berlin, when a crowd flung stones at the windows of the British Embassy, the German emperor apologized to the British ambassador. In Austria-Hungary, where the government was so badly in need of positive proof that the assassination of Francis Ferdinand had been on the orders of the Serbian government, no torture was used on the conspirators and at the end of their trial Princip and several of his companions were held to be too young to be executed and were sentenced instead to imprisonment. More extraordinary still, the Serbian Commander-in-Chief, Marshal Putnik, who was actually in Austria for medical treatment at the time of the crisis, was contacted by the police in July and hastily sent back to Serbia. As Sir Edward Grey remarked at the time, the lamps were going out all over Europe; yet it was typical of the old order to ensure at least that they went out with dignity.

[1]See p. 258.

VI

THE ECLIPSE OF NINETEENTH-CENTURY
EUROPE 1914–21

25

THE GREAT WAR 1914–18

1. The failure of the offensives 1914

FEW wars have been so terrible in their course or so dramatic in their consequences as the war of 1914–18. In the savage pattern of the twentieth century it now has its place simply as 'the first World War'—the forerunner of the second; but for the generation that grew up after 1918 it was 'the Great War', an event of unparalleled horror that seemed to have left the participants numbed by the very memory of it. For four years millions of men faced each other in trenches across a shattered No-man's-land; they were smashed by shell-fire, shot, burnt, and gassed; wounded men hung for days on the barbed wire between the lines until they died, and hundreds of thousands were mown down in long murderous offensives that achieved virtually nothing. The Great War was the war of the unknown civilian soldier, and the thunder of the artillery barrages and the rattle of the machine-guns were like some requiem for the civilization of the nineteenth century.

One man, at least, had foreseen the type of war that would come. 'Everybody will be entrenched in the next war. It will be a great war of entrenchment. The spade will be as indispensible to the soldier as his rifle. . . . Your soldiers may fight as they please, the ultimate decision is in the hands of famine.' But the author of this remarkable prophecy made in 1899 was a civilian, a banker of Warsaw, and certainly no professional soldier would have envisaged such a turn of events in August 1914. The prevailing belief was in the swift 'knock-out blow' and in the eyes of the professional the whole issue would be resolved in a race to launch the various plans of operations. All these schemes, however, were upset by one miscalculation. The period of armed peace since 1871 had deprived any single country of that overwhelming superiority which the 'knock-out blow' demanded. The Dual Alliance and the Entente Powers had created something of a balance and, even after this had failed to preserve the peace, the crude military balance remained. The contending forces were too equally matched, the 'knock-out blows' were inconclusive, and the outcome was to be a long desperate war of attrition.

Purely in terms of statistics the Entente Powers with their combined population of 238 million had a considerable preponderance; on the other hand, the 120 million of Germany and Austria-Hungary were centrally placed and their forces could thus enjoy closer coordination and greater flexibility of movement between the eastern and western fronts. The German army, probably the best in Europe, mustered 87 infantry divisions and 10 divisions of cavalry, while the *Landwehr* provided approximately a further 22 divisions. Austria-Hungary's army was sizeable—49 infantry divisions and 11 divisions of cavalry—but hampered by the usual Habsburg difficulties in that orders had to be given in eight or nine languages and the political reliability of some of the troops—Czechs and Serbo-Croats—was uncertain. On 2 August 1914 Turkey had signed an alliance with Germany, but although she gave shelter to the two German cruisers, the *Goeben* and the *Breslau*, and closed the Straits to commercial shipping on 26 September, it was not until the end of October that she took definite action against Russia with the bombardment of Odessa. The Young Turk party in Constantinople were convinced that Germany would win the war and reckoned that Turkey could make a useful contribution, since her 36 divisions could harass Russia in the south, while the closing of the Straits severed an important Russian line of communication with the west.

Of the Entente Powers France had what was probably the most effective army with 62 infantry divisions and 20 divisions of cavalry; Russia certainly had the largest—114 infantry divisions and 40 divisions of cavalry—although there were doubts about their quality; the British Expeditionary Force of 6 divisions was certainly the most highly trained of all, a purely professional army, but far too small for the coming struggle. Indeed, Belgium could muster as many divisions, and Serbia almost double, not all well armed but with the advantage of the recent experience of the Balkan wars. In naval strength, however, Great Britain had a fair lead over Germany in modern battleships and a far greater one in the older types of ship, although German submarine strength was later to be a considerable threat.

The campaigns of 1914 were to be the most fluid and significant of the whole war; none of the initial offensives succeeded and out of their failure the pattern of the next four years of hostilities was established.

In the west all depended upon the great German sweep through Belgium and France in accordance with a modified version of the Schlieffen plan. Could France be knocked out of the war in six weeks before Germany had to turn back to the east? In fact, there had already been considerable activity in the east long before the issue had been settled in the west. The first clash between the Russians and Germans took place in the middle of August, when two Russian armies began to advance through the pine forests and marshes of East Prussia—a gallant effort on the part of the Russians, since they undertook this move before their mobilization was completed simply in response to a plea from the French.

This Russian thrust into East Prussia was begun by General Rennenkampf's First Army, which routed the German forces at Gumbinnen on 20 August. At the same time General Samsonov's Second Army, which the Masurian lakes separated from Rennenkampf by some forty miles, began to move north towards Tannenberg. At this point the German commander Prittwitz expressed such alarm on the telephone to Supreme Headquarters at Coblenz that Moltke decided to replace him by Hindenburg and his Chief of Staff Ludendorff. Afterwards Hindenburg always enjoyed the credit for the victory over the Russian forces, yet before he and Ludendorff had arrived, a new plan drawn up by a local staff officer, Max Hoffmann, had already been set in motion. It was certainly daring. The bulk of the German forces facing Rennenkampf were to be switched away to the south-west in the hope that they might inflict a decisive defeat on Samsonov's Second Army before Rennenkampf realized that he could advance unopposed. The manoeuvre, carried out partly by train and partly on foot, was successfully completed, and after several days of fighting near Tannenberg the Germans had shattered Samsonov's army and taken 90,000 prisoners. Hindenburg now had to rush his forces north again to meet Rennenkampf and during the first fortnight of September the battle of the Masurian lakes, although not as overwhelming a victory as Tannenberg, resulted in the retreat of the Russians, of whom some 30,000 were taken prisoner. 'Up to now,· with our inferior numbers,' wrote Hoffmann, 'we have defeated about fifteen Russian army corps and eight divisions, and we are not finished yet.'

The Austrians had been rather less successful. On 12 August Potiorek had launched a great invasion of Serbia—retribution for Sarajevo—but during several months of ferocious fighting the Serbs under Marshal Putnik threw the Austrians back, invaded Bosnia themselves, fell back before a new onslaught, and finally recovered to drive the Austrians north of the Danube by the middle of December. In August the other group of Austrian armies under Conrad von Hötzendorff advanced north towards Lublin and then after several weeks of mobile warfare were gradually pushed back into Galicia. By 10 September the Russian Grand Duke Nicholas was poised for a great enveloping movement on the right wing which would probably have destroyed the Austrian forces, had not Conrad heard of the plan in advance owing to the remarkable Russian habit of sending important messages by wireless uncoded. As it was, he was able to retire in time, but he could not rest free from the threat of encirclement until he had withdrawn as far west as the river Dunajec which he reached by the beginning of October.

Meanwhile, in the west, the most decisive drama of all had been played out. Here a million and a half German troops were committed to that great wheeling operation through Belgium and France which had obsessed their General Staff for so long. The German Second Army under von Bülow captured Liège, the essential preliminary to the advance of the northernmost First Army under von Kluck, who occupied Brussels on 20 August, while the Belgian forces fell back on Antwerp.

As the great line of German armies moved towards the Franco-Belgian frontier, the French produced their reply in the form of the famous Plan XVII. This was to meet attack with attack, to thrust into the north of Lorraine at the hinge of the German swing, but although the French assault which began on 14 August was serious, the German Fourth and Fifth armies had succeeded in repulsing it after a week's hard fighting. By the end of the month French forces facing the First and Second Armies were falling back towards Paris and the British Expeditionary Force under Sir John French had to retire with them, although the effectiveness of British fire power enabled them to give a good account of themselves at Mons.

It was now that the campaign reached a crucial stage. The plan that von Schlieffen had devised[1] had always assumed that the extreme right wing of the German sweep would swing south only when it was well to the west of Paris, whose defending forces would then be swiftly enveloped. In the last days of August, however, three decisions changed the whole character of the attack on France. First, four divisions were detached from the western front and sent to the eastern, despite the fact that the Tannenberg operation was already launched. Second, the German centre and left began an advance on Verdun with the result

[1] See p. 309.

that the German line now seemed to be attempting a gigantic pincer operation. Third, and most significant of all, on 30 August, von Kluck, finding that a serious gap was already developing between his First

THE WESTERN FRONT 1914–18

Army and von Bülow's Second, decided to wheel south while he was still east of Paris.

The apparent abandonment of the Schlieffen plan by Moltke was afterwards blamed for the eventual failure of the German attack. Certainly Moltke had departed from it by sending away four divisions and strengthening the left sufficiently for the attack on Verdun at a time when he needed every possible reinforcement on the right; yet it would be wrong to blame Moltke for the inherent weaknesses in the plan itself, since even with total concentration of all forces on the right wing it had always been very doubtful whether the German Army could be strong enough to sustain a sweep of so wide a radius as to pass to the west of Paris; the Schlieffen plan was in reality a staff officer's pipe dream to which time had given an almost religious air of inviolability.

Whatever was to blame, von Kluck had no option. The need to regain contact with von Bülow, already badly shaken at Guise on 29 August, forced him to turn south towards the Marne with Paris on his right. This might mean that he could roll up the retreating French forces from the flank; equally, his own flank was now exposed to attack from Paris. It was Galliéni, Military Governor of Paris, who first saw this opportunity and on 4 September flung the French Sixth Army into the assault on von Kluck's flank; and although Joffre, the French Commander-in-Chief, took a little time to digest the implications of this new situation, a French counter-attack soon developed against the German Second and Third Armies which had already crossed the Marne. Joffre's hope was to isolate von Kluck, and on 7 September the British Expeditionary Force and the left wing of the French Fifth Army began to advance into the gap that was widening between the German First and Second Armies. By now Moltke, far back at Luxemburg and only in fitful wireless communication with his commanders, was desperately anxious at the thought of an Allied break-through, and after a rapid tour of the various army headquarters had been made by one of his staff officers on 8 and 9 September, the German forces began to pull back to the river Aisne.

On 14 September Erich von Falkenhayn, the Prussian Minister of War, replaced Moltke as supreme commander, and there now followed a series of attempts by each side to outflank the other to the north until the sea was reached. At the end of October and in the first weeks of November German forces made tremendous efforts to break through to the Channel ports, but failed to do so despite the appalling losses inflicted on the British and French at the first battle of Ypres. Gradually the opposing lines of armies settled down to digging themselves in, and the separate lengths of trench began to link up in an elaborate system of dugouts, reserve lines, and communication trenches running intermittently from the Channel to the Swiss frontier.

M

Thus in Europe no attack was successful, yet no repulse was final. Overseas the results were more decisive. In South Africa, Botha, the Prime Minister, was able to contain and then to crush German forces in German South-West Africa; Togoland was overrun by British, French, and Belgian troops and only in Tanganyika did the Germans manage to put up a sustained resistance. In the Pacific, Japan, Australia, and New Zealand helped themselves to the German island colonies, while on the shores of the Persian Gulf Indian Army troops established themselves around Basra. At sea, the sinking of two British cruisers at the battle of Coronel off the Chilean coast in November was followed a month later by the destruction of almost the entire German naval force in those waters, near the Falkland Isles, and by the end of the year, with German cargo boats taking refuge in neutral ports, the British could at least feel that they still ruled the waves.

2. The deadlock 1915-17

For the next three years trench warfare predominated on the eastern and the western fronts. In the east, however, there was room for manoeuvre and the lines oscillated over considerable distances, whereas in the west only frontal assault was possible and advances costing tens of thousands of lives were to be measured in hundreds of yards. The Germans were for the most part content to hold a defensive position on French and Belgian territory. In April 1915 their attack on the British salient east of Ypres was simply an experiment in the use of poison gas, since Falkenhayn was already committed to a major offensive on his eastern front in that year. Even so, the second battle of Ypres was sufficiently fierce for the total casualties on both sides to amount to more than a hundred thousand, and enabled the Germans to flatten out most of the salient, thereby gaining the high ground from which they were to observe the British positions outside Ypres for the next two-and-a-half years. Apart from this the only other major assault by the Germans in the west was the attempt to take Verdun between February and July 1916; the concentration of so much artillery on a narrow front made this a hellish struggle, as the Germans fought to gain the outlying forts and the French under General Pétain put up a resistance of extra-ordinary tenacity which cost them 315,000 casualties as against the Germans' 281,000.

The other major assaults on the western front in these years were launched by the French and the British, and with minor variations there is an appalling similarity about them all. For the attackers it meant an immense artillery bombardment which was supposed to shatter the opposing artillery and machine-gun posts, break a gap through the barbed wire entanglements, and cow the enemy manning the opposite trenches. Under such conditions no surprise was possible; the preliminary bombardment and the cutting of the gaps in the wire made the precise point of the intended attack all too obvious, and when the extended lines of infantry climbed out of their trenches, weighed down with every form of weapon and equipment, and plodded, very often knee deep in mud, towards their objective, they were simply mown down by the enemy machine-gun posts in concrete pill-boxes which had usually survived the bombardment.

In 1915 Joffre attempted to break in on either side of the German bulge—from Champagne in the south and Artois in the north—and by the end of the summer the French had lost 190,000, the Germans 178,000, and the British 60,000 after being committed at Festubert in May and at Loos in September. In 1916, when Sir Douglas Haig had taken over from Sir John French and Pétain was badly in need of relief at Verdun, an assault along the line of the Somme by fourteen British divisions and five French on 1 July resulted in the most appalling slaughter, in which the British lost in a single day over 57,000 men, including 19,000 dead—the flower of a generation that had volunteered in the early months of the war—and even by the middle of November the greatest advance was no more than five miles on a front of twenty miles.

There was worse to follow in 1917. In April General Nivelle, who had now replaced Joffre, launched a great offensive in the region of Reims, hoping for a quick break-through northwards. He was to be assisted by a British attack east from Arras during which the Canadians captured Vimy Ridge. The French army fought hard and effectively, but no break-through was achieved and the loss of 187,000 men, coupled with the mistrust of the French politicians, resulted in Nivelle's dismissal. Pétain now took over, while Foch became Chief of the General Staff. The collapse of the Nivelle offensive had given Haig his chance to press for his own scheme of a British assault east of Ypres aiming at a break-through north-east to Ostend and Zeebrugge, and between 1 July and 10 November the British forces edged their way forward a distance of 9,000 yards along the ridge that commanded their positions outside Ypres; the weather always broke for each attack, and the low-lying Flanders soil, soaked with rain and pulverized by millions of shells, became a quagmire in which, during the last stages of the advance on Passchendaele, movement was almost impossible without duckboards. Men actually drowned in the mud and the total cost of the advance, all of which was lost the following spring, was 240,000 men according to Haig's supporters, 400,000 according to his critics.

The real wonder of the first World War is that men could stand so much. It is true that after the Nivelle offensive the French army was partially incapacitated by a mutiny which Pétain had rapidly to stamp out—a period of weakness which Haig was able to use as an added justification for the continuation of the third battle of Ypres—but in the main men continued to walk forward to certain death throughout this terrible deadlock. The debate over the generalship on the western front has raged ever since. The principal defence of the generals has been that since the line was continuous, no other form of attack was possible, and that since the German positions were of such strength and depth, a break-through soon became impossible and the only aim left was to kill as many of the enemy as possible in a war of attrition. Within these limits it has been suggested that they developed new tactical methods from experience of the enemy, and with the invention of the tank introduced a totally new feature of modern war. Yet when all this is allowed, the great storm of criticism that broke upon the generals in the inter-war years, when the ex-servicemen were free to speak their minds, remains essentially unanswered. A war of attrition on such a scale was no less than an abandonment of military art, a senseless massacre in which men continued to be sent forward to their deaths in thousands long after it was clear that the offensive had failed. Indeed, towards the end of 1917 Lloyd George was holding reserves in England for fear that Haig would fling them away in one more blood bath. And whatever the difficulties of the situation may have been, there was little excuse for the gulf that existed between the soldiers in the trenches and the General Staff launching their attacks from their desks. 'Did we really send men to fight in that?' cried one general who first saw the swamp at Passchendaele the day after the battle had ended. And he burst into tears.

In fact, the generals' defence lends force to a second school of thought that Great Britain as a maritime power should never have allowed her armies to become sucked into the Flanders mud simply to form part of the French defence, and that she should have retained mobility for her forces by mounting a series of amphibious operations. Before 1914 there had been little thought along these lines; the military conversations

with the French after Algeciras had been purely concerned with shipping the expeditionary force to France, and although the French, as
early as 1906, had agreed that the British should command at sea, a
naval Staff was not created at the Admiralty until Winston Churchill
had become First Lord. In any case, the initial German attack and the
continuing threat to Paris robbed the British of any chance to take the
initiative in combined operations, binding them increasingly to the side
of their French allies, who naturally saw the presence of German armies
on their soil in a more simple light.

There was only one serious strategic attempt made by the British to
open up a new flank—the Gallipoli expedition of 1915 inspired
primarily by Winston Churchill—and this failed largely through the
constant demand for troops on the western front. The object of the
attack was grandiose; Turkey was to be knocked out of the war; with
the opening of the Straits more direct contact with Russia would be
established, and Bulgaria, still hanging back from commitment in a
wavering neutrality, would probably join the Allies. The method, however, was unfortunate in that it envisaged an attempt by a naval force
to penetrate the narrow mine-strewn waters of the Dardanelles un-
supported by military forces, and to cross the Sea of Marmora to Constantinople whose bombardment was to bring about the collapse of the
Turkish government. When this attempt failed on 18 March, a military
force was landed a month later on the Gallipoli peninsula, but the loss
of surprise and the fanatical defence by the Turkish army, recently reorganized by the German military mission under Liman von Sanders,
made it impossible to advance and all forces were withdrawn at the
end of the year. It had been a daring and imaginative campaign and, but
for certain errors in command, might have succeeded; as it was, 500,000
Allied forces had been involved, of whom half had become casualties—
all apparently to no purpose—and for many years afterwards the
Gallipoli expedition was to give a bad name to those who had been
associated with the planning of it.

On the eastern front[1] the struggle remained for some time indecisive,
but never so static as in the west. In 1915, while Joffre battered unavailingly against the bulge in the west, Falkenhayn was forced to turn
to the aid of the Austrians. In May Mackensen, on a plan suggested by
Conrad von Hötzendorff, broke through the Russian line at Gorlice in
Galicia, taking over 100,000 prisoners, and there developed a stupen-
dous advance all along the front. On 5 August Warsaw fell to the

[1] See map, p. 357.

Central Powers, much of Lithuania was taken and by December the line ran from Riga due south to the Carpathians—an advance of 300 miles in eight months with the capture of 300,000 prisoners and more than 3,000 guns.

Nor was this the only achievement of the Central Powers on the eastern front that year. Both sides had been hoping to win over Bulgaria; the Entente Powers had offered her Macedonia, but the Central Powers were prepared to raise the bid with Greek and Rumanian territory as well, and in September King Ferdinand, drawing his own conclusions from a comparison of the success of the eastern offensive with the deadlock in Gallipoli, threw in his lot with the Central Powers. The principal significance of his decision was that in the second week of October German and Austrian forces were able to invade Serbia from Bulgarian territory in the east as well as from across the Danube in the north, and despite skilful manoeuvring Putnik, the Serbian Commander-in-Chief, was inevitably forced to retreat. The Allies sent one British and one French division to Salonica from the Gallipoli force, but the difficulty of the terrain and the equivocal attitude of Greece, whose King Constantine was pro-German, made it unlikely that they would be able to do much to assist the Serbs, who eventually made their escape to the coast of Albania where Allied ships conveyed them to Corfu.

The Entente Powers thus had no military success in 1915 with which they could match these achievements of their opponents, but in the diplomatic field they did at least gain Italy. As over their ultimately unsuccessful negotiations with Bulgaria, the problem for the Entente statesmen was the incompatibility of Serbian and Italian aims. The Russian minister Sazanov's earlier offer of Macedonia to Bulgaria was bound to mean heavy compensation for Serbia on the Adriatic coast and that in turn clashed with the aims of the Italians, who were making control of the eastern coast of the Adriatic the price of their alliance. Eventually, however, Sazanov demanded no more than southern Dalmatia for Serbia. Fortunately for the Entente Powers all this took place before the battle of Gorlice had broken the Russian front; thus the Italian government was still in a hurry to join in the war, in case it should end before they had established a claim to a share of the spoil. The treaty that was finally signed in April 1915 promised them Trieste, the Istrian peninsula and northern Dalmatia, as well as more hypothetical regions in Asia Minor and among the German colonies in Africa. On 23 May Italy declared war on Austria-Hungary and the

Italian army embarked upon a long unsuccessful assault on the Austrian positions in the mountainous region to the east of the Venetian plateau.

In 1916 there was another spectacular swing in the fortunes of the military. In March a Russian attack in the north, made in response to an appeal by the French, now hard pressed at Verdun, was a disastrous failure causing them 110,000 casualties. In May it was the Italians who appealed for help when they were pushed back by the Austrians, and on 4 June General Brusilov, commanding the south-western sector, launched a great offensive before which the Austrian Fourth and Seventh Armies began to break up. Other Russian generals to the north were unable to support him, but Brusilov pushed on magnificently on his own for 150 miles as he thrust into the Bukovina and by October he had captured 400,000 prisoners and some 500 guns. This was a highly significant achievement, for the Germans had to rush forces from the western front and the Austrians halted their offensive against the Italians.

Yet even this good news for the Entente Powers was to be clouded over by another disastrous development. In October 1914 Rumania, in return for the promise of gaining Transylvania from Hungary after the war, had come to an agreement with Russia whereby she would observe benevolent neutrality. The effect of the Brusilov offensive, however, was to fire her ambition still further, and in August 1916 she signed a treaty with Russia and France which gave her the Bukovina and the Banat as well as Transylvania, on the understanding that the Allies would keep the Bulgarian army engaged—the British and French from Salonica, the Russians through the Dobruja—so that the Rumanians would be free to concentrate on invading Transylvania. In fact, they had left it too late, for the full strength of the Brusilov offensive was by now almost spent. In September a force of Germans, Bulgarians, and Turks under Mackensen thrust north into the Dobruja, and the Rumanian army itself which had triumphantly invaded Transylvania was flung back by German and Austrian divisions under Falkenhayn, who had just been replaced as Chief of the General Staff by Hindenburg. By the end of the year the Rumanians had lost over 300,000 men—half of them prisoners—and retained no more of their country than the northern province of Moldavia.

The Entente Powers had certainly been unfortunate in their satellites —Serbia overrun in 1915, Rumania virtually knocked out in 1916, Italy clearly in danger of becoming a liability—and now in 1917, the year of the Nivelle offensive and the third battle of Ypres in the west,

Russia herself was to succumb to revolution and defeat. The first revolution in March brought about the abdication of the Tsar, but not
Russia's immediate withdrawal from the war.[1] A July offensive under
Brusilov, in which the Rumanians joined, met with some initial success, but by the beginning of August the Germans were beginning to
counter-attack effectively and even before the revolution of the
Bolsheviks in November paralyzed any further war effort, it was clear
that the Russian forces would be incapable of much more. And with
this realization there came the news of a great Italian rout at Caporetto
on 24 October, when the Austrians, strengthened with German reinforcements, broke through and put the Italians into a flight which
could only be checked at the Piave river.

The war at sea in these years was less spectacular than the land battles,
yet highly significant for the combatants. It demonstrated in particular
the ability of the British navy to maintain an effective blockade of the
Central Powers, at the same time keeping open the sea lanes through
which the newly devised convoys of merchant shipping were able to
pass despite the ferocious German submarine campaign. The one major
action between the enemy fleets took place on 31 May 1916—the
battle of Jutland—when the German High Seas Fleet under von Scheer
tried to lure Jellicoe's battleships into torpedo range and then returned
to port—after which the caution of both admirals made any further
serious encounter unlikely.

In the Near and Middle East the Allied forces met with gradual success against the Turks. The British advance on Baghdad in 1915 was
unsuccessful and ended in the recapture of Kut el Amara by the Turks
in April 1916. In June, however, a revolt of the Arabs against their
Turkish overlords clearly offered a great opportunity which was seized
by a young peace-time archaeologist, Colonel T. E. Lawrence, one of
the very few figures in this war to fire the popular imagination. In
March 1917 Baghdad was occupied by the British. In Palestine General
Allenby finally broke through the defences of Beersheba and Gaza and
on 9 December took Jerusalem. To the pious and the romantic this
might seem to lend an air of crusade to the efforts of the Allies; it did
not disguise the fact that by the end of 1917 the Allied cause was still
not in particularly good shape.

[1] See p. 352.

3. The climax of the war 1917–18

Four principal factors combined to bring the war to a climax in 1918. First, the entry of the United States in April 1917 began to bring about an appreciable increase of fresh troops on the western front. Second, the Bolshevik revolution in Russia in November 1917 was followed in March 1918 by the Treaty of Brest Litovsk, whereby the new Russian government conceded complete victory to the Central Powers. Third, this success on the eastern front enabled Germany to swing all her forces into a great western offensive in March 1918. Fourth, when this offensive had spent itself by the middle of the summer, the Allied armies, now greatly reinforced, were able to take advantage of the loosening of the whole front, and in August, after the assault had been contained, began to drive the Germans back in a retreat that ended with the armistice in November.

The Germans really had only themselves to blame for the entry of the United States into the war. It is true that American objections to the thought of fighting on the side of Russian autocracy were ended by the outbreak of the March revolution, but this in itself would not have drawn the United States in, since anti-interventionist feeling was strong and President Wilson had been re-elected to a second term of office in 1916 on the understanding that his government would continue to follow a policy of neutrality. Two events at the beginning of 1917 brought about the rapid reversal of this attitude. In January the German Foreign Minister, Zimmermann, dispatched a telegram in code to the German minister in Mexico City in which he described his plans for stimulating a Mexican invasion across the Rio Grande in the event of the United States entering the war; this message was intercepted by the British, decoded, and after being passed on to Washington, actually appeared in the American press. Then on 1 February the German government, after having given due warning, embarked upon an un-restricted submarine campaign in which their U-boats were prepared to sink the merchant ships of any country which approached the shores of the western Allies. The Germans had previously been cautious over offending American opinion—particularly after American lives had been lost on board the British liner *Lusitania* sunk in the Atlantic in 1915—and until now the Americans had been more irritated by the incon-venience caused to their shipping by the British search for contraband in the imposition of the Allied blockade. The ferocity of the new German campaign, however, involving the sinking of 600,000 tons in March

M 2

alone, very rapidly swung American opinion round to accepting a decision that Wilson knew was inevitable, and on 2 April 1917 the United States formally declared war on Germany.

If Great Britain and France had gained an ally in the west, it was nevertheless some time before her contribution could be effective and meanwhile they were to lose their principal ally in the east. The Bolshevik party, which seized power in St Petersburg in November 1917,[1] had sworn to take Russia out of the war. 'This government', announced Lenin, 'solemnly declares its resolution to conclude at once a peace . . . equally just to all nations and nationalities without exception.' By the second week of December the Bolsheviks were already in negotiation with the Germans and Austrians at Brest Litovsk and after some delay due to the harshness of the demands made by the Central Powers peace was formally signed on 3 March 1918. Thus Russia, whose support of Serbia in 1914 had brought France and then Great Britain into this appalling struggle, passed out of the war. Still, until this moment she had certainly been a good ally. Her threat to Germany's eastern frontier had helped to save France in 1914 and in the following years her millions of peasant soldiery had held down as many enemy divisions as the French, British, and Belgian forces were containing in the west.

For Ludendorff this cessation of hostilities in the east released a vast number of troops whom the German railway system could now switch to the west for an all-out offensive before the Allies had been too strongly reinforced by the new American contingents. This was launched on 21 March against the British section of the line between Arras and St Quentin, and although the British had attempted to copy the extremely flexible German method of defence in depth, fog assisted the Germans in pressing through[2] and within a few days the situation seemed so desperate that a conference was summoned under the French President, Poincaré, at Doullens on 26 March. Pétain expressed a gloomy belief that the British would be broken 'in the open field'—an interesting anticipation of his pessimism in 1940[3]—but on Haig's initiative Foch was given a unified command as *Général-en-Chef des Armées Alliées en France*.

By now Bapaume and Peronne had been given up, but although the

---

[1] See p. 355.

[2] In the west the Germans seem constantly to have had the advantage of the weather—as, for example, during the third battle of Ypres.

[3] See p. 459.

Allies had suffered some 240,000 casualties, the Germans had already lost as many and the railway junction of Amiens had not yet been reached. Ludendorff turned next to the valley of the Lys south of Ypres and on 9 April a new thrust drove the line back as far as Armentières— an advance which imposed a withdrawal from the Passchendaele ridge whose capture had cost the British so many thousands of lives in 1917. By 11 April the situation had become so grim that Haig, a man to whom memorable phrases did not normally come easily, issued his famous order of the day: 'With our backs to the wall and believing in the justice of our cause each one must fight on to the end.' This was, in fact, the last battle in the war for the Channel ports and by the end of April after the most furious fighting the Flanders line still held.

Ludendorff now turned to the south, and in May attacked between Soissons and Reims. By 3 June German forces had crossed the Marne and Paris lay only fifty-six miles distant. Ludendorff's real aim was to draw off the Allied reserves southwards, so that he might then renew the Flanders attack, and in July he thrust forward once more on either side of Reims, but once again the French line, although pushed back, did not break. Furthermore, Ludendorff had struck so heavily in making this feint that he had to pause before turning to the Armentières front again; thus the Allies gained the time to seize the initiative and to justify an Intelligence commentary of January 1918: 'The German accession of morale is not of a permanent character and is not likely to stand the strain of an unsuccessful attack with consequent losses. . . . If Germany attacks and fails, she will be ruined.'

Already in May, at the height of the German onslaught, Haig had given instructions for the preliminary study for an offensive in the area of Amiens, and on 8 August an assault whose preparation had been carefully kept secret was launched by the British Fourth and the French First Armies. It met with overwhelming success; on that one day— which Ludendorff described as 'the black day of the German army in the history of the war'—the Germans suffered some 26,000 casualties, and from this time on, as the French and the Americans joined in the attack to the south, the German line was constantly in retreat. 'We have nearly reached the limit of our powers of resistance,' said William II at a meeting with the military leaders on 11 August; 'the war must be ended.' The struggle was still to continue, however, with appallingly heavy casualties as the Allies continued to press the line back towards the frontier.

By the end of September Bulgaria had surrendered and Allenby, now north of Damascus, had routed the Turks, while the Italians having successfully resisted an Austrian offensive in June made a great thrust in October aimed at Vittorio Veneto. Meanwhile, negotiations with Germany had begun; Foch received the German delegates in his train in the forest of Compiègne and after a little argument the armistice was finally signed early on 11 November. At eleven o'clock that morning the fire of artillery and machine-guns gradually died away across the battlefields of western Europe. In four years the civilization of the nineteenth century had been blown to shreds; a whole generation of young men had been massacred in anonymous millions, and although the ordinary soldier on that November morning might listen in unbelieving relief to the first silence of peace, the British and the French now found themselves victorious after a struggle which had gone on too long for victory to have any sweetness.

26

THE INTERNAL CONSEQUENCES OF WAR

1. The acceleration of collectivism

'SEIN oder Nichtsein, das ist hier die Frage.'[1] Thus William II addressed the German nation in August 1914. The quotation may have a self-conscious exaggerated ring; yet it was not in itself inappropriate. For this was not simply the outbreak of a war with precise limited objectives—like most of those of the nineteenth century; it was nothing less than a crisis of national existence.

It was consequently hardly surprising that in such a war demands should accelerate the general tendency towards collectivism. On both sides it involved the granting of emergency powers to the governments, and in Germany and Austria-Hungary this greater authority was concentrated more and more in the hands of the army. By 1917 the German military chiefs could virtually make and break a Chancellor at will. In Vienna the *Reichsrat*, prorogued in March 1914, did not meet again until May 1917, and considerable administrative powers were given to the Habsburg military authorities in regions such as Bohemia and Moravia, even though they were a very great distance from the front. Among the western Allies parliamentary institutions remained actively critical. In France, after his assumption of power in November 1917, Georges Clemenceau wielded enormous power in the last desperate year of the war, but at least the politicians did not succumb to the generals, as they did in Germany, although the long feud between Lloyd George, who became British Prime Minister in 1916, and Field Marshal Haig illustrated the peculiar limitations that the circumstances of a major war imposed upon the civil authority.

On both sides there was an intensive organization of social and economic life. The Allied blockade, the German U-boat campaign, and all the requirements for maintaining vast armies in the field necessitated an extraordinary degree of State control of industry. In May 1915 Albert Thomas in France and Lloyd George at the Ministry of

[1] 'To be, or not to be—that is the question.'

Munitions in Great Britain were put in charge of the supply of shells which were in such demand on the western front. In Germany Walter Rathenau was responsible for a vast mobilizing of German industry and labour to overcome with various forms of *ersatz* (substitute) material the deficiencies created by the blockade. In November 1916 all this activity was brought under the control of the *Kriegsamt*, a department of the Ministry of War, and in December a National Service Law made men between the ages of seventeen and sixty liable to be directed into the forces or the factories.

All these developments were the work of governments determined to employ every possible means in the struggle for victory, and in so far as they accustomed the individual to a further surrender of his freedom of action to the needs of the community, they were to be of lasting significance. The more dramatic aspects of the internal consequences of war, however, were to be seen towards the end, as the three great dynasties of Romanov, Habsburg, and Hohenzollern collapsed amid the ruin of the political and social framework of central and eastern Europe.

2. Two revolutions in Russia: March and November 1917

Twice during the recent past Russia's defeat in war had been followed by revolutionary domestic change. The tragedy of these reforms was that, although remarkable in themselves at the time of their inauguration, they never developed sufficiently to create a basis for a new social stability. A rapidly rising population had undone much of the benefits of the emancipation of the serfs after the Crimean war and there had not yet been time for the more recent land reforms of Stolypin[1] to give the peasantry a vested interest in the existing structure of government and society. Similarly, the national *Duma*, granted by the Tsar after Russia's defeat by Japan and the revolution of 1905, had been carefully relegated to acting in an advisory capacity and there had been little opportunity for middle-class liberals to gain experience in government. Thus, when the military disasters of 1914 and 1915 on the eastern front faced Tsarism with a new crisis, this failure to cultivate the social groups who might have acted as a bulwark against more radical forces meant that Nicholas II had virtually nowhere to turn, even if he had been willing to do so. This explains why there was no moderate phase in the

[1] See p. 292.

Russian revolution; the question of establishing a constitutional monarchy never really arose and the struggle was waged principally between competing brands of Socialism.

The royal couple presented one more unfortunate example of a devoted husband married to a narrow-minded dominating woman whose determination that he should be a king was to bring disaster on them both. In the war, during Nicholas's absence at supreme headquarters, Alexandra was really able to enjoy power herself—a fact which destroyed whatever chances there may have been for the liberal deputies in the *Duma* to gain a government which had their confidence. In September 1915 the *Duma* was prorogued and governmental decisions came increasingly under the influence of an unsavoury monk, Rasputin, who managed to combine a reputation for mystical piety with a life of utter immorality and who had convinced Alexandra that he could exercise some guardian power over her son Alexis when his life was endangered by haemophilia. In February 1916 Rasputin virtually nominated his own Prime Minister, Stürmer, who also took over the Ministry of Foreign Affairs on Sazanov's dismissal in the following July. Eventually, when there were distinct signs of unrest among the soldiers and the workers, the *Duma* was recalled in November; here the liberals denounced the utter inadequacy of the government, but it was the court aristocracy who took the most dramatic step with their assassination of Rasputin in December. This was an appropriately dramatic episode, yet typically inconclusive. Rasputin was poisoned, then shot, and his body finally thrust beneath the ice of the Neva, but although there were rumours of an impending palace revolution, nothing ever happened. The *Duma*, which was to meet in February 1917 to discuss a full programme of reform, was postponed, and so the last days of Romanov rule slipped away until the power of taking the initiative was finally lost.

As in 1848, the Russian revolution of March 1917 broke out without any immediate stimulation or leadership. On 8 March[1] there was rioting at the bakers' shops in St Petersburg; later, when the police opened fire on the crowds, there followed a general strike, and during the next couple of days the soldiers showed themselves increasingly unreliable. So far all this commotion was simply the result of war weariness, an outburst of popular anger at the shortages at home and the bad

---

[1] On 23 February, according to the Russian calendar, which was still based on the Julian or Old Style, by now thirteen days behind the rest of Europe. After their accession to power the Bolsheviks modernized the Russian system in February 1918.

news from the front. But now, again as in 1848, the realization of the weakness of the authorities suddenly dawned, and the political groups began hastily to organize themselves in a race to take advantage of the situation. In the afternoon of 11 March the *Duma*, which had just been officially dissolved by the Tsar, formed a provisional committee representing all parties, while a little later a Soviet of factory workers also met in St Petersburg. By the evening the government's loss of control was so plain that the Grand Duke Cyril sent a telephone message to the *Duma*'s provisional committee suggesting that they should assume power. Accordingly, by 14 March the committee had established a new government under Prince Lvov and on the following day Tsar Nicholas II abdicated in favour of his brother Grand Duke Michael, who, however, decided not to accept until he had received an official invitation from some kind of constitutional assembly.

For the moment it might seem as if the struggle for power in St Petersburg lay between the liberal–conservative elements in the provisional government and the left-wing Soviet. In fact, Prince Lvov's administration represented a *via media* which had few roots in popular feeling; the real opponents of the Soviet were soon to be found in the right-wing aristocratic groups who looked to a military *coup* for a restoration of power. With discipline disintegrating fast in the army— assisted by the dissemination of Bolshevik propaganda—this was not a very serious threat. The real issue was the complexion of opinion within the Soviet and it was only towards the end of the autumn that Lenin judged that political feeling here had swung sufficiently towards the Bolsheviks for them to launch their own *coup*.

Meanwhile, throughout the spring and summer of 1917, a succession of coalitions strove to exploit the opportunity that chance had let drop into their lap. Lvov's government was determined to push on with the war, but the abolition of the death sentence and the mounting rate of desertions made this highly problematical for the army commanders; Lvov also declared local government totally decentralized, thereby undermining most of the existing organs of government, and announced the forthcoming election of a constituent Assembly which would decide the question of the ownership of land. The state of anarchy which now seemed imminent was not displeasing to the extremists, who saw it as a safeguard against any effective counter-revolutionary action, but beyond this the Bolsheviks were for the moment simply feeling their way.

Indeed, at the time of the outbreak the majority of the Bolshevik

leaders had been far from St Petersburg, where the young Molotov, a
member of the Russian bureau of the central committee, had simply
issued a party manifesto and resumed the publication of *Pravda*. It was
not until the end of March that Stalin and Kamenev returned from
Siberia, not until May that Trotsky arrived from the United States.
The most spectacular event of all was the journey of Lenin in April with
a small party of Bolsheviks including Zinoviev, Radek, and Luna-
charsky from neutral Switzerland across Germany and thence by ship
to Sweden. The motive of the German government in allowing this
was simple, since the Bolsheviks were sworn to take Russia out of the
war. 'Since we are interested that influence of radical wing gains the
upper hand in Russia,' commented the Foreign Minister, Zimmermann,
'I consider travel permission through Germany perhaps appropriate.'
And so this group of Russian revolutionaries was hurriedly transported
across Germany in two sealed railway carriages like dangerous germs
to be injected into the body politic of the enemy, although it is doubtful
whether even the Germans imagined that they would so quickly take
effect.

   Lenin himself wasted no time. At the Finland station at St Petersburg
he was met by members of the Bolshevik party as well as the President
of the Soviet and on the following day proclaimed the 'April theses'—
'not a parliamentary republic—a return to that from the Soviet of
Workers' deputies would be a step backwards—but a republic of
Soviets of Workers, Poor Peasants and Peasants' Deputies throughout
the country, growing from below upwards'. This was the doctrine of
the uninterrupted revolution which Lenin had developed after the split
with the Mensheviks in 1903.[1] For the moment it was clear that he
would have to bide his time, since the provisional government was
still nominally in control, and although the Bolsheviks had now seized
on the slogan 'all power to the Soviets', the St Petersburg Soviet was
still largely under Menshevik and Social Revolutionary influences. In
Russia in 1917, however, time was on the side of the Bolsheviks. They
stood for peace and for the immediate distribution of the estates among
the peasantry—two popular cries—and the oscillation of revolutionary
violence between right and left naturally lent encouragement to more
extreme views.

   In the provisional government a coalition with Liberals and moderate
Socialists had been formed, but this eventually collapsed in July with
the failure of the Russian military offensive, and an abortive rising by

[1] See p. 259.

workers and sailors at St Petersburg on 16 July swung the government back towards dependence upon right-wing elements. Kerensky, a Social Revolutionary, who at the beginning of the revolution was both a member of the *Duma* and Vice-President of the St Petersburg Soviet and who had been appointed Minister of Justice and later Minister of War in the provisional government, eventually attempted to form a new administration of his own. Although the Bolshevik leaders had disapproved of the July rising, Kerensky knew perfectly well that they were hard at work undermining the discipline of the army, and their party was now virtually proscribed; *Pravda* was banned, Trotsky and others were arrested, and Lenin went into hiding in Finland.

Yet no sooner had Kerensky shown that he intended to stand firm against the Bolsheviks than he was confronted with the threat of a counter-revolutionary action, when, after the fall of Riga to the Germans on 3 September, the Russian Commander-in-Chief, General Kornilov, decided to attempt a march on St Petersburg. To meet the threat Kerensky had to fall back on the Bolsheviks; their Red Guards were now mobilized and their political agitation had the most decisive effect on Kornilov's troops, who melted away. Kornilov himself was placed under arrest.

Kerensky continued to rule, yet the two incidents of July and September had revealed the utter weakness of his position. To check the forces of the extreme left he had to rely upon the right, while to resist the attempts at counter-revolution he was driven back to dependence upon the Bolsheviks. At the same time the careful work of preparation carried on by the Bolsheviks since the outbreak in March was greatly assisted by the disastrous continuation of the war and Kornilov's unsuccessful *coup*. By the middle of September they had a majority in the Moscow Soviet, while Trotsky, now released from prison on bail, had been elected President of the St Petersburg Soviet.

To Lenin it seemed clear that the moment to act had come. He spurned the idea put forward by Zinoviev and Kamenev that the central committee of the Bolshevik party should wait for the long promised Constituent Assembly, which by now was almost certain to be a fairly radical body. Instead, he wished the party to strike immediately on the eve of an All-Russian Congress of Soviets, due to meet on 7 November, which could then be presented with a *fait accompli*. This time, unlike most revolutions of the previous hundred years, the rising was not simply a spontaneous outbreak without leadership. It was a carefully planned *coup* timed by Lenin to coincide with the greatest likelihood of acquiescence on the part of the populace. The operation was organized by Trotsky from the Smolny Institute, the headquarters of the revolutionary military committee, and carried out by the Red Guards and regular regiments who on the night of 6 November rapidly occupied the strategic points of the city. Lenin emerged from hiding to find the battle virtually won, and on the morning of 7 November Kerensky fled from the city. In the same month as the British were dying in their thousands to gain the swamp and ruins of Passchendaele, the Bolsheviks had captured control of the government of Russia at the cost of a handful of casualties.

That evening the Congress of Soviets met in the hall of the Institute. The Winter Palace was still holding out and the delegates could hear the guns of the cruiser *Aurora* and of the fortress of Peter and Paul bombarding it—with blanks—as the Bolshevik leaders announced what they had accomplished. With a majority of almost two-thirds they had little to fear from this gathering. Lenin declared that peace would be negotiated with the Central Powers at once and that 'landlord property is abolished forthwith without compensation'. A Council of People's Commissars was set up on the next day including Lenin at the head, Trotsky as Commissar for Foreign Affairs and Stalin as Commissar for Nationalities. Thus the Bolsheviks had little intention of sharing the power that they had won; they would not form a coalition with Mensheviks and Social Revolutionaries, who accordingly walked out of the Congress. 'You are bankrupt,' cried Trotsky after them; 'you have played out your role. Go where you belong: to the dust heap of history.' Still less did the Bolsheviks mean to surrender to the democratically elected Constituent Assembly, which met at last on 18 January 1918. When it became clear that the Bolshevik party was in a minority, a sailor commanding the military guard informed the president that he had been told to close the meeting 'because the guard is tired'. The instructions actually came from Lenin and the Constituent Assembly did not meet again.

There is a tendency for left-wing historians to use such phrases as 'the logic of history' when speaking of Lenin's extraordinary success in 1917. In fact, history is profoundly illogical and the victory of the Bolsheviks is more easily explained in simple practical terms. The absence of a widespread liberal bourgeois class with some experience of government made a left-wing success more likely in Russia than elsewhere, once the conditions of wartime had shattered the royal autocracy. And among the left wing it was Lenin's disciplined group who could act with confidence at a time when there was a power vacuum at the heart of the government of Russia. There was, however, a price to be paid, if so small a group was to maintain its position. 'This intricate task cannot be solved by placing above the proletariat a few well-picked people,' Trotsky had written in 1904, '. . . or one person invested with power to liquidate or degrade.' Yet by 1917 Trotsky was a Bolshevik and the dictatorship of the party was soon to become consolidated under the stress of civil war.

The Bolsheviks were now free to open their attack on capitalism with a doctrinaire programme that was pushed to impracticable extremes. Banks were abolished; all forms of private trading were prohibited, and the management of factories was handed over to councils of workers. But the most startling aspect of their rule was their attitude towards the non-Russian nationalities to whom they intended to give independence. Their hope was that these emancipated peoples would then carry out their own Socialist revolutions and a new link be established with Russia through a community of political outlook. In fact, they were to be disappointed in this, owing partly to the resistance of local anti-Bolshevik interests, and partly to the presence of the German army to whom they had to surrender enormous areas of the Russian western borderland.

In Finland Stalin announced the attitude of the new Russian government at a Finnish Social Democrat congress held at Helsinki some three weeks after the November revolution, and on 6 December 1917, a newly elected Parliament took him at his word by declaring Finnish independence, which was accepted by the Russian Bolsheviks early in 1918. The real struggle was still to come. Would this new republic under the presidency of P. E. Svinhufvud survive in the face of the efforts of Finnish Bolsheviks supported by the Russian government from across the frontier? Towards the end of January 1918 Bolshevik groups had gained control of Helsinki, and for the next five weeks the most that the right-wing forces could do under General Mannerheim, who had recently returned from the Rumanian front, was to consolidate their position in the western province of Ostrobothnia. In March, however, they began to advance; at the same time a German Baltic Division under General von der Goltz landed at Hanko in the extreme south-west of Finland and moved along the coast towards Helsinki, and by the middle of May the Bolshevik threat to the new republic of Finland had been ended.

It was naturally the terms of the peace with Germany that involved

THE TREATY OF BREST LITOVSK, MARCH 1918

Map labels:

FINLAND

Stockholm
Hanko
St Petersburg
ESTONIA
Riga
LATVIA
R U S S I A
Moscow
Orel
Voronezh
Kursk
Don
Tannenberg
Brest
Litovsk
Warsaw
Kholm
Kiev
GERMANY
Lublin
Dnieper
U K R A I N E
Lemberg
Gorlice
BUKO-VINA
Vittorio Veneto
AUSTRIA-HUNGARY
Piave
Caporetto
RUMANIA
SERBIA
BULGARIA
ALBANIA
Salonika
T U R K E Y
Dardanelles
Smyrna
Dodecanese
Cyprus
Crete
Damascus
Jerusalem
Gaza

Scale 0 ——— 400 Miles

///// Territory lost by Russia

——— Western boundary of the Ukrainian Republic (Treaty of 9 February 1918)

——— Furthest extent of the Central Powers' occupation of Russia and the Ukraine by May 1918

358 ECLIPSE OF NINETEENTH-CENTURY EUROPE 1914-21

Russia in the most striking concessions of territory. Before the end of the year the Bolsheviks had opened negotiations with the Germans and in the bleak fortress of Brest Litovsk Trotsky, representing the new masters of Russia, faced the representatives of the old order in central Europe—Prince Leopold of Bavaria, the Commander-in-Chief, General Hoffmann, his Chief of Staff, Kühlmann and Count Czernin, the German and Austrian Foreign Ministers. The terms demanded were so heavy that not even Trotsky as a Bolshevik sworn to make peace could accept them, and he left the conference with the meaningless formula 'no peace, no war'. The Germans simply continued their advance unopposed—'the most comic war I have ever experienced', wrote Hoffmann—and on 19 February, after an agonized debate in the Central Committee, the Russians decided to sue for peace.

The Germans could now put up their price, and the result was a *Diktat* more overwhelming than anything which the Allies in the west were to impose on Germany in just over a year's time. Russia was to demobilize entirely, and in addition to the surrender of Poland, the Ukraine, and Courland which had been in the original terms, Estonia, Latvia,[1] and Finland were to be evacuated by Russian troops and Russia was to guarantee 'a speedy and orderly return' of eastern Anatolia to Turkey. To all this the Bolsheviks finally gave their consent and the Treaty of Brest Litovsk was signed on 3 March 1918. Before this the Germans had already been working to undermine the establishment of Bolshevik influence in the Ukraine. Here in 1917 a nationalist government had been set up under Hrushevsky, but as with Svinhufvud's government in Finland there was soon a serious clash with Bolshevik elements and the Central Powers were quick to seize their chance in February 1918. At the same time as the Bolsheviks were setting up a Ukranian Soviet government, national delegates were signing a separate peace treaty at Brest Litovsk, and within a few weeks German forces had overrun the Ukraine and a pro-German Ukrainian government had been established under the Hetman Skoropadsky.

The German victory in the east was now rounded off with a peace treaty with Rumania. The eastern slopes of the Transylvanian mountains were to be given to Hungary, the Dobruja to Bulgaria, Bessarabia to Russia. Thus Rumania was deprived of the Black Sea coast and Germany's lease of her oil wells for ninety years pointed to the

[1] By the supplementary treaty of 27 August Russia agreed to relinquish Estonia and Latvia entirely.

confidence with which the Central Powers could now turn to the great western offensive of 1918.

For the Bolsheviks, however, peace with Germany only rid them of one of their opponents. General Kornilov had managed to escape from arrest and now moved to the south of Russia where he took command of a White Russian (i.e. anti-Bolshevik) force, until he was killed in action and General Denikin took over. Farther east, Social Revolutionary members of the Constituent Assembly, indignant at their dismissal by the Bolsheviks, organized themselves under Chernov on the lower Volga. They had a considerable hold also on Siberia and Vladivostok, while in Manchuria General Horvat had established a conservative government. In the summer of 1918 the Allies, highly dubious of Bolshevism, landed a combined military force at Murmansk and authorized Admiral Kolchak to coordinate the various forces of resistance in Siberia. The most remarkable feature of the whole scene was the Czech army corps organized by Professor Masaryk from the prisoner-of-war camps in Russia and now on its way to France via Vladivostok.[1] Strung out across Siberia they held much of the Trans-Siberian railway and they were so effective in their attacks that in July 1918 Ekaterinburg seemed likely to fall to them. Here the Tsar and his family were interned and the Bolsheviks afterwards claimed that they had no time to organize a swift evacuation; on the other hand, they dare not let their opponents rescue Nicholas, whose presence would rally many waverers to the side of the anti-Bolshevik forces. Thus the entire royal family was done to death in a cellar—'butchered' according to liberal and right-wing historians, 'executed' according to the left. Yet even without this rallying point the resistance to Bolshevism was to continue for long and it was ironical that the Bolsheviks who had claimed to bring an end to war should continue to be deeply engaged in a ferocious struggle for survival long after the cease-fire had sounded in the west.

3. The last of the Habsburg Empire

In eastern Europe the beginning of the war appeared to suggest one more phase in the old struggle between German and Slav. This naturally raised the question of the dependability of the various nationalities under Habsburg rule, but although the Austrian army did not enjoy any great military triumphs—except for the rout of the Italians at

[1] See p. 362.

Caporetto—there was little sign of any political disintegration during the first two-and-a-half years of the war.

The south Slavs within the Empire might certainly have represented a considerable danger on the Serbian front, but for the fact that the Croats had a considerable mistrust of the Serbs and disliked the Italians still more. What was even more striking was that the Poles, whose independence had been one of the great lost causes of nineteenth-century Europe, continued to support their existing political masters. Thus in Russian Poland a National Democrat party under Dmowski still looked towards St Petersburg in the hope of gaining local autonomy, while in Austrian Galicia Josef Pilsudski, who also stood for Polish independence, actually raised forces to fight on behalf of the Habsburgs. Not even when the Central Powers had overrun Warsaw and eastern Poland in the offensive of 1915 was this division healed. Only the promise of a united independent Poland would have won the Poles of Russian Poland over to the side of the Central Powers, and on this Germany and Austria-Hungary did not see entirely eye to eye. At first the Germans held back because they were still hoping for a separate peace with Russia, who would hardly be agreeable to such a territorial loss. There was, too, the question whether the new Poland would be orientated towards Germany or Austria-Hungary. The Habsburg proposal —sometimes known as the Austro-Polish solution—was to incorporate Galicia and Russian Poland in one political territory whose inhabitants would have their own parliament. This would, in fact, have amounted to a new form of 'trialism' within the Empire. It suited the German Austrians, who saw that the existence of a Polish parliament would draw off the Polish element in the *Reichsrat* and leave them in greater control in Vienna; it did not suit the Magyars, who saw it as a modification of their own special position within the Dual Monarchy. The German government, however, preferred a solution which would turn Poland rather more towards them, and since Austria's military dependence on Germany had soon become undeniable, a manifesto issued by the two Powers in November 1916 virtually established the German plan; a Polish Council of State included Pilsudski as head of the ministry of war, but real power lay with the German Governor-General in Warsaw.

The danger from the south Slavs and the Poles had been that they might turn to compatriots outside the Empire. The weakness of the Czechs was that they had no one to whom they might look across the frontiers, and since their territories lay much closer to the heart of the

Habsburg dominions—unlike Galicia or Croatia—their only hope of obtaining independence lay in the total disintegration of the Empire. At first, the majority of Czech politicians did not regard this as remotely possible, since they anticipated either an Austrian victory or, at the most, a compromise peace; besides, among many of them there remained the old fear of 1848 that complete freedom from Habsburg rule would simply lay them open to German domination. Indeed, the German parties within the Empire—except for the Social Democrats— were already repeating by Easter 1915 their earlier proposals whereby Galicia and Dalmatia should be given up and the rest of Austria including the Czech territories became a unitary germanized State. Czech radicals, however, did not allow themselves to be restrained by these factors. Thomas Masaryk, a professor of philosophy at Prague University moved to Italy in December 1914, and nine months later Eduard Beneš, his former pupil, who had been placed under police surveillance, managed to leave the country on a forged passport. From now on, communication between the Czech exiles and their former colleagues at home was extremely fitful, but to radicals like Masaryk and Beneš it seemed essential that there should be spokesmen for the Czechs among the western Allies.

For the first two years of the war, however, nationalist aspirations seemed unlikely to hinder seriously the war effort of the multi-national Empire—the obverse of the failure of the international ideals of the Socialists to prevent the opening of hostilities in 1914. Thus the Emperor Francis Joseph, who died in November 1916 at the age of eighty-six, was at least spared the final disruption. He had come to the throne at a time when the Empire had seemed on the verge of collapse; his life ended with the incompatibilities of the Habsburg inheritance still unresolved, with the entire Continent drawn into an appalling war on account of them; and under his successor Karl, the nephew of Francis Ferdinand,[1] the Empire was only to survive a further two years.

It was the news of the Russian revolution in March 1917 that awoke a fresh excitement among the Habsburg peoples. The *Reichsrat*, which the Emperor had re-opened as a liberal gesture in May 1917, became the forum for renewed nationalist claims—Ruthenes demanding a Ukrainian state separate from the Polish territories, Slovenes demanding an autonomous state of Serbs, Croats, and Slovenes, Czechs demanding 'the transformation of the Habsburg monarchy into a federal

[1] See Genealogical table, p. 480.

state consisting of free and equal national states'. At the same time, outside the Empire, Masaryk had made contact with the provisional government in Russia and in May arrived in St Petersburg to organize the creation of a Czech army corps from among the Czech prisoners-of-war, of whom the Russians had taken some 210,000. In August Brusilov agreed to its formation, and as a result of Masaryk's visits to the camps about 39,000 volunteers were raised. The advent of the Bolsheviks to power, however, made it impossible for these troops to be used on an eastern front which had almost ceased to exist, and it was agreed that they should now proceed to France to continue the fight there. By March 1918 they were sufficiently organized to begin the long journey across Siberia to Vladivostok, which was the only possible route open to them, but by May they had come into conflict with local Russian Bolsheviks and before long Czech units had taken possession of much of the Trans-Siberian railway.[1]

Meanwhile, the Central Powers' treaty with the Ukraine in February 1918[2] had infuriated the Poles, since it was clear that they were being sacrificed to German interests. Kholm was surrendered to the Ukraine, Eastern Galicia and the Bukovina were to form a separate crownland with its own administration, Lithuania was to be re-created and the Prussian frontier to be extended farther east. To the Poles this was simply another partition; whole military units deserted to Russia and there seemed little likelihood of any further cooperation between the Poles and the Central Powers. Pilsudski himself had already been interned in July 1917 for refusing an oath which would have made his troops part of the German forces.

Thus the various interests which had believed it best to acquiesce during the first two years of the war were everywhere becoming more restless, aggravated by the poor food situation due to the Allied blockade. Prisoners returning from Russia were infected with ideas of revolution, and in January 1918 there were mass strikes and a naval mutiny in the Adriatic. Furthermore, the Allies were by now beginning to see that they could make the same use of the discontent of the Habsburg peoples as the Germans had made of Lenin, with the added advantage that the nationalist leaders were middle-class men strongly antagonistic to Bolshevism. In April a congress of 'suppressed nationalities' was held at Rome; agreements between Italian and Yugoslav representatives were published; on 3 June the British, French, and Italian premiers at the Supreme War Council at Versailles issued a declaration

[1] See p. 359.   [2] See p. 358.

that 'a united and independent Polish state with free access to the sea' would be an essential condition of peace. On 29 June the French government accepted the Czechs' National Council as the 'first basis of the future government' and on 14 August the British recognized the Czechs as an Allied nation.

Thus, as the German army wore itself out in its last great offensive in France, the Allies had already committed themselves to policies which were bound to mean the break-up of the Habsburg dominions, and by the autumn the various peoples of the Empire were taking the law into their own hands. On 28 October the Czech National Council assumed powers of government in Prague; on 29 October the Slovaks declared their readiness to be part of a Czechoslovak state; on the same day in the south, Serbs, Croats, and Slovenes proclaimed their new state Yugoslavia. On 31 October the Emperor Karl appointed by telephone Count Károlyi, a liberal aristocrat, as Prime Minister of Hungary and on 3 November Károlyi announced the complete independence of Hungary. And so, while the armies of the Allies were still many miles distant, the Habsburg Empire, rehabilitated at the Congress of Vienna in 1815, jarred yet not shattered by the emergence of Italy and Germany some fifty years later, finally fell to pieces at the end of a war which had destroyed so much else of Europe, and the last of the Emperors crossed the Swiss frontier by train into exile.

4. The German revolution 1918

In Germany there was a serious clash between two different conceptions of war aims. One group was prepared to consider a negotiated peace which was not to include any annexations of territory by Germany. This was a predominantly civilian outlook and by 1917 the Chancellor, Bethmann Hollweg, wished to link it with proposals for constitutional reform both in the Imperial system and in the Prussian franchise. These ideas not merely gained the support of the Democrats and the Centre Party under Matthias Erzberger; they created a split within the Social Democrats (SPD). One section—known as Majority Socialists—supported the government on these conditions and was therefore ready to vote war credits, in contrast to the left wing of the party—Independent Socialists—who were determined to oppose the continuation of the war.

Ranged against the politicians who were content to return to the *status quo ante bellum* the military leaders and great industrialists created a formidable opposition. They stood positively for a vast annexationist programme, the ultimate of pan-Germanism, including expansion along the Baltic coast and into Belgium, the creation of a system of client states stretching as far east as Persia, and the development of a German Mittelafrika. After the appointment of Hindenburg as Chief of the General Staff with Ludendorff as his Quarter-Master-General in August 1916, their influence over the government of Germany increased markedly. Their determination to create a satellite Polish state in the declaration of 5 November 1916[1] ended the chances of any negotiated peace with Tsarist Russia; their insistence on embarking on unrestricted submarine warfare in January 1917 was to bring the United States rapidly on to the side of the Allies, and in July 1917 they were able to secure the dismissal of Bethmann Hollweg, who was replaced first by Georg Michaelis, and then by Count von Hertling. Most striking of all, their power was to be seen in the negotiation of the Treaty of Brest Litovsk and the separate agreement with the Ukraine.

Naturally, these ambitions all assumed victory in war. In the offensive of March 1918, however, Ludendorff had only enough strength for tactical success, not enough for a strategic break-through, and since the annexationist policy of Germany's military rulers precluded any possibility of a negotiated peace, the Allies fought on with their backs to the wall. With the Allied assault near Amiens on 8 August Ludendorff knew that the last gamble had failed. The retreat went on across the eastern territories of France and through Belgium, until at the beginning of October he was forced to acknowledge that an armistice could no longer be delayed.

There followed during the last month of the war a most remarkable transformation of the system of government in Germany. Prince Max of Baden who was appointed Chancellor on 3 October, opened negotiations with the Allies on the same day and formed a government out of conservative and liberal groups including the Majority Socialists. He had, however, to convince the Americans as well as the left wing of his own supporters that the rule of the war-lords was now a thing of the past, and a 'revolution from above' was speedily organized. In future, German governments were to be fully responsible to the Reichstag; deputies were to be eligible as ministers, and the military were to be subordinated to the civil authority. In short, Germany was to become a parliamentary democracy, and if only William II had been

[1] See p. 360.

prepared to abdicate—as Prince Max begged him to do—the Hohen-zollern monarchy might still have survived.

Throughout October, as the German line was pressed back towards the frontier, notes continued to be exchanged between Prince Max and President Wilson over the Fourteen Points which Wilson had issued in January 1918 as the basis for a peace settlement. On 26 October Prince Max dismissed Ludendorff and three days later William II, still clinging to his crown, turned to Spa where the army headquarters was now established. But by this time the news that Germany was suing for peace had begun to awaken more revolutionary forces, which the politicians with their eyes on the Russian scene had been hoping to forestall with the 'revolution from above'. On 3 November the German navy at Kiel mutinied on being ordered out for one last hopeless battle against the British. On 6 November Cuxhaven, Bremen, and Hamburg were partly under the control of workers' and soldiers' councils, and on the same day Kurt Eisner, an Independent Socialist, led a demonstration in Munich which resulted in the occupation of public buildings and the proclamation of a Bavarian republic. Soon there were similar scenes of excitement in Cologne, Frankfurt, Stuttgart, and Leipzig, and on 7 November the Majority Socialists declared that they would not con-tinue to support Prince Max's government unless William II announced his abdication within forty-eight hours.

The struggle reached its climax on 9 November. Prince Max in despair proclaimed the abdication of William II before the German emperor had actually given his consent, but when, despite this, the Majority Socialists withdrew from the government and joined forces with the Independent Socialists, he handed over the Chancellorship to Friedrich Ebert, a Majority Socialist who had little liking for extreme revolution. The situation was already tense in Berlin; Karl Liebknecht on the steps of the Imperial Palace was proclaiming a Soviet régime, and it was in order to preserve the shaky existence of the constitutional government that Philip Scheidemann, another Majority Socialist, until recently a member of Prince Max's cabinet, hastily countered Liebknecht with the proclamation of a German republic from a window of the Reichstag building.

At this point in the story there is a striking parallel with the events of the previous year in St Petersburg. Disaster at the front had led to the collapse of the monarchy and now the constitutional forms of govern-ment which had emerged were swinging rapidly towards the extreme left. Yet in Germany, although the outcome seemed still to hang in the balance, there were several factors that made the emergence of a Bolshevik dictatorship highly unlikely.

First, the development of commerce and industry had naturally greatly increased the strength of the German middle class, who, since the 1830s, had been endeavouring to cultivate a political life of their own. When on 14 November the leaders of the workers' and soldiers' councils in Dresden and Leipzig announced the collapse of bourgeois capitalism, they were really guilty of wishful thinking. Capitalism had not collapsed, and the widespread discontent was aimed chiefly at the military hierarchy, officialdom, and the stringent conditions of wartime—not at a capitalist form of society. A second factor was the absence of anarchy in Germany; the country had not been overrun, the civil service was still functioning, and the army was falling back on its own frontier in reasonable order.

The most significant factor of all, however, was the bargain struck between the General Staff of the army and the new government. On the night of 9 November, as Ebert sat in the Chancellery listening to the noise of the street demonstrations and wondering how long his government could survive in the face of a Bolshevik onslaught, the telephone suddenly rang. It was General Gröner, Ludendorff's successor, speaking from Spa. In a short dramatic conversation these two men— Gröner, the son of an N.C.O., and Ebert, the son of a tailor—made their pact designed to save from Bolshevism the Empire still technically ruled by a Hohenzollern. The government would support the maintainance of military discipline and guarantee the means of supply for the army; the army would support the existence of the government and suppress the forces of Bolshevism. It was almost as if General Kornilov and Kerensky had joined forces against the Russian Bolsheviks in 1917.

That Ebert, a Socialist, should take this chance of alliance with a military clique who in the last years of the war had come close to gaining control over the government of Germany, is the measure of his dislike of the extreme left. For Gröner the agreement is more easily understandable. He knew that the Majority Socialists at least were hardly a revolutionary force; the General Staff badly needed some sort of national authority to which they could turn against the soldiers' councils; furthermore, at this very moment the armistice delegation was in contact with the Allies at Compiègne and to the military it was vital that some sort of civil government should be in existence to shoulder the responsibility for the defeat.

On 10 November—one day before the official cease-fire—the Emperor William II agreed at last to go into exile in Holland, and the rule of the Hohenzollerns in Germany was now officially replaced by that of a constitutional republic. Only to this extent was the German revolution a revolution at all. Its implications were purely political, its tendencies conservative, and the fact that it had established a government of Socialists was more than balanced by the uneasy alliance of that government with the military hierarchy.

27

THE AFTERMATH OF WAR 1919-21

1. Peace-making with the Central Powers

O N 18 January 1919 the Peace Conference was officially
opened at Paris. This was essentially a meeting of the victors,
including some thirty-two separate delegations, but none
representing either the neutrals or the defeated Powers. Originally it
had been intended to follow the pattern of peace-making in 1814—a
swift conclusion of terms with the enemy countries, followed by a
general European Congress to redraw the political map of the Continent; it soon became apparent, however, that nothing so clear-cut was
going to emerge from the confusion of what Arthur Balfour described
as 'a rough and tumble affair'.

It would perhaps be unjust to stress the unfavourable comparison
between Vienna and Versailles. Unlike their predecessors of 1814, the
principal statesmen of 1919 were committed to satisfying the demands
of the nationalist movements rampant in eastern Europe, whose
spokesmen were quick to assert their claims in the absence of any
German or Austrian representatives. Nor could the peace-makers
ignore the forces of democracy, dependent as they were on their own
electorates whose fury was constantly stimulated by a virulent press.
It was also highly significant that for the first time the United States
was to play a leading part in a European settlement, and the scope of the
treaty with Germany was inevitably widened by President Wilson's
determination that it should include his great scheme for a League of
Nations. Lloyd George and Clemenceau might differ over the details
of the peace; they were as one in their acceptance of the cynical
workings of European diplomacy. But for President Wilson this was
to be the opening of a new era of sweetness and light in international
relations. With all the New World's suspicion of the trickery of the
Old, he was determined to set right the complexities of central and
eastern Europe at a stroke. He saw himself, said Lloyd George, as 'a
missionary whose function it was to rescue the poor European heathen
from their age-long worship of false and fiery gods'. The French press,

which lampooned him mercilessly, did not even allow him the credit of his idealism. 'He speaks like Jesus Christ,' remarked Clemenceau, 'but he acts like Lloyd George.'

Democratic procedures were responsible for some delay in the assembling of the conference after the armistice of November 1918. In Great Britain the issues raised by the ending of hostilities, heightened by the light-headedness of war exhaustion, threatened to wreck the uneasy coalition government which Lloyd George had led since 1916, and as war-time conditions had kept the existing House of Commons unchanged for over eight years, the Prime Minister decided on a general election in December. There was certainly time for this, since President Wilson, whose personal representative at Paris, Colonel House, had failed to dissuade him from attending the conference, could not sail from the United States until he had delivered the annual presidential address to Congress on 2 December, and after his arrival on 14 December there followed a month of informal conversations in London, Paris, and Rome. Delay was perhaps not undesirable; it might allow a little time for the angry bitterness of war to subside, and as Clemenceau pointed out to Lloyd George, 'it is not a bad plan to let the German revolution settle down for a while in order that we may know before proceeding what we have before us'.

Indeed, in Germany the whole form of future government still hung in the balance. On 16 December a Soviet Congress had met in the hall of the Prussian Diet in Berlin and demanded the dismissal of Hindenburg and the surrender of the organization and discipline of the army to the soldiers' councils. On 23 December Ebert and his cabinet were actually besieged in the Chancellery, and for a time it seemed as if the provisional government of Germany was, after all, about to suffer the fate of Kerensky in St Petersburg in November 1917. A frantic telephone call from Ebert brought a military force from Potsdam to their rescue, but although the besiegers had actually withdrawn before its arrival, the German generals still exacted a price for their support. The Independent Socialists were to be excluded from the provisional government, and Ebert appointed as Minister of National Defence Gustav Noske, a right-wing Socialist whose suppression of the naval mutiny at Kiel in November 1918 made him acceptable to the General Staff. By the beginning of 1919 the first units of a volunteer Free Corps had been formed out of the old Imperial Army, and in the second week of January, under the command of General von Lüttwitz, they put down the extreme left Spartakists in

N

a series of bloody engagements during which the leaders Karl Liebknecht and Rosa Luxemburg were killed. This removal of the immediate threat of Communism in Germany now enabled Ebert to
organize the election of a National Assembly on the basis of universal
suffrage. On 6 February this met at Weimar, where, under the presidency of Ebert and with a Social Democrat, Philip Scheidemann, as
Chancellor, work was begun on devising a republican constitution.
Before this task had been completed, however, the new German
government learnt with a sudden shock the terms that the Allies were
resolved to impose.

At Paris the major decisions had been taken by an inner council of
the five major belligerent Powers—the United States, Great Britain,
France, Italy, and Japan. Clemenceau presided and had the advantage
of being able to speak English, whereas neither Wilson nor Lloyd
George could speak French. Japan soon dropped out, and Orlando, the
Italian premier, withdrew his delegation in April in protest at Wilson's
direct appeal to the Italians over his head to accept a frontier line which
would exclude Fiume on the Adriatic coast. Lloyd George was particularly concerned with the question of the German colonies, since
many of these had already been taken in possession by the Dominions.
For Clemenceau, who as a young man had watched the Prussian
army besieging Paris and whose country had now been ravaged by
four years of war, the sole aim of victory was to ensure that Germany
might never again invade France. French demands for an autonomous
republic to be carved out of German territory on the left bank of the
Rhine and for a permanent Allied control of the four Rhine bridge-
heads brought about the major crisis of the conference; the resistance
of both Wilson and Lloyd George, however, eventually forced a
compromise, and on 7 May the German delegates who had arrived at
Versailles could be presented with the statement of the terms that the
Allies had agreed to impose on Germany.

Both the refusal to negotiate and the nature of the terms themselves
were profoundly abhorrent to the Germans. Alsace and Lorraine, including all State property therein, were to be ceded to France, and the
districts of Eupen and Malmédy to Belgium; in Slesvig a plebiscite was
to decide the position of the Danish–German frontier. In the east the
new state of Poland was granted the provinces of Posen and West
Prussia, thus giving her access to the sea—the controversial Polish corridor—although Danzig was to have the separate status of a Free City.
Memel and the surrounding region was to be detached from East Prussia

Scale 0 ⊢ ⊢ ⊢ ⊢ 400 Miles

////// Territory lost by Germany |||||| Territory lost by Russia
········· Eastern limit of demilitar-   ≈≈≈≈ Former frontier of
ised zone in Germany   Austria-Hungary
———— Curzon Line

EUROPE IN 1921

to provide a port for Lithuania, and a small strip of territory was to be given up to Czechoslovakia. The German colonies were simply shared out among the Allies. South Africa gained South-West Africa, Australia German New Guinea, New Zealand Samoa, and Japan the northern Pacific islands, while Great Britain, France, and Belgium received the remainder of German possessions in Africa—all these territories being held technically under a mandate from the League of Nations.[1]

There were also stern measures to ensure against the revival of German military power. The army was to be reduced to 100,000 men, based on voluntary enlistment for a period of service of twelve years; it was to have no tanks, heavy artillery, or aircraft, and the fortifications of Heligoland were to be dismantled. The General Staff was to be dissolved. The navy was to have no U-boats, and its heaviest vessels were to consist of six battleships of 10,000 tons. In addition to this, French fears were quietened by an Allied occupation of the Rhineland for fifteen years and by a permanent demilitarization of both banks of the river.

Debatable though they may be, the fears of the French and the requirements of the new states in eastern Europe go far to explain these terms of the settlement. The justification of the economic clauses, however, rested almost entirely on the assumption of Germany's war guilt, which actually formed Article 231 of the treaty. It was argued that in causing the war Germany had wrought appalling havoc on the other Powers and that now she must pay. In compensation for the destruction of her own coal-mines France was to administer the Saar district with its annual output of 17,000,000 tons of coal under a League of Nations commission for the next fifteen years. All the victors, however, were each determined to press their account until the final figure to be demanded seemed likely to be so large that it was left to later negotiation—a festering sore which would jeopardize international relations and European economy for years to come.

During the next six weeks the German government struggled to escape its fate. It was useless. Beyond agreeing to a plebiscite in Upper Silesia the Allies were adamant. Scheidemann and his cabinet resigned rather than accept such terms, but Ebert in consultation with Hindenburg and Gröner knew that a continuation of the war in the west could only end in defeat and that the subsequent domestic turmoil would deliver Germany into the hands of either a Communist government or

[1] See p. 380.

a right-wing dictatorship of army officers. Scheidemann was replaced as Chancellor by a Social Democrat, Gustav Bauer, and eventually the Assembly agreed by a large majority to accept the treaty.

On 28 June—five years to the day after the assassination of Francis Ferdinand at Sarajevo—the ceremony of signing took place in the Hall of Mirrors in Louis XIV's palace of Versailles, where forty-eight years previously the German Empire had been proclaimed. 'Faites entrer les Allemands,' came Clemenceau's command, when the representatives of the victorious Powers were duly assembled. The two German delegates were led in; they signed, and shortly afterwards with hardly a word spoken were escorted out again. 'Oui,' said Clemenceau with tears in his eyes, 'c'est une belle journée.' It was perhaps understandable that for the French this was the supreme moment of triumph, but there were many that day who had doubts about its wisdom.

For the next two decades the Treaty of Versailles was to be a source of deep anger for the Germans. They spoke of it as a *Diktat* through which they had been deprived of any chance of negotiation, and they resented the heaviness of its terms which they claimed went far beyond the original Fourteen Points. They could certainly argue that the partition of the German colonies by the victors was inconsistent with 'a free open-minded and absolutely impartial adjustment of colonial claims'. The principle of national self-determination had deprived them of some seven million inhabitants; yet the treaty had positively forbidden the inclusion of German Austria within the frontiers of Germany. The general disarmament which had been proposed seemed to apply only to Germany, and the admission of war guilt appeared to lay them open to absurdly heavy reparations.

In fact, any defeated country, whether it negotiates or not, has to accept the conditions that the victor demands. Great Britain and France had both made reservations over the Fourteen Points, and in any case the terms which Germany had imposed on Russia at Brest Litovsk in March 1918 deprived her of any moral right to complain of Versailles; indeed, in comparison with her allies, Austria-Hungary and Turkey, Germany had kept the bulk of her territory intact and those regions which had been removed from her were of mixed population and had mostly been the fruit of conquest. She had lost roughly 13% of her lands and economic potential, but the revival of German power in the 1930s would hardly suggest that these territorial changes had permanently maimed her.

The fundamental significance of Versailles, however, was emotional rather than rational. Allied statesmen, urged on by the pressure of public opinion, had made peace in a spirit of revenge. The cries of 'il faut en finir,' 'hang the Kaiser', and 'squeezing the German lemon until the pips squeak' were indicative of the desire not merely for a guarantee of future security, but for the national humiliation of Germany. Similarly, the Germans, confronted with disaster less than a year after their overwhelming victory in the east, accepted the inevitable in a spirit of sullen resentment. The actual thought of military defeat, the loss of overseas colonies, and the surrender of land to the Poles and the Czechs were a constant hurt to national pride; four years of war followed by the upheaval of social revolution were bound to mean a long painful period of recovery and readjustment for the entire Continent; yet the Germans saw every difficulty in subsequent years as a further indignity that they alone must suffer as a result of the hated Treaty of Versailles.

Two other treaties were concluded by the Allies in 1919. With the signing of the Treaty of Saint-Germain on 10 September, Austria was reduced to a tiny rump in the German-speaking Alpine lands. Trieste, Istria, and the southern half of the Tyrol were surrendered to Italy; she was severed from Hungary, and the subject peoples of the rest of the old Habsburg dominions were free to go their own way. Vienna, the only reminder of her past Imperial greatness, had become the capital of a small European republic, its industry hampered by the loss of the minerals and raw materials on which it had formerly drawn, its frontiers harassed by the ambitions of new nation states. Two months later, on 27 November, Bulgaria made her peace with the Allies by the Treaty of Neuilly, which simply confirmed the territorial losses which she had suffered at the end of the second Balkan war in 1913.

2. The emergence of the new nation states in eastern Europe

Of the enemy countries there remained Hungary and Turkey. Before settlement could be reached with them, however, the Allies had had to grapple with the countless problems created by the collapse of four Empires, whose existence had been the mainstay of an entire political and social system. When Bismarck commented in 1878 that the duty of the Powers was to consider the peace of Europe rather than the happiness of the Bulgarians, he had spoken with the voice of the nineteenth century. Now, in 1919, the assumptions on which central and eastern Europe had previously been governed were no longer valid. This time legitimacy was to be based not on dynastic right, but on national self-determination; the Allies were to supervise a new 'springtime of the nations', an 1848 in which the emancipated peoples would be free to pursue their conflicting national aims without the fear of any immediate retribution.

This was an appallingly difficult task. It involved problems of securing strategically defensible frontiers and a workable economy within each of the new states, and was complicated by one further consideration that the statesmen of 1919 did share with their predecessors of 1814. Both were haunted by the fear of social revolution; thus, just as the men of the Congress of Vienna were prompted by a desire to shore up an aristocratic social system against the ambitions of a middle class inspired by the doctrines of the French Revolution, so the victors of 1919 attempted to contain the Communism of Russia through the establishment of liberal parliamentary democracies in the new states that were emerging from the ruin of eastern Europe.

Over the creation of Czechoslovakia the main difficulty had been for Czechs and Slovaks to reach agreement, but when the Slovaks were at last persuaded that they would enjoy full national autonomy within a federal state, Dr Beneš and Professor Masaryk, the Czech leaders, were able to present a powerful case to the western Allies. At the end of the war the Czechs were accordingly granted the right to occupy Bohemia and Moravia, until the Peace Conference assembled. The Hungarians were determined to resist the loss of Slovakia, and a week after an armistice had been signed at Padua on 3 November, they invaded Slovakia and drove out the Czechs. In March 1919, however, the Allies forced them to withdraw, and by the treaty that was finally signed in September 1919 a Czechoslovak State was brought into existence including the whole of Slovakia, as well as several purely Magyar districts, and Ruthenia, whose people had elected to join the new state on the basis of local autonomy.

Rumania's conclusion of a separate peace with the Central European Powers in January 1918 had released the western Allies from their secret treaty of 1916, whereby she had been due to receive a considerable area of Hungarian territory, but despite the unpopularity of the Rumanian Prime Minister, Bratianu, at the Peace Conference, they agreed in response to the wishes of a majority of the population that Bessarabia, the districts of the Dobruja and the Bukovina, as well as the whole of Transylvania, should be included within the frontiers of Rumania.

In Hungary, however, Count Károlyi's government had lost support after the enforced withdrawal from Slovakia in March 1919, and in the hope of gaining the friendship of Russia the Socialists combined with the Communists under Bela Kun, who proclaimed a Soviet republic. The Allies' demand for the surrender of Transylvania to Rumania was rejected and in the early summer Hungarian forces reoccupied Slovakia and checked the advance of the Rumanian army westwards. Their resistance did not last long. Russia was not in a position to help and the attempt of the Communists to turn the great estates into cooperative farms disappointed the Hungarian peasantry, whose hopes had been raised by an earlier Social Democrat decree that the land would be divided among them. In June Slovakia had to be evacuated again and in August—to the relief of the western Powers—Bela Kun fled before the Rumanian army, which proceeded to occupy Budapest until November, when it finally withdrew behind the frontiers laid down by the treaty.

It has sometimes been said that no one was the victor in the first World War. This may well have been true of the Powers who were brought into it indirectly, but for Serbia, who saw the whole struggle as one between herself and Austria-Hungary, the issue was more simple. Austria-Hungary had lost and paid the price in disruption, and in the Balkans there emerged an enlarged Serb–Croat–Slovene state, the Kingdom of Yugoslavia, including some 250,000 Magyars along its northern frontier, many Albanians living in Montenegro, and the Italians of Fiume on the Adriatic coast.

Thus the successes of Czechoslovakia, Rumania, and Yugoslavia in pressing their claims before the Allies all involved Hungary in serious losses, and only a plebiscite held in December 1920 saved her from having also to surrender the Burgenland on her western frontier to Austria.

The settlement of the lands that had lain under Tsarist rule was complicated by the course of the Soviet government's struggle in Russia. Only in Finland was the situation relatively straightforward. Finnish independence had already been recognized by the Bolshevik government in January 1918; under General Mannerheim the Finnish Whites had overcome the Reds in the civil war of that spring, and her constitutional form of government gave her a firm basis on which to put her affairs in order. Finland's principal need at this time was to re-establish friendly relations with the west, which had been jeopardized by her use of a German expeditionary force against the Bolsheviks and, in October 1918, by the Finnish Diet's election of Prince Frederick Charles of Hesse, William II's brother-in-law, as King of Finland. By the end of the year, however, these western suspicions had been quietened by the appointment of Mannerheim as Regent, since he had strongly opposed the German election, and after the establishment of a new republican government and a general election in the spring of 1919, Finland's international situation seemed to be satisfactorily stabilized. The balance of forces on the south coast of the Baltic naturally concerned her, but she took no part in any direct attack on Russia, since the White Russians, who were pressing for her support, would give no guarantee of confirming the independence which she had already gained.

South of the Gulf of Finland the turmoil was inevitably greater. The position of the German Baltic barons was naturally challenged alike by Estonian and Latvian nationalists and by Bolsheviks, and both had been savagely suppressed by the German army advancing eastwards in the first months of 1918. On the collapse of Germany in the west, however, Bolshevik forces returned and in December 1918 Estonian and Latvian Soviet Republics were officially recognized by Russia. The appearance of British naval units in the Baltic soon brought about the collapse of these régimes and new national non-Communist governments, established in Estonia in January 1919 and in Latvia in May, combined their armies to resist the Germans who, under the command of General von der Goltz, were still attempting to establish an occupation. Riga was successfully defended and later in the year Allied intervention forced von der Goltz to withdraw to East Prussia, when all Baltic forces were placed under the command of a young British officer, Lieutenant Colonel Alexander.

In Poland the problem of independence was confused at the end of the war by the existence of two separate governments, one under Pilsudski at the head of the Polish Regency Council which the Central Powers had set up in 1916, the other under the pro-Russian Dmowski whose National Committee had been recognized by the Allies in Paris. It was the great pianist Paderewski who managed to weld the two into a workable organization, and in January 1919 a Polish parliament was elected by universal suffrage. Poland's western frontier was largely defined by the terms of the Treaty of Versailles, leaving only the disputed area of Upper Silesia to be settled by a plebiscite.

N 2

To the north and east, however, Pilsudski was determined to establish Poland's claims by force of arms. In April 1919 Vilna, which the Lithuanians had established as their own capital, was seized, and throughout the rest of the year Polish forces thrust into Eastern Galicia where the Ukrainians put up a fierce but unavailing resistance to them.

These Polish successes on the eastern front in 1919 are partly explained by the presence of the anti-Bolshevik forces that were occupying the attention of the Red Army in Russia during this year. In March Kolchak[1] had made a fresh attempt to strike up towards the Volga, but by the end of April had been pushed back by General Kamenev in the direction of the Urals. No sooner had this threat been met than Denikin began a great thrust north and west through the Ukraine, captured Kiev, Kursk, Voronezh, and Orel, and by October appeared to be coming within striking distance of Moscow. At the same time General Judenich launched an assault through Estonia on St Petersburg. For the Bolsheviks it was the supreme crisis of their struggle for survival, but in Trotsky they had the man to rise to the challenge. He organized his reinforcements, prepared a plan for the defence of St Petersburg street by street, argued the Politbureau into accepting it, and fired his commanders with such determination that by November the armies of Judenich and Denikin, whose lines of communication had become seriously over-extended, were in full retreat.

After this the survival of the Soviet government in Russia was no longer in question. Denikin was driven out of his base in the Crimea: in February 1920 Kolchak, who had by now fallen back east of the Urals, was surrendered to the Bolsheviks and executed, and the Allied expeditionary forces at Archangel and Vladivostok were withdrawn. The new non-Communist governments of Estonia and Latvia still held firm; on the other hand, they had given little support to the White Russians and the Bolsheviks decided to accept the situation, as they had done over Finland, by concluding peace treaties with them in 1920.

There remained the problem of Poland. Like the Finns and the Baltic peoples the Poles had been cautious over giving direct assistance to the White Russians, whom they did not trust to recognize their independence. Pilsudski, however, had no wish to accept the eastern frontier suggested by the Allies—known later as the Curzon line.[2] after the British Foreign Secretary who had proposed it—which came close

---

[1] See p. 359.   [2] See map, p. 371.

to that of 1815, and in April 1920 he embarked upon a new attack in the hope of gaining the old 1772 frontier. For six months the fortune of war swung to and fro. The Poles reached Kiev, but the Red Army, now able to concentrate all its forces on a single front, pushed them back until it stood before Warsaw. The Poles made frantic appeals to the Allies; the French general Weygand was sent to them from Paris, and on 16 August Pilsudski won a great victory by the Vistula. A second Polish advance began, and on 12 October Lenin decided to cut his losses with an armistice, followed in March 1921 by the Treaty of Riga which established the frontier some two hundred miles to the east of the Curzon line. For the Lithuanians this Polish success was disastrous, since Vilna and the region around it, known as the Suwalki triangle, was placed under a Polish military occupation which was able to ensure that in the subsequent plebiscite the territory became part of Poland.

In the extreme south-east of Europe it had been agreed at Paris that Albania should receive a part of Epirus on her southern frontier, and after a little difficulty with the occupying forces of Italy and Yugoslavia an independent government was established under Ahmed Zogu as Prime Minister. Concessions to Greece, which included most of Thrace and a large area of Smyrna in Asia Minor, where there was a considerable Greek population, were all part of the Allies' settlement with Turkey—the Treaty of Sèvres signed in August 1920—whereby the Ottoman Empire suffered a fate similar to that of Austria-Hungary. She was to lose all her Arab territories in Africa and Asia; some, such as Arabia, were to receive outright independence; others were to be governed under a type of mandate which left them considerable control over their domestic affairs, Syria being entrusted to France, Transjordania, Iraq, and the Sheikhdoms of the Persian Gulf to Great Britain.

The effect of these terms was to add tremendous support to a Turkish nationalist movement under Mustapha Kemal, which had already so threatened the Sultan's position that the Allies had had to occupy Constantinople in March 1920. Kemal's reply to the publication of the Treaty of Sèvres was a military attack on British and Greek forces in Asia Minor, and the Allies agreed with the Greek Prime Minister, Venizelos, that Greek reinforcements should be sent in. At this point, however, the whole course of political and military events was changed by a most remarkable chance. In June 1917 the Allies had forced through the deposition of Constantine, the pro-German King of

Greece,[1] who was succeeded by his son Alexander. In October 1920, however, Alexander died as a result of a bite by his pet monkey. In the general election that followed, Venizelos was defeated and the pro-German Constantine was restored to the Greek throne. The outcome was to be disastrous for Greece. The Allies at once withdrew their support. By November 1922 the forces of Mustapha Kemal had taken over the government of Turkey and driven the Greeks from Smyrna, and in the final settlement by the Treaty of Lausanne in August 1923 the Allies made their peace with Turkey, confirming the expulsion of the Greeks from Asia Minor and restoring to her the eastern half of Thrace and several islands near the entrance to the Dardanelles.

3. The League of Nations

'It is not done well,' remarked Dr Johnson of a dog walking on its hind legs, 'but you are surprised to find it done at all.' The same judgement might be made of the settlement of central and eastern Europe after the war. There could be no fundamental solution to the problems of the nineteenth century; the new frontiers had simply been superimposed upon them, and at best the Allies had managed to tidy up a chaotic map. Some of the new states were composite creations out of different national groups—Czechs, Slovaks, and Ruthenians in Czechoslovakia; Serbs, Croats, and Slovenes in Yugoslavia. Class divisions aggravated by differences of language complicated the national unity of others—Swedes in southern Finland, German-speaking landowners in the Baltic states. Many were dissatisfied with the frontiers that had been allotted to them; most included national minorities under their rule—German Sudetenlanders and Magyars within Czechoslovakia, Austrians of the southern Tyrol within Italy, Ukrainians, Germans, and Lithuanians within Poland, Magyars, Germans, and Albanians within Yugoslavia—all resentful of their new condition and determined to preserve their own identity.[2]

Of these it was the German problem which was to be the most significant for the future. 'I cannot conceive any greater cause of future war,' Lloyd George had written in a memorandum in March 1919, 'than that the German people, who have certainly proved themselves one of the most vigorous and powerful races in the world, should be

---

[1] See Genealogical table, p. 482.　　[2] See Appendix 8, p. 489.

surrounded by a number of small states, many of them consisting of people who have never previously set up a stable government for themselves, but each of them containing large masses of Germans clamouring for re-union with their native land.'

There was, nevertheless—in the west, at least—a strange sense of hopeful idealism which must have produced a sardonic smile from the ghost of Metternich. There were two reasons for this optimism. The first was purely wishful thinking; the World War had been so appalling that it must never, and therefore could never, happen again. The second was slightly more practical in that the Allies believed that through the establishment of a League of Nations all future disagreements could be settled by negotiation. The congresses of nineteenth-century Europe have sometimes been regarded as an anticipation of such a scheme, but in fact these had been no more than occasional gatherings of the great Powers to safeguard their own interests; the happiness of the Bulgarians had played no part in them. The conception of the League of Nations was totally different; it aimed at a concert of governments of the whole world, in which all the member States were pledged to apply economic and, if necessary, military sanctions against any apparent aggressor, thus ensuring a system of collective security for great and small alike. The preservation of peace was no longer to depend upon the *ad hoc* arrangements of the Powers concerned, but upon a permanent assembly at Geneva with an International Court of Justice at The Hague. The League was to supervise the protection of national minorities, the government of the mandated territories, the Saar and the Free City of Danzig, and through a variety of subordinate bodies, such as the International Labour Organization, was to develop organs of international cooperation to deal with questions of health, working conditions, and white slavery.

So much scorn has been poured on the ultimate failure of the League that it would be as well to suggest some of the points in its favour. It was certainly a positive and gallant attempt, strongly supported by many high-minded Europeans, to move away from the anarchy of power politics, and if as a pioneering attempt it did suffer from many inadequacies, it nevertheless provided a body of experience from which it was possible to design a more effective international organization after the second World War. For a few years, at least, it was able to adjudicate over minor frontier disputes, and in the less spectacular non-political spheres its achievement was quite considerable.

The efficacy of an international political organization, however, must depend upon the extent to which each state is prepared to surrender some part at least of its national sovereignty, and the weakness of the League lay in the fact that it was entirely based upon the rights and existence of independent nation states. Despite the insistence of the French, it did not even possess an international force of its own, relying simply upon the voluntary cooperation of its members. Small issues it might be able to resolve, but in any major crisis involving the great Powers it was eventually to find itself ignored. The dream of the idealists had been of an international parliament. But the League was never a parliament; it was not even a confederation. Worse still, even its impartiality was in some doubt. Seeing Germany and Russia excluded from membership and the Covenant of the League written into the peace treaties, many countries regarded the League as little more than an instrument of policy for the western Powers. And after March 1920 this meant only Great Britain, France, and Italy, for in that month the United States Senate, shrinking from any further commitment in Europe, refused to ratify the Treaty of Versailles and thereby rejected American participation in the President's own scheme.

VII

THE CRISIS OF LIBERAL DEMOCRACY 1921-45

28

THE 1920S: (1) THE REHABILITATION OF EUROPE

ONLY very gradually did the grass grow back over the tortured land of the battlefields, amid the deserted pill-boxes and the rusting barbed wire; and on the minds of men the scars of the first World War lasted still longer. For all the belligerents the cost had been appalling—for Great Britain and the Empire a million dead, France well over a million, Germany perhaps two million, Austria-Hungary a million, Italy half a million, and the United States 81,000; for Russia, who had probably suffered worst of all, the final figure cannot be established. During the next twenty years the horror of the Great War was to be a constant theme of reminiscence; a curiosity to know how it could ever have happened created a great reading public for the memoirs of statesmen and generals, and led to a wide-spread mood of pacifism reflected in the great war novels and plays—Sherriff's *Journey's End*, Hemingway's *A Farewell to Arms*, Barbusse's *Le Feu*, and Remarque's *Im Westen Nichts Neues*. The men who had fought and lived to see the end were dominated by one thought. Such a war must never in any circumstances happen again, and the fruit of their teaching to their children was to be seen in a famous motion carried at an Oxford Union debate in 1933 that 'This House will in no circumstance fight for its King and Country.'

Throughout the entire Continent the World War was like some great divide cutting off one epoch from another. Of course, it had not actually created the problems of industrial labour relations, the growth of collectivism in all forms of government, the turbulence of nation-alism, or the development of new forces outside Europe, all of which had well established antecedents before 1914. Yet it had so accelerated them that the world seemed utterly changed. The new fashions in clothes, the introduction of wireless in the home, the first solo flights across the Atlantic and to Australia, the appearance of the cinema, and, by the end of the decade, the first 'talkies', all helped to strengthen this sense of a break with the past. Men talked of recovery with a nostalgia for the pre-war days, but the gap could not be bridged. Even when prosperity did return after 1925, there was something shallow and feverish about it, like the jazz sweeping in from the New World or the excitements of university students who felt that they had missed the war—the symptoms of a society that had lost its bearings, as depicted in the early novels of Evelyn Waugh and in Christopher Isherwood's *Goodbye to Berlin.*

1. New governments and societies

Before 1914 it could be assumed that any new state would adopt the title of a principality or a kingdom, and Greece, Belgium, Rumania, Bulgaria, Norway, and Albania had each in their turn added to the number of crowned heads in Europe. It was symbolic of the revolution of the time that every state created after 1918 should declare itself a republic—with the exception of Yugoslavia, which the Serbs regarded as an extension of the kingdom of Serbia. One might also have expected the form of their governments to be federal, in view of the promises that had been made to the various national groups within the new frontiers; yet the only countries to organize themselves on a federal basis were Germany and Austria, whose populations were by far the most homogeneous. Nearly all the rest, conscious of the need to emphasize their political identity, established a unitary system which naturally tended to benefit the dominant national group in each country. Thus, in Yugoslavia local government was modelled on the French pattern of *départements*; in Poland, although some recognition was accorded to the old historic divisions, the system was fundamentally centralized, and in Czechoslovakia the projected autonomy for Slovakia and Ruthenia soon succumbed to control from Prague. The treatment of minorities was seldom harsh, but the question was always liable to cause animosity, and in each of the three countries official posts fell increasingly into the hand of Serbs, Poles, and Czechs. The most liberal solution was to be seen in Finland. The League of Nations had rejected Sweden's plea for possession of the Åland Islands, but although they remained Finnish, the Swedish-speaking population were granted autonomy by the Finnish government, while on the mainland Swedes and Finns shared complete equality of civil rights.

Now that the Treaty of Riga in 1921 had checked the immediate fear of international Communism, central and eastern Europe had become littered with highly technical paper constitutions. Parliamentary democracy was the rule. Reigning kings had become constitutional monarchs and the new republics had established elected presidents. With the exception of Czechoslovakia and the federal governments of Germany and Austria the legislatures were single chamber assemblies and were everywhere elected by universal suffrage. In Poland, Czechoslovakia, and the Baltic states these new systems had to be devised in their entirety; elsewhere, they emerged through modifications of forms of government already in existence, but in all the new countries their roots were shallow and the problems with which they had to deal enormous.

In Germany the constitution of the Weimar Republic was adopted by the National Assembly on 11 August 1919. On paper, at least, this offered Germany a strikingly democratic system of government, in marked contrast to the subterfuge of the Empire of 1871. The legislature was to be bi-cameral—the lower House, the Reichstag, elected every four years on a basis of proportional representation by universal suffrage for men and women who had reached the age of twenty; the upper House, the *Reichsrat*, consisting of representatives of the regional governments. The head of the State was to be a President elected on a popular vote to hold office for seven years, although a referendum proposed by a two-thirds majority in each House could bring about his removal. On the other hand, the President, too, had the right of appeal to the electorate, since he could dissolve the Reichstag, provided that the government concurred, and he could temporarily veto legislation while the issue was decided by a national referendum. The Chancellor was appointed by the President to form a government, but these ministers remained responsible to the Reichstag. The position of the army within this system was of fundamental significance, since under the Empire the Officer Corps had been bound by a personal allegiance to the Emperor quite apart from the normal ties of citizenship. The President was now technically Supreme Commander of the armed forces, but the oath of allegiance was simply taken to the constitution, and the Reichstag had secured the sole right of declaring war.

This new system of government for Germany, drawn largely from the experience of other constitutional states, might well seem like the long awaited realization of the hopes of the German liberals of 1848. Not merely had Germany at last a democratic government with as many safeguards for its preservation as a legal document could devise;

she had, too, established a stronger central control over the various regions—now known as *Länder*—than either the men of 1848 had envisaged or Bismarck had achieved in 1871; the new constitution really completed the unification of Germany.

There were a few weak points. Proportional representation was to encourage the growth of a multiplicity of small political parties that would add to the difficulties of parliamentary government. The short life of the Second Republic in France should have been a warning against the election of a President by a popular vote,[1] and certain emergency powers that enabled the President to select a Chancellor without the sanction of the Reichstag were to create a loophole through which Adolf Hitler was eventually to come to power. Yet the ultimate strength of a constitution lies in the political sense and good-will of the men who govern within it, and the final collapse of the Weimar Republic was due to the inadequacies of individuals rather than to the clauses of a single document.

As in the political sphere, social change immediately after the war was more marked in the east than elsewhere in Europe. In Great Britain, France, and Germany, and to a lesser extent in Italy and Scandinavia, industrialism had already before 1914 created a great urban proletariat, and a new hierarchy of wealth had gradually become intertwined with the old landed aristocracy which, although now less self-assured, still enjoyed considerable margins of security. The war accelerated, but did not radically alter this process, and even in Germany after 1918 the aristocracy, although deprived of much of their former political influence, still retained their estates and their social position.

In eastern Europe the pattern of development was far more varied. The people of these lands were primarily peasantry whose backward methods of farming could barely keep pace with a steadily rising population. In Serbia, Bulgaria, and Greece land reforms before the war had already created a society of small independent farmers. Now in Yugoslavia, Czechoslovakia, and Rumania similar measures broke up the large estates which had been in the possession of Magyar and German landlords, but the division of the spoil was carried out largely in the interest of the dominant groups in these new countries and the

---

[1] The German government was certainly aware of the dangers of a popular election in the summer of 1919. Contrary to the provisions of the new constitution, Ebert was elected President in August by the National Assembly which assumed the functions of the Reichstag until the election of June 1920.

national minorities fared badly. Part of the motive force behind these changes was the need felt by the governments to satisfy their peasantry in the face of the Communist experiment in Russia. In Poland and Hungary, however, the fear of Communism had precisely the reverse effect. The Poles had been at war with Russia until 1921; Hungary had for a few months in 1919 had a Soviet régime under Bela Kun, and the consequence of the right-wing reaction after these experiences was to preserve the great landed estates, so that throughout the inter-war years the vast hereditary properties of the old noble families, such as the Esterházy and the Festetics in Hungary or the Radziwill and the Potocki in Poland, survived virtually untouched.

The change in the character of the middle class in these regions after the war was still more striking. Previously only in Bohemia and Greece had a powerful bourgeois class established its hold over commerce, the professions, and the bureaucracy. In Croatia and Rumania the bourgeois had at least managed to move into the professions, but in Poland and Hungary these had remained the preserve of the aristocracy. No middle class existed in Serbia, Slovakia, and Bulgaria, which had been almost entirely peasant lands, while in Albania society was purely tribal. Hardly anywhere in these regions had commerce been controlled by the local populations. In Hungary it was shared between a German and a Jewish trading class; elsewhere, it was almost entirely in the hands of the Jews.

Once independence had been gained, however, the new governments began to foster their own economic interests. The effect of this was twofold. Contrary to the provisions of the Fourteen Points, it led to the raising of tariffs, as each state protected its own produce from foreign competition; and secondly, the growth of a national commercial class attempting to enter what had been a Jewish preserve led to a new fury of anti-Semitism to which the governments often lent their support.

2. The problem of reparations and war debts

The strain and expense of war, the new scene in eastern Europe, and the readjustments in the colonial field had naturally entailed a serious dislocation of world economy. There was in addition the question of a settlement of accounts among the belligerents. Great Britain and France had lent considerable sums to their European allies, but the situation was complicated by the fact that both had also incurred considerable debts of their own. From the United States and Great Britain France had borrowed almost three times as much as she had lent, while Great Britain had borrowed from the United States slightly less than half. Shortly after the war the British proposed an all-round cancellation of debts with a direct payment of German reparations to the United States, but the suggestion was acceptable to neither the French who were determined not to lose their share of German reparations, nor to the Americans who were the principal creditor nation. 'They hired the money, didn't they!' remarked President Coolidge, and the most that could be achieved in this direction was a general reduction in the total amounts to be repaid. Thus, an acrimonious situation was prolonged, adding a sense of urgency to the demand for reparations from Germany, so that the western Powers might be able in turn to meet their own liabilities. Only the Russians managed to escape from this imbroglio by the simple means of disowning all debts of the Tsarist government.

A decision over the total amount of reparations had not been reached at the time of the peace-making, Germany simply being required to make an interim payment of £1,000 million. In March 1921, when Germany had defaulted over this, the Allies occupied Düsseldorf, Duisburg, and Ruhrort on the east side of the Rhine, and on 27 April the Reparations Commission followed up by announcing the total figure that would be exacted from Germany—£6,600 million in gold to be paid off in annual instalments. Not surprisingly this brought about the downfall of a German government already deep in domestic difficulties, but in May its successor had to accept the demand.

The wisdom of the Allies' policy over reparations has often been seriously questioned. Certainly there was nothing unusual in the payment of an indemnity by a defeated nation, and the appalling devastation that France and Belgium had suffered gave them a perfectly good case for compensation. Yet the very size of the payment demanded was without precedent and was to have disastrous political and economic consequences for victors and vanquished alike. As Bernard Shaw pointed out in a later broadcast, there were no gold mines in Germany; all payment must depend ultimately upon the sale of goods and services abroad and this could only be achieved by the stimulation of German foreign trade; the financial profit that Germany might thereby gain would then be drained off in the form of reparations. Thus, foreign rivals would be faced with a far greater German competition without any corresponding increase in consuming power on the German home market, where they might have been able to retaliate. This aspect of reparations was of particular significance for the British, who depended utterly on their overseas trade; it mattered less to the French, whose economy was more self-contained and who were concerned with the immediate question of repairing the material damage of the war.

This divergence of views between Great Britain and France became apparent almost at once when, in 1922, the German government requested a moratorium on cash payments. The British were prepared to grant this, but the French refused and in January 1923, when Germany defaulted once more, French and Belgian troops crossed the Rhine to occupy the Ruhr, the heart of German industry, to undertake the direct supervision of continued payment. The German government replied by proclaiming a policy of non-cooperation throughout the occupied area, giving financial aid to strikers and indefinitely suspending all further reparations payments to France and Belgium. Casualties were suffered in many clashes between French soldiers and Germans, and ill-feeling became still further inflamed when in the course of the year French generals attempted to foster in the Palatinate a local separatist movement whose supporters eventually expelled the officials of the Weimar Republic. The British had already refused to participate in the occupation of the Ruhr, and their disagreements with the French came to a head in January 1924, when they were outvoted in the Allied High Commission, which proceeded to recognize an autonomous government for the Palatinate. In fact, strong British pressure led to the abandonment of the separatist movement and the German government, recently harassed by an unsuccessful coup in Bavaria,[1] was assisted in its suppression by the Rhinelanders themselves, most of whom had seen the movement as no more than a French stratagem.

This unhappy outbreak of Franco-German hostility, involving a considerable deterioration in Anglo-French relations, was accompanied by the final collapse of the German currency. The value of the German mark had already begun to decline during the war, and by 1920 it had dropped from a pre-war level of 20 to the pound sterling to 250. Then in the last months of 1921 it fell again to 1,000 and in the following year it had plunged to 35,000. The French occupation of the Ruhr

[1] See p. 399.

and the economic deadlock that ensued completed the ruin, and by August 1923 the mark had become completely worthless—20 million to the pound—a situation of which any collector of German postage stamps will have seen the evidence.

This collapse of the mark was to some extent due to the circumstances of war and defeat, but there is little doubt that the German government was fundamentally responsible for the final catastrophe, since more and more paper money had been issued despite the failure to balance the national budget. The consequences varied greatly for different sections of the community. There was positive gain for financiers who had access to foreign currency and for industrialists who could pay off their debts in worthless marks; landowners and small business men could on the whole manage to keep afloat. Wage-earners, poor before, became still poorer, but the greatest revolution was suffered by that section of the middle class who depended for their place in society on their salaries and the income from the investment of their private savings, which were now virtually wiped out. It was a most appalling blow for the most stable element of society and it was eventually to cost the Weimar Republic dear. Thousands became destitute, and from their despair the Communist and Nazi parties were later to draw a powerful reinforcement.

Inflation, hunger, and the industry of the country at a standstill as a result of the policy of passive resistance in the Ruhr—this was the scene that confronted Gustav Stresemann, when he took office as German Chancellor in August 1923. Although a monarchist and a conservative at heart, he believed that for the moment the only hope of German recovery lay in the survival of the Republic, and in September he abandoned the policy of non-cooperation in the Ruhr and resumed payment of reparations. The Allies, who had become seriously alarmed at the situation in Germany, responded at once to this first step by Stresemann; the British Prime Minister, Stanley Baldwin, appealed to the United States to collaborate in a new settlement, and in January 1924 a committee under an American general, Charles G. Dawes, was set up in Paris to examine ways of setting German finances aright and to devise a more sensible approach to the problem of reparations.

The Dawes Committee presented its report in April. It advised a German currency reform which would establish the Reichsmark at 20 to the pound, the bank of issue being free from governmental interference. To prime the pump Germany would receive a foreign loan of £40 million and a more moderate scale of annual instalments of reparations was to be introduced with payments made in German currency. These suggestions were discussed at London in July, and here Stresemann was fortunate in that a Labour administration under Ramsay MacDonald had been formed in Great Britain at the beginning of the year, while in France a radical government under Édouard Herriot had taken over after the fall of Poincaré in May. The left wing in Great Britain and France were inclined to be more conciliatory towards Germany, and the recommendations of the Dawes Committee were accepted without great difficulty. In October 1924 the foreign loan was floated, much of it being raised in the United States, and in November French and Belgian troops were finally withdrawn from the Ruhr.

Although the course of domestic life had been less cataclysmic than in Germany, every country had passed through a lean period of recovery during the years immediately following the war. Austria and Hungary had both suffered from inflation. Great Britain's markets for her exports were now being seriously attacked by American and Japanese competition, and the raising of tariffs, due to the general sense of economic insecurity, added to her difficulties, while in France the preservation of the value of the franc had been a matter of constant political concern.

The year 1925, however, marks the beginning of a new upward trend in the whole economy of Europe, and during the next four years international trade increased by 20%. A nostalgia for the formulae of pre-war prosperity led most countries to a somewhat theoretical return to the gold standard. France began now to feel the benefit of a revolution in her industrial output brought about by the stimulus of war, followed by the recovery of Alsace and Lorraine and the development of hydro-electric power. In Italy the national economy was placed on a firmer footing through a corporative system of State control under Mussolini.[1] In Germany the Dawes plan was successful in re-creating a sound currency and a flood of foreign capital, mostly in the form of short-term loans raised in the United States, enabled her industry to be re-organized and her reparations payments to be met. Many of her industrialists had made fortunes out of the inflation, and in the subsequent period of stability there was a marked increase in that tendency to form great combines which had been noticeable in Germany before the war—the concentration of chemical industries in I. G. Farben in 1925, the creation of a steel trust, the *Vereinigte Stahlwerke A.G.* in

[1] See p. 403.

1926, and a growing empire of electrical engineering in the Siemens concern. The effect of this German recovery was widespread, since it provided a market for the agricultural produce of the countries of eastern Europe. It was natural that a new sense of optimism should encourage the belief that the effects of the war were safely over, but, in fact, the whole of this sudden prosperity rested fundamentally on enormous loans from the United States, and it would last just as long as the flow of credit held out.

29

THE 1920s: (2) THE MAINTENANCE OF
THE VERSAILLES SETTLEMENT

1. The new democracies' struggle for survival

'IT has long been clear to me,' wrote Jacob Burckhardt in 1882, 'that the world is moving towards the alternatives between complete democracy and absolute lawless despotism, and the latter would certainly not be run by the dynasties which are too soft-hearted, but by supposedly military commands.' The eclipse of the old monarchical system had now brought this issue out into the open, and the economic instability of the post-war years was thus particularly unfortunate for the new parliamentary governments throughout central and eastern Europe, still at a highly experimental stage and threatened by the rise of two different types of authoritarianism.

The crisis of international Socialism in July 1914[1] had finally set a gulf between the Social Democrats and the more extreme Socialists. Each to some extent betrayed its original principles. The Social Democrats had now positively accepted the notion of working for gradual reform through constitutional processes in a bourgeois society; the extreme Socialists accepted the pattern of the dictatorship of the Bolshevik party which had been established in Russia, and since Moscow provided a firm base from which their efforts might be directed, the possibility of Communism loomed constantly over Europe as an alternative to which the masses might turn if the parliaments proved unable to cope with the problems of a free economy.

It was the fear of such an eventuality that in a time of economic crisis caused landowners, army officers, industrialists, and disappointed bourgeois to look towards another form of authoritarian rule. The general programme of Fascism was a right-wing dictatorship pledged to maintain the existing order of society, and in this sense some conservatives could see it as performing the function of the old monarchies. In Italy, Rumania, and Greece, for example, Fascist governments were later established through the connivance of the reigning sovereigns,

[1] See p. 329.

while in Germany and Spain some of Hitler's and Franco's supporters hoped that it would open the way to a royalist restoration. In other ways Fascism included aspects of the left. Like Communism, it demanded an absolute power of government to which the people in their own interest must resign their freedom, and in varying degrees it stood for the planning of a national economy. Yet the extravagances of Fascism went far beyond the spirit of nineteenth-century monarchy or Socialism. If anything, it was a type of Bonapartism carried out with all the technical resources of the twentieth century and inspired by an ugly fanaticism; the concentration on the personality of the leader, the mobilization of every kind of theatrical device to convey a sense of power, the creation of private armies with their own uniforms and insignia, the mammoth youth movements, and the stimulation of an aggressive nationalism—all were like a perversion of nineteenth-century romanticism, a practical realization of those wilder emotions fostered by a lunatic fringe in the years before the outbreak of the war.

In Great Britain and France the left-wing governments which had come to power at the height of the crisis in Germany in 1924 did not last long. The British general election of October 1924 gave a strong majority to the Conservatives under Stanley Baldwin and by 1926 Poincaré had re-established himself in France. This swing to the right was prompted by a new sense of prosperity, but although British and French parliamentary institutions were never seriously threatened in this period, class antagonism rose to new heights in the crushing of the General Strike in Great Britain in 1926 and in the fury of the French radicals at the control exercised by an oligarchy of shareholders in the Bank of France.

In Germany the new Federal Republic not merely had to face the turbulence of the immediate post-war period; it suffered also from a profound psychological handicap. There could be no doubt that in the late summer of 1918 the German Army had sustained a crushing defeat, and the fact that the General Staff accepted this is plainly indicated by their refusal to contemplate a resumption of hostilities in the spring of 1919, when the terms of the Treaty of Versailles were made known. Yet the army had nevertheless withdrawn to the frontier in reasonable order and since no fighting had taken place on German soil, it was easy for the civilian to accept the myth that the army itself had never been defeated, only betrayed by revolution at home—the *Dolchstoss*, the stab in the back. The General Staff were naturally only too anxious to propagate this myth and unfortunately gained considerable support from Friedrich Ebert himself, when he reviewed German troops at the Brandenburger Tor in Berlin in December 1918: 'I salute you who return unvanquished from the field of battle.' Thus, since the army claimed to be blameless, the Assembly of the new Republic which had accepted the terms of the treaty was burdened with all the odium of national surrender. This meant more than an unhappy start for democracy in Germany; for certain individuals closely associated in the public mind with events at the end of the war it meant personal danger. Extreme nationalists never forgave them. In 1921 an attempt was made on the life of Philip Scheidemann; in the same year Erz-berger, the president of the German armistice commission, was murdered, and in 1922 Walter Rathenau, the Foreign Minister, was shot down in Berlin.

Ebert remained President until his death in 1925, but although the Social Democrats were the strongest party in the Reichstag, successive Chancellors had to rely upon a coalition of groups in order to maintain a government, and in these circumstances the Socialists were unable to overcome the resistance of the conservative elements to a policy of nationalization in industry and agriculture. The most significant feature of these early years of the Republic was its dependence upon the army, and this may partly explain the fact that whereas any Communist movement was crushed with the utmost severity, the leaders of right-wing nationalist outbreaks were usually treated with considerable leniency.

The crushing of the Spartakists in Berlin in January 1919 was followed by a revolutionary upheaval in Bavaria. On the abdication of the Wittelsbach king, Kurt Eisner had set up a Social Democrat régime in Munich, but after his assassination three months later a Majority Socialist government under Johannes Hoffmann failed to prevent the establishment of a Soviet republic. On this, Noske, the Minister of Defence in Berlin, sent in regular army forces who, in May 1919, assisted by troops of the local Free Corps, put down the Communists in an action that involved the deaths of several hundreds and re-established the Hoffmann government.

In March 1920, however, the army showed itself less inclined to act against the threat of an extreme right-wing *coup* by Dr Kapp, sup-ported by General von Lüttwitz and several staff officers. The position of the government had been weakened by the Allies' recent presentation of their first list of war criminals—some 900 names including the German Crown Prince, two Field Marshals and two former Chancellors, who were to be surrendered for trial—and when a march on Berlin by the extremists seemed imminent, Noske found that the army chiefs were not prepared to involve their forces in the clash. 'Would you force a battle at the Brandenburger Tor,' demanded General von Seeckt, 'between troops who a year and a half ago were fighting shoulder to shoulder against the enemy?' Faced with the withdrawal of the army into neutrality, the President, the Chancellor and his cabinet fled to Dresden and thence to Stuttgart, where they proclaimed a general strike. Thus it was not the power of the military, but of the trade unions, coupled with the political ineptitude of Dr Kapp, that brought to an end within four days the régime which he and von Lüttwitz attempted to set up in Berlin.

The failure of the Kapp *putsch* did convince the army, now entrusted to the command of General von Seeckt, that for the time being the interests of Germany demanded an active support of the Republic, and during the next great period of unrest, in 1923, they remained true to this policy. The French occupation of the Ruhr and the German counter-measures of passive resistance had at first brought the whole nation behind the government at Berlin, but when in August Stresemann decided to bring this resistance to an end, the fury of the extremists seemed once again to threaten the life of the Republic. Prussian nationalists plotted the occupation of Berlin. In Saxony, Thuringia, Hamburg, and the Ruhr, Communists appeared about to gain the upper hand. In Bavaria the Hoffmann government, which had fallen at the time of the Kapp *putsch*, had been succeeded by a series of right-wing administrations giving protection to many extreme nationalist movements which now came to the fore. The Bavarian situation was complicated, however, in that the local authorities under the influence of Gustav von Kahr were thinking in terms of separatism with a restoration of the Wittelsbach monarchy, while the National Socialist German Workers' Party, with whom they were closely associated, was aiming at an authoritarian régime which would unite the whole of Germany.

The leader of this Nazi party, as it came to be known, was Adolf Hitler. Contrary to later propaganda which always stressed his rise from utter poverty, Hitler, the son of an Austrian customs official, had grown up in modest lower middle-class surroundings. After his father's death he left school without passing his final exams and spent an idle three years, supported by his mother at Linz, while he made unsuccessful attempts to enter the Academy of Fine Arts and the School of Architecture at Vienna. His mother died at the end of 1908 and Hitler settled in Vienna, which had completely captivated him, but he still managed to avoid any regular employment, eking out an existence with odd jobs and selling little sketches of the city. During the next four years he certainly sank to the lowest level of society, dependent on doss-houses and soup kitchens, an odd remote individual, reading voraciously, brooding over a world that had rejected him, and nursing a growing sense of German nationalism and a hatred for the Slavs and the Jews, who peopled the polyglot capital of the Habsburg empire.

In 1913 he went to Munich, where on the outbreak of war he volunteered for service in a Bavarian regiment. The violence of war suited the melancholy nihilism of his nature; during four years on the western front he rose to the rank of corporal, was twice wounded and twice decorated for bravery—on the second occasion with the Iron Cross, First Class, an award seldom given to uncommissioned ranks. In November 1918 he was discharged from hospital, where he had been recovering from temporary blindness after a gas attack, and in 1919 was posted to a regiment in Munich as an educational officer, after a violent speech against the Jews had attracted the attention of his military superiors.

It was through this new work that Hitler came to realize his own powers of demagogy and to see in political life an outlet for the hatred and megalomania that consumed him. When in the course of his activities he came across a small German Workers' Party which had been founded by Anton Drexler, a locksmith, he decided to join in order to take it over for his own ends, and within two or three years this strange figure with his lank black hair, his tooth-brush moustache, and his burning compelling eyes had imposed himself upon the political life of Bavaria. He preached against the monstrosity of Versailles, the corruption and weakness of the Weimar Republic, the threat of Communist Russia, the folly of democracy, and the wickedness of the Jews; he demanded a new strong united Germany. No politician ever made such a clean breast of all his intentions; none ever came so close ultimately to achieving them. He collected around him a number of post-war misfits who surrendered to the driving will of this new leader—Rudolph Hess, a student of economics at Munich, Hermann Goering, a war hero of the German Air Force, Alfred

Rosenberg, who had grown up in Tsarist Russia, and Joseph Goebbels, an unsuccessful novelist. He began to amass funds through the army, manufacturers, Goering's wife, and Putzi Hanfstaengel, who financed the party's newspaper the *Völkische Beobachter*; he raised a private army, the *Sturmabteilung*, the S.A., who with their brown-shirt uniform and their insignia of the swastika kept order at his own meetings and broke up the meetings of others. And in 1923 he gained the support of General Ludendorff, who had been living near Munich in disgruntled retirement since the failure of the Kapp *putsch* and whose name might add strength to a movement that aimed at nothing less than the overthrow of the Republic.

In fact, the government weathered the storm in the autumn of 1923 with greater ease than in 1920. 'Will the army stick to us, General?' President Ebert had asked before announcing the end of passive resistance in the Ruhr. 'The army, Mr President,' replied von Seeckt, 'will stick to me.' His answer, although not entirely reassuring for the head of a constitutional government, was strictly in the tradition of Prussian history and at least this time the army did not hold back. The threatened revolt in Berlin was crushed on von Seeckt's orders and in Saxony army commanders arrested the Communist and Socialist members of the government and disbanded the militia.

In Bavaria von Kahr, who had taken over as State Commissioner, and General von Lossow, the local military commander, were still prepared to ignore the orders of Berlin and in November were actually planning a restoration of the Wittelsbach monarchy. Their hands, however, were forced, when in a famous scene at a meeting in the Bürgerbräu cellar, Hitler, who was determined to wreck any separatist movement, forced them to participate in his proclamation of a new nationalist government for Germany. Hitler, however, was relying on bluff; as soon as they were out of the cellar, von Kahr and von Lossow hastened to put themselves on the side of the legitimate government, and when on the next day the Nazis attempted a march through Munich led by Hitler and Ludendorff, their column was broken up by rifle fire from the police, and Hitler and Ludendorff were placed under arrest.

The Munich *putsch* had been a hasty and ill-prepared affair and Hitler had acted contrary to his own principle of working alongside rather than against the major forces in power—mainly because of his desire to forestall the separatists. He was, however, able to take advantage of his trial to make one speech after another, all reported in the national press, denouncing the government from the dock and offering an eventual alliance with the army. 'The *Reichswehr* remains as untarnished as before. One day the hour will come when the *Reichswehr* will stand at our side, officers and men.' Even when confronted with this open declaration of war on the Republic, the judges remained true to the Weimar policy of leniency towards those who had erred in the direction of right-wing nationalism. There were too many Germans who believed in their hearts at least some of the accusations that Hitler voiced; even von Seeckt himself had said after a meeting with Hitler six months before the events in Munich: 'We were one in our aim; only our paths were different.' Hitler thus received the mildest sentence that the court could give—five years of fortress detention, from which he was to be released on parole after six months.

The return of economic stability after 1924 and the general prosperity in the second half of the decade naturally enabled the German Republic to consolidate its position; as in Great Britain and France a reviving sense of optimism was reflected in a slight swing to the right, and in 1925, on the death of Ebert, Hindenburg, who in his old age had become a German father-figure, was elected President. Of the two extremes that had once threatened the continued existence of parliamentary government, Communism and Fascism were both dormant during these years, although on the right, two forces remained at work which were to be of considerable significance for the future.

First, Hitler during his short spell of confinement was able to write a large part of his autobiography, *Mein Kampf*, which was as much a manifesto as the story of his life, and on his release quickly regained the leadership of the party which in his absence had fallen a prey to squabbling factions. As a more reliable element than the S.A., he formed his own bodyguard, the *Schutzstaffel*, the S.S., bound to him by a personal oath of loyalty, and in 1929 placed it under the command of a Bavarian chicken-farmer, Heinrich Himmler. On the whole, however, these were years of only gradual growth for the Nazis—from 49,000 in 1926 to 108,000 in 1928.

The second force was the German Army which, under the skilful direction of von Seeckt, was being reorganized on a far wider basis than that envisaged by the Treaty of Versailles. Although the treaty had stipulated that its size should not be greater than 100,000 men, of whom only 4,000 were to be officers, it had made no mention of the number of N.C.O.s. Von Seeckt took advantage of this to concentrate on the training of leaders, creating some 40,000 N.C.O.s out of 96,000 other ranks, who were to be rehearsed for far higher command than their rank would suggest, and the smallness of the force based on voluntary enlistment enabled him to insist upon the highest standards of physique and education. The General Staff simply continued to exist under another name and set to work almost at once on a new revolutionary technique of war based on mobility, the use of armour, and air support which was to bring about the remarkable German victories in the early years of the second World War. Plans were made for the ultimate equipping of 63 divisions—later reduced to 21, although even this was three times greater than the number allowed by the Treaty of Versailles; much of this was covered by secret business agreements in Austria, Switzerland, Sweden, Spain, the Netherlands, and Italy, but in Germany also the Krupp works made a pact, in January 1922, with the German Ministry of Defence 'jointly to circumvent . . . the provisions of the Treaty of Versailles'. Commercial aviation, gliding clubs, and para-military organizations such as labour battalions and the Prussian police force were all used to the same end, and in 1922 the Treaty of Rapallo[1] with the Soviet Union enabled von Seeckt to set up tank and flying schools in Russia. It was an essay in evasion which far surpassed the achievement of Scharnhorst and Gneisenau after the disaster of Jena in 1806, although it did not entirely escape the notice of the Allied Commissions which remained stationed in Germany until 1927. It would indeed be hard to imagine two more different personalities—Hitler, the fanatical rabble-rouser who was to turn the organization of gangsterdom into a theory of State, and von Seeckt, the immaculate be-monocled Prussian aristocrat, the epitome of the German General Staff—yet the work of these two men was to have a decisive influence upon the later fortunes of Germany. 'When Hitler came to power in 1933,' said a German staff officer in a broadcast in 1941, 'he found all the technical preparations for rearmament ready, thanks to the *Reichswehr*.'

It was understandable that the German Republic, born in the shadow of defeat, should have such a stormy history during its early years. Yet the country which first succumbed to Fascism shortly after the war had been on the winning side and had had a parliamentary form of government since its unification in 1860. The close of the war had confronted Italy with problems which a succession of Prime Ministers were quite unable to solve. Rising prices, coupled with unemployment

[1] See p. 407.

o

due to the closing down of many war industries, created a scene of working-class unrest that seemed to herald the advent of Communism. The inclusion of Fiume within the frontiers of Yugoslavia roused the anger of the nationalists, and in September the Italian poet D'Annunzio, who saw himself as a latter-day Garibaldi, launched a private expedition to take Fiume, where he established his own régime, and it was over a year before the Italian government under a new premier, Giolitti, had the courage to bring about his withdrawal.

The real force of extreme right-wing nationalism, however, found expression not in D'Annunzio's romantic crusade, but in the rapidly developing Fascist party. The leader of this movement, Benito Mussolini, unlike Lenin, Trotsky, and Hitler, really was of humble origin. The son of a blacksmith, he had been educated in a Catholic seminary, from which he was expelled after stabbing another pupil; after a short spell as a schoolmaster, he had drifted into politics, and in the years before the war was editor of a Marxist newspaper. During the war he swung round in favour of intense nationalism, and when in the elections of 1919 he failed to gain any success against the great party machines of the Christian Democrats and the Socialists, he began to build up his own organization which, like Hitler's, included a private army of black-shirted hooligans. In North Italy the constant strikes and unrest brought him many clients among the industrialists and wealthy farmers, and it was here that he resolved to concentrate his power rather than in Parliament, where even in the elections of 1921 his party only gained 35 seats out of 535.

By 1922 the north Italian cities and countryside had become a scene of ferocious gang warfare; in August Fascist squads virtually took control of Milan and ejected the local Socialist administration, and soon they had established themselves in Ferrara, Cremona, Ravenna, Parma, and Leghorn. In Rome one government after another had failed to come to grips with this open lawlessness, but in October 1922 decisive action could be postponed no longer, when it became known that the Fascists were planning a march on Rome. There seemed good reason to suppose that the army would support the constitutional government in this time of crisis and the premier, Facta, resolved upon a proclamation of martial law, but at this point King Victor Emmanuel made a fateful intervention. He refused to sign the decree. He, too, had lost all faith in the existing system of government; reckoning that the Fascists could at least establish strong rule in the defence of property, he sent an invitation by telegram to Mussolini to form an administration, and only on this was Mussolini prepared to give the word for action; the march on Rome duly took place after the real battle had already been won—nothing more than a rather unnecessary piece of theatre—and Mussolini himself travelled comfortably from Milan by train.

The incongruity of the short corpulent heavily jowled figure who throughout the 1920s and 1930s proclaimed a new Caesarism from the balcony of the Palazzo Venezia, and the contrast between his imperialist pretensions and the utter fiasco of the Italian campaigns in the second World War inevitably create a faintly ludicrous impression that obscures some of the positive achievements of Italian Fascism. Since the blackshirts had been the principal law-breakers, their advent to power certainly ensured a restoration of order, and the authority of the State did impose a new discipline on industrial relations and facilitate a considerable programme of public works including the draining of the Pontine marshes. Indeed, the usual comment of foreign visitors was that if Mussolini's régime was not democratic, at least he had succeeded in making the trains run to time. Despite the almost insuperable conditions of poverty in the south, the system of the corporative State did place Italian economy on a firmer footing although, like Nazi rule in Germany in the 1930s, it was aided by a general European recovery shortly after the beginning of the régime.

The collapse of democratic government in the 1920s was not restricted to Italy. In 1923, in Spain, Primo de Rivera[1] replaced the *Cortes* by a military dictatorship, and three years later the Portuguese republic, undermined by financial instability, succumbed to the authoritarian rule of General Carmona. There was, too, a radical transformation of the scene in Poland. The Polish parliament, like the old Diet in the days of the monarchy, had been granted very extensive powers by the constitution of 1919, and in 1926, after a succession of governments had proved themselves incapable of dealing with a growing economic crisis, Pilsudski marched on Warsaw, ejected the legitimate government and organized the election of a National Assembly which gave its consent to a new constitution seriously restricting the powers of parliament and greatly increasing those of the executive. This change at once alarmed the Lithuanians, who feared that it would lead to a more aggressive Polish foreign policy, and they accordingly granted far greater executive powers to their own President. In Bulgaria an enlightened policy of land reform and friendship

[1] See p. 243.

with Yugoslavia came to an end with the murder of the Prime Minister, Stamboliiski in 1923, and was followed by a growing influence from the right-wing nationalist groups, while in 1929 the constant antagonism between Croats and Serbs in Yugoslavia led King Alexander to set up what was virtually a royal dictatorship.

In all these other instances the desertion of the democratic principle resulted quite simply from the incompetence and weakness of parliamentary institutions, when the problems of government, the social divisions, and the general sense of insecurity proved too much for the working of democracy which had been so suddenly established. It was not due to any positive Fascist doctrine, still less to any real threat of Communism. Indeed, not merely was the foreign policy of Russia quiescent at this time; her own domestic scene did not present a picture of Communism at all. The devastation which she had suffered during the war and the civil war that followed had confronted the Communist government with an appalling problem. The collapse of industry and communications and the refusal of the peasants to co-operate, led to a famine in the cities which spread to the Ukraine and the Crimea, when the government seized the grain stores. The consequence was that Lenin took the remarkable decision, with the introduction of the New Economic Policy, to revert to a system of private enterprise. The Communist government retained control over political life, the press, the major industries and education, and continued its persecution of the churches, but trade, factories, and farming were all to be allowed to operate for personal profit. Russian missions were sent abroad to try to attract foreign capital, and amid an atmosphere of economic independence the towns began to thrive again and a class of wealthy peasantry emerged.

There was also a significant change in the Communist attitude towards the rest of the world. Trotsky continued to demand the encouragement of universal revolution, but this policy was rejected by the triumvirate that took over on Lenin's death in 1924—Stalin, Kamenev, and Zinoviev. Stalin, a Georgian, who had spent long years of secret conspiracy in Tsarist Russia and had now attained a considerable position of influence as General Secretary of the party, had been largely responsible for drawing up the new constitution of the State—a Union of Soviet Socialist Republics—which allowed a certain measure of local government for the non-Russian peoples, while retaining a strong central control through the party. He was determined to concentrate on 'Socialism in one country'—Russia—and

Trotsky fought a long duel with him over this question, but eventually in 1929 had to leave the country, although he continued to intrigue from abroad until his murder in Mexico in 1940. This was not the only victory for Stalin. By the end of the decade he had strengthened his position within the Politburo, set up his own supporter Molotov as premier and, abandoning the New Economic Policy which had by now served its purpose, embarked upon the second stage of the Communist revolution. The resistance of the wealthier peasantry—the Kulaks—was ruthlessly broken in order to impose the system of collective farms; the first Five Year Plan for industry was laid down and it was soon clear that the liberal phase had lasted no longer in Russia than it had in some of the shakier democracies.

2. Diplomacy in the 1920s

Although national frontiers had assumed a new complexity since 1919, the relationship of the great Powers had undergone a remarkable simplification. Austria-Hungary had disintegrated, Germany could hardly play an independent role, and Russia, ostracized by non-Communist countries, wished simply to barricade herself against interference, while she set her domestic affairs in order. With the withdrawal of the United States into isolationism, Great Britain and France remained the two Powers whose will could be decisive throughout the Continent. Each was committed to the maintenance of the existing situation—the policy of Metterich after 1815—but whereas the British, their fears of German naval rivalry now allayed, could relax with a sense of security that lent strength to the heart-felt desire for the avoidance of further war and discouraged involvement in any system of alliances, the French preferred to follow a far more active policy designed to safeguard them against any revival of German power.

This nervousness of the French was not entirely without foundation. At Versailles they had desisted from their scheme for depriving Germany of all territory west of the Rhine only on the understanding that the Franco-German frontier would be guaranteed by a defensive pact with the United States and Great Britain. Reliance on the United States, however, was ruled out after the American Senate had refused to ratify the Treaty of Versailles, and this was followed in 1922 by the failure of negotiations with the British, who would offer assistance 'only in the event of a German army actually crossing the French frontier'. Their sole remaining safeguard now was the Covenant of the League of Nations—a somewhat dubious guarantee, since several of the member states were already having second thoughts over the application of sanctions against an aggressor acting outside their own spheres of interest.

Faced with the danger of isolation, the most obvious step for the French would have been a return to the 1894 alliance with Russia, had it not been for the changed situation in eastern Europe. One of the aims of the western statesmen in 1919 had been to devise a *cordon sanitaire* of small states that would bar the way to any expansion westwards by Soviet Russia, and the disadvantage of such a scheme for France was that it also precluded any direct intervention by Russia against Germany. As early as 1916 Arthur Balfour had predicted that if Poland were to be re-created, 'France would be at the mercy of Germany in the next war, for this reason that Russia could not come to her aid without violating the neutrality of Poland.'[1] Thus France was now forced to look elsewhere. In 1920 a military alliance was concluded with Belgium, but her main efforts were directed towards signing a series of treaties with countries immediately to the east of Germany—with Poland in 1921, with Czechoslovakia in 1924, with Rumania in 1926, and with Yugoslavia in 1927. This was far from creating a unified system of defence against Germany, whereby each would act on behalf of the others. It is true that after the war Czechoslovakia, Rumania, and Yugoslavia had formed a 'little *entente*', but this was mainly to guard against any attempt by Hungary to regain her lost territories, while Yugoslavia was concerned with her quarrel with Italy over Fiume. Poland did share French fears of a German national revival, but she was equally suspicious of Russian and Lithuanian designs upon her frontier. This diversity of aims naturally militated against the likelihood of any concerted action against Germany, whose great bulk in the centre of Europe separating France from her allies was at the same time the *raison d'être* and the fundamental weakness of the French system.

The geographical position of Germany had always been a prime factor in her foreign policy, enabling her to look either east or west. Even now after her defeat the choice was still open to her. The dominant position of Great Britain and France at the end of the war naturally inclined many of the statesmen of the Weimar Republic to think that friendship with the west was an indispensable preliminary

[1] For the relevance of this judgement in the 1930s, see pp. 423, 439.

to her recovery; on the other hand, the coolness with which the west regarded both Russia and Germany was a circumstance that tended to throw these two countries together. In April 1922 a general economic conference between Russia and the western Powers at Genoa ran into difficulties over Russia's demand for a cancellation of war debts and her refusal to grant compensation for the nationalization of private property after the Revolution, and in the same month Germany and Russia concluded the Treaty of Rapallo which re-established diplomatic and commercial relations between the two countries. This at once awoke the suspicions of the western Powers—and with reason, for the easterners' school of thought in Germany was already advocating a positive Soviet alliance. In September 1922 General von Seeckt presented a masterly statement of this view, suggesting nothing less than a new partition of Poland with Russia. 'The restoration of the frontier between Russia and Germany is a necessary condition before both sides can become strong. The 1914 frontier between Russia and Germany should be the basis of any understanding between the two countries.' This was simply to revive the policy which had governed Prussian and, later, German relations with Russia from the time of Frederick the Great until William II's abandonment of the Bismarckian system before 1914—a basic theme in German foreign policy which was to find expression again in the German–Soviet pact of August 1939 on the eve of the second World War. At this time von Seeckt was primarily concerned with making local arrangements for facilitating the reconstruction of his army,[1] and his hopes of establishing a definite political alliance were disappointed when Stresemann, who became Foreign Minister[2] in 1924, decided to concentrate on the improvement of Germany's relations with the west.

In 1925 Stresemann's policy culminated in the signing of the Treaties of Locarno. This new stage in international relations had been preceded by two attempts on the part of the French to strengthen their defence by revising the machinery of the League of Nations. In 1923 they had strongly supported a draft Treaty of Mutual Assistance which was based on the assumption that a state of general security must precede any scheme for world-wide disarmament. The plan was to make military sanctions *obligatory* for member states against any country stigmatized as an aggressor by the Council of the League; on

[1] See p. 401.
[2] He was Chancellor for only a few months, but he remained Foreign Minister in successive governments until his death in 1929.

the other hand, this duty to intervene was to be restricted to those states situated in the continent where the aggression had taken place. The terms of the treaty naturally suited the French with their new system of alignments to the east of Germany, but for the British the complication of the Commonwealth made such a sub-division of regional responsibilities unacceptable and the proposal lapsed. In 1924, however, a meeting between the two Prime Ministers, Ramsay MacDonald and Herriot, at Geneva led to a reformulation of the scheme. The main purpose of the Geneva Protocol was to strengthen the League's power of intervention in two ways. The existing arrangement precluded any action by the League, if the Council were not unanimous or if a dispute came within the domestic jurisdiction of one of the parties. The Protocol now laid down a system whereby disputes in either of these cases would be bound to be subject to some form of arbitration, although it made no mention of obligatory military sanctions. Once again, the French pressed for acceptance of the scheme, since any dispute over treaty revision was specifically excluded from its terms and hence any enforcement of the settlement of 1919 would not be at the mercy of arbitration. And once again consideration for the Commonwealth caused the British to hold back, since they saw that it would give the Japanese an opportunity to demand the right of immigration into Australia, New Zealand, and Canada, whose governments had prohibited their entry. In March 1925 Austen Chamberlain, Foreign Secretary in the new Baldwin administration in Great Britain, accordingly announced his country's rejection of the Geneva Protocol.

Faced with the failure of these two schemes to harness the League of Nations to the requirements of her own security, France now returned to more traditional forms of diplomacy and in the course of 1925 negotiations with Great Britain and Germany led, in October, to an important conference at the Swiss lakeside resort of Locarno, where agreement was reached over a set of treaties that were signed in London at the end of the year. These included mutual guarantees of the Franco-German and Belgo-German frontiers between Great Britain, France, Belgium, Germany, and Italy, while Germany signed arbitration treaties with Poland and Czechoslovakia, both of whom were to be reinsured by treaties of mutual defence with France in the case of German aggression.

The election of Hindenburg as President of the German Republic after the death of Ebert in February 1925, and the fall of the Herriot government in France in April, had at first seemed likely to make agreement more difficult, but despite the resistance of the easterner school of thought in Germany Stresemann managed to gain the necessary support from Hindenburg and the Reichstag for this alignment with the west, and Briand, the new French Foreign Minister, worked in such harmony with Austen Chamberlain that for the next four years this triumvirate of Foreign Ministers was able to give some substance to the spirit of concord with which public opinion associated the Locarno pact. There were, nevertheless, two serious weaknesses in the treaties of 1925. First, they implied that the Versailles settlement was inadequate on its own to maintain the existing situation. Second, the absolute guarantee of Germany's western frontiers in contrast to the arbitration treaties with Poland and Czechoslovakia suggested that Great Britain, at least, accepted the fact that Germany's eastern frontiers were less firm than those in the west.

This distinction between Germany's possible attitudes towards the east and the west was emphasized during negotiations in 1926 over her entry into the League of Nations. It was originally proposed that she should join Great Britain, France, Italy, and Japan as a permanent member of the Council, but when Poland, Spain, and Brazil were also to be given permanent seats, German protests resulted in Poland becoming only a semi-permanent member, and Spain and Brazil withdrew from the League. This resistance to equality of status for Poland coincided with a renewal, in April, of the Treaty of Rapallo between Germany and Russia, whereby each agreed to remain neutral in the event of the other being attacked, and it was abundantly clear that the Locarno pact had not entirely laid the ghost of the German easterners' policy.

Still, Locarno, coupled with returning prosperity, did usher in a short period of stability which greatly heartened the pacifism of the idealists. It marked also the heyday of the League of Nations as an effective instrument for the settlement of international disputes. Admittedly it had been ignored by Mussolini when, in 1923, the death of Italian commissioners at the hands of bandits on the Greco-Albanian frontier had been followed by the bombardment of Corfu by the Italian fleet, but in subsequent years it was able to intervene with a modicum of success in frontier disputes between Turkey and Iraq over Mosul in 1924, between Bulgaria and Greece in 1925, and between Poland and Lithuania in 1927, when the two Presidents, Pilsudski and Voldemaras, confronted each other at Geneva. It could not escape

o 2

notice that none of these disputes touched on serious interests of the great Powers; yet the League's success did help to foster the idealistic optimism which found its most resplendent expression in the Briand–Kellogg pact of 1928, an agreement which originated in a private negotiation between France and the United States and to which sixty-five states ultimately adhered. This was a solemn renunciation of war 'as an instrument of national policy', a statement as typical of the hopes of the 1920s as were the various provisos that enabled most national policies to remain unchanged. It could not obscure the fact that although most countries had reduced their armed forces in the interests of economy, little headway had been made in the interminable discussions over an organized general disarmament.

The sense of goodwill engendered by Locarno did, however, enable Germany to take a significant step towards national recovery. In June 1929 the Young Committee, named after its American chairman, proposed a slight modification of the annual payment of reparations, which was to be transferred to German control, and when this had been accepted at an international conference at The Hague in August, the western Powers decided to demonstrate their faith in Germany with a complete evacuation of the Rhineland almost five years before the date stipulated by the Treaty of Versailles. This decision marked the crowning success of Stresemann's policy. The Inter-Allied Disarmament Commission had already been withdrawn in 1927, and now, with the evacuation of the Allied forces, the German government had assumed the principal responsibility for the observance of the de-militarized zone and for the continued payment of reparations. Stresemann did not live to see the outcome of his work. He died in October 1929; the French government fell in November, and the Baldwin administration in Great Britain had already fallen in the previous May. The removal of the triumvirate of Foreign Ministers—Chamberlain, Briand, and Stresemann—coincided with the end of an epoch, for by the following summer, when the Allied occupation forces were finally moving out of the Rhineland, the Continent was already feeling the effects of the great slump and a new period of international relations was about to open, quite remote from the happy optimism of the Locarno period.

30

THE GREAT DEPRESSION 1929-33

1. Economic disaster

IN 1929 the economy of the entire world outside Russia was stricken by a period of depression more dramatic and widespread in its political consequences than any similar crisis in the nineteenth century. The fundamental causes of this catastrophe remain the subject of some debate, but it seems probable that they lie in the cumulative effects of the over-production of raw commodities such as foodstuffs throughout the 1920s. The irony of the story is that there were still many regions in the world where poverty and hunger were endemic. The farmer with his living to make, however, had to depend upon those markets where he could sell, and since these were ultimately limited in their demand, an excess of agricultural produce soon led to falling prices. It was in order to check this decline that produce was actually kept off the market, with the result that world stocks of food left over at the end of the year rose from 8·8 million tons in 1925 to 15·9 million tons in 1929. This drop in agricultural prices naturally meant a considerable reduction in the purchasing power of the farming population, but although this was in turn bound to affect the market for industrial goods, the inevitable time-lag in the economic process enabled the industrial world to continue to enjoy the boom of the later half of the 1920s and the shock was thus all the greater when it eventually came.

This disparity of tendencies within the economy was most marked in the United States. American agricultural prices had been falling since 1926, yet in the world of industrial investment optimism continued to soar. The average price of stock rose by 25% in 1928 and by a further 35% in 1929, an orgy of speculation in which a great deal of much-needed capital was attracted away from Europe. An example of the corresponding output is provided by the automobile industry, which in the single year 1929 produced nearly five-and-a-half million cars. Then with appalling suddenness the industrialists awoke to the fear that the market might become saturated; production had to be checked and the consequent sense of doubt turned almost at once into a great panic to withdraw investments. On one day, 24 October 1929, thirteen million shares were sold on Wall Street, the financial centre of the U.S.A.; one firm after another crashed as their credit failed, and by the end of the month American investors who had sold too late had lost some 40,000 million dollars. Unemployment mounted, purchasing power collapsed, and so the avalanche rolled on into utter disaster.

It has been seen how throughout the nineteenth century Europe had grown increasingly sensitive to the vicissitudes of American economy,[1] and in the 1920s, as never before, her fate was utterly dependent upon the prosperity of the United States. The immediate consequence of the Wall Street crash was that the American business man in his frantic need of capital could lend no more to Europe and even began to call in his existing short-term loans. With this enormous source of credit suddenly cut off, European banks had to meet their obligations in gold, which accelerated the drop in prices already falling through the catastrophic shrinking of American purchasing power, and so Europe, too, became caught up in the vicious circle of depression—pessimism leading to the withdrawal of capital, with the consequent bankruptcies and unemployment which spread pessimism still further.

In Austria the *Kreditanstalt*, a bank whose name was a byword for financial stability, was near collapse by May 1931 and was only saved for the moment by an advance of 150 million schillings from the Bank of England. German economy had hinged almost entirely on foreign loans; in 1927 and 1928, for instance, she had borrowed almost five times as much as was due in reparations payments. By July 1931 the *Reichsbank* had exhausted its reserves of foreign paper money and in three weeks £50 million in gold had been drained from the country. In the same month the *Darmstädterbank* had to close, and in November came the collapse of a great Berlin bank. There were few savings or reserves in Germany with which to meet the crisis, and the figures for trade between 1929 and 1932 tell their own story, exports dropping from £630 million to £280 million, imports from £670 million to £230 million. By the summer of 1931 the Bank of England was losing gold at the rate of £2½ million a day, and in one week at the end of July £21 million were withdrawn. In September Great Britain left the gold standard, which by this time had become purely theoretical throughout most of Europe, and the consequent fall in the value of

[1] See pp. 100, 252.

sterling brought the pound to 30 per cent below par. France did not feel the full shock until 1932 owing to the greater self-sufficiency of her economy, but in the agricultural regions of eastern Europe, which depended upon their export of foodstuffs, the fall in prices meant growing debts for the small peasant farmers.

The social scene was of a modern industrial world that had run calamitously to a halt through a breakdown in the machinery of credit and financial exchange. Small businesses were caught up in the ruin of great ones; thousands of investors lost everything, and in the industrial towns millions of unemployed workers wandered about the streets outside the gates of the silent empty factories. In 1932 there were nearly 6 million workless in Germany, nearly 3 million in Great Britain, and nearly 14 million in the United States. By 1933 France had 1,300,000, while the American figure had risen to 15 million.

Although the disaster was world-wide, international cooperation played only a small part in the attempts to find a solution. There were certain regional agreements, such as the Oslo group formed by the Scandinavian countries or the British Commonwealth discussions at Ottawa in 1932. And an end was brought, not before its time, to the senseless cycle of payments that had been in operation since the end of the war. In July 1932 the Lausanne Convention cancelled all further reparations in return for a single payment by Germany of £150 million in 5% redeemable bonds. The United States had announced in June 1931 a moratorium for one year on all war debts, but when payment was due to be resumed in December 1932, France, indignant at the cancellation of reparations, defaulted, although Great Britain, while making no demand on her own debtors, paid her full instalment in gold to the United States. In 1933 Great Britain could make only a token payment and most other countries defaulted, except Finland, who paid her instalment in full; in 1934 the whole process finally petered out.

Beyond this all attempts at general cooperation were defeated by the continued pursuit of individual national interests. In August 1930, at the conference of Warsaw, the Danubian states had failed in their efforts to persuade the governments of Europe to establish a system of tariffs which would protect their agricultural produce from American competition, and at Stresa in 1932 another scheme for protection among themselves was eventually undermined by German and Italian suspicions over the possible growth of French economic influence in the Balkans. In 1931 French objections prevented the creation of a

Customs Union between Germany and Austria, and in June 1933 a World Economic Conference at London came to nothing when the American government, who had left the gold standard in April, refused to agree over a policy of currency stabilization.

In the main, each country tried to work out its own solution for itself. This took the form generally of protecting home production by higher tariffs, at the same time attempting to improve the chances of selling abroad by a devaluation of the currency. This highly competitive approach to the problem was to have a continuing effect upon economic relations; even as late as 1938 tariff walls were still hampering the full development of trade and foreign investment among the great Powers, and there was a general abandonment of the gold standard by most European countries in the early 1930s.

In the United States the new President, Franklin D. Roosevelt, inaugurated his policy of the New Deal. Government controls encouraged certain sections of the economy, while monetary inflation was used to promote higher prices; a vast programme of public works was started to reduce the millions of unemployed, and schemes for a minimum wage and social insurance were introduced to alleviate the worst distress. In Great Britain in 1931 part of the Labour administration formed a coalition with the Conservatives in a National government which cut State expenditure by 10% and embarked upon a policy of Protection with Imperial preference for the Commonwealth countries—the final repudiation of the nineteenth-century gospel of Free Trade. France preferred to rely upon a quota system of imports, and Germany and Italy both turned to the development of national self-sufficiency, whereby they would be less dependent upon foreign production, although this policy was as much due to political and military requirements as to the needs of the economic situation. Fortunately for them all, there comes a point in any slump when the curve of depression ceases to sink so sharply and after 1933 signs of returning confidence were to be seen in the gradual revival of industry and agriculture aided by these government measures.

2. The political consequences

Economic recovery might eventually reduce the vast numbers of unemployed; it could not, however, undo the psychological and political consequences of the great slump. With all the technical resources of the twentieth century at its disposal an unrestricted system of free enterprise had completely broken down, depriving millions throughout the world of their livelihood, and such a catastrophe inevitably gave rise to a fierce questioning of the very principles that had emerged from the turmoil of the nineteenth century. The idea that governments should simply concern themselves with the liberty of the individual through parliamentary institutions, entrusting the general prosperity to *laissez-faire* capitalism now appeared utterly inadequate. Men and women caught up in an economic disaster that they could not explain knew only that they wanted firm efficient leadership, and it was natural that their angry despair should bring about a sudden strengthening of the forces of Communism and Fascism which had been quiescent in the democracies during the last half of the 1920s.

In Great Britain, France, Switzerland, Belgium, the Netherlands, Scandinavia, and Czechoslovakia parliamentary systems survived the ordeal, although there was now a new awareness of the extent to which governments must watch over economic developments, and the antagonism between right and left became considerably sharpened. This last effect was particularly marked in France, where governments changed with even greater rapidity than usual, while in Czechoslovakia the Sudeten Germans, who maintained that they had been victimized by the Czech administration during the slump, began to organize themselves under the leadership of Konrad Henlein, a gymnastics instructor, whose party, the Sudeten German Home Front, gained the support of 62% of the German voters in Czechoslovakia in the elections of 1935.

The existing dictatorships, through their power to suppress opposition and their greater control over State economy were on the whole strengthened in their position. In Italy Mussolini survived the depression without difficulty; in Poland a junta of army colonels continued authoritarian rule after Pilsudski's death in 1935, and in Yugoslavia King Alexander was able to put down any popular stirrings caused by economic distress. In Portugal Salazar, who had been Finance Minister since 1928, took over as Prime Minister in 1932, formed an administration of experts and turned the parliament into nothing more than an advisory Chamber. 'The people', remarked Salazar, 'have less need of being sovereign than of being governed'—a comment which would have been heartily endorsed by the monarchs of the nineteenth century.

Spain provided the only instance of a dictatorship actually undermined by the depression. Primo de Rivera[1] had already lost the support

[1] See p. 403.

of the Universities and the intellectuals, and when he found that with the onset of the slump he no longer had the confidence of the army, he left Spain for Paris. In 1931 municipal elections revealed such an overwhelmingly republican vote that King Alfonso XIII also quitted the country and a new liberal constitution was devised with a single-chamber Assembly elected by universal suffrage for men and women over the age of twenty-two. The Church was disestablished, the Jesuits expelled, and a system of primary education organized, and in 1932 laws were passed restricting the power of the army and inaugurating land reforms whereby small holdings could be leased to the peasantry.

In contrast to this anti-clerical leftward tendency in Spain, the majority of changes consequent on the depression in Europe were in the direction of a right-wing authoritarianism, either through an outright surrender to Fascism as a defence against resurgent Communism, or through attempts to bolster up a wavering parliamentary régime. In Rumania, where King Carol II returned to the throne in 1930, strong-arm government was established through the Iron Guard. In Bulgaria a military dictatorship was finally set up in 1934; in the same year the executive power was greatly strengthened in Latvia and Estonia, and in Greece General Metaxas became dictator in 1936 with the consent of King George II, who had recently been restored to his throne.[1]

In Austria the emotions of economic distress seemed to place the survival of parliamentary government at the mercy of three antagonistic armed forces—the *Schutzbund* of the Social Democrats, the Austrian Nazis, and the right-wing *Heimwehr*, the private army of Prince von Starhemberg. The gains made by the Austrian Nazis in the municipal elections of May 1932 were emphasized by the spreading of rioting and gang warfare, and in March 1933, after Hitler's advent to power in Germany, the Chancellor, Dr Dollfuss, whose diminutive size earned him the name of *Millimetternich* among his opponents, decided to rule by decree, relying upon the support of Starhemberg's *Heimwehr*. In June the Nazi party was prohibited and, after conversations with Mussolini, Dollfuss announced his intention to set up a corporative State on an authoritarian basis. This was virtually a declaration of war on the Social Democrats, and in February 1934 the left-wing forces were crushed after three days of fighting between the *Heimwehr* and the *Schutzbund*, during which the besieged working-class district of Vienna was bombarded with artillery.

[1] See Genealogical table, p. 482.

The most disastrous aspect of the great depression was to be seen in Germany, where Adolf Hitler emerged as Chancellor in January 1933 —not as the result of a revolutionary *coup*, but by presidential appointment in accordance with the provisions of the Weimar constitution. This superficially 'respectable' rise to power was due to a combination of unfortunate circumstances. When in July 1930 Heinrich Brüning, leader of the Catholic Centre party and Chancellor since the previous March, put his programme for cutting government expenditure before the Reichstag, he was unable to gain a majority. With the numbers of German unemployed mounting to three million, Brüning felt justified in asking President Hindenburg to invoke Article 48 of the constitution, whereby his measures could be enforced by presidential decree. Hindenburg complied, but since the Reichstag strongly objected to this action, Brüning and his successors throughout the depression were henceforth to remain dependent upon the whim of the President.

This first factor has a considerable bearing on the second. The Weimar Republic had now come close to the position of the short-lived Second Republic in France; too few of the men in authority had any deep faith in its survival. The most significant figure behind the scenes at this time, General Kurt von Schleicher, was hoping for a perpetuation of presidential rule, backed by the strength of the army, and by the autumn of 1931 Brüning himself was thinking in terms of a restoration of the Hohenzollern monarchy within a constitutional framework— mainly as a means of robbing the Nazis of some of their support. Thus, it was not Hitler alone who was envisaging a radical alteration of the system of government; yet the atmosphere of intrigue in a situation in which the Chancellor depended purely upon the President's support robbed these conservatives of the chance of finding a firm alternative which would enable them to stand against the Nazis.

The third overwhelmingly significant factor was the enormous gains that the Nazis had made as a result of the depression. 'Never in my life', said Hitler, 'have I been so well disposed and inwardly contented as in these days.' Indeed he might be, for when in September 1930 Brüning, hoping to gain a more amenable Reichstag, rashly asked for a dissolution, the Nazis won six-and-a-half million votes in the subsequent election, increasing the number of their seats from 12 to 107. What suited Hitler almost as well was the four-and-a-half million votes gained by the Communists, a fact of which he made good use in wooing some of the army officers, and more particularly industrialists such as the steel magnates, Fritz Thyssen and Albert Vögler, Georg von

418   THE CRISIS OF LIBERAL DEMOCRACY 1921-45

Schnitzler, a director of I.G. Farben, Cuno of the Hamburg-Amerika line, and von Schroeder, a Cologne banker, all of whom made considerable contributions to the party funds. These negotiations were typical of Hitler's technique of aligning himself with the real centres of power, but they had to be kept secret from radicals in the Nazi party such as Gregor Strasser who still believed that Hitler was aiming at a genuine social revolution.

These new funds which enabled Goebbels to organize a prodigious nation-wide publicity campaign, the violent tactics of the S.A., the fear of Communist revolution, and the presence of nearly six million unemployed, all combined to bring the Nazi party to the peak of its popularity in 1932. In March Hindenburg, standing for re-election as President against Hitler, just failed to gain the necessary absolute majority and was successful only in a second election in April in which Hitler nevertheless won nearly thirteen-and-a-half million votes. In the same month local elections in Prussia, whose territory comprised two-thirds of the whole of Germany, made the Nazis the strongest party in the Diet.

By this time von Schleicher had decided to get rid of Brüning, who had already alarmed Hindenburg with a proposal that the bankrupt estates of East Prussia should be taken over by the State with compensation for the owners and distributed to the landless peasantry. Still relying on his presidential prerogative, Hindenburg now chose Franz von Papen as Brüning's successor in the hope that he could come to terms with the Nazis—a task which was inescapable after the Reichstag elections in July 1932 when they became the most powerful party in the Assembly with 230 seats. A working agreement proved impossible, however, since Hitler was demanding the Chancellorship for himself, and although a second Reichstag election in November reduced the Nazi seats to 196, von Papen reckoned that he could not carry on without a declaration of a state of emergency. Von Schleicher refused to support him in this and on von Papen's resignation became Chancellor himself. With the offer of the Vice-Chancellorship to Gregor Strasser he hoped to win the Nazis to his side, but after Hitler had forced Strasser to resign from the party, von Schleicher did not last long. On 4 January 1933 von Papen, determined to get his own back, met Hitler at the house of von Schroeder in Cologne, and when von Schleicher failed to gain the trade unions and the peasantry in an attempt to form a coalition in the face of continued Nazi opposition, he resigned on 28 January.

The Nazis were still open to the highest bidder and von Papen who, as the President's personal favourite, was entrusted with the negotiations, had to make haste to forestall any further manoeuvres by von Schleicher. Hitler, it was agreed, should have the Chancellorship, but only two other members of the party should have seats in the cabinet— Frick as Minister of the Interior and Goering as Minister without Portfolio. With von Papen as Vice-Chancellor and General Blomberg as Minister of Defence, as well as six other cabinet posts at their disposal, it was the hope of the conservatives behind the scenes that they could effectively smother the independent action of the Nazis, at the same time as gaining their cooperation. In this they sadly misjudged the man with whom they had to deal, and the appointment of Adolf Hitler as Chancellor on 30 January 1933 was to have the most fateful consequences for Germany and for the world.

31

THE END OF COLLECTIVE SECURITY
1933–8

1. Hitler's destruction of the Treaty of Versailles

THE Weimar Republic did not long survive Hitler's appointment as Chancellor. It had always been his intention to establish the dictatorship of the Nazi party from a position of power within the State, and the first step was to secure a Reichstag that would be amenable to its own destruction. Having carefully failed to come to terms with the Catholic Centre party, he was able to convince Hindenburg that there would have to be one more dissolution, and in the subsequent election Hitler declared openly that he would ask for the suspension of parliamentary government for the next four years. 'The struggle is a light one now,' wrote Goebbels in his diary, 'since we are able to employ all the means of the State. Radio and press are at our disposal.' They had more than that. Goering as Prussian Minister of the Interior formed an auxiliary police force of 25,000 S.A. men and 15,000 S.S. who carried out a campaign of violence against all opposing parties, in which at least fifty people were killed and many hundreds injured. Then, on the night of 27 February, a further opportunity presented itself when the Reichstag building was gutted by fire. A young Dutchman, van der Lubbe, was arrested on the spot and the Nazis announced at once that he had been the dupe of Communist conspirators. The Communists returned the charge against the Nazis and for many years the democratic world believed that the fire was the work of the S.A. attempting to create a Communist scare. In fact, it now seems probable that van der Lubbe was really acting on his own account, but whatever the truth may be, the fire provided Hitler with the excuse to issue a decree on 28 February suspending the Weimar constitution's guarantee of individual liberty and thus enabling the Nazis to intensify their activities against their opponents.

The elections in March gave the Nazis 288 seats which with the support of Hugenburg's Nationalist party only ensured them a bare majority, but the arrest of most of the Communist deputies under the decree of 28 February and an unwise agreement by the Catholic Centre party to work in cooperation with the Nazis supplied Hitler with the two-thirds majority necessary for a constitutional amendment. At the first meeting of the Reichstag in the Kroll Opera House nothing could stop the passage of the Enabling Bill which would free the government from all forms of constitutional and parliamentary control for a period of four years. 'I do not want your votes,' sneered Hitler at the Social Democrats, the only party that had the courage to oppose him in a hall lined with S.A. men, and when the Bill was carried by 441 votes to 94, the Nazis burst exultantly into the Horst Wessel song. As in France in 1851, a republican constitution had been destroyed by the head of the government himself, but Hitler's achievement in 1933 was even more remarkable than Louis Napoleon's, for in Germany democracy had been officially stifled by parliamentary consent.

The way was now open to a process of *Gleichschaltung* (coordination) which finally established the supreme rule of the Nazi party. In the provinces the Nazis were already strongly represented in the *Länder* assemblies, and even before the passing of the Enabling Bill Frick as Minister of the Interior had appointed Reich Police Commissars who ejected the local governments. At the beginning of April their place was taken by Reich governors, all of whom were Nazis nominated by Hitler, and in January 1934 the remaining functions of local government were finally declared to be under the central administration in Berlin. Already by July 1933 all other political parties had been banned—including the Catholic Centre who could now only rely on a Concordat which the Nazi government concluded with the Vatican promising to leave the Roman Church unmolested. At the same time the trade unions were put under government control, while their leaders who resisted were beaten up and thrust into concentration camps at Oranienburg and Dachau.

Thus far, Hitler had revealed how easily the forces of uninhibited gangsterism could kick aside the restraints with which the conservatives had hoped to curb the will of their newly appointed Chancellor. Yet for all his ruthlessness in dealing with his political opponents, Hitler knew well that there were two sections of the community with whose support he could not yet dispense—the industrialists and the army. And here he was to be increasingly embarrassed by the crude menace of the S.A. under their commander Ernst Roehm. These brownshirts had believed that the success of the party would be followed by a social revolution in which the jobs and positions of profit at present still in the hands of the old order would be theirs for the asking. Hitler, however, had no intention of pandering to their wishes at the cost of his good relations with his new friends. The S.A. had by now served his purpose, and when their impatience had almost led to an open breach, he resolved to make an end. During a short sea trip on the pocket battleship *Deutschland* in April 1934, he struck a bargain with General von Blomberg whereby the army would support him in gaining the Presidency on Hindenburg's death, while he would ensure that the S.A. ceased to be a danger to the existing social order.

Both sides honoured the pact. On 29 June Hitler arrived at Munich by air to superintend the execution of S.A. leaders, while Himmler and Goering carried out a similar purge in Berlin; for the next thirty-six hours the firing squads of the S.S. shot down the men who had been among Hitler's closest associates during the struggle for power— seventy-seven according to Hitler himself, four hundred and one according to the *White Book* published in Paris. Roehm, three S.A. *Obergruppenführer* and Gregor Strasser all perished—as well as a number of political opponents including General von Schleicher, his wife, and two of von Papen's assistants. Von Papen himself probably only escaped death on account of his position as Vice-Chancellor and his close friendship with Hindenburg. The General Staff offered their congratulations on such a speedy solution to the problem, and when Hindenburg finally died on 2 August, they did not shirk their part of the bargain. Hitler, it was agreed, should combine the offices of President and Chancellor, and was now to be supreme Commander-in-Chief of the armed forces. Thus the surrender of the army followed on that of the Reichstag and this new triumph for Hitler was rounded off by a plebiscite in which almost 90% of the electorate gave their assent.

Hitler had never made any secret of the fundamental aims of his foreign policy. In contrast to Bismarck he believed fervently in *Grossdeutschland* and was consequently not interested in simply regaining the frontiers of 1914; 'they were temporary frontiers', he had written in *Mein Kampf*, 'established in virtue of a political struggle that had not been brought to a finish', and this revival of old German ambitions naturally implied that the memory of the Treaty of Brest Litovsk was to be as significant a factor for the future as the hatred of the Versailles settlement. For the moment, however, he had to proceed with caution, and during the first few years of his Chancellorship, before the possession of a strong army made him more careless of the risk of war, Hitler, despite his lack of formal training, displayed a remarkable diplomatic skill, assisted by a gambler's instinct.

First, he was determined to rearm. Germany, he claimed, was the only country that had really disarmed. She had no aggressive intentions, but he must insist that she could only accept continued restrictions on the size of her forces as part of an agreed international programme. As he well knew, this was a fairly safe stipulation. Great Britain and the United States had already run their military machines down to a mere shadow, and French activity was entirely concerned with defence; yet the official Disarmament Conference had utterly failed to arrive at a general formula, and with this excuse, in October 1933, Hitler finally withdrew Germany from the Conference and from the League of Nations. Thus he could now begin to rearm openly in direct contravention of the terms of the Treaty of Versailles, and he had struck his attitude of moral righteousness with such insight that when Winston Churchill stated in the House of Commons in 1934 that the German *Luftwaffe* would equal the strength of the R.A.F. by 1935, the warning went unheeded. In Germany he had overwhelming support, for rearmament meant employment for the workless, a greater army for the General Staff, and, above all, a gesture of defiance at the victors of the first World War.

His second step was the announcement of a ten-year non-aggression pact with Poland in January 1934. The Poles had already begun to lose confidence in their alliance with France, since the French government had rejected their suggestion for a preventive war against Germany in March 1933, and they turned now to bolstering their position by friendship with her instead. From a German point of view the pact was certainly not in accordance with the policy outlined by von Seeckt in 1921,[1] but for Hitler it was simply a temporary measure. In terms of propaganda it was a useful advertisement of his peaceful intentions, while at the same time it struck a blow at the French security system in eastern Europe. More important, it left him free to deal with affairs nearer home, and until the quarrel over Danzig in 1939 the Polish pact remained the linchpin of Hitler's foreign policy.

In 1934, however, he did suffer a couple of setbacks. In Austria the local Nazi party had been making their own plans for taking over the government, and on 25 July they attacked the Chancellery at Vienna, shot down Dr Dollfuss and occupied the radio station. The Austrian

[1] See p. 407.

authorities, however, succeeded in frustrating the *coup*, and when Mussolini openly supported them by strengthening his forces on the Austro-Italian frontier, Hitler had publicly to disown any German interest in the conspiracy. The murderers of Dollfuss, who had fled to Germany, were surrendered and the German minister at Vienna was replaced by von Papen, who as a conservative and a Roman Catholic might quieten Austrian suspicions of German designs on their country.

Since the evacuation of the Rhineland the French had already shown their mistrust of German ambitions in embarking upon the construction of a vast fortification known as the Maginot Line running between the Belgian and Swiss frontiers, and now Louis Barthou, their Foreign Minister, made a tour of eastern Europe attempting to repair the damage done to the French system by the German–Polish pact. His efforts to create some sort of eastern Locarno agreement were hindered by Poland's suspicion of the Soviet Union, but in September he did succeed in gaining Russia's admission to the League of Nations. In October, however, Barthou died from his wounds when King Alexander of Yugoslavia on a State visit to France was assassinated at his side in Marseilles, and although his successor, Pierre Laval, did not immediately abandon the policy of eastern alliances against possible German expansion, he chose to concentrate on reaching agreement with Italy by a treaty in January 1935 settling some of their colonial differences and guaranteeing the independence of Austria.

For his next achievement Hitler had only to abide by the Treaty of Versailles, when in January 1935 the fifteen-year separate administration of the Saar expired and a plebiscite gave an overwhelming vote in favour of reunion with Germany. In March, however, Hitler took a more hazardous step when he announced the introduction of conscription which would give Germany an army of thirty-six divisions with 550,000 men. Even the German General Staff would probably have preferred a smaller army to manage at the beginning of a programme of rearmament, but Hitler claimed as justification the fact that the French had just greatly increased their own military forces by doubling their length of service. Diplomatic reactions among the other Powers to this open defiance of the Treaty of Versailles were almost immediate. In April at Stresa Great Britain, France, and Italy mutually confirmed the treaties of Locarno; the League of Nations censured this new step by Germany, and in May France concluded a pact with Russia for mutual assistance. At the same time Russia made a similar pact with Czechoslovakia on the understanding that Russian support would follow on a French initiative.

Hitler at once set to work to remove all suspicions and in a masterly speech—given before the meaningless Reichstag, and really for foreign consumption—he drew on all the vocabulary of the League of Nations to protest his utter horror at the thought of war and to emphasize the harmlessness of German policy. At the same time he was able to make skilful use of the very fears that he had aroused to break up the apparent unity of this new front against Germany. In June an Anglo-German naval agreement was signed, limiting the tonnage of the German fleet to 35% of the British, although U-boat construction was to be allowed to reach 100% of British submarine strength. It seemed a peaceful move and it certainly reassured the British, yet it was utterly disastrous for the maintenance of the Stresa front, since Great Britain had consulted neither France nor Italy, who regarded the agreement as an open recognition of Germany's right to rearm.

The complete disunity of Germany's opponents was finally revealed in October 1935 when Mussolini embarked upon the invasion of Abyssinia.[1] The measures proposed by the League of Nations appeared utterly ineffectual; the hesitations of Great Britain and France in their attitude towards this Italian attack undermined the hopes for any positive action in accordance with the doctrine of collective security, and with this object lesson before him Hitler resolved to go forward with the greatest gamble of his life—the military reoccupation of the Rhineland.

The ruling laid down in the Treaty of Versailles that the Rhineland as well as the territory fifty kilometres to the east of the Rhine should remain permanently demilitarized had been restated in the Locarno pact of 1925 and confirmed in 1929 at the time of the final withdrawal of the Allied occupation forces. Hitler, however, had already shown that he was prepared to ignore the Treaty of Versailles by his open announcement of German rearmament, and he had seen that the Franco-Soviet treaty of May 1935 could be denounced as an aggressive alliance in contravention of the Locarno pact. The final ratification of the Franco-Soviet treaty by the French Chamber gave him the excuse that he needed. On 7 March 1936 German troops marched into the demilitarized zone of the Rhineland at the same time as Hitler informed the western Powers that as a consequence of French diplomatic action he regarded Germany as no longer bound by the Locarno pact,

[1] See p. 427.

although he was careful to make a specific exception of the arbitration treaties with Poland and Czechoslovakia.

In purely military terms it was a suicidal move, for the French, Poles, and Czechs could between them mobilize 190 divisions in war, and it was hardly surprising that the German General Staff were absolutely appalled at the risk. 'I ran into General von Blomberg,' wrote an American correspondent in his diary on the night of 7 March; 'his face was white, his cheeks twitching.' Yet in the event Hitler's reading of the political scene proved correct. The French General Staff, obsessed by now with a purely defensive strategy behind the Maginot Line, were as cautious and pessimistic as their German counterparts over an offensive operation in the Rhineland. Flandin, the French Foreign Minister, was determined on resistance, but the British government, more concerned over the Abyssinian war at this time, held him back from presenting an ultimatum and insisted that the question should be settled at a diplomatic level. In any case, the most that Great Britain could promise in the way of active aid was two divisions fifteen days after the opening of hostilities. Russia and Poland, conscious of these hesitations in the west, also held back; clearly nothing would happen unless France took the first step alone and this she would not do.

Still, if judgement is to be passed, it can be said that at least a part of the French government had wanted to act. In Great Britain both government and public opinion flatly refused to countenance the thought of military intervention; such a prospect had awoken unhappy memories of the French occupation of the Ruhr in 1923 and there was even a certain sympathy with the German action. 'After all, they're only going into their own back garden,' was a comment that appealed strongly, and among the right wing—already suspicious of the French treaty with Soviet Russia—there was always the lurking thought that a powerful Germany would act as a bulwark against Communist expansion.

There is now little doubt that the reoccupation of the Rhineland could have been successfully resisted, as Hitler had every reason to know. 'The forty-eight hours after the march into the Rhineland,' he said long afterwards, 'were the most nerve-racking in my whole life.' The occupation had been carried out with purely token forces and the French General Staff had wildly over-estimated the strength of the German army. It is harder to assess what the political consequences of an Anglo-French intervention might have been. It is, of course, tempting to imagine that it might have led to the overthrow of Hitler, but it is equally possible that German patriotic sentiment might have rallied to him, just as the Weimar Republic had enjoyed its greatest popularity at the time of the passive resistance to the French occupation of the Ruhr. On the other hand, the German generals were beginning to have second thoughts about Hitler by this time and a failure in the Rhineland might have strengthened their hand sufficiently to get rid of him.

As it was, Hitler had enormously bettered his position at home and on the Continent as a whole. He had proved his generals wrong and had demonstrated to the world the weakness of the forces that opposed him. Not merely had he watched the west lose a supreme opportunity to check him; he could ensure that in future such an opportunity would not recur, for Germany was now free to construct the Siegfried Line of fortifications along her western frontier, creating, as Winston Churchill said in the House of Commons, 'a barrier across Germany's front door which will leave her free to sally out eastwards and south-wards by the other doors'. With this single outrageous gamble Hitler had turned Germany's back on the past and opened the way to the future, and when in January 1937 he officially withdrew his country's signature from the Treaty of Versailles, he was doing no more than registering what was already a *fait accompli*.

2. The Abyssinian war 1935-6

The Anglo-German naval pact and the Franco-Soviet treaty had certainly played a considerable part in weakening the united front that the British and the French might have presented to Hitler when he sent his troops into the Rhineland. The principal factor in the under-mining of the policy of collective security, however, was Mussolini's invasion of Abyssinia in October 1935.

Like most European Powers who had entered the race for colonial acquisitions Italy had found that the profits of empire were to be measured more in terms of prestige than of actual economic gain. The organization of her settlements in Libya was costing her 107 million lire in 1921 and as much as 530 million lire by 1930. Somaliland and Eritrea, however, seemed more promising, since their geographical position might enable her to establish economic influence over Abys-sinia, with whom she accordingly fostered good relations. It was due to

Italian representations that Abyssinia in 1923 was made a member of the League of Nations, and in 1928 a treaty of friendship was signed between the two countries. Unfortunately Mussolini's hopes were disappointed when the Emperor Haile Selassie showed that he wished to encourage other competitors and concluded a commercial treaty with Japan in 1930. Shortly after this disillusionment Mussolini began to consider the possibility of war which would not only establish Italian control throughout Abyssinia, but would also provide his régime with the glory of a cheap victory which would wipe out the memory of the Italian defeat at the hands of the Abyssinians at Adowa in 1896.[1]

There followed, inevitably, an incident—a skirmish at the oasis of Wal-Wal within Abyssinian territory in December 1934, after which the Italian government demanded an indemnity and the Emperor appealed to the League of Nations. Neither Great Britain nor France was charitably disposed towards the idea of Italian control over Abyssinia—Great Britain, because she did not wish the sources of the Nile, fundamental to Egyptian economy, to fall into their hands; France, because of her own economic interests there. Yet two other factors placed great obstacles in the way of giving whole-hearted support to the Emperor. First, the dangerously low level to which the British had run down their military machine and the concentration of the French on the defence of their eastern frontier would make direct resistance to an Italian expeditionary force extremely problematical; second, the foreign policy of Laval at that time was based on gaining the friendship of Italy in order that Mussolini might continue to guarantee Austria's independence against Germany, as he had done at the time of Dollfuss's murder in July 1934, and the Franco-Italian treaty of January 1935[2] had given some encouragement to these hopes.

It was this ambivalence of attitude that was to bedevil all subsequent policy throughout the crisis. Mussolini was clearly not going to desist and did his best to delay the appointment of arbitrators, while building up his forces in Eritrea and Italian Somaliland. Yet Hitler's announcement of conscription in Germany in March 1935 made it even more essential for the west that Mussolini should not be driven into his arms, and when Great Britain, France, and Italy met at Stresa in April the Abyssinian question was tactfully left unmentioned—from which Mussolini assumed a general acquiescence. Thus, when in June Anthony Eden proposed the cession of the Abyssinian province of Ogaden to

[1] See p. 277.   [2] See p. 424.

Italy, offering to compensate Abyssinia with the use of a port in British Somaliland, Mussolini rejected the suggestion and in August refused to allow the dispute to be settled by the League of Nations. Finally, on 2 October 1935 Italian forces invaded Abyssinia.

The reaction of the League a fortnight later was to impose a moderate form of economic sanctions, but since the embargo did not include the two vital commodities, coal and oil, this measure was largely ineffectual. In any case, Russia continued to supply Italy, and as neither Germany nor the United States were members of the League, they were not bound by the ruling. Thus, while these half-hearted measures made very little impact on Mussolini's war effort, they did rouse his anger sufficiently against Great Britain and France to cause him to denounce the Franco-Italian treaty and the Stresa agreements.

In fact, the only obstacle to Italian success during the opening months of the campaign was their own military incompetence. The Abyssinian army remained intact and it was becoming doubtful whether the Italians would gain control of the railway line to the capital Addis Ababa before the rainy reason in 1936. Yet, despite the time gained by this long-drawn-out resistance and strong public opinion in Great Britain in favour of full sanctions, the British and French diplomats continued to struggle to find some way of attaining the contradictory ends of forcing the Italians to stop, at the same time as regaining their friendship. Already in September 1935 Sir Samuel Hoare and Pierre Laval had agreed that there should be no military sanctions, mainly because the British naval authorities had expressed strong doubts over their ability to hold the Suez canal against the Italian fleet, and in December the Hoare–Laval pact proposed further concessions that would have given approximately two-thirds of Abyssinia to Italy; the remaining third would be allowed a small outlet to the sea which even *The Times*, although hardly an advocate of resistance to the dictators, described as 'a corridor for camels'.

The Hoare–Laval pact came to nothing. In Great Britain there was an outcry of indignation and Hoare himself had to resign. Nor would Mussolini settle for two-thirds, when he believed that he could gain all without any resistance from the Powers. The Italian army met with greater success in 1936 after the commander, De Bono, had been replaced by Badoglio, and the use of aerial bombardment and poison gas against tribesmen armed with spears soon put the issue beyond doubt. Addis Ababa was occupied by Italian troops at the beginning of May and the Emperor was forced to flee. Thus, at a cost of 1,537

Italians killed in action Mussolini added the largest of the remaining independent territories of Africa to his empire, and with the ending of sanctions in July the world officially accepted this new state of affairs.

The whole of the Abyssinian episode was an appalling political defeat for Great Britain and France and meant nothing less than the utter bankruptcy of the League of Nations and the ideal of collective security. By antagonizing Italy and yet failing to resist her, the two western Powers had fallen hopelessly between two stools and their evident lack of firmness of purpose had shown Hitler that he might safely risk the reoccupation of the Rhineland at a moment when they were unhappily involved elsewhere. Furthermore, the collapse of the Stresa agreements naturally caused Mussolini to turn to friendship with Hitler. By a treaty signed in October 1936 their two countries were in future to cooperate over foreign policy, and a year later, after Mussolini had paid an official visit to Germany, he joined the Anti-Comintern Pact which Germany and Japan had already formed against Russia. This was mainly to Hitler's advantage, since good relations with Italy suggested that Austria might not be able to rely upon continued Italian support against Germany. For Mussolini, on the other hand, the immediate gain from his Abyssinian adventure was negligible and the eventual outcome disastrous. The Italian administration of Abyssinia proved extremely corrupt and by 1939 Italy's trade with all her African colonies only amounted to 2% of her total trade. Even the prestige of success did him little good, for his flouting of Great Britain and France gave him an ill-founded opinion of his own strength, and his friendship with Hitler was the beginning of a policy that was to culminate in the invasion and defeat of his country and an ignominious death for himself.

3. The growing cleavage of opinion: the Spanish civil war 1936-9

The ruthlessness with which Hitler had established the supremacy of the Nazi party has sometimes led commentators to exaggerate the extent to which a single monolithic totalitarian rule had been set up in Germany. In fact, as one historian has suggested, the leading Nazis formed a court rather than a government, whose members constantly intrigued against each other, setting up agencies whose functions overlapped and conflicted, while running parallel with the existing institutions of State administration.

Nevertheless, the imprint of the new forces in power was apparent in almost every side of social life. Under Dr Schacht there was a remarkable return to full employment aided by a programme of public works and the policy of rearmament, and the year 1936 saw the inauguration of a four-year economic plan. The principal domestic concern of the Nazis was the inculcation of their ideology. Under the control of the party, education was to concentrate on the fanning of German nationalism and the racial mystique of Aryanism. During the first five years of the régime nearly 3,000 professors and instructors were dismissed from their posts; many more, however, felt compelled to conform and in the autumn of 1933 almost a thousand took a public vow in support of Hitler. 'True physics is the creation of the German spirit,' wrote the director of the Institute of Physics at Dresden, '. . . in fact, all European science is the fruit of Aryan, or, better, German thought.' 'In reality,' said Professor Lenard of Heidelberg University, 'science, like every other human product, is racial and conditioned by blood.' Para-military youth organizations proliferated, and as early as May 1933 sections of the student population were sufficiently enthusiastic to participate in a great burning of books written by liberals, pacifists, and Jews, casting into the flames the works of Thomas Mann, Stefan Zweig, Remarque, Freud, and Einstein as well as those of H. G. Wells, Gide, Zola, and Proust. For the schools, textbooks were vetted and often re-written, although this was to some extent a gradual process and it was not until 1944 that the Nazis finally imposed a single history textbook to be used in all schools in Germany—*Der Weg zum Reich*—which naturally brought the story to a triumphant climax with the rise of the Third Reich, listing in heavy type the names of all those who had fallen during the Munich *putsch* of 1923.

At first, the Roman Catholics had pinned their hopes to the Concordat of July 1933, while the Protestant churches, accustomed to the authority of the State and to the anti-Semitism in Luther's writings, were divided in their attitude towards Hitler. By 1937, however, Catholics and Protestants alike had reacted against increasing interference with their publications and religious and educational activities, and thousands of Catholic priests and nuns and Protestant pastors, including Dr Niemöller, were arrested and dispatched to concentration camps.

The fate of the Jews was still worse. In 1933 they were excluded from holding public office and from the professions of journalism, teaching, and the civil service, in 1934 from the stock exchange, and in 1938 from law and medicine. The Nuremberg laws of 1935 deprived them of German citizenship, forbade Jewish–Aryan marriages, and prohibited any Jew from employing female Aryan servants under the age of thirty-five. This was the doctrine which the later success of Hitler's foreign policy was to carry beyond the frontiers of Germany; the first consequences of his acquisition of Austria in 1938, for instance, included the looting of Jewish possessions and the forcing of Jews out of their homes to scrub the streets and descended to such trivialities as forbidding them to sit on public seats in the parks. Naturally, while international opinion had still to be considered, Hitler could not yet give full rein to his hatred which, during the second World War, was to lead to the mass extermination of some five million European Jews.

Yet, for all the unpopularity of the spectacle of a police state with its control of the courts of law and the stories of the concentration camps at Dachau, Buchenwald, and Sachsenhausen under the supervision of the S.S., the predominating impression that foreign tourists gained was of a country finding new confidence in itself, and the holding of the Olympic Games at Berlin in 1936 gave Hitler his chance to advertise the blessings of the Nazi régime, the great new roads (the *Reichs autobahnen*), the improved amenities for German workers, and the general sense of returning prosperity.

Meanwhile, in the east of Europe, another police state, the sworn foe of Nazism, was pursuing its destiny with enigmatic ruthlessness. With the new policy of the collectivization of farms and the organization of Russian industry through a series of five-year plans, Stalin was now using the dictatorship of the Bolshevik party to impose the second stage of the Communist revolution. This was designed to create a completely Socialist State in which all the major forms of property were to be in the hands of the State or of large corporations such as the collective farms. It is, of course, here that the fundamental difference between Nazism and Communism lies, since Nazism, despite its allusions to Socialism, simply provided a framework of authoritarianism within which private enterprise could flourish; it is true that Hitler intended industry and the army ultimately to serve his purpose, but that purpose was fundamentally racial and national, whereas Soviet Russia officially spurned all forms of racialism and regarded foreign policy purely as a means for the safeguarding and eventual extension of its social system.

There were, nevertheless, several striking points of similarity between German Nazism and Russian Communism in the 1930s. In both cases

the ruling party had its own separate existence, its organization corresponding at all levels with the heirarchy of governmental departments. Education in both countries was in the hands of the State, both
highly doctrinaire and stressing the importance of youth movements,
although in Russia instruction was positively anti-religious, whereas in
Germany the gulf between the Party and the Churches was simply the
incidental outcome of the realization of Nazi paganism. Russia might
eschew any kind of racial discrimination, but she too had her scape-
goats. The task of rapid modernization in Soviet Russia involved the
most appalling difficulties, yet any failure was automatically regarded as
wilful, and when progress was insufficiently rapid during the first
five-year plan, foreign engineers and technicians were arrested and
brought up for trial on charges of sabotage. The most striking point of
similarity was to be seen in the treason trials between 1935 and 1938,[1]
when many of the leading Bolsheviks of the early days of the revolution—including Zinoviev, Kamenev, Bukharin, and Rykov—were
charged with treason, condemned, and executed. The most sinister
aspect of these trials was the way in which these confirmed and devoted
Communists confessed their full guilt before the court. Torture or the
promise of reprieve may have played some part in this, although a
more ingenious solution has been suggested in Arthur Koestler's novel
Darkness at Noon. Certainly nothing could have been more indicative
of the power of the dominating authorities in the Party, and the
discrediting of these founder members of the movement was followed
by a purge of the army in which seven generals were shot and hundreds
of officers dismissed. Thus, just as Hitler smashed the S.A. and continued to work for the suborning of the German General Staff, so
Stalin rid himself of the centres of political and military opposition and
consolidated his own position of power as General Secretary of the
Communist party.

The existence of these two fundamentally opposed forms of police
state naturally affected political feelings in the western democracies,
creating a growing cleavage of opinion between right and left. Many
of the right, although doubtful of many aspects of Fascism, saw Germany and Italy as efficient powerful states which could offer an
effective resistance to Communism; on the left many liberals and mild
Socialists, regarding the immediate background of slump, unemployment, and hunger marches as the final condemnation of *laissez-faire*

[1] There is an eye-witness account of the trials in Fitzroy Maclean's *Eastern Approaches*.
P

capitalism, leaned increasingly in the direction of Communist Russia, who seemed to be the only non-Fascist country that was prepared to take an unambiguous stand against the racialism and national aggressiveness of the right-wing dictatorships of Germany and Italy.

The practical outcome of these attitudes varied. In Great Britain they played their part in the formation of views throughout the country, but they had only a minor effect on the official policies of the parties. The conservatives were governed by many other motives than fear of Communism in attempting the appeasement of the Fascist countries,[1] while the Labour party, as was natural for Socialists who accepted the principle of parliamentary constitutionalism, was equally mistrustful of the political implications of revolutionary Communism.

In France and Spain, however, the clash between the two views was translated into direct political action. On the French right wing a number of organizations had been formed of a Fascist type—*Action française*, the oldest of them, which included Charles Maurras, Léon Daudet, and Jacques Bainville, *Croix de feu* led by Colonel de la Roque, and *Solidarité Française*—all authoritarian, appealing to ex-servicemen and strongly anti-Communist and anti-Semitic. The membership of each of the groups was no more than about 100,000, but in 1934 a domestic crisis revealed the lengths to which they might be prepared to go. At the beginning of that year members of the French government were known to have been involved in the fraudulent transactions of a Russian–Jewish business man, Serge Stavisky, and when Stavisky who was due for trial was discovered dead in his villa at Chamonix, apparently through suicide, the right-wing leagues launched a great attack on the government in Paris, declaring that he had been killed in order that embarrassing disclosures might be avoided. On 6 February they fought a pitched battle with the police in the Place de la Concorde in an attempt to break through to the Palais Bourbon where the Assembly had its seat. Constitutional government survived this test, but the left wing, mindful of the lessons offered by Italy and Germany, took warning. In January 1936 Radicals, Socialists, and Communists combined to form a party, the *Rassemblement Populaire Français*, and when the elections of April 1936 gave them a majority, a new government under Léon Blum embarked on a series of left-wing measures, including a forty-hour week, holidays with pay for workers, and the nationalization of munition factories. Employers had to agree to a

[1] See pp. 438–40.

system of collective negotiation and to wage increases, and the right-wing leagues were outlawed.

In Spain the cleavage between right and left was equally marked in the new freedom of political life that the constitution of 1931 [1] allowed. Governments had risen and fallen with the speed customary in countries that had just embarked upon an experiment in constitutional rule, but the elections of February 1936 revealed the formation of two composite groups: on the left, Republicans, Socialists, Syndicalists, Anarchists, and Communists combined to create a Popular front; on the right, the Falange Española was supported by the Roman Catholic Church, the army, and the industrialists. In these elections the right gained slightly more votes, but owing to the workings of the electoral system the left actually held a majority in the assembly, the *Cortes*. The outcome was the opening of the civil war in Spain, when a military rising in Spanish Morocco under General Franco in July 1936 was followed by rapid successes on the mainland. By November Franco's forces were established in the south, west, and north of Spain and had set up a new government at Burgos, while the Republicans had withdrawn the seat of the official government to Barcelona and centred their resistance on Catalonia, Valencia, and the two Basque provinces of the north.

Within Spain itself the struggle was only incidentally one between Fascism and Communism. On the right the principal elements were the military and the monarchists, although they naturally included Fascist organizations; nor was the left primarily Communist. Yet to the Powers of Europe it appeared such a struggle. None of them could remain indifferent to it, partly because of Spain's geographical position, partly because both sides in the war were in urgent need of men and supplies. Germany and Italy both favoured Franco-Italy, because she hoped to establish naval bases in the Balearic Isles and to weaken Great Britain's hold on Gibraltar; Germany, because a victory for Franco might create embarrassment for France on her southern frontier—an attitude reminiscent of Bismarck's dabbling in the question of the Spanish succession in 1870. Naturally the consequence of these aims was to swing the western democracies away from supporting Franco, but the presence of Communists among the Republicans inhibited the British government in particular from sending help to the forces that were resisting him. In France, Blum would have liked to intervene on the side of the left, but divisions in his cabinet as well as the attitude of

[1] See pp. 415-16.

the British compelled him to compromise with a scheme for a general guarantee of non-intervention, and in August 1936 an agreement was signed to this effect by Great Britain, France, Germany, Italy, and Russia.

In fact, none of the dictatorships honoured the agreement. In November Mussolini and Franco reached an understanding over economic support and political collaboration in the western Mediterranean, and before long thousands of rifles and machine-guns were being shipped from Italy to Franco. By January 1937 there were 44,000 Italian troops in Spain and by the following October 60,000. In March 1937 Franco came to a similar agreement with Hitler, whereby he was to have the services of German pilots and technicians together with a great deal of war material. This violation of the principle of non-intervention naturally provided the Soviet government with all the justification that it needed to announce openly in October that Russian help would be sent to the Republican forces. In France the extreme left of the *Rassemblement Populaire* advocated direct intervention on behalf of the Republicans—as eventually did the Labour party in Great Britain—but the governments of the western democracies remained unwilling to make what seemed to be a choice between a Communist and a Fascist cause.

In Spain the war had almost reached a stalemate by the end of 1937 after Franco had been checked at Madrid and Teruel, but in 1938 the superiority of his forces in numbers and equipment due to the assistance of Germany and Italy enabled him to strike through to the east coast. Barcelona fell in January 1939, Madrid in March, and in April Franco declared that hostilities were officially at an end.

Although the bitterness of the struggle had left Spain far too exhausted to participate in any further warfare, the victory of Franco certainly seemed to represent an overwhelming success for the Fascist dictators. In March 1939 he formed a definite alliance with Germany and Italy, and France was now faced with the possibility of a hostile neighbour beyond the Pyrenees. The prospects for the west of regaining Italian friendship were more remote than ever; the efforts of Neville Chamberlain, who in May 1937 had replaced Baldwin as Prime Minister in Great Britain, met with little success in drawing Italy away from her involvement with Germany, and resulted only in the resignation of Anthony Eden, the Foreign Secretary.

These considerations were naturally important, yet the two most significant aspects of the Spanish Civil war were emotional rather than diplomatic. First, it provided an object lesson in a new form of total war; the ferocity of the fighting, the sufferings of the civilian population, the bombing of cities such as Guernica, the activity of resistance groups behind the lines, all gave a glimpse of the fate that might one day engulf the entire Continent. Second, to many for whom Spain in these years appeared like an arena in which the two extremes of left and right were at last in open conflict, it seemed that there could no longer be any further neutrality in the crisis of ideological loyalty, and with this hardening of opinions over Fascism many of those of more moderate outlook in the western countries, watching the gradual advance of Franco's armies, knew at last in their hearts where their ultimate decision lay.

32

GERMANY'S ADVANCE EASTWARDS
1938-9

B Y the beginning of 1938 the initiative appeared to be firmly in
the hands of the Powers of the Anti-Comintern Pact. The
Japanese invasion of Manchuria in 1931, the Italian conquest of
Abyssinia, the German reoccupation of the Rhineland, and the supply-
ing of General Franco in the Spanish Civil war, all suggested that the
objections of Great Britain and France might be safely defied and the
authority of the League of Nations ignored. Certainly the smaller
countries of Europe interpreted events in this light. In eastern Europe,
except for Czechoslovakia, they began to trim their sails towards
Berlin; the Netherlands and the Scandinavian nations announced that
they could not in future shape their policy in accordance with the
requirements of collective security, while in 1936 Belgium had already
officially abandoned her alliances in order to revert to strict neutrality.

British and French reactions to the aggressiveness of the dictators took
two forms. By 1936 they had both reluctantly begun to rearm. For
Great Britain the importance of air defence seemed to the experts to
loom as large as the question of naval superiority had done before 1914,[1]
but this time there was a striking difference, since the British had
already lost their lead and plans had to be made for an expansion of the
R.A.F. which would enable it to catch up with the German *Luftwaffe*.
At the same time work was begun under the Tizard committee on the
operational development of radar—perhaps the greatest single factor
in the salvation of the country in 1940. The French, obsessed with the
thought of German invasion, concentrated their efforts on the Maginot
Line, but these purely defensive measures naturally only added to the
apprehensiveness of their eastern allies.

The principal policy of the west remained one of appeasement. This
simply allowed the dictators to have almost everything their own way,
so that Hitler was able in 1938 to absorb Austria and the Czech
Sudetenland, and in 1939 Slovakia and the Memelland, until his

[1] See pp. 314, 322, 325.

attempt to gain Danzig led to the outbreak of the second World War. Appeasement eventually became so discredited that the word itself retained a pejorative flavour long after the end of the war, but at the time it was a policy which had the support of a considerable body of public opinion in the west. The fundamental reason for this lay in the appalling memory of the first World War. 'Never again' was the all-consuming thought of the western democracies—particularly among ex-servicemen whose families were by now reaching military age. And for the British there was in addition a confused sense of guilt over the Treaty of Versailles, strengthened by their irritation with the French in the 1920s. They were consequently not entirely unconvinced by Hitler's arguments over German minorities, and it was not until the partition of the non-German regions of Czechoslovakia in March 1939 that the electorates of Great Britain and France awoke to the belated realization that paying the Danegeld—or, rather, making others pay—meant no limit to what would ultimately be demanded.

Appeasement, however, was based on practical considerations as well as emotional. British mildness in their relations with the Italians over the Abyssinian war was due mainly to a desire to prevent a German–Italian alliance which would add to their problems in the Mediterranean. Over Germany the predominating consideration in 1938 and 1939 was not merely the general military weakness of the west, but also the fact that the Siegfried Line, flanked by a neutral Belgium and Switzerland, shut Great Britain and France out from any effective intervention that might prevent Hitler's expansion east-wards. The only hope seemed to lie in the creation of a league of states in eastern Europe who would stand firm with the west against Ger-many, but by now the eastern states, increasingly impressed by Hitler's handling of the west, preferred to play his game for him in furthering their individual ends; thus Poland and Hungary each annexed Czech territory in 1938, and Hungary did so again in March 1939.

In the last analysis any firm resistance would depend upon some form of western agreement with Russia—a recreation of the Triple Entente of 1907—but here national and political considerations acted as a powerful brake. The right wing in both Great Britain and France remained highly suspicious of Communist Russia and even saw Nazi Germany as a dam raised against the Bolshevik flood, as Hitler in a speech in 1936 had suggested that they would; 'better Hitler than Blum' was the comment of some French conservatives. In eastern

Europe the mistrust of Russia was even stronger; in the crisis of September 1938 the Czechs did not relish the idea of dependence on the Red Army and in any case neither Poland nor Rumania would have allowed it a free passage through their lands to defend Czechoslovakia; in the summer of 1939, when the German demands on Poland were mounting, the Poles were adamant that there could be no alliance with Russia.

Thus, throughout these crises Neville Chamberlain, the British Prime Minister, was haunted by the thought that even if general war in resistance to Hitler did ensue, nothing could be done to save the country over whom it had broken out. In 1938 there was in addition the realization that public opinion, particularly in the Commonwealth, was as yet unprepared to accept the appalling consequences of an outbreak of war, and that in any case the west was still lagging too far behind in rearmament to bring effective pressure to bear on Germany. On this last point it has sometimes been argued that the surrender of the Sudetenland at Munich in 1938 was simply an attempt to gain time. Chamberlain was not so Machiavellian. He was certainly aware of the desperate need to be able to argue from a position of strength, but he still hoped after Munich that war might be averted. In this he clearly misjudged Hitler; on the other hand, when war was finally forced upon him over the Danzig crisis in 1939, his earlier efforts to preserve peace did at least ensure him the full support of public opinion, and the immediate fall of Poland and the military disasters for the west in 1940 would suggest that his appreciation of the difficulties that had prompted his policy of appeasement had not been entirely unrealistic.

1. The Austrian Anschluss, March 1938

Hitler's own avowal in *Mein Kampf* had made it clear that the first stage in his revision of the frontiers of 1919 would be the absorption of Austria within Germany. There is, however, little to indicate that the actual circumstances of the *Anschluss* (union) of March 1938 were due to any long premeditated plan; it seems probable that Hitler was content to rely upon the activity of the Austrian Nazi party to bring about such a union with Germany by peaceful invitation, but, as was his way, he was always ready to seize an opportunity which the growing tension might present. The Austrian Chancellor, von Schuschnigg, had hoped to buy time with an agreement with Germany in July 1936, at the same time vainly trying to strengthen Austria's ties with the 'little *entente*,'[1] but when his police unearthed plans for an Austrian Nazi *coup d'état* in January 1938, he decided that the moment had arrived for a new negotiation with Hitler. Von Papen, the German ambassador at Vienna, was recalled at the beginning of February, but on hearing of von Schuschnigg's willingness to come to terms, Hitler sent him back to Vienna, where a meeting was arranged between the two Chancellors at the Berghof, Hitler's residence in the Obersalzberg. Their conversations on 12 February consisted of no less than a series of demands by Hitler that Austrian Nazis should be reinstated in their official posts, that Seyss-Inquart, one of their leading members, should become Minister of the Interior—consequently with control over the police—and that close economic and military relations should be established between the two countries. Von Schuschnigg, impressed by the presence of German generals at the Berghof, duly gave way. 'I am happy to be able to tell you, gentlemen,' Hitler announced in the Reichstag on 20 February, 'that during the past few days a further understanding has been reached with a country that is particularly close to us for many reasons.' Four days later, however, von Schuschnigg made it clear in a speech of his own before the Austrian *Bundestag* that a halt must be called to German demands and on 8 March he announced a plebiscite on the question of union with Germany.

Hitler did not hear of this until 10 March and it seems that he was taken by surprise. The result of the plebiscite, due to be held on Sunday 13 March, would almost certainly deprive him of his argument that the Austrians were longing for reunion with Germany and he was determined to forestall it. Three German army corps and the air force were mobilized at once and Prince Philip of Hesse was dispatched to Mussolini with a letter to dissuade him from rallying to the support of Austria, as he had done at the time of the murder of Dollfuss. On 11 March Goering demanded through Seyss-Inquart that the plebiscite should be called off, but when von Schuschnigg finally agreed, this was followed by an ultimatum that Seyss-Inquart must replace Schuschnigg as Chancellor. Throughout the rest of that day President Miklas stubbornly refused to acquiesce, but in the evening Seyss-Inquart under German instructions sent a telegram to Berlin asking for military assistance to put down disorder in Austria, and when later that night Prince Philip of Hesse telephoned from Rome to say that

[1] See p. 406.

P 2

Mussolini had agreed not to resist German action, Hitler knew that the way was open. 'Please tell Mussolini that I shall never forget him for this.' Any other resistance he was prepared to brush aside, and during a vast reception at the *Haus der Flieger* in Berlin Goering listened unmoved to the indignation of the British ambassador and quietened the anxiety of the Czech minister, giving his word of honour 'that Czechoslovakia has nothing to fear from the Reich'.

Shortly before midnight President Miklas finally surrendered, but the orders for an occupation had already been given, and early on 12 March German forces crossed the frontier into Austria, where local Nazi groups were now taking over the local administration. On 13 March union with Germany was proclaimed and on the next day Hitler arrived at Vienna to take possession of the capital in which he had once lived in poverty and degradation. He might indeed feel triumphant. At the price of abandoning the Tyrolese to continued rule under Italy he had taken the first step in realizing the old dream of *Grossdeutschland*, and Austria with a population of seven million, resources of iron, steel, and magnesite, and frontiers that opened a door to the Balkans, was now to be no more than a province of the German Reich.

Plebiscites in Germany and Austria—held under government auspices and naturally overwhelmingly in favour of the *Anschluss*— were mainly for the purpose of conciliating foreign opinion, but in fact reactions abroad to the *coup* were remarkably slight. Poland and Czechoslovakia acquiesced, while France at this time was actually without a government. In Great Britain the public felt vaguely that the Austrians were German anyway, and despite the warning sounded by Winston Churchill in the House of Commons, there was no sense of outrage when the British government contented itself with an official protest.

2. The Sudetenland crisis and the Munich Pact, August–September 1938

There could be little doubt where the next blow would fall. The successful accomplishment of the Austrian *Anschluss* awoke a great excitement among the Sudeten Germans in Czechoslovakia, and before the end of March their leader Konrad Henlein was in consultation with Hitler, Ribbentrop, and Hess in Berlin. Immediately after the Austrian crisis Neville Chamberlain had turned down any suggestion of a British guarantee for Czechoslovakia, as well as a Russian proposal for a four-Power conference, and when Henlein in a speech at Karlsbad on 24 April outlined eight points demanding autonomy for the Sudeten-landers, it seemed as if there might be very little western resistance to Nazi plans.

Then suddenly in the middle of May Hitler encountered unexpected difficulties. The Czechs, suspicious of German troop-movements near their frontiers, mobilized part of their forces; the British and French governments supported them with the strongest diplomatic warnings, while the Russians reassured the French that they would stand by the agreements of May 1935 in defence of Czechoslovakia. Thereupon Hitler decided to hold back, but this momentary interference with his policy only confirmed him in his hatred of the Czechs as Slav *Unter-menschen*; on 30 May he informed the General Staff that 'it is my unalterable decision to smash Czechoslovakia by military action in the near future', and gave orders for the preparation of a military invasion by 1 October.

Throughout the summer, as the tension over the Sudetenland con-tinued to mount, the British and French governments attempted to mediate, asking Hitler to moderate his demands and putting pressure on the Czechs to make concessions to the Sudetenlanders. On 4 September President Beneš granted Henlein's eight points, but by now Hitler was convinced that the west would not fight, and a week later at the Nuremberg Party Rally he launched a savage attack on the Czech President. 'The Germans in Czechoslovakia are neither defence-less, nor are they deserted, and people should take notice of that fact.'

Then, when the crisis was at its height, Neville Chamberlain announced on 13 September his intention of flying to Germany to initiate direct conversations with Hitler. There is little now that can be said in defence of the Munich agreement to which these negotiations led; yet there is an inescapable sense of drama in the extraordinary pertinacity of this old man, setting off with his umbrella in an attempt to soften the bitter realities of central European power politics. It was the first flight that he had ever made and the German Chancellor did not even bother to meet him at the airport.

At Berchtesgaden Hitler stated an outright demand that the Sudeten-land be ceded to Germany. Back in London Chamberlain and the French decided to agree to a transference of territory where the population was more than 50% German, and the Czechs were forced to accept this. On 22 September Chamberlain returned to Germany by air, this time to Godesberg on the Rhine, only to find that Hitler now wanted more. The Poles and the Hungarians must also receive concessions and the Sudetenland must be placed under immediate German military occupation. These fresh demands seemed to wreck even Chamberlain's hopes of avoiding war. The British cabinet refused to accept them, the French government called up 600,000 reservists, and the Czechs had already mobilized during the Godesberg conversations. These were facts that Hitler did not ignore; his General Staff were already advocating extreme caution, and he had himself noticed the atmosphere of gloom among the crowds in Berlin. At any rate, despite a virulent speech against the Czechs on 26 September, he did not break off negotiations with London, and when the French put forward a proposal involving slight modifications of his Godesberg demands, Mussolini, who dreaded the possibility of being dragged into a European war, was prompted by the British to persuade him to accept this as a basis for discussion. And so on 29 September Hitler, Mussolini, Chamberlain, and Daladier met in conference in the *Führerbau* at Munich and reached an agreement that gave Hitler almost the whole of what he had demanded. The Czechs were not invited and their ambassador was afterwards simply informed by Chamberlain and Daladier that they would have to submit.

Thus, in an ultimately fruitless attempt to preserve European peace Great Britain and France abandoned Czechoslovakia to the German dictator. The Czechs were compelled to give up the horseshoe-shaped western edge of their frontier which contained all their mountain fortifications, and nearly a million Czechs who lived among the German Sudetenlanders found themselves under Nazi rule. Immediately afterwards Poland seized the Teschen district, while Hungary extended her own frontier northwards[1]—each glad to settle grievances that had rankled since the end of the war. In his own way Hitler had harnessed local national animosity to his policy as effectively as the Habsburgs had done in the past.

For France Munich was a flagrant breach of a treaty of alliance. Great Britain had had no treaty with the Czechs; on the other hand, she had taken the initiative in organizing the surrender. It had been open to the British government to create a firm diplomatic front with France and Russia, yet they refused to contemplate cooperation with the Soviet Union; they would not even commit themselves to joining

[1] See maps, pp. 371, 446-7.

France against Germany, unless she was actually invaded by German forces. Instead, by conscious choice Chamberlain preferred to negotiate with Germany on the assumption of Hitler's good faith, and it was not unnatural that the Russians should suspect the forming of a European alignment that would eventually leave them to face a German on-slaught in isolation.

Unhappy though it was, however, not every criticism that has been made of Munich is entirely sound. It has been claimed, for example, that Hitler was only bluffing. It is true that the German General Staff were strongly opposed to war and at the Nuremberg trials after the war General Keitel declared that they would not have been strong enough to fight in September 1938. Yet Hitler had continually over-ruled his General Staff. The secrecy of his partial mobilization on 27 September does not suggest bluff; he had been in a black mood at Munich and his remark to the S.S. afterwards that 'that fellow Chamberlain has spoiled my entry into Prague' implied that he really had been hoping for an excuse 'to smash Czechoslovakia'. Mussolini's attitude may have given him cause to think, but if the west had stood firm in refusing concessions, it is impossible to see how he could have retreated from the public statements that he had already made.

Another criticism that the Germans have constantly stressed since 1945 is that the west's surrender to Hitler at Munich wrecked the chances of a plot that was being hatched among German generals and politicians who were hoping to oust the Nazis. Certainly there was a tentative scheme to get rid of Hitler in September 1938, of which the British government was aware through secret emissaries from Ger-many, but they could hardly be expected to shape their policy simply on the strength of such information. One must not underestimate the technical difficulties, the personal risk, and the struggle of divided loyalties involved in any attempt to supplant Hitler; yet if Munich did ruin a plan to remove him, it is legitimate to ask why the eventual resistance of the west twelve months later did not favour a similar *coup*. In fact, none materialized until July 1944 and was then a failure—as indeed the doubts and perplexities of the conspirators suggest it would have been in September 1938, even if it had been attempted.

Of course, it is possible that Hitler might have succumbed to a *coup d'état*. Certainly on that assumption Munich can be blamed for the appalling holocaust of the second World War. It seems much more probable, however, that if the west had supported Czechoslovakia, Hitler would have remained in power and that war would have ensued.

Sudetenland

Territory gained by Hungary
1938-40

European countries neutral
during second world war

UNITED
KINGDOM

Trondheim

NORWAY

SWEDEN

DENMARK

Lübeck

Liverpool

Bremen

Hamburg

Coventry

Berlin

London

Dunkirk

Arnhem

Plymouth

Boulogne

Rotterdam

Cherbourg

Arras

Paris

Reims

SAAR

BOHE
MORAV

Tours

Munich

Vienna

Berchtes
gaden

Bordeaux

Vichy

SWITZERL'D

UNOCCUPIED
FRANCE 1940-42

Burgos

Marseilles

ITALY

Rome

PORTUGAL

Madrid

Barcelona

Anzio

SPAIN

Valencia

Naples

Balearic Is

Salerno

Gibraltar

Algiers

Casablanca

Oran

Tunis

Syracuse

Malta

MOROCCO

ALGERIA

LIBYA

Scale 0 ⌐———————⌐ 400 Miles

FINLAND   KARELIA   ▬▬▬ *Furthest line of German*
Viipuri   (ceded to   *advance Oct. 1942*
          Russia 1940) ▬ ▬ ▬ *German advance in 1941*
     Leningrad   ×××××× *French Maginot line*
Hanko   ESTONIA   —·—·— *Partition line in Poland*
    Novgorod   *1939*

LATVIA

emel LITHUANIA   Moscow

E.   Smolensk
PRUSSIA
Warsaw   Brest   Voronezh
      Litovsk
                   Stalingrad   Volga
P O L A N D   Kiev   Kharkov
           Dnieper   Don
OVAKIA   Rostov
Budapest TRAN-
NGARY   SYLVANIA
elgrade   RUMANIA   Yalta
YUGO-
SLAVIA   BULGARIA

ALBANIA   T U R K E Y
anto   GREECE

                       SYRIA

Cape   IRAQ
Matapan   Cyprus
Crete

                   Port   PALESTINE
Tobruk   Sidi Barrani   Said   TRANS-
Benghazi   JORDAN
        El   Suez   S A U D I
     Alamein   Cairo   A R A B I A
El Agheila   E G Y P T

Beyond that it is difficult to speculate. The French General Staff were highly pessimistic over their chances of penetrating the Siegfried Line; 'une bataille de la Somme modernisée', General Gamelin predicted gloomily. The thirty-six divisions of the Czech army, aided by their Sudetenland fortifications, would have given a good account of themselves, but they would have had to fight without any immediate aid. Despite her protestations to the contrary Russia might have been content to remain neutral while the European Powers exhausted themselves in war, but even if she had been prepared to throw in her lot with the west and if the Czechs had accepted her support, Poland and Rumania would have resisted the passage of the Red Army through their territories. Indeed, the Czechs would have been fortunate if Poland and Hungary had not joined in the attack against them, and on the face of it there is every likelihood that war in September 1938 would have given Hitler possession of the whole of Czechoslovakia in a matter of weeks.

3. The destruction of Czechoslovakia, March 1939, and the change in western policy

'We have sustained a total and unmitigated defeat', declared Winston Churchill in the House of Commons, yet despite the revolt of a small section of the conservatives at Westminster, there is little doubt that the majority of the public in Great Britain and France were conscious of an overwhelming sense of relief. They preferred to believe that 'it is peace in our time', as Chamberlain announced from the windows of Downing Street on his return from Munich, and for a short while events gave some encouragement to this wishful thinking. In December a Franco-German declaration was issued confirming the agreement at Munich; in January 1939 Chamberlain and his Foreign Secretary, Lord Halifax, paid an official visit to Italy, while in Spain it was clear that the civil war was almost at an end.

It was not long, however, before disillusionment finally dawned. After Munich President Beneš had resigned and left the country, and Czechoslovakia had been converted into a federal state with autonomy for Slovakia and Ruthenia, except over matters of defence and foreign policy. This soon led to domestic disputes until, early in March 1939, President Hacha, Beneš' successor, dismissed the two premiers of Slovakia and Ruthenia, one of whom, Father Tiso of

Slovakia, appealed to Hitler in Berlin. Once again Hitler, although taken by surprise at the time, seized the chance when it came. A German demand for Slovak independence brought President Hacha to Berlin, where, through the same techniques as had been employed against von Schuschnigg the year before, he was browbeaten into placing the whole of Czechoslovakia under German protection. Almost at once Bohemia and Moravia, where military occupation had already begun, were annexed to Germany, Slovakia became a German protectorate, and Ruthenia was handed over to the Hungarians. As Hitler announced in delight, Czechoslovakia had ceased to exist, and he followed up this advance a week later by forcing Lithuania to yield the Memelland to East Prussia, and by concluding a trade agreement with Rumania which would ensure oil supplies for Germany.

The west took no direct action, using the excuse that the changes had come about with the consent of the Czech and Lithuanian governments. Yet these events in March 1939 were to be of momentous significance in the history of Europe, for with this further annexation Hitler unwittingly created an extraordinary revolution in official and public opinion in the west. Now, even the most pacific-minded realized at last that the issue of German minorities was merely a screen for a consistent march eastwards which only diplomatic or military pressure could halt. The destruction of Czechoslovakia had finally demonstrated the utter bankruptcy of the policy of appeasement. 'Is this, in fact, a step in the direction of an attempt to dominate the world by force?' demanded Chamberlain in a speech at Birmingham on 17 March. However mild, his question sounded a new note. A week later Great Britain and France agreed that they would resist any German aggression in the Netherlands, Belgium, or Switzerland, and at the end of the month Chamberlain stated in the House of Commons that Great Britain would stand with France in supporting Poland with whom Hitler was already beginning to pick a quarrel over Danzig.

This remarkable change of attitude on the part of the west was confirmed almost immediately by Mussolini, when on Good Friday Italian troops began the occupation of Albania. It was a fairly pointless operation, since Albania was economically already in Italy's pocket; indeed, Ahmed Zogu had been able to have himself proclaimed King Zog in 1928 mainly because of Italian support. Mussolini, however, with a Fascist dictator's concern for prestige, was jealous of Hitler's recent successes and was, furthermore, anxious over the growth of German influence in the Balkans. In their new mood the British and the French at once gave guarantees of support to Greece and Rumania and made similar offers to the Netherlands, Switzerland, and Denmark who, however, rejected them. Then, on 26 April, for the first time in her history Great Britain, as a result of French persuasion, introduced universal military conscription. The length of service was only to be six months and made little immediate difference to the state of the British forces, yet as a symbol it marked the extraordinary alteration in general feeling since the previous September.

4. Danzig, and the outbreak of war, September 1939

'It would be wrong', wrote the German ambassador in London on 18 March, 'to cherish any illusions that a fundamental change had not taken place in Britain's attitude towards Germany,' but if Hitler saw this, it had little effect on his actions in the summer of 1939. At the beginning of April his General Staff had already received orders to prepare for a campaign against Poland, and in a speech in the Reichstag at the end of the month he demanded the return of Danzig to Germany, at the same time denouncing the German–Polish non-aggression pact of 1934 and the Anglo-German naval agreement of 1935. On 22 May the so-called Pact of Steel between Germany and Italy was published, each promising to support the other in war and to collaborate over the acquisition of *Lebensraum*. On the next day Hitler outlined his plans before an audience of senior officers. 'We cannot expect a repetition of the Czech affair. There will be war. Our task is to isolate Poland. The success of this isolation will be decisive . . . there must be no simultaneous conflict with the western Powers.' A week later Mussolini secretly informed Hitler that despite the Pact of Steel Italy could do nothing for the next three years. This was of little significance to Hitler, however, since the over-riding diplomatic consideration now was not Italy, but Russia.

There is little doubt that the west could have gained a Russian alliance that summer. On 16 April the Russians had actually proposed a three-Power agreement with Great Britain and France, including Poland as well, if possible, but the offer had been rejected because the west, suspicious themselves of Russian designs, knew well the fears that Poland, Rumania, Finland, and the Baltic states entertained of a Communist advance westwards. Critics in the House of Commons urged an immediate alliance. 'You are in it up to the neck already,' declared Winston

Churchill, 'and the question is how to make your system effective, and effective in time.' Indeed, the only hope of saving Poland was an Anglo-French–Russian alliance, but the Poles would not hear of it, and after the rejection of their offer of 16 April the Soviet government was confirmed in its conviction that the western Powers were hoping to leave Russia to face Germany alone. On 3 May the pro-western Russian Foreign Minister, Litvinov, was replaced by Molotov and, throughout the summer, negotiations with the west continued at a snail's pace. On 29 June the west did agree to the ominous Russian proposal that if the alliance were formed, it should include a guarantee of Finland and the Baltic States, but subsequent military conversations in August broke down over the Polish refusal to allow Russian bases in Poland.

This failure on the part of the west to come to terms with Russia played into the hands of Germany. It might seem that there could be nothing more incongruous than a pact between a Nazi and a Communist government, yet there were arguments in favour of it on both sides. For Germany it would simply be a reversion to the policy of the nineteenth century which von Seeckt had advocated in 1921, and it would effectively seal the fate of Poland; for Russia it would enable her to gain the spheres of influence which her negotiations with the west did not seem likely to provide. For both it would be a cynical bargain whereby each manoeuvred for a better position in the war that each knew would one day break out between them. Initially, contacts were established through trade talks in May, but by July conversations in Berlin were moving in the direction of a political alliance and on 29 August Ribbentrop arrived by air at Moscow to complete the negotiations. That same night the treaty of alliance between Russia and Germany was finally signed. The first part which was made public was simply a non-aggression pact; the second part was a secret agreement over the division of the spoil. Poland was to be partitioned roughly along the line originally proposed by Lord Curzon as her eastern frontier in 1920.[1] Lithuania and Vilna were to come within the German sphere of influence, Finland, Estonia, and Latvia within the Russian, while Germany agreed to turn a blind eye to Russian interests in the Rumanian province of Bessarabia.

Hitler was naturally overjoyed at the news of the Molotov–Ribbentrop pact and hailed his Foreign Minister on his return from Moscow as 'a second Bismarck'. Indeed, both Hitler and the statesmen of the west had taken action as soon as they had known that the signing of

[1] See p. 378.

the pact was imminent. On 22 August Hitler had lectured his generals on the certainty of war with Poland. 'I am only afraid,' he said, 'that some *Schweinehund* will make a proposal for mediation.' On the same day the British cabinet met to issue a *communiqué* that a Soviet–Nazi pact 'would in no way affect their obligation to Poland', and immediately afterwards Chamberlain dispatched a personal letter to Hitler to the same effect. This left Hitler unmoved, but on 25 August the announcement of a definite Anglo-Polish treaty, coupled with a further warning from Mussolini that Italy would be unable to give Germany direct military support, did cause him to hesitate and he ordered a temporary postponement of the attack on Poland.

During these last few days of peace Chamberlain, despite his mistrust of Hitler, was still hoping for some compromise agreement, but for Hitler this seemed no more than an opportunity to detach the west from Poland. He insisted that he had no designs on the British Empire, but over the immediate issue he demanded that a Polish plenipotentiary should be sent to Berlin with powers to accept whatever Germany wanted. This would clearly mean a repetition of the interviews that Hitler had held previously with Schuschnigg and Hacha, and the British government would not countenance it, although they still urged the Poles to continue to negotiate. On 31 August Hitler came to his fateful decision. He issued the final directive to his supreme commander and on 1 September German forces invaded Poland.

To the growing dismay of the British House of Commons the reaction of the west was not immediate. There were reasons for this. Mussolini had made one last frantic attempt at mediation and the coordination of British and French military measures was not easy to arrange by telephone. The principal difficulty was the demand of the French General Staff for a delay of forty-eight hours in which they could carry out their mobilization without interference from German air attack. By 2 September, however, members of all parties in the House of Commons had grown so impatient that Chamberlain forced the French to overrule their generals and at eleven o'clock on 3 September, after Nevile Henderson had presented an ultimatum at Berlin, a state of war existed between Great Britain and Germany. A French declaration followed later the same day.

Thus, after having for so long failed to face up to the realities of Hitler's aims, the west had at last committed themselves to calling a halt to German expansion. It was an unavoidable step, yet the diplomatic follies of previous years now placed them in a position far worse than in 1914. This time Italy was far more closely linked with Germany; worse still, the Molotov–Ribbentrop pact had freed Germany from the likelihood of a prolonged war on two fronts. As it turned out, this was to have disastrous consequences for Russia as well as for the west. Russia's aim had been to keep Germany embroiled with the west, just as she had suspected the west hoped to see Germany and herself exhausting each other's energies in the east. In the event she over-estimated the strength of the west, and the Russo-German alliance enabled Hitler to concentrate all his forces on knocking France out of the war in the summer of 1940, after which he was able to turn them against Russia in 1941.

Even when one makes all due allowance for contemporary prejudice, it is hard to see how Germany can escape the full burden of responsibility for the outbreak of the second World War. This was of course largely the work of one man. There was little sense of jubilation among the German public or the professionals; indeed, it might be argued that war broke out in 1914 because the German General Staff had too much power, and in 1939 because they had too little. There is no doubt that Hitler had envisaged war with Poland, but it may have been that he had still hoped that the west would not honour their pledge. 'The men of Munich will not take the risk', he had said in the middle of August according to General Halder's diary. The postponement of the German attack on 25 August suggests that another Munich might have suited him perfectly well, and Hitler's interpreter's account clearly indicates great surprise at the British ultimatum. Yet all these considerations are largely academic. Hitler was simply determined to get his own way either by the complete surrender of his opponents or, if need be, by general war when the balance of forces was greatly in his favour.

The causes of the war, however, rest on something more than the whim of one man, for the roots of Hitler's ambition stretch back into the nineteenth century. His annexations during the previous eighteen months had been no more than a ruthless pursuit of the *Grossdeutschland* ideal, inflated with the pan-Germanism of the second half of the nineteenth century. It had been this prospect that had caused the Bohemians in 1848 to pin their hopes to the survival of the Habsburg Empire. 'If the Austrian Empire did not exist,' Palacky had said, 'it would be necessary to create it.' But after 1918 the Austrian Empire had existed no longer and all that had been created in its stead had been a jumble of nation states, too weak to stand alone, too discordant to stand together. In 1848 the springtime of nations had lasted little more than a year; after Versailles the collapse of Germany and Russia had given them a brief life of twenty years, but now they were to become the victims or the satellites of Nazi Germany, and then, after 1945, of Communist Russia. Nearly a century after the year of revolutions Palacky's assessment of the situation in central Europe was still valid.

33

THE SECOND WORLD WAR 1939-45

EVEN after the outbreak of the second World War the memory of the first retained its hold upon men's minds. This time there were no illusions; the war was not going to be over by Christmas and the thought of the previous carnage imposed a sense of caution alike on Gamelin and von Brauchitsch, the French and German Commanders-in-Chief. But whereas in Germany Hitler was able to brush this aside, the memory of the devastation that the French had suffered was to contribute greatly to that loss of morale which brought about their early defeat, and later, even when victory for the Allies seemed ultimately assured, the western leaders still continued to be haunted by the fear that the lines would settle down into a static conflict of attrition.

In fact, the whole character of the second World War was to be utterly different from the first—more diverse, fast moving, sometimes more desperate, but never as heart-breaking as the 1914-18 deadlock. It was fought out over a vast theatre stretching from the Pyrenees to the Volga and ended with the complete overrunning of Germany by the western and Russian armies; it became linked with another great struggle, when Japan attempted to challenge British and American power in south-east Asia and the Pacific—truly a world war. It was, strangely enough in a totalitarian epoch, a war that allowed the individual a greater range of personal exploits—in the resistance movements, the paratroop landings, and the new techniques of combined operations. It never did become static, but it was fought with an utter savagery on the eastern front and the air bombardment of cities involved the indiscriminate slaughter of hundreds of thousands of civilians—although this was small compared with the ruthless extermination of five million Jews by the Nazis, who could now give free rein to their racial doctrines. A single chapter cannot do justice to the immensity of this conflict, yet the general pattern of the war is fundamentally a simple one. Until the autumn of 1942 the German armies achieved one victory after another until they held an area greater than that ever before ruled by Germany, equalling the Napoleonic empire at its height; after the autumn of 1942 they knew only defeat as the combined forces of Great Britain, the United States, and Russia thrust them back to ruin and unconditional surrender.

1. The German victories 1939–42

A. THE DEFEAT OF POLAND AND FRANCE: SEPTEMBER 1939–JUNE 1940

During the first eight months of the war Great Britain and France made no move in the west. Had they been ready, their greatest opportunity would have been in September 1939, when the requirements for the German attack on Poland had left only 42 weak divisions in the Siegfried Line against 72 available French divisions. Such a possibility did not last long, for the Polish campaign was over in less than a month —a startling example of the new technique of *blitzkrieg* which the German General Staff under von Seeckt had first envisaged in the 1920s. The Polish army, outnumbered two to one, overwhelmed by German air power and the speed of the armoured Panzer divisions, was cut through and encircled by a three-pronged thrust from East Prussia, Pomerania, and Silesia, and on 20 September the battle of the Vistula completed its destruction.

At the same time the Russians were moving in for their share of the bargain and by 19 September had carried out the occupation of eastern Poland. Stalin was now determined to extend his defences as far west as possible and after a further agreement with Hitler, who could not for the moment object, Russian bases were established in Estonia, Latvia, and Lithuania. At the end of October, still in pursuit of this policy, Russia demanded the Karelian isthmus and the port of Hanko from Finland, and when this was refused, the Russian army crossed the Finnish frontier on 30 November. For three-and-a-half months the Finns under Marshal Mannerheim put up a remarkable resistance to the invader. The spectacle of a tiny country of four million inhabitants fighting alone against the might of Soviet Russia aroused tremendous sympathy in the west, but the British and French governments had inevitably to concentrate on their own war effort; Sweden was determined to remain neutral and Germany remained passive as a matter of policy, since she was still relying on her economic agreements with Russia. Thus, only 11,500 foreign volunteers ever reached

Finland, and although the Russian army was successfully repulsed in December, Mannerheim was unable to check a break-through on the Karelian isthmus in February 1940. The winter war finally ended on 12 March, when a peace treaty granted Russia the isthmus and the whole province of Viipuri as well as a border territory to the north and a thirty-year lease of the port of Hanko.

Scandinavia was also to be the scene of the next step in the major war, when on 9 April Hitler launched his forces into neutral Denmark and Norway. The Danes made no resistance, while the Norwegians fought back unavailingly. British forces, who were hurriedly landed along the coast a week later, failed to reach Trondheim and although Narvik was recaptured from the Germans, it had eventually to be abandoned. The fundamental cause of Hitler's occupation of Norway was Germany's need of Swedish iron ore. This had been brought down by sea through Norwegian territorial waters, and the objections of the British, who finally began to lay minefields there, seemed to point to possible interference in a region which would threaten Germany's strategic right flank. With the successful conclusion of the military operation Hitler had produced a decisive answer to this problem, but he could hardly have anticipated one immediate consequence. In the House of Commons at Westminster Neville Chamberlain came under fierce attack from all sides over the ineffectiveness of the Norwegian campaign, and on 10 May a coalition government was formed under Winston Churchill who was to continue to lead the nation until the end of the war.

On the same day the storm burst in the west, when the German armies suddenly violated the neutrality of Belgium, the Netherlands, and Luxemburg. Despite the opening of the dykes the Dutch were rapidly overrun, Rotterdam was mercilessly bombed from the air and on 15 May the Dutch army capitulated. At the same time in Belgium the Germans had reached the line of the Maas and a break-through near Sedan suddenly revealed the nature of their plan. This was not to be the wide-sweeping right flank movement of 1914; the main thrust had come farther south skirting the Maginot Line and as it broke through the Allied front, threatened to isolate the British and French forces to the north, which had advanced eastwards from their prepared positions to link up with the Belgian army. The question was whether the German Panzers would manage to keep open this gap in the Allied lines and swinging round towards the Channel ports complete the encirclement of the northern forces.

General Weygand now took over as French Commander-in-Chief from General Gamelin and an attempt was made to close the gap, but achieved no more than a slight British advance to the south of Arras. On 23 May Boulogne fell and it seemed as if the whole of the northern armies were doomed. They were, in fact, to be spared as a result of two highly significant decisions. On 24 May the order was given for the German armour to the west of the Allies to halt, although whether this emanated from Hitler or from von Rundstedt has been debated by the generals ever since. And on 25 May Lord Gort, commander of the British Expeditionary Force, doubtful how much longer the Belgians would remain in the war, decided on his own initiative to call off the thrust south and to make for the sea. This was an act of extreme moral courage, and although the French have regarded it as desertion, it was certainly justified by the facts of the political and military situation; indeed, it may be considered one of the great decisions of the war, for if the northern forces had been broken up in the open field, as seemed only too likely, Great Britain would have lost the major part of her army without which it might not have been possible to continue the struggle after the fall of France. It is vital in war to know when to retreat, as the German generals were to learn to their cost in the Russian campaigns of 1943 and 1944.

Gort's decision had been taken only just in time. The German armoured thrust from the west was renewed on 26 May and King Leopold's capitulation on the next day left a great gap on the eastern flank which the Belgians had been holding. The situation was only saved by the defence of Calais to the last round and the extraordinarily skilful withdrawal operation fought by General Brooke enabling the northern forces to fall back on Dunkirk. The R.A.F. managed to hold off the bulk of the German air attack; the sea remained calm, and from the harbour and the bomb-racked beaches of Dunkirk the British navy, aided by every kind of small craft which had put out in response to an Admiralty appeal, succeeded during nine days in bringing back to England 338,000 British and Allied troops.

Meanwhile, the situation in France had deteriorated sharply. On 10 June Mussolini, hoping for a share of the spoils, declared war, but even at this stage the Italians were unable to shake the French resistance in the Alpine regions. Elsewhere, however, the speed of the German penetration, the psychological shock of their massive air power, and the confusion of refugees blocking the roads had all created a sense of inevitable defeat. By 11 June the Germans had reached the Seine, while another thrust southwards was soon to cut off the one-third of the French army still manning the Maginot Line; and on 12 June the government declared Paris an open city and moved to Tours and thence to Bordeaux.

The question now was: how long would France remain in the war? Winston Churchill, who flew to Tours on 13 June, tried every means to persuade the French government to continue the fight, if need be from North Africa. Two British divisions had been sent back to northern France after Dunkirk; there was long discussion over holding a redoubt in Brittany, and at the end he even proposed an indissoluble union between the two countries. It was all in vain. There were strong defeatist elements at work among the French, despairing of any assistance from the United States and mistrustful of Great Britain, who refused to sacrifice her remaining twenty-five fighter squadrons, the last line of her own defence; they were in any case convinced that the British would themselves make peace with Germany. Paul Reynaud, Prime Minister since March, would have been prepared to carry on, but on 16 June he was forced to resign and a new government under Marshal Pétain requested an armistice on the next day. British forces were now left to fend for themselves, but 156,000 were re-embarked, mainly from Cherbourg, and on 18 June General de Gaulle, who as Under-Secretary for National Defence had favoured a continuation of hostilities, was flown from Bordeaux to London, where that same night he broadcast an appeal to the French nation.

Otherwise, the prospect was dark indeed. On 22 June the French Armistice Commission had to sue for peace at Compiègne on the very spot and in the same railway carriage—unearthed by the Germans from a Paris museum—in which Foch had presented his terms in November 1918. All except the south-eastern segment of France was to be under German occupation and all French forces were to be disarmed, while the armistice with Italy signed immediately afterwards stipulated the demilitarizing of zones in the south of France, Tunisia, Algeria, and French Somaliland. Thus, only seven-and-a-half years after he had become German Chancellor Adolf Hitler had finally torn the Treaty of Versailles to shreds and the defeat of Imperial Germany had been avenged by the ex-corporal of the Kaiser's army.

B. THE ISOLATION OF GREAT BRITAIN: JUNE 1940–JUNE 1941

By the end of June 1940 the Continent lay under Germany's control from east of the Vistula to the Pyrenees. She had, in addition, drawn in Italy as an active partner and she still retained a somewhat uneasy friendship with Russia; Spain was dallying with thoughts of a German alliance which might give her Gibraltar; there remained the unknown factor of the French fleet. Against this colossus of power Great Britain stood alone, in far worse plight than during the Napoleonic war. Her sea routes on which she depended utterly for food and supplies were seriously threatened, and her army, although saved from Dunkirk, lacked all its armament and equipment which had had to be left behind in France. It was a historic moment in every sense, for, had Great Britain surrendered, as Hitler hoped she would, Nazi rule would have been consolidated throughout Europe and with the total force of German arms free to concentrate in the east the eventual attack on Russia might well have resulted in a German victory. It was the British determination to continue the war that made such a concentration impossible. 'Hitler knows', said Winston Churchill in the House of Commons in June, 'that he will have to break us in this island, or lose the war,' and under his magnificent leadership the whole land was consumed with a singleness of purpose remote from the days of appeasement. The man-power and industry of the country were placed on a war footing; local defence volunteers prepared to fight for every village, if invasion should come, and the government showed that it was prepared to stop at nothing, when French warships in north African ports which refused to place themselves beyond the reach of Germany were attacked and disabled.

The dominating thought in Great Britain that summer was the imminent prospect of invasion. On 2 July Hitler had already given his order for such an operation, but as his service chiefs well knew, the successful crossing of the Channel depended upon command of the air. Throughout July the German air force concentrated on Channel shipping, and then in August the familiar pattern of *blitzkrieg* was repeated as the attack shifted to the airfields of the British fighter squadrons. Here the vital phase of the battle of Britain was fought out, and by the middle of September the British fighter command under Sir Hugh Dowding had inflicted the first major defeat on Goering's *Luftwaffe*; at the same time incessant bombing raids were being carried out on the invasion barges forming up in French and Belgian ports, and on 17 September the German assault which had been scheduled for a few days later had to be postponed, while in October it was finally called off until the following spring. This change of plan was marked by the shifting of the German air attacks to the large cities. London was bombed almost nightly throughout the winter; Southampton, Plymouth, Bristol, and Liverpool all suffered, and on 14 November the centre of Coventry was utterly destroyed; nearly 22,000 civilians had been killed in these attacks by the end of the year, and a further 19,000 perished in 1941.

Meanwhile, Mussolini was determined to seize his chance in Africa. In August Italian forces invaded British Somaliland and on 13 September Marshal Graziani began an advance along the north African coast into Egypt as far as Sidi Barrani[1]. British forces were too small to retaliate immediately, but on 11 November the Fleet Air Arm carried out a great bombing attack on the Italian navy at Taranto. Then on 9 December General Wavell began his own advance on Graziani, and by March 1941 had reached Benghazi and El Agheila, capturing the bulk of the Italian forces. After this, however, hostilities in Greece caused serious reductions in Wavell's forces, which had in any case been far less than the Italians, and the arrival of General Rommel and a German armoured corps forced him to retire to Egypt. Farther south, the British had occupied Eritrea in April and after a short campaign in Abyssinia the Emperor Haile Selassie was once again able to enter his capital, Addis Ababa, on 5 May 1941.

At the same time the war at sea had centred on the maintenance of supplies—an appalling struggle in which the German U-boats sank nearly four million tons of British, Allied, and neutral shipping in 1940 and slightly more in 1941. The situation seemed even more desperate when in the spring of 1941 the German heavy battleship, *Bismarck*, was at large in the Atlantic and it was not until 27 May that an all-out effort by sea and air succeeded in sinking her. The other major function of the British navy was to impose a blockade, yet with all the Continent at Hitler's disposal this could hardly be effective. Nothing could check the trade of neutrals such as Turkey, Spain, Portugal, and Switzerland with Germany; Russia was still delivering supplies in accordance with the agreements of 1939, and Sweden was even allowing unarmed soldiers as well as supplies to pass through her territory.

The most significant developments of this period, however, lay outside the immediate war areas. In the United States public opinion had become greatly excited at the sight of Great Britain holding the fort against an entire continent dominated by Nazism. By special agreement American destroyers had been handed over for British

[1] See map, pp. 446–7.

use in the autumn of 1940, and in January 1941 President Roosevelt introduced a 'Lease-Lend' bill in Congress which was greatly to facilitate the supply of material to Great Britain.

In eastern Europe Russia was continuing to make good use of her opportunities. While Germany had been embroiled in the campaign in France, she had set up Communist governments in Estonia, Latvia, and Lithuania and in June Rumania was forced to surrender Bessarabia and northern Bukovina to her. Eastern European interests remained incorrigibly parochial to the end, for in August Rumania had to give up the south of the Dobruja to Bulgaria, as well as two-thirds of Transylvania to Hungary through German mediation. Then on 28 October Mussolini, still hungry for glory, launched an attack on Greece, but by the end of 1940 had suffered such a repulse at the hands of the Greek forces under General Metaxas that in the early months of the next year he had become dependent, as in North Africa, upon German help. Hitler's troops could reach Greece through Rumania and Bulgaria, but with Yugoslavia partly surrounded the moment seemed to have come for a pact with the Regent Prince Paul, which was duly signed towards the end of March 1941. This was at once followed, however, by an anti-German *coup d'état* in Belgrade with the result that on 6 April the German army invaded Yugoslavia and Greece simultaneously. Breaking through on the Bulgarian frontier they forced the outnumbered Yugoslav forces to capitulate on 17 April, and their mounting attack on Greece eventually overran the Greek defence, despite the support of 58,000 British troops who were sent to their aid from Egypt. The Greek government withdrew to Crete, but here in May a German airborne landing succeeded in capturing the island and the evacuation of British forces was considerably less effective than it had been from Greece. Indeed, the only British success in these months had been a naval encounter off Cape Matapan on 28 March, when four Italian cruisers and three destroyers had been sunk; apart from that, the whole of the British intervention in Greece seemed to be just one more episode in a tale of disaster and retreat.

C. THE GERMAN INVASION OF RUSSIA AND THE ENTRY OF THE UNITED STATES INTO THE WAR

On 22 June 1941 Hitler embarked upon the most fateful venture of his career when he suddenly declared war on Russia. One hundred and fifty German divisions, twenty of which were armoured, began an advance into Soviet territory, striking south towards Kiev and the

Ukraine, through White Russia towards Smolensk and Moscow, and through the Baltic states towards Leningrad. This decision of Hitler's was taken against the advice of most of his generals and political associates, who believed that the war should be won in the west before Germany embarked upon the new campaign. Hitler, however, was adamant. He mistrusted the recent gains that Russia had been making in eastern Europe; he hoped for the rapid defeat of Russia, which would finally deprive Great Britain of any chance of an eventual alliance with her, and he reckoned that the territorial gains would more than compensate for the disruption of Russo-German economic agreements.

Except on this last point he was utterly wrong. The lack of Soviet resistance to the growth of German influence in Rumania and Bulgaria hardly suggested any imminent danger, and despite British warnings the Russian army was taken by surprise. On the other hand, once the battle had been joined, the Russian resistance at the front and behind the German lines was so fierce that a rapid victory was soon out of the question; thus, instead of depriving Great Britain of an ally, he actually drove Russia into her arms. On the same day as the German invasion Churchill announced on the radio: 'Any man or State who fights against Nazidom will have our aid', and on 13 July a pact of mutual assistance was signed between the two countries, while in September the United States also agreed to supply Russia. Soon convoys sailing the perilous Arctic route north of Scandinavia began to bring a steady stream of British and American war material to Murmansk and Archangel, and by the end of 1942, 3,276 tanks and 2,665 aircraft had been delivered—at a cost of sixty-four ships sunk by German air and U-boat attack.

By December 1941 the German armies had thrust their way far east of the Crimea; farther north, they had reached the Don and were only thirty miles from the suburbs of Moscow, while Leningrad held out under siege. Then winter, still the Russians' greatest ally, came to their aid, and in the early months of 1942 the Germans were pushed back in a series of counter-attacks. Field Marshal von Brauchitsch was dismissed by Hitler, who took over personal command himself, and then when the spring enabled the Germans to make a new offensive, Field Marshal von Bock swept forward in the south into the Caucasus, although Voronezh on the Don and Stalingrad on the Volga still defied him.

Meanwhile, the British had gained their most significant alliance. Under the guidance of President Roosevelt the United States had been slanting her neutrality increasingly in the interest of Great Britain, and in August 1941 he and Churchill had met in mid-Atlantic to devise the Atlantic Charter which, in answer to the Nazi New Order in Europe, guaranteed the freedom of the nations of the world. It was, however, Japan that finally precipitated the Americans into the war. The Japanese had already taken advantage of the defeat of France to occupy French Indo-China in the summer of 1941, and on 7 December they launched a devastating air attack on American naval forces in Pearl Harbor in Hawaii. For the United States this meant war with Japan and with her Axis allies; for Winston Churchill it meant at last the formation of the Grand Alliance which had been his principal hope since the desperate summer of 1940. That same month he was in Washington; a Combined Chiefs-of-Staffs Committee was established to ensure close cooperation in the Anglo-American war effort, and the whole mighty power of American industry was turned over to the defeat of Hitler.

Certainly the ultimate prospect had changed beyond belief; yet the immediate outcome was to be a further series of disasters. On Christmas Day 1941 Hong Kong fell to the Japanese; the Americans lost Wake Island and Guam in the Pacific, and in January 1942 the Dutch East Indies were overrun. On 15 February Singapore itself was forced to surrender; by May American resistance in the Philippine Islands had been crushed, and it was only the American naval victory in the Coral Sea on 4 May that saved Australia from the immediate threat of invasion.

Nor was the news any better elsewhere. In North Africa General Auchinleck, who had assumed command in June 1941, was able to clear the German forces from Cyrenaica by December, but had to withdraw in January 1942 when Rommel was reinforced. In May a new German attack on the British positions met with success, and although Auchinleck was able to check the rout, the British had by July fallen back on El Alamein only 150 miles from Cairo. In these last six months three million tons of Allied shipping had been sunk; the Japanese had strengthened their hold on south-east Asia and the Pacific, von Bock's great thrust was reaching into the Caucasus, and the British stood at bay on the last line of defence before the Suez canal. Thus the late summer of 1942 marks the blackest moment in the fortunes of the Allied Powers, and Hitler's success was now at its height.

2. Germany in Europe

Between 1940 and 1944 almost the entire Continent lay at Hitler's disposal and in that time he was able to translate into deadly reality the most lunatic racialist dreams that had haunted central Europe in the late nineteenth century. The frontiers of Germany herself, which now included the pre-1914 Polish territories, were simply those of *Grossdeutschland*. Belgium and the occupied parts of France remained under military government owing to the war situation, but countries which were thought to be suitably Aryan—Norway, Denmark, and the Netherlands—were placed under their own Nazi administration. It was not until August 1943 that strikes in Copenhagen caused Hitler to appoint a Reich Commissioner for Denmark, and in the meantime Himmler was recruiting a considerable proportion of foreign Nordic elements in the S.S. This basis of racialism naturally meant that there could be no question of an Aryan partnership in the east. Here the local populations were to be treated as a slave class providing the labour for a string of German colonies stretching through the Baltic lands and in the south reaching as far as the Urals. 'There should be one master only for the Poles—the Germans', said Hitler in 1940. 'Two masters side by side, cannot and must not exist. Therefore all representatives of the Polish intelligentsia are to be exterminated.' In fact, the stupid brutality of the Germans when they first entered the Russian border areas in 1941 deprived them of the support of many who would have welcomed release from Communism.

Plunder was the immediate reward of victory. From food and raw materials to blankets and fur coats the Germans lived on Europe for four years, and when in 1945 the invading armies of the Allies reached Germany after passing through the under-nourished occupied countries, they found the Germans the best-fed people on the Continent. In addition to this, nearly five million foreign workers were conscripted and transported to Germany. The more fortunate of these were housed in large camps in the countryside where they supplied the farms with labour; others were despatched to factories where their treatment was so bad that thousands did not survive.

The most iniquitous aspect of Hitler's rule was, of course, the concentration camps to which Jews, political prisoners, and resistance fighters were sent to be worked to death or used for medical experiments. Between 1937 and 1945 some 239,000 people were sent to

Q

Buchenwald, of whom more than 33,000 died. There was also a particular category of extermination camp—as at Auschwitz in Poland or Mauthausen in Austria—where a highly methodical organization accounted for the death of about five million Jews, principally in gas chambers—not the hot-blooded excitement of a local *pogrom*, but a cold efficient plan devised with bureaucratic thoroughness to kill every Jew in Europe.

In the grip of all this horror there was little that the conquered countries could do in their own defence. There was, however, in all of them a growing resistance movement which towards the end of the war in France, Norway, and Yugoslavia had placed whole areas under their effective control, and which in small countries whose topography did not lend itself to such achievements concentrated on the rescue of Jews and assistance to Allied agents and escaping prisoners of war. The risk was appalling, for capture usually meant torture and death; German reprisals often took the form of the shooting of hostages, and in June 1942 the entire village of Lidice in Czechoslovakia was wiped out after the Nazi governor Heydrich had been assassinated. Such methods of retaliation naturally inspired hatred, but they also created mixed feelings over resistance activity, particularly since the most effective elements in the partisan movement were very often Communist; in any case, despite the extraordinary heroism of the resistance, the Continent could only await the outcome of a world conflict in which by the summer of 1942 the hopes for an Allied victory still seemed extremely remote.

3. The defeat of Germany 1942-5

In the autumn of 1942, however, the Allies won two overwhelming victories, at El Alamein and Stalingrad, which together mark the turning point in the course of the war. In August Churchill and General Brooke, Chief of the Imperial General Staff since November 1941, had stopped at Cairo on their way to a conference at Moscow and appointed General Alexander as Commander-in-Chief with General Montgomery in command of the Eighth Army. At the end of the month Montgomery defeated a flanking attack by Rommel at Alam Halfa and continued to prepare for his own assault as reinforcements of American Sherman tanks began to arrive from the long journey round the Cape. On 23 October the battle of El Alamein opened with a tremendous artillery barrage and a frontal assault, reminiscent of the offensives in the first World War, and after twelve days of heavy fighting Rommel was in full retreat, having suffered nearly 60,000 casualties. This great victory was followed almost at once on 8 November by an American landing in Morocco and Algeria under the command of General Eisenhower.

Hitler reacted at once to the resurgence of Allied power in the Mediterranean; Vichy France was occupied, although the French fleet avoided capture by scuttling itself in the harbour of Toulon, and by the middle of November 18,000 German troops had moved into Tunis. None of this could alter the fact that Rommel was now caught between two advancing armies; on 20 March 1943 he was defeated again by Montgomery at Mareth; throughout April there was hard fighting on the German western flank in Tunis, and in May the end came with the capture of a quarter of a million Axis soldiers.

Within a month of El Alamein the Russians sprang their trap on the German forces besieging Stalingrad. On 19 November 1942 thrusts from the north and the south linked up, and although the Germans on Hitler's orders continued a desperate resistance in the appalling winter conditions, Field Marshal von Paulus had eventually to surrender on 31 January 1943. To the north Leningrad was relieved, but in the south the German forces did succeed in escaping from a second trap in the Caucasus, and in March 1943 the Russian offensive was temporarily halted, when Field Marshal von Manstein recaptured Kharkov.

This turn in the fortunes of the Allies naturally necessitated a reconsideration of future western strategy, and at an Anglo-American conference at Casablanca in January 1943 General Brooke was able to gain agreement on its general form. The plan was to concentrate on the Mediterranean with an assault on Italy. This might knock Mussolini out of the war; it would certainly draw more German divisions into Italy and from the point of view of supply it would enable the Allies to dispense with the long route round the Cape. Thus shipping would be freed and the German Command forced to divide their forces, both essential preliminaries to the launching of a cross-Channel invasion on the mainland of the Continent.

At first things moved quickly. In July and August Sicily was overrun, and in Rome a new government formed under Marshal Badoglio after the arrest of Mussolini on 25 July, eventually signed an armistice with the Allies at Syracuse on 3 September. On the same day an Anglo-American landing in the south of Italy in Calabria and at Salerno met with initial success, but the German forces under Field Marshal Kesselring who now held Italy virtually captive began a long stubborn resistance in a countryside ideally suited to defence. Throughout the remainder of 1943 the weary struggle went on, as Alexander edged his way northwards. On 1 October Naples was taken; the rivers Sangro and Garigliano were crossed, but although the Allies attempted to leap-frog up the western coast with a landing at Anzio in January 1944, it was not until May that they were able to link up, and then at last, on 4 June, Alexander's troops entered Rome, which had been declared an open city.

Meanwhile, in Russia a German summer offensive in 1943 had been successfully resisted and with the autumn the Russian advance was renewed. On 25 September Smolensk was taken, by October they had reached the Dnieper and by February 1944 they were all to the west of Novgorod and were thrusting out in the south. Many factors contributed to these victories. The rapid industrialization of Russia with the five-year plans of the 1930s, aided by the influx of supplies from the west in the Arctic convoys, had enabled the Russians to equip their armies in a way that had been impossible in the first World War. The Germans were faced with mounting demands for troops on their Mediterranean front, and their generals in Russia were hamstrung by the insistence of Hitler, their Commander-in-Chief, that there should never be a strategic withdrawal while there was still time.

Of course, for the Germans all this fighting was on foreign soil. At home, however, their great cities were now coming under an air bombardment far more concentrated and destructive than anything that they themselves had been able to launch in the early years of the war. Throughout 1943 and 1944 the British and American bomber commands wrought appalling havoc, although the effect on German industrial output was afterwards found to have been far less than had been imagined, owing to the remarkable organization of dispersal and prefabrication by Albert Speer, Hitler's Minister of Armaments Production. Still, the air bombardment certainly hampered the full development of the German war effort, at the same time as the Allies were gradually gaining the upper hand on the U-boats attacking their supply lines in the Atlantic.

All these efforts were the essential prelude to the invasion of the Continent from the southern shore of England, and on 6 June 1944— D Day—British, Canadian, and American forces under the command of General Montgomery duly made a landing at various points along the coast of Normandy. Aided by naval and air superiority and by a multiplicity of remarkable devices including a floating harbour, the Allies were able to build up their forces in the bridgehead, and in July, while the British in the eastern sector held the bulk of the German armour, the Americans broke out at the western end, swept south and then north to join up with the British and to catch a considerable portion of Rommel's forces in the 'Falaise pocket'. With the Germans in full retreat, the Allies kept up the pursuit across northern France into Belgium, while in August a landing in the south of France completed the liberation of the French.

The situation was now desperate for Germany. Hitler's secret weapon—the V.1, a pilotless flying bomb—was ready for use too late to have any effect upon the invasion armies, which by September had taken a quarter of a million prisoners; fifty-five German divisions were held down on the Italian and Mediterranean fronts; Russia was continuing to advance into Poland and the Baltic states, and in September Finland finally signed an armistice with her. On 20 July a group of German officers, prompted by the sense of inescapable doom, attempted to assassinate Hitler and to take over the government of the country with the intention of suing for peace in the west. The attempt failed, and in the orgy of executions that followed, Hitler not merely wiped out thousands in Germany who represented a latent opposition to Nazi rule, but also completed his subjugation of the German Officer Corps. It is the paradox of the history of the Third Reich that Hitler's power in Germany had never been so great as it was in the last ten months of the war. Dislike of Nazism and the war policy there may have been; the fact remains that after July 1944 generals and soldiers alike fought on bitterly for Hitler to the end.

In September the Allies suffered their first set-back when an attempt by the British to leap-frog across the Maas and the upper and lower Rhine with airborne landings was checked at Arnhem, and the Allies were still holding the line of the Maas, when von Rundstedt attempted one last counter-attack through the Ardennes on 16 December in an effort to cut through to Antwerp. The attack was held and after this the Germans had really shot their bolt. By now the Russians were thrusting into Rumania and Bulgaria, Yugoslavia had largely been

470

EUROPE AFTER 1945

freed by the partisan army of the Communist Marshal Tito, and on 12 February 1945 the Russians captured Budapest.

At this point European statesmen were well aware that the post-war political scene in Europe was already in the making. Stalin's motives in directing this southern thrust along the Danube through the Balkans suggested nothing less than the re-emergence of the old Eastern Question. Indeed, the main hope of the Germans now was that the realization of this by the west would at last shatter their alliance with Russia. 'They had not counted on our defending ourselves step by step and holding them off in the west like madmen,' said Goering in January, 'while the Russians drive deeper and deeper into Germany.' The Allies, however, had no intention of playing into the Germans' hands in this way, and the only outcome of the prolonged resistance in the west was eventually to place far more of eastern Germany under Russian control. Winston Churchill had long been uneasy about the possible extent of Russian gains, for as early as November 1943 he had proposed at the Teheran Conference that the Allied forces in Italy should push on northwards up into Austria and the Hungarian plainland. Castlereagh and Metternich would have understood his concern, but such a campaign would not have been easy from a military point of view, and Stalin was by now confident of victory on his own front and therefore wanted no western army interfering in eastern Europe. He pressed instead for an Allied landing in the south of France, which duly took place in August 1944 with forces drawn from Italy where the advance was inevitably slowed down.

The only other chance of forestalling the Russians lay in breaking into Germany and ending the war in the autumn of 1944, while the Red Army was still some way to the east. Montgomery believed that a concentrated thrust through Holland in September could not have been resisted, but Eisenhower, who had now assumed supreme command, favoured an advance on a broad front, and thus the Arnhem venture lacked the strength to take the Allies over all the water obstacles that separated them from Germany and the end did not come until the following spring. The debate over these decisions still continues. It is clear that the landing in the south of France suited Stalin, and subsequent statements by German generals have lent support to Montgomery's plan for the September thrust. On the other hand, the problem of supply may well have been decisive. The Channel ports were still holding out under siege, and with a line of communications stretching back as far as Cherbourg the Allied armies benefited greatly from gaining the south of France, while the invasion of Germany in the autumn of 1944 would have been a hazardous undertaking before Antwerp had been captured.

In February 1945 the Allies met in conference at Yalta in the Crimea. Here it was agreed that the old Curzon line should be the eastern frontier of Poland, who was to be compensated with territory in the west up to the rivers Oder and Neisse, and that the Poles should have free elections, although these were not to be supervised by an international force. Churchill was by no means happy about these new frontiers for Poland, nor about the arrangements for the elections, but President Roosevelt was anxious to secure Russian support in the Japanese war and, in any case, Stalin was by now in something of the position of Alexander I at the Congress of Vienna. 'His Imperial Majesty', wrote Castlereagh to Lord Liverpool on the Polish problem in October 1814, 'insinuated that the question could only end in one way, as he was in possession.' And in 1950 Edward R. Stettinius, the American Secretary of State at the time of the Yalta meeting, commented: 'What, with the possible exception of the Kuriles, did the Soviet Union receive at Yalta which she might not have taken without any agreement?' Indeed, Stalin was even able to stake a claim to ten million dollars in German reparations, despite the British insistence that no figure should be mentioned.

The war was now moving into its last phase. The German effort in the Ardennes enabled the Russians to advance into eastern Germany early in 1945. In March, when the western Allies crossed the Rhine, the British moved north on to Bremen and Hamburg, crossed the Elbe to capture Lübeck twenty-four hours ahead of the Russians, and sent a small holding force by air to Copenhagen in order to make sure of Denmark. The Americans swept through the centre and the south of Germany, but held back on the Czech border, honouring the agreement that the Russians should take Prague. In April Alexander was victorious in the valley of the Po, and Mussolini, who had been rescued by the S.S. after his arrest and set up as a puppet dictator in north Italy, was captured by Italian partisans and shot. By 25 April the Russians had surrounded Berlin and five days later Hitler, still in his bunker below the grounds of the Chancellery, committed suicide.

Admiral Doenitz, whom he had appointed as his successor, did not have long in which to enjoy a somewhat embarrassing inheritance. On 2 May nearly a million Germans surrendered to Alexander in Italy; on 4 and 5 May there were local surrenders of the German troops facing the British and American forces in Germany and Austria, and on 7 May General Jodl and Admiral von Friedeburg signed a formal document of unconditional surrender at General Eisenhower's head-quarters at Reims before representatives of the United States, Great Britain, Russia, and France. The German nightmare of the ultimate consequence of war on two fronts had finally come to pass; the armies of her enemies had met in the middle of Europe and the Third Reich was no more.

CONCLUSION

I N May 1945 almost the entire continent of Europe was in utter
ruin. From the Volga across the plains of Russia and Poland to
east Germany town after town had been laid waste in the fighting,
while the path of the war was marked by destruction throughout the
length of Italy and in Normandy and the south of the Netherlands. In
Germany great cities had been transformed unbelievably into enormous
mountains of rubble, her railway and road systems had been completely wrecked by bombing, and the girders of her smashed bridges
poked forlornly from the rivers. All civil government had broken down
and Germany lay at the mercy of her invaders and, worse still, of the
forced labour workers from the east who roamed the countryside
pillaging, burning, and killing in an orgy of revenge. To this was
added the revelation of the appalling conditions in the concentration
and extermination camps and the fury of the occupied peoples as they
turned on their own nationals who had collaborated with the Nazis.

In June 1938 von Weizsäcker, the State Secretary at the German
Foreign Office, had warned Ribbentrop of all these consequences. 'The
decision about our aims in the east would once again have to be fought
for in the west and be confirmed by a dictated peace in London and
Paris. . . . We have no military recipe for defeating France and Britain.
. . . The war would therefore end in our exhaustion and defeat. The
common loser with us would be the whole of Europe, the victors
chiefly the non-European continents and the anti-social powers.' It
was a highly accurate prediction. The United States would not this
time retire to her own hemisphere; the havoc which Europe had
wrought upon herself opened the way to the emergence of new independent states in Asia and Africa, and the presence of the Red Army
as far west as the Elbe created a new element in the political tension
throughout the Continent. At the same time, the end of the Japanese
war in August 1945 with the dropping of the atom bombs on Hiro-
shima and Nagasaki marks the beginning of a new era in world history
under the shadow of a destructive force far greater than anything
previously conceived. Thus, the dwindling of Europe's significance in
relation to the rest of the world might well suggest that by 1945 her
old feuds would play little further part in the history of mankind.

And yet the remarkable recovery of Europe in the post-war period, aided by American generosity, points to her extraordinary resilience, a dynamic of political ferment and cultural diversity which not even two terrible wars have stifled and which still fosters the animosities that have been her undoing. Indeed, no single year can ever mark the beginning of a totally different period. The statesmen of 1814 could never blot out the fact that the Napoleonic Empire had existed; the peace-makers of 1919 were haunted by the problems with which Metternich and the Habsburgs had earlier had to struggle. Even at the height of the second World War governments paid their respects to the past; in 1940 a leading Hungarian Communist was released by Hungary in exchange for the battle flags seized by the Russian armies in 1849, and in the same year Hitler attempted to win over the French by returning the remains of 'Napoleon II', the Duke de Reichstadt, to Paris. And in the post-war period, although the world scene now presents a vastly different context, the old antagonisms remain in the fear of Russian expansion and in the hatred of German and Slav, strengthened by the actions of the Nazis during the war. Nationalism is still the most potent force in European relations—still stronger than Socialism, as the break between Stalin's Russia and Tito's Yugoslavia would suggest—and since geography does not change, foreign policy continues to repeat the various patterns of earlier decades; the division of Europe by the Iron Curtain is not so remote from the alignment that created the secret treaty of January 1815.

Certainly the impact of Socialism has hastened the political and social transformation of the Continent; yet here too the implications are not as new as one might imagine. The issue of western democracy and eastern authoritarianism, which helped to shape so much of the history of nineteenth-century Europe, is still with us today, and political ideology, when translated into practice, has constantly to come to terms with the existing circumstances that are rooted in the past. As in human nature, Europe can never escape from the forces of her heredity; Louis XIV and the sovereigns of the eighteenth century would have found nothing strange in the cult of personality, and it is perhaps not inappropriate that the rulers of the new Socialist republics should reside in the former palaces of the *ancien régime*.

APPENDIXES

ROYAL GENEALOGICAL TABLES

N.B. The family trees have been very much simplified. The dates beneath the
Sovereigns refer to their reigns.

FRANCE: THE HOUSES OF BOURBON AND BOURBON-ORLEANS

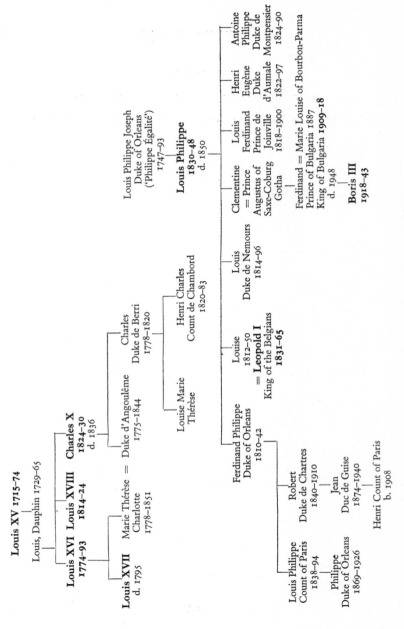

FRANCE: THE HOUSE OF BONAPARTE

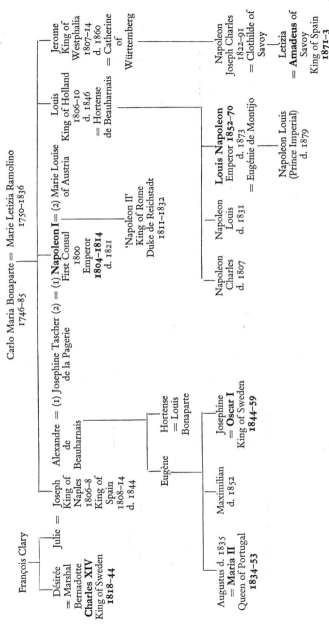

Carlo Maria Bonaparte = Marie Letizia Ramolino
1746–85   1750–1836

François Clary

Julie = Joseph
King of
Naples
1806–8
King of
Spain
1808–14
d. 1844

Désirée
= Marshal
Bernadotte
Charles XIV
King of Sweden
1818–44

Alexandre = (1) Josephine Tascher (2) = (1) **Napoleon I** = (2) Marie Louise
de   de la Pagerie   First Consul   of Austria
Beauharnais   1800
                                             Emperor
                                             1804–1814
                                             d. 1821

Eugène

Hortense
= Louis
Bonaparte

Josephine
= **Oscar I**
King of Sweden
1844–59

Maximilian
d. 1852

Augustus d. 1835
= **Maria II**
Queen of Portugal
1834–53

'Napoleon II'
King of Rome
Duke de Reichstadt
1811–1832

Louis
King of Holland
1806–10
d. 1846
= Hortense
de Beauharnais

Jerome
King of
Westphalia
1807–14
d. 1860
= Catherine
of
Württemberg

Napoleon
Charles
d. 1807

Napoleon
Louis
d. 1831

Louis Napoleon
Emperor **1852–70**
d. 1873
= Eugénie de Montijo

Napoleon Louis
(Prince Imperial)
d. 1879

Napoleon
Joseph Charles
1822–91
= Clothilde of
Savoy

Letizia
= **Amadeus** of
Savoy
King of Spain
1871–3

AUSTRIA: HOUSE OF HABSBURG

BAVARIA: HOUSE OF WITTELSBACH

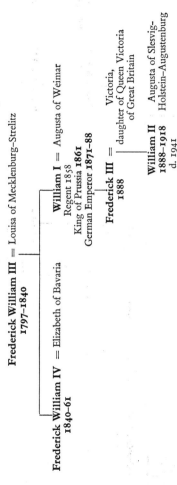

PRUSSIA: THE HOUSE OF HOHENZOLLERN

Frederick William III = Louisa of Mecklenburg–Strelitz
1797–1840

Frederick William IV = Elizabeth of Bavaria
1840–61

William I = Augusta of Weimar
Regent 1858
King of Prussia 1861
German Emperor 1871–88

Frederick III = Victoria,
1888 daughter of Queen Victoria
of Great Britain

William II = Augusta of Slesvig–
1888–1918 Holstein–Augustenburg
d. 1941

R

DENMARK: THE HOUSE OF OLDENBURG

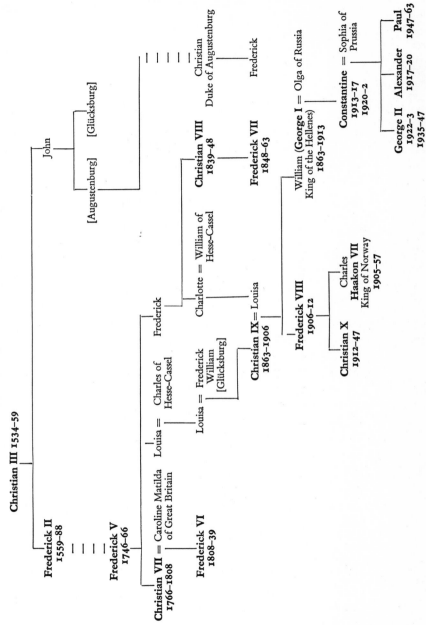

ITALY: THE HOUSE OF SAVOY

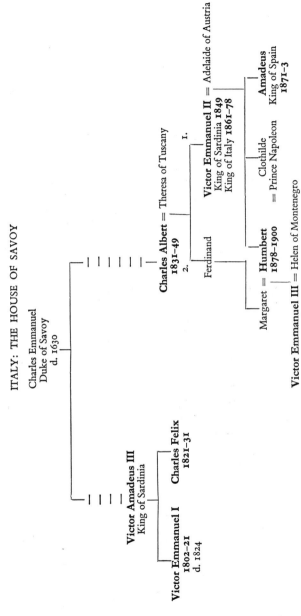

RUSSIA: THE HOUSE OF ROMANOV

Paul = Sophia Dorothea of
1796–1801   Württemberg

Alexander I = Elizabeth of Baden   Constantine   Nicholas I = Charlotte of Prussia
1801–25   d. 1831   1825–55

Alexander II = Marie of Hesse-Darmstadt
1855–81

Alexander III = Marie of Denmark
1881–94

Nicholas II = Alexandra of Hesse   Michael
1894–1917
ex. 1918

Alexis

APPENDIX 2
POPES

Elected	Title	Family Name
1800	Pius VII	Chiaramonti
1823	Leo XII	Della Genga
1829	Pius VIII	Castiglion
1831	Gregory XVI	Cappellari
1846	Pius IX	Mastai-Ferretti
1878	Leo XIII	Pecci
1903	Pius X	Sarto
1914	Benedict XV	Della Chiesa
1922	Pius XI	Ratti
1939	Pius XII	Pacelli

APPENDIX 3
PRESIDENTS OF THE FRENCH THIRD REPUBLIC
1871–1940

Adolphe Thiers	1871–3
Marshal MacMahon	1873–9
Jules Grévy	1879–87
Sadi Carnot	1887–94
Jean-Paul Casimir Périer	1894–5
Félix Faure	1895–9
Emile Loubet	1899–1906
Armand Fallières	1906–13
Raymond Poincaré	1913–20
Paul Deschanel	1920
Alexandre Millerand	1920–4
Gaston Doumergue	1924–31
Paul Doumer	1931–2
Albert Lebrun	1932–40

APPENDIX 4

FRENCH ELECTORAL SYSTEMS 1814–1945

See also: P. Campbell, *French Electoral Systems and Elections 1789–1957*. (1958)

No. of seats	Deputies' Qualifications Tax	Age	Years of tenure	Electors' Qualifications Tax	Age	Type of constituency	Size of electorate
1814 258	1,000 fr.	40	5 (annual election of ⅕)	300 fr.	30	Single-member (scrutin d'ar-rondissement)	88,000–110,000 (1814–30)
1815 402 (395)[1]		25					
1816 258		40					
1817					25	Multi-member (scrutin de liste)	
1820 430						Single-member (172 additional deputies elected by chief tax-payers)	
1824			7 (no ⅕)				
1830–1 459	500	30	5	200[2]	25	Single-member	166,000–241,000 (1830–48)
1848 900[3]	—	21	—	Manhood[4] suffrage 21		Multi-member	8 million
1849 750[5]		25	3				10 million[6]
1850				3-year residential			7 million
1852 261[7]			6			Single-member	
1857 267							
1863 283							
1869 292							
1871 768 (738)[8]	—	25				Multi-member	10 million
1875 533[9]			4			Single-member	
1881 541[10]							
1885 569						Multi-member	
1889 560						Single-member	
1919–20 610[11]						Multi-member	
1927 593[12]						Single-member	12 million
1944				Female suffrage			25 million
1945 586							

[1] Reduction after territorial losses by the second Treaty of Paris.   [2] As well as members of the Institut de France and a small number of retired army officers paying 100 francs in tax.   [3] Including 4 for Algeria and 12 for colonies.   [4] Including soldiers and sailors.   [5] Including 4 for Algeria and 7 for colonies.   [6] Increase of 2 million since 1848 owing to the completion of the registers.   [7] 1 seat per 35,000 electors during the Second Empire.   [8] Reduction after the loss of Alsace and Lorraine.   15 for Algeria and colonies.   [9] Including 7 for Algeria and colonies.   [10] Representation of Algeria and colonies raised to 16.   [11] After regaining Alsace and Lorraine.   [12] Representation of Algeria and colonies raised to 19.

GERMAN CHANCELLORS AND PRESIDENTS
1871–1945

1. The German Reich.

   Chancellors:

   Prince Otto von Bismarck 1871–90
   Count Leo von Caprivi 1890–4
   Prince Chlodwig zu Hohenlohe-Schillingsfürst 1894–1900
   Prince Bernhard von Bülow 1900–9
   Theobald von Bethmann Hollweg 1909–17
   Dr Georg Michaelis, July–October 1917
   Count Georg von Hertling, October 1917–September 1918
   Prince Max of Baden, October–November 1918
   Friedrich Ebert, November 1918–February 1919

2. President of the National Assembly:

   Friedrich Ebert, February–August 1919

3. The Weimar Republic.

   Presidents:

   Friedrich Ebert 1919–25
   Field Marshal Paul von Hindenburg 1925–34

   Chancellors:

   P. Scheidemann (SPD) February 1919
   G. Bauer (SPD) June 1919
   H. Müller (SPD) March 1920
   K. Fehrenbach (Centre) June 1920
   J. Wirth (Centre) May 1921
   W. Cuno (non-party) November 1922
   G. Stresemann (People's) August 1923
   W. Marx (Centre) November 1923
   H. Luther (non-party) January 1925
   W. Marx (Centre) May 1926
   H. Müller (SPD) June 1928
   H. Brüning (Centre) March 1930
   F. von Papen (non-party) May 1932
   K. von Schleicher (non-party) December 1932
   A. Hitler (Nat. Soc.) January 1933

4. The Third Reich.

   Chancellor:

   A. Hitler, who assumed the Presidency as well in August 1934

APPENDIX 6

SEATS HELD BY THE PRINCIPAL PARTIES IN THE GERMAN REICHSTAG ELECTIONS 1919–33

Source: K. S. Pinson, *Modern Germany: its History and Civilization.* (1954)

	Jan. 1919	June 1920	May 1924	Dec. 1924	May 1928	Sept. 1930	July 1932	Nov. 1932	Mar. 1933	Nov. 1933
Majority Socialists	165	102	100	131	153	143	133	121	120	—
Independent Socialists	22	84								
Communists	—	4	62	45	54	77	89	100	81	—
Centre party	91	64	65	69	62	68	75	70	74	—
Bavarian People's party	—	21	16	19	16	19	22	20	18	—
Democrats	75	39	28	32	25	20	4	2	5	—
Wirtschaftspartei	4	4	10	17	23	23	2	1	—	—
Nationalists	44	71	95	103	73	41	37	52	52	—
Landbund	—	—	10	8	3	3	2	2	1	—
People's party	19	65	45	51	45	30	7	11	2	—
National Socialists	—	—	32	14	12	107	230	196	288	661

APPENDIX 7

POPULATIONS

Figures given in millions.

	Great Britain	France	Italy	Habsburg Empire	Germany	Russia
1815	18	29	18		26	43
1830	24	32	21		30	50
1840	26	33	22·4		31	55
1850	27·6	35·8	24·3	30·7	35·9	57
1860	29	37·4	25	31·7	38	63
1870	31	37	26	35·8	41	77
1880	35	37	28	38	45	89
1890	38	38	30	41	49	95
1900	41	39	32	45	56	103
1910	45	39	35	50	65	111
1920	42	40	38		58	
						147 (1926)
1930	44	42	42		65	170 (1939)
			42 (1936)		86 (1939)[1]	
1940		40				64 (1945)[2]
	48 (1951)					

[1] This includes the acquisition of Austria, the Sudetenland, Bohemia, Moravia, and Memel.

[2] After the Treaty of Potsdam in 1945.

APPENDIX 8

THE MIXED POPULATIONS IN THE NEW EASTERN EUROPEAN STATES AFTER 1919

Source: H. Seton-Watson, *Eastern Europe between the Wars 1918–1941.* (1945)
Figures given in thousands.

Date of census	Poland 1921	Czecho-slovakia 1921	Hungary 1920	Rumania 1930	Yugo-slavia 1921	Bulgaria 1934	Austria 1923
Poles	18,814	76		35			
Ruthenians	3,898	462	1	500			
Jews	2,110	181	161[1]	778	68[2]	28	
Germans	1,059	3,124	551	714	506		6,273
Russians	1,116			174		12	
Lithuanians	69						
Czechs	31	} 8,761			} 176[3]		94
Slovaks			142	27			5
Magyars		745	7,147	1,464	468		25
Rumanians		14	24	11,545	231	16	
Croats			37		} 8,912		} 47
Serbs			17	53			
Slovenes			6		1,020		43
Bulgarians				351		5,275	
Turks				222		618	
Albanians					440		
Italians					13		
Armenians						23	
Gypsies				133		81	

[1] According to the census of 1941.
[2] According to the census of 1931.
[3] This figure also includes Ruthenians.

APPENDIX 9

EMIGRATION FROM EUROPE TO THE UNITED STATES 1831–1930

Source: S. E. Morison and H. S. Commager, *The Growth of the American Republic.* (1942)

Countries refer to the last place of permanent residence.

Figures given in thousands.

	1831–40	1841–50	1851–60	1861–70	1871–80	1881–90	1891–1900	1901–1910	1911–20	1921–30
Austria–Hungary				8	73	354	593	2,145	896	
France	45·5	77	76	36	72	50·5	31	73	62	49·5
Germany	152·5	434·5	951·5	787·5	718	1,453	505	341·5	144	412
Great Britain[1]	283	1,048	1,338	1,042·5	985	1,463	660	865	487·5	551
Italy	2	2	9	12	56	307	652	2,046	1,109·5	455
Russia	0·5	0·5	1·5	4·5	52	265	602	1,597	922	78·5
Total European	495·5	1,597·5	2,452·5	2,046·5	2,262	4,731·5	3,559	8,136	4,376·5	2,478

[1] Including Ireland.

APPENDIX 10

COAL, IRON, AND STEEL PRODUCTION OF THE GREAT POWERS 1850–1944

Sources: A. J. P. Taylor, *The Struggle for Mastery in Europe 1848-1918.* (1954)

Encyclopaedia Britannica. (1959 edn.)

Figures given in millions of metric tons.[1]

	1850	1860	1870	1880	1890	1900	1910	1914	1920[2]	1929[2]	1935	1944
COAL												
Germany	6	12	34	59	89	149	222	277	275	348	319	404
Austria–Hungary	1·2	2·3	8·6	15	26	39	47	47	11[3]	11	12	15
France	5	8·3	13·3	19·4	26·1	33·4	38·4	40	37	57	52	29
Great Britain	57	81	112	149	184	228	268	292	265	250	249	216
Russia		0·15	0·75	3·2	6	16·2	24·9	36·2	12	34	121	130
PIG-IRON												
Germany		0·9	1·3	2·5	4·1	7·5	9·5	14·7	6·9	13·2	12·6	14·2
France	0·5		1·2	1·7	2	2·7	4	4·6	3·4	10·2	5·7	2·8
Great Britain	2·2	3·9	6	7·8	8	9	10	11	8	7·6	6·4	6·7
Russia			0·4	0·4	0·9	2·9	3	3·6	0·11	3·9	12·4	7·6
STEEL												
Germany			0·3	0·7	2·3	6·7	13·8	14	8·4	16	16·1	16·2
France			0·3	0·4	0·7	1·6	3·4	3·5	3	9·5	6·2	3
Great Britain			0·7	1·3	3·6	5	5·9	6·5	9	9·6	9·8	12·1
Russia					0·4	1·5	3·5	4·1	0·1	4·9	12·3	11·8

[1] 1 metric ton = 1,000 kg. = 19 cwt. 12 oz. 5 dwt.

[2] The figures for coal in 1920 are based on an average for the years 1920-4, and in 1929 on an average for the years 1925-9.

[3] After the creation of the Republic of Austria in 1919.

GLOSSARY OF PLACE-NAMES

Place-names loom large in Continental emotions. An inhabitant of Lausanne once expressed indignation to the author at the English habit of calling Lac Léman the Lake of Geneva; after the Anglo-French crisis of 1898 (see p. 277) the name of Fashoda was changed to Kodok, so that further mention of the place might not awaken unpleasant memories, and at the beginning of the first World War the German-sounding St Petersburg was changed by the Russians to Petrograd. Since 1945 an ideological element has been added to the confusion in eastern Europe with the naming of cities after leading Communists. For example, Königsberg in East Prussia is now Kaliningrad, and the cartographer has to keep pace with the shifts in the official Russian interpretations of recent history. For the student of nineteenth-century Europe, however, the principal significance of place-names is that they reflect the rivalries of linguistic nationalism. A dispassionate viewpoint would demand an anglicized form, but too often a satisfactory one does not exist, and the following glossary simply gives the alternative forms of the place-names that occur in the text.

Danzig (German)	Gdansk (Polish)	
Dorpat (German)	Tartu (Estonian)	Yuryev (Russian)
Fiume (Italian)	Rijeka (Yugoslav)	
Gorizia (Italian)	Görz (German)	Goriska (Yugoslav)
Hanko (Finnish)	Hangö (Swedish)	
Helsinki (Finnish)	Helsingfors (Swedish)	
Kaunas (Lithuanian)	Kovno (Russian)	

Königgrätz: The battle of 1866 is sometimes called Sadowa, particularly by French historians. This is not an alternative place-name, but simply another town not far from Königgrätz.

Laibach (German)	Ljubljana (Yugoslav)	
Lemberg (German)	Lwow (Polish)	Lvov (Russian)
Memel (German)	Klaypeda (Lithuanian)	
Olmütz (German)	Olomouc (Czech)	
Porvoo (Finnish)	Borgå (Swedish)	
Posen (German)	Poznan (Polish)	
Pressburg (German)	Pozsony (Hungarian)	Bratislava (Czech)
Ragusa (Italian)	Dubrovnik (Yugoslav)	
Reval (German)	Talinn (Estonian)	

Slesvig-Holstein: This involves a particular difficulty, since a hyphenated form implies the German nationalist view of the indivisibility of the duchies, while the separation of the two supports the Danish claim. I have retained the hyphen, since this seems to be customary in English, but have used the

Danish Slesvig rather than the German Schleswig (although one historian has suggested Sleswick as an earlier English form).

Teschen (German)   Těšin (Czech)   Cieszyn (Polish)
Vilna (German)   Vilnyus (Lithuanian)   Wilno (Polish)
Viipuri (Finnish)   Viborg (Swedish)   Vyborg (Russian)

GLOSSARY OF TECHNICAL TERMS

Anschluss: Union, usually referring to that of Germany and Austria, accomplished in 1938. See p. 440.

Ausgleich: The Compromise of 1867, creating Austria-Hungary. See p. 224.

Barshchina: Compulsory labour performed by privately owned Russian serfs.

Blitzkrieg: Lightning war, a German technique of attack in the second World War, based on close cooperation of infantry, armour, and air power.

Bundesrat: Federal Council representing the states in the German Reich of 1871 (see pp. 224, 284), and the cantons in the Swiss constitution of 1848.

Bundesstaat: Any federal organization in which the central government has definite power over the member states: e.g. Switzerland after 1848, and the German Reich of 1871. This is in contrast to a *Staatenbund*, a confederation in which the member states enjoy far greater independence: e.g. the German and Swiss Confederations of 1815.

Bundestag: (1) Diet of the German Confederation of 1815. See p. 33. (2) Federal Parliament of Austria after 1918.

Consulta: An advisory council.

Cortes: Spanish Parliament.

Diet: A general term to describe a representative assembly of: (1) the states of a confederation, or (2) a single country, usually meeting in the form of three or four Estates of the realm (*Stände* in German). See p. 34.

Duma: Russian national Parliament established after the revolution of 1905. See p. 290.

Landtag (plur. -e): A provincial Diet.

Métayage: A system of farming whereby the owner of the land and the farmer shared the profits.

Mir: The community of the peasant village in Russia.

Obruk: Payment made in cash or in kind by Russian serfs for the right to farm.

Reichsrat: (1) Austrian constitutional assembly whose powers were gradually increased in the second half of the nineteenth century. (2) Upper House representing the provincial governments in the constitution of the Weimar Republic. See p. 386.

Reichstag: Lower representative House in the constitutions of the North German Confederation of 1867, the German Reich of 1871, and the Weimar Republic.

Reichswehr: The German army.

Riksdag: Swedish Diet. The four Estates were transformed into a bi-cameral Parliament in 1866, but the institution retained the same name.

Risorgimento: Resurgence, the Italian word applied to the movement of Italian nationalism.

Staatenbund: See Bundesstaat.

Staatsrat: Council of State.

Storting: Norwegian Parliament.

Zemstvo (plur. -va): District or provincial assembly established by Tsar Alexander II in Russia in 1864. See p. 229.

Zollverein: Customs Union. See p. 61.

FURTHER READING

A. Bibliographies

A. BULLOCK and A. J. P. TAYLOR. *Select Lists of Books on European History 1815–1914*, 2nd edn. Oxford U.P., 1957.

W. N. MEDLICOTT. *Modern European History 1789–1945.* (Historical Association Pamphlet.)

B. General Works

A. J. GRANT and H. TEMPERLEY, *History of Europe in the 19th and 20th Centuries, 1789–1950.* 6th edn. rev. by L. M. Penson. Longmans, 1952.

D. THOMSON. *Europe since Napoleon*, 2nd edn. Longmans, 1962.

E. BARKER, G. N. CLARK, and P. VAUCHER, eds. *The European Inheritance.* Vol. III. Oxford U.P. 1954.

E. L. WOODWARD. *War and Peace in Europe 1815–70.*

The following series each contain several volumes on the period:

The New Cambridge Modern History. Cambridge University Press.

The Rise of Modern Europe. Harper; Hamish Hamilton.

Peuples et Civilisations. Presses Universitaires de France.

Clio: Introduction aux Études Historiques. Presses Universitaires de France.

C. Diplomatic

OFFICIAL DOCUMENTS:

A. OAKES and R. B. MOWAT, eds. *Great European Treaties of the 19th Century.* 2nd edn. Oxford U.P. 1921.

H. W. V. TEMPERLEY and L. M. PENSON. *Foundations of British Foreign Policy, from Pitt to Salisbury.* Cambridge U.P., 1938.

R. H. LORD. *Origins of the War of 1870.* Harvard U.P., 1924.

G. BONNIN. *Bismarck and the Hohenzollern Candidate for the Spanish Throne.* Chatto, 1958.

A. F. PRIBRAM, *The Secret Treaties of Austria-Hungary 1879–1914.* Harvard U.P.; Oxford U.P., 1920.

A. B. KEITH. *Speeches and Documents on International Affairs 1918–37.* 2 vols. Oxford U.P., 1938 (World's Classics).

SECONDARY SOURCES:

P. RENOUVIN. *Histoire des Relations Internationales: Le XIXe siècle. 2 vols.*, 1954–5; *le XXe siècle. 2 vols.* Hachette, 1958.

A. J. P. TAYLOR. *The Struggle for Mastery in Europe 1848–1918.* Oxford U.P., 1954 (Oxford History of Modern Europe).

C. K. WEBSTER. *The Congress of Vienna, 1814–1815.* Bell, 1934.

W. E. MOSSE. *The European Powers and the German Question 1848–71.* Cambridge U.P., 1958.

A. F. PRIBRAM. *England and the International Policy of the Great Powers 1871–1914.* Oxford U.P., 1931. Ford Lectures.

W. L. LANGER. *The Diplomacy of Imperialism 1890–1902. 2 vols.* New York, 1935.

L. ALBERTINI. *The Origins of the War of 1914*, trans. I. M. Massey. 3 vols. Oxford U.P., 1952–7.

G. M. GATHORNE-HARDY. *A Short History of International Affairs 1920–39.* 4th edn. Oxford U.P. for R.I.I.A., 1950.

L. B. NAMIER. *Diplomatic Prelude 1938–9.* Macmillan, 1948.

D. Economic

J. H. CLAPHAM. *The Economic Development of France and Germany 1815–1914.* 4th edn. Cambridge U.P., 1936.

W. O. HENDERSON. *The Industrial Revolution on the Continent 1800–1914.* F. Cass, 1961.

L. H. JENKS. *The Migration of British Capital.* Cape, 1938.

W. ASHWORTH. *A Short History of the International Economy, 1850–1950.* Longmans, 1952.

W. A. LEWIS. *Economic Survey 1919–39.* Allen & Unwin, 1949.

E. Religious and Ideological

ORIGINAL WRITINGS:

J. J. ROUSSEAU. *Du contrat social* (1762) (various translations).

J. G. FICHTE. *Reden an die deutsche Nation* (1808). Trans. R. F. Jones and G. H. Turnbull, The Open Court Publishing Co., 1922.

L. BLANC. *L'organisation du travail* (1839). English edn. Sir J. A. R. Marriott, 1913.

G. MAZZINI. *The Duties of Man* (1844–58). Everyman's Library.

NAPOLEON III. *Des idées napoléoniennes* (1838) trans. as *The Mind of Napoleon*. Pennsylvania U.P., 1955.

K. MARX. *Das Kapital* (1867–94) (various translations).

K. MARX and F. ENGELS. *The Communist Manifesto* (1848) (various translations).

SECONDARY SOURCES:

A. R. VIDLER. *The Church in an Age of Revolution*. Penguin 1961. (Pelican History of the Church.)

E. E. Y. HALES. *The Catholic Church in the Modern World*. Eyre & Spottiswoode and Burns Oates, 1958.

R.I.I.A. *Nationalism*. Oxford U.P., 1939.

P. HENRY. *Le problème des nationalités*. 2nd edn. Armand Colin, 1949.

J. ANCEL. *Slaves et Germains*. 2nd edn. Armand Colin, 1947.

R. W. SETON-WATSON. *Racial Problems in Hungary*. Constable, 1908.

G. de RUGGIERO. *European Liberalism*, trans. R. G. Collingwood. Oxford U.P., 1927.

J. PLAMENATZ. *German Marxism and Russian Communism*. Longmans, 1954.

R. N. CAREW HUNT. *The Theory and Practice of Communism*. 5th edn. Bles, 1956.

I. BERLIN. *Karl Marx*. 2nd edn. Oxford U.P., 1948 (Home Univ. Lib.).

J. JOLL. *The Second International 1889–1914*. Weidenfeld, 1955.

A. B. COBBAN. *Dictatorship: Its History and Theory*. Cape, 1939.

E. HELLER. *The Disinherited Mind*. Bowes, 1959.

F. National Histories
France

MEMOIRS:

F. R. de CHATEAUBRIAND. *Mémoires d'outre-tombe* (1849–50), ed. A. H. Thompson, Cambridge U.P., 1920.

A. de MUSSET. *Confession d'un enfant du siècle* (1836).

G. SAND. *Histoire de ma vie* (1854–5) adaptation de Noelle Roubaud, Librairie Stock 1960.

NASSAU SENIOR. *Conversations with Thiers and Guizot*. 2 vols. Hurst, 1878.

V. HUGO. *Choses vues* (1887–1900). Collection Nelson.

A. de TOCQUEVILLE. *Souvenirs* (1893); as *Recollections*, ed. J. P. Mayer. Harvill, 1948.

E. RENAN. *Souvenirs d'enfance et de jeunesse* (1892). Paris. Calmann Lévy. Trans. C. B. Pitman. Routledge, 1929.

R. BALDICK, ed. *Pages from the Goncourt Journal*. Oxford U.P., 1962.

NOVELS:

H. de BALZAC. *Le Colonel Chabert* (1832); *Le Père Goriot* (1834); *César Birotteau* (1838) (all in various translations).

G. FLAUBERT. *L'éducation sentimentale* (1869) trans. Goldsmith. Dent (Everyman's Library).

E. ZOLA. *Germinal* (1885); *La terre* (1877) (various translations).

A. FRANCE. *Ile des pingouins* (1908).

M. PROUST. *A la recherche du temps perdu* (1913–27) trans. C. K. Scott Moncrieff as *Remembrance of Things Past*, Chatto (1922–31).

G. DUHAMEL. *Le notaire du Havre.* Mercure de France, 1933.

SECONDARY SOURCES:

J. P. T. BURY. *France 1814–1940*, 3rd edn. (including an appendix with the successive French constitutions) Methuen, 1954.

D. W. BROGAN. *The Development of Modern France 1870–1939.* Hamish Hamilton, 1939.

E. L. WOODWARD. *French Revolutions.* Oxford U.P., 1934.

J. PLAMENATZ. *The Revolutionary Movement in France 1815–71.* Longmans, 1952.

P. CAMPBELL. *French Electoral Systems and Elections 1789–1957.* Faber, 1958.

A. R. VIDLER. *Prophecy and Papacy: A Study of Lamennais, The Church and the Revolution.* S.C.M., 1954.

DUFF COOPER. *Talleyrand.* Cape, 1932.

D. O. EVANS. *Social Romanticism in France 1830–48.* Oxford U.P., 1952.

T. E. B. HOWARTH. *Citizen King. The Life of Louis Philippe.* Eyre & Spottiswoode, 1961.

F. A. SIMPSON. *The Rise of Louis Napoleon.* 3rd edn. Longmans, 1950. *Louis Napoleon and the Recovery of France, 1848–56.* 3rd edn. Longmans, 1951.

T. ZELDIN. *The Political System of Napoleon III.* Macmillan, 1958.

M. HOWARD. *The Franco-Prussian War.* Hart-Davis, 1961.

F. H. BRABANT. *The Beginnings of the Third Republic in France.* Macmillan, 1940.

J. HAMPDEN JACKSON. *Clemenceau and the Third Republic.* English U.P., 1946. (Teach Yourself History.)

D. THOMSON. *Democracy in France*, 3rd edn. Oxford U.P. for R.I.I.A., 1958.

Austria

ORIGINAL WRITINGS:

P. QUENNELL and D. POWELL, eds. *Private Letters of Princess Lieven to Prince Metternich 1820–26.* Murray, 1946.

LORD SUDLEY, ed. *The Lieven–Palmerston Correspondence 1828–56.* Murray, 1943.

S. ZWEIG. *The World of Yesterday.* Cassell, 1943.

SECONDARY SOURCES:

A. J. P. TAYLOR. *The Habsburg Monarchy 1809–1918.* Hamish Hamilton, 1948.

H. von SRBIK. *Metternich.* F. Bruckmann A.G., 1921–6.

G. de BERTIER de SAUVIGNY. *Metternich and his Times,* trans. P. Ryde. Darlon, 1962.

A. J. MAY. *The Habsburg Monarchy 1866–1914.* Harvard U.P.; Oxford, 1951.

I. EISENMANN. *Le Compromis austro-hongrois de 1867.* 1904.

Z. A. B. ZEMAN. *The Break-up of the Habsburg Empire 1914–18.* Oxford U.P., 1961.

C. A. GULICK. *Austria from Habsburg to Hitler.* 2 vols. Univ. of California Press, 1948.

Germany

ORIGINAL WRITINGS:

O. von BISMARCK. *Reflections and Reminiscences. Gedanken und Erinnerungen,* ed. A. M. Gibson, Cambridge U.P., 1940. In German.

G. RITTER, ed. *The Schlieffen Plan,* trans. A. and E. Wilson. O. Wolff, 1958.

PRINCE MAX of BADEN. *Memoirs,* trans. W. M. Calder and C. W. H. Sutton. Constable, 1928.

A. HITLER. *Mein Kampf* (1925–27) (various translations). Full edn. trans. J. Murphy, Hurst and Blackett, 1939.

NOVELS:

T. MANN. *Buddenbrooks,* trans. H. L. Porter. Secker 1937. Penguin 1957.

F. KAFKA. *The Trial,* trans. W. and E. Muir. Secker, 1956; *The Castle,* trans. W. and E. Muir. Secker, 1930.

SECONDARY SOURCES:

E. J. PASSANT, and others. *A Short History of Germany 1815–1945*. Cambridge U.P., 1959.

K. S. PINSON. *Modern Germany: Its History and Civilization*. Macmillan, New York, 1954.

G. A. CRAIG. *The Politics of the Prussian Army 1640–1945*. Oxford U.P., 1955.

T. S. HAMEROW. *Restoration, Revolution, Reaction: Economics and Politics in Germany 1815–71*. Princeton U.P., 1958.

W. O. HENDERSON. *The Zollverein*. Cambridge U.P., 1939.

H. FRIEDJUNG. *The Struggle for Supremacy in Germany*, trans. A. J. P. Taylor and M. L. McElwee. Macmillan, 1935.

R. D'O BUTLER. *The Roots of National Socialism*. Faber, 1941.

V. VALENTIN. *1848: Chapters of German History*. Trans. E. T. Scheffauer. Allen & Unwin, 1940.

J. DROZ. *Les Révolutions allemandes de 1848*. Presses Universitaires de France, 1949.

A. J. P. TAYLOR. *Bismarck: The Man and the Statesman*. Hamish Hamilton, 1955.

E. EYCK. *Bismarck and the German Empire*. Allen & Unwin, 1950.

E. L. WOODWARD. *Great Britain and the German Navy*. Oxford U.P., 1935.

A. ROSENBERG. *The Birth of the German Republic*, trans. I. F. D. Morrow. Oxford U.P., 1931.

R. COPER. *Failure of a Revolution: Germany in 1918–1919*. Cambridge U.P., 1955.

J. W. WHEELER-BENNETT. *The Nemesis of Power: The German Army in Politics 1918–1945*. Macmillan, 1953.

A. BULLOCK. *Hitler*. Odhams, 1952.

H. MAU and H. KRAUSNICK. *German History 1933–45*, trans. A. and E. Wilson. O. Wolff, 1959.

Italy

ORIGINAL WRITINGS:

A. MANZONI. *The Betrothed*, trans. Colquhoun. Dent (Everyman's Library).

G. S. ABBA. *The Diary of one of Garibaldi's Thousand*, trans. E. R. Vincent. Oxford U.P., 1962.

G. DILAMPEDUSA. *The Leopard*. English trans. Harvill. Collins, 1960.

O. RUSSELL. *The Roman Question: extracts from despatches from Rome 1858–1870*, ed. N. Blakiston. Chapman, 1962.

SECONDARY SOURCES:

A. J. WHYTE. *The Evolution of Modern Italy, 1715–1920.* Blackwell, 1944. *The Political Life and Letters of Cavour 1848–61.* Oxford U.P., 1930.

E. E. Y. HALES. *Mazzini and the Secret Societies.* Eyre & Spottiswoode, 1956. *Pio Nono.* 2nd edn. Eyre & Spottiswoode, 1956.

D. MACK SMITH. *Cavour and Garibaldi in 1860.* Cambridge U.P., 1954; *Garibaldi.* Hutchinson, 1957; *Italy 1860–1960.* Univ. of Michigan Press, 1959.

Russia

NOVELS AND PLAYS:

L. N. TOLSTOY. *The Cossacks,* trans. V. Traill. Hamish Hamilton, new edn., 1949. *Resurrection,* trans. L. and A. Maude. Oxford U.P., 1916. (World's Classics.)

I. TURGENEV. *A Sportsman's Sketches,* trans. Dent., 1932; *On the Eve; Smoke; Literary Reminiscences* (including several short stories); *Virgin Soil; Fathers and Sons; A Month in the Country* (all in various translations).

N. GOGOL. *Dead Souls.* (1842) trans. G. Reavez. Oxford U.P. (World's Classics); trans. C. J. Hogarth. Dent (Everyman's Library); *The Inspector General,* trans. D. J. Campbell. Heinemann.

F. DOSTOEVSKY. *The House of the Dead.* Trans. C. Garnett. Heinemann, 1915. *Crime and Punishment* (various translations).

A. TCHEKOV. *The Cherry Orchard; Uncle Vanya; The Three Sisters* (various translations).

B. PASTERNAK. *Doctor Zhivago.* Collins, 1958.

SECONDARY SOURCES:

B. PARES. *A History of Russia.* Rev. edn. Cape, 1955.

J. D. CLARKSON. *A History of Russia, from the Ninth Century.* Longmans, 1962.

R. HARE. *Portraits of Russian Personalities between Reform and Revolution.* Oxford U.P., 1959.

W. E. MOSSE. *Alexander II and the Modernization of Russia.* English U.P., 1959 (Teach Yourself History).

H. SETON-WATSON. *The Decline of Imperial Russia 1855–1914.* New edn. Methuen, 1952.

B. H. SUMNER. *Russia and the Balkans 1870–80.* Oxford U.P., 1937.

N. BERDYAEV. *The Origin of Russian Communism.* Bles, 1937.

. H. CHAMBERLIN. *The Russian Revolution.* 2 vols. Macmillan, New York, 1952.

C. E. HILL. *Lenin and the Russian Revolution.* English U.P., 1947 (Teach Yourself History).

E. H. CARR. *The Bolshevik Revolution 1917–23.* Macmillan, 1950.

I. DEUTSCHER. *Stalin.* Oxford U.P., 1949.

G. F. KENNAN. *Russia and the West under Lenin and Stalin.* Hutchinson, 1961.

Eastern Europe

C. A. MACARTNEY and A. W. PALMER. *Independent Eastern Europe.* Macmillan, 1962.

H. SETON-WATSON. *Eastern Europe between the Wars 1918–41.* Cambridge U.P., 1945.

C. A. MACARTNEY. *Hungary and her Successors 1919–37.* Oxford U.P., 1937. *Hungary: a short history.* Edinburgh U.P., 1962.

W. F. REDDAWAY, ed. *Cambridge History of Poland 1697–1935.* Cambridge U.P., 1941.

H. W. V. TEMPERLEY. *History of Serbia.* Bell, 1917.

J. REMAK. *Sarajevo.* Weidenfeld, 1959.

R. WEST. *Black Lamb and Grey Falcon.* Macmillan, 1942.

R. W. SETON-WATSON. *History of the Roumanians.* Cambridge U.P., 1936.

E. S. FORSTER. *Short History of Modern Greece 1821–1956.* 3rd edn. Methuen, 1957.

A. J. TOYNBEE and R. KIRKWOOD. *Turkey.* Benn, 1926. Nations of the Modern World.

A. J. TOYNBEE. *A Study of History.* 10 vols. Oxford U.P., 1935–54. Vol. VIII, pp. 216–72 (on Turkey).

Scandinavia

B. J. HOVDE. *The Scandinavian Countries 1720–1865.* 2 vols. Cornell U.P., 1950.

J. DANSTRUP. *History of Denmark.* Bailey, 1949.

K. LARSEN. *History of Norway.* Princeton U.P.; Oxford, 1948.

I. ANDERSSON. *History of Sweden,* trans. C. Hannay. Weidenfeld, 1956.

J. HAMPDEN JACKSON. *Finland,* 2nd edn. Allen & Unwin.

Other Western Countries

LOW COUNTRIES:

H. PIRENNE. *Histoire de Belgique*. Vols. VI and VII. 1926, 1932.
G. J. RENIER. *The Dutch Nation*. Allen & Unwin, 1944.
B. H. M. VLEKKE. *Evolution of the Dutch Nation*. Dobson, 1951.

SWITZERLAND:

C. HUGHES, ed. *The Federal Constitution of Switzerland*. Oxford U.P., 1954.
J. BURCKHARDT. *The Letters of Jacob Burckhardt*, ed. A. Dru. Routledge, 1955.
E. BONJOUR, H. S. OFFLER, and G. R. POTTER. *A Short History of Switzerland*. Oxford U.P., 1952.

SPAIN AND PORTUGAL:

H. V. LIVERMORE. *History of Spain*. Allen & Unwin, 1958.
G. BRENAN. *The Spanish Labyrinth*. Cambridge U.P., 1943.
E. ALLISON PEERS. *The Spanish Tragedy 1930–36*. Methuen, 1936.
H. THOMAS. *The Spanish Civil War*. Eyre and Spottiswoode, 1961.
G. L. STEER. *The Tree of Gernica*. Hodder & Stoughton, 1938.
G. ORWELL. *Homage to Catalonia*. Secker, 1938.
H. V. LIVERMORE. *History of Portugal*. Cambridge U.P., 1947.

G. Special Topics

THE REVOLUTIONS OF 1848:

F. FEJTÖ, ed. *The Opening of an Era: 1848*. Wingate, 1948.
F. PONTEIL. *1848*. 2nd edn. Armand Colin, 1947.
A. WHITRIDGE. *Men in Crisis: The Revolutions of 1848*. Scribner's, 1950.
L. B. NAMIER. *1848: The Revolution of the Intellectuals*. Oxford U.P., 1944.

THE FIRST WORLD WAR:

C. R. M. F. CRUTTWELL. *History of the Great War 1914–18*, 2nd edn. Oxford U.P., 1936.
C. FALLS. *The First World War*. Longmans, 1960.
W. S. CHURCHILL. *The World Crisis 1911–1918*. 4 vols. Butterworth, 1923–9.
F. P. CHAMBERS. *The War behind the War, 1914–1918: the history of the political and civilian fronts*. Faber, 1939.
A. MOOREHEAD. *Gallipoli*. Hamish Hamilton, 1956.
J. W. WHEELER-BENNETT. *Hindenburg. The Wooden Titan*.

THE PEACE SETTLEMENT OF 1919:

J. W. WHEELER-BENNETT. *The Forgotten Peace: Brest Litovsk, March 1918.* Macmillan, 1938.
HAROLD NICOLSON. *Peacemaking 1919.* Rev. edn. Constable, 1945.
D. LLOYD GEORGE. *The Truth about the Peace Treaties.* 2 vols. Gollancz, 1938.
G. CLEMENCEAU. *Grandeur and Misery of Victory.* Harrap, 1930.
J. M. KEYNES. *The Economic Consequences of the Peace.* Macmillan, 1919.
E. MANTOUX. *The Carthaginian Peace, or the Economic Consequences of Mr. Keynes.* Oxford U.P., 1946.

THE SECOND WORLD WAR:

J. F. C. FULLER. *The Second World War 1939–1945,* 3rd edn. Eyre & Spottiswoode, 1954.
C. FALLS. *The Second World War, a Short History,* 3rd edn. Methuen, 1950.
W. S. CHURCHILL. *The Second World War.* 6 vols. Cassell, 1948–52.
C. WILMOT. *The Struggle for Europe.* Collins, 1952.
E. SPEARS. *Assignment to Catastrophe.* 2 vols. Heinemann, 1954.
C. de GAULLE. *War Memoirs.* 1954–9.
F. MACLEAN. *Eastern Approaches.* Cape, 1949.
LORD ALANBROOKE. *The Turn of the Tide,* ed. A. Bryant. Collins, 1957; *Triumph in the West,* ed. A. Bryant. Collins, 1959.
A. and V. M. TOYNBEE, ed. *Hitler's Europe.* Oxford U.P. for R.I.I.A., 1954.
H. R. TREVOR ROPER. *The Last Days of Hitler.* 3rd edn. Macmillan, 1956.

H. Miscellaneous

MAPS:

J. RAMSAY MUIR. *Historical Atlas, Medieval and Modern,* 8th edn. G. Philip, 1959.
J. F. HORRABIN. *An Atlas of Current Affairs* (covers much of the inter-war years).
I. RICHARDS, J. B. GOODSON, and J. A. MORRIS. *A Sketch-map History of the Great Wars and after, 1914–60.* Rev. edn. Harrap, 1961.

PHOTOGRAPHS.

H. and A. GERNSHEIM. *Historic Events 1839–1939.* Longmans, 1960.

The topography and architecture of Europe is captured in the various collections of photographs by M. Hürlimann. See also:

S. SITWELL, ed. *Great Houses of Europe.* Weidenfeld and Nicolson, 1961.

H. R. HITCHCOCK. *Architecture: 19th and 20th Centuries.* Penguin 1958. (Pelican History of Art.)

COLLECTIONS OF ESSAYS

L. B. NAMIER. *Vanished Supremacies.* Hamish Hamilton, 1958.

A. J. P. TAYLOR. *From Napoleon to Stalin.* Hamish Hamilton, 1950.

A. O. SARKISSIAN, ed. *Studies in Diplomatic History and Historiography in honour of G. P. Gooch.* Longmans, 1961.

R. PARES and A. J. P. TAYLOR, eds. *Essays presented to Sir Lewis Namier.* Macmillan, 1956.

The *Problems in European Civilization* series (D. C. Heath; Harrap) includes the following:

1848—A Turning Point?; The Outbreak of the First World War—Who was Responsible?; The Russian Revolution and Bolshevik Victory—Why and How?; The Versailles Settlement—Was it foredoomed to Failure?; The Nazi Revolution—Germany's Guilt or Germany's Fate?

INDEX

Treaties and Congresses are listed together alphabetically. Dates after rulers refer to their reigns. Ranks attained after 1945 are omitted.